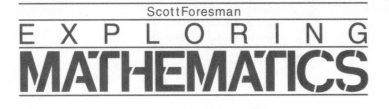

ScottForesman

EXPLORING MATHEMATICS

AUTHORS

L. Carey Bolster
Coordinator of Mathematics
Baltimore County Public Schools
Towson, Maryland

Clem Boyer
Coordinator of Mathematics, K-12
District School Board of Seminole County
Sanford, Florida

Thomas Butts
Associate Professor,
Mathematics Education
University of Texas at Dallas
Richardson, Texas

Mary Cavanagh
Math/Science Coordinator
Solana Beach School District
Solana Beach, California

Marea W. Channel
Mathematics Resource Teacher
Los Angeles Unified School District
Los Angeles, California

Warren D. Crown
Associate Professor of
Mathematics Education, Rutgers,
The State University of New Jersey
New Brunswick, New Jersey

Jan Fair
Mathematics Department
Allan Hancock College
Santa Maria, California

Robert Y. Hamada
District Mathematics Specialist, K-12
Los Angeles Unified School District
Los Angeles, California

Margaret G. (Peggy) Kelly
Associate Professor
California State University, San Marcos
San Marcos, California

Miriam Leiva
Professor of Mathematics
University of North Carolina at Charlotte
Charlotte, North Carolina

Mary Montgomery Lindquist
Callaway Professor of Mathematics Education
Columbus College
Columbus, Georgia

William B. Nibbelink
Professor, Division of Early Childhood and
Elementary Education, University of Iowa
Iowa City, Iowa

Linda Proudfit
University Professor of Mathematics
and Computer Education, Governors State
University, University Park, Illinois

Cathy Rahlfs
Mathematics Coordinator
Humble Independent School District
Humble, Texas

Rosie Ramirez
Assistant Principal
Highland Elementary School
Silver Spring, Maryland

Jeanne F. Ramos
Assistant Principal
Nobel Middle School
Northridge, California

Gail Robinette
Vice-Principal
Fresno Unified School District
Fresno, California

David Robitaille
Head, Department of Mathematics
and Science Education
University of British Columbia
Vancouver, British Columbia,
Canada

James E. Schultz
Project LITMUS
University of Georgia
Athens, Georgia

Richard Shepardson
Professor, Division of Early Childhood
and Elementary Education
University of Iowa
Iowa City, Iowa

Jane Swafford
Professor of Mathematics
Illinois State University, Normal, Illinois

Benny Tucker
Dean, School of Education and Human Studies
Union University
Jackson, Tennessee

John Van de Walle
Professor of Education
Virginia Commonwealth University
Richmond, Virginia

David E. Williams
Former Director of Mathematics Education
School District of Philadelphia
Philadelphia, Pennsylvania

Robert J. Wisner
Professor of Mathematics
New Mexico State University
Las Cruces, New Mexico

Multicultural Reviewers

Cherry McGee Banks
University of Washington
Seattle, Washington

Armando Ayala
Director of Bilingual Education
Placer County, California

Diane Deckert Jost
Field Museum of Natural History, Chicago, Illinois

Patricia Locke
(Ta Wacin Waste Win)
Lakota, Chippewa Educator
Wakpala, South Dakota

Vicky Owyang Chan
Multicultural Educator
Fremont, California

Seree Weroha
Kansas State University, Manhattan, Kansas

Efrain Melendez
Dakota School, Los Angeles, California

Linda Skinner
Choctaw Educator, Edmond, Oklahoma

ScottForesman
A Division of HarperCollinsPublishers

Editorial Offices: Glenview, Illinois   Regional Offices: Sunnyvale, California • Tucker, Georgia • Glenview, Illinois • Oakland, New Jersey • Dallas, Texas

CONTRIBUTING AUTHOR

Janet K. Scheer
Director of Field Services for Mathematics
Scott, Foresman and Company
Glenview, Illinois

CONSULTANTS

Reading
Robert A. Pavlik
Professor, Reading/Language Arts Department
Cardinal Stritch College
Milwaukee, Wisconsin

At-Risk Students
Edgar G. Epps
Marshall Field Professor of Urban Education
Department of Education
University of Chicago
Chicago, Illinois

Limited-English-Proficient Students
Walter Secada
Department of Curriculum and Instruction
University of Wisconsin
Madison, Wisconsin

Mainstreaming
Roxie Smith
Associate Provost
Northwestern University
Evanston, Illinois

Gifted Students
Christine Kuehn Ebert
Associate Professor of Education
University of South Carolina
Columbia, South Carolina

CRITIC READERS

Mary P. Brown
Master Teacher, Math Specialist
Winston-Salem, North Carolina

Joyce Buratti
Hoover School
Oklahoma City, Oklahoma

Bruce C. Burt
East Bradford Elementary School
West Chester, Pennsylvania

Desdra J. Butler
Los Angeles Unified School District
Los Angeles, California

Howard Cohn
Lone Star Elementary School
Jacksonville, Florida

Rachel Carter Cole
Johns Hopkins University
Baltimore, Maryland

Laura Dunn
St. Brendan School
San Francisco, California

Ruth Elliott
Hopkinsville Middle School
Hopkinsville, Kentucky

Herlinda Garza
Zavala Elementary School
Corpus Christi, Texas

Ruth Harbin
Olathe District Schools
Olathe, Kansas

Barbara J. Kane
Bridgewater-Raritan Schools
Bridgewater, New Jersey

Norma P. Lowe
Daniel E. Morgan School
Cleveland, Ohio

Carol Newman
Broward County Schools
Fort Lauderdale, Florida

Clara Parker
Fayette County Public Schools
Lexington, Kentucky

Henry W. Richard
Governor Wolf School
Bethlehem, Pennsylvania

Barbara F. Wallace
The John B. Russwurm School
New York, New York

Acknowledgments appear after the index.

ISBN: 0-673-45525-4

3456789-DR-99989796959493

Contents

xi   **Welcome to *Exploring Mathematics***

Chapter 1 Place Value, Addition, and Subtraction

2	Number-Sense Project Chapter Opener
4	Place Value
6	Comparing and Ordering Whole Numbers
8	Rounding Whole Numbers
10	**Problem Solving:** Using a Problem-Solving Guide
12	Estimating Sums
14	**Activity:** Adding Whole Numbers
16	Mental Math for Addition
18	**Problem Solving:** Give Sensible Answers MIDCHAPTER CHECKUP
20	**Problem-Solving Workshop:** Number-Sense Project, Explore with a Computer, Real-Life Decision Making, Explore as a Team
22	Adding Larger Numbers EXPLORE MATH
24	Estimating Differences
26	Subtracting Whole Numbers
28	Mental Math for Subtraction SKILLS REVIEW
30	Subtracting Larger Numbers EXPLORE MATH
32	**Problem-Solving Strategy:** Write an Equation CHOOSE A STRATEGY
34	Missing Addends
36	Chapter Review
37	Cumulative Skills Review
38	Reteaching
40	More Practice
42	Enrichment: Roman Numerals
43	Chapter Review/Test

Chapter 2 Multiplication

44	Number-Sense Project Chapter Opener
46	**Activity:** Multiples
48	Mental Math for Multiples of 10, 100, and 1,000
50	Multiplying by a One-Digit Number
52	**Problem-Solving Strategy:** Draw a Diagram EXPLORE MATH
54	Multiplyng by a Multiple of 10 or 100 READING MATH
56	Mental Math for Multiplication
58	Choosing a Computation Method MIDCHAPTER CHECKUP
60	**Problem-Solving Workshop:** Number-Sense Project, Explore as a Team, Math-at-Home Activity, Math Laugh
62	Estimating Products SKILLS REVIEW
64	**Problem Solving:** Deciding When an Estimate Is Enough
66	Multiplying by a Two-Digit Number
68	**Problem-Solving Strategy:** Choose an Operation CHOOSE A STRATEGY
70	Multiplying by a Three-Digit Number
72	Chapter Review
73	Cumulative Skills Review
74	Reteaching
76	More Practice
78	Enrichment: Lattice Multiplication
79	Chapter Review/Test

Chapter 3 Measurement and Geometric Figures

80 Number-Sense Project Chapter Opener
82 Customary Units of Length
84 Equal Customary Measures of Length
86 Metric Units of Length
88 Equal Metric Measures of Length
90 Perimeter
MIDCHAPTER CHECKUP
92 **Problem-Solving Workshop:** Number-Sense Project, Explore with a Computer, Real-Life Decision Making, Visual-Thinking Activity
94 Finding Area by Counting Squares
96 **Activity:** Area of Squares and Rectangles
98 **Problem-Solving Strategy:** Make a Table
CHOOSE A STRATEGY

100 Area of Triangles
EXPLORE MATH
102 **Problem Solving:** Use Data From a Picture
SKILLS REVIEW
104 Time
106 Temperature: Celsius and Fahrenheit
108 Chapter Review
109 Cumulative Skills Review
110 Reteaching
112 More Practice
114 Enrichment: Numbers Greater Than And Less Than Zero
115 Chapter Review/Test

Data File 116
Cumulative Review/Test 118

Chapter 4 Division with One-Digit Divisors

120 Number-Sense Project Chapter Opener
122 Dividing Whole Numbers
124 **Problem-Solving Strategy:** Try and Check
CHOOSE A STRATEGY
126 Mental Math and Estimating Quotients
MIDCHAPTER CHECKUP
128 **Problem-Solving Workshop:** Number-Sense Project, Explore with a Computer, Explore as a Team
130 Dividing Larger Numbers
132 Zeros in the Quotient
134 Finding Averages
EXPLORE MATH

136 **Problem-Solving Strategy:** Write an Equation
SKILLS REVIEW
138 **Activity:** Missing Factors
140 Chapter Review
141 Cumulative Skills Review
142 Reteaching
144 More Practice
146 Enrichment: Short Division
147 Chapter Review/Test

Chapter 5   Division with Two-Digit Divisors

148 Number-Sense Project Chapter Opener

150 Mental Math for Division

152 Estimating Quotients
READING MATH

154 **Activity:** One-Digit Quotients

156 Adjusting the Quotient

158 Using Rounded Divisors
MIDCHAPTER CHECKUP

160 **Problem-Solving Workshop:**
Number-Sense Project, Real-Life
Decision Making, Visual-Thinking Activity,
Math-at-Home Activity, Math Laugh

162 Two-Digit Quotients
EXPLORE MATH

164 **Problem Solving:** Interpret the
Remainder
CHOOSE A STRATEGY

166 Three-Digit Quotients
SKILLS REVIEW

168 Zeros in the Quotient

170 **Problem-Solving Strategy:**
Choose an Operation
CHOOSE A STRATEGY

172 Chapter Review

173 Cumulative Skills Review

174 Reteaching

176 More Practice

178 Enrichment: Divisibility Rules

179 Chapter Review/Test

Chapter 6   Geometric Solids and Measurements

180 Number-Sense Project Chapter Opener

182 **Activity:** Investigating Solid Shapes

184 Finding Volume by Counting Cubes

186 Volume

188 Customary Units of Capacity

190 Metric Units of Capacity
MIDCHAPTER CHECKUP

192 **Problem-Solving Workshop:**
Number-Sense Project, Explore as a
Team, Math-at-Home Activity

194 Customary Units of Weight

196 Metric Units of Mass
SKILLS REVIEW

198 **Problem-Solving Strategy:**
Try and Check

200 Computing with Customary Measures
EXPLORE MATH

202 **Problem Solving:**
Use Data From a Table
CHOOSE A STRATEGY

204 Chapter Review

205 Cumulative Skills Review

206 Reteaching

208 More Practice

210 Enrichment: Polyominoes

211 Chapter Review/Test

Chapter 7 Addition and Subtraction of Decimals

212 Number-Sense Project Chapter Opener

214 Tenths and Hundredths

216 Activity: Thousandths

218 Place Value
EXPLORE MATH

220 Comparing and Ordering Decimals
MIDCHAPTER CHECKUP

222 Problem-Solving Workshop:
Number-Sense Project, Explore with a
Computer, Explore as a Team

224 Problem-Solving Strategy: Use
Logical Reasoning

226 Rounding Decimals

228 Estimating Sums and Differences
SKILLS REVIEW

230 Problem Solving: Too Much or Too
Little Information
CHOOSE A STRATEGY

232 Adding Decimals

234 Subtracting Decimals

236 Chapter Review

237 Cumulative Skills Review

238 Reteaching

240 More Practice

242 Enrichment: Prime and Composite
Numbers

243 Chapter Review/Test

Data File 244

Cumulative Review/Test 246

Chapter 8 Multiplication of Decimals

248 Number-Sense Project Chapter Opener

250 Extending Place Value

252 Activity: Multiplying a Decimal by a
Whole Number
SKILLS REVIEW

256 Problem-Solving Strategy: Choose
an Operation
CHOOSE A STRATEGY

258 Mental Math for Multiplying by 10, 100,
or 1,000

260 Estimating Products
MIDCHAPTER CHECKUP

262 Problem-Solving Workshop:
Number-Sense Project, Explore with a
Computer, Real-Life Decision Making

264 Multiplying by a Decimal

266 Multiplying Decimals: Zeros in the
Product
EXPLORE MATH

268 Activity: Exploring Division of Decimals

270 Problem Solving: Multiple-Step
Problems
CHOOSE A STRATEGY

272 Chapter Review

273 Cumulative Skills Review

274 Reteaching

276 More Practice

278 Enrichment: Equal Metric Measures

279 Chapter Review/Test

Chapter Patterns and Coordinate Graphing

280 Number-Sense Project Chapter Opener

282 Patterns
SKILLS REVIEW

284 **Activity:** Number Patterns

286 Number Relationships
EXPLORE MATH

288 **Problem-Solving Strategy:** Find a Pattern
MIDCHAPTER CHECKUP

290 **Problem-Solving Workshop:** Number-Sense Project, Explore with a Computer, Explore as a Team, Math-at-Home Activity

292 Locating Points with Ordered Pairs

294 **Problem Solving:** Use Data from a Graph
CHOOSE A STRATEGY

296 Number Relationships and Ordered Pairs
READING MATH

298 Chapter Review

299 Cumulative Skills Review

300 Reteaching

302 More Practice

304 Enrichment: Prime Factorization

305 Chapter Review/Test

Chapter 10 Fraction Concepts

306 Number-Sense Project Chapter Opener

308 Fractions

310 Equal Fractions

312 Fractions in Lowest Terms
EXPLORE MATH

314 Mixed Numbers
SKILLS REVIEW

316 Improper Fractions, Quotients, and Mixed Numbers
MIDCHAPTER CHECKUP

318 **Problem-Solving Workshop:** Number-Sense Project, Explore with a Computer, Real-Life Decision Making, Explore as a Team

320 Fractions and Estimation
READING MATH

322 **Problem-Solving Strategy:** Work Backward
CHOOSE A STRATEGY

324 **Activity:** Finding the Least Common Denominator

326 Comparing and Ordering Fractions

328 Fractions and Decimals

330 **Problem Solving:** Interpret the Remainder
CHOOSE A STRATEGY

332 Chapter Review

333 Cumulative Skills Review

334 Reteaching

336 More Practice

338 Enrichment: Terminating and Repeating Decimals

339 Chapter Review/Test

Chapter 11 Exploring Addition and Subtraction of Fractions

340 Number-Sense Project Chapter Opener
342 Adding Fractions: Same Denominator
344 Subtracting Fractions: Same Denominator
346 Adding and Subtracting Mixed Numbers: Same Denominator
348 Adding Mixed Numbers: Renaming Sums
350 Subtracting from a Whole Number
352 Subtracting Mixed Numbers with Renaming
MIDCHAPTER CHECKUP
354 Problem-Solving Workshop: Number-Sense Project, Explore with a Computer, Explore as a Team
356 Adding and Subtracting Fractions: Related Denominators
358 Problem Solving: Use Alternate Strategies
CHOOSE A STRATEGY

360 Activity: Adding Fractions: Different Denominators
EXPLORE MATH
364 Subtracting Fractions: Different Denominators
SKILLS REVIEW
366 Adding Mixed Numbers: Different Denominators
368 Subtracting Mixed Numbers: Different Denominators
370 Problem-Solving Strategy: Solve a Simpler Problem
CHOOSE A STRATEGY

372 Chapter Review
373 Cumulative Skills Review
374 Reteaching
376 More Practice
378 Enrichment: Betweenness for Fractions
379 Chapter Review/Test

Data File 380
Cumulative Review/Test 382

Chapter 12 Exploring Multiplication of Fractions

384 Number-Sense Project Chapter Opener
386 Using Pictures to Multiply Fractions
388 Multiplying Fractions
SKILLS REVIEW
390 Activity: Multiplying Fractions and Whole Numbers
MIDCHAPTER CHECKUP
394 Problem-Solving Workshop: Number-Sense Project, Real-Life Decision Making, Critical-Thinking Activity, Math-at-Home Activity
396 Mixed Numbers as Improper Fractions
398 Multiplying Mixed Numbers
EXPLORE MATH
400 Problem Solving: Use Data from a Table
CHOOSE A STRATEGY

402 Exploring Division by Fractions
404 Problem-Solving Strategy: Choose an Operation
CHOOSE A STRATEGY

406 Chapter Review
407 Cumulative Skills Review
408 Reteaching
410 More Practice
412 Enrichment: Shortcut in Multiplying Fractions
413 Chapter Review/Test

Chapter **13** Statistics, Graphing, and Probability

414 Number-Sense Project Chapter Opener

416 **Problem Solving:** Collecting Data
CHOOSE A STRATEGY

418 Organizing Data
SKILLS REVIEW

422 **Activity:** Making a Broken-Line Graph

424 Reading and Interpreting a Line Graph

426 **Activity:** Making a Line Graph
MIDCHAPTER CHECKUP

428 **Problem-Solving Workshop:**
Number-Sense Project, Explore with a
Computer, Real-Life Decision Making,
Math-at-Home Activity

430 **Problem-Solving Strategy:**
Make a Graph
CHOOSE A STRATEGY

432 Circle Graphs
SKILLS REVIEW

434 Line Plots in Statistics

436 Outcomes

438 **Activity:** Experiments
EXPLORE MATH

440 Fractions and Probability

442 Chapter Review

443 Cumulative Skills Review

444 Reteaching

446 More Practice

448 Enrichment: Order of Operations

449 Chapter Review/Test

Chapter **14** Geometry

450 Number-Sense Project Chapter Opener

452 Solid Shapes
SKILLS REVIEW

456 Polygons

458 Basic Geometric Ideas

460 **Activity:** Triangles

462 Angles

464 Using a Protractor
EXPLORE MATH
MIDCHAPTER CHECKUP

468 **Problem-Solving Workshop:**
Number-Sense Project, Explore with a
Computer, Explore as a Team, Math-
at-Home Activity, Math Laugh

470 Quadrilaterals

472 **Activity:** Circles

474 Circumference

476 Congruent Figures

478 **Problem-Solving Strategy:** Draw
a Diagram

480 Symmetry

482 Similar Figures
READING MATH

484 **Problem Solving:** Find a Pattern
CHOOSE A STRATEGY

486 Chapter Review

487 Cumulative Skills Review

488 Reteaching

490 More Practice

492 Enrichment: Surface Area

493 Chapter Review/Test

Chapter 15 Ratio, Proportion, and Percent

494 Number-Sense Project Chapter Opener
496 Meaning of Ratio
498 **Activity:** Equal Ratios
500 Finding Equal Ratios
SKILLS REVIEW
502 Proportions
504 **Problem-Solving Strategy:** Write an Equation
506 **Problem-Solving Workshop:** Number-Sense Project, Explore with a Computer, Real-Life Decision Making, Explore as a team, Visual-Thinking Activity
508 **Activity:** Ratios and Percents
MIDCHAPTER CHECKUP
510 Percents and Fractions
EXPLORE MATH

512 Percents and Decimals
514 Finding a Percent of a Number
READING MATH
516 Estimating a Percent of a Number
EXPLORE MATH
518 **Problem Solving:** Too Much or Too Little Information
CHOOSE A STRATEGY

520 Chapter Review
521 Cumulative Skills Review
522 Reteaching
524 More Practice

526 Enrichment: Making a Circle Graph
527 Chapter Review/Test

Data File 528
Cumulative Review/Test 530

Review
532 Whole Numbers Through Hundred-Thousands
533 Comparing and Ordering Numbers
534 Addition and Subtraction Basic Facts
535 Adding and Subtracting Money
536 Addition and Subtraction Families of Facts
537 Multiplication Basic Facts
538 Measuring in Inches
539 Measuring in Centimeters
540 Division Basic Facts
541 Multiplication and Division Families of Facts
542 Meaning of Equal Fractions
543 Pictographs
544 Bar Graphs
545 Broken-Line Graphs

Independent Study Handbook
546 How to Use a Calculator
548 Problem-Solving Help File
550 Mental Math Strategies
552 Estimation Strategies
554 Math Study Skills
556 Working in Groups
557 Tables
558 Glossary
552 Index

WELCOME TO
EXPLORING
MATHEMATICS

Mathematics is valuable and interesting. The next ten pages describe some of the ways your book will help you explore and discover more of the wonders of mathematics.

Your book will help you build your
Math Power

Build your math power by doing
Problem Solving and Critical Thinking

You'll need to use your math to solve problems all your life. So, as you solve problems in your book, you will do more than find answers. You will also learn how to think mathematically.

In Chapter 1, tell the page numbers where you first find these.

1 "Problem-Solving Guide"
- Understand
- Plan and Solve
- Look Back

2 "Tips for Problem Solvers"

3 An exercise called "Critical Thinking"

Build your math power by looking for
Connections

Your book will help you explore connections between mathematics, the real world, and other school subjects. Multicultural connections show the part mathematics plays in many cultures and societies.

4 On what page does "Multicultural Connection" first appear at the top of the page?

5 On page 31, find a problem that involves a consumer decision.

Build your math power by working on
Number Sense and Using Data

1 Find a chapter that begins with a Number-Sense Project about kites of different shapes. Then find where this project is continued. (Hint: Find the Problem-Solving Workshop within the chapter.) On what page is the project continued?

2 On page 12, Example A estimates the sum by using what estimation strategy?

3 On what page is the Data File that you'll use with Exercise 35 on page 72?

Scott, Foresman
GRAPHING and
PROBABILITY
WORKSHOP

Press Return.

Build your math power by using
Calculators and Computers

4 On page 250, what math topic does a calculator help you learn?

5 On page 319, what math topic does a computer help you learn?

6 What pages in the Independent Study Handbook explain how to use a calculator?

7 Which exercises on page 59 ask you to tell whether or not you would use a calculator?

Use your book to help you

Do Your Best

To do your best,
Expect to Succeed

When you want to learn something, it helps to believe in yourself. Whether you are learning a sport, a musical instrument, or mathematics, a positive attitude can make a big difference.

To do your best,
Build Your Understanding

When you understand what you're doing, you do it better and remember it longer. So it pays to study the "Build Understanding" part of the lessons.

1 On page 24, why is it easy to see what new math word is being taught?

To do your best, learn ways to do

Independent Study

One of the most important things you can learn from a math book is how to learn math even when a teacher is not there to help.

2 On page 7, look to the right of the words "Check Understanding." On what page can you find another example for that lesson?

3 On page 7, look to the right of the word "Practice." On what page can you find more practice for that lesson?

4 There is an Independent Study Handbook in the back of your book. On what page does the "Math Study Skills" section begin?

5 Name the first and last words defined in the glossary on page 559.

Your book will help you experience

Active Learning

You'll learn math by doing
Math Activities

Activities help you understand math. Some activities use materials that help you show numbers, measure objects, do experiments, explore shapes, or solve problems.

1 What materials are used in the activity on page 46?

2 Use your "Math Sketcher" or a ruler to draw pictures that show $\frac{1}{2}$ of three shapes.

Doing math includes
Reading, Writing, Talking, Listening

Reading, writing, talking, and listening in math class will help you think mathematically.

3 In Chapter 1, tell the page number where these first occur.

"Talk About Math"

"Write About Math"

A good way to learn is by
Working in Groups

In real life and in math class, people can often solve problems better by working together.

4 How many students should work together in a group to do the "Area of Squares and Rectangles" activity on page 96?

5 In the "Explore As a Team" on page 20, what is the "Tip for Working Together"?

To have a math adventure, catch the spirit of
Exploration

Be a Math Explorer and discover new things. Look for patterns, check out your hunches, and try different approaches to problems.

6 What lesson in Chapter 9 explores number patterns by folding paper and drawing steps?

7 In the "Explore Math" on page 23, what are you asked to do in Problems 20–24?

A key ingredient to learning math is
Enjoying Math

Your book will help you
Enjoy Math at School

The explorations in your book will help you discover and enjoy the wonders of mathematics.

1 In Chapter 3, what page asks you to explore the area of squares and rectangles by counting squares?

2 Use a sheet of grid paper. See how many different figures you can cut out having exactly 5 squares.

To make math a part of your life

Enjoy Math at Home

Outside of school, share math ideas with others and continue to explore math your whole life.

3 In the Math-at-Home activity on page 61, what type of activity is suggested?

4 What is the name of the family game suggested in the Problem-Solving Workshop in Chapter 9?

5 Play this Estimation game with someone at home. Use a bag full of items such as peanuts, beans, bottlecaps, or pennies. Each player guesses how many items will fit in a spoon. The player with the closest estimate scores 1 point. Repeat this estimation activity with other containers, such as a jar lid, a cup, a saucer, a handful. The player with the most points wins.

Place Value, Addition, and Subtraction

1

Did You Know: The United States is made up of people from many cultures. In 1910, about 10 of every 1,000 Americans were born in a different country. In 1980, about 2 of every 1,000 Americans were born in a different country. In 1989, about 4 of every 1,000 Americans were born in a different country.

Number-Sense Project

Estimate
If you ask 5 older people to estimate the population of your state, what do you think will be the greatest estimate?

Gather Data
Ask 5 older people to estimate the population of your state. Record their estimates.

Analyze and Report
List the estimates in order from greatest to least. Write a sentence comparing your prediction to the greatest estimate you recorded.

Place Value

Build Understanding

A. In 1986, the Internal Revenue Service collected $782,251,812,000 in taxes. The commas separate this number into *periods.*

Taxes Collected by IRS

Year	Amount
1984	$680,475,229,000
1985	$742,871,541,000
1986	$782,251,812,000
1987	$886,290,590,000

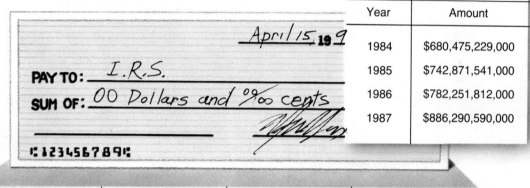

billions period			millions period			thousands period			ones period		
hundred-billions	ten-billions	billions	hundred-millions	ten-millions	millions	hundred-thousands	ten-thousands	thousands	hundreds	tens	ones
7	8	2	2	5	1	8	1	2	0	0	0

782,251,812,000

782 billion, 251 million, 812 thousand

seven hundred eighty-two billion, two hundred fifty-one million, eight hundred twelve thousand

B. *Standard form*
108,507

Expanded form
100,000 + 8,000 + 500 + 7

■ **Talk About Math**   Read aloud each of the numbers in the table. Why is it necessary to include the zeros when you write these numbers?

Check Understanding

For another example, see Set A, pages 38–39.

1. Tell what the 6 means in 168,475,043.

2. Write 5,403,008,925 in words.

3. Write 92 million, 48 thousand, 28 in standard form.

Practice

For More Practice, see Set A, pages 40–41.

Tell which digits are in the millions period in each number.

4. 843,909,002 **5.** 52,555,821,905 **6.** 80,752,224 **7.** 4,254,896

8. 71,893,784 **9.** 7,587,321 **10.** 9,584,717 **11.** 43,984,111,301

Tell what the 8 in each number means.

12. 5,790,823 **13.** 45,678,421 **14.** 3,845,241 **15.** 8,000,657,221

16. 4,927,683 **17.** 1,931,098 **18.** 84,725,042 **19.** 7,891,523,446

Write each number in words.

20. 6,009 **21.** 105,320 **22.** 40,600,709

23. 3,051,003 **24.** 452,005,020 **25.** 100,000,000,000

Write in standard form. **Remember** to use commas where needed.

26. 5 thousand, 243 **27.** 52 million, 523 thousand, 342

28. 800,000 + 30,000 + 50 + 9 **29.** 3,000,000 + 8,000 + 400 + 9

Write each number in expanded form.

30. 840,005 **31.** 30,907,030 **32.** 48,009,700,820 **33.** 5,002,050,600

34. 705,080 **35.** 67,008,029 **36.** 467,089,006 **37.** 7,302,008,019

Problem Solving

Solve each problem.

38. Use the table at the top of page 4. If $100 billion more was collected in 1988 than 1987, what was the total for 1988?

39. What is the largest 6-digit number? the smallest 6-digit number? Find the difference between the numbers.

40. **Critical Thinking** My thousands digit is twice my hundreds digit. The sum of my tens and ones digit is my thousands digit. My hundreds digit is 2 more than my tens digit. My tens digit is greater than 1 and less than 3. What 4-digit number am I?

Comparing and Ordering Whole Numbers

Build Understanding

A. Which park is larger, Katmai or Glacier Bay?

Compare 3,716,000 and 3,225,284.

What do you notice about the digits in the millions place? What do you notice about the digits in the hundred-thousands place?

same

3,716,000 ⠿ 3,225,284

7 hundred-thousands is more than 2 hundred-thousands.

3,716,000 > 3,225,284

> means "is greater than."
< means "is less than."

Katmai National Park is larger than Glacier Bay National Park.

Alaska is the largest state in the United States.

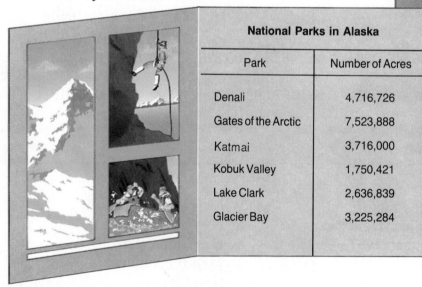

National Parks in Alaska

Park	Number of Acres
Denali	4,716,726
Gates of the Arctic	7,523,888
Katmai	3,716,000
Kobuk Valley	1,750,421
Lake Clark	2,636,839
Glacier Bay	3,225,284

B. List the numbers 52,384, 52,525, and 50,981 in order from least to greatest.

50,981   52,384   52,525

50,981 < 52,384
52,384 < 52,525

■ **Talk About Math** Discuss ways to help you remember which symbol means "is greater than" and which symbol means "is less than."

Check Understanding

For another example, see Set B, pages 38–39.

Compare these numbers. Use >, <, or =.

1. 589 ⬚ 582   **2.** 3,765 ⬚ 3,981   **3.** 4,089 ⬚ 4,809   **4.** 61,020 ⬚ 61,020

Practice

For More Practice, see Set B, pages 40–41.

Compare these numbers. Use >, <, or =.

5. 754 ⬚ 745

6. 607 ⬚ 760

7. 5,891 ⬚ 6,857

8. 7,942 ⬚ 7,942

9. 38,924 ⬚ 38,752

10. 59,387 ⬚ 59,984

11. 380,521 ⬚ 392,521

12. 30,210 ⬚ 30,210

13. 450,369 ⬚ 540,369

List the numbers in order from least to greatest.

14. 785   724   758

15. 983   872   827

16. 207   270   200

17. 8,457   8,472   7,484

18. 3,045   3,542   3,425

19. 8,542   8,540   85,420

20. 35,426   35,624   35,246

21. 72,584   72,589   72,857

22. 53,002   5,302   53,302

23. 980,651   908,561   980,165

Problem Solving

Use the table at the beginning of the lesson.

24. Which park is the largest? How can you tell?

25. Which park is the smallest? Explain how you know.

26. List the parks in order from the largest to the smallest.

27. 🖩 **Calculator**   Find the total number of acres in the Alaskan parks.

28. Bryce Canyon in Utah is 35,835 acres. Is Bryce Canyon larger or smaller than any of the parks in Alaska? Is the difference more or less than 1 million acres?

Rounding Whole Numbers

Build Understanding

A. American Indians used baskets to carry food, store water, play games, and carry children. Each tribe had its own design and style of basket making. A book about Indian baskets pictured 324 different types of baskets. To the nearest hundred, how many baskets were shown?

324 is between 300 and 400, but it is closer to 300.

To the nearest hundred, 300 baskets were pictured in the book.

The Cherokee used dye from walnuts and bloodroot to color their baskets.

B. Round each number to the nearest thousand.
18,458   18,925   18,512

Each number is between 18,000 and 19,000.

What digit can help you round to the nearest thousand?

18,458	**18,925**	**18,512**
The hundreds digit is less than 5. The thousands digit stays the same.	The hundreds digit is greater than 5. Add 1 to the thousands digit.	The hundreds digit is 5. Add 1 to the thousands digit.
18,000	**19,000**	**19,000**

■ **Talk About Math** Explain how to round 2,500 to the nearest thousand.

Check Understanding

For another example, see Set C, pages 38–39.

1. The digit in the ___?___ place helps to round to the nearest hundred.

2. To the nearest ___?___, 48,215 rounds to 50,000.

Round 83,852 to the nearest

3. ten-thousand.   4. thousand.   5. hundred.   6. ten.

Practice

For More Practice, see Set C, pages 40–41.

Round to the nearest ten.

7. 56   **8.** 73   **9.** 185   **10.** 398   **11.** 5,142   **12.** 3,778

13. 359   **14.** 1,077   **15.** 456   **16.** 7,238   **17.** 4,621   **18.** 8,342

Round to the nearest hundred.

19. 136   **20.** 350   **21.** 483   **22.** 1,291   **23.** 4,549   **24.** 4,550

25. 827   **26.** 1,293   **27.** 491   **28.** 6,099   **29.** 2,249   **30.** 6,352

Round to the nearest thousand.

31. 743   **32.** 5,789   **33.** 7,062   **34.** 524   **35.** 12,382   **36.** 71,500

Round to the nearest ten-thousand.

37. 8,875   **38.** 37,951   **39.** 78,928   **40.** 45,000   **41.** 9,842

Problem Solving

Solve each problem.

42. Cherokee women weave split cane around 16 ribs to make a small basket. Round this number to the nearest ten.

43. There were 586 tribal groups listed in a book of American Indians. Round this number to the nearest ten, hundred, and thousand.

44. According to an 1835 United States census, there were 16,542 Cherokees living east of the Mississippi River. Round this number to the nearest thousand.

A woman from the Oconaluftee Indian Village in North Carolina uses 15 splints for the base of her basket.

45. Critical Thinking Write a number with a 5 in the tens place that rounds to 8,000 when rounded to the nearest hundred.

9

Using a Problem-Solving Guide

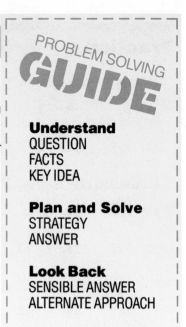

Understand
QUESTION
FACTS
KEY IDEA

Plan and Solve
STRATEGY
ANSWER

Look Back
SENSIBLE ANSWER
ALTERNATE APPROACH

Build Understanding

Solving a problem is like taking a journey. There may be more than one road that leads to an answer. Some roads turn out to be dead ends. Sometimes you need to turn back and start over. The Problem-Solving Guide is like a map that can help you find your way.

The Silver Boot Award is given to campers who hike 250 miles in a month. Jim has hiked 140 miles so far this month. How many more miles does he need to hike to earn a Silver Boot?

Understand

QUESTION
What are you asked to find?

FACTS
What facts are given?

KEY IDEA
How are the facts
and question related?

Plan and Solve

STRATEGY
What can you do to solve
the problem?

ANSWER
Give the answer in a sentence.

Look Back

SENSIBLE ANSWER
Did you check your work?

ALTERNATE APPROACH
Is there another way to get
the same answer?

Understand

QUESTION How many more miles does Jim have to hike?

FACTS Jim has hiked 140 miles. He has to hike a total of 250 miles.

KEY IDEA One part of the 250 miles is 140 miles. Find the other part.

Plan and Solve

STRATEGY Subtract to find the number of miles Jim has to hike.

$$\begin{array}{r} 250 \\ -140 \\ \hline 110 \end{array}$$

ANSWER Jim needs to hike 110 miles more.

Look Back

SENSIBLE ANSWER Add 110 to the number of miles Jim has already hiked. $140 + 110 = 250$. The answer checks.

■ **Talk About Math** Can you think of a different way to solve the problem?

Check Understanding

1. What are the three steps of the Problem-Solving Guide?

Answer each exercise about the problem at the right.

2. What are you asked to find?

3. What label will you use for the answer to show what the number represents?

> On a hiking trip, Jim and his two friends hiked 15 miles the first day, 10 miles the second day, and 4 miles the third day. How much farther did they hike on the first day than on the second day?

Practice

Answer each exercise about the problem at the right.

4. What facts are given?

5. What facts are not needed to solve the problem?

6. Rewrite the problem in your own words.

7. The answer is 38. Give this answer in a sentence.

8. Complete this sentence. "I know that the answer to Exercise 7 makes sense for this problem because . . . ."

> A canteen costs $15. A backpack costs $23. Hiking boots cost $65. How much will it cost for Leon to buy a canteen and a backpack?

Solve each problem. Use the Problem-Solving Guide to help you.

9. Chuck bought lunches for a one-day hike along the Delaware River. Each lunch cost $4. What is the total cost of lunch for 21 hikers?

10. The total distance of a three-day hike in the Pocono Mountains is 75 miles. What would be the average number of miles hiked per day?

Estimating Sums

Build Understanding

Tumi needs to order name tags for two workshops. She has reservations of 3,168 for Saturday and 2,764 for Sunday. Name tags come in packs of 1,000. How many packs should she order?

Since an exact total is not needed, use an estimation strategy to find an estimate.

A. Estimate by *finding a range.*

Round down:
$$3{,}168 + 2{,}794$$
$$\downarrow \qquad \downarrow$$
$$3{,}000 + 2{,}000 = 5{,}000$$

Round up:
$$3{,}168 + 2{,}794$$
$$\downarrow \qquad \downarrow$$
$$4{,}000 + 3{,}000 = 7{,}000$$

The actual number of tags needed will be between 5,000 and 7,000.

C. Estimate $48 + 47$ by *comparing to a reference point.*

Each addend is less than 50. The sum must be less than $50 + 50$ or 100.

B. Estimate by *rounding* both addends to the same place and add.

Round to the nearest thousand:
$$3{,}168 + 2{,}764$$
$$\downarrow \qquad \downarrow$$
$$3{,}000 + 3{,}000 = 6{,}000$$

She will need about 6,000 tags.

Gayle Tumi

■ **Talk About Math** Suppose you have estimated the sum of two numbers. What can you say about the actual sum if both numbers were rounded down? If both numbers were rounded up?

Check Understanding

For another example, see Set D, pages 38–39.

1. Estimate $2{,}859 + 6{,}051$ by finding a range.   4,000

2. Estimate $7{,}654 + 1{,}821$ by rounding to the same place.   10,000

Practice

For More Practice, see Set D, pages 40–41.

Estimate each sum. Tell which strategy you used.

3. 59 + 58   **4.** 498 + 391   **5.** 5,852 + 6,071   **6.** 3,825 + 3,157

7. 37 + 41   **8.** 689 + 193   **9.** 3,028 + 2,971   **10.** 2,941 + 4,708

11. 18 + 79   **12.** 97 + 596   **13.** 3,211 + 5,902   **14.** 491 + 486

15. 29 + 32 + 31   **16.** 298 + 342 + 687   **17.** 513 + 225 + 401

Choose the best estimate for each sum.

18. 489 + 312

   8,000   800   700

19. 322 + 287 + 315

   9,000   900   800

20. 386 + 294

   500   600   700

21. 46 + 44 + 47 + 49

   2,000   20   200

22. 379 + 423

   8,000   800   700

23. 189 + 176

   200   400   500

24. 3,759 + 3,549

   6,000   8,000   600

25. 203 + 192 + 219 + 197

   200   2,000   800

26. 578 + 192

   800   600   700

Mixed Practice

Round 46,259 to the nearest

27. ten-thousand.   **28.** thousand.   **29.** hundred.   **30.** ten.

List the numbers in order from least to greatest.

31. 609   960   690   **32.** 4,003   3,004   3,040   **33.** 709   907   870

Problem Solving

Solve each problem.

34. Jack said that the actual sum for 577 + 483 is more than 900 but less than 1,100. Do you agree? Which strategy did he use?

35. Sally agreed with Jack but said that the actual sum is closer to 1,100. What strategy did she use?

36. Benita said that the sum of 893 and 768 is less than 1,500. Do you agree? Explain why or why not.

37. Andy said that the answer to 29 + 34 + 27 + 32 is close to 150. Is that a reasonable estimate?

Adding Whole Numbers

Build Understanding

The two sentences at the right are alike in some way. How are they alike?

The letters in each sentence read the same, forward or backward. These are called *palindromes*. Here are some numbers that are palindromes:

323   1,331   265,562

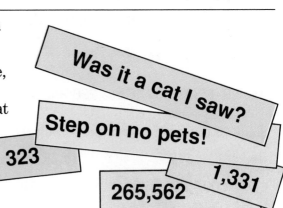

Was it a cat I saw?

Step on no pets!

323

1,331

265,562

Exploring Palindromes
Groups: 3-6 students

A. a. Start with the number 263. Reverse the digits to create another number. Then add.

b. If the sum is not a palindrome, reverse the digits and add again. Continue reversing the digits and adding until the result is a palindrome.

c. How many additions did it take to make a palindrome?

B. a. Make several palindromes. Start with 2- or 3-digit numbers. Keep track of how many additions it took to make each palindrome.

b. Share your results with the others in your group. Who found the palindrome that took the most additions to make?

■ **Write About Math**   Explain how you would use place value to help do the renamings for the addition in Example A.

Check Understanding

For another example, see Set E, pages 38–39.

For each exercise, which statement at the right is needed to find the answer? Then give the sum.

1. 387
 + 531

2. 7,326
 + 813

3. 58
    14
 + 23

4. 9,526
 + 3,471

a. 10 hundreds = 1 thousand
b. 10 tens = 1 hundred
c. 10 thousands = 1 ten-thousand
d. 10 ones = 1 ten

5. **Estimation** Len said that the actual sum for 4,942 + 2,816 was 8,758. Is this answer reasonable? Explain your reasoning.

6. How is finding $25.36 + $51.91 like adding two 4-digit numbers?

Practice

For More Practice, see Set E, pages 40–41.

For each exercise, estimate the sum. Then find the actual sum.

7.   76
 + 23

8.   35
 + 54

9. 236
 + 62

10. 174
 + 413

11. 689
 + 110

12. 53
 + 28

13. 94
 + 25

14. 173
 + 142

15. 628
 + 207

16. 273
 + 84

17. 1,234
 +   354

18. 6,743
 +   239

19. 8,230
 +   294

20. 7,483
 +   508

21. 5,118
 + 3,225

22. 7,356
 + 1,229

23. 6,692
 + 2,213

24. $12.50
 + 31.25

25. $54.25
 + 12.18

26. $20.53
 + 8.91

27. 29 + 32 + 24

28. 52 + 31 + 46

29. 253 + 121 + 316

30. 1,320 + 545 + 324

31. 1,523 + 4,005 + 258

32. 1,009 + 2,110 + 3,237

Problem Solving

33. **Estimation** The sum of which two of these palindromes is closest to 7,000?

 5,665   2,772   1,441

34. **Number Sense** Use each of the digits 1 through 7 once to write a 4-digit number plus a 3-digit number that gives the greatest possible sum.

15

Mental Math for Addition

Build Understanding

Here are some mental math strategies
to use when adding.

A. Look for numbers that you can **_break
apart_** into numbers that are easy to add.

54 + 23 = 77   Think: 23 = 20 + 3
                             54 + 20 = 74
                             74 + 3 = 77

B. Look for **_combinations_** that give
numbers that are easy to add, such as
numbers that add up to 10 or 100.

┌──10──┐
7 + 18 + 3 = 28   (42 + 75) + 25 = 142
                    └──100──┘

You can change the order of the addends
and get the same sum. This is the
commutative property of addition.

┌──10──┐   ┌─10─┐
7 + 18 + 3 = 7 + 3 + 18   Think: 7 + 3 = 10
         = 28   10 + 18 = 28

You also can change the grouping of the
addends and get the same sum. This
is the **_associative property of addition._**

      ┌─100─┐   ┌─100─┐
(42 + 75) + 25 = 42 + (75 + 25)   Think: 75 + 25 = 100
             = 142   42 + 100 = 142

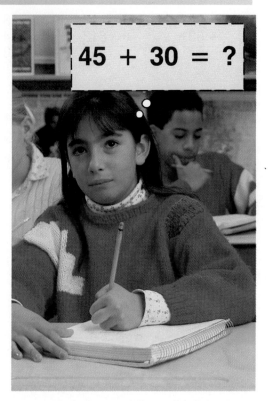

45 + 30 = ?

■ **Write About Math**
Explain how to do
Example A if you
break 54 apart
instead of 23.

Check Understanding

For another example, see Set F, pages 38–39.

1. Find 8 + 5 + 2 + 6 + 4 using
combinations of numbers.

2. Find 154 + 322 by breaking apart
one addend.

16

Practice

For More Practice, see Set F, pages 40–41.

Use mental math to find each sum.
Tell which strategy you used.

3. 76 + 47 + 24   **4.** 103 + 465   **5.** 589 + 301   **6.** 102 + 99

7. 68 + 32   **8.** 45 + 33   **9.** 12 + 85 + 88   **10.** 84 + 58 + 16

11. 526 + 372   **12.** 27 + 48 + 73   **13.** 352 + 234   **14.** 50 + 74 + 50

15. 271 + 328   **16.** 10 + 57 + 90   **17.** 511 + 743   **18.** 20 + 483 + 80

19. Choose two of the exercises above. Explain why
you chose the strategy you used.

Use mental math to choose the correct sum.

20. 9 + 8 + 1 + 12

    20   30   40

21. 27 + 231

    257   258   268

22. 642 + 205

    842   847   805

23. 236 + 52

    238   288   289

24. 64 + 13 + 36

    103   93   113

25. 104 + 93

    194   197   198

26. 83 + 25 + 75

    73   93   183

27. 173 + 124

    97   297   292

28. 25 + 373 + 75

    273   473   474

29. 542 + 237

    777   779   879

30. 25 + 54 + 75

    64   144   154

31. 403 + 763

    1,066   1,163   1,166

Problem Solving

Solve each problem.

32. Mental Math   Luis said he could use mental
math to add 317 + 483. What strategy would you
use? Explain your thinking and give the sum.

33. Estimation   Raul said that the answer to
25 + 446 + 75 is close to 550. Is this a reasonable
estimate? Explain the method Raul used the get
this answer. Find the sum.

Take risks. Try your
hunches. They often work.

Give Sensible Answers

PROBLEM SOLVING
GUIDE

Understand
QUESTION
FACTS
KEY IDEA

Plan and Solve
STRATEGY
ANSWER

Look Back
SENSIBLE ANSWER
ALTERNATE APPROACH

Build Understanding

Sean and his friends went skating at the Central Roller-Rama on Friday. Which choice is the most sensible for the time they skated?

$\frac{1}{4}$ hour $2\frac{1}{2}$ hours   5 hours

Understand   How long did Sean and his friends skate? The group skated on Friday night. The rink is open from 7:30 to 11:00 P.M. Determine which of the choices is the most sensible.

Plan and Solve   The rink is open for only $3\frac{1}{2}$ hours on Friday nights. One fourth hour is only 15 minutes.

Consider the three choices. The only reasonable choice that is less than $3\frac{1}{2}$ hours is $2\frac{1}{2}$ hours.

Sean and his friends skated for $2\frac{1}{2}$ hours.

Look Back   SENSIBLE ANSWER   The other choices are not sensible.

Sean and his friends could not have skated for longer than the rink was open. So 5 hours is not a sensible answer.

Unless there were some kind of emergency that would force the group to leave early, they probably would not skate for only $\frac{1}{4}$ hour. So $\frac{1}{4}$ hour is not a sensible answer.

CENTRAL
ROLLER-RAMA
FRIDAY
7:30 PM – 11:00 PM
SATURDAY & SUNDAY
12 NOON – 11:00 PM

■ **Talk About Math**   How did the context of this problem affect the answer? What could Sean and his friends have done instead of skating so $\frac{1}{4}$ hour would have been the sensible answer?

Check Understanding

1. Choose the most sensible answer. How many people were skating at the rink on Friday night?

   3 people   50 people   700 people

2. Explain why the other two choices are not sensible.

Practice

Choose the most sensible answer. Explain why the other choices are not sensible.

3. Sean rented a pair of skates. How much was the skate rental fee?

   $2 $20 $200

4. What was the temperature in the roller rink?

   20°F   72°F   105°F

5. A Roller-Rama T-shirt costs $5 more than skate pompons. How much do pompons cost?

   $3 $20 $35

6. Sean's brother drove Sean and his friends home from the rink. How many people were in the car?

   1 person   2 people   5 people

Solve each problem.

7. Forty people paid $3.00 each to ride a charter bus to the rink. How much did it cost to charter the bus?

8. For lunch, Lee spent $0.75 for lemonade, $1.50 for pizza and $0.50 for a pretzel. How much did he spend in all?

Midchapter ✓ Checkup

1. What does the 6 mean in 265,291?

2. Use >, <, or =.
   18,429 ▦ 18,249

3. Round 24,581 to the nearest thousand.

4. Use mental math to find 39 + 58.

5. Estimate 8,295 + 357. Then find the actual sum.

6. Liz bought a movie ticket. How much change could she have received from $5? Choose the most sensible answer.
   $8 $4.95 $3

7. If the three choices were not given for Exercise 6, what other fact would you need to know to solve the problem?

Explore as a Team

1. Discuss how you might estimate the number of squares or parts of squares in Drawing A.

   a. You may count only up to 10 squares before you estimate.

   b. Ask yourselves questions like: Does the drawing include more than 10 squares? 20 squares? 30 squares? 100 squares?

2. **Estimate** the number of squares in Drawing A.

3. **Estimate** the number of squares or parts of squares in Drawing B. (You may count up to 25 squares only before you estimate.)

4. What questions did you ask yourselves before making your estimate?

5. Use 1-centimeter-square paper to make a drawing.

6. **Estimate** the number of squares you will include in your drawing. After you have made the drawing, count the actual number of squares. Secretly record the total.

7. **Estimate** the number of squares or parts of squares in your teammates' drawings. After estimating, compare the actual number of squares with your estimates.

Drawing A

Drawing B

TIPS FOR
WORKING TOGETHER

Involve your whole group. Help everyone to participate.

Real-Life Decision Making

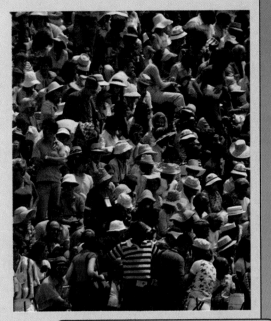

Consider crowds such as these:

a. in a park

b. in the auditorium

c. at recess

d. in a football stadium

1. Discuss situations in which you would estimate the number of people in a crowd. When would you need to know the exact number of people in a crowd?

2. Evaluate how far off your estimate could be if you were writing a newspaper article about a crowd.
10? 25? 200? 1,000? 5,000? 20,000?

Explore with a Computer

Use the *Graphing and Probability Workshop Project* for this activity.

1. Find the differences between the height and reach of the students in your class. As a team, use a tape measure to measure each person's height and reach in inches.

2. At the computer, enter the data into a table.

3. Display the information using the **Bar Graph** option.

4. Compare the results for each student.

Number-Sense Project

Look back at pages 2-3.

1. The actual population in 1900 was approximately 75,995,000. Which estimate in the table is closest?

2. What do you think the actual population of the United States is today?

Estimates of U.S. population in 1900	
1.	1,300,000
2.	500,000,000
3.	10,000,000
4.	2,000,000
5.	25,000,000

3. How could you find the current estimated population of the United States?

21

Adding Larger Numbers

Build Understanding

A. The observation level of Toronto's CN Tower is 1,136 feet above the ground. The tower with its antenna continues upward for another 679 feet. What is the height of the CN Tower?

Find 1,136 + 679.
Estimate: 1,100 + 700 = 1,800

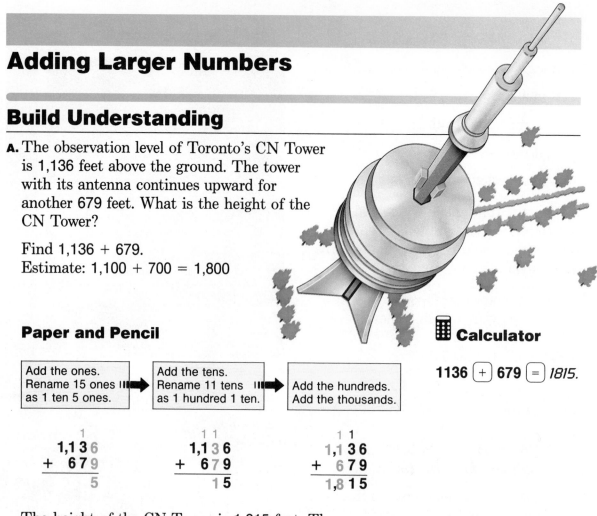

Paper and Pencil

Add the ones. Rename 15 ones as 1 ten 5 ones.	Add the tens. Rename 11 tens as 1 hundred 1 ten.	Add the hundreds. Add the thousands.

$$\begin{array}{r} {\scriptstyle 1} \\ 1,13\,6 \\ +\ \ 67\,9 \\ \hline 5 \end{array}$$

$$\begin{array}{r} {\scriptstyle 1\ 1} \\ 1,1\,3\,6 \\ +\ \ 6\,7\,9 \\ \hline 1\,5 \end{array}$$

$$\begin{array}{r} {\scriptstyle 1\ 1} \\ 1,1\,3\,6 \\ +\ \ 6\,7\,9 \\ \hline 1,8\,1\,5 \end{array}$$

▦ Calculator

1136 ⊕ 679 ⊜ *1815.*

The height of the CN Tower is 1,815 feet. The estimate shows that the answer is reasonable.

B. Estimation Use *front-end digits with adjusting.*

Use front-end digits.

2̲73 + 4̲12 + 1̲48
↓   ↓
2̲00 + 4̲00 + 1̲00 = 700

Then adjust the estimate.
73 + 12 + 48 > 100

The sum is more than 800.

C. Mental Math Use *compensation.*

Change one number to make it easy to add. Then change the other number.

29 + 1 = 30	45 − 1 = 44	30 + 44
29	+ 45	= 74

Change both numbers to make them easy to add. Then change the answer.

98 + 2 = 100	97 + 3 = 100	200 − 5
98	+ 97	= 195

■ **Talk About Math** Explain how you would use mental math to find $3.25 + $2.60 + $4.75 + $1.45.

Check Understanding

For each exercise, estimate the sum. Then give the sum.
Which statements at the right are needed to find the answer?

1. 2,868
   + 2,043

2. 8,237
   + 8,369

3. 824
    341
   + 516

4. 31,328
   + 19,925

a. 10 hundreds = 1 thousand
b. 10 tens = 1 hundred
c. 10 thousands = 1 ten-thousand
d. 10 ones = 1 ten

5. **Mental Math**   Use mental math to find 298 + 327.

Practice

For each exercise, estimate the sum. Then find the actual sum.

6. 4,009
   + 3,171

7. 21,467
   + 6,425

8. 87,027
   + 23,058

9. 41,666
   + 22,335

10. 51,008
    + 27,165

11. 27,463
    + 10,008

12. 14,298
    + 3,506

13. $307.96
    + 408.73

14. $642.54
    +   88.79

15. $142.67
    + 238.54

Mental Math   Find each sum using mental math.

16. 124 + 59

17. 197 + 196

18. $8.65 + $1.35

19. $32.05 + $3.95

Problem Solving

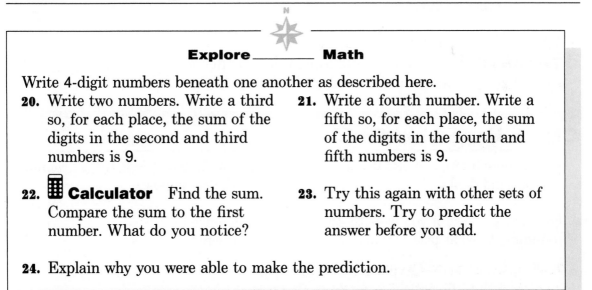

Explore ————— Math

Write 4-digit numbers beneath one another as described here.

20. Write two numbers. Write a third so, for each place, the sum of the digits in the second and third numbers is 9.

21. Write a fourth number. Write a fifth so, for each place, the sum of the digits in the fourth and fifth numbers is 9.

22. ▦ **Calculator** Find the sum. Compare the sum to the first number. What do you notice?

23. Try this again with other sets of numbers. Try to predict the answer before you add.

24. Explain why you were able to make the prediction.

Estimating Differences

Build Understanding

Here are some estimation strategies to use when estimating differences.

A. Estimate 3,217 − 1,229 *using front-end digits.*

3,217 − 1,229
↓   ↓
3,000 − 1,000 = 2,000

The actual difference should be about 2,000.

B. Estimate 693 − 219 by *rounding* both the minuend and subtrahend to the same place.

693 − 219   Round to the
↓   ↓   nearest hundred.
700 − 200 = 500

The actual difference should be about 500.

3,217 minuend
− 1,229 subtrahend
? difference

■ **Talk About Math** Why would using front-end digits not have been a good strategy to use with the numbers in Example B?

Check Understanding

For another example, see Set G, pages 38–39.

1. Estimate 9,581 − 4,623 using front-end digits.

2. Estimate 5,841 − 2,104 by rounding to the same place.

For each exercise, if you were to estimate the difference by rounding, to what place would you round the numbers?

3. 98 − 57   4. 592 − 45   5. 4,730 − 285

Practice

For More Practice, see Set G, pages 40–41.

Estimate each difference. Tell which strategy you used.

6. 82 − 23 **7.** 78 − 49 **8.** 585 − 329 **9.** 717 − 521

10. 73 − 51 **11.** 788 − 408 **12.** 621 − 424 **13.** 813 − 389

14. 6,642 − 2,591 **15.** 8,472 − 5,924 **16.** 5,217 − 1,388 **17.** 7,246 − 984

18. 9,304 − 4,210 **19.** 3,562 − 1,908 **20.** 6,031 − 2,726 **21.** 2,059 − 1,103

Choose the best estimate for each difference.

22. 91 − 32

    30 50 60

23. 87 − 39

    30 50 60

24. 623 − 384

    100 200 300

25. 894 − 321

    400 500 600

26. 7,157 − 4,852

    1,000 2,000 3,000

27. 5,827 − 952

    4,000 5,000 6,000

28. 91 − 68

    20 30 40

29. 798 − 211

    400 500 600

30. 6,928 − 4,219

    1,000 2,000 3,000

31. 794 − 521

    200 300 400

32. 3,216 − 2,111

    1,000 1,500 2,000

33. 7,871 − 3,128

    3,000 4,000 5,000

Problem Solving

Solve each problem.

34. Kazuko said the actual difference between 472 and 295 is close to her estimate of 300. Does this seem reasonable? Explain.

35. Brenda said the actual difference between 4,376 and 2,977 was close to her estimate of 1,000. Do you agree? Explain why or why not.

36. **Critical Thinking** Suppose you estimate a difference where the minuend rounds up and the subtrahend rounds down. Will the actual difference be less than or greater than the estimate? Explain your reasoning.

37. **Use Data** Use the table on page 6 to determine how much larger the park at Lake Clark is than the park at Kobuk Valley.

Subtracting Whole Numbers

Build Understanding

A. Moroccan crafts are known world wide for their beauty and textures. The *Souk* or market, is where many Moroccans shop. Tourists also love to visit the *Souk*.

Slippers, called *babouches,* are worn inside Moroccan homes. Salaama makes *babouches,* and sells them in the *Souk*.

She sold 118 pairs of slippers during the tourist season and only 45 pairs the next month. How many more did she sell during the tourist season?

Find 118 − 45.

Estimate: 120 − 50 = 70

Moroccan *babouches* are displayed in the *Souk*.

Subtract the ones.	Rename 1 hundred. Then there will be 11 tens. Subtract the tens.

$$\begin{array}{r} 118 \\ -\ 45 \\ \hline 3 \end{array} \qquad \begin{array}{r} 0\ 11 \\ \cancel{1}\cancel{1}8 \\ -\ 45 \\ \hline 73 \end{array}$$

Salaama sold 73 more pairs of *babouches* during the tourist season.

B. Mental Math Multiples of 10 and 100 are easy to subtract mentally.

642 − 200 = 442

Think: 6 hundreds − 2 hundreds = 4 hundreds. The numbers in the ones and tens places remain the same.

Talk About Math Explain how you can use addition to check subtraction.

Check Understanding

For each exercise, which statement at the right is needed to find the answer? Then give the difference.

| a. 1 hundred = 10 tens |
| b. 1 ten = 10 ones |
| c. 1 thousand = 10 hundreds |

1. 84
   − 37

2. 529
   − 74

3. 7,062
   − 5,431

4. 8,463
   − 5,431

Practice

For each exercise, estimate the difference. Then find the actual difference. **Remember** to check your work.

5. 87
   − 29

6. 98
   − 32

7. 584
   − 300

8. 607
   − 293

9. 5,735
   − 824

10. 9,704
   − 5,000

11. 5,468
   − 3,124

12. $27.08
   − 14.24

13. $32.58
   − 11.24

14. $154.38
   − 42.75

15. 792 − 400

16. 7,596 − 342

17. 6,270 − 4,155

18. 400 − 32

19. 619 − 42

20. 3,096 − 805

21. 8,621 − 730

22. 37,091 − 129

Mixed Practice Find each answer. **Remember** to watch the signs.

23. 852
   + 183

24. 527
   − 313

25. 2,539
   − 627

26. 7,624
   − 3,483

27. 5,437
   + 5,622

28. 1,023 + 409

29. 8,960 − 598

30. 12,539 + 1,825

31. 9,006 − 2,541

32. $32.59 + $19.62

33. $62.59 − $31.24

34. $31.60 − $20.00

Problem Solving

35. Number Sense Use each of the digits 1 through 7 once to write a 4-digit number minus a 3-digit number that gives the *greatest* possible difference.

36. Critical Thinking The difference of two numbers is 100. The sum is 1,000. What are the numbers?

37. Estimation Does rounding or using front-end digits give a better estimate for Exercise 8? Explain.

38. Estimation Is 2,036 a reasonable difference for 5,827 − 3,791? Explain your reasoning.

Mental Math for Subtraction

Build Understanding

Ellen Logan is the manager of a store that sells party supplies. She often uses mental math when taking inventory.

Here are some mental math strategies to use when subtracting mentally.

A. Look for numbers where you can use *compensation.*

Change one number to make it easy to subtract. Then change the other number.

177 + 2 = 179   98 + 2 = 100   179 − 100

177 − **98** = **79**

Change one number to make it easy to subtract. Then change the answer.

97 + 3 = 100   65 + 3

165 − **97** = **68**

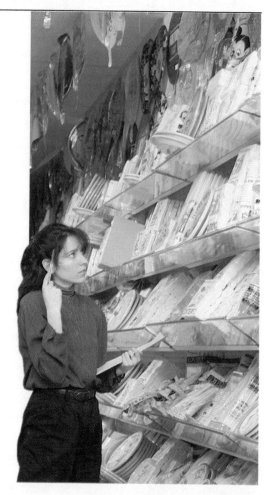

B. Look for numbers that you can **break apart** into numbers that are easy to subtract. This works best when there is no renaming.

67 − **24** = **43**   Think: 20 + 4 = 24
67 − 20 = 47
47 − 4 = 43

■ **Talk About Math** Explain how Ellen could use mental math to find $10.00 − $5.75.

Check Understanding

For another example, see Set H, pages 38–39.

1. Find 94 − 68 using compensation. Explain your thinking.

2. Find 254 − 32 by breaking apart one number.

3. Explain how to use mental math to find $20.00 − $15.99.

4. Explain why you can use mental math to find 359 − 40.

Practice

For More Practice, see Set H, pages 40–41.

Use mental math to find each difference.
Tell which strategy you used.

5. 84 − 40   **6.** 275 − 99   **7.** 872 − 521   **8.** 729 − 300

9. 68 − 32   **10.** 539 − 396   **11.** 786 − 432   **12.** 917 − 299

13. 59 − 24   **14.** 888 − 521   **15.** 852 − 397   **16.** 979 − 748

17. 143 − 96   **18.** 736 − 498   **19.** 978 − 623   **20.** 87 − 32

Mixed Practice   Find each answer.
Remember to watch the signs.

21. 288 − 98   **22.** 286 + 97   **23.** 1,497 − 231   **24.** 7,583 + 398

25. $1.43 − $0.96   **26.** 6,838 + 5,790   **27.** 747 + 242   **28.** 834 − 22

29. 285 − 98   **30.** $7.45 + $12.09   **31.** 893 − 281   **32.** $5.00 − $2.92

Problem Solving

Solve each problem.

33. Ellen counted 185 bags of balloons. Each bag contained either all red or all blue balloons. If there were 100 bags of red balloons, how many bags of blue balloons were there?

34. Ellen found 98 packs of white note pads, and 14 packs of yellow note pads on the shelves. How many packs of note pads were there all together?

35. Ellen knows that 82 + 18 = 100. How will this help her use mental math to give change to a customer who paid for items costing $5.82 with a $10 bill?

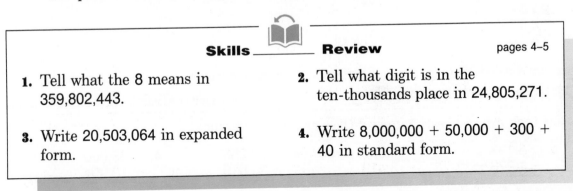

Skills _____ **Review**   pages 4–5

1. Tell what the 8 means in 359,802,443.

2. Tell what digit is in the ten-thousands place in 24,805,271.

3. Write 20,503,064 in expanded form.

4. Write 8,000,000 + 50,000 + 300 + 40 in standard form.

Subtracting Larger Numbers

Build Understanding

A. Giants Stadium seats 76,891 people. In Chicago, Soldier Field seats 65,793 people. How many more fans can watch a football game in Giants Stadium than in Soldier Field?

Find 76,891 − 65,793.

Estimate: 77,000 − 66,000 = 11,000

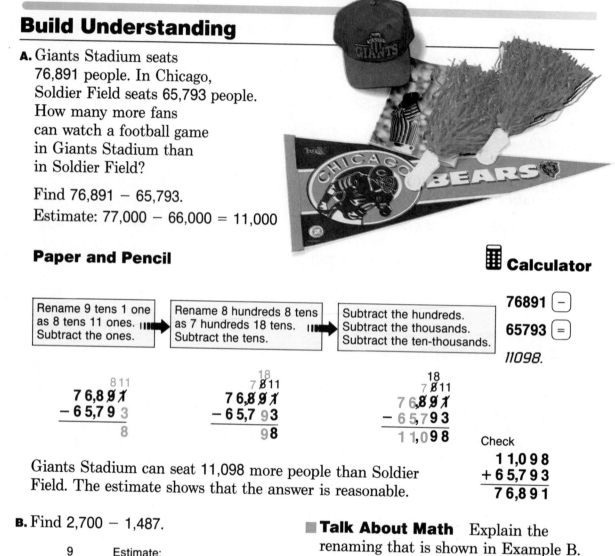

Paper and Pencil

Rename 9 tens 1 one as 8 tens 11 ones. Subtract the ones.	Rename 8 hundreds 8 tens as 7 hundreds 18 tens. Subtract the tens.	Subtract the hundreds. Subtract the thousands. Subtract the ten-thousands.

$$\begin{array}{r} {}^{8\,11} \\ 76{,}89\cancel{1} \\ -\,65{,}79\;3 \\ \hline 8 \end{array}$$

$$\begin{array}{r} {}^{18} \\ {}^{7\,\cancel{8}11} \\ 76{,}\cancel{8}9\cancel{1} \\ -\,65{,}7\;93 \\ \hline 98 \end{array}$$

$$\begin{array}{r} {}^{18} \\ {}^{7\,\cancel{8}11} \\ 7\,6{,}\cancel{8}9\cancel{1} \\ -\,6\,5{,}793 \\ \hline 1\,1{,}098 \end{array}$$

Calculator

76891 ⊖

65793 ⊜

11098.

Giants Stadium can seat 11,098 more people than Soldier Field. The estimate shows that the answer is reasonable.

Check

$$\begin{array}{r} 11{,}098 \\ +\,65{,}793 \\ \hline 76{,}891 \end{array}$$

B. Find 2,700 − 1,487.

$$\begin{array}{r} {}^{9} \\ {}^{6\,\cancel{1}010} \\ 2{,}\cancel{7}\cancel{0}\cancel{0} \\ -\,1{,}487 \\ \hline 1{,}213 \end{array}$$

Estimate:
2,700 − 1,500 = 1,200

■ **Talk About Math** Explain the renaming that is shown in Example B.

Check Understanding

For another example, see Set I, pages 38–39.

For each exercise, estimate and then give the difference.

1. 5,192
  − 1,223

2. 4,037
  − 3,419

3. 70,258
  − 34,619

4. 33,000
  − 19,004

Practice

For More Practice, see Set I, pages 40–41.

For each exercise, estimate and then give the difference.

5. 9,711
− 3,645

6. 38,704
− 9,295

7. 81,008
− 64,029

8. 32,436
− 21,647

9. 54,782
− 26,295

10. 3,692
− 980

11. 6,923
− 5,742

12. 8,008
− 4,340

13. 12,258
− 9,800

14. 7,230
− 5,904

15. 42,601
− 18,407

16. 50,007
− 34,160

17. 60,207
− 24,819

18. 80,059
− 43,962

19. 15,030
− 5,987

Mixed Practice   Find each answer. **Remember** to watch the signs.

20. 92,516
+ 38,745

21. 37,005
− 15,129

22. 12,000
− 7,859

23. 74,612
+ 99,953

24. 95,817
− 87,908

25. 35,797
+ 68,980

26. 12,524
− 5,781

27. 6,610
− 2,389

28. 72,163
+ 49,409

29. 27,005
− 17,971

Problem Solving

Solve the problem.

30. The Ruiz family planned to spend $100 to
see the Giants play football. They spent
$54.75 on tickets, $18.29 on food, and
$17.50 on transportation. Did they have any
money left over? If so, how much?

Explore ———— Math

31. Write a 4-digit number with the
first digit greater than the fourth
and the second digit less than the
third.

32. Reverse the digits to create
another number. Then subtract.

33. Reverse the digits of the
difference. Then add.

34. Try this several times with other
4-digit numbers.

35. Describe the pattern you see in
your answers.

36. For Ex. 31, why can't the first
digit be less than the fourth?

Write an Equation

Build Understanding

The two-day Highland School Health Fair was a big success. On Thursday, 312 people attended the fair. Another 259 people attended on Friday. What was the total attendance at the fair?

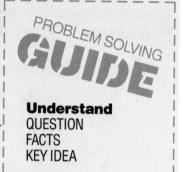

PROBLEM SOLVING GUIDE

Understand
QUESTION
FACTS
KEY IDEA

Plan and Solve
STRATEGY
ANSWER

Look Back
SENSIBLE ANSWER
ALTERNATE APPROACH

Understand The fair lasted two days. There were 312 people on the first day and 259 people on the second day. The total attendance is the sum of the attendance for both days.

Plan and Solve STRATEGY To find the total attendance, add the attendance for each of the two days. An *equation* is a number sentence that can be used to show how the parts of the problem are related. *Write an equation* using t, where t is a *variable* standing for the total attendance. A variable is a letter or symbol that stands for a number. Then solve the equation.

Thursday's attendance		Friday's attendance		Total attendance
312	+	259	=	t

Estimate: $300 + 300 = 600$

Paper and Pencil

$$\begin{array}{r} 312 \\ +259 \\ \hline 571 \end{array} \quad t = 571$$

Calculator

$312 \boxed{+} 259 \boxed{=} 571.$

$t = 571$

ANSWER There were 571 people at the fair.

Look Back The answer is reasonable because the answer is close to the estimate.

■ **Talk About Math** Could you solve the problem using this equation: $259 + 312 = t$? Explain why or why not.

Check Understanding

The planning committee expected 500 people to attend the fair. How many more people attended than were expected?

1. Which equation can you use to solve this problem?

   a. $500 + 571 = n$ **b.** $571 - 500 = n$

2. Solve the equation and give the answer in a sentence.

Practice

Write an equation. Then find the answer.

3. Eye tests were given to 208 people on Thursday. On Friday, 185 people had their eyes tested. How many fewer people had their eyes tested on Friday?

4. The dental display booth had 575 toothbrushes to give as prizes. At the end of the fair, there were 98 toothbrushes left. How many were given away?

5. The heart rate of one fifth grader was 72 beats per minute. After she rode an exercise bike, her rate was 128 beats per minute. How much did her rate increase?

6. The snack booth sold 485 bran muffins. Of these, 248 were sold individually and the rest were sold with fruit salad. How many were sold with fruit salad?

7. During the two days, the snack booth sold 247 glasses of orange juice, 245 glasses of milk, and 108 glasses of grapefruit juice. How many glasses were sold in all?

8. Hearing tests were given to 179 people on Thursday. On Friday, 74 more people were tested than on Thursday. How many people were tested on Friday?

Choose a _____ Strategy

Rainbow Math   The numbers in the red and blue parts of the rainbow count double.

9. What 3 numbers give a total sum of 120?

10. What 5 numbers give a total sum of 122?

11. What 5 numbers give a total sum of 158?

34
26
4
8

A
L
G
E
B
R
A

Missing Addends

Build Understanding

The fourth and fifth graders at Meyer School went to
Orchestra Hall to see a concert. There were 98 fifth graders.
All together there were 173 students on the trip. How many
fourth graders were there?

	Number of fifth graders		Number of fourth graders		Total number of students
Use this equation. How can it be solved?	**98**	+	x	=	**173**
Subtract to find the missing addend.			x	=	173 − 98
			x	=	75

$$\begin{array}{r} 173 \\ -98 \\ \hline 75 \end{array}$$

There were 75 fourth graders.

■ **Write About Math**   You can use families
of facts to help find a missing addend.
Which fact in the family below would help
you find y in $7 + y = 16$?

$7 + y = 16$ $16 - 7 = y$
$y + 7 = 16$ $16 - y = 7$

Write a family of facts for the equation in
the example above.

Check Understanding

For another example, see Set J, pages 38–39.

Find the missing addend. Use families of facts to help.

1. $45 + x = 82$ **2.** $y + 53 = 101$ **3.** $134 = 78 + s$ **4.** $92 = m + 35$

Practice

For More Practice, see Set J, pages 40–41.

Find the missing addend.

5. $25 + w = 45$ **6.** $a + 34 = 68$ **7.** $100 = 14 + b$ **8.** $22 = c + 15$

9. $x + 17 = 45$ **10.** $67 = 41 + r$ **11.** $138 = s + 94$ **12.** $87 + n = 192$

13. $p + 59 = 148$ **14.** $q + 363 = 787$ **15.** $784 = t + 137$ **16.** $517 + u = 638$

17. $56 + f = 3,000$ **18.** $809 = 63 + g$ **19.** $54 + h = 1,098$ **20.** $k + 70 = 2,139$

21. $x + 77 = 321$ **22.** $e + 51 = 450$ **23.** $606 = 280 + t$ **24.** $390 + a = 506$

Calculator Find the missing addend.

25. $2,496 = 712 + z$ **26.** $317 + v = 1,548$ **27.** $918 = 421 + x$

28. $4,002 = y + 1,642$ **29.** $m + 3,165 = 3,916$ **30.** $2,043 + n = 6,571$

31. $q + 38,176 = 67,145$ **32.** $98,176 + r = 142,631$ **33.** $380,162 = s + 145,002$

Problem Solving

Solve each problem.

34. Orchestra Hall seats 2,560 people. It was sold out for this performance. In addition to the 173 students, how many other people were in the audience?

35. The concert tickets and transportation cost $1,384. It was paid out of the $2,000 school activity account. How much was left after this expense?

36. There were 105 orchestra members performing on stage. Later, the chorus performed with the orchestra. Then there were 223 performers on stage. How many people were in the chorus?

37. In the orchestra, the violin players and the 21 players of other stringed instruments make up the 67 members of the string section. How many violin players are there?

38. A student pass to attend 3 concerts costs $15. The ticket cost for one concert is $6.50. Is it cheaper to buy the pass than to buy 3 separate tickets? If so, how much money would a student save? What reasons are there why someone would not want to buy the pass?

Skills Review

Write each number in expanded form.

1. 650,032 **2.** 43,085,070

List the numbers in order from least to greatest.

3. 405   450   400

4. 75,304   75,430   75,043

Round to the nearest hundred.

5. 368   **6.** 2,504   **7.** 6,850

Estimate each sum or difference.
Tell which strategy you used.

8. 87 − 39   **9.** 214 + 485

Estimate. Then find the actual sum or difference.

10. 45   **11.** 775   **12.** 3,725
    + 24   − 85   + 970

13. 68   **14.** 186   **15.** 7,052
    − 39   + 172   − 2,430

16. 34,092   **17.** 86,993
     + 23,041   − 49,234

18. 47,508   **19.** 16,800
     − 4,385   + 7,123

Use mental math to find each sum or difference. Tell which strategy you used.

20. 6 + 18 + 4   **21.** 645 + 221

22. 75 − 42   **23.** 345 − 98

Find the missing addend.

24. $23 + n = 45$ **25.** $158 = 45 + n$

Problem-Solving Review

Solve each problem.

26. In 1790 the population of the United States was 3,929,213. Round the number to the nearest million.

27. How many songs an hour can a radio station play? Which is a reasonable answer? Why?

5   15   35

28. Use the digits, 0, 3, 4 and 7 to write the least number possible.

29. At the first game of a baseball doubleheader, the attendance was 56,221. Before the second game, 1,927 people left. How many fans stayed for the second game?

30. The continental shelf of the Northeast Atlantic Ocean covers 1,162,250 square miles. For the Northwest Atlantic, the area is 486,360 square miles. How much larger is the area for the Northeast Atlantic?

31. Date File Use the map on pages 116–117. Find the difference in height between Longs Peak and Mt. Julian.

32. Make a Data File Use a map of North and South America. Make a list of places that are about 1,000 miles, 2,000 miles, 3,000 miles and so on, up to 10,000 miles away from your town.

Tell what the 5 in each number means.

1. 645,320   **2.** 503,498,000   **3.** 120,058,292   **4.** 85,987,000

Write each number in expanded form.

5. 4,507,200   **6.** 785,040,060   **7.** 500,720   **8.** 99,730,020,000

Compare these numbers. Use >, <, or =.

9. 608 ▒ 680   **10.** 5,756 ▒ 5,756   **11.** 34,249 ▒ 34,421

List the numbers in order from least to greatest.

12. 4,512   4,215   4,152   **13.** 75,329   75,392   753,920

Round 24,536 to the nearest

14. ten-thousand.   **15.** thousand.   **16.** hundred.   **17.** ten.

Estimate each sum or difference. Tell which strategy you used.

18. $49 + 47$ **19.** $788 - 312$ **20.** $521 + 391$ **21.** $8,343 - 3,380$

Estimate. Then find the actual sum or difference.

22.	97 + 22	**23.**	65 − 25	**24.**	752 + 339	**25.**	709 − 488	**26.**	6,109 + 5,980
27.	8,430 − 540	**28.**	12,198 + 3,806	**29.**	3,821 − 1,154	**30.**	32,446 + 55,982	**31.**	51,320 − 29,170
32.	$10.15 + 6.90	**33.**	$72.80 − 9.78	**34.**	$65.50 + 13.85	**35.**	$56.25 − 23.75	**36.**	$402.10 + 207.15

37. $62 + 19 + 38$ **38.** $914 - 395$ **39.** $187 + 204 + 791$

40. $6,420 - 318$ **41.** $3,502 + 482$ **42.** $8,000 - 6,950$

Use mental math to find each sum or difference. Tell which strategy you used.

43. $65 + 23$ **44.** $87 - 35$ **45.** $3 + 76 + 7$ **46.** $545 - 98$

Find the missing addend.

47. $42 + n = 65$ **48.** $n + 18 = 30$ **49.** $125 = n + 35$ **50.** $815 = 343 + n$

Reteaching

Set A   pages 4–5

Billions period			Millions period			Thousands period			Ones period		
hundred-billions	ten-billions	billions	hundred-millions	ten-millions	millions	hundred-thousands	ten-thousands	thousands	hundreds	tens	ones
1	0	6	0	2	5	4	0	0	0	0	0

The number 10,602,540,000 is read ten billion, six hundred two million, five hundred forty thousand.
Remember that the comma separates each group of three digits, or period.

Give the standard form. **Remember** to use zeros as placeholders.

1. 285 million, 806 thousand

2. 9 billion, 3 million, 80 thousand, 912

Set B   pages 6–7

Compare 46,469 and 46,584. The ten-thousands digits and the thousands digits are the same in both numbers. So compare the hundreds.

Since 4 < 5, then 46,469 < 46,584.

Remember that > means greater than and < means less than.
Compare these numbers. Use >, <, or =.

1. 647 ▒ 649   **2.** 48,030 ▒ 48,303

Set C   pages 8–9

Round 14,287 to the nearest thousand. To round to the nearest thousand, look at the hundreds digit. Since 2 is less than 5, the thousands digit stays the same.

So 14,287 rounds to 14,000.

Remember to add 1 to the digit in the place to be rounded if the digit to its right is 5 or more. Round to the nearest thousand.

1. 3,429   **2.** 14,192   **3.** 804

Set D   pages 12–13

Estimate the sum by rounding to the nearest thousand.

$$
\begin{array}{rcl}
4{,}9\,1\,3 & \rightarrow & 5{,}0\,0\,0 \\
+\,7{,}0\,8\,6 & \rightarrow & +\,7{,}0\,0\,0 \\
\hline
 & & 1\,2{,}0\,0\,0
\end{array}
$$

Remember that the digit in the place to be rounded stays the same if the digit to its right is less than 5. Estimate each sum.

1. 6,215 + 5,831   **2.** 7,902 + 7,092

Set E   pages 14–15

Estimate the sum. Find the actual sum.

$$
\begin{array}{rcl r}
 & & & 1 \\
7{,}2\,9\,6 & \rightarrow & 7{,}0\,0\,0 & 7{,}2\,9\,6 \\
+\,2{,}6\,4\,2 & \rightarrow & +\,3{,}0\,0\,0 & +\,2{,}6\,4\,2 \\
\hline
 & & 1\,0{,}0\,0\,0 & 9{,}9\,3\,8
\end{array}
$$

Remember that the actual sum will be less than the estimate if both addends are rounded up.
Estimate the sum. Find the actual sum.
1. 283 + 174   **2.** 5,309 + 3,102

Set F pages 16–17

Using combinations can help you to find a sum using mental math. Look for numbers whose sum is 10 or 100.

$$68 + 75 + 32 = 100 + 75$$
$$= 175$$

Remember you can add numbers in any order. Use mental math to find each sum.

1. 39 + 84 + 61   **2.** 44 + 97 + 56

3. 81 + 19 + 48   **4.** 76 + 27 + 73

Set G pages 24–25

Estimate 6,413 − 3,806 by rounding both the minuend and the subtrahend to the nearest thousand.

$$\begin{array}{r} 6{,}413 \rightarrow 6{,}000 \\ -\,3{,}806 \rightarrow -4{,}000 \\ \hline 2{,}000 \end{array}$$

Remember when estimating by rounding to round the numbers to the same place. Estimate each difference.

1. 86 − 57   **2.** 431 − 276

3. 629 − 318   **4.** 6,809 − 4,570

Set H pages 28–29

Use mental math to find 364 − 97. Change 97 to 100 in order to make it easier to subtract.

$$364 - 100 = 264$$

Since you added 3 to 97, add 3 to this answer, 264. So

$$364 - 97 = 267$$

Remember that if you add a number to the subtrahend, you must add the same amount to the difference. Use mental math to find each difference.

1. 179 − 98   **2.** 86 − 48

3. 147 − 38   **4.** 238 − 27

Set I pages 30–31

Find 18,546 − 9,752.

Estimate: 19,000 − 10,000 = 9,000

Rename to show 10 more tens.

$$\begin{array}{r} {}^{4}{}^{14} \\ 1\,8{,}\cancel{5}\cancel{4}6 \\ -\ 9{,}752 \\ \hline 94 \end{array}$$

Rename to show 10 more hundreds.

$$\begin{array}{r} {}^{14} \\ {}^{7}{}^{\cancel{4}}{}^{14} \\ 1\,8{,}\cancel{5}\cancel{4}6 \\ -\ 9{,}752 \\ \hline 8{,}794 \end{array}$$

Remember to estimate the difference to be sure your answer makes sense. Estimate the difference. Then find the actual difference.

1. 8,924   **2.** 46,275   **3.** 14,000
    − 4,675   − 32,489   − 6,532

Set J pages 34–35

Use subtraction to find the missing addend in this addition equation.

$$\begin{aligned} 83 + f &= 276 \\ f &= 276 - 83 \\ f &= 193 \end{aligned}$$

Remember that it is helpful to think of a family of facts to find a missing addend. Find the missing addend.

1. 46 + z = 90   **2.** k + 68 = 135

3. 374 = w + 298   **4.** 733 + n = 1,038

More Practice

Set A   pages 4–5

Tell which digits are in the millions period in each number.

1. 108,627,831   **2.** 31,846,225,006   **3.** 14,396,025   **4.** 4,027,834

Tell what the 6 in each number means.

5. 4,630,147   **6.** 3,486,091   **7.** 6,107,052   **8.** 719,060,005

Write in standard form.

9. 14 thousand, 38   **10.** 3 million, 80 thousand, 452

Write each number in words and in expanded form.

11. 407,003   **12.** 2,400,070   **13.** 320,000,900   **14.** 5,060,008,000

Set B   pages 6–7

Compare these numbers. Use >, <, or =.

1. 649 ▦ 647   **2.** 4,286 ▦ 4,301   **3.** 53,102 ▦ 53,012

List the numbers in order from least to greatest.

4. 436   463   419   **5.** 2,305   2,053   2,530

Set C   pages 8–9

Round to the nearest ten and to the nearest hundred.

1. 83   **2.** 145   **3.** 551   **4.** 249   **5.** 4,036   **6.** 3,091

Round to the nearest thousand and to the nearest ten-thousand.

7. 8,483   **8.** 16,544   **9.** 52,426   **10.** 12,420   **11.** 68,035

Set D   pages 12–13

Estimate each sum. Tell which strategy you used.

1. 64 + 86   **2.** 419 + 624 + 733   **3.** 3,821 + 7,125

Choose the best estimate for each sum.

4. 279 + 486
   600   700   800

5. 107 + 92 + 101 + 96
   300   3,000   400

6. 4,820 + 6,021
   10,000   11,000   1,100

Set E   pages 14–15

For each exercise, estimate the sum. Then find the actual sum.

1.	**2.**	**3.**	**4.**	**5.**
68	147	374	5,528	7,629
+ 19	+ 39	+ 138	+ 391	+ 3,392

Set F   pages 16–17

Use mental math to find each sum. Tell which strategy you used.

1. 76 + 96   **2.** 68 + 41   **3.** 32 + 47 + 68   **4.** 86 + 59 + 14

Use mental math to choose the correct sum.

5. 12 + 13 + 14   **6.** 426 + 563   **7.** 153 + 95
    29 39 49   983 986 989   148 184 248

Set G   pages 24–25

Estimate each difference. Tell which strategy you used.

1. 93 − 54   **2.** 679 − 442   **3.** 523 − 325   **4.** 7,394 − 4,833

Choose the best estimate for each difference.

5. 74 − 45   **6.** 438 − 296   **7.** 6,246 − 3,908
    20 30 400   100 200 300   2,000 3,000 4,000

Set H   pages 28–29

Use mental math to find each difference. Tell which
strategy you used.

1. 657 − 432   **2.** 387 − 96   **3.** 429 − 299   **4.** 59 − 36

5. Choose one of the exercises above. Explain why you
chose the strategy you used.

Set I   pages 30–31

For each exercise, estimate the difference. Then find the
actual difference.

1. 8,617 − 4,705	**2.** 26,842 − 8,356	**3.** 74,064 − 35,206	**4.** 43,562 − 32,683	**5.** 85,626 − 76,337

Mixed Practice   **Remember** to watch the signs.

6. 73,468 + 37,654	**7.** 49,006 − 31,238	**8.** 14,000 − 6,483	**9.** 48,391 + 86,829	**10.** 78,625 − 69,816

Set J   pages 34–35

Find the missing addend.

1. $29 + b = 43$ **2.** $317 + p = 508$ **3.** $3,006 = x + 2,086$

Calculator   Find the missing addend.

4. $n + 49,268 = 62,497$ **5.** $86,695 + d = 103,708$

Enrichment

Roman Numerals

The Roman numeral system was used many years ago to name numbers.
The basic symbols are:

I	V	X	L	C	D	M
(1)	(5)	(10)	(50)	(100)	(500)	(1,000)

Study these samples.

1	I	19	XIX	39	XXXIX	200	CC
2	II	20	XX	40	XL	300	CCC
3	III	21	XXI	41	XLI	400	CD
4	IV	24	XXIV	44	XLIV	500	D
5	V					600	DC
6	VI	29	XXIX	50	L		
7	VII	30	XXX	60	LX	900	CM
8	VIII	31	XXXI	70	LXX	1,000	M
9	IX	34	XXXIV	80	LXXX		
10	X			90	XC		
11	XI			100	C		

Write each Roman numeral in standard form. Follow these examples.

LXVIII	XCII	CDXLII	MMCMXCIX
60 + 8	90 + 2	400 + 40 + 2	2,000 + 900 + 90 + 9
68	**92**	**442**	**2,999**

1. XV   2. XXXVII   3. XLIX   4. LXVIII   5. LXXIV

6. LXXXIX   7. XCV   8. XCIX   9. CXVI   10. CXL

11. CDIX   12. MCXV   13. MDCLXI   14. MDCCL   15. MCMXL

16. Section XII   17. King Louis XIV   18. Chapter XXIX

19. Date on a building: MDCCCXXIV   20. Book copyright date: MCMXLIX   21. Movie copyright date: MCMXCI

Chapter 1 Review/Test

1. What does the 7 in 7,000,826,354 mean?

2. List the following numbers in order from least to greatest:

   47,189   47,028   40,008

3. Round 89,127 to the nearest ten-thousand.

Choose the best estimate.

4. 689 + 788

   150   1,300   1,500

5. 5,168 − 2,850
   1,000   2,000   3,000

For each exercise, estimate the sum or difference. Then find the actual sum or difference.

6. $\begin{array}{r} 6,224 \\ + 2,198 \end{array}$ 7. $\begin{array}{r} 28,168 \\ + 39,667 \end{array}$

8. $\begin{array}{r} 7,821 \\ - 1,587 \end{array}$ 9. $\begin{array}{r} 40,007 \\ - 22,188 \end{array}$

Use mental math to choose the correct sum or difference.

10. 72 + 65 + 35

    162   172   272

11. 683 − 199

    482   384   484

Find the missing addend.

12. 38 + n = 89

13. n + 3,078 = 5,924

14. Name the three steps of the Problem-Solving Guide.

15. Mr. Donovan bought 4 baseball tickets costing $12 each. What was the total cost?

16. Pablo said that the sum of 687 and 792 is more than 1,300. Do you agree? Why or why not?

17. Choose the most sensible answer.

    Amy bought a sandwich. How much change could she have received from $10?

    $9.95 $6.95 $12.25

Read the problem below. Then answer the question.

On Monday, Sarah sold 78 papers. On Tuesday, she sold 92 papers, and on Wednesday, she sold 50 papers. How many more did she sell on Tuesday than on Monday?

18. Which equation can you use to solve the problem?

    a. 78 + 92 = n
    b. 78 + 92 + 50 = n
    c. 92 − 78 = n
    d. 92 − 50 = n

19. **Write About Math** Explain the mental-math strategy you used in Exercise 11.

Multiplication

2

Did You Know: The average American watches 968 hours of television a year. That is just over 40 days.

Number-Sense Project

Estimate
Predict how many hours of television you watch in a week. Is it more than 24 hours?

Gather Data
Keep a record of how many hours you watch television during a week.

Analyze and Report
Summarize your results. Make a chart or graph to display your data. Compare your results with another student.

Multiples

Build Understanding

The *Lightning Bolt* roller coaster leaves the station every 6 minutes. The *Thunder Wave* leaves every 4 minutes. If they start at the same time, how long before they both leave the station again at the same time?

A. Exploring Multiples
Materials: Grid paper, scissors
Groups: Small groups of 2-4

a. Cut strips of paper that are each 1 unit wide. Make some 6 units long to represent the time for *Lightning Bolt*. Make some 4 units long for *Thunder Wave*.

b. Put the 6-unit strips end to end. Put the 4-unit strips end to end next to the row of 6-unit strips. Line up the beginnings of both rows.

c. For each row, how many units are in 1 strip? in 2 strips? in 3 strips? What do these numbers represent for each roller coaster?

d. Find the first place where ends of strips from both rows line up. How many units from the start is this? What does this tell you about the two roller coasters?

e. Find other places where ends of strips line up. How many units from the start are they? If you add more strips, can you continue to find more places where the strips line up?

B. If *Lightning Bolt* runs 3 times, how long will it take before it leaves again?

3 × 6 = 18   Since each run takes the same
              amount of time, you multiply.
Factor Factor Product

It will take 18 minutes. The number 18 is a ***multiple*** of 6. Here are some multiples of 6.

6	12	18	24	30	36
1 × 6	2 × 6	3 × 6	4 × 6	5 × 6	6 × 6

c. Multiples of 6 and 4 tell when each roller coaster leaves its station. The *common multiples* of 6 and 4 tell when the roller coasters leave their stations at the same time.

Multiples of 6 *(Lightning Bolt):*   6   12   18   24   30   36   42   48   54 . . .

Multiples of 4 *(Thunder Wave):*   4   8   12   16   20   24   28   32   36 . . .

The *least common multiple* of 6 and 4 is 12. So it takes 12 minutes from the start before the roller coasters leave at the same time again.

■ **Write About Math**   Describe how you can tell if a number is even or odd.

Check Understanding

For another example, see Set A, pages 74–75.

1. List six multiples of 9.

2. What is the greatest multiple of 9?

3. List three common multiples of 9 and 3.

4. Find the least common multiple of 9 and 3.

Practice

For More Practice, see Set A, pages 76–77.

List five multiples of the following numbers.

5. 2   **6.** 3   **7.** 5   **8.** 7   **9.** 8   **10.** 9   **11.** 10   **12.** 12   **13.** 15

List three common multiples for each pair of numbers.

14. 2 and 4   **15.** 3 and 6   **16.** 6 and 8   **17.** 3 and 4   **18.** 5 and 10

19. 7 and 4   **20.** 5 and 6   **21.** 2 and 9   **22.** 8 and 12   **23.** 8 and 10

24. Find the least common multiple for each pair of numbers in Exercises 14–23.

Problem Solving

25. For *Lightning Bolt* and *Thunder Wave,* how many runs did each make in 12 minutes?

26. Critical Thinking   Does every pair of whole numbers have a common multiple?

27. Is there a greatest common multiple of 6 and 8? Explain why or why not.

A
L
G
E
B
R
A

28. If the variable c can stand for any whole number greater than one, then $7 \times c$ is always a multiple of what number?

Mental Math for Multiples of 10, 100, and 1,000

Build Understanding

On December 17, 1903, near Kitty Hawk, N.C., Wilbur and Orville Wright were the first to fly a power-driven airplane. The plane was a single engine biplane named *Flyer*. The longest flight made that day reached a speed of about 30 miles per hour (mi per h). How does this compare with the speed of other planes?

Approximate Speed of Selected Aircraft (in miles per hour)

Wright Brothers' *Flyer*	30 mi per h
Light plane (single engine)	200 mi per h
Propeller plane (four engines)	400 mi per h
Jet (twin engines)	500 mi per h
Jumbo jet (four engines)	600 mi per h
Supersonic transport	1,500 mi per h

How far can a jumbo jet travel in 3 hours?

Think of 3 lengths of 600 miles each. Add to find the answer.

600 + 600 + 600 = 1,800

Or, since you know the rate for one hour, you can multiply the number of hours and the rate to get the total distance. Use mental math.

3 × 600 = 1,800   3 × 6 hundreds = 18 hundreds

■ **Talk About Math**   How far can a supersonic transport travel in 1 hour? in 0 hours? What does this tell you about multiplying by 1 and multiplying by 0?

Check Understanding

For another example, see Set B, pages 74-75.

Complete each with *tens*, *hundreds*, *thousands*, or *ten-thousands*.

1. 30 × 600 = 18 ___?___   **2.** 30 × 60 = 18 ___?___   **3.** 6,000 × 30 = 18 ___?___

Copy and complete.

4. 4 × 3,000 = ▦▦,000   **5.** 80 × 50 = 4,▦▦0   **6.** 500 × 20 = ▦▦,000

Multiply using mental math.

7. 1,000 × 80   **8.** 400 × 1   **9.** 100 × 100   **10.** 0 × 800

Practice

For More Practice, see Set B, pages 76–77.

Multiply. **Remember** to use mental math.

11. 50 × 7   **12.** 9 × 20   **13.** 30 × 1   **14.** 10 × 1,000

15. 90 × 40   **16.** 600 × 7   **17.** 0 × 300   **18.** 60 × 70

19. 1 × 4,000   **20.** 800 × 600   **21.** 5 × 800   **22.** 100 × 1,000

23. 50 × 6,000   **24.** 9,000 × 0   **25.** 52 × 1,000   **26.** 9 × 3,000

27. 200 × 800   **28.** 500 × 200   **29.** 7 × 1,000   **30.** 60 × 9,000

Problem Solving

Use the data at the beginning of the lesson.

31. How far does a propeller plane travel in 3 hours?

32. How far does a jumbo jet travel in 5 hours?

33. Which plane can travel 3 times as fast as a jet?

34. Which plane can travel 20 times as fast as the Wrights' *Flyer*?

35. Write a problem that can be answered by using some of the data about airplane speeds.

36. Find four pairs of factors with a product of 400. The factors should each have only one nonzero digit.

49

Multiplying by a One-Digit Number

Build Understanding

A. A *ristra* is a string of red chile peppers. It is hung on doorways and in kitchens in Mexico, Central America, and Southwestern United States as a sign of welcome. One type of ristra uses 127 peppers. How many peppers are needed to make 6 of these ristras?

Multiply to find the number of peppers needed. Find 6 × 127.

Estimate: Round 127 to the nearest hundred. Then multiply.
6 × 100 = 600.

Multiply the ones. 6 × 7 ones = 42 ones Rename 42 ones as 4 tens 2 ones.	Multiply the tens. 6 × 2 tens = 12 tens 12 tens + 4 tens = 16 tens Rename 16 tens as 1 hundred 6 tens.	Multiply the hundreds. 6 × 1 hundred = 6 hundreds 6 hundreds + 1 hundred = 7 hundreds
4 12**7** × 6 —— 2	1 4 12**7** × 6 —— 6 2	1 4 1**2**7 × 6 —— 7 6 2

It takes 762 peppers to make 6 ristras. The answer is reasonable because 762 is close to 600.

B. Find 8 × 3 × 5.

Multiply two factors.	Then multiply by the third factor.
8 × 3 = 24	2 4 × 5 —— 1 2 0

C. Find 3 × $2.98.

Think of $2.98 as 298 cents.
Write the answer in dollars and cents.

$$\begin{array}{r} 298 \\ \times \quad 3 \\ \hline 894 \end{array} \qquad \begin{array}{r} \$2.98 \\ \times \quad 3 \\ \hline \$8.94 \end{array}$$

■ **Talk About Math** In Example A, how did you know that your estimate would be less than the actual answer?

Check Understanding

For another example, see Set C, pages 74–75.

Copy and complete.

1. 27 tens = ▦ hundreds ▦ tens   **2.** 35 hundreds = ▦ thousands ▦ hundreds

Multiply.

3. 5 × 2,056   **4.** 4 × $5.26   **5. Mental Math** Use mental math to find the product of 3 × 5 × 4.

Practice

For More Practice, see Set C, pages 76–77.

Multiply. **Remember** to estimate to tell if the answer is reasonable.

6. 17 × 8	**7.** 87 × 3	**8.** 40 × 6	**9.** 75 × 7	**10.** 861 × 5
11. 579 × 7	**12.** 403 × 8	**13.** 640 × 3	**14.** 261 × 9	**15.** 376 × 4
16. 2,413 × 2	**17.** 3,592 × 9	**18.** 7,053 × 4	**19.** 4,006 × 6	**20.** 6,040 × 5
21. $0.45 × 4	**22.** $8.20 × 9	**23.** $4.97 × 3	**24.** $5.59 × 6	**25.** $7.08 × 7

26. 4 × 3 × 9   **27.** 7 × 1 × 5   **28.** 5 × 7 × 6   **29.** 8 × 8 × 8   **30.** 3 × 0 × 7

31. 8 × 2 × 5   **32.** 6 × 2 × 9   **33.** 1 × 8 × 1   **34.** 7 × 8 × 9   **35.** 4 × 4 × 4

Problem Solving

36. Hot sauce is used in many Mexican recipes. It is made from ground cayenne pepper, water, and salt. Find the cost of 6 bottles if one costs $1.19.

37. Critical Thinking Luis has 4 times as many jalapeño peppers as chile peppers. If he buys four more of each type, he will have 3 times as many jalapeño peppers as chile peppers. How many of each type of pepper does Luis have now?

In Indonesia, red chili peppers are used to decorate a rice cone dish called Nasi Kuning Lengkap.

Draw a Diagram

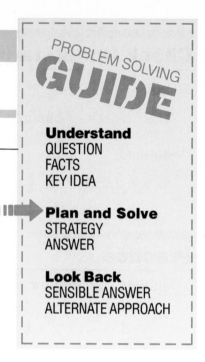

PROBLEM SOLVING GUIDE

Understand
QUESTION
FACTS
KEY IDEA

▌▌▌➡ **Plan and Solve**
STRATEGY
ANSWER

Look Back
SENSIBLE ANSWER
ALTERNATE APPROACH

Build Understanding

Kenji is shopping for a new bike. He can choose between three models: the Falcon, the Eagle, and the Hawk. Each model comes in two colors: red and silver. How many choices for a new bike does Kenji have?

Understand   You need to find the number of different choices. There are three different models and two different colors for each model. You need to count each model matched with each color.

▌▌▌➡ **Plan and Solve**   STRATEGY   To consider the choice of colors for each model of bike, one by one, you can *draw a diagram*. A **tree diagram** will show each model matched with each color.

Models	Colors	Choices
Falcon	red	red Falcon
	silver	silver Falcon
Eagle	red	red Eagle
	silver	silver Eagle
Hawk	red	red Hawk
	silver	silver Hawk

ANSWER   Kenji has six possible choices for a new bike.

Look Back   Be sure that all the colors were listed with each model and that all models were listed.

■ **Talk About Math**   Would the answer be different if you started your diagram by first listing the colors and then listing the type of models for each color?

Check Understanding

Tires come in two types: gumwall or blackwall. Each tire comes in four colors: white, black, blue, or red.

1. List the types of tires.

2. For each type, list the colors.

3. Make a tree diagram to show all the different tire combinations.

4. How many different choices for tires are there?

Practice

5. Handlebars are made from two different materials and come in three different styles. How many choices are there for handlebars?

Materials	Styles
steel	standard
chrome	high-rise
	racing

6. The pedal assembly comes in two styles of crank and two styles of pedal. How many choices are there for pedal assemblies?

Cranks	Pedals
1-piece	rubber platform
3-piece	metal trap

7. Bike saddles come in standard, racing, or touring styles. Each style comes in red or black. How many choices is this?

8. The combination for a bike lock has two digits. Each digit can be 1, 2, 3, or 4. How many combinations are there?

Explore ———— Math

Look back at the information in this lesson and your answers.

9. How many bike choices were there? How many models? colors?

10. How many tire choices were there? How many types? colors?

11. How many handlebar choices were there? How many materials? styles?

12. Describe how you might find the number of possible choices without drawing a tree diagram.

13. How many bike choices would there be if each model came in three colors?

14. How many tire choices would there be if each tire type came in five colors?

Multiplying by a Multiple of 10 or 100

Build Understanding

A. An Airedale needs about 20 pounds of dog food a week. At this rate, how many pounds of dog food will an Airedale need in a year?

Since the rate is the same each week, multiply the rate and the number of weeks (52) in a year to find the total amount. Find 20 × 52.

Estimate: Using front-end digits, the product will be about 20 × 50 = 1,000.

Multiply by 0 ones. 0 × 52 = 0	Multiply by 2 tens. 2 tens × 52 = 104 tens

```
    52          52
  × 20        × 20
  ----        -----
     0        1,040
```

An Airedale will need about 1,040 pounds of dog food. The answer is reasonable because it is close to the estimate.

B. Find 200 × 368.

Multiply by 0 ones.	Multiply by 0 tens.	Multiply by 2 hundreds.

```
   368        368         368
 × 200      × 200       × 200
 -----      -----       ------
     0         00       73,600
```

■ **Write About Math** Write a rule for multiplying by a multiple of 10 or 100. Then try your rule on the product 300 × 320.

St. Bernard

40 lb

25 lb

German Shepherd

20 lb

Airedale

10 lb

Cocker Spaniel

2 lb

Chihuahua

Weekly Dog Food Requirements
(in pounds)

Check Understanding

For another example, see Set D, pages 74–75.

Multiply.

1. 4 × 614   **2.** 40 × 614   **3.** 400 × 614

Practice

For More Practice, see Set D, pages 76–77.

Multiply. **Remember** to estimate to tell if the answer is reasonable.

4. $\begin{array}{r} 47 \\ \times\,30 \\ \hline \end{array}$
5. $\begin{array}{r} 31 \\ \times\,70 \\ \hline \end{array}$
6. $\begin{array}{r} 65 \\ \times\,90 \\ \hline \end{array}$
7. $\begin{array}{r} 38 \\ \times\,50 \\ \hline \end{array}$
8. $\begin{array}{r} 24 \\ \times\,40 \\ \hline \end{array}$
9. $\begin{array}{r} 72 \\ \times\,20 \\ \hline \end{array}$

10. $\begin{array}{r} 940 \\ \times\,50 \\ \hline \end{array}$
11. $\begin{array}{r} 728 \\ \times\,80 \\ \hline \end{array}$
12. $\begin{array}{r} 502 \\ \times\,30 \\ \hline \end{array}$
13. $\begin{array}{r} 622 \\ \times\,80 \\ \hline \end{array}$
14. $\begin{array}{r} 708 \\ \times\,40 \\ \hline \end{array}$
15. $\begin{array}{r} 815 \\ \times\,60 \\ \hline \end{array}$

16. $\begin{array}{r} 416 \\ \times\,200 \\ \hline \end{array}$
17. $\begin{array}{r} 325 \\ \times\,500 \\ \hline \end{array}$
18. $\begin{array}{r} 907 \\ \times\,400 \\ \hline \end{array}$
19. $\begin{array}{r} 989 \\ \times\,200 \\ \hline \end{array}$
20. $\begin{array}{r} 605 \\ \times\,700 \\ \hline \end{array}$
21. $\begin{array}{r} 500 \\ \times\,300 \\ \hline \end{array}$

22. 70×66
23. 50×30
24. 57×300
25. 300×208

26. 400×511
27. 200×856
28. 800×143
29. 60×251

30. 500×782
31. 90×73
32. 700×842
33. 84×600

Problem Solving

Use the information about dog food at the beginning of the lesson.

34. Dog food costs $0.79 per pound. How much will it cost to feed a cocker spaniel for one week?

35. How much more will it cost to feed a St. Bernard for one week than a cocker spaniel?

36. **Calculator** Find the amount of food an Airedale and a German shepherd would eat in one year.

37. How much will it cost to feed 8 German shepherds for one week if their food costs $1.26 per pound?

Reading ———— Math

Numbers and Symbols Match each situation on the left with the most likely expression on the right.

1. A St. Bernard eats more than a German shepherd.

   a. $4 \times \$0.79 = \$3.16$

2. After buying a can of dog food, Juanita received some change.

   b. $\$1.00 - \$0.79 = \$0.21$

3. Ann bought a few cans of dog food.

   c. $40 > 25$

55

Mental Math for Multiplication

Build Understanding

Here are some mental math strategies to use when multiplying mentally.

A. Look for **combinations** that give numbers that are easy to multiply, such as numbers that give multiples of 10 or 100.

$$\overset{\displaystyle \overset{20}{\overbrace{\qquad}}}{4 \times 9 \times 5} = 180$$

You can change the order of the factors and get the same product. This is the **commutative property of multiplication.**

$$4 \times 9 \times 5 = 4 \times 5 \times 9$$

B. Look for numbers that you can **break apart** into numbers that are easy to multiply.

Multiply each part, and then add the products back together.

$$\underset{\underset{8 \times 23}{\uparrow}}{\overset{20 + 3}{}} = \overset{8 \times 20}{160} + \overset{8 \times 3}{24}$$
$$= 184$$

This is the **distributive property.**

$$8 \times 23 = (8 \times 20) + (8 \times 3)$$

You can change the grouping of the factors and get the same product. This is the **associative property of multiplication.**

$$\overset{\displaystyle \overset{100}{\overbrace{\qquad}}}{(29 \times 4) \times 25} = 2{,}900$$

You can change the grouping of the factors and get the same product. This is the **associative property of multiplication.**

$$(29 \times 4) \times 25 = 29 \times (4 \times 25)$$

C. Look for numbers where you can use **compensation.**

Change a difficult factor into the difference of two easy factors. Multiply each part, and then subtract to compensate.

$$\underset{\underset{5 \times 29}{\uparrow}}{\overset{30 - 1}{}} = \overset{5 \times 30}{150} - \overset{5 \times 1}{5}$$
$$= 145$$

■ **Talk About Math** Explain how you can use the mental math strategy in Example C to find $4 \times \$4.99$.

Check Understanding

For another example, see Set E, pages 74–75.

1. Find 4 × 6 × 25 using combinations of numbers.

2. Find 8 × (50 × 3) using combinations of numbers.

3. Find 3 × 53 by breaking apart one factor. Explain your thinking.

4. Find 8 × 19 using compensation. Explain your thinking.

Practice

For More Practice, see Set E, pages 76–77.

Use mental math to find each product. Tell which strategy you used.

5. 12 × 3

6. 29 × 2

7. 9 × 5 × 4

8. 6 × 21

9. 4 × 39

10. 5 × 7 × 6

11. 5 × 66

12. 98 × 4

13. 8 × 199

14. 205 × 4

15. 2 × 17 × 5

16. 2 × 9 × 50

17. 4 × 8 × 25

18. 4 × 26

19. 8 × $4.03

20. 8 × $2.97

21. 197 × 2

22. 52 × 9

23. 81 × 7

24. 5 × 7 × 6

25. 2 × 17 × 50

26. 5 × 499

27. $10.11 × 6

28. 10 × 63 × 10

29. Choose four of the exercises above. Explain why you chose the strategy you used.

30. Find 4 × 59 two ways. Explain which way you think is easier and why.

Problem Solving

Remember to use mental math when it is helpful.

31. The pet shop sells rawhide bones for $3.98 each. How much will it cost to buy four of them?

32. **Critical Thinking** A leash costs $4.25. A collar costs $1.50 more than a leash. How much will it cost to buy a collar and a leash?

TIP$ FOR PROBLEM SOLVERS

Be flexible. If you get stuck, try another idea.

4.25

Choosing a Computation Method

Greenbriar
Theater Ticket Prices
Adults $6.00
Under 12 . . . . $3.50
Seniors $4.75

Build Understanding

Three friends went to the Greenbriar Mall. After shopping for a while, they wanted to see a movie. Their tickets for the movie would cost $3.50 each. Between them they had $10. The three girls decided to see if they could afford a movie.

Patient Penelope reached for a notebook and wrote:

$$\begin{array}{r} \overset{1}{} \\ \$3.50 \\ \times \quad 3 \\ \hline \$10.50 \end{array}$$

Merry Martha scratched her head and thought:

$3 \times \$3 = \$9 \quad 3 \times \$0.50 = \$1.50$

$\$9 + \$1.50 = \$10.50$

Careful Carolyn took out her calculator and entered:

$3 \;\boxed{\times}\; 3 \;\boxed{\cdot}\; 5 \;\boxed{=}\; \mathit{10.5}$

"We don't have enough money!" they all agreed. But they could not agree on whose computation method was most appropriate. What do you think?

Here are some general guidelines to help you choose a computation method.

When an exact answer is needed,
• use *mental math* if you can find the exact answer in your head.
• use *paper and pencil* if you cannot do it in your head easily.
• use a *calculator* if there are many numbers or the numbers are complicated.

■ **Talk About Math** Do you think Carolyn got her answer faster than Penelope did? Discuss when you might find it easier or faster to use paper and pencil rather than a calculator.

Check Understanding

For another example, see Set F, pages 74–75.

1. What method would you choose to total the ticket sales for the day if you were the theater manager? Explain your thinking.

2. What method would you choose to figure the change from $20 for seven tickets that cost $2 each? Explain your thinking.

Practice

For More Practice, see Set F, pages 76–77.

Tell which computation method you would use. Then find each answer.

3. 20×40

4. $1,939 + 5,386$

5. $7 \times \$1.10$

6. $854 - 399$

7. 5×348

8. $5,000 - 924$

9. 30×90

10. $224 + 105$

11. $\$96.83 + \$64.57$

12. $4 \times \$10.25$

13. $25 \times 478 \times 4$

14. $184 - 79$

15. $7 \times \$16.28$

16. $5,201 + 379$

17. 8×302

18. $920 - 278$

Problem Solving

Tell which computation method you would use. Then find each answer. Use the information about ticket prices given at the beginning of the lesson.

19. The lobby has 4 walls of movie posters with 10 posters on each wall. How many posters are there?

20. Can a family of two adults and two children under 12 see a movie for under $20? Explain your answer.

21. Attendance at six showings of a new movie was 186, 179, 191, 182, 187, and 189. How many people attended?

22. There were 213 boxes of popcorn sold at the first show and 426 sold at the second. How many more were sold at the second show?

23. The theater has 408 seats. What is the greatest amount that could be collected from a sold-out movie?

Midchapter ✓ Checkup

Multiply using mental math.

1. 4×30 **2.** $5 \times 7 \times 4$

Multiply.

3. 8×74 **4.** 924×300

5. List three common multiples of 2 and 3. Then give the least common multiple.

6. Would you use paper and pencil, mental math, or a calculator to find 8×947?

7. Tents come in cabin or dome models. Each model comes in canvas or nylon. How many choices are there? Draw a tree diagram.

Problem Solving WORKSHOP

Explore as a Team

The numbers 1, 4, and 9 are *square numbers*. We can show them as squares.

$1 \times 1 = 1$

$2 \times 2 = 4$

$3 \times 3 = 9$

TIPS FOR **WORKING TOGETHER**

When you are unsure, ask someone in your group for help or say you don't understand.

1. Discuss the dot arrangements. How are they the same? How are they different?

2. Use counters to find the next two square numbers.

3. Invent ways to "mark off" and record square numbers. Here are some examples for 9.

$9 = 3 \times 3$

$9 = 4 + 2 + 2 + 1$
$9 = 4 + (2 \times 2) + 1$

$9 = 1 + 3 + 5$

$9 = 1 + 2 + 3 + 2 + 1$

4. Try to "mark off" and record the next two square numbers. Discuss the patterns you find in the recording of square numbers.

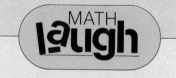

MATH Laugh

What tools do we use in arithmetic?

ANSWER: Multipliers

Number-Sense Project

Look back at pages 44-45.
The chart at the right shows the number of hours that Jeffrey watched television during a week.

1. About how many hours of television does Jeffrey watch per month?

2. About how many hours of television does Jeffrey watch in a year?

3. Write a sentence telling how Jeffrey's yearly total compares to yours.

Day	Television Viewing
Monday	1 hour
Tuesday	1 hour
Wednesday	2 hours
Thursday	1 hour
Friday	3 hours
Saturday	5 hours
Sunday	2 hours

Math-at-Home Activity

Gather Data Take a survey of 12 people who live with or near you. Ask them to guess a, b, or c for the following census question.

At the time of the first census, in 1790, about how many people were living in the United States?

a. *500,000* **b.** *4 million*

c. *100 million*

● 0–100,000
● 100,001–200,000
● 200,001–300,000
● 300,001+

United States Population in 1790

500,000
4 million
100 million

0 2 4 6 8 10 12

Number of people choosing each answer

Estimating Products

Build Understanding

Here are some estimation strategies to use when estimating products.

A. Estimate 17 × 305 by *rounding* both factors so each has only one nonzero digit.

17 × 305
↓   ↓
20 × 300 = 6,000

The actual product is about 6,000.

B. Estimate 58 × 24 by *finding a range.*

Round down.   Round up.

58 × 24   58 × 24
↓   ↓   ↓   ↓
50 × 20 = 1,000 60 × 30 = 1,800

The actual product will be between 1,000 and 1,800.

C. Estimate 26 × 4 using *compatible numbers.*

Substitute a number that is close to an original number and can be multiplied easily.

26 × 4   25 × 4 = 100

The actual product should be close to 100.

■ **Talk About Math** If you estimate a product by rounding, what can you say about the actual product if both factors round down? if both factors round up? if one factor rounds down and one rounds up?

Check Understanding

For another example, see Set G, pages 74–75.

1. Estimate 59 × 784 using rounding.

2. Estimate 625 × 297 by finding a range.

3. Estimate 98 × 7 using compatible numbers.

4. For Exercise 1, will the actual product be less than or more than the estimate?

Practice

For More Practice, see Set G, pages 76–77.

Estimate each product. For Exercises 5–8, find a range. For Exercises 9–24, use any strategy given on page 62. Tell which strategy you used.

5. 81 × 38　　　**6.** 29 × 31　　　**7.** 98 × 17　　　**8.** 205 × 42

9. 8 × 59　　　**10.** 6 × 197　　　**11.** 59 × 687　　　**12.** 2 × 49 × 8

13. 4 × 6 × 26　　**14.** 8 × 24　　　**15.** 45 × 85　　　**16.** 14 × 199

17. 28 × 416　　**18.** 85 × 630　　**19.** 2 × 73 × 51　　**20.** 48 × 885

21. 5 × 304　　　**22.** 9 × 172　　　**23.** 18 × 440　　　**24.** 2 × 52 × 4

25. Choose two of Exercises 9–24. Explain why you chose the strategy you used.

26. Estimate 14 × 98 using rounding and compatible numbers. Explain which gives a closer estimate and why.

Choose the better estimate for each product.

27. 32 × 485

　　12,000　　15,000

28. 89 × 72

　　5,600　　6,300

29. 307 × 81

　　24,000　　32,000

Problem Solving

30. Kazuko said that 346 × 28 is between 6,000 and 12,000. Give a better estimate.

31. How can you tell that 27,824 is a more reasonable answer for 752 × 37 than 21,824?

32. Use Data Use the information about ticket prices on page 58. Would $50 be enough to pay for nine senior citizens to see a movie? Explain.

33. Do you think 20 × 100 or 18 × 100 will give a better estimate for 18 × 99? Explain why.

Skills _____ Review　　　pages 6-7

Compare these numbers. Use >, <, or =.

1. 538 ▦ 583　　　**2.** 947 ▦ 938　　　**3.** 5,049 ▦ 5,409

List the numbers in order from greatest to least.

4. 849　857　728　　**5.** 957　1,089　846　　**6.** 648　693　629

Deciding When an Estimate Is Enough

PROBLEM SOLVING GUIDE

Understand
QUESTION
FACTS
KEY IDEA

Plan and Solve
STRATEGY
ANSWER

Look Back
SENSIBLE ANSWER
ALTERNATE APPROACH

Build Understanding

The Olivers are planning a raft trip down the Colorado River through the Grand Canyon. It will cost them $1,102.50 each for the seven-day trip. Will $5,000 cover the cost for the four of them to make this trip?

Understand QUESTION Is $5,000 enough for four people?

FACTS The rate for one person is $1,102.50. There are 4 people.

KEY IDEA Since the problem is not asking for the exact cost for four people, an estimate may be enough.

An estimate is enough if:
• you cannot get exact amounts, or
• an exact answer does not make sense, or
• you do not need an exact answer and you are certain that an estimate will answer the question.

Plan and Solve Since the rate is the same for everyone, you would multiply the rate by 4 to find the exact answer. To estimate the product, think:

$1,102.50 is less than $1,200, so 4 × $1,102.50 is less than 4 × $1,200.   4 × 1,200 = 4,800

The raft trip for the Olivers will cost less than $4,800, so $5,000 will cover the cost of the trip.

Look Back An estimate was enough to solve this problem because the exact cost will be less than the estimate, and the estimate is less than $5,000.

The Grand Canyon extends 277 miles in northwest Arizona.

■ **Talk About Math** If you were sending a check as payment for your family to take a raft trip, would an estimate of the total cost be enough? Explain.

Check Understanding

Suppose the Olivers decide that they can spend no more than $4,500 on the trip.

1. **Estimation** Will the exact cost of the Olivers' raft trip be more or less than $4,400?

2. **Estimation** Will the exact cost of the Olivers' raft trip be more or less than $4,800?

3. Is the estimate of the range given in Problems 1 and 2 enough to tell if the Olivers can make the trip?

4. What must you do to see if the exact cost of the trip is no more than $4,500?

Practice

5. A two-day trip down the river costs $435.75. Round-trip fare to the canyon costs $372. Will $1,000 cover the entire cost? Tell whether an estimate is enough.

6. Is an estimate enough to tell if $800 will cover the entire cost for the situation in Problem 5? Explain.

7. Raft tours are offered for 18 weeks of the year. If all the rafts are full, 39 people can take the tours each week. Can 900 people take the tours during the year? Tell whether an estimate is enough.

8. For the situation in Problem 7, is an estimate enough to tell how many people can take the raft tours during the year? Explain.

Explain each answer. Would an estimate be enough to decide

9. how far you hiked on a hiking trip?

10. whether you have enough money to pay for your lunch?

11. how much allowance you will earn during the summer?

12. how much you plan to spend on souvenirs during your vacation?

Multiplying by a Two-Digit Number

Build Understanding

A. How long would a train of 37 covered hopper cars be, not counting the engine and caboose?

Since all the cars are the same length, multiply. Find 37 × 54.

Estimate: 40 × 50 = 2,000

```
    5 4
  × 3 7      30 + 7
  -------
    3 7 8    7 × 54
  1 6 2 0    30 × 54
  -------
  1,9 9 8
```

The train would be 1,998 feet long. The answer is reasonable because it is close to the estimate.

	Covered hopper car 54 ft
	Open-top hopper car 44 ft
	Tank car 50 ft
	Two-level rack car 94 ft
	Boxcar 44 ft
	Piggyback flatcar 92 ft
	Refrigerator car 60 ft
	Stock car 44 ft

B. Find 84 × 673.

Paper and Pencil

```
    6 7 3
  ×   8 4      80 + 4
  -------
  2 6 9 2      4 × 673
  5 3 8 4 0    80 × 673
  ---------
  5 6,5 3 2
```

Calculator

84 ⊗ 673 ⊜ *56532.*

■ Talk About Math

Discuss how this diagram relates to the multiplication in Example A.

Check Understanding

For another example, see Set H, pages 74–75.

Tell whether you would use paper and pencil, mental math, or a calculator. Then find each product.

1. 40×97
2. 27×582
3. $39 \times \$0.47$
4. $82 \times \$5.35$

Practice

For More Practice, see Set H, pages 76–77.

Tell whether you would use paper and pencil, mental math, or a calculator. Then find each product.

5.
$$48 \times 63$$
6.
$$52 \times 20$$
7.
$$30 \times 51$$
8.
$$75 \times 44$$
9.
$$80 \times 49$$
10.
$$86 \times 60$$

11.
$$284 \times 53$$
12.
$$408 \times 20$$
13.
$$830 \times 65$$
14.
$$907 \times 19$$
15.
$$211 \times 80$$
16.
$$238 \times 85$$

17. 76×81
18. 12×203
19. 38×600
20. 54×360

21. $31 \times \$0.82$
22. $23 \times \$7.10$
23. $30 \times \$4.99$
24. $75 \times \$2.00$

Mixed Practice   Use paper and pencil or a calculator to find each answer. **Remember** to watch the signs.

25.
$$381 - 274$$
26.
$$738 + 81$$
27.
$$203 \times 6$$
28.
$$937 - 61$$
29.
$$731 \times 12$$
30.
$$826 + 957$$

31.
$$606 + 459$$
32.
$$8,463 - 5,388$$
33.
$$628 \times 3$$
34.
$$372 \times 53$$
35.
$$2,361 + 9,979$$
36.
$$2,178 - 854$$

Problem Solving

Use the information at the beginning of the lesson.

37. What is the length of 42 piggyback flatcars?

38. What is the length of 24 open-top hopper cars?

39. **Estimation**   Which is closer to the length of 28 two-level rack cars, 1,800 feet or 2,700 feet?

40. **Number Sense**   Is the product even or odd if you multiply two odd numbers? two even numbers? one even and one odd?

41. What is the length of 52 refrigerator and 52 tank cars?

42. What is the length of 21 stock cars and 30 boxcars?

Choose an Operation

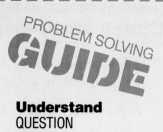

Build Understanding

Jesse owns a dairy store that sells milk, cheese, yogurt, and frozen yogurt. Last month, the store sold 12 times as much low fat milk as whole milk. There were 156 gallons of whole milk sold. How many gallons of low fat milk did the store sell last month?

PROBLEM SOLVING GUIDE

Understand
QUESTION
FACTS
KEY IDEA

Plan and Solve
STRATEGY
ANSWER

Look Back
SENSIBLE ANSWER
ALTERNATE APPROACH

Understand How many gallons of low fat milk were sold? Jesse sold 156 gallons of whole milk and 12 times as much low fat milk. One amount is a multiple of the other.

Plan and Solve STRATEGY Since the amount of low fat milk sold is a multiple of the amount of whole milk sold, you multiply. Find 12 × 156.

Paper and Pencil

$$
\begin{array}{r}
156 \\
\times\ 12 \\
\hline
312 \\
1560 \\
\hline
1,872
\end{array}
$$

Calculator

12 ⊗ 156

⊜ *1872.*

ANSWER The store sold 1,872 gallons of low fat milk last month.

Look Back The answer is sensible since:
12 × 156 is about 12 × 150.
12 × 150 is 12 × 100 plus half of 12 × 100.
So, 12 × 150 = 1,200 + 600 = 1,800.

■ **Talk About Math** Decide which method you would have used for the computation in the example—paper and pencil, calculator, or mental math. Explain why you chose the method you would use.

Check Understanding

How much milk, whole and low fat, did Jesse's store sell all together?

1. Will you add, subtract, or multiply?   **2.** Find the answer.

3. Explain why you chose the operation you used.

Practice

Tell whether to add, subtract, or multiply. Then solve the problem.

4. The store sold 501 quarts of vanilla frozen yogurt and 437 quarts of chocolate. How much more vanilla than chocolate was sold?

5. Each shelf in the dairy case holds 15 rows of milk cartons. Each row has 5 cartons. There are 25 shelves. How many cartons of milk can the dairy case hold?

6. A gallon of frozen yogurt is enough to make 32 cones. How many cones can Jesse make if he has a gallon each of 8 different flavors?

7. Whole milk sells for $1.78 a gallon. A gallon of skim milk sells for $0.27 more. What is the cost of a gallon of skim milk?

8. Each person in the U.S. drinks about 25 gallons of milk per year. At this rate, how many gallons would a fifth-grade class of 26 drink in a year?

9. If milk costs $1.78 a gallon and each person in the U.S. drinks 25 gallons per year, how much does the average person spend on milk in a year?

Choose a 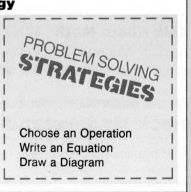 **Strategy**

Pretty Petunias

10. Kim is planting 4 petunias of different colors in a long pot. The white petunia is closer to the purple petunia than to the red petunia. The purple petunia is just to the left of the pink petunia. The red petunia is on the right. From left to right, what is the order of the colors?

PROBLEM SOLVING
STRATEGIES

Choose an Operation
Write an Equation
Draw a Diagram

Multiplying by a Three-Digit Number

Build Understanding

Most people of the world rely on milk as a food source. Milk is produced by dairy cows, goats, camels, llamas, sheep, and water buffalo. In the U.S., there are about 11 million cows which produce about 17 billion gallons of milk each year.

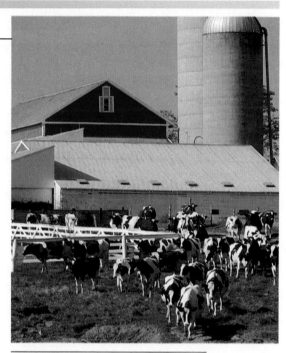

There are more Holsteins in the U.S. than any other breed of dairy cattle.

A. A herd of Holstein cows needs 720 pounds of hay and 645 pounds of grain each day. How many pounds of grain does the herd need in one year?

The herd needs the grain at the same rate each day, so multiply. There are 365 days in one year. Find 365 × 645.

Estimate: 400 × 600 = 240,000

$$
\begin{array}{r}
645 \\
\times 365 \\
\hline
3225 \\
38700 \\
193500 \\
\hline
235,425
\end{array}
\quad
\begin{array}{l}
300 + 60 + 5 \\
5 \times 645 \\
60 \times 645 \\
300 \times 645
\end{array}
$$

The herd needs 235,425 pounds of grain each year. The answer is reasonable because it is close to the estimate.

B. Find 109 × 247.

$$
\begin{array}{r}
247 \\
\times 109 \\
\hline
2223 \\
24700 \\
\hline
26,923
\end{array}
$$

Estimate using compatible numbers.
100 × 250 = 25,000
The product is about 25,000.

■ **Talk About Math**   What estimation strategy was used in Example A? Do you think that finding a range would have given a better estimate?

Check Understanding

For another example. see Set I, pages 74–75.

Use paper and pencil or a calculator to multiply.

1. 420 × 347   **2.** 800 × 614   **3.** 237 × 846   **4.** 215 × 459

Practice

For More Practice, see Set I, pages 76–77.

Use paper and pencil or a calculator to multiply.
Remember to estimate to tell if the answer is reasonable.

5. 291 × 400	**6.** 202 × 125	**7.** 563 × 325	**8.** 433 × 102	**9.** 604 × 500	**10.** 562 × 722
11. 909 × 230	**12.** 722 × 502	**13.** 413 × 210	**14.** 499 × 300	**15.** 862 × 593	**16.** 508 × 430

Estimation Estimate to choose the most reasonable answer.

17. 806 × 257   **a.** 127,142   **b.** 167,142   **c.** 207,142   **d.** 277,142

18. 489 × 312   **a.** 12,000   **b.** 150,000   **c.** 400,000   **d.** 16,000

19. 673 × 585   **a.** 293,705   **b.** 313,705   **c.** 393,705   **d.** 423,705

20. 329 × 760   **a.** 250,000   **b.** 24,000   **c.** 204,000   **d.** 260,000

Mixed Practice Use paper and pencil or a calculator
to find each answer. **Remember** to watch the signs.

21. 706 − 422	**22.** 3,491 + 5,488	**23.** 5,608 × 23	**24.** 670 × 451	**25.** 364 + 979
26. 453 + 866	**27.** 185 × 207	**28.** 4,920 − 3,169	**29.** 608 × 106	**30.** 72,804 + 21,642

Problem Solving

Solve each problem.

31. A Holstein cow gives an average of 1,714 gallons of milk each year. A Jersey cow gives 616 gallons less. How much does a Jersey cow give?

32. Wisconsin is the leading dairy state. It has twice as many dairy cows as California. If California has 1,336,000 dairy cows, how many does Wisconsin have?

Choose which way you would write each problem if you were using paper and pencil to find the product. Then explain why you chose as you did.

33. 305 × 346   **a.** 346
               × 305   **b.** 305
            × 346

34. 800 × 492   **a.** 800
               × 492   **b.** 492
            × 800

Skills Review

List three common multiples of the following.

1. 2 and 6   **2.** 3 and 4

Find the least common multiple of

3. 6 and 8.   **4.** 2 and 3.

Estimate each product. Tell which strategy you used.

5. 4×49 **6.** 495×31

Multiply. Remember to estimate to tell if the answer is reasonable.

7. $\begin{array}{r} 70 \\ \times\ 4 \\ \hline \end{array}$ **8.** $\begin{array}{r} 93 \\ \times\ 6 \\ \hline \end{array}$ **9.** $\begin{array}{r} 472 \\ \times\ 5 \\ \hline \end{array}$

10. $\begin{array}{r} 508 \\ \times\ 8 \\ \hline \end{array}$ **11.** $\begin{array}{r} 1,628 \\ \times\ 3 \\ \hline \end{array}$ **12.** $\begin{array}{r} 2,060 \\ \times\ 7 \\ \hline \end{array}$

13. $\begin{array}{r} 46 \\ \times 50 \\ \hline \end{array}$ **14.** $\begin{array}{r} 73 \\ \times 17 \\ \hline \end{array}$ **15.** $\begin{array}{r} 602 \\ \times\ 49 \\ \hline \end{array}$

16. $\begin{array}{r} 350 \\ \times\ 88 \\ \hline \end{array}$ **17.** $\begin{array}{r} 158 \\ \times\ 36 \\ \hline \end{array}$ **18.** $\begin{array}{r} 601 \\ \times 400 \\ \hline \end{array}$

19. $\begin{array}{r} 702 \\ \times 620 \\ \hline \end{array}$ **20.** $\begin{array}{r} 139 \\ \times 505 \\ \hline \end{array}$ **21.** $\begin{array}{r} 395 \\ \times 124 \\ \hline \end{array}$

Use mental math to find each product. Tell which strategy you used.

22. $2 \times 8 \times 5$ **23.** 400×700

24. 5×99 **25.** 308×2

Tell which computation method you would use. Then find each answer.

26. 50×30 **27.** $6,000 - 957$

28. $245 + 304$ **29.** $\$87.96 - \$49.58$

Problem-Solving Review

Solve each problem.

30. How much did Janice pay for 3 birthday cards that cost $1.25 each?

31. You can see the rock opera *Frankie* on Thursday, Friday, or Saturday. You can buy a ticket for $8, $12, or $20. How many choices are there for seeing the show?

32. Vince bought a $7.60 gift and a $0.90 card. How much change did he get back from $10.00?

33. At an air show, plane rides cost $37.50 per person. Is $200 enough to buy five tickets?

34. Find the cost of 26 weeks of *Magic Magazine*, a weekly magazine. Find the cost of 52 weeks.

Magic Magazine	
26 weeks	$0.54 per issue
52 weeks	$0.47 per issue

35. **Data File** Use the chart of animal champions on pages 116-117 to find the slowest reptile in the world. How many feet can it travel in 8 minutes? What is the fastest land animal? How fast can it travel?

36. **Make a Data File.** Find the meaning of each of the numbers on the face of a dollar bill. Show your findings by making a drawing of the bill and labeling it.

Write in standard form. Remember to use commas where needed.

1. 6 thousand, 389

2. 75 million, 590 thousand, 149

3. 800,000 + 4,000 + 200 + 6

4. 30,000,000 + 600,000 + 50,000 + 90

Estimate. Then compute.

5.   95
    + 45

6.   54
    − 39

7.   50
    × 4

8.   207
    + 59

9.   439
    − 85

10.   357
    + 429

11.   402
    × 8

12.   750
    − 245

13.   583
    × 5

14.   6,490
    + 705

15.   3,498
    − 1,900

16.   56,124
    + 10,978

17.   810
    × 200

18.   375
    × 26

19.   98,005
    − 29,049

20. 31 + 47 + 50

21. 2 × 7 × 5

22. 4,000 − 398

23. 755 − 289

24. 1,450 + 298

25. 9 × 8 × 0

List the numbers in order from least to greatest.

26. 345   354   305

27. 1,243   1,234   1,324

28. 7,058   7,508   7,085

29. 5,678   6,587   56,780

Use mental math to compute.

30. 40 × 60

31. 8 × 1,000

32. 5 × 17 × 2

33. 32 + 24

34. 4 × 49

35. 725 − 99

Tell whether you would use paper and pencil, mental math, or a calculator to solve.

36. 5 × 307

37. 4,500 − 725

38. $26.98 + $45.79

39. 158 + 35

40. 2 × 235 × 50

41. 3 × 125

List three common multiples of the following.

42. 2 and 5

43. 3 and 6

44. 6 and 4

45. 2 and 6

Find the least common multiple of the following.

46. 2 and 4

47. 7 and 2

48. 3 and 8

49. 6 and 9

Reteaching

Set A   pages 46–47

Find the least common multiple of 6 and 10.

List the first few multiples of 6 and of 10.

Multiples of 6: 6, 12, 18, 24, ⟨30⟩, 36

Multiples of 10: 10, 20, ⟨30⟩, 40, 50

The least common multiple is 30.

Remember that the least common multiple of two numbers is the least number that is a multiple of both numbers.

Find the least common multiple of

1. 3 and 4.   **2.** 2 and 8.

3. 6 and 9.   **4.** 8 and 10.

Set B   pages 48–49

A twin-engine jet can fly about 500 miles per hour. How far can it go in 4 hours?

Add: $500 + 500 + 500 + 500 = 2,000$

Multiply: $4 \times 500 = 2,000$

  4×5 hundreds = 20 hundreds

Remember that multiplication is repeated addition.
Multiply using mental math.

1. 40×6 **2.** 40×60

3. 500×5 **4.** $60 \times 8,000$

Set C   pages 50–51

Find 148×6.

Rename 48 ones as 4 tens 8 ones.

```
   4
 1 4 8
×    6
─────
     8
```

Rename 28 tens as 2 hundreds 8 tens.

```
 2 4
 1 4 8
×    6
─────
   8 8
```

```
 2 4
 1 4 8
×    6
─────
 8 8 8
```

Remember to estimate the product to see if the answer is reasonable.
Multiply.

1.   19
       × 8

2.   77
       × 6

3.   328
       ×   5

4. 304×4 **5.** $5,607 \times 3$

Set D   pages 54–55

Find 300×137.

Multiply by 0 ones.

```
 1 3 7
×3 0 0
─────
     0
```

Multiply by 0 tens.

```
 1 3 7
×3 0 0
─────
   0 0
```

Multiply by 3 hundreds.

```
 1 3 7
×3 0 0
──────
4 1,1 0 0
```

Remember to put as many ending zeros in the product as there are in the two factors.

Multiply.

1. 346×200 **2.** 891×400

Set E   pages 56–57

Find 4×27.

Break apart 27 into $20 + 7$.
Multiply each part by 4.
$4 \times 20 = 80$ $4 \times 7 = 28$

Now add the two products.
$80 + 28 = 108$

Remember that some numbers are easy to multiply after you break them apart. Use the break-apart strategy to find each product mentally.

1. 41×6 **2.** 33×4

3. 62×8 **4.** 306×9

Set F pages 58–59

When an exact answer is needed,

- use mental math if you can find the exact answer in your head.
- use paper and pencil if you cannot do it in your head easily.
- use a calculator if there are many numbers or the numbers are complicated.

Remember that paper and pencil can sometimes be as fast as a calculator.

Tell which computation method you would use. Then find each answer.

1. 8×687 2. $297 + 148$

3. 40×90 4. $382 - 167$

Set G pages 62–63

Estimate 47×489.

Round each factor so each has only one nonzero digit.

47×489
$\downarrow \quad \downarrow$
$50 \times 500 = 25,000$

Remember to add 1 to the digit in the place to be rounded if the digit to its right is 5 or more.

Estimate each product by rounding.

1. 7×48 2. 5×95

3. 64×483 4. 56×271

Set H pages 66–67

Find 578×62.

Estimate: 600 × 60 = 36,000

$$
\begin{array}{r}
578 \\
\times \quad 62 \\
\hline
1156 \\
34680 \\
\hline
35,836
\end{array}
\quad
\begin{array}{l}
62 = 60 + 2 \\
2 \times 578 \\
60 \times 578
\end{array}
$$

Remember that the actual answer will be less than the estimate if both factors are rounded up.

Tell whether you would use paper and pencil, mental math, or a calculator. Then find each product.

1.	36	2.	62	3.	58
	$\times 28$		$\times 30$		$\times 22$

4. 307×50 5. 670×54

Set I pages 70–71

Find 423×528.

Estimate: 400 × 500 = 200,000

$$
\begin{array}{r}
423 \\
\times 528 \\
\hline
3384 \\
8460 \\
211500 \\
\hline
223,344
\end{array}
\quad
\begin{array}{l}
528 = 500 + 20 + 8 \\
8 \times 423 \\
20 \times 423 \\
500 \times 423
\end{array}
$$

Remember to estimate the product to tell if the answer is reasonable.

Use paper and pencil or a calculator to multiply.

1.	692	2.	837	3.	808
	$\times 300$		$\times 255$		$\times 504$

4.	506	5.	715	6.	962
	$\times 483$		$\times 320$		$\times 243$

More Practice

Set A pages 46–47

List five multiples of the following numbers.

1. 4   **2.** 6   **3.** 9   **4.** 7   **5.** 8

List three common multiples of the following.

6. 2 and 7   **7.** 3 and 6   **8.** 6 and 10   **9.** 8 and 12

10. Find the least common multiple for the numbers in Exercises 6–9.

Set B pages 48–49

Multiply. **Remember** to use mental math.

1. 40×8 **2.** 30×10 **3.** 500×9 **4.** 50×60

5. 700×900 **6.** 40×300 **7.** $64 \times 1{,}000$ **8.** $30 \times 7{,}000$

Set C pages 50–51

Multiply. **Remember** to estimate to tell if the answer is reasonable.

1. $\begin{array}{r} 18 \\ \times\ 9 \\ \hline \end{array}$ **2.** $\begin{array}{r} 46 \\ \times\ 5 \\ \hline \end{array}$ **3.** $\begin{array}{r} 80 \\ \times\ 7 \\ \hline \end{array}$ **4.** $\begin{array}{r} 782 \\ \times\ 4 \\ \hline \end{array}$ **5.** $\begin{array}{r} 609 \\ \times\ 3 \\ \hline \end{array}$

6. $\begin{array}{r} 6{,}580 \\ \times\ 6 \\ \hline \end{array}$ **7.** $\begin{array}{r} 5{,}004 \\ \times\ 8 \\ \hline \end{array}$ **8.** $\begin{array}{r} 3{,}648 \\ \times\ 4 \\ \hline \end{array}$ **9.** $\begin{array}{r} \$0.62 \\ \times\ 9 \\ \hline \end{array}$ **10.** $\begin{array}{r} \$5.10 \\ \times\ 8 \\ \hline \end{array}$

Set D pages 54–55

Multiply. **Remember** to estimate to tell if the answer is reasonable.

1. $\begin{array}{r} 53 \\ \times\ 20 \\ \hline \end{array}$ **2.** $\begin{array}{r} 49 \\ \times\ 40 \\ \hline \end{array}$ **3.** $\begin{array}{r} 87 \\ \times\ 50 \\ \hline \end{array}$ **4.** $\begin{array}{r} 26 \\ \times\ 60 \\ \hline \end{array}$ **5.** $\begin{array}{r} 660 \\ \times\ 40 \\ \hline \end{array}$

6. $\begin{array}{r} 821 \\ \times\ 70 \\ \hline \end{array}$ **7.** $\begin{array}{r} 504 \\ \times\ 30 \\ \hline \end{array}$ **8.** $\begin{array}{r} 685 \\ \times\ 600 \\ \hline \end{array}$ **9.** $\begin{array}{r} 307 \\ \times\ 300 \\ \hline \end{array}$ **10.** $\begin{array}{r} 451 \\ \times\ 500 \\ \hline \end{array}$

Set E pages 56–57

Use mental math to find each product. Tell which strategy you used.

1. 9×41 **2.** 306×7 **3.** $8 \times 9 \times 5$ **4.** $2 \times 14 \times 5$

5. 6×195 **6.** $4 \times 6 \times 25$ **7.** $4 \times \$8.07$ **8.** 7×199

9. Choose three of the exercises above. Explain why you chose the strategy you used.

Set F   pages 58–59

Tell which computation method you would use.
Then find each answer.

1. 6 × 438

2. 346 − 208

3. 8,000 − 648

4. 80 × 70

5. $103.46 + $73.84

6. 5 × $20.20

7. 263 − 49

8. 20 × 392 × 5

Set G   pages 62–63

Estimate each product. Tell which strategy you used.

1. 48 × 52

2. 9 × 37

3. 19 × 104

4. 8 × 205

5. 38 × 492

6. 408 × 64

7. 4 × 82 × 24

8. 9 × 28 × 11

9. Choose two of the exercises above. Explain why you
chose the strategy you used.

Choose the better estimate for each product.

10. 41 × 312
12,000   16,000

11. 32 × 98
2,700   3,000

12. 408 × 68
28,000   30,000

Set H   pages 66–67

Tell whether you would use paper and pencil, mental
math, or a calculator. Then find each product.

1.   39
    × 53

2.   40
    × 82

3.   238
    × 45

4.   306
    × 18

5. $6.20
    × 24

Mixed Practice   **Remember** to watch the signs.

6.   408
   × 7

7.   683
   − 367

8.   846
   × 14

9.   783
   − 92

10.   539
   + 768

Set I   pages 70–71

Use paper and pencil or a calculator to multiply.
Remember to estimate to tell if the answer is reasonable.

1.   438
   × 300

2.   647
   × 135

3.   303
   × 352

4.   566
   × 106

5.   318
   × 410

Estimation   Estimate to choose the most reasonable answer.

6. 509 × 386   **a.** 156,474   **b.** 196,474   **c.** 176,474   **d.** 206,474

7. 376 × 418   **a.** 127,168   **b.** 137,168   **c.** 147,168   **d.** 157,168

8. 627 × 892   **a.** 639,284   **b.** 589,284   **c.** 559,284   **d.** 489,284

Enrichment

Lattice Multiplication

Lattice multiplication is a way of multiplying that is based on an ancient calculating instrument.

Lattice multiplication is based on "Napier's Rods" which were used in the 16th century.

To find 482 × 63, make a lattice as shown here.

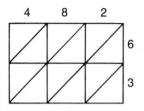

Next, multiply the digits of the two factors. Record the products in the lattice.

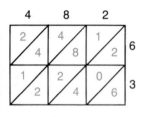

Finally, add along the diagonals within the lattice.

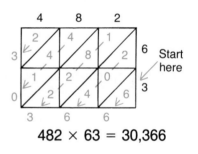

482 × 63 = 30,366

Lattices can be any size. Try these. Copy each lattice, and find the product.

1. 47 × 58

2. 258 × 367

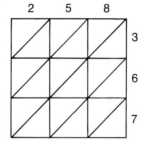

Find each answer using lattice multiplication.

3. 53 × 64   **4.** 27 × 16   **5.** 38 × 246   **6.** 293 × 824   **7.** 814 × 452

1. List three common multiples of 3 and 4.

Multiply.

2. 9×87

3. $2,386 \times 5$

4. 18×60

5. 705×700

6. $\begin{array}{r} 295 \\ \times\ 57 \\ \hline \end{array}$

7. $\begin{array}{r} 863 \\ \times\ 82 \\ \hline \end{array}$

8. $\begin{array}{r} 524 \\ \times\ 18 \\ \hline \end{array}$

9. $\begin{array}{r} 706 \\ \times 795 \\ \hline \end{array}$

10. Complete with *tens, hundreds, thousands,* or *ten-thousands.*

    $70 \times 40 = 28 \underline{\quad?\quad}$

11. Copy and complete.

    48 tens = ▦ hundreds ▦ tens

Multiply using mental math.

12. 700×6

13. 800×700

14. 12×4

15. $2 \times 18 \times 5$

Choose the best estimate for each product.

16. 79×42

    2,800   3,200

17. 609×23

    12,000   18,000

Tell which computation method you would use. Then find each answer.

18. 80×60

19. 7×123

20. A car travels at an average rate of 60 miles per hour for 4 hours. How far does the car travel?

21. One car comes with black, brown, or blue upholstery. The material can be vinyl or leather. How many choices are there? Make a tree diagram to show your answer.

22. Connie can earn $38 a week at her part-time job. She is saving to go to a computer camp that costs $600. If she works for 22 weeks, will she save enough to go to camp? Tell whether an estimate is enough.

Read this problem. Then answer the questions below.

The Gonzalez family spent $532 on home heating last year. This year they spent $670. How much did heating costs increase this year?

23. Which do you need to find for this problem?

    a. The family's total heating costs for the two years
    b. How much greater this year's costs were than last year's
    c. The cost per month for heating

24. Solve the problem.

25. **Write About Math**   In Exercises 16 and 17, explain the method of estimation you used.

Measurement and Geometric Figures

Did You Know: The first ribbon factory in the United States was started in Philadelphia in 1815. Around 1865, most ribbon in the United States was produced in the Paterson, New Jersey, area.

Number-Sense Project

Estimate
Estimate how many inches of ribbon it took to wrap this present and make the bow.

Gather Data
Wrap a piece of ribbon around an object such as a book, a basketball, or a stuffed animal. Remember the actual length you use. Ask ten people to estimate the length of the ribbon.

Analyze and Report
Record the estimates you collect. Record whether the estimates were greater or less than the actual length and by how much. Compare your results with those of other students.

Customary Units of Length

Build Understanding

Macie paints signs on trucks and vans. Some letters may be only a few inches tall while other letters could be a foot or more tall.

Inches, feet, yards, and miles are *customary units of length.*

A. One *inch* (in.) is about the length of a paper clip.

One *foot* (ft) is about the length of a notebook.

One *yard* is about the distance from a doorknob to the floor.

One *mile* is about the length of 5,280 notebooks placed end to end.

B. Macie used a ruler to measure the heights of the two letters on this page. She said each letter measured $2\frac{1}{4}$ inches. Did she measure correctly?

You can tell by looking at the two letters that their heights are not the same. Macie did measure correctly, however. Both letters are $2\frac{1}{4}$ inches to the nearest $\frac{1}{4}$ inch.

■ **Talk About Math** What would the two letters measure to the nearest $\frac{1}{8}$ inch?

Check Understanding

Estimation Choose the most sensible measure.

1. Height of a ladder
   a. 8 in. **b.** 8 ft **c.** 8 mi

2. Width of a paint brush
   a. $2\frac{1}{2}$ in. **b.** $2\frac{1}{2}$ yd **c.** $2\frac{1}{2}$ ft

Practice

Estimation Tell whether you would use inches, feet, yards, or miles to measure each of the following.

3. Height of a woman

4. Distance from home to school

5. Length of a spoon

6. Distance from the earth to the moon

7. Width of a backyard

8. Length of a kitchen table

Use the Math Sketcher to measure each segment to the nearest $\frac{1}{4}$ inch and $\frac{1}{8}$ inch.

9. _____

10. _____

11. _____

12. _____

13. _____

14. _____

Use the Math Sketcher to draw a line of each length.

15. $1\frac{1}{2}$ inches

16. $2\frac{3}{8}$ inches

17. $3\frac{1}{4}$ inches

18. $2\frac{3}{4}$ inches

19. $1\frac{7}{8}$ inches

20. 5 inches

Problem Solving

21. The letters on the door of a truck are 2 inches tall. How tall will the letters on the side of the truck be if they are 10 times as tall?

22. Macie charges $10.50 for each letter she paints on a truck. How much will she charge to write ACE TRUCKING FIRM?

23. **Visual Thinking** Macie needed to paint three large letters on the side of a truck. Each of the three letters could be 2 feet wide and still leave the following amounts of blank space: 1 foot before the first letter, 1 foot after the last letter, and 6 inches between letters. How long was the side of the truck?

24. Macie charges $12 for capital letters and $8 for lowercase letters. How much will she charge to paint Tucknott Tires?

Equal Customary Measures of Length

Build Understanding

What do you notice about these pairs of words?

little—small   far—distant   strong—powerful

The two words that make up each pair are synonyms, or words that mean almost the same thing. With synonyms, you have different ways to describe the same thing.

A. "Five feet" and "60 inches" are two different ways to describe the same length.

> 1 foot = 12 inches
> 1 yard = 3 feet
> 1 mile = 5,280 feet
> 1 mile = 1,760 yards

One foot is 12 inches, or the length of some rulers. Something that is 5 feet long is like 5 rulers, or $5 \times 12 = 60$ inches.

B. Is 500 yards the same as 1,500 feet?

1 yard = 3 feet

You can think of 500 yards as 500 groups of 3 feet.

500 × 3 = 1,500

500 yards is the same as 1,500 feet.

C. Which is longer, 6 feet 10 inches or 77 inches?

1 foot = 12 inches

You can think of 6 feet as 6 groups of 12 inches.

6 × 12 = 72

6 feet 10 inches is 10 inches longer.

72 + 10 = 82

6 feet 10 inches, or 82 inches, is longer than 77 inches.

■ **Talk About Math**   Why do you multiply when you change a larger unit, like feet, to a smaller unit, like inches?

Check Understanding

For another example, see Set A, pages 110–111.

Read this story. Then match each measure in Exercises 1–4 with an equal measure from the story.

Tamara and her grandfather drove to the river to go fishing. Tamara's grandfather parked the truck and said, "The river is not far from here—only about *900 feet*. When I was a boy, I used to walk *5,280 yards* to school every day." Then Tamara asked her grandfather how big the biggest fish he ever caught was. He said, "It was *1 foot 9 inches* long." Tamara wondered what it would be like to be *76 inches* tall, just like her grandfather.

1. 3 miles   **2.** 6 feet 4 inches   **3.** 21 inches   **4.** 300 yards

Practice

For More Practice, see Set A, pages 112–113.

Change each measure to inches.

5. 7 ft   **6.** 7 ft 5 in.   **7.** 2 yd   **8.** 12 ft   **9.** 128 ft

Change each measure to feet.

10. 8 yd   **11.** 2 mi   **12.** 8 yd 2 ft   **13.** 2 yd   **14.** 96 in.

Write each measure as yards and feet.

15. 27 ft   **16.** 72 in.   **17.** 22 ft   **18.** 4 ft 24 in.   **19.** 5 ft

Write each measure as feet and inches.

20. 18 in.   **21.** 45 in.   **22.** 4 yd   **23.** 6 ft 21 in.   **24.** 7 yd 30 in.

Number Sense   Choose the larger measure.

25. 32 in. or 2 ft   **26.** 15 yd or 15 ft   **27.** 56 in. or 4 ft 7 in.

28. 2 yd or 7 ft   **29.** 5 yd or 20 ft   **30.** 3 mi or 15,000 ft

Problem Solving

31. An article stated that the new mall would be "3 football fields long." A football field is 100 yards long. How many feet long will the new mall be?

32. Brian saw an advertisement for 66-inch-long extension cords. Would one of these cords be long enough to reach an outlet that is 5 feet away?

Metric Units of Length

Build Understanding

Michael couldn't understand why none of the wrenches in his dad's toolbox would fit the bolt on his bike.

Later, his father explained it. The wrenches were designed for bolts with measures involving customary units, like $\frac{1}{2}$ inch, $\frac{3}{4}$ inch, and $\frac{5}{16}$ inch. The measure of the head of the bolt on Michael's bike involved metric units.

A. Here are some common *metric units of length*.

One *millimeter* (mm) is about the thickness of a dime.

One *centimeter* (cm) is about the length of the fingernail on your little finger.

A soup can is about 1 *decimeter* (dm) tall.

A baseball bat is about 1 *meter* (m) long.

One thousand baseball bats placed end to end would be about 1 *kilometer* (km) long.

B. Michael measured these two bolts and told his dad that they were both 3 centimeters long. Did Michael measure correctly?

You can see that the top bolt is longer than the bottom bolt. Michael measured correctly, however. The length of both bolts is 3 centimeters to the nearest centimeter.

You can also measure to the nearest millimeter. The top bolt is 34 millimeters. The bottom bolt is 28 millimeters.

■ **Talk About Math**   How many millimeters long is the longest line that you could draw that would measure 5 centimeters if measured to the nearest centimeter?

Check Understanding

Estimation   Choose the most sensible measure.

1. Length of a nail
   a. 8 cm   **b.** 8 km   **c.** 8 dm

2. Width of a button
   a. 12 m   **b.** 12 km   **c.** 12 mm

3. Length of a board
   a. 2 m   **b.** 2 cm   **c.** 2 mm

4. Distance from home to school
   a. 1 dm   **b.** 1 cm   **c.** 1 km

Practice

Estimation   Tell whether you would use centimeters, meters, or kilometers to measure each of the following.

5. Length of a backyard

6. Width of a watchband

7. Length of a river

8. Width of a dollar bill

9. Length of a brick

10. Width of a car

11. Height of a woman

12. Length of a spoon

13. Width of a house

Use the Math Sketcher. Measure to the nearest centimeter and to the nearest millimeter.

14. _____

15. _____

16. _____

17. _____

18. _____

19. _____

20. _____

21. _____

Use the Math Sketcher. Draw a line of each length.

22. 42 mm   23. 8 cm   24. 2 dm   25. Between 5 and 8 cm

26. 2 cm   27. 75 mm   28. 100 mm   29. 4 cm 7 mm

Problem Solving

30. How many millimeters long is the shortest line you could draw that would measure 5 centimeters if measured to the nearest centimeter?

31. Name two classroom objects you would measure in each unit.

   millimeter   centimeter   meter

Equal Metric Measures of Length

Build Understanding

A purple martin birdhouse is divided into separate sections so the birds can nest in groups called *colonies*.

A. Roger's aunt owns Rosie's Posies, a garden shop. She asked Roger to help her display a new purple martin birdhouse she has for sale. The instructions said that the birdhouse should be 450 centimeters above the ground. The pole Roger wants to use is 4 meters long. Is it long enough?

> 1 meter = 10 decimeters
> 1 meter = 100 centimeters
> 1 meter = 1,000 millimeters
> 1,000 meters = 1 kilometer

Since 1 meter is 100 centimeters, 4 meters is 4 × 100 centimeters, or 400 centimeters.

The birdhouse needs to be 450 centimeters above the ground, and the pole is only 400 centimeters long. The pole is not long enough.

B. The height of the birdhouse is 6 decimeters. What is the height in centimeters?

Since 1 decimeter is 10 centimeters, 6 decimeters is 6 × 10 centimeters, or 60 centimeters.

The height of the birdhouse is 60 centimeters.

C. The openings to the birdhouse are 7 centimeters apart. How many millimeters is that?

One centimeter is 10 millimeters, so 7 centimeters is 7 × 10 millimeters, or 70 millimeters.

The openings are 70 millimeters apart.

■ **Talk About Math** For Example A, if Roger had found a pole that was 4,200 millimeters long, would it have been long enough? Explain.

Check Understanding

For another example, see Set B, pages 110–111.

Use the information on page 88 to fill in the blanks.

1. 1 cm = ▦ mm   **2.** 1 dm = ▦ cm   **3.** 1 ▦ = 100 cm = ▦ mm

4. If 1,000 millimeters is 1 meter, how many millimeters is 9 meters?

5. If 100 centimeters is 1 meter, how many centimeters is 22 meters?

Practice

For More Practice, see Set B, pages 112–113.

Write each measure in millimeters.

6. 35 cm   **7.** 7 m   **8.** 4 dm   **9.** 4 m   **10.** 10 dm   **11.** 8 cm

12. 12 m   **13.** 8 dm   **14.** 50 cm   **15.** 22 dm   **16.** 40 m   **17.** 106 cm

Write each measure in centimeters.

18. 15 dm   **19.** 39 m   **20.** 2 km   **21.** 6 m   **22.** 5 km   **23.** 4 dm

24. 4 m   **25.** 11 dm   **26.** 6 km   **27.** 80 m   **28.** 9 dm   **29.** 10 km

30. 24 dm   **31.** 41 m   **32.** 12 km   **33.** 30 dm   **34.** 100 m   **35.** 60 mm

Number Sense   Tell which of these is the larger measure.

36. 67 m or 720 km   **37.** 67 m or 720 cm   **38.** 239 mm or 239 cm

39. 239 mm or 23 cm   **40.** 42 dm or 3 m   **41.** 42 m or 3 dm

42. Write the lengths 8 m, 800 mm, and 8 cm in order from shortest to longest.

Problem Solving

Read for the facts to solve the problems.

43. A wren birdhouse is 22 centimeters tall. How many millimeters is that?

44. Rosie's delivery van goes about 2,000 km each month. How many kilometers is that every year?

45. Rosie's store has two bird baths. One is 5 centimeters deep and the other is 45 millimeters deep. Which is deeper? By how much?

46. If Roger filled the 45 millimeter deep bird bath with 3 centimeters of water, how many millimeters from the top would the water be?

Perimeter

Build Understanding

3 ft

5 ft

5 ft

3 ft

The **perimeter** of the window, or the distance around, is the sum of the lengths of all four sides of the window.

Irene used a tape measure to measure the length of each side of the window. Then Irene added the measures of the sides to find the perimeter.

The perimeter of the window is 3 ft + 5 ft + 3 ft + 5 ft, or **16 feet**.

■ **Talk About Math** How would you have found the perimeter of this window if some of the measurements had been in inches?

Check Understanding

For another example, see Set C, pages 110–111.

Measure the length of each side in centimeters. Then find the perimeter of each figure.

1.

2.
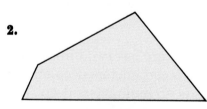

Practice

For More Practice, see Set C, pages 112–113.

Find the perimeter of each figure. **Remember** to label the unit of measure.

3. 15 in. / 8 in. / 8 in. / 15 in.

4. 7 cm / 7 cm / 7 cm / 7 cm / 7 cm / 7 cm

5. 5 yd / 6 yd / 4 yd / 8 yd

6. A rectangle:
length 4 cm
width 3 cm

7. A rectangle:
length 35 mm
width 35 mm

8. A rectangle:
length 3 in.
width 2 in.

9. A triangle:
1 in., 2 in., 3 in.

10. A five-sided figure:
each side 25 mm

11. A triangle:
3 cm, 4 cm, 5 cm

Problem Solving

12. A rectangular window is
3 feet long and 2 feet wide.
What is its perimeter?

13. Another window is 32 inches
long and 26 inches wide.
What is its perimeter?

14. If the window on page 90 was
10 feet tall instead of 5 feet,
what would the perimeter be?

15. What is the perimeter of a
figure that has six equal sides
each 3 ft 4 in.?

16. ▦ **Calculator** Sealer is used around the perimeter
of a window. A tube of sealer will seal 125 feet.
Will one tube be enough to seal 8 windows that
are each 5 feet long and 2 feet wide?

✓

Midchapter _____ **Checkup**

Choose the most sensible measure for each of the following.

1. Width of a door
   a. 1 km   **b.** 1 mm   **c.** 1 m

2. Length of a car
   a. 12 ft   **b.** 12 in.   **c.** 12 mi

3. Choose the larger measure.
3 ft or 38 in.

4. Find the perimeter.
13 m / 5 m / 12 m

Problem-Solving Workshop

Real-Life Decision Making

You are at the zoo with 1 adult and another child. The three of you want to take each ride once. You have $12 and some coupons that allow two people to ride for the price of one.

1. What is the least the Elephant Ride will cost if you use the pay adult price coupon?

2. What is the least the Bus Tour will cost if you use the pay child price coupon?

3. Decide which coupon you will use on which ride.

PAY ADULT PRICE
CHILD RIDES FREE
Good on any zoo ride
2 for 1

PAY CHILD PRICE
ANOTHER CHILD RIDES FREE
Good on any zoo ride
2 for 1

ZOO RIDES

	Sky Ride	Elephant Ride	Bus Tour
ADULT	$2.25	$1.50	$3.00
CHILD	$1.75	$0.75	$2.00

Explore with a Computer

Use the *Geometry Workshop* Project for this activity.

1. Suppose you want to make a rectangle that has a perimeter of 24 units. How many different size rectangles can you make?

2. Use the **Draw** option to make the rectangles. Record the length, width, and perimeter of each one.

3. Use the **Measure** option to check your answers.

```
File Edit Draw Measure Extras Help
MEASURES
pABCD  24.00



Perimeter of:|
Type a label. Then press Return.
```

Number-Sense Project

Look back at pages 80-81.

1. This table shows the estimates Ben collected for the length of a cord he tied around a box.

Estimate	Under by	Over by
20 ft	12 ft	
18 ft	14 ft	
60 ft		28 ft
33 ft		1 ft
50 ft		18 ft
30 ft	2 ft	
50 ft		18 ft
24 ft	8 ft	
30 ft	2 ft	
26 ft	6 ft	

a. How long was Ben's cord?

b. Write a summary telling how accurate the 10 estimates that Ben collected were.

c. Were the people who estimated too high more accurate than those who estimated too low?

Visual-Thinking Activity

You have built a fence in the shape of a square. There are 4 fence posts on each side. How many posts did you use altogether?

Finding Area by Counting Squares

Build Understanding

Lenny's mother is designing a new park for the city. She drew a plan showing the park's buildings, monuments, and playgrounds on grid paper.

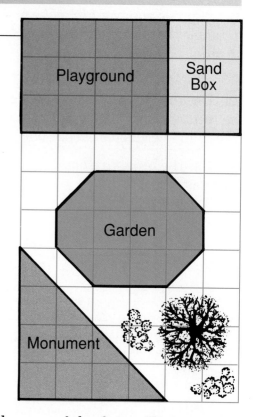

A. Lenny counted 12 shaded squares labeled "playground."

 The length of each side of this square is 1 centimeter. The **area** of the square is 1 **square centimeter** (1 cm²).

Each square shown on the grid paper is 1 square centimeter.

On the plan, the playground covers three rows of 4 square centimeters.

The area of the playground on the plan is 12 square centimeters.

B. What is the area of the monument on the plan? There are 6 whole squares and 4 half squares.

4 half squares equal 2 whole squares.

The area of the monument is 6 cm² + 2 cm², or 8 cm².

C. Find the area of the figure. Each square represents 1 **square inch** (1 sq in.). There are 4 whole squares and 8 half squares.

2 half squares equal 1 whole square, so 8 half squares equal 4 whole squares.

The area of the figure is 4 sq in. + 4 sq in., or 8 square inches.

■**Talk About Math** Is it possible for two figures with different shapes to have the same area? Explain.

Check Understanding

For another example, see Set D, pages 110–111.

Find the area of each shaded figure on the plan on page 94. Each square is 1 square centimeter. **Remember** to label the unit of measure.

1. Sandbox   **2.** Garden   **3.** Sandbox and playground together

Practice

For More Practice, see Set D, pages 112–113.

Find the area of each figure. Each square represents 1 square inch.
Remember to label the unit of measure.

4.   **5.**   **6.**

Find the area of each figure. Each square is 1 cm^2.

7.   **8.**   **9.**

Problem Solving

Critical Thinking   Use grid paper for Exercises 10–13.

10. Show all the different ways you can put together four square inches so the perimeter is 10 inches.

11. Show all the different ways you can put together four square inches so the perimeter is 8 inches.

12. How are the units used to measure the area of a figure different from the units used to measure the perimeter of a figure?

13. If the length of a rectangle is increased from 4 cm to 5 cm, how does this affect the area?

> **TIPS** FOR PROBLEM SOLVERS
>
> **Don't give up.** Some problems take longer than others.

Area of Squares and Rectangles

Build Understanding

A. A Square Deal
Materials: Pieces of paper 1 inch square
Groups: Groups of 4 students

a. Arrange your squares into the figures shown.

b. All of the figures are *rectangles*. The two rectangles with four equal sides are *squares*.

c. Find the area of each square or rectangle by counting.

d. Think about the figures as rows of small squares. For example, the top figure has 1 row containing 5 squares. Write the number of rows each of the figures has and the number of squares in each row.

e. For each figure, multiply the number of rows by the number of squares in each row.

f. Compare your answers in Step e with your answers in Step c. What do you notice?

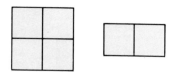

B. Each square in this figure represents 1 square foot. What area is represented by this figure?

There are 2 rows.
Each row contains 3 squares.

$2 \times 3 = 6$

The area represented by the figure is 6 square feet.

Check You can count 6 squares, so the answer checks.

■ Talk About Math
Tell how you can find the area of a square or rectangle if the length and width are given.

Check Understanding

For another example, see Set E, pages 110–111.

1. How many rows of 1-foot squares would fit in the rectangle?

2. How many squares would be in each row?

3. What is the area of the rectangle?

2 ft

8 ft

Practice

For More Practice, see Set E, pages 112–113.

Use the Math Sketcher to measure the length and width of each figure in inches. Then find the area of the figure.

4.

5.

Use the Math Sketcher to measure the length and width of each figure in centimeters. Then find the area of the figure.

6.

7.

8.

Use the Math Sketcher to draw the rectangle with the given dimensions. Then find the area of the figure.

9. Length 3 in.; width 2 in.

10. Length 5 in.; width 3 in.

11. Length 4 in.; width 4 in.

12. Length 4 in.; width 2 in.

13. Length 6 cm; width 2 cm

14. Length 7 cm; width 7 cm

15. Length 5 cm; width 4 cm

16. Length 12 cm; width 1 cm

Problem Solving

Solve each problem.

17. Estimation Measure the front of your math book to the nearest inch. Then find its approximate area.

18. Critical Thinking Do you think a rectangle twice as long and twice as wide as the one pictured will have an area twice as large? Explain.

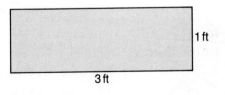

1 ft

3 ft

Make a Table

Build Understanding

Harvey has 24 yards of chicken wire. He will use 1-yard sections of the wire to fence in a rectangular garden. Harvey wants to have the largest possible area. How should he arrange the fence?

PROBLEM SOLVING GUIDE

Understand
QUESTION
FACTS
KEY IDEA

Plan and Solve
STRATEGY
ANSWER

Look Back
SENSIBLE ANSWER
ALTERNATE APPROACH

Understand   QUESTION   What is the largest rectangular area that can be made from 24 yards of chicken wire?

FACTS   Each side must be a whole number of yards since the fence is to be built in 1-yard sections.

KEY IDEA   The perimeter of the garden must be 24 yards.

Plan and Solve   STRATEGY   Use a table to make an organized list.

ANSWER   The garden measuring 6 yards long and 6 yards wide has the largest area for a 24-yard perimeter.

Width (yd)	Length (yd)	Perimeter (yd)	Area (sq yd)
1	11	1 + 11 + 1 + 11 = 24	1 × 11 = 11
2	10	2 + 10 + 2 + 10 = 24	2 × 10 = 20
3	9	3 + 9 + 3 + 9 = 24	3 × 9 = 27
4	8	4 + 8 + 4 + 8 = 24	4 × 8 = 32
5	7	5 + 7 + 5 + 7 = 24	5 × 7 = 35
6	6	6 + 6 + 6 + 6 = 24	6 × 6 = 36
7	5	7 + 5 + 7 + 5 = 24	7 × 5 = 35

Look Back   SENSIBLE ANSWER   The largest rectangular area for Harvey's garden uses all 24 yards of fence and is 6 yards wide and 6 yards long.

■ **Talk About Math**   Does the table include all possibilities?
Why does it stop with the width at 7 yards? Explain.

Check Understanding

1. Suppose Harvey has only 20 yards of fencing.
   Make a table to show the possible gardens.

2. What is the area of the largest
   rectangular garden Harvey could put
   20 yards of fencing around?

3. What are the shapes of the largest
   gardens for both 24 yards of fencing
   and 20 yards of fencing?

Practice

Lupe has 12 meters of chicken wire. She will use 1-meter
sections of the wire to fence in her garden.

4. What is the area of the largest
   rectangular garden Lupe could
   build a fence around?

5. What is the area of the largest
   rectangular garden Lupe could
   enclose if she used the wall of a
   barn for one side of the garden?

Mark is planning a rectangular garden with an area of 40 sq ft.
He will use 1-foot sections of wire to fence the garden.

6. What are the dimensions of the
   garden that needs the least
   amount of fencing?

7. What are the dimensions of the
   garden that needs the least amount
   of fencing if Mark uses the wall of
   his house for one side of the garden?

Choose a ——— Strategy

Neighborly Fences   One piece of chicken wire
is 28 meters long. Another piece of chicken wire
is 36 meters long. Each piece of chicken wire is
to be made into a fence with 1-meter sections.

8. Could these two lengths of chicken wire fence
   two gardens with the same area? Explain.

PROBLEM SOLVING
STRATEGIES

Choose an Operation
Write an Equation
Draw a Diagram
Make a Table

Area of Triangles

Build Understanding

Kites around the world come in many shapes and sizes. Chinese kites are often shaped like dragons, fishes, birds, and butterflies.

The simplest flat kite is made up of a diamond shape. Each of the four sections of the diamond kite at the right is a different color. Find the area of each section.

A. Each section of the kite is a *triangle*. The two top triangles are the same size. If you put them together, they form a rectangle.

The area of the rectangle is 8 in. × 14 in., or 112 sq in.

The area of each of the top triangles is half of 112 sq in., or 56 sq in.

B. The two bottom triangles also form a rectangle.

The area of the rectangle they form is 14 in. × 26 in., or 364 sq in.

The area of each of the bottom triangles is half the area of the rectangle, or 182 sq in.

Kites are the oldest form of aircraft. They were used over 2,000 years ago in both China and Greece.

■ **Talk About Math** What is the area of the triangle inside this rectangle? Explain how you got your answer.

4 cm

18 cm

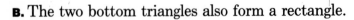

Snake kites are popular in Thailand.

Check Understanding

For another example, see Set F, pages 110–111.

For Exercises 1–3, draw a sketch that will help you find the area
of each triangle. Then give the area in Exercise 3.

1.

3 ft

6 ft

2.

8 dm

5 dm

3.

6 in.

15 in.

Practice

For More Practice, see Set F, pages 112–113.

Find the area of each triangle. **Remember** to label each unit of measure.

4. The triangle in Exercise 1   **5.** The triangle in Exercise 2

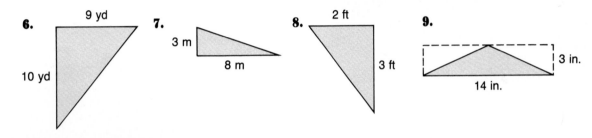

6.

9 yd

10 yd

7.

3 m

8 m

8.

2 ft

3 ft

9.

3 in.

14 in.

Problem Solving

Kim made a diamond kite. The rectangle formed by the 2 top triangles was
12 in. by 14 in. The one formed by the bottom triangles was 14 in. by 20 in.

10. Draw a diagram of
the diamond kite.

11. Find the areas of
the four triangles.

12. Find the area of
the whole kite.

13. Critical Thinking What must be true about two triangles if they
form a rectangle when put together?

Explore _____ Math

This Japanese kite has two crossbars that are 60 cm
long. The crossbars intersect in the middle.

14. Find the area of each small triangle
15. What is the total area of the kite?
16. What do you notice about this kite?

Kites from different
regions of Japan
have different shapes.

Use Data from a Picture

Build Understanding

Matt Allison is a roofing contractor. What is the area of this roof?

27 ft

22 ft

69 ft

55 ft

33 ft

96 ft

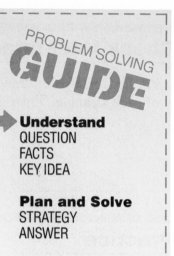

PROBLEM SOLVING GUIDE

Understand
QUESTION
FACTS
KEY IDEA

Plan and Solve
STRATEGY
ANSWER

Look Back
SENSIBLE ANSWER
ALTERNATE APPROACH

Understand

QUESTION   What is the area of the roof?

FACTS   The measurements of the roof are shown.

KEY IDEA   Think of the roof as two rectangles.

Plan and Solve

STRATEGY   Find the area of each rectangle. Then add to find the total area.

Area of large rectangle
96 ft × 33 ft = 3,168 sq ft

Area of small rectangle
27 ft × 22 ft =   594 sq ft

Total area   **3,762 sq ft**

ANSWER   The area of the roof is 3,762 sq ft.

Look Back   ALTERNATE APPROACH   You could divide the figure into two different rectangles. Then find the area of each.

27 ft   22 ft

69 ft

55 ft

33 ft

96 ft

■ **Write About Math** Explain how to find the area of the roof in the example if you think of the roof as a rectangle with a small rectangle missing from it.

Check Understanding

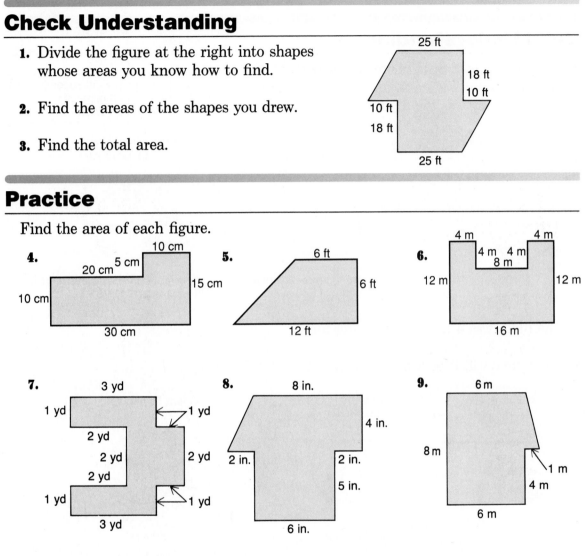

1. Divide the figure at the right into shapes whose areas you know how to find.

2. Find the areas of the shapes you drew.

3. Find the total area.

Practice

Find the area of each figure.

4.

5.

6.

7.

8.

9.

10. Suppose the shape of the figure in Example 7 were enlarged to one square with a length of 4 yards. How would the area of the roof change?

11. Draw a figure that is not a rectangle with an area that is twice the area of the figure in Exercise 4.

Skills _____ **Review**   pages 8–9

Round each number to the nearest hundred.
1. 8,456 **2.** 29,491 **3.** 3,924 **4.** 984 **5.** 49,999

Time

Build Understanding

A. Soo Kim schedules flights at the airport. One flight started at 7:45 A.M. and ended at 12:15 P.M. How long was the flight?

1 minute (min) = 60 seconds (sec)
1 hour (h) = 60 minutes
1 day (da) = 24 hours

Start at 7:45 A.M.

Count the hours from 7:45 A.M. to 11:45 A.M.

There are 4 hours between 7:45 A.M. and 11:45 A.M.

Count the minutes from 11:45 A.M. to 12:15 P.M.

There are 30 minutes between 11:45 A.M. and 12:15 P.M.

The flight was 4 hours 30 minutes long.

B. What time will it be 9 hours 35 minutes after 8:20 P.M.?

Start at 8:20 P.M.

Count 9 hours past 8:20 P.M.

5:20 A.M.

Count 35 minutes past 5:20 A.M.

5:55 A.M.

The time will be 5:55 A.M.

C. Write 5 hours 25 minutes in minutes.

Multiply the number of hours and the number of minutes in each hour.

Add the rest of the minutes.

5 h 25 min = 325 min

■ **Talk About Math** Does A.M. mean from midnight to noon? What does P.M. mean?

Check Understanding

For another example, see Set G, pages 110–111.

1. What is the length of time from 4:25 A.M. to 6:10 A.M.?

2. What time will it be 3 hours 25 minutes after 10:15 P.M.?

3. Write 3 minutes 45 seconds in seconds.

Practice

For More Practice, see Set G, pages 112–113.

What is the length of time from

4. 8:25 A.M. to 10:30 A.M.?

5. 3:35 P.M. to 6:15 P.M.?

6. 10:40 A.M. to 2:00 P.M.?

7. 9:45 P.M. to 6:15 A.M.?

Remember to label A.M. or P.M. What time will it be

8. 2 h 5 min after 3:50 P.M.?

9. 5 h 35 min after 6:35 A.M.?

10. 7 h 45 min after 4:10 P.M.?

11. 3 h 20 min before 5:45 A.M.?

Solve each problem. **Remember** to label the unit of time.

12. Write 3 hours in minutes.

13. Write 15 minutes in seconds.

14. Write 7 hours 19 minutes in minutes.

15. Write 8 days 14 hours in hours.

16. Write 9,300 seconds in minutes and hours.

17. Write 86 hours in days and minutes.

Problem Solving

On the first Sunday in April, most areas in the U.S. change from standard time to *daylight savings time.* The clocks are set *ahead* one hour. In the fall, when standard time resumes, the clocks are set *back* one hour.

18. On the first Sunday in April, an airline passenger was surprised to find that he had missed his flight by almost 1 hour. What do you think happened?

19. **Critical Thinking** It is 5:45 A.M. daylight savings time, the first Sunday in April. What time was it 6 hours and 45 minutes ago?

Temperature: Celsius and Fahrenheit

Build Understanding

A. The temperature is 30 degrees Celsius (30°C). Rachel is wearing shorts and a T-shirt. Should she put on heavier clothing before going outside?

In most places of the world, *degree Celsius* is the unit of measure used for temperature. In the United States, *degree Fahrenheit* is the unit of measure used for temperature.

On the Celsius thermometer, 30 degrees is the same as 86 degrees on the Fahrenheit thermometer (86°F). Rachel does not need to change her clothes.

B. Give the temperature.

▒▒▒°F

The temperature is −5°F.

▪ **Talk About Math** Not all thermometers are marked for every degree. Suppose a thermometer was marked for every 2 degrees. Explain how you would read this thermometer.

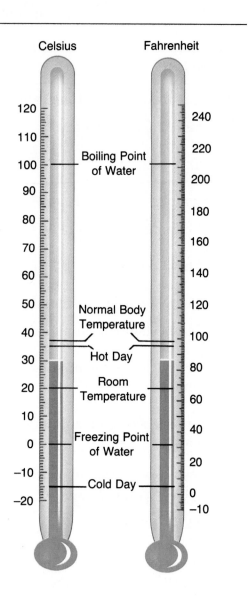

Check Understanding

For another example, see Set H, pages 110–111.

Estimation Choose the more sensible temperature.

1. The temperature for swimming
  35°C   60°C

2. The temperature for ice skating
  29°F   65°F

Practice

For More Practice, see Set H, pages 112–113.

Estimation   Choose the more sensible temperature.

3. Cold day
$20°C$ $-20°C$

4. Hot cocoa
$20°C$ $80°C$

5. Classroom
$23°C$ $70°C$

6. Freezing water
$32°F$ $50°F$

7. Melting butter
$30°F$ $100°F$

8. Boiling water
$100°F$ $212°F$

Give the temperature shown on each thermometer.

| **9.** | **10.** | **11.** | **12.** | **13.** | **14.** |
| °C | °C | °C | °F | °F | °F |

Problem Solving

15. The radio said it was $-20°C$ in Duluth, Minnesota, and $-10°C$ in Winnipeg, Canada. Which city had the colder temperature?

16. Estimation   Ham should be cooked to an internal temperature of $50°$. Would this be degrees Celsius or degrees Fahrenheit?

17. Estimation   The printing in a cookbook is smudged. Should soup be heated to $60°F$ or $160°F$ in a microwave oven?

18. Use Data   If you were going to put gutters around the roof on page 102, how many feet of gutter would you need?

19. A microwave oven has been programmed to defrost and cook a 5-pound beef roast. It takes 8 minutes per pound to defrost and 7 minutes per pound to cook. How many minutes will defrosting and cooking take?

Skills Review

Use a ruler. Measure the line above to the nearest.

1. $\frac{1}{8}$ inch.　　**2.** millimeter.

Use ruler to draw a line of each length.

3. $5\frac{3}{4}$ inches　　**4.** 10 centimeters

Choose the larger measure.

5. 34 in. or 3 ft　　**6.** 2 yd or 5 ft

7. 2 km or 500 m　　**8.** 7 mm or 5 cm

9. Find the perimeter.

6 cm　10 cm　8 cm

10. Find the area. Each square is 1 cm.

11. Measure the length of each side in centimeters. Find the area.

12. Find the area of the triangle in Exercise 9.

What time will it be

13. 3 h 25 min after 5:15 P.M.

14. 2 h 15 min before 4:30 A.M.

Choose the more sensible temperature.

15. Hot day　　40°F or 90°F

16. Freezing water　　0°C or 30°C

Problem-Solving Review

Solve each problem.

17. Jumbo the elephant is 10 feet tall. How many inches tall is Jumbo?

18. Mrs. Reiner's house is on a lot shown by the diagram. What is the perimeter of her lot?

180 ft

120 ft

19. If Mrs. Reiner puts a fence around her lot 3 feet inside the edge, how many feet of fence does she need?

20. The Harris family left home for the beach at 7:00 A.M. They returned home at 4:40 P.M. How long were they away from home?

21. Can Mrs. Lee buy two $0.89 pens and two $1.79 books for $5.00?

22. **Data File** Greg is 5 ft 2 in. tall and weighs 109 lb. Jane is 4 ft 6 in. tall and weighs 80 lbs. Use the chart on pages 116-117 to find the baseball bat each person should buy.

23. **Make a Data File** Look up the regulation length and width of fields or courts for some sports. Make a table showing length, width, perimeter, and area.

Use mental math to compute.

1. 70×5 **2.** 300×600 **3.** $102 + 89$ **4.** 4×203

5. $3 + 28 + 7$ **6.** $563 - 98$ **7.** 6×34 **8.** $598 - 200$

Tell whether you would use inches, feet, yards, or miles to measure each of the following.

9. Height of a tree   **10.** Length of a pencil

11. Distance between two cities   **12.** Length of the classroom

Round 70,652 to the nearest

13. ten-thousand.   **14.** thousand.   **15.** hundred.   **16.** ten.

Find the least common multiple of the following.

17. 3 and 4   **18.** 2 and 8   **19.** 2 and 3   **20.** 9 and 6

What is the length of time from

21. 8:15 P.M. to 11:10 P.M.   **22.** 11:30 A.M. to 3:45 P.M.

Estimate. Then compute.

23. $\begin{array}{r} 87 \\ \times\ 3 \\ \hline \end{array}$ **24.** $\begin{array}{r} 304 \\ \times\ 7 \\ \hline \end{array}$ **25.** $\begin{array}{r} 5,300 \\ -\ 245 \\ \hline \end{array}$ **26.** $\begin{array}{r} 85 \\ \times 21 \\ \hline \end{array}$ **27.** $\begin{array}{r} 315 \\ \times\ 90 \\ \hline \end{array}$

28. $\begin{array}{r} 470 \\ \times\ 55 \\ \hline \end{array}$ **29.** $\begin{array}{r} 65,490 \\ +\ 28,045 \\ \hline \end{array}$ **30.** $\begin{array}{r} 571 \\ \times 400 \\ \hline \end{array}$ **31.** $\begin{array}{r} 901 \\ \times 830 \\ \hline \end{array}$ **32.** $\begin{array}{r} 256 \\ \times 127 \\ \hline \end{array}$

Use a ruler to draw a line of each length.

33. $2\frac{1}{4}$ in.   **34.** $4\frac{3}{8}$ in.   **35.** 6 cm   **36.** 38 mm

Find the perimeter of each figure. For Exercise 39 you need to measure the length of each side of the triangle in centimeters.

37.   **38.**   **39.**

40. Find the area of the triangle in Exercise 37.

Reteaching

Set A   pages 84–85

Change 3 miles to feet.

The chart on page 84 shows that
1 mile = 5,280 feet.

So 3 miles = 3 × 5,280 or 15,840 feet.

Remember to multiply when changing a
larger unit to a smaller unit.

Change each of the measures as described.
Use the equal measures given in the chart
on page 84.

1. 9 feet to inches

2. 6 yards to feet

3. 2 miles to yards

Set B   pages 88–89

Write 5 centimeters in millimeters.

Since 1 centimeter = 10 millimeters,
5 centimeters is 5 × 10 or 50 millimeters.

Remember that since 1 centimeter equals
10 millimeters and 10 centimeters equals
1 decimeter, 1 decimeter equals
100 millimeters.

Use the chart of equal metric measures on
page 88 if necessary.

Write each measure in millimeters.

1. 45 cm   **2.** 6 dm   **3.** 3 m

Write each measure in centimeters.

4. 12 dm   **5.** 6 m   **6.** 3 km

Set C   pages 90–91

Find the perimeter
of this figure.
Add the lengths of
the sides:

15 cm
9 cm   9 cm
9 cm   9 cm

15 cm + 9 cm + 9 cm + 9 cm + 9 cm
or 51 cm

Remember to label the unit of measure.

For Exercise 1, measure each side in
centimeters. Then find the perimeter. For
Exercise 2, use the measurements given to
find the perimeter.

1.   **2.**
                                        4 in.
                                2 in.   2 in.
                                        4 in.

Set D   pages 94–95

Find the area.
Each square represents
1 square inch.

Think: There are 5 whole squares and
4 half squares. 4 half squares equals
2 whole squares. So the area is

5 + 2 = 7 sq in.

Remember that area is measured in
square units.

Find the area of each figure. Each square
represents 1 sq in.

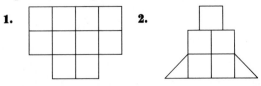

1.   **2.**

Set E   pages 96–97

This rectangle is 2 cm long and 1 cm wide.

The area is 2 × 1 or 2 cm².

Remember that the area of a figure is the number of square units needed to cover the figure.

Measure the length and width of each figure in centimeters. Then find the area of the figure.

1.

2.

Set F   pages 100–101

Find the area of this triangle.

Think of the triangle as one half of a rectangle.

9 in.

6 in.

Rectangle: 9 × 6 = 54 sq in.
Triangle: one half of 54 sq in., or 27 sq in.

Remember that you can sketch a rectangle to help you find the areas of these triangles.

Find the area of each triangle.

1. 10 in.   4 in.   **2.** 12 ft   4 ft

Set G   pages 104–105

The drive to the mountains began at 9:15 A.M. We arrived 4 hours 10 minutes later. What time did we arrive?

Count 4 hours   Count 10 minutes
past 9:15 A.M.   past 1:15 P.M.

We arrived at 1:25 P.M.

Remember that A.M. means from midnight to noon. P.M. means from noon to midnight.

What time will it be

1. 3 hours 15 minutes before 1:30 P.M.?

2. 6 hours 35 minutes after 7:15 A.M.?

3. 3 hours 25 minutes after 10:10 P.M.?

Set H   pages 106–107

On this thermometer, every two degrees is marked. What temperature is shown?

The color in the thermometer is 4 marks above 20°C.

30°C
20°C
10°C
0°C

Since every 2 degrees is marked, the temperature is 4 × 2 or 8 degrees above 20°C, or 28°C.

Remember that not all thermometers are marked for every degree. Give the temperature shown on each thermometer.

1.

10°C
5°C
0°C

2.

40°F
35°F
30°F

More Practice
Set A   pages 84–85

Change each of the measures in Exercises 1–4 to inches.

1. 8 ft   **2.** 4 ft 9 in.   **3.** 4 yd   **4.** 146 ft

Change each measure to feet.

5. 7 yd   **6.** 3 mi   **7.** 10 yd 2 ft   **8.** 6 yd

Number Sense   Choose the larger measure.

9. 14 in. or 3 ft   **10.** 6 yd or 16 ft   **11.** 52 in. or 4 ft 6 in.

Set B   pages 88–89

Write each measure in millimeters.

1. 45 cm   **2.** 6 m   **3.** 5 dm   **4.** 10 m   **5.** 9 dm   **6.** 30 cm

Write each measure in centimeters.

7. 12 dm   **8.** 44 m   **9.** 4 km   **10.** 60 m   **11.** 7 km   **12.** 10 dm

Number Sense   Tell which of these is the larger measure.

13. 94 m or 500 km   **14.** 188 mm or 18 cm   **15.** 9 dm or 96 cm

Set C   pages 90–91

Find the perimeter of each figure. For Exercises 1 and 2 you need to measure the length of each side in centimeters.

1.   **2.**   **3.** 12 in., 12 in., 12 in., 12 in.   **4.** 9 cm, 9 cm, 9 cm, 9 cm, 9 cm

Set D   pages 94–95

Find the area of each figure. Each square represents 1 cm².

1.   **2.**   **3.**   **4.**

Set E pages 96–97

Measure the length and width of each figure in inches.
Then find the area of the figure.

1.

2.

Measure the length and width of each figure in
centimeters. Then find the area of the figure.

3.

4.

Set F pages 100–101

Find the area of each triangle. **Remember** to label each
unit of measure.

1. 6 ft 10 ft

2. 12 cm 3 cm

3. 28 in. 4 in.

Set G pages 104–105

What is the length of time from

1. 6:20 P.M. to 10:10 P.M.?

2. 11:50 A.M. to 4:55 P.M.?

3. Write 5 hours in minutes.

4. Write 3 minutes 18 seconds in seconds.

What time will it be

5. 4 hours 20 minutes after 1:10 P.M.?

6. 6 hours 45 minutes after 7:15 P.M.?

Set H pages 106–107

Estimation Choose the more sensible temperature.

1. Bath water
   10°C   35°C

2. Snow skiing
   25°F   65°F

3. Hot soup
   30°C   80°C

Give the temperature shown on each thermometer.
Remember to determine the number of degrees each mark represents.

4. −10°C −15°C

5. 30°C 20°C

6. 0°F −5°F −10°F

7. 50°F 40°F 30°F

113

Enrichment

Numbers Greater Than and Less Than Zero

Most thermometers show temperatures both above and below 0°. Numbers above zero are greater than 0°. Numbers below zero are less than 0° and are written with a negative sign. A temperature of 5 degrees below zero is written as −5°.

By counting degrees on the thermometer, you can find the new temperature after it rises or falls.

Temperature at 7:00 A.M. was −5°. It rose 11° during the day. Count up 11 degrees from −5°. The new temperature is 6°.

Temperature at 7:00 P.M. was 3°. It fell 7° during the night. Count down 7 degrees from 3°. What is the new temperature?

The number line below is like a thermometer turned on its side. The numbers less than 0 are at the left of 0. You can use the number line to add and subtract. Think of a rise or fall in temperature.

Find −7 + 3.

Add 3 to −7.
Move 3 units to
the right from −7.
−7 + 3 = −4

Find 6 − 9.

Subtract 9 from 6.
Move 9 units to
the left from 6.
6 − 9 = −3

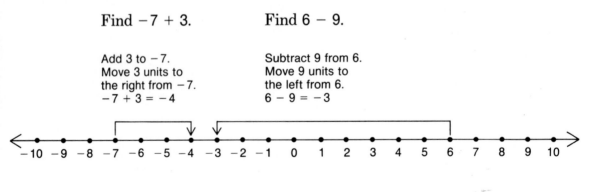

The temperature at 6:00 A.M. was −2°.
Find the new temperature if it

1. rises 1°.　　**2.** falls 3°.　　**3.** rises 6°.　　**4.** falls 8°.

Use the number line to add or subtract.

5. −6 + 2　　**6.** −3 + 4　　**7.** −4 + 4　　**8.** −8 + 0　　**9.** −1 + 7

10. 4 − 7　　**11.** 1 − 5　　**12.** 0 − 2　　**13.** −1 − 5　　**14.** −6 − 4

Chapter 3 Review/Test

Choose the most sensible measure.

1. Length of a hammer

   a. 13 in.   **b.** 13 ft   **c.** 13 mi

2. Width of a nail

   a. 2 m   **b.** 2 km   **c.** 2 mm

Change each measure to feet.

3. 5 yd   **4.** 3 mi

Write each measure in centimeters.

5. 17 m   **6.** 12 dm

Use a ruler.

7. Measure the line to the nearest $\frac{1}{4}$ inch.

8. Draw a line that is 36 mm long.

Which is larger?

9. 38 in. or 3 feet

10. 57 m or 600 cm

11. Find the perimeter.

12. Find the area. Each square represents 1 sq in.

13. Measure the length and width in centimeters. Then find the area.

14. Find the area of the triangle.

15. Write 6 hours 12 minutes in minutes.

16. Which is the more sensible temperature for a hot day, 32°C or 32°F?

17. An eraser is 5 centimeters long. How many millimeters is this?

18. One room is 20 feet long and 12 feet wide. Another room is 18 feet long and 16 feet wide. Which has the greater perimeter?

19. Collette is making a rectangular pen for her puppy. She has 24 feet of fencing. What is the area of the largest pen she can make?

20. Which is an appropriate method to use in finding the area of the lot shown below?

   a. Add 100 × 40 and 20 × 10.
   b. Add 100 × 50 and 20 × 10.
   c. Add 100 × 50 and 80 × 10.
   d. Add the lengths of all the sides.

21. **Write About Math** Two rectangles have the same area, but different perimeters. Explain how this can happen.

Data File

1. Animal Champions

Fastest		
Bird	Indian Swift	200 miles per hour
Land animal	Cheetah	70 miles per hour
Ocean swimmer	Sailfish	68 miles per hour

Slowest		
Fish (marine)	Sea Horse	$10\frac{1}{2}$ inches per minute
Animal	Snail	2 to 3 ft per minute
Mammal	Three-toed Sloth	6 to 8 ft per minute
Reptile	Tortoise	15 ft per minute

1. List
The fastest and slowest speed of some kinds of animals are listed here.

2. Tables
Batter's height is given in feet (') and inches (").

3. Map
The elevation of peaks in Rocky Mountain National Park are on this map.

4. Graph
The graph shows the growth in world population from 1450 to 1980.

5. Chart
The chart shows the size of bat used by some major league baseball players.

2. Baseball Bat Sizes

Boys

Batter's weight in lb	Batter's height							
	3'5"-3'8"	3'9"-4'	4'1"-4'4"	4'5"-4'8"	4'9"-5'	5'1"-5'4"	5'5"-5'8"	5'9"-6
under 60	27"	28"	29"	29"				
61-70	27"	28"	29"	29"	30"			
71-80	28"	28"	29"	30"	30"	31"		
81-90	28"	29"	29"	30"	30"	31"	32"	
91-100	28"	29"	30"	30"	31"	31"	32"	
101-110	29"	29"	30"	30"	31"	31"	32"	
111-120	29"	29"	30"	30"	31"	31"	32"	
121-130	29"	30"	30"	30"	31"	32"	33"	33"
131-140	29"	30"	30"	31"	31"	32"	33"	34"
141-150		30"	30"	31"	31"	32"	33"	34"
151-160		30"	31"	31"	32"	32"	33"	34"
Over 160			31"	31"	32"	32"	33"	34"

4. World Population Growth

Millions

5,000	
4,500	1980: 4,469,934,000
4,000	
3,500	1970: 3,677,837,000
3,000	
2,500	1950: 2,501,000,000
2,000	
1,500	1850:
1,000	1,091,000,000
500	

AD 1450   1650   1850

1980

From Road Atlas.
Copyright © 1990 by Rand McNally & Company. R.L. 90-S-32. Reprinted with permission.

3. Rocky Mountain National Park

5. Bat Facts

Name	Length (inches)	Weight (ounces)
Henry Aaron	35–36	32–34
Ernie Banks	Varied	32
Yogi Berra	35	33
George Brett	34½	32
Jose Canseco	35	35
Roberto Clemente	Varied	40–42
Alvin Dark	Varied	28
Joe DiMaggio	36	34–35
Lou Gehrig	34	38 +
Tony Gwynn	32	30
Rogers Hornsby	34–35	37–39
Reggie Jackson	34½	33
Ted Kluzewski	35	35–39
Mickey Mantle	35	32–34
Willie Mays	35	33–34
Dale Murphy	34½	32
Stan Musial	34½	32–33
Dave Parker	35½	34½
Frank Robinson	36	35
Pete Rose	34–36	31–35
Al Rosen	36	36
Babe Ruth	35–36	37–54
Mike Schmidt	35	32½
Willie Stargell	36½	38
Darryl Strawberry	35	33
Ted Williams	33–35	32–34
Carl Yastrzemski	35	33

Girls

Batter's weight in lb	Batter's height 3'10"-4'	4'1"-4'4"	4'5"-4'8"	4'9"-5'	5'1"-5'4"	5'5"-5'9"
under 40	26"	27"	28"			
40-45	27"	28"	29"	30"		
46-50	27"	28"	29"	30"		
51-60	27"	28"	29"	30"	31"	
61-70	28"	29"	30"	31"	32"	
71-80	28"	29"	30"	31"	32"	33"
81-90	29"	30"	31"	32"	33"	33"
91-100	29"	30"	31"	32"	33"	34"
101-110		30"	31"	32"	33"	34"
111-120		31"	32"	33"	34"	34"
121-130		31"	32"	33"	34"	34"
Over 130			32"	33"	34"	34"

117

1. What does the 6 in 6,000,124,008 mean?

a. 6 billions   c. 6 ten-millions
b. 6 millions   d. 6 ten-billions

2. Round 76,524 to the nearest ten-thousand.

a. 70,000   c. 77,000
b. 76,000   d. 80,000

3. Choose the best estimate.

489 + 308

a. 800   c. 8,000
b. 700   d. 1,000

4. Subtract.

15,000
− 9,724

a. 6,724   c. 6,276
b. 5,276   d. 5,724

5. Find the missing addend.

$n + 92 = 150$

a. 58   c. 242
b. 48   d. 68

6. Which number is a common multiple of 5 and 6?

a. 15   c. 24
b. 30   d. 25

7. Multiply.

800 × 700

a. 560   c. 56,000
b. 5,600   d. 560,000

8. Multiply.

137
× 85

a. 11,545   c. 10,545
b. 11,645   d. 10,645

9. Multiply.

536
× 324

a. 173,564   c. 173,664
b. 174,664   d. 162,624

10. Choose the best estimate.

28 × 495

a. 1,500   c. 8,000
b. 15,000   d. 10,000

11. Choose the most sensible measure.

Height of a table

a. 3 in.   c. 3 yd
b. 6 ft   d. 30 in.

12. Change 30 yd to feet.

a. 90 ft   c. 10 ft
b. 360 ft   d. 300 ft

13. Write 90 meters in centimeters.

   a. 9 cm   **c.** 9,000 cm
   b. 900 cm   **d.** 90,000 cm

14. Find the perimeter.

   a. 22 ft   **c.** 112 ft
   b. 44 ft   **d.** 224 ft

15. Find the area of the rectangle.

   a. 16 sq in.   **c.** 9 in.
   b. 18 sq in.   **d.** 17 in.

16. Write 2 hours 20 minutes in minutes.

   a. 220 minutes   **c.** 120 minutes
   b. 140 minutes   **d.** 80 minutes

17. Find the area of the triangle.

   a. 100 sq ft   **c.** 50 sq ft
   b. 200 sq ft   **d.** 60 sq ft

18. Choose the operation that could be used to solve this problem. Then solve the problem.

In a field there are 27 rows of corn. Each row has 36 corn plants. How many corn plants are in the field?

   a. Addition; 63 corn plants
   b. Multiplication; 972 corn plants
   c. Subtraction; 9 corn plants
   d. Division; 862 corn plants

19. Find the area of the figure.

   a. 1,000 m^2 **c.** 140 m^2
   b. 700 m^2 **d.** 1,300 m^2

Read the problem below. Then answer the question.

In the fifth grade there are 112 students, and 60 of the students are girls. How many boys are in the fifth grade?

20. Which equation can you use to solve the problem?

   a. $112 + 60 = n$
   b. $n + 112 = 60$
   c. $112 \times 60 = n$
   d. $n + 60 = 112$

Division with One-Digit Divisors

4

Did You Know: In international parachuting contests the jumpers try to hit a 10-centimeter disk in the drop zone. Parachutes are used to deliver cargo. Airplanes and helicopters drop food and medicine by parachute.

Number-Sense Project

Estimate

In a "drop the paper clip" contest, how accurate do you think you will be? Estimate in centimeters how close a paper clip will land to an X on a piece of paper. Drop the paper clip from a height of 1 meter.

Gather Data

Bend the paper clip into different shapes and experiment to find the shape that is easiest to drop near the target. Then drop the paper clip 5 times. Record the distance from the X for each drop.

Analyze and Report

Add the distances from the target for your 5 trials. The sum is your total error. Compare your results with those of other students.

121

Dividing Whole Numbers

Build Understanding

A. There were 114 students in the Choral Club. The students were divided equally into 4 groups. How many students were in each group? How many were left? Find 114 ÷ 4.

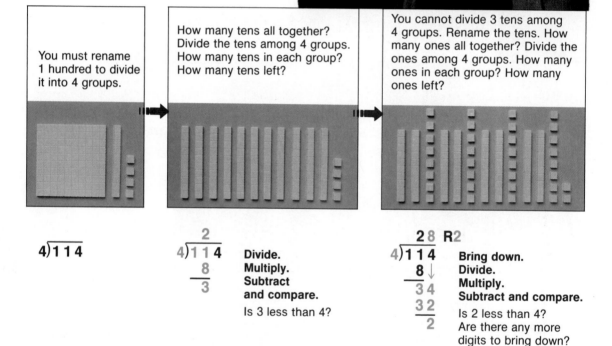

You must rename 1 hundred to divide it into 4 groups.

How many tens all together? Divide the tens among 4 groups. How many tens in each group? How many tens left?

You cannot divide 3 tens among 4 groups. Rename the tens. How many ones all together? Divide the ones among 4 groups. How many ones in each group? How many ones left?

4)114

$$\begin{array}{r} 2 \\ 4\overline{)114} \\ 8 \\ \hline 3 \end{array}$$

Divide.
Multiply.
Subtract and compare.
Is 3 less than 4?

$$\begin{array}{r} 28 \text{ R2} \\ 4\overline{)114} \\ 8\downarrow \\ \hline 34 \\ 32 \\ \hline 2 \end{array}$$

Bring down.
Divide.
Multiply.
Subtract and compare.
Is 2 less than 4?
Are there any more digits to bring down?

There were 28 students in each group with 2 students left.

B. You can check division using multiplication.

Quotient → **3 R4** ← Remainder
Divisor → 8)28 ← Dividend

Check

$$\begin{array}{r} 3 \\ \times 8 \\ \hline 24 \\ + 4 \\ \hline 28 \end{array}$$

← Quotient
← Divisor

← Remainder
← Dividend

■ **Talk About Math**
If the divisor is 6, what can you say about the remainder? Explain your thinking.

Check Understanding

For another example, see Set A, pages 142–143.

Divide.

1. 7)31   **2.** 6)84   **3.** 8)286

4. If the divisor is 7, what can you say about the remainder?

Practice

For More Practice, see Set A, pages 144–145.

Divide. **Remember** to check your work.

5. $2\overline{)19}$ **6.** $9\overline{)65}$ **7.** $5\overline{)37}$ **8.** $4\overline{)39}$ **9.** $5\overline{)48}$ **10.** $3\overline{)29}$

11. $4\overline{)75}$ **12.** $5\overline{)94}$ **13.** $6\overline{)96}$ **14.** $8\overline{)94}$ **15.** $7\overline{)84}$ **16.** $8\overline{)714}$

17. $6\overline{)215}$ **18.** $4\overline{)358}$ **19.** $7\overline{)616}$ **20.** $3\overline{)230}$ **21.** $5\overline{)418}$ **22.** $5\overline{)613}$

23. $75 \div 8$ **24.** $87 \div 5$ **25.** $615 \div 8$ **26.** $839 \div 9$ **27.** $411 \div 3$ **28.** $522 \div 6$

29. $35 \div 7$ **30.** $78 \div 7$ **31.** $41 \div 9$ **32.** $420 \div 8$ **33.** $108 \div 5$ **34.** $288 \div 7$

35. $800 \div 3$ **36.** $94 \div 8$ **37.** $608 \div 5$ **38.** $726 \div 6$ **39.** $394 \div 4$ **40.** $828 \div 9$

41. $891 \div 8$ **42.** $74 \div 5$ **43.** $335 \div 3$ **44.** $582 \div 5$ **45.** $819 \div 9$ **46.** $407 \div 5$

Mixed Practice **Remember** to watch the signs.

47. $994 + 58$ **48.** $676 \div 9$ **49.** 6×342 **50.** $492 - 165$ **51.** $61 \div 7$

52. 8×700 **53.** $732 + 571$ **54.** $435 \div 8$ **55.** $502 - 57$ **56.** $8,016 + 9,023$

57. $444 \div 5$ **58.** 14×58 **59.** $735 \div 3$ **60.** 348×21 **61.** $2,063 - 1,480$

Problem Solving

Solve each problem.

62. The practice room has 8 chairs per row. If 97 students filled as many rows as possible, how many rows were filled? How many students were in the incomplete row?

63. The audience for the Choral Concert filled 24 rows of the auditorium. There were 20 seats in each row. How many people attended the concert?

64. Ron said he divided by 7 and got an answer of 15 R7. Is this correct? Why or why not?

65. What are the possible remainders if you divide by 5?

Critical Thinking Will there always be a remainder if you

66. divide an even number by an odd number?

67. divide an odd number by an even number?

Try and Check

Build Understanding

You are applying for a job at the Who-Done-It Detective Agency. Before you can be hired, you have to take a test to show your mystery-solving abilities. Can you solve this mystery?

The product of two numbers is 48. The sum of the numbers is 19. What are the numbers?

PROBLEM SOLVING
GUIDE

Understand
QUESTION
FACTS
KEY IDEA

▶ **Plan and Solve**
STRATEGY
ANSWER

Look Back
SENSIBLE ANSWER
ALTERNATE APPROACH

Understand   Two numbers multiplied together give 48. The same two numbers added together give 19. You need to find the two numbers.

▶ **Plan and Solve**   STRATEGY   You can *try and check* pairs of numbers until you find the pair that works. Find two numbers whose product is 48. Check to see what their sum is. Continue trying and checking until you find the correct numbers.

1 × 48 = 48	Does 1 + 48 = 19?
2 × 24 = 48	Does 2 + 24 = 19?
3 × 16 = 48	Does 3 + 16 = 19?

ANSWER   The numbers are 3 and 16.

Look Back   Could you solve this problem by trying numbers whose sum is 19 and checking to find a product of 48?

■ **Talk About Math**   Could you solve this problem by randomly picking numbers? Why was it helpful to try and check in an organized manner?

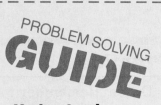

Fingerprinting became a method of indentification in the 1880s.

Check Understanding

The product of two numbers is 40. The sum of the numbers is less than 15. What are the numbers?

1. List all the pairs of numbers that have a product of 40.

2. Check the sum of the numbers in each pair. Give each sum.

3. What pairs of these numbers have a sum less than 15?

Practice

Solve each problem.

4. The product of two numbers is 20. The sum of the numbers is 12. What are the numbers?

5. The sum of two numbers is 10. The difference is 2. What are the numbers?

6. What two numbers have a quotient of 3 and a difference of 8?

7. What two numbers have a product of 32 and a quotient of 2?

8. What two numbers have a sum that is a multiple of 5 and a product of 36?

9. What two pairs of numbers have a product of 72 and a sum that is less than 20?

10. As a detective, you can work mornings, afternoons, or evenings. During each shift you can work in or out of the office. How many choices are there?

11. It takes Phil 25 minutes to drive to the Agency. He begins work at 1 P.M. What time should he leave home if he wants to arrive at work 15 minutes early?

Choose a ▦ Strategy

12. *Time Ticks Away* The test for the detective job took 3 hours 45 minutes. What time did the test start, and what time did it end? Use each of the digits 0, 1, 2, 3, 5, and 6 once to write the starting and ending times.

PROBLEM SOLVING
STRATEGIES

Choose an Operation
Write an Equation
Draw a Diagram
Make a Table
Try and Check

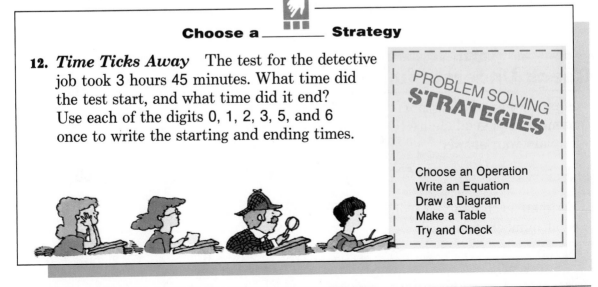

Mental Math and Estimating Quotients

Build Understanding

Here is an estimation strategy to use when estimating quotients. Substitute numbers that are close to the original numbers for the divisor, the dividend, or both. Choose numbers that can be easily divided using mental math. Then divide these **compatible numbers.**

Track-and-field trophies are packed 9 to a box. About how many boxes are needed for 468 trophies?

Estimate 468 ÷ 9 using compatible numbers.

468 ÷ 9

450 ÷ 9 = 50	About 50 boxes
500 ÷ 10 = 50	About 50 boxes
470 ÷ 10 = 47	About 47 boxes
480 ÷ 8 = 60	About 60 boxes

Since there can be more than one way to choose compatible numbers, all these estimates are reasonable.

■ **Talk About Math** Explain how knowing 45 ÷ 9 helped to choose a pair of compatible numbers.

Check Understanding

For another example, see Set B, pages 142–143.

Suppose you are to estimate 503 ÷ 6. Tell if each pair of numbers is a good choice for compatible numbers. Explain your answer.

1. 500 ÷ 6   **2.** 500 ÷ 5   **3.** 480 ÷ 6   **4.** 500 ÷ 10

Estimate each quotient using compatible numbers. Tell what numbers you used.

5. 60 ÷ 7   **6.** 550 ÷ 9   **7.** 295 ÷ 6   **8.** 568 ÷ 8

Practice

For More Practice, see Set B, pages 144–145.

Estimate each quotient using compatible numbers. Tell what numbers you used.

9. 41 ÷ 5   **10.** 55 ÷ 8   **11.** 28 ÷ 6   **12.** 70 ÷ 9   **13.** 43 ÷ 6

14. 22 ÷ 7   **15.** 16 ÷ 9   **16.** 84 ÷ 9   **17.** 22 ÷ 5   **18.** 30 ÷ 8

19. 228 ÷ 4   **20.** 640 ÷ 9   **21.** 405 ÷ 5   **22.** 566 ÷ 7   **23.** 487 ÷ 6

24. 278 ÷ 9   **25.** 711 ÷ 8   **26.** 650 ÷ 8   **27.** 188 ÷ 2   **28.** 231 ÷ 3

29. 492 ÷ 5   **30.** 180 ÷ 8   **31.** 604 ÷ 6   **32.** 803 ÷ 9   **33.** 480 ÷ 7

Mixed Practice   Estimate each quotient or product using compatible numbers. Tell what numbers you used. Then find each quotient or product.

34. 97 × 6   **35.** 206 ÷ 4   **36.** 469 ÷ 6   **37.** 8 × 27   **38.** 356 ÷ 8

39. 157 ÷ 5   **40.** 791 × 21   **41.** 404 ÷ 8   **42.** 41 × 62   **43.** 290 ÷ 7

Problem Solving

44. Find three different pairs of compatible numbers to estimate 621 ÷ 9. Tell which numbers you used and give the estimates.

45. **Use Data**   Use the information about weekly dog food requirements on page 54. For about how many weeks could you feed a Chihuahua with 81 pounds of dog food?

TIPS FOR PROBLEM SOLVERS

Be confident so you can do your best.

Midchapter ✓ **Checkup**

Estimate using compatible numbers. Then divide

1. 59 ÷ 7   **2.** 268 ÷ 4   **3.** 429 ÷ 6   **4.** 538 ÷ 9

5. Use try and check to find two numbers that have a sum of 11 and a product of 24.

Explore as a Team

TIPS FOR
WORKING TOGETHER

Be a good tutor. Make up similar problems or easier ones to help someone understand.

JONES
ERSON

1. How many letters are in the longest last name of someone in your class? Shortest name?

2. Predict the average number of letters in the last names of your classmates.

3. Each member of your group writes his or her last name on a strip of squares, one letter to a square. Cut out the names and tape them together in one strip.

4. Count the number of last names in that strip. Fold the strip into that many equal parts. If there are four names, fold it into four equal parts. There should be the same number of letters in each part. Count the number of letters in each part. This is the average number of letters of the last names in your group.

5. What is the average number of letters of the last names in your group? (Do not count partial letters.)

6. Compare your group's results with those of other groups.

Problem Solving WORKSHOP

Explore with a Computer

Use the *Spreadsheet Workshop Project* for this activity.

1. At the computer, type two numbers whose sum is 15. What is their product? What other combinations of numbers add up to 15? What happens to the product each time you change these numbers? Keep a record of your results. What happens to the product as the first addend becomes larger and the second addend smaller?

2. What two numbers have a product of 144 and a sum of 25?

3. What two numbers have a product of 36 and a sum of 13?

4. What two numbers have the same product and sum?

Number-Sense Project

Look back at pages 120-121. Michelle did the paper clip drop. The table shows her result for 5 trials.

1. What was the total distance from the target for her 5 trials?

2. If she made 5 more trials, would you expect her total distance from the target to be about 20 cm or 50 cm? Why?

Trial	Distance from Target in Centimeters
1	8 cm
2	14 cm
3	9 cm
4	9 cm
5	1 cm

3. If you did the experiment, write a summary comparing your accuracy with Michelle's.

Dividing Larger Numbers

Build Understanding

Suppose you are the Commissioner of Public Works of the city of Frozen Tundra. How much would your city be paying per ton for road salt if you purchased 5 tons?

Since each ton costs the same, divide the 5-ton price by the number of tons. Find 3,695 ÷ 5.

Estimate: Use compatible numbers.
3,500 ÷ 5 = 700
Will the answer be more or less than $700?

Road Salt	
Number of tons	Price
1	$ 895
2	$1,695
3	$2,395
4	$2,995
5	$3,695

$$\begin{array}{r} 7 \\ 5\overline{)3,695} \\ 35 \\ \hline 1 \end{array}$$
Divide.
Multiply.
Subtract and compare.

$$\begin{array}{r} 73 \\ 5\overline{)3,695} \\ 35\downarrow \\ \hline 19 \\ 15 \\ \hline 4 \end{array}$$
Bring down.
Divide.
Multiply.
Subtract and compare.

$$\begin{array}{r} 739 \\ 5\overline{)3,695} \\ 35 \\ \hline 19 \\ 15\downarrow \\ \hline 45 \\ 45 \\ \hline 0 \end{array}$$
Bring down.
Divide.
Multiply.
Subtract and compare.

The cost per ton is $739.

■ **Talk About Math** When you estimated the answer above, how did you know that the answer would be more than the estimate?

Check Understanding

For another example, see Set C, pages 142-143.

Each exercise refers to steps in the example above.
Replace the blanks with *hundred(s)*, *ten(s)*, or *one(s)*.

1. In the first step, 36 __?__ are divided by 5 to give 7 __?__ with 1 __?__ left.

2. In the second step, 1 __?__ 9 __?__ becomes 19 __?__. There are 4 __?__ left.

Divide.

3. 3)129   **4.** 3)442   **5.** 5)359   **6.** 5)2,567

Practice

For More Practice, see Set C, pages 144-145.

Tell whether you would use paper and pencil or mental math. Then find each quotient.

7. 6)150 **8.** 5)240 **9.** 8)375 **10.** 3)693 **11.** 4)924

12. 3)881 **13.** 8)2,549 **14.** 2)1,599 **15.** 5)1,358 **16.** 7)3,577

17. 6)5,480 **18.** 8)1,768 **19.** 8)7,133 **20.** 6)1,889 **21.** 6)5,166

22. 669 ÷ 6 **23.** 4,009 ÷ 6 **24.** 6,741 ÷ 7 **25.** 4,203 ÷ 9 **26.** 8,848 ÷ 4

27. 2,954 ÷ 8 **28.** 5,208 ÷ 7 **29.** 4,441 ÷ 9 **30.** 1,822 ÷ 2 **31.** 4,390 ÷ 5

32. 6,639 ÷ 3 **33.** 2,569 ÷ 8 **34.** 1,477 ÷ 7 **35.** 4,871 ÷ 9 **36.** 5,690 ÷ 8

37. 3,050 ÷ 7 **38.** 2,230 ÷ 2 **39.** 7,008 ÷ 6 **40.** 6,811 ÷ 5 **41.** 9,696 ÷ 8

Mixed Practice **Remember** to watch the signs.

42. 58 × 84 **43.** 123 + 794 **44.** 589 ÷ 6 **45.** 7,819 − 5,486

46. 752 ÷ 8 **47.** $14.98 − $0.63 **48.** 200 × 65 **49.** 76,484 + 52,773

50. 482 × 182 **51.** 4,233 ÷ 5 **52.** 3,046 × 8 **53.** $26.88 + $55.31

Problem Solving

54. There was $738 budgeted for new stop signs. Each sign costs $9. How many signs can be bought?

55. For Exercise 54, suppose that $745 was budgeted for the signs. What does the remainder represent?

56. How much more does it cost per ton to buy road salt one ton at a time than to buy it in a 5-ton load?

57. **Estimation** Which is closer to 68, 4 × 29 or 417 ÷ 6?

Zeros in the Quotient

Build Understanding

A. The Lincoln Junior High Pep Club sold school T-shirts to raise money for new soccer uniforms. They collected $848 from the sales. If each T-shirt sold for $8, how many T-shirts did they sell?

Since each T-shirt cost the same, divide the total by the cost per T-shirt. Find 848 ÷ 8.

Estimate: Use compatible numbers. 800 ÷ 8 = 100

```
    1
8)848        Divide.
  8          Multiply.
  0          Subtract and
             compare.
```

```
    1 0
8)848        Bring down.
  8 ↓        Divide. You cannot
  0 4        divide 4 tens among
             8 groups.
             Write 0 in the quotient.
```

```
    1 0 6
8)848        Bring down.
  8 ↓        Divide.
  0 4 8      Multiply.
    4 8      Subtract and
      0      compare.
```

The Pep Club sold 106 T-shirts.

B. Find $5.70 ÷ 3.

Think of $5.70 as 570 cents.
Write the answer in dollars and cents.

```
   1 9 0
3)570
  3
  27
  27
  0 0
```

```
  $1.9 0
3)$5.7 0
  3
  27
  27
  0 0
```

Has your school ever sold T-shirts to raise money for school activities?

■ **Talk About Math** For Example B, explain why it is necessary to write zero in the quotient.

Check Understanding

For another example, see Set D, pages 142-143.

Divide.

1. 8)165   **2.** 3)841   **3.** 4)$12.32   **4.** 6)3,604

Practice

For More Practice, see Set D, pages 144–145.

Tell whether you would use paper and pencil or mental math.
Then find each quotient.

5. $6\overline{)365}$ **6.** $8\overline{)246}$ **7.** $7\overline{)770}$ **8.** $8\overline{)808}$ **9.** $4\overline{)435}$

10. $7\overline{)4,956}$ **11.** $6\overline{)4,321}$ **12.** $3\overline{)1,517}$ **13.** $6\overline{)4,863}$ **14.** $2\overline{)1,201}$

15. $8\overline{)\$32.24}$ **16.** $5\overline{)\$45.05}$ **17.** $9\overline{)\$57.60}$ **18.** $3\overline{)\$25.20}$ **19.** $7\overline{)\$35.21}$

20. 4,509 ÷ 9   **21.** 2,418 ÷ 8   **22.** 1,400 ÷ 7   **23.** $6.18 ÷ 6   **24.** 4,340 ÷ 7

25. 1,000 ÷ 4   **26.** 1,813 ÷ 3   **27.** $15.50 ÷ 5   **28.** $64.32 ÷ 8   **29.** 3,960 ÷ 9

30. 3,643 ÷ 7   **31.** 2,402 ÷ 6   **32.** 8,170 ÷ 9   **33.** 6,008 ÷ 6   **34.** $71.05 ÷ 7

Mixed Practice   **Remember** to watch the signs.

35. 208 ÷ 5   **36.** 824 + 926   **37.** 18 × 57   **38.** $16.09 + $21.97

39. 1,280 − 571   **40.** 8 × 4,059   **41.** 7,473 ÷ 9

Problem Solving

Solve each problem.

42. The school paid $510 for 3 soccer trips. Each trip
costs the same amount. Find the cost of each trip.

Calculator   Complete each key sequence. Tell the
letter of the operation key that is the last one you can press
so that the answer has fewer than five digits. Give that answer.

43. 49 $\boxed{×}^{a}$ 87 $\boxed{+}^{b}$ 629 $\boxed{÷}^{c}$ 2 $\boxed{×}^{d}$ 4 $\boxed{+}^{e}$ 357 $\boxed{−}^{f}$ 82 $\boxed{÷}^{g}$ 3 $\boxed{=}^{h}$

44. 381 $\boxed{+}^{a}$ 594 $\boxed{÷}^{b}$ 5 $\boxed{×}^{c}$ 16 $\boxed{+}^{d}$ 5928 $\boxed{−}^{e}$ 827 $\boxed{×}^{f}$ 2 $\boxed{+}^{g}$ 827 $\boxed{=}^{h}$

Number Sense   Use the numbers to the left of the equal sign.
Insert the operation sign shown in brackets to form a true equation.

Example: 1 0 5 5 = 21 [÷] becomes 105 ÷ 5 = 21.

45. 6 0 6 6 = 101 [÷]   **46.** 1 0 0 8 = 800 [×]   **47.** 1 8 1 8 6 = 95 [−]

Finding Averages

Build Understanding

What is the average attendance for the four home games played so far by the Washington High football team?

Suppose that the same total number of people attended the four games but they were divided equally so that the same number attended each game. The number at each game is the average attendance.

To find the *average,* add to find the total. Then divide the sum by the number of addends.

| Washington High School Home Football Games ||
Opponent	Attendance
Jefferson High	3,262
Lincoln High	2,248
Madison High	2,000
Roosevelt High	1,810

Paper and Pencil

```
  3,262        2,330
  2,248     4)9,320
  2,000        8
+ 1,810       13
  9,320       12
              12
              12
              12
               00
```

Calculator

3262 $+$ 2248 $+$

2000 $+$ 1810 $÷$

4 $=$ *2330.*

The average attendance was 2,330.

Talk About Math Will the average attendance increase or decrease if the attendance at the fifth home game is 1,000? if the attendance at the fifth home game is 3,000? Explain your thinking.

Check Understanding

For another example, see Set E, pages 142–143.

1. Which game had the least attendance? Was the average more or less than this?

Find the average of each group of numbers.

2. 13   4   2   9   7   **3.** 15   45   39   21   **4.** 7   12   9   19   8

Practice

For More Practice, see Set E, pages 144–145.

Use paper and pencil or a calculator to find the average of each group of numbers.

5. 2 7 4 5 7   **6.** 2 8 9 14 7   **7.** 18 12 10 12

8. 11 17 11 13   **9.** 14 15 26 21   **10.** 51 49 48 28

11. 156 129 144   **12.** 256 284 276   **13.** 5,254 1,226 3,351

14. 7 9 11 22 6   **15.** 94 88 81 101   **16.** 688 791 1,011

17. 411 878 655   **18.** 121 72 208 91   **19.** 2,650 2,983 2,953

20. 18 13 21 28   **21.** 1,881 712 200 491   **22.** 22 8 19 8 14 7

Problem Solving

23. If only 630 people attended the fifth home game, what would be the average attendance?

24. If the team scored 168 points in 8 games, what was their average score per game?

25. Critical Thinking Can the average of a group of numbers be greater than the largest number? smaller than the smallest number? Explain.

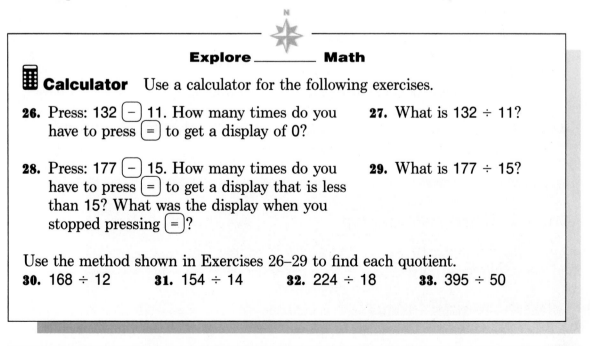

Explore _____ Math

Calculator Use a calculator for the following exercises.

26. Press: 132 ⊟ 11. How many times do you have to press ⊟ to get a display of 0?

27. What is 132 ÷ 11?

28. Press: 177 ⊟ 15. How many times do you have to press ⊟ to get a display that is less than 15? What was the display when you stopped pressing ⊟?

29. What is 177 ÷ 15?

Use the method shown in Exercises 26–29 to find each quotient.
30. 168 ÷ 12   **31.** 154 ÷ 14   **32.** 224 ÷ 18   **33.** 395 ÷ 50

A
L
G
E
B
R
A

Write an Equation

Build Understanding

People in all cultures have relied on animals at some time or another for transportation. Camels are still used to cross deserts because they can travel long distances without water. If it takes a caravan 8 days to cross 192 miles of the Australian outback, how many miles does the caravan average each day?

PROBLEM SOLVING
GUIDE

Understand
QUESTION
FACTS
KEY IDEA

➤ **Plan and Solve**
STRATEGY
ANSWER

Look Back
SENSIBLE ANSWER
ALTERNATE APPROACH

Understand You need to find how many miles the caravan travels each day if it travels the same distance each day.

➤ **Plan and Solve**

STRATEGY *Write an equation* using r for the average distance traveled each day. Then solve the equation.

Distance traveled	Number of days	Average distance traveled each day
192	÷ 8	= r

Estimate:

$200 \div 8 = 25$

Paper and Pencil

$$\begin{array}{r} 24 \\ 8)\overline{192} \\ \underline{16} \\ 32 \\ \underline{32} \\ 0 \quad r = 24 \end{array}$$

▦ **Calculator**

$192 \boxed{÷} 8 \boxed{=} \; 24.$

$r = 24$

ANSWER The caravan travels an average of 24 miles each day.

Look Back The answer is reasonable because it is close to the estimate.

■ **Talk About Math** Explain how to check the division in the problem above.

A millet caravan in Niger Republic heads for Agadez.

Check Understanding

A wagon train can travel 6 miles in one day. How far can it travel in 30 days?

1. Which equation can you use to solve this problem?

   a. $30 \div 6 = w$ **b.** $6 \times 30 = w$

2. Solve the equation and give the answer in a sentence.

Practice

Write an equation. Then find the answer using paper and pencil or a calculator.

3. Arabs have used camels for more than 3,000 years. At an oasis, a camel can drink about 26 gallons of water in 10 minutes. About how many gallons of water could 3 camels drink in 10 minutes?

4. American Indians used dogs and horses to pull a *travois*. A strong dog can pull a load of 75 pounds. A horse can pull 300 pounds. How many more pounds can a horse pull than a dog?

A team of 7 to 10 sled dogs can haul 600 to 1,000 pounds.

5. A sled dog team can travel 9 miles per hour at top speed. At this rate, how many hours will it take to travel 45 miles?

6. The Iditarod Trail was an Alaskan mail and delivery route. Today, the Iditarod Trail Sled Dog Race is the longest dog race in the world. If a dog team travels 79 miles each day, it will complete the race in 2 weeks. About how long is the race?

Skills _____ **Review**

pages 14–15, 22–23, 26–27, 30–31

Add or subtract. **Remember** to watch the signs.

1. $245 + 83$

2. $943 - 72$

3. $604 - 375$

4. $8{,}749 - 3{,}868$

5. $5{,}926 + 3{,}829$

6. $35{,}284 + 8{,}391$

7. $29{,}016 - 3{,}825$

8. $98{,}347 - 29{,}492$

9. $34{,}258 + 95{,}114$

▶ Missing Factors

Build Understanding

A. Multiply or Divide?
Materials: 100 centimeter cubes
Groups: 4 students each

Number of groups	×	Number in each group	=	Total number
	×		=	
	×		=	

a. Each group splits into two teams, Team A and Team B. Each team should make a table like the one shown at the right.

b. Team A organizes some of the cubes into 3 to 9 groups with the same number of cubes in each group. Team A can use some or all of the cubes. Team B should not see what Team A is doing. Team A records the information on its record sheet.

c. Team A gives the cubes it used to Team B with a clue that tells how many groups to use. Team B records the total number of cubes and the number of groups on its record sheet. Team B groups the cubes to find the correct number in each group, records the information, and compares its record with Team A's record.

d. What operation is Team B showing when it organizes the cubes in this way?

e. The teams switch roles and go through the steps again with a different number of cubes. The teams should do this several times.

B. Find the missing factor in $3 \times g = 42$.

Divide to find the missing factor.

$3 \times g = 42$

$g = 42 \div 3$

$g = 14$

$$\begin{array}{r} 14 \\ 3\overline{)42} \\ \underline{3} \\ 12 \\ \underline{12} \\ 0 \end{array}$$

■ **Write About Math** You can use families of facts such as the family shown at the right to find a missing factor. Which fact would help you to find x in $4 \times x = 56$?

Write a family of facts for the equation in Example B.

$$4 \times x = 56$$
$$56 \div 4 = x$$
$$x \times 4 = 56$$
$$56 \div x = 4$$

Check Understanding

For another example, see Set F, pages 142–143.

Find the missing factor. Use families of facts to help.

1. $j \times 7 = 98$ **2.** $864 = a \times 8$ **3.** $7 \times w = 3{,}549$

Practice

For More Practice, see Set F, pages 144–145.

Find the missing factor. Use paper and pencil or a calculator.

4. $3 \times b = 57$ **5.** $n \times 3 = 87$ **6.** $252 = 9 \times y$

7. $v \times 8 = 544$ **8.** $8 \times r = 688$ **9.** $x \times 6 = 2{,}364$

10. $1{,}981 = 7 \times m$ **11.** $4{,}445 = n \times 5$ **12.** $4 \times a = 3{,}488$

13. $t \times 6 = 3{,}288$ **14.** $3 \times c = 1{,}236$ **15.** $3{,}928 = 4 \times y$

16. $9 \times s = 9{,}873$ **17.** $5{,}515 = m \times 5$ **18.** $3 \times d = 7{,}047$

Calculator   Find the missing factor.

19. $37 \times x = 185$ **20.** $4{,}526 = 73 \times n$ **21.** $4{,}234 = h \times 58$

Mixed Practice   Find the missing addend or the missing factor.

22. $618 = j + 104$ **23.** $6 \times t = 4{,}266$

24. $k \times 9 = 1{,}953$ **25.** $1{,}922 + n = 7{,}648$

Problem Solving

26. What is the missing factor if $8 \times n$ is as close as possible to 83?

27. What is the missing factor if $c \times 8$ is as close as possible to 162?

28. What is the missing factor if $6 \times x$ is the least multiple of 6 that is greater than 65?

29. What is the missing factor if $6 \times m$ is a multiple of 6 that is between 181 and 191?

30. Critical Thinking For each equation in Exercises 4–9, write a division fact you could use to help you solve for the variable.

31. Critical Thinking Write a problem you could solve by using one of the equations in the family of facts at the bottom of page 138.

Skills Review

Divide. Then check your work.

1. $3\overline{)17}$ **2.** $5\overline{)48}$ **3.** $8\overline{)652}$

4. $51 \div 6$ **5.** $754 \div 9$

Estimate each quotient using compatible numbers.

6. $186 \div 2$ **7.** $150 \div 6$

8. $352 \div 5$ **9.** $697 \div 7$

10. $238 \div 4$ **11.** $805 \div 9$

Tell whether you would use paper and pencil or mental math. Then find each quotient.

12. $2\overline{)124}$ **13.** $7\overline{)327}$

14. $5\overline{)1,664}$ **15.** $8\overline{)6,488}$

16. $3\overline{)122}$ **17.** $4\overline{)880}$

18. $6\overline{)2,438}$ **19.** $9\overline{)907}$

Find the average of each group of numbers.

20. 4   7   5   8   6

21. 12   19   15   18

22. 44   51   57   48

23. 398   357   379

Find the missing factor.

24. $4 \times n = 64$ **25.** $t \times 5 = 225$

26. $354 = d \times 6$ **27.** $520 = 8 \times s$

28. $f \times 82 = 574$ **29.** $182 = g \times 14$

Problem-Solving Review

Solve each problem.

30. Van has 97 flower bulbs. If he plants the same number of bulbs in each of 6 rows, how many bulbs will be in each row? How many will be left over?

31. What two numbers have a product of 91 and a sum of 20?

32. There are 5,280 feet in 1 mile. If 4 people run a mile relay race, how far should each person run?

33. A baseball and a basketball cost a total of $27.88. The baseball costs $6.90. How much does the basketball cost?

34. If a football costs $14.75, how much will 6 footballs cost?

35. In the past 4 days, Roger practiced the piano for 55 min, 65 min, 40 min, and 72 min. Find his average practice time.

36. You have 22 meters of fencing in 1-meter sections. What is the greatest rectangular area you can enclose?

37. **Data File** Find the average cost of flying roundtrip from Chicago to the cities shown on the chart on pages 244–245.

38. **Make a Data File** Find out how old the past 8 United States presidents were when they became president. What was the average age?

Compare. Use >, <, or =.

1. 835 ▦ 853   **2.** 8,976 ▦ 8,976   **3.** 45,390 ▦ 45,039

Choose the better estimate.

4. 4,762 + 2,815   **5.** 48 × 392   **6.** 206 ÷ 7
   6,000   8,000   20,000   2,000   20   30

Which is larger?

7. 18 in. or 2 ft   **8.** 4 yd or 50 in.   **9.** 10 ft or 3 yd

10. 34 km or 410 m   **11.** 350 cm or 3 m   **12.** 700 mm or 7 cm

Estimate. Then compute.

13.   507   **14.**   67   **15.**   722   **16.**   572   **17.**   65
      × 6   + 45   × 30   − 81   × 14

18. 754 + 109   **19.** 62 × 200   **20.** 7)38   **21.** 2 × 5 × 7

22. 3)67   **23.** 8)682   **24.** 6,275 − 425   **25.** 9 × 6 × 0

26. 5)698   **27.** 503 × 210   **28.** 6)660   **29.** 23 + 17 + 35

Use a ruler to measure the line to the nearest

30. $\frac{1}{4}$ inch.   **31.** $\frac{1}{8}$ inch.   **32.** centimeter.   **33.** millimeter.

Find the area of each figure. For Exercise 36, measure the length and width of the rectangle in centimeters.

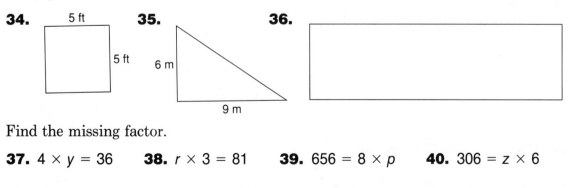

34. 5 ft / 5 ft   **35.** 6 m / 9 m   **36.**

Find the missing factor.

37. $4 \times y = 36$ **38.** $r \times 3 = 81$ **39.** $656 = 8 \times p$ **40.** $306 = z \times 6$

Find the average of each group of numbers.

41. 6 2 5 6 1   **42.** 19 11 13 17   **43.** 345 298 308

Reteaching

Set A   pages 122–123

Find 327 ÷ 6.

```
    5              Quotient →  5 4 R3
6)327        Divisor → 6)3 2 7  ← Dividend
  30                     30↓
   2                      27
                          24
                           3  ← Remainder
```

Remember to check the quotient by multiplying the quotient times the divisor and adding the remainder. This number and the dividend should be the same.

Divide.

1. 2)17   2. 8)33

3. 7)51   4. 4)31

5. 5)39   6. 4)254

7. 6)417   8. 8)628

9. 9)795   10. 5)439

Set B   pages 126–127

Estimate 344 ÷ 9 using compatible numbers.

Choose numbers close to 344, 9, or both, that are easy to divide.

Think: 350 ÷ 10 = 35
        or 360 ÷ 9 = 40

Remember that there is more than one way to choose compatible numbers.

Estimate each quotient using compatible numbers.

1. 238 ÷ 6   2. 408 ÷ 7

3. 316 ÷ 4   4. 278 ÷ 5

5. 512 ÷ 9   6. 543 ÷ 8

7. 369 ÷ 7   8. 416 ÷ 6

9. 511 ÷ 5   10. 387 ÷ 9

Set C   pages 130–131

Find 5,968 ÷ 8.

Estimate: Use compatible numbers.
        5,600 ÷ 8 = 700

```
      7 4 6
8)5,9 6 8
  5 6↓|
    3 6 |
    3 2↓
      4 8
      4 8
        0
```

Remember to estimate the quotient first to see if your answer is reasonable.

Tell whether you would use paper and pencil or mental math. Then find each quotient.

1. 5)450   2. 6)486

3. 7)440   4. 4)873

5. 8)648   6. 9)3,799

7. 6)1,478   8. 7)2,718

9. 9)4,797   10. 5)4,386

Set D   pages 132–133

Find 832 ÷ 4.

Estimate: Use compatible numbers.
$$800 ÷ 4 = 200$$

```
    2          20          208
4)8 3 2    4)8 3 2     4)8 3 2
  8          8↓           8 ↓
  ─          ──           ──
  0          0 3          0 3 2
                           3 2
                           ──
                            0
```

Remember to write zeros in the quotient when needed. Tell whether you would use paper and pencil or mental math. Then find each quotient.

1. 4)323   2. 6)606

3. 7)4,221   4. 5)2,850

5. 3)1,229   6. 4)1,603

7. 8)4,165   8. 6)5,344

Set E   pages 134–135

Find the average of this group of numbers.

41   52   48   43

To find the average:
  first, add to find the total,
  then divide the sum by the
  number of addends.

```
  4 1         4 6 ← Average
  5 2      4)1 8 4
  4 8        1 6
+ 4 3        ──
─────         2 4
1 8 4         2 4
              ──
               0
```

Remember that the average of a group of numbers cannot be greater than the largest number or smaller than the smallest number.

Use paper and pencil or a calculator to find the average of each group of numbers.

1. 7   5   4   8   6

2. 185   196   151   168

3. 2,341   1,846   2,860

Set F   pages 138–139

Find the missing factor in

$4 \times n = 208$.

Divide by 4 to find the missing factor.

$n = 208 ÷ 4$

```
    5 2
4)2 0 8
  2 0
  ──
  0 8
    8
    ─
    0
```
$n = 52$

Remember that it is helpful to think of a family of facts. Find the missing factor.

1. $5 \times n = 185$

2. $n \times 3 = 93$

3. $288 = n \times 8$

4. $7 \times n = 3,073$

5. $2,892 = 6 \times n$

Independent Study **RETEACHING**

More Practice

Set A   pages 122–123

Divide. **Remember** to check your work.

1. $3\overline{)17}$ 2. $8\overline{)59}$ 3. $6\overline{)38}$ 4. $5\overline{)36}$ 5. $4\overline{)29}$

6. $9\overline{)84}$ 7. $6\overline{)84}$ 8. $7\overline{)91}$ 9. $4\overline{)86}$ 10. $5\overline{)89}$

11. $4\overline{)298}$ 12. $5\overline{)328}$ 13. $6\overline{)326}$ 14. $7\overline{)579}$ 15. $8\overline{)554}$

16. $6\overline{)567}$ 17. $4\overline{)390}$ 18. $5\overline{)423}$ 19. $8\overline{)634}$ 20. $9\overline{)569}$

21. $84 \div 9$ 22. $78 \div 7$ 23. $706 \div 8$ 24. $507 \div 6$

Set B   pages 126–127

Estimate each quotient using compatible numbers.

1. $37 \div 6$ 2. $17 \div 5$ 3. $34 \div 9$ 4. $31 \div 4$

5. $66 \div 8$ 6. $328 \div 8$ 7. $180 \div 9$ 8. $155 \div 5$

9. $219 \div 3$ 10. $287 \div 7$ 11. $168 \div 8$ 12. $240 \div 5$

13. $196 \div 9$ 14. $430 \div 8$ 15. $558 \div 8$ 16. $619 \div 7$

17. $341 \div 7$ 18. $717 \div 9$ 19. $536 \div 6$ 20. $338 \div 5$

21. Choose two of the exercises above. Explain why you chose the compatible numbers you used.

Set C   pages 130–131

Tell whether you would use paper and pencil or mental math. Then find each quotient.

1. $8\overline{)176}$ 2. $6\overline{)283}$ 3. $5\overline{)320}$ 4. $9\overline{)738}$ 5. $7\overline{)226}$

6. $4\overline{)946}$ 7. $8\overline{)3,289}$ 8. $6\overline{)1,866}$ 9. $2\overline{)1,359}$ 10. $5\overline{)4,207}$

11. $6\overline{)2,597}$ 12. $8\overline{)5,752}$ 13. $7\overline{)1,575}$ 14. $3\overline{)1,783}$ 15. $5\overline{)4,643}$

16. $4\overline{)3,347}$ 17. $6\overline{)3,889}$ 18. $9\overline{)6,417}$ 19. $7\overline{)4,379}$ 20. $8\overline{)6,586}$

Set D   pages 132–133

Tell whether you would use paper and pencil or mental math. Then find each quotient.

1. $7\overline{)426}$
2. $6\overline{)304}$
3. $9\overline{)457}$
4. $8\overline{)872}$
5. $3\overline{)624}$

6. $6\overline{)5,430}$
7. $2\overline{)1,618}$
8. $9\overline{)1,807}$
9. $4\overline{)1,840}$
10. $8\overline{)3,247}$

11. $8\overline{)\$56.24}$
12. $6\overline{)\$13.20}$
13. $3\overline{)\$10.50}$
14. $6\overline{)\$19.20}$
15. $2\overline{)\$18.16}$

Mixed Practice   Remember to watch the signs.

16. $738 + 862$
17. 17×48
18. $1,470 - 482$

19. $7 \times 3,046$
20. $309 \div 6$
21. $6 \times 2,108$

22. $946 + 485$
23. $2,376 - 1,469$
24. $8,345 \div 9$

Set E   pages 134–135

Use paper and pencil or a calculator to find the average of each group of numbers.

1. 8   7   5   6   4
2. 15   10   12   11
3. 16   12   18   10

4. 18   13   14   15
5. 19   14   21   18
6. 52   45   44   47

7. 151   133   154
8. 280   255   248
9. 4,263   1,819   1,367

Set F   pages 138–139

Find the missing factor.

1. $4 \times n = 96$
2. $n \times 2 = 86$
3. $432 = 8 \times n$

4. $n \times 6 = 318$
5. $9 \times n = 711$
6. $n \times 7 = 2,009$

7. $3,415 = n \times 5$
8. $2,748 = n \times 4$
9. $n \times 6 = 5,544$

10. $n \times 8 = 5,528$
11. $7 \times n = 8,442$
12. $3,174 = 3 \times n$

Calculator   Find the missing factor.

13. $43 \times n = 387$
14. $3,886 = 67 \times n$
15. $5,056 = 79 \times n$

16. $n \times 53 = 4,081$
17. $5,762 = n \times 86$
18. $7,644 = n \times 91$

Enrichment

Short Division

With one-digit divisors, you can save time and space by using the short form of division.

This shows the long form and the short form for $2,402 \div 7$.

Long form

```
    3              34             343 R1
7)2,402        7)2,402        7)2,402
  21             21             21
  ‾‾             ‾‾             ‾‾
   3             30             30
                 28             28
                 ‾‾             ‾‾
                  2             22
                                21
                                ‾‾
                                 1
```

Short form

```
    3              3 4            3 4 3 R1
7)2,4³0 2      7)2,4³0²2      7)2,4³0²2
```

Divide. Use the short form.

1. $3\overline{)46}$ **2.** $8\overline{)395}$ **3.** $4\overline{)274}$ **4.** $6\overline{)745}$ **5.** $5\overline{)548}$

6. $7\overline{)751}$ **7.** $8\overline{)6,592}$ **8.** $3\overline{)1,362}$ **9.** $5\overline{)3,025}$ **10.** $8\overline{)4,163}$

11. $9\overline{)3,457}$ **12.** $7\overline{)5,106}$ **13.** $9\overline{)3,656}$ **14.** $8\overline{)4,237}$ **15.** $9\overline{)3,821}$

16. $7\overline{)2,656}$ **17.** $7\overline{)6,734}$ **18.** $4\overline{)2,987}$ **19.** $5\overline{)3,212}$ **20.** $8\overline{)9,673}$

Chapter 4 Review/Test

Divide.

1. $5\overline{)93}$ **2.** $7\overline{)226}$

3. $6\overline{)5{,}321}$ **4.** $9\overline{)4{,}188}$

5. $4\overline{)521}$ **6.** $8\overline{)1{,}601}$

Estimate each quotient using compatible numbers.

7. $26 \div 3$ **8.** $65 \div 8$

9. $252 \div 5$ **10.** $598 \div 6$

Find the average of each group of numbers.

11. 3   5   8   12

12. 54   80   91   95   100

13. 1,238   1,367   1,520

Find the missing factor.

14. $4 \times n = 84$

15. $x \times 6 = 228$

16. $9 \times a = 2{,}322$

17. If the average of 5 numbers is 9, could the largest number be 8? Explain.

Solve each problem.

18. Miss Watkins bought 4 new tires for $268. What was the cost of each tire?

19. Use try and check to find two numbers that have a sum of 17 and a product of 30.

20. Use the table below to find the average daily sales for the days shown.

Daily Sales

Monday	$786
Tuesday	$824
Wednesday	$767
Thursday	$825
Friday	$1,028

Read this problem. Then answer the questions below.

A machine produces 88 parts per hour. How many parts can the machine produce in 8 hours?

21. Which sentence could be completed to answer the question?

   a. The machine produces ▦ parts in 1 hour.

   b. The machine takes ▦ hours to produce 88 parts.

   c. In 8 hours the machine produces ▦ parts.

22. Write an equation and solve the problem.

23. **Write About Math** When you divide a number by 8, what is the greatest remainder you can get? Explain your answer.

Division with Two-Digit Divisors

Did You Know: Tolls are not only charged on roads, but they are also charged on some bridges, canals, and ferries.

Number-Sense Project

Estimate
Estimate how much money will be collected by 4 automatic toll gates during 1 hour of heavy traffic. Each car must pay a toll of 25¢.

Gather Data
Make your estimate and then gather estimates from 4 other people.

Analyze and Report
Compare your results with those of other students. Are there any patterns in the estimates? Do people in any age group tend to estimate higher than people in other groups?

149

Mental Math for Division

Build Understanding

A. Sgt. Wilson is a forest ranger. One of his duties is to collect information on bears. During a 20-day span of time, there were 140 bear sightings. What was the average number of sightings per day for this time?

Find 140 ÷ 20 using mental math.

Here is a mental math strategy you can use when dividing mentally. Look for *special numbers* that are easy to divide.

140 ÷ 20 = 7   Think: 14 ÷ 2 = 7
So, 14 tens ÷ 2 tens = 7

The average number was 7 bear sightings per day.

B. Find 6,000 ÷ 30 mentally using special numbers.

6,000 ÷ 30 = 200

Think: 600 tens ÷ 3 tens = 200.

■ **Write About Math** Write a multiplication sentence that will help you find 2,400 ÷ 20 mentally.

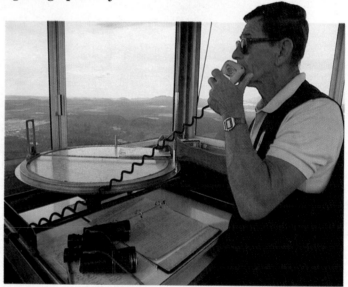

Check Understanding

For another example, see Set A, pages 174–175.

Copy and complete.

1. 4,000 ÷ 10 = ▦00   **2.** 800 ÷ 40 = 2▦   **3.** 1,000 ÷ 50 = ▦▦

4. Find 180 ÷ 60 using special numbers.

150

Practice

For More Practice, see Set A, pages 176–177.

Use mental math to find each quotient.

5. 400 ÷ 40   **6.** 80 ÷ 20   **7.** 240 ÷ 80   **8.** 250 ÷ 50

9. 600 ÷ 60   **10.** 490 ÷ 70   **11.** 9,000 ÷ 30   **12.** 6,300 ÷ 90

13. 320 ÷ 80   **14.** 180 ÷ 30   **15.** 10,000 ÷ 20   **16.** 230 ÷ 10

17. 350 ÷ 70   **18.** 36,000 ÷ 40   **19.** 300 ÷ 60   **20.** 8,100 ÷ 90

21. 5,600 ÷ 70   **22.** 1,800 ÷ 90   **23.** 6,100 ÷ 10   **24.** 540 ÷ 60

25. 24,000 ÷ 80   **26.** 1,600 ÷ 40   **27.** 400 ÷ 50   **28.** 1,200 ÷ 20

29. 160 ÷ 80   **30.** 270 ÷ 90   **31.** 800 ÷ 40   **32.** 320 ÷ 10

33. 450 ÷ 50   **34.** 480 ÷ 60   **35.** 12,340 ÷ 10   **36.** 30,300 ÷ 30

37. 2,020 ÷ 20   **38.** 3,090 ÷ 30   **39.** 4,550 ÷ 50   **40.** 14,070 ÷ 70

Problem Solving

Use the information in the table. There are 30 days in April and June and 31 days in May. **Remember** to use mental math when it is helpful.

41. What was the average number of bear sightings reported per day in April at the North Camp?

42. What was the average number of bear sightings reported per day in April at the South Camp?

43. How many bear sightings were reported in May in Ridge Park?

44. What is the average number of bear sightings reported per day in June in Ridge Park?

Ridge Park Bear Sightings			
Camp	April	May	June
North	0	0	0
South	60	50	20
East	51	160	35
West	26	40	5

Estimating Quotients

Build Understanding

How many coins do you think the average person carries each day? One day, data was gathered from 31 people. Together they had a total of 157 coins. About how many coins did each person have?

Estimate 157 ÷ 31.

You can use **compatible numbers** as an estimation strategy when estimating quotients.

Substitute numbers that are close to the original numbers for the divisor, the dividend, or both. Choose numbers so you can divide easily.

157 ÷ 31   Think: 150 ÷ 30 = 5

Each person had about 5 coins.

■ **Write About Math**   Often there can be more than one way to choose compatible numbers when estimating a quotient. List the compatible numbers that could be used for 358 ÷ 46 and for 4,581 ÷ 64.

Check Understanding

For another example, see Set B, pages 174–175.

Suppose you are to estimate the quotient of each of the given numbers divided by 60. What compatible number would you use for the given number?

1. 358   **2.** 661   **3.** 1,187   **4.** 6,258

5. Name some 2-digit numbers that would be compatible with 4,000 in 4,000 ÷ ▦▦.

Estimate each quotient. Tell what compatible numbers you used.

6. 345 ÷ 49   **7.** 421 ÷ 21   **8.** 4,611 ÷ 47   **9.** 8,109 ÷ 87

Practice

For More Practice, see Set B, pages 176–177.

Estimate each quotient. Tell what compatible numbers you used.

10. 33)346 **11.** 47)244 **12.** 81)326 **13.** 17)123 **14.** 71)500

15. 43)290 **16.** 34)357 **17.** 22)175 **18.** 92)944 **19.** 57)418

20. 554 ÷ 59 **21.** 498 ÷ 49 **22.** 349 ÷ 62 **23.** 251 ÷ 39

24. 816 ÷ 79 **25.** 389 ÷ 41 **26.** 634 ÷ 82 **27.** 341 ÷ 73

28. 7,209 ÷ 78 **29.** 3,179 ÷ 83 **30.** 2,438 ÷ 49 **31.** 2,917 ÷ 63

32. 8,221 ÷ 41 **33.** 6,053 ÷ 59 **34.** 8,905 ÷ 31 **35.** 5,426 ÷ 62

Problem Solving

36. If 21 people had 137 coins, give an estimate of about how many coins each person had.

37. How much change will you get if you pay a $17.42 grocery bill with a twenty-dollar bill?

38. **Critical Thinking** If you have $5 in quarters, how many quarters do you have?

39. If you have 3 quarters, 2 dimes, 4 nickels, and 8 pennies, how much money do you have?

Reading ———— Math

A
L
G
E
B
R
A

▶ *Numbers and Symbols*   A bicycle club planned to ride a total of ___a___ miles on a trip Saturday. They plan to cover ___b___ miles in the morning. How many miles will they have left for the afternoon?

1. Describe what *a* represents.   **2.** Describe what *b* represents.

3. Which tells how to solve the problem?   *a + b*   *a − b*   *a ÷ b*

The members of the club keep a record of the number of miles they ride each month. There are ___c___ members. In June, the members rode a total of ___d___ miles. What is the average number of miles each member rode in June?

4. Describe what *c* represents.   **5.** Describe what *d* represents.

6. Which tells how to solve the problem?   *c ÷ d*   *c × d*   *d ÷ c*

One-Digit Quotients

Build Understanding

A. Division
Materials: Place-value materials
Groups: 4 students

a. You are to find the number in each group if 112 is divided equally into 18 groups. First show the number 112 with place-value materials.

b. Can you divide 1 hundred into 18 groups? Trade 1 hundred for 10 tens. Do you have enough tens to divide them into 18 groups?

c. Trade the tens for ones and divide. How many are in each group? Record your results.

d. Model several other division problems. Decide the number to divide and the number in each group. Use dividends of 120 or less and two-digit divisors. Record your results.

B. Find 178 ÷ 21.

$$\begin{array}{r} 8 \\ 21\overline{)178} \end{array}$$

Divide.
To find 178 ÷ 21, think: what is 17 ÷ 2? 8

$$\begin{array}{r} 8\ \text{R}10 \\ 21\overline{)178} \\ \underline{168} \\ 10 \end{array}$$

Multiply.
Subtract and compare.

■ **Talk About Math** In Example B, explain why the 8 is placed above the digit in the ones place of the dividend.

Check Understanding

For another example, see Set C, pages 174–175.

Divide.

1. 15)87 **2.** 31)96 **3.** 23)138 **4.** 71)570 **5.** 81)729

Practice

For More Practice, see Set C, pages 176–177.

Tell whether you would use paper and pencil or mental math.
Then find each quotient.

6. $32\overline{)39}$ 7. $23\overline{)98}$ 8. $37\overline{)74}$ 9. $20\overline{)87}$ 10. $12\overline{)49}$

11. $11\overline{)58}$ 12. $12\overline{)38}$ 13. $21\overline{)79}$ 14. $21\overline{)98}$ 15. $52\overline{)417}$

16. $40\overline{)98}$ 17. $31\overline{)87}$ 18. $50\overline{)350}$ 19. $42\overline{)336}$ 20. $54\overline{)165}$

21. $51\overline{)153}$ 22. $30\overline{)201}$ 23. $83\overline{)664}$ 24. $43\overline{)175}$ 25. $40\overline{)210}$

26. $58\overline{)182}$ 27. $87\overline{)451}$ 28. $60\overline{)305}$ 29. $62\overline{)251}$ 30. $74\overline{)166}$

31. $71 \div 30$ 32. $69 \div 21$ 33. $87 \div 76$ 34. $218 \div 50$ 35. $105 \div 35$

36. $505 \div 72$ 37. $719 \div 94$ 38. $222 \div 30$ 39. $869 \div 91$ 40. $407 \div 67$

41. $684 \div 85$ 42. $547 \div 60$ 43. $416 \div 52$ 44. $675 \div 75$ 45. $321 \div 40$

Mixed Practice   **Remember** to watch the signs.

46. 6×85 47. $592 + 608$ 48. $814 - 327$ 49. $604 \div 7$ 50. $8{,}244 + 3{,}008$

51. $734 \div 88$ 52. 24×80 53. $542 \div 6$ 54. 46×118 55. $3{,}651 - 407$

Problem Solving

56. Liza watched a 90-minute television program. Write this time in hours and minutes.

57. Ed is 49 inches tall. Write this height in feet and inches.

58. **Use Data**   Use the information in the table on page 151. What was the total number of bear sightings reported in April for Ridge Park?

Estimation   Louis used compatible numbers to estimate $2{,}485 \div 55$.

59. What compatible numbers did he use if his estimate was 50?

60. What compatible numbers did he use if his estimate was 40?

Adjusting the Quotient

Build Understanding

A. Mrs. Saito's science class was conducting experiments with eggs. There were 184 eggs to be shared equally among 23 students. How many eggs was this per student?

Find 184 ÷ 23.

The shell of an egg contains pores so water and gases can pass through it.

Estimate: Use compatible numbers. 180 ÷ 20 = 9

Paper and Pencil

```
      9
23)184
  207
```
Divide.
Think:
What is 18 ÷ 2? 9
Multiply.
207 is greater than 184.

```
      8
23)184
  184
    0
```
Try 8.
Multiply.
Subtract and compare.

🖩 Calculator

184 ÷ 23 = 8.

Each student received 8 eggs.

B. Find 418 ÷ 42.

```
42)418
```
Divide.
Think:
What is 41 ÷ 4? 10
Since 10 × 42 is 420, there are less than 10.

```
      9 R 40
42)418
  378
   40
```
Try 9.
Multiply.
Subtract and compare.

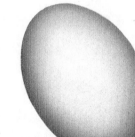

C. 🖩 **Calculator** Find 532 ÷ 56.

532 ÷ 56 = 9.5

■ **Talk About Math** For Example A, explain where the number 207 came from and describe what it tells you about the quotient.

Check Understanding

For another example, see Set D, pages 174–175.

Refer to the problem at the right.

1. How was 6 selected for the quotient? **2.** Explain why 6 will not work.

```
      6
14)68
  84
```

Divide.

3. 28)112 **4.** 12)90 **5.** 76)149 **6.** 12)57 **7.** 37)344

Practice

For More Practice, see Set D, pages 176–177.

Use paper and pencil or a calculator. Show each answer as a quotient with a whole-number remainder (if there is one) or as a decimal with one digit after the decimal point.

8. $27\overline{)135}$ **9.** $29\overline{)116}$ **10.** $12\overline{)96}$ **11.** $68\overline{)375}$ **12.** $47\overline{)329}$

13. $38\overline{)228}$ **14.** $12\overline{)59}$ **15.** $14\overline{)55}$ **16.** $36\overline{)295}$ **17.** $26\overline{)159}$

18. $29\overline{)68}$ **19.** $58\overline{)103}$ **20.** $57\overline{)415}$ **21.** $96\overline{)642}$ **22.** $13\overline{)93}$

23. $15\overline{)53}$ **24.** $48\overline{)452}$ **25.** $19\overline{)49}$ **26.** $78\overline{)767}$ **27.** $86\overline{)832}$

28. $87 \div 26$ **29.** $38 \div 18$ **30.** $98 \div 14$ **31.** $127 \div 45$ **32.** $108 \div 58$

33. $222 \div 37$ **34.** $869 \div 91$ **35.** $644 \div 85$ **36.** $400 \div 55$ **37.** $377 \div 91$

38. $456 \div 95$ **39.** $328 \div 46$ **40.** $549 \div 63$ **41.** $64 \div 38$ **42.** $267 \div 28$

Problem Solving

Eggs are sized by weight. The table at the right gives information about egg classifications.

43. What is the minimum weight for 1 dozen medium eggs? 4 dozen large eggs?

44. If 5 dozen eggs weighed 150 ounces, what kind of eggs were they?

45. The age of an egg can be tested using a float test. A fresh egg will sink to the bottom of a container and rest on its side. If 184 eggs were tested and 135 of them sank and rested on their sides, how many eggs were not fresh?

46. Critical Thinking Jack has fewer than 3 dozen eggs. If he divides the eggs evenly among 2, 3, or 4 friends, there is one left over. But if he divides them among 5 friends, there are no extras. How many does he have?

Egg Classifications

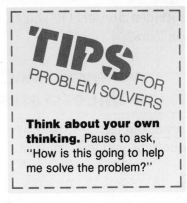

Weight class	Minimum weight per dozen
Small	18 ounces
Medium	21 ounces
Large	24 ounces
Extra Large	27 ounces
Jumbo	30 ounces

TIPS FOR PROBLEM SOLVERS

Think about your own thinking. Pause to ask, "How is this going to help me solve the problem?"

Using Rounded Divisors

Build Understanding

A. As you saw in the last lesson, sometimes you need to adjust your first try for the quotient because the quotient is too big. Sometimes it is helpful to round the divisor and use the rounded divisor to find the quotient.

Find 259 ÷ 38.

```
      6 R31
38)259      Divide.
   228      Think: 38 rounds to 40.
    31              What is 25 ÷ 4? 6
            Multiply.
            Subtract and compare.
```

When you use a rounded divisor to find the quotient, *be sure to use the actual divisor* when you multiply.

B. Sometimes when a rounded divisor is used, the first try for the quotient is too small, and the quotient must be adjusted.

Find 198 ÷ 28.

```
      6              Divide.
28)198              Think: 28 rounds to 30.
   168                      What is 19 ÷ 3? 6
    30              Multiply.
                    Subtract and compare.
                    30 is greater than 28,
                    so 6 is too small.
```

```
      7 R2
28)198      Try 7.
   196      Multiply.
     2      Subtract and compare.
```

■ **Talk About Math** For both Examples A and B, tell what quotient you would have tried if you did not use a rounded divisor. Do you think it is helpful to use rounded divisors?

Check Understanding

For another example, see Set E, pages 174–175.

For Exercises 1-4, use rounded divisors. Tell what quotient you will try first. Then give the answer.

1. 48)139   **2.** 21)162   **3.** 39)196   **4.** 426 ÷ 58

Practice

For More Practice, see Set E, pages 176–177.

Use paper and pencil or a calculator. Show each answer
as a quotient with a whole-number remainder (if there is
one) or as a decimal with one digit after the decimal point.

5. $37\overline{)293}$ **6.** $77\overline{)691}$ **7.** $68\overline{)233}$ **8.** $19\overline{)146}$ **9.** $18\overline{)125}$

10. $89\overline{)573}$ **11.** $47\overline{)421}$ **12.** $56\overline{)501}$ **13.** $58\overline{)243}$ **14.** $48\overline{)153}$

15. $199 \div 39$ **16.** $150 \div 17$ **17.** $125 \div 16$ **18.** $274 \div 67$

Mixed Practice   Tell whether you would use paper and pencil,
a calculator, or mental math. Then find each answer.

19. $8{,}000 + 2{,}351$ **20.** $3{,}421 - 2{,}985$ **21.** 42×97 **22.** $364 \div 4$

23. 5×804 **24.** $6{,}525 \div 8$ **25.** $372 \div 81$ **26.** $458 + 927$

27. 342×9 **28.** $6{,}000 \div 30$ **29.** $984 \div 27$ **30.** 348×129

Problem Solving

31. Mental Math   Which of the following will help
you find $10{,}000 \div 200$ mentally?

200×500 200×50

32. Number Sense   Find the missing digits
in the division problem at the right.
There is no remainder.

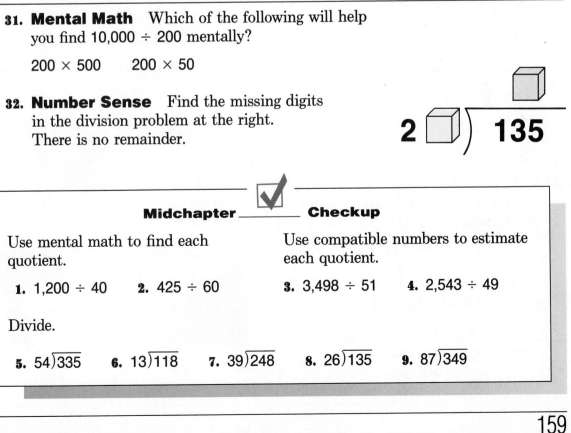

$2\,\square\,\overline{)135}$

Midchapter ✓ Checkup

Use mental math to find each
quotient.

1. $1{,}200 \div 40$ **2.** $425 \div 60$

Use compatible numbers to estimate
each quotient.

3. $3{,}498 \div 51$ **4.** $2{,}543 \div 49$

Divide.

5. $54\overline{)335}$ **6.** $13\overline{)118}$ **7.** $39\overline{)248}$ **8.** $26\overline{)135}$ **9.** $87\overline{)349}$

Problem Solving WORKSHOP

Number-Sense Project

Look back at pages 148-149.
A group of several students organized their data in three rows, one row for each age group.

1. How many adults did these students interview?

2. How many people in all did these students interview?

3. How many adults estimated that less than $100 was collected in an hour?

4. If $3,024.00 was collected in a day, what was the average amount per hour?

5. One type of automatic toll gate allows 1 car to pass every 4 seconds. If the toll is $0.25 per car, how much money would be collected in 1 hour by 4 of these gates during heavy traffic?

Age Group	Number Surveyed	Estimate Under $100	$100–$199	$200–$299	Over $300
Pre-Teen	III	I			II
Teenager	HH HH I			IIII	HH
Adult			HH I	II	

Visual Thinking Activity

Here are four views of the same cube.

1. What color is opposite red?

2. What color is opposite orange?

MATH laugh

Why is SMILES the longest word in the English language?

ANSWER:
Because there is a mile between the two Ss.

Real-Life Decision Making

On June 1, you have $70 to spend on your summer vacation. You get $5 a week allowance. You plan to ride horses at Gallager's Stables 10 to 15 times during the summer. You also need money for the movies and other summer activities.

1. If you pay separately for each horseback ride, what is the least amount of money you will spend?

2. If you buy a summer pass but ride only 10 times, how much money will be wasted?

3. If you buy a summer pass and ride 15 times, how much money will you save?

4. Decide how you will spend your money during summer vacation.

Movies
Children 12 or under $3   Adults $6

Gallager's Stables
2-hour ride $5
Summer Pass $65

Math-at-Home Activity

Take a survey of 9 people who live with or near you. Ask them if they think the same side of the moon always faces earth. Graph the results.

Does Same Side of Moon Always Face Earth?

Yes									
No									
	1	2	3	4	5	6	7	8	9

Number of answers

Two-Digit Quotients

Build Understanding

The drive from St. Louis to New Orleans is about 768 miles. If you used 24 gallons of gasoline on this trip, how many miles per gallon did you average?

Find 768 ÷ 24.

Estimate: Use compatible numbers. 800 ÷ 20 = 40   Will the answer be more or less than the estimate?

Each car in the U.S. uses an average of about 700 gallons of gasoline each year.

Paper and Pencil

```
      3
24)768
   72
    4
```
Divide.
Think:
24 rounds to 20.
What is 7 ÷ 2? 3
Multiply.
Subtract and compare.

```
     32
24)768
   72 ↓
    48
    48
     0
```
Bring down.
Divide.
Think:
What is 4 ÷ 2? 2
Multiply.
Subtract and compare.

Calculator

768 ÷ 24 = *32.*

You averaged 32 miles per gallon.

■ **Talk About Math**   When you estimated the answer above, how did you know that the answer would be less than the estimate?

Check Understanding

For another example, see Set F, pages 174–175.

1. **Estimation**   Use compatible numbers to estimate the answers to Exercises 2-5.

Divide.

2. 32)544   3. 42)3,913   4. 27)605   5. 3,087 ÷ 58

Practice

For More Practice, see Set F, pages 176–177.

Use paper and pencil or a calculator. Show each answer as a
quotient with a whole-number remainder (if there is one) or as
a decimal with one digit after the decimal point. **Remember**
to estimate to tell if the answer is reasonable.

6. 20)920   **7.** 30)840   **8.** 43)995   **9.** 70)5,844   **10.** 80)3,511

11. 71)999   **12.** 38)871   **13.** 28)653   **14.** 73)4,535   **15.** 54)1,739

16. 611 ÷ 18   **17.** 968 ÷ 39   **18.** 2,325 ÷ 68   **19.** 1,989 ÷ 58

Problem Solving

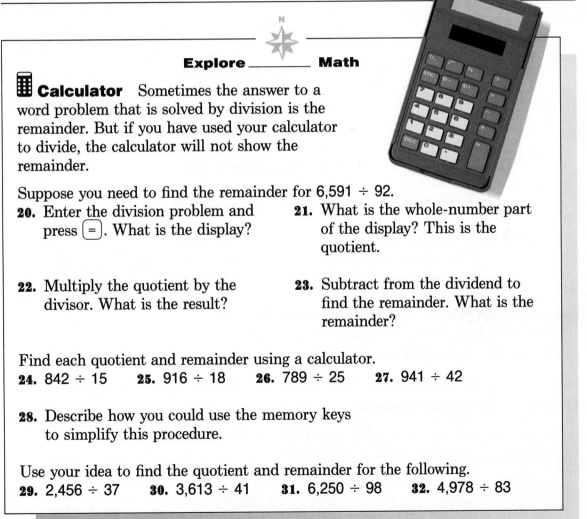

Explore ———— Math

Calculator   Sometimes the answer to a
word problem that is solved by division is the
remainder. But if you have used your calculator
to divide, the calculator will not show the
remainder.

Suppose you need to find the remainder for 6,591 ÷ 92.

20. Enter the division problem and
press $\boxed{=}$. What is the display?

21. What is the whole-number part
of the display? This is the
quotient.

22. Multiply the quotient by the
divisor. What is the result?

23. Subtract from the dividend to
find the remainder. What is the
remainder?

Find each quotient and remainder using a calculator.
24. 842 ÷ 15   **25.** 916 ÷ 18   **26.** 789 ÷ 25   **27.** 941 ÷ 42

28. Describe how you could use the memory keys
to simplify this procedure.

Use your idea to find the quotient and remainder for the following.
29. 2,456 ÷ 37   **30.** 3,613 ÷ 41   **31.** 6,250 ÷ 98   **32.** 4,978 ÷ 83

Interpret the Remainder

PROBLEM SOLVING
GUIDE

Build Understanding

Connie has 250 telephone books to deliver. The books are packaged 18 books to a carton. How many cartons does Connie need to complete the order?

Understand
QUESTION
FACTS
KEY IDEA

Plan and Solve
STRATEGY
ANSWER

Look Back
SENSIBLE ANSWER
ALTERNATE APPROACH

Understand   How many cartons does Connie need? There are 18 books in a carton. Connie needs a total of 250 books. You need to find how many 18s there are in 250.

Plan and Solve   STRATEGY   To find how many groups of 18 are in 250, use division.

$$\begin{array}{r} 13 \ \text{R16} \\ 18\overline{)250} \end{array}$$

The quotient tells that 13 full cartons of books are needed. The remainder of 16 means you need 16 more books. So, you need one more carton to complete the order, even though you will not use all 18 books in the carton.

ANSWER   Connie needs 14 cartons of books.

Look Back   Since Connie needs 250 books, 13 cartons of 18 books is not enough because $13 \times 18 = 234$. Since $14 \times 18 = 252$, 14 cartons is enough.

■ **Talk About Math**   What question could you ask for the situation above that would use the quotient as the answer? the remainder as the answer?

Check Understanding

Use paper and pencil or a calculator to solve each problem. Tell what you would do with the remainder.

1. If 250 names are printed in an office directory and each page holds 18 names, how many pages will be filled?

2. There were 250 directories to be packed. As many full cartons of 18 directories as possible were packed. How many directories were left over?

3. There are 250 guests invited to a phone company banquet. They will be seated at tables that can each seat 18. How many tables are needed to seat all the guests?

Practice

Use paper and pencil or a calculator to solve each problem.

4. Telephones are packaged 20 to a crate. The Kelso Building needs 150 telephones. How many crates have to be opened to fill the order?

5. If the installer uses as many full crates of 20 phones as he can, how many more phones will he need for the 150-phone order?

6. How many 12-foot sections of telephone wire can be cut from a 508-foot roll of wire?

7. How much will be left after as many 12-foot sections as possible have been cut from a 508-foot roll?

8. A telephone company truck can carry 55 telephone poles. How many truck loads will be needed to carry 692 poles?

9. Wall phones are packed 15 to a carton. The installer used as many full cartons as he could for an order of 76 wall phones. He took the rest from another full carton. How many phones were left in the partially used carton?

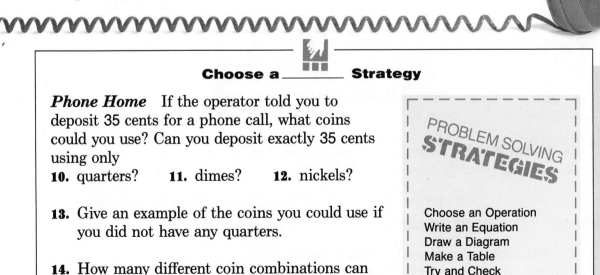

Choose a ⬛ **Strategy**

Phone Home If the operator told you to deposit 35 cents for a phone call, what coins could you use? Can you deposit exactly 35 cents using only

10. quarters? **11.** dimes? **12.** nickels?

13. Give an example of the coins you could use if you did not have any quarters.

14. How many different coin combinations can you use?

PROBLEM SOLVING
STRATEGIES

Choose an Operation
Write an Equation
Draw a Diagram
Make a Table
Try and Check

Three-Digit Quotients

Build Understanding

Every year, as a public health service, a local television station sponsors cholesterol testing. This year, the station set up 21 sites for testing. There were 8,673 people tested. What was the average number of people tested at each site?

Find 8,673 ÷ 21.

Estimate: Use compatible numbers.
   8,000 ÷ 20 = 400

Paper and Pencil

```
      4              41             413
21)8,673       21)8,673        21)8,673
   84             84↓             84
    2             27              27
                  21              21↓
                   6             63
                                 63
                                  0
```

Calculator

8673 ÷
21 = *413.*

Each site averaged 413 people tested. This is a reasonable answer because it is close to the estimate.

■ **Talk About Math** Describe how you would check your answer for the problem above.

Check Understanding

For another example, see Set G, pages 174–175.

1. **Estimation** Use compatible numbers to estimate the answers to Exercises 2-5.

2. 32)6,880   3. 18)2,359   4. 32)5,381   5. 4,603 ÷ 37

Practice

For More Practice, see Set G, pages 176–177.

Use paper and pencil or a calculator. Show each answer as a quotient with a whole-number remainder (if there is one) or as a decimal with one digit after the decimal point. **Remember** to estimate to tell if the answer is reasonable.

6. 40)8,745   **7.** 60)7,479   **8.** 27)6,641   **9.** 44)9,597   **10.** 62)7,936

11. 23)7,498   **12.** 52)8,049   **13.** 31)8,412   **14.** 22)9,331   **15.** 42)9,385

16. 5,885 ÷ 34   **17.** 9,583 ÷ 43   **18.** 3,977 ÷ 27   **19.** 9,583 ÷ 57

Problem Solving

20. Last year, 5,967 people had their cholesterol checked at 17 sites. What was the average number of people checked at each site?

21. The station donated $5 to a heart fund for every person checked. Since 8,673 people were checked, what was the total donation?

22. One site checked a total of 1,631 people in 3 days. An odd thing happened. On each of the 3 days, the number checked was double the number from the day before. How many people were checked on each of the 3 days?

Skills	Review		pages 46-71

Multiply.

1. 800 × 400   **2.** 320 × 1,000   **3.** 20 × 500   **4.** 2 × 9 × 5

5. (31 × 25) × 4   **6.** 4 × 32   **7.** 8 × 725   **8.** 3,462 × 9

9. 5 × 421   **10.** 50 × 85   **11.** 629 × 300   **12.** 30 × 508

13. 29 × 53   **14.** 82 × 621   **15.** 307 × 921   **16.** 761 × 508

Zeros in the Quotient

Build Understanding

A person's family name may describe a place or a job, or it may have a meaning in another language. Many Japanese names have two parts. The name Morita means *forest-rice field*. In English-speaking countries, Smith is the most common name. It means *worker with metal*.

A. In the telephone book of a large city, there are 4,908 Smiths listed. There are 12 pages in this section. On the average, how many Smiths are on each page?

Find 4,908 ÷ 12.

How many Smiths do you know?

Estimate: Use compatible numbers.
$$5,000 ÷ 10 = 500$$

Paper and Pencil

```
      4
12)4,9 0 8
   48
    1
```

```
     40
12)4,9 0 8
   48↓
    10
     0
    10
```
Think:
What is 10 ÷ 12? 0
Write 0 in the quotient.

```
    409
12)4,9 0 8
   48
    10
     0↓
    108
    108
      0
```

 Calculator

4908 ÷ 12 =

409

There are about 409 names on each page.

B. Find 7,624 ÷ 38.

```
   2 0 0 R24
38)7,6 2 4
   76↓
    0 2
     0↓
     2 4
      0
     2 4
```
Think:
What is 2 ÷ 38? 0
Write 0 in the quotient.

What is 24 ÷ 38? 0
Write 0 in the quotient.

■ **Talk About Math** If you had worked Example A and got 49 as the answer, how would you have known that it was not the correct answer? Would estimation have helped you?

Check Understanding

For another example, see Set H, pages 174–175.

Estimation Use compatible numbers to estimate each quotient. Then find the answer.

1. $64\overline{)3{,}857}$ 2. $37\overline{)8{,}152}$ 3. $49\overline{)9{,}823}$ 4. $8{,}532 \div 21$ 5. $5{,}831 \div 56$

Practice

For More Practice, see Set H, pages 176–177.

Use paper and pencil or a calculator. Show each answer as a quotient with a whole-number remainder (if there is one) or a decimal with one digit after the decimal point.

Remember to estimate to tell if the answer is reasonable.

6. $73\overline{)2{,}953}$ 7. $57\overline{)1{,}155}$ 8. $42\overline{)9{,}664}$ 9. $28\overline{)9{,}815}$ 10. $34\overline{)7{,}041}$

11. $33\overline{)6{,}878}$ 12. $32\overline{)9{,}619}$ 13. $19\overline{)3{,}808}$ 14. $48\overline{)1{,}471}$ 15. $29\overline{)9{,}879}$

16. $28\overline{)2{,}888}$ 17. $77\overline{)4{,}629}$ 18. $31\overline{)6{,}222}$ 19. $17\overline{)6{,}874}$ 20. $35\overline{)7{,}175}$

21. $40\overline{)3{,}226}$ 22. $12\overline{)8{,}458}$ 23. $62\overline{)6{,}560}$ 24. $53\overline{)4{,}794}$ 25. $16\overline{)8{,}151}$

26. $9{,}104 \div 44$ 27. $5{,}402 \div 18$ 28. $9{,}217 \div 23$ 29. $6{,}530 \div 62$

Problem Solving

Solve each problem.

30. More than 104 million people have the family name Chang. It is the most common name in the world. Chang means *mountain* in Chinese. Write 104 million in standard form.

31. A complete Spanish name has three parts. The first name is given at birth, the middle name is the father's family name, and the last name is the mother's family name. The middle name is used for the phone book. There are 1,275 Garcias listed in 11 columns of a phone book. On the average, how many Garcias are listed in each column?

In China, a person's family name is written before his or her individual name.

32. **Critical Thinking** Explain how addition could be used to solve a subtraction equation such as $p - 15 = 9$.

Choose an Operation

Build Understanding

When the McGee family travels by car, they record the different vanity license plates they see. When they get home, they add the license plates to an alphabetical master list that they keep with their computer. The list has 462 license plates on it. It is 14 pages long. On the average, how many plates are listed on each page?

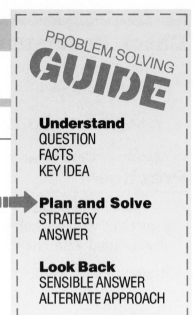

PROBLEM SOLVING
GUIDE

Understand
QUESTION
FACTS
KEY IDEA

➤ **Plan and Solve**
STRATEGY
ANSWER

Look Back
SENSIBLE ANSWER
ALTERNATE APPROACH

Understand   You need to find how many plates are listed on each page. There are a total of 462 plates listed on 14 pages. You need to find how many plates there are in each of the 14 groups.

➤ **Plan and Solve**   STRATEGY   Since you are finding the average number of plates, you divide.

Paper and Pencil

$$14\overline{)462} \quad \begin{array}{r} 33 \\ \hline \end{array}$$

```
         33
    14)462
       42
       ──
        42
        42
        ──
         0
```

Calculator

462 ÷ 14 = *33.*

ANSWER   On the average, there are 33 plates listed on each page.

Look Back   Be sure to check your work.
14 × 33 = 462. The answer is correct.

■ **Talk About Math**   Does the answer above mean that there are exactly 33 plates listed on each page?

Check Understanding

After their latest trip, the McGees' list grew from 462 plates to 491 plates. How many plates did they see on this trip?

1. Will you add, subtract, multiply, or divide?

2. Find the answer.

3. Explain why you chose the operation you used.

Practice

Tell whether to add, subtract, multiply, or divide. Then solve the problem using paper and pencil or a calculator.

4. Later, the McGees found a list of 38 plates in their car. When they added these to the 491 plates already listed, how many did they have in all?

5. If a state sets aside $15 of the profit from each vanity plate for the construction of rest stops, how many vanity plates need to be sold to total $6,450 for rest stops?

6. In one state, it costs $50 for a vanity plate. The cost for a regular plate is $24. How much more does a vanity plate cost?

7. If the McGees collect an average of 125 license plates each year, how many plates will they have after 10 years?

Choose a ___ Strategy

Day	Number of plates
Friday	20 or 30
Saturday	17
Sunday	twenty something
Monday	21

How Many Was That? Mitzi McGee was trying to remember the number of vanity plates they saw on each day of a 4-day trip. She knew that they averaged 24 plates each day. The table shows what she remembers about the number for each day.

8. What was the total number of plates seen on the 4-day trip?

What was the number of plates seen

9. on Sunday?   **10.** on Friday?

Skills Review

Use mental math to find each quotient.

1. 600 ÷ 60   **2.** 320 ÷ 40

3. 180 ÷ 30   **4.** 9,000 ÷ 90

5. 8,000 ÷ 20   **6.** 5,400 ÷ 90

Estimate each quotient. Tell what compatible numbers you used.

7. 461 ÷ 45   **8.** 423 ÷ 81

9. 812 ÷ 39   **10.** 3,054 ÷ 28

11. 7,429 ÷ 24   **12.** 6,602 ÷ 32

Divide. Show each answer as a quotient with a whole number remainder (if there is one) or as a decimal with one digit after the decimal point.

13. $63\overline{)71}$ **14.** $26\overline{)86}$

15. $30\overline{)94}$ **16.** $79\overline{)435}$

17. $24\overline{)482}$ **18.** $17\overline{)31}$

19. $87\overline{)854}$ **20.** $55\overline{)109}$

21. $33\overline{)421}$ **22.** $40\overline{)920}$

23. $67\overline{)3,722}$ **24.** $29\overline{)1,500}$

25. $45\overline{)9,555}$ **26.** $50\overline{)8,352}$

27. $99\overline{)8,925}$ **28.** $17\overline{)3,405}$

Tell what quotient you would try first if you used rounded divisors. Then give the answer.

29. $21\overline{)183}$ **30.** $44\overline{)350}$

31. $77\overline{)708}$ **32.** $19\overline{)118}$

Problem-Solving Review

Solve each problem.

33. If you have 4 quarters, 3 dimes, and a nickel, how much money will you have left after paying $0.52 for a muffin?

34. If 1 wheel on a pictograph represents 70 cars, how many wheels represent 1,715 cars?

35. How many 8-ounce hamburgers can you make with 216 ounces of hamburger?

36. In 1961 a manned balloon reached a height of 113,740 feet. In 1966 another balloon reached a height of 123,800 feet. How much higher did the second balloon go?

37. Mrs. Kouros ran an average of 45 minutes each day for 3 days. If she ran 50 minutes the first day and 50 minutes the second day, how many minutes did she run the third day?

38. **Data File** If you could watch meteor showers each night they are visible during one year, what is the average number of meteors per hour you would see? Use the chart on page 244–245.

39. **Make a Data File** Find the price per case and the price per item for at least 4 different items that come in cases. Make a table to show the name of the item, the number of items per case, and the prices.

Choose the most sensible measure.

1. Length of a pencil
7 in.   7 ft   7 yd

2. Distance from home to school
3 ft   3 yd   3 mi

3. Height of a door
6 ft   6 yd   6 mi

4. Length of a man's finger
8 cm   8 m   8 km

5. Height of a flag pole
9 mm   9 m   9 km

6. Width of a stamp
23 mm   23 cm   23 m

Estimate each quotient. Tell what compatible numbers you used.

7. $647 \div 65$ **8.** $312 \div 61$ **9.** $238 \div 62$ **10.** $913 \div 88$

11. $4{,}201 \div 39$ **12.** $3{,}597 \div 92$ **13.** $8{,}877 \div 92$ **14.** $1{,}052 \div 99$

Use mental math to compute.

15. 9×50 **16.** $400 + 365$ **17.** 980×0 **18.** $60 \div 3$

19. $700 \div 7$ **20.** $738 - 99$ **21.** $320 \div 4$ **22.** $900 \div 9$

23. $164 \div 4$ **24.** 7×140 **25.** 4×102 **26.** $800 \div 20$

Use the figure for Exercises 27–29.
27. Measure the length and width of the figure in centimeters.

28. Find the area of the figure.

29. Find the perimeter of the figure.

Find the missing addend or factor.

30. $f + 16 = 56$ **31.** $144 = 4 \times h$ **32.** $750 = 25 + q$ **33.** $2 \times n = 284$

Estimate. Then compute.

34. $\begin{array}{r} 14{,}256 \\ + 25{,}906 \end{array}$ **35.** $\begin{array}{r} 570 \\ \times\ \ 6 \end{array}$ **36.** $\begin{array}{r} 32{,}500 \\ -\ 4{,}125 \end{array}$ **37.** $\begin{array}{r} 1{,}234 \\ \times\ \ \ 5 \end{array}$ **38.** $\begin{array}{r} 303 \\ \times\ 40 \end{array}$

39. $5)\overline{124}$ **40.** $35 + 525$ **41.** $8)\overline{6{,}234}$ **42.** $23)\overline{87}$ **43.** $40)\overline{140}$

Find the average of each group of numbers.

44. 5 2 1 4 3   **45.** 54 43 57 42   **46.** 298 305 285

Reteaching

Set A pages 150–151

Find 360 ÷ 90.

Look for special numbers.

When both numbers end in zero, you can cross out the zeros.   36Ø ÷ 9Ø

Then divide: 36 ÷ 9 = 4

360 ÷ 90 = 4

Remember, you can cross out zeros only if both numbers end with zero.

Use mental math to find each quotient.

1. 420 ÷ 60   **2.** 280 ÷ 70

3. 810 ÷ 90   **4.** 560 ÷ 80

5. 2,800 ÷ 40   **6.** 4,500 ÷ 50

Set B pages 152–153

Estimate 334 ÷ 82 using compatible numbers.

Choose numbers that are close to 334, 82, or both. Think: 8 × 4 = 32. Replace 82 with 80 and 334 with 320.

320 ÷ 80 = 4

So 334 ÷ 82 is about 4.

Remember that there is more than one way to choose compatible numbers.

Estimate each quotient. Tell what compatible numbers you used.

1. 551 ÷ 79   **2.** 372 ÷ 92

3. 419 ÷ 64   **4.** 623 ÷ 71

Set C pages 154–155

Find 257 ÷ 32.

```
      8 R1
3 2)2 5 7      To find 257 ÷ 32,
    2 5 6      think: what is 25 ÷ 3? 8
        1
```

Remember that the remainder must be less than the divisor.

Tell whether you would use paper and pencil or mental math. Then find each quotient.

1. 23)69   **2.** 33)298

3. 52)423   **4.** 40)370

Set D pages 156–157

Find 339 ÷ 43.

```
      8
4 3)3 3 9      Think: What is 33 ÷ 4? 8
    3 4 4
```

Since 344 is greater than 339, try 7 in the quotient.

```
      7 R38
4 3)3 3 9
    3 0 1
      3 8
```

Remember to estimate the quotient first to see if your answer is reasonable.

Use paper and pencil or a calculator. Show each answer as a quotient with a whole-number remainder (if there is one).

1. 26)156   **2.** 31)304

3. 13)67   **4.** 32)254

5. 46)272   **6.** 64)301

Set E   pages 158–159

Find 249 ÷ 47.

Round the divisor. Use the rounded divisor to find the quotient.

Think: 47 rounds to 50.
What is 24 ÷ 5? 4

```
         4
 4 7)2 4 9    Since 61 is greater
     1 8 8    than 47, try 5
     ─────    in the quotient.
       6 1
```

```
             5 R14
 4 7)2 4 9
     2 3 5
     ─────
       1 4
```

Remember to use the actual divisor when you multiply and not a rounded divisor.

Use paper and pencil or a calculator. Show each answer as a quotient with a whole-number remainder (if there is one).

1. 68)364   **2.** 37)283

3. 27)168   **4.** 56)462

Set F   pages 162–163

Find 792 ÷ 44.

```
       1
 4 4)7 9 2    What is
     4 4      7 ÷ 4? 1
     ───
     3 5
```

```
         1 8
 4 4)7 9 2
     4 4 ↓
     ─────
     3 5 2    What is
     3 5 2    35 ÷ 4? 8
     ─────
         0
```

Remember to use a rounded divisor to help you find the quotient.

Use paper and pencil or a calculator. Show each answer as a quotient with a whole-number remainder (if there is one).

1. 32)416   **2.** 40)960

3. 63)718   **4.** 54)1,415

Set G   pages 166–167

Find 6,275 ÷ 26.

```
       2
 2 6)6,2 7 5
     5 2
     ───
     1 0
```

```
         2 4
 2 6)6,2 7 5
     5 2 ↓
     ─────
     1 0 7
     1 0 4
     ─────
         3
```

```
           2 4 1 R9
 2 6)6,2 7 5
     5 2     │
     ─────   │
     1 0 7   │
     1 0 4 ↓
     ───────
         3 5
         2 6
         ───
           9
```

Remember to estimate first to be sure the answer is reasonable.

Use paper and pencil or a calculator. Show each answer as a quotient with a whole-number remainder (if there is one).

1. 30)6,452   **2.** 34)7,177

3. 42)8,970   **4.** 53)5,892

Set H   pages 168–169

Find 7,368 ÷ 24.

```
       3
 2 4)7,3 6 8
     7 2
     ───
       1
```

```
         3 0
 2 4)7,3 6 8
     7 2 ↓
     ─────
       1 6
         0
     ─────
       1 6
```

```
           3 0 7
 2 4)7,3 6 8
     7 2     │
     ───     │
       1 6   │
         0 ↓
       ─────
       1 6 8
       1 6 8
       ─────
           0
```

Remember to write zeros in the quotient as needed.

Use paper and pencil or a calculator. Show each answer as a quotient with a whole-number remainder (if there is one).

1. 23)4,780   **2.** 42)8,728

3. 66)9,288   **4.** 16)9,637

More Practice
Set A   pages 150–151

Use mental math to find each quotient.

1. $600 \div 60$ 2. $280 \div 70$ 3. $480 \div 80$ 4. $240 \div 30$

5. $720 \div 90$ 6. $360 \div 60$ 7. $8,000 \div 40$ 8. $420 \div 70$

9. $3,600 \div 40$ 10. $210 \div 30$ 11. $2,700 \div 90$ 12. $4,800 \div 60$

Set B   pages 152–153

Estimate each quotient. Tell what compatible numbers you used.

1. $476 \div 61$ 2. $393 \div 48$ 3. $652 \div 83$ 4. $591 \div 57$

5. $272 \div 37$ 6. $789 \div 82$ 7. $356 \div 63$ 8. $776 \div 38$

9. $4,314 \div 72$ 10. $3,460 \div 47$ 11. $5,719 \div 83$ 12. $4,825 \div 51$

13. $8,186 \div 38$ 14. $9,135 \div 31$ 15. $4,901 \div 64$ 16. $2,912 \div 42$

Set C   pages 154–155

Tell whether you would use paper and pencil or mental math. Then find each quotient.

1. $41\overline{)85}$ 2. $32\overline{)98}$ 3. $20\overline{)68}$ 4. $33\overline{)74}$ 5. $21\overline{)88}$

6. $30\overline{)67}$ 7. $21\overline{)84}$ 8. $63\overline{)379}$ 9. $60\overline{)420}$ 10. $57\overline{)231}$

11. $80\overline{)642}$ 12. $73\overline{)440}$ 13. $52\overline{)315}$ 14. $44\overline{)276}$ 15. $82\overline{)578}$

Set D   pages 156–157

Use paper and pencil or a calculator. Show each answer as a quotient with a whole number remainder (if there is one) or as a decimal with one digit after the decimal point.

1. $24\overline{)94}$ 2. $14\overline{)126}$ 3. $16\overline{)128}$ 4. $23\overline{)160}$ 5. $37\overline{)259}$

6. $46\overline{)368}$ 7. $24\overline{)174}$ 8. $34\overline{)219}$ 9. $54\overline{)369}$ 10. $19\overline{)82}$

11. $48\overline{)348}$ 12. $73\overline{)507}$ 13. $59\overline{)413}$ 14. $34\overline{)256}$ 15. $86\overline{)579}$

16. $42\overline{)409}$ 17. $87\overline{)325}$ 18. $63\overline{)495}$ 19. $76\overline{)511}$ 20. $53\overline{)421}$

Set E pages 158–159

Use paper and pencil or a calculator. Show each answer
as a quotient with a whole number remainder (if there is
one) or as a decimal with one digit after the decimal point.

1. 47)256   **2.** 29)198   **3.** 18)161   **4.** 38)243   **5.** 19)125

6. 69)485   **7.** 57)470   **8.** 85)342   **9.** 38)316   **10.** 76)532

Mixed Practice Tell whether you would use paper and pencil,
a calculator, or mental math. Then find each answer.

11. 426 ÷ 6   **12.** 37 × 58   **13.** 476 + 589   **14.** 9,000 ÷ 30

Set F pages 162–163

Use paper and pencil or a calculator. Show each answer
as a quotient with a whole number remainder (if there is
one) or as a decimal with one digit after the decimal point.

1. 40)920   **2.** 20)740   **3.** 34)821   **4.** 60)4,468   **5.** 30)2,572

6. 24)858   **7.** 67)802   **8.** 38)745   **9.** 34)1,479   **10.** 53)3,758

11. 763 ÷ 16   **12.** 933 ÷ 46   **13.** 3,444 ÷ 46   **14.** 5,420 ÷ 62

Set G pages 166–167

Use paper and pencil or a calculator. Show each answer
as a quotient with a whole number remainder (if there is
one) or as a decimal with one digit after the decimal point.

1. 80)8,963   **2.** 40)5,851   **3.** 38)8,092   **4.** 22)6,864   **5.** 46)6,079

6. 31)6,609   **7.** 26)6,275   **8.** 48)5,718   **9.** 54)9,637   **10.** 28)7,365

11. 7,348 ÷ 65   **12.** 8,038 ÷ 34   **13.** 8,833 ÷ 27   **14.** 9,707 ÷ 77

Set H pages 168–169

Use paper and pencil or a calculator. Show each answer
as a quotient with a whole number remainder (if there is
one) or as a decimal with one digit after the decimal point.

1. 46)3,689   **2.** 16)9,637   **3.** 23)4,780   **4.** 24)2,528   **5.** 43)8,908

6. 32)6,535   **7.** 28)8,665   **8.** 25)5,086   **9.** 19)3,239   **10.** 89)9,125

11. 5,632 ÷ 27   **12.** 9,696 ÷ 94   **13.** 8,515 ÷ 34   **14.** 7,180 ÷ 66

Enrichment

Divisibility Rules

Here are ways you can tell if a whole number is divisible by 2, 3, 5, 9, or 10.

2 A number is divisible by 2 if the ones digit is 0, 2, 4, 6, or 8.

86 is divisible by 2 because the ones digit is 6.

3 A number is divisible by 3 if the sum of the digits is divisible by 3.

876 is divisible by 3 because $8 + 7 + 6 = 21$, and 21 is divisible by 3.

5 A number is divisible by 5 if the ones digit is 5 or 0.

805 is divisible by 5 because the ones digit is 5.

9 A number is divisible by 9 if the sum of the digits is divisible by 9.

828 is divisible by 9 because $8 + 2 + 8 = 18$, and 18 is divisible by 9.

10 A number is divisible by 10 if the ones digit is 0.

940 is divisible by 10 because the ones digit is 0.

Copy and complete the table. The check marks show that 3,285 is divisible by 3, 5, and 9.

		Divisible by				
	Number	2	3	5	9	10
	3,285		✔	✔	✔	
1.	630					
2.	762					
3.	856					
4.	810					
5.	2,685					
6.	5,814					
7.	32,004					
8.	74,010					
9.	431,204					
10.	602,265					
11.	4,277,133					
12.	5,009,407					
13.	7,961,590					
14.	9,951,413					

15. If a number is divisible by 6, it is divisible by both 2 and 3. Describe how you can tell if a number is divisible by 6.

16. Tell which of the numbers in Exercises 1-14 are divisible by 6.

Chapter 5 Review/Test

Use mental math to find each quotient.

1. 500 ÷ 50   **2.** 60 ÷ 20

3. 630 ÷ 90   **4.** 3,200 ÷ 80

Use compatible numbers to estimate each quotient.

5. 562 ÷ 71   **6.** 4,520 ÷ 49

Divide. Show each answer as a quotient with a whole-number remainder (if there is one).

7. 35)‾40   **8.** 25)‾50

9. 71)‾230   **10.** 60)‾425

11. 39)‾137   **12.** 48)‾216

13. 42)‾505   **14.** 39)‾2,269

15. 17)‾5,457   **16.** 33)‾5,117

17. 42)‾841   **18.** 18)‾5,425

19. Suppose you want to find 216 ÷ 28 by using a rounded divisor. Which is the correct method?

   a. Think: 28 rounds to 30.
   How many 3s in 21?
   b. Think: 216 rounds to 220.
   How many 2s in 22?

Solve each problem.

20. Sophie is 51 inches tall. Write this height in feet and inches.

21. A hotel offers its guests free trips to the airport by van. The van carries 14 passengers. If 62 people need rides, what is the least number of trips the van can make?

22. Eggs are packaged in cartons of 12 each. If a farmer has collected 520 eggs, how many cartons can be completely filled?

23. A computer printer will print 51 lines on each page. There are 1,530 lines to be printed. How many pages will be filled?

Read this problem. Then answer the questions below.

On a vacation trip, the Jimenez family traveled an average of 264 miles per day. They were gone for 12 days. How many miles did they travel?

24. One student got an answer of 22 miles for this problem. Is this answer reasonable? Why or why not?

25. Solve the problem.

26. **Write About Math**   Explain how you chose the compatible numbers you used in Exercise 6.

Geometric Solids and Measurement

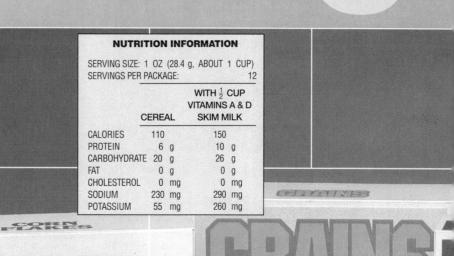

6

NUTRITION INFORMATION

SERVING SIZE: 1 OZ (28.4 g, ABOUT 1 CUP)
SERVINGS PER PACKAGE: 12

	CEREAL	WITH $\frac{1}{2}$ CUP VITAMINS A & D SKIM MILK
CALORIES	110	150
PROTEIN	6 g	10 g
CARBOHYDRATE	20 g	26 g
FAT	0 g	0 g
CHOLESTEROL	0 mg	0 mg
SODIUM	230 mg	290 mg
POTASSIUM	55 mg	260 mg

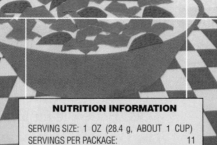

NUTRITION INFORMATION

SERVING SIZE: 1 OZ (28.4 g, ABOUT 1 CUP)
SERVINGS PER PACKAGE: 11

	CEREAL	WITH $\frac{1}{2}$ CUP VITAMINS A & D SKIM MILK
CALORIES	110	150
PROTEIN	2 g	6 g
CARBOHYDRATE	26 g	32 g
FAT	0 g	0 g
CHOLESTEROL	0 mg	0 mg
SODIUM	125 mg	190 mg
POTASSIUM	30 mg	230 mg

Number-Sense Project

Estimate

Predict how much of a difference there is in the number of calories in a 1-ounce serving of different breakfast cereals. Are there:
a. no differences?
b. small differences?
c. considerable differences?

Gather Data

Look at the boxes of 3 different types of cereal. Record the number of calories, grams of sucrose and other sugars, and milligrams of sodium in a 1-ounce serving of each cereal.

Analyze and Report

Make a table to show the data you collected. Write a summary statement telling how the cereals you checked differ in calories, sugars, and sodium per serving.

NUTRITION INFORMATION		
SERVING SIZE: 1 OZ (28.4 g, ABOUT 1 CUP)		
SERVINGS PER PACKAGE:		12
		WITH $\frac{1}{2}$ CUP VITAMINS A & D
	CEREAL	SKIM MILK
CALORIES	100	140
PROTEIN	2 g	6 g
CARBOHYDRATE	24 g	30 g
FAT	0 g	0 g
CHOLESTEROL	0 mg	0 mg
SODIUM	290 mg	350 mg
POTASSIUM	35 mg	240 mg

NUTRITION INFORMATION		
SERVING SIZE: 1 OZ (28.4 g, ABOUT 1 CUP)		
SERVINGS PER PACKAGE:		16
		WITH $\frac{1}{2}$ CUP VITAMINS A & D
	CEREAL	SKIM MILK
CALORIES	110	150
PROTEIN	2 g	6 g
CARBOHYDRATE	24 g	30 g
FAT	1 g	1 g
CHOLESTEROL	0 mg	0 mg
SODIUM	200 mg	260 mg
POTASSIUM	40 mg	240 mg

Investigating Solid Shapes

Build Understanding

Mikoko likes to use cubes to display photographs she has taken. She hangs some of the cubes from the ceiling to display them.

A. Cut It Out

Materials: 1-inch grid paper,
Math Sketcher, scissors

Groups: 4 students

A ***cube*** is a figure with six flat, square sides called ***faces.***

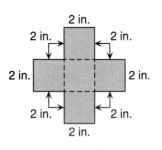

2 in.
2 in. ← → 2 in.
2 in. | 2 in.
2 in. ← → 2 in.
2 in.

a. Draw a figure like the one at the left on grid paper. If you cut the figure out and fold along the dotted lines, will you get a cube?

b. What can you add to this figure so that when you cut it out and fold it, you will get a cube?

c. Make the change. Cut out and fold the figure. Did you get a cube?

B. These shapes are ***rectangular prisms.*** When the 12 ***edges*** of the shape are the same length, the prism is a cube.

■ **Talk About Math** Could you make a solid cube with an odd number of smaller cubes? Explain.

Check Understanding

For another example, see Set A, pages 206–207.

Tell whether each of these shapes is a *cube, rectangular prism, both,* or *neither.*

1.

2.

3.

4.

Practice

For More Practice, see Set A, pages 208–209.

Tell whether each object is shaped like a *cube,* a *rectangular prism, both,* or *neither.*

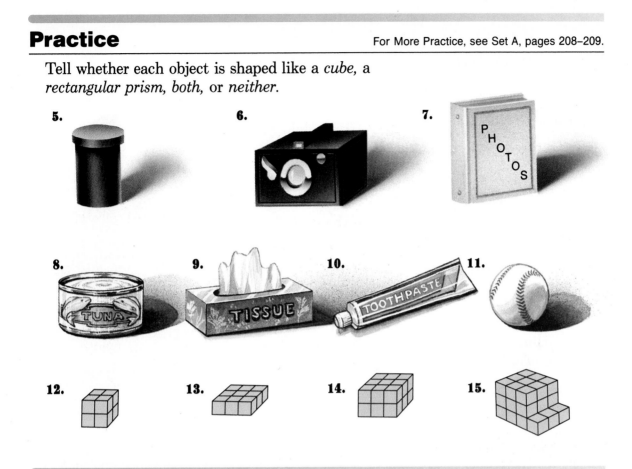

5.

6.

7.

8.

9.

10.

11.

12.

13.

14.

15.

Problem Solving

Critical Thinking   Write true or false for each statement. Explain your thinking.

16. All cubes are rectangular prisms.

17. All rectangular prisms are cubes.

Visual Thinking   Mikoko used this figure to display her photographs. How many faces of the small cubes can be seen if Mikoko places the figure on the floor

18. in the middle of the room?

19. in the corner of the room?

Solve the problem.

20. Describe the different rectangular prisms that could be made from 48 small cubes.

Finding Volume by Counting Cubes

Build Understanding

How is the word *volume* used in each sentence below?

Our encyclopedia has sixteen *volumes*.

Would you turn down the *volume* of the stereo?

One word can have several different meanings. In the top sentence, *volume* means *book in a set*. In the bottom sentence, *volume* means *loudness*.

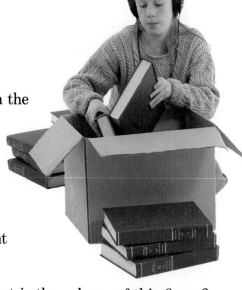

A. In mathematics, ***volume*** is the measure of the amount of space inside a solid figure.

One way to find the volume of a figure is to count the number of cubes that will "fill" the figure.

B. Each edge of this cube measures 1 inch. The volume of this cube is 1 ***cubic inch*** (1 cu in.).

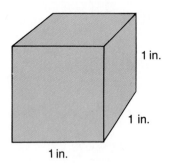

1 in.

1 in.

1 in.

Each edge of this cube measures 1 centimeter. The volume of this cube is 1 ***cubic centimeter*** (1 cm³).

1 cm

1 cm

1 cm

C. What is the volume of this figure? Each cube represents 1 cubic inch.

Count the number of cubes in the top layer. There are 20 cubes.

Since there are 3 layers, there are 3 × 20, or 60, cubes.

The volume is 60 cubic inches (60 cu in.).

■ **Write About Math** Explain how you can find the number of cubes in the top layer without counting.

Check Understanding

For another example, see Set B, pages 206–207.

Each cube represents 1 cubic centimeter.
Find the volume by counting the cubes.

1.   **2.**   **3.** 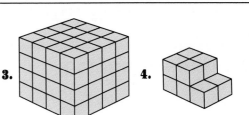   **4.**

Practice

For More Practice, see Set B, pages 208–209.

Each cube represents 1 cubic centimeter. Find the
volume of each figure by counting cubes. **Remember** to
write the unit of measure.

5.   **6.**   **7.**   **8.**

Each cube represents 1 cubic inch. Find the volume of
each figure by counting cubes. **Remember** to write the
unit of measure.

9.   **10.**   **11.**

Problem Solving

Critical Thinking   Solve each problem.

12. Which is larger, a box with a
volume of 64 cubic inches or a
box with a volume of 64 cubic
centimeters? Explain.

13. Look at Exercises 1 and 3. If you
double the width, the length,
and the height of a prism, how
will the volume change?

Volume

Build Understanding

A. Robert works at Sanchez Office Supply. He is stacking plastic storage crates on an area of the floor that is 6 feet long and 3 feet wide. Robert has enough storage crates to make 4 complete layers. What is the volume of the stack?

In the diagram, each small cube represents 1 cubic foot. The stack is 6 feet long, 3 feet wide, and 4 feet high. Find the number of cubes in the top layer.

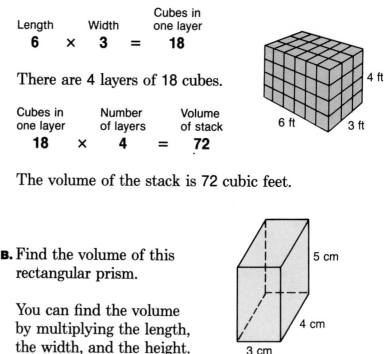

Length		Width		Cubes in one layer
6	×	3	=	18

There are 4 layers of 18 cubes.

Cubes in one layer		Number of layers		Volume of stack
18	×	4	=	72

The volume of the stack is 72 cubic feet.

B. Find the volume of this rectangular prism.

You can find the volume by multiplying the length, the width, and the height.

Length		Width		Height		Volume
4	×	3	×	5	=	60

The volume of the figure is 60 cubic centimeters.

■ **Talk About Math** Would the volume of the figure in Example B be different if the figure were turned over so a different face was on the bottom? Why or why not?

186

Check Understanding

For another example, see Set C, pages 206–207.

Find the volume of each rectangular prism.

1.

12 cm   7 cm   5 cm

2. Length: 9 inches
Width: 5 inches
Height: 3 inches

Practice

For More Practice, see Set C, pages 208–209.

Find the volume of each rectangular prism.

3. 5 yd, 5 yd, 3 yd

4. 10 cm, 17 cm, 8 cm

5. 11 mm, 15 mm, 17 mm

Tell whether you would use paper and pencil, mental math,
or a calculator to find the volume of each rectangular
prism. Then find the volume.

6. Length: 13 ft
Width: 11 ft
Height: 12 ft

7. Length: 14 cm
Width: 4 cm
Height: 14 cm

8. Length: 15 in.
Width: 10 in.
Height: 10 in.

9. Length: 23 m
Width: 18 m
Height: 20 m

10. Length: 76 cm
Width: 50 cm
Height: 20 cm

11. Length: 84 m
Width: 26 m
Height: 30 m

Problem Solving

12. Will 4,000 cubic inches of packing material fit
into a box 20 inches long, 18 inches wide, and
9 inches high?

13. **Critical Thinking** Each box of computer
paper is 11 inches long and 10 inches wide. The
volume of each box is 1,320 cubic inches. How
tall is each box?

TIPS FOR PROBLEM SOLVERS

**Brainstorm to get
started**—one idea will
lead to another.

187

Customary Units of Capacity

Build Understanding

1 pt = 2 c	
1 qt = 2 pt	
1 qt = 4 c	
1 gal = 4 qt	

Holds about
one *cup*
(1 c)

Holds about
one *pint*
(1 pt)

Holds about
one *quart*
(1 qt)

Holds about
one *gallon*
(1 gal)

A. Shelley wanted to buy 2 gallons and one quart of milk. How many quart containers would Shelley have to buy?

The chart shows that one gallon equals 4 quarts.
Multiply the number of gallons by 4.
Then add the additional quart.

She would need to buy 9 quarts of milk.

$$\begin{array}{r} 4 \\ \times 2 \\ \hline 8 \\ +1 \\ \hline 9 \end{array}$$

B. Write 7 cups in pints and cups.

The chart shows that 1 pint is equal to 2 cups.
Divide the number of cups by 2. The remainder is the number of cups left over.

$$\begin{array}{r} 3 \\ 2\overline{)7} \\ 6 \\ \hline 1 \end{array}$$

7 c = 3 pt 1 c

■ **Talk About Math** In Example A, how many pint containers would Shelley need?

Check Understanding

For another example. see Set D, pages 206–207.

1. How many quarts in 2 gallons?

2. How many quarts in 6 pints?

3. Write 3 qts 1 pt as pints.

4. Write 11 cups in pints and cups.

Practice

For More Practice, see Set D, pages 208–209.

Estimation Would you use

5. cups or gallons to measure the amount of water in a bathtub?

6. cups or quarts to measure the amount of soup in a bowl?

7. pints or gallons to measure the amount of water a washing machine can hold?

8. cups or gallons to measure the amount of water needed to fill a kitchen sink?

Number Sense Tell which measure is larger.

9. 3 pt or 1 qt   **10.** 16 c or 2 qt   **11.** 1 gal or 5 qt   **12.** 7 pt or 1 gal

Estimation Choose the most sensible measure.

13. Glass of juice   **14.** Pitcher of lemonade   **15.** Baby bottle

   1 c   1 qt   1 gal   8 c   8 qt   8 gal   1 c   1 qt   1 gal

Write each measure in pints.

16. 8 c   **17.** 2 gal 3 qt   **18.** 12 qt   **19.** 1 gal   **20.** 8 qt 1 pt

Write each measure in quarts.

21. 16 pt   **22.** 7 gal   **23.** 8 c   **24.** 5 gal   **25.** 10 gal 3 qt

Write each measure in quarts and pints.

26. 9 pt   **27.** 25 pt   **28.** 34 c   **29.** 1 gal 2 c   **30.** 4 pt 2 c

Problem Solving

31. Shelley is making tomato soup. A 1-pint can of tomato juice costs $0.90. A 1-quart can costs $1.65. Which is the better buy for one quart of juice?

32. Shelley bought three 1-quart cans of tomato juice. How much did the tomato juice cost?

33. Shelley mixed 3 quarts of tomato juice with 3 pints of milk. How many cups of soup does this make?

Metric Units of Capacity

Build Understanding

Jason Schwartz works at a zoo. Sometimes he has to feed baby animals whose mothers cannot take care of them.

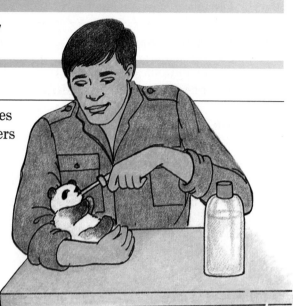

A. The eyedropper Jason uses to feed very small animals holds about 1 *milliliter* (1 mL) of liquid.

The bottled water Jason drinks comes in a 1-*liter* (1 L) container.

One liter is 1,000 milliliters.

B. Estimation A plastic drinking cup holds about 250 milliliters. About how many cups of water could Jason pour from the 1-liter container?

One liter is 1,000 milliliters. Each time Jason pours a cup of water from the bottle, there are 250 milliliters less in the bottle.

1,000 − 250 − 250 − 250 − 250 = 0

Jason could pour about 4 cups from the 1-liter container.

C. How many milliliters is 16 liters?

Sixteen liters is
16 × 1,000 milliliters,
or 16,000 milliliters.

D. How many liters is 3,000 mL?

1,000 mL = 1 L

$$\begin{array}{r} 3 \\ 1{,}000\overline{)3{,}000} \\ 3{,}000 \\ \hline 0 \end{array}$$

Divide the number of milliliters by 1,000 to find the number of liters.

3,000 mL = 3 L

■ **Talk About Math** One cubic centimeter holds 1 milliliter of water. How many liters will 1,000 cubic centimeters hold?

Check Understanding

For another example, see Set E, pages 206–207.

Number Sense Tell which quantity is larger.

1. 951 L or 951 mL   **2.** 6 L or 5,699 mL   **3.** 2,500 mL or 3 L

Practice

For More Practice, see Set E, pages 208–209.

Estimation Would you use milliliters or liters to measure the amount of liquid each container can hold?

4. Hot water tank   **5.** Ice cube tray   **6.** Bird's water dish

Estimation Choose the more sensible measure.

7. Glass of milk

25 mL   250 mL

8. Pitcher of water

3 L   300 L

9. Sink

1 L   10 L

Mental Math Write each measure in milliliters.

10. 3 L   **11.** 9 L   **12.** 15 L   **13.** 20 L

Problem Solving

Calculator Solve each problem.

14. How many full cups of water can Jason pour from his 1-liter bottle if his cup holds about 190 mL?

15. How much water will be left in the bottle?

Midchapter ✓ **Checkup**

1. Tell whether this figure is a cube, a rectangular prism, or neither.

2. Count the cubes to find the volume. Each cube represents 1 cubic inch.

3. Find the volume of this rectangular prism.

3 cm
4 cm
6 cm

Complete.

4. 8 qt = ▦ gal

5. 9 L = ▦ mL

Problem Solving WORKSHOP

Explore as a Team

1. Use cubes to make a new building shaped like the original Building A, but doubling its dimensions (length, width, and height).

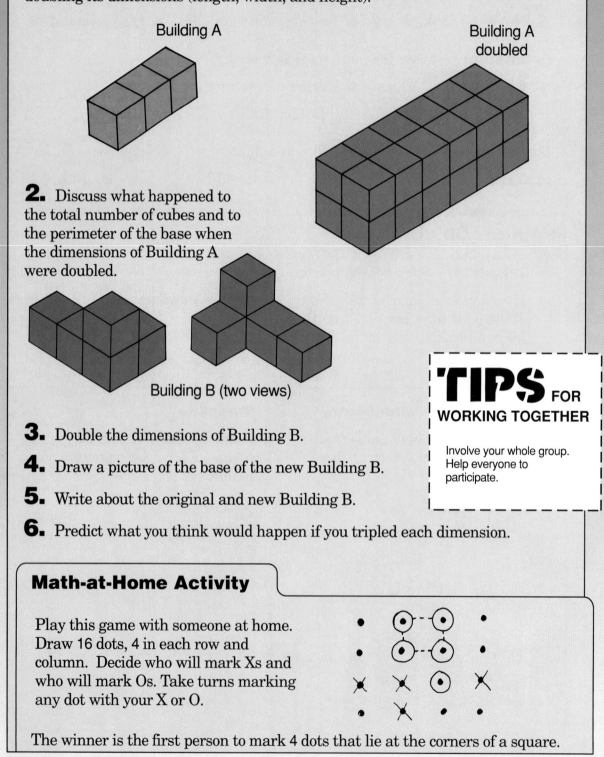

Building A

Building A doubled

2. Discuss what happened to the total number of cubes and to the perimeter of the base when the dimensions of Building A were doubled.

Building B (two views)

3. Double the dimensions of Building B.

4. Draw a picture of the base of the new Building B.

5. Write about the original and new Building B.

6. Predict what you think would happen if you tripled each dimension.

TIPS FOR
WORKING TOGETHER

Involve your whole group. Help everyone to participate.

Math-at-Home Activity

Play this game with someone at home. Draw 16 dots, 4 in each row and column. Decide who will mark Xs and who will mark Os. Take turns marking any dot with your X or O.

The winner is the first person to mark 4 dots that lie at the corners of a square.

Number-Sense Project

Look back at pages 180-181.

Two students collected the data shown in the tables below.

1. Which cereal has the greatest number of calories per serving?

2. If a person is trying to limit sugar intake, which cereals should be avoided?

3. In these samples is there a greater difference between cereals in calories, sugar, or sodium?

4. Is it important to pay attention to these differences? Why?

Student 1

Type/Brand of cereal	Amount of each ingredient per 1-ounce serving		
	Calories (without milk)	Sucrose and other sugars	Sodium
Brand A	100	5 g	160 mg
Brand B	90	0 g	0 mg
Brand C	110	9 g	280 mg

Student 2

Type/Brand of cereal	Amount of each ingredient per 1-ounce serving		
	Calories (without milk)	Sucrose and other sugars	Sodium
Brand D	120	12 g	250 mg
Brand E	90	5 g	200 mg
Brand F	130	15 g	150 mg

Customary Units of Weight

Build Understanding

In Korea, people eat many different kinds of vegetables. One favorite is Kimch'i, a pickled vegetable dish made by mixing cabbage, radishes, garlic, and red peppers.

Two red peppers weigh about 1 **pound.**
A radish weighs about 1 **ounce.**

A. Yung Hoh bought 2 pounds and 3 ounces of radishes. How many ounces is that?

1 pound (lb) = 16 ounces (oz)
2,000 pounds = 1 ton (T)

Use the chart above. Since 1 pound equals 16 ounces, multiply the number of pounds by 16. Then add the number of ounces to to find the total ounces.

$$\begin{array}{r} 16 \\ \times\ 2 \\ \hline 32 \\ +\ 3 \\ \hline 35 \end{array}$$

2 pounds 3 ounces is 35 ounces.

B. Yung Hoh also bought a cabbage that weighed 37 ounces. Write 37 ounces in pounds and ounces.

Use the chart above.

Divide the number of ounces by 16. The remainder is the number of ounces left over.

37 oz = 2 lb 5 oz

■ **Talk About Math** Name some animals or objects that weigh more than a ton.

Kimch'i vegetables are pickled in pots like these. In the winter, Kimch'i is buried in the frozen ground to keep it fresh until spring.

Check Understanding

For another example, see Set F, pages 206–207.

1. Write 3 lb 5 oz in ounces.

2. Write 19 oz in pounds and ounces.

Practice

For More Practice, see Set F, pages 208–209.

Estimation Would you use ounces, pounds, or tons to weigh a

3. pair of glasses?   **4.** bicycle?   **5.** bus?

Estimation Choose the most sensible measure.

6. Telephone

4 oz   4 lb   4 T

7. Elephant

5 oz   5 lb   5 T

8. Apple

6 oz   6 lb   6 T

Write each measure in ounces.

9. 4 lb   **10.** 20 lb   **11.** 8 lb 9 oz   **12.** 25 lb 12 oz

Write each measure in pounds.

13. 6 T   **14.** 368 oz   **15.** 128 oz   **16.** 10 T

Write each measure in pounds and ounces.

17. 23 oz   **18.** 81 oz   **19.** 216 oz   **20.** 498 oz

21. 148 oz   **22.** 374 oz   **23.** 92 oz   **24.** 674 oz

25. 354 oz   **26.** 75 oz   **27.** 777 oz

Problem Solving

28. Futari is an African dish made with squash, yams, coconut milk, cinnamon, and cloves. The recipe uses $1\frac{1}{2}$ pounds of yams. How many ounces is that?

29. Estimation A Creole vegetable dish is made with stewed tomatoes and okra. One okra weighs about 2 ounces. About how many are in a 3-pound bag?

30. Use Data Use the chart on page 157. Write the minimum weight of one dozen jumbo eggs in pounds and ounces.

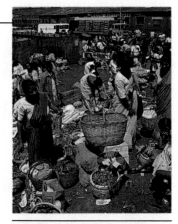

In India, fruits, vegetables, and herbs are sold in stores and open-air markets.

Metric Units of Mass

Build Understanding

A healthy diet includes plenty of fruits and vegetables.

A. A grape is about 1 *gram* (1 g). A bunch of bananas is about 1 *kilogram* (1 kg).

One kilogram is 1,000 grams.

B. How many grams is 3 kilograms?

Three kilograms is 3 × 1,000 grams, or 3,000 grams.

c. How many kilograms is 17,000 grams?

1,000 g = 1 kg

```
       17
1,000)17,000
      17000
          0
```
Divide the number of grams by 1,000 to find the number of kilograms.

■ **Talk About Math**   A thousand meters is a kilometer. A thousand grams is a kilogram. What do you think *kilo-* means?

A healthy diet includes 4 servings of fruits and vegetables daily.

Check Understanding

For another example, see Set G, pages 206–207.

Number Sense   Tell which quantity is larger.

1. 42 g or 42 kg   **2.** 6 kg or 5,232 g   **3.** 4 kg or 4,822 g

4. Estimation   Would you use grams or kilograms to measure a large bag of potatoes?

5. Estimation   Choose the more sensible measure for a melon.

5 g   5 kg

Practice

For More Practice, see Set G, pages 208–209.

Estimation Would you use grams or kilograms to measure each of the following?

6. Tomato

7. Bag of apples

8. Bunch of parsley

9. Baby

10. Sack of potatoes

11. Bologna

Estimation Choose the more sensible measure.

12. Strawberry
15 g   15 kg

13. Banana
225 g   225 kg

14. Bag of oranges
3 g   3 kg

Write each measure in grams.

15. 2 kg

16. 28 kg

17. 75 kg

18. 57 kg

19. 1 kg 34 g

Write each measure in kilograms.

20. 3,000 g

21. 7,000 g

22. 12,000 g

23. 15,000 g

24. 23,500 g

Mixed Practice Choose the more sensible measure.

25. Length of car
12 in   12 ft

26. Pitcher of juice
10 c   10 qt

27. Bowl of soup
500 mL   500 L

Problem Solving

Solve each problem.

28. If a whole watermelon is 6 kilograms and you cut off a 450-gram slice, how much remains?

29. Each bunch of grapes is about 180 grams. Would 10 bunches be more than or less than 1 kilogram?

30. A bunch of bananas is about 1 kilogram. If the bunch contains 4 bananas, about how many grams is each banana?

Skills ____ **Review**   pages 14–71

Add, subtract, or multiply.

1. 523 + 251

2. 938 − 33

3. 4,809 − 711

4. 519 + 3,265

5. 4 × 56

6. 19 × 91

7. 78 × 68

8. 208 × 118

Try and Check

Build Understanding

Megan has 60 pounds of camping gear to put in 4 packs. She wants 3 packs to be of equal weight and the fourth to weigh less than 10 pounds. Which items should she put in each of the 4 packs?

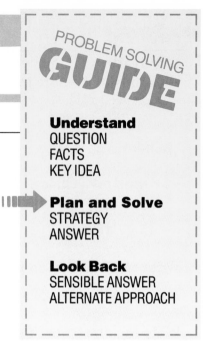

PROBLEM SOLVING
GUIDE

Understand
QUESTION
FACTS
KEY IDEA

Plan and Solve
STRATEGY
ANSWER

Look Back
SENSIBLE ANSWER
ALTERNATE APPROACH

Understand

QUESTION   Which items should she put in each pack?

FACTS   The table gives the number of items and the weight of each item. Megan has 4 packs. One pack has to weigh less than 10 pounds. The other 3 packs have to be of equal weight.

KEY IDEA   Try to make 3 groups of equal weight and see if the fourth group weighs less than 10 pounds.

Camping Gear

Item	Number of items	Weight of each item
Mess kits	4	16 oz
Food sacks	2	12 lb
Craft kits	2	5 lb
Stove	1	3 lb
Tent	1	8 lb
First-aid kit	1	32 oz
Sports kit	1	9 lb

Plan and Solve

STRATEGY   Convert all the weight to pounds. Then list each item and its weight on a slip of paper. Try different groupings of the items. Since the 2 food sacks weigh 12 pounds each, put 1 food sack in Pack 1 and 1 food sack in Pack 2. Then try to find other items that total 12 pounds and put them in Pack 3. Repeat the process with the items of less weight.

ANSWER

Pack 1		Pack 2		Pack 3		Pack 4	
Food sack	12	Food sack	12	Sports kit	9	Tent	8
Craft kit	5	Craft kit	5	Stove	3	Mess kit	1
				First-aid kit	2		
				Mess kit	1		
				Mess kit	1		
				Mess kit	1		

Look Back   SENSIBLE ANSWER   The weight of each of the first three packs is 17 pounds. The fourth pack weighs 9 pounds, which is less than 10 pounds. The answer is sensible.

■ **Write About Math**   Show how you could make each of the four packs have equal weight.

Check Understanding

Use the information on page 198 for Exercises 1–5.
Write the weight of each item in pounds.

1. First-aid kit

2. Mess kit

3. Could both food sacks be put in the same pack? Explain.

4. Could the 3 packs of equal weight contain only 12 pounds? Explain.

5. Show another way Megan could arrange the items in the packs.

Practice

For Problems 6–10, refer to the Example.

6. Put the stove, the first-aid kit, and a mess kit in Pack 4. Separate the remaining gear so that Packs 1, 2, and 3 are of equal weight.

7. If you put the first-aid kit and the sports kit together in a pack, is it possible to separate the remaining gear so that each of two packs weighs 20 pounds and each of two packs weighs 10 pounds? Explain.

On the trip home from camping, Megan's packs weighed 24 pounds less than when she started.

8. Why would the packs be 24 pounds lighter than before?

9. How much does the remaining gear weigh?

10. Show how Megan could arrange the remaining items to make each pack equal in weight.

Computing with Customary Measures

Build Understanding

A. Raoul works in a hardware and lumber store. A customer wants a wooden closet rod cut into 2 pieces. One piece must be 8 feet 3 inches long, and the other piece must be 2 feet 10 inches long. What is the smallest length that the original rod can be?

Find 8 feet 3 inches + 2 feet 10 inches.

Add the inches.
Add the feet.

8 ft   3 in.
+ 2 ft 10 in.
Rename the answer.
13 in. = 1 ft 1 in.

10 ft 13 in. = 11 ft 1 in.

B. Find 12 lb 4 oz − 6 lb 9 oz.

Rename to
subtract ounces.
12 lb 4 oz = 11 lb 20 oz

Subtract ounces.
Subtract pounds.

12 lb 4 oz	=	**11 lb 20 oz**
− 6 lb 9 oz	=	**6 lb 9 oz**
		5 lb 11 oz

C. Find 3 × 7 gal 3 qt.

Multiply quarts.
Multiply gallons.

7 gal 3 qt
×   3
Rename the answer.
9 qt = 2 gal 1 qt

21 gal 9 qt = 23 gal 1 qt

D. Find 8 ft 4 in. ÷ 5.

Write 8 feet 4 inches in inches. Then divide. Rename the answer.

8 ft 4 in. = 100 in.

100 in. ÷ 5 = 20 in.

20 in. = 1 ft 8 in.

■ **Write About Math** Explain how you could use mental math to find 3 hours 30 minutes ÷ 3.

Check Understanding

For another example, see Set H, pages 206–207.

Find each answer. **Remember** to watch the signs.

1. 4 ft 16 in.
        − 1 ft 19 in.

2. 5 pt 1 c
        + 1 pt 2 c

3. 4 gal 3 qt
        ×   2

4. 4 qt
        − 1 qt 3 c

Practice

For More Practice, see Set H, pages 208–209.

Find each answer. **Remember** to watch the signs.

5. 3 gal 1 qt
        + 7 gal 3 qt

6. 8 ft 6 in.
        − 4 ft 8 in.

7. 6 ft 5 in.
        ×   4

8. 6 qt
        − 3 qt 3 c

9. 6 h 40 min
        + 8 h 35 min

10. 7 yd 1 ft
        −   4 ft

11. 9 h 15 min
        ×   3

12. 5 qt 3 c
        − 2 qt 2 c

13. 6 yd 2 ft 7 in.
        ×   5

14. 8 h 20 min
        − 6 h 45 min

15. 14 min 20 sec
        + 7 min 32 sec

16. 3 gal 2 qt × 7

17. 3 gal ÷ 2

18. 7 h 23 min + 45 min

19. 5 h 55 min ÷ 5

20. 2 yd 15 in. ÷ 3

21. 5 ft 11 in. × 7

22. 5 ft 8 in. × 3

23. 5 h 20 min ÷ 5

24. 5 gal ÷ 2

Problem Solving

25. Raoul has two 5-ft boards. How many shelves can he make that are each 14 inches long? Will he have any lumber left?

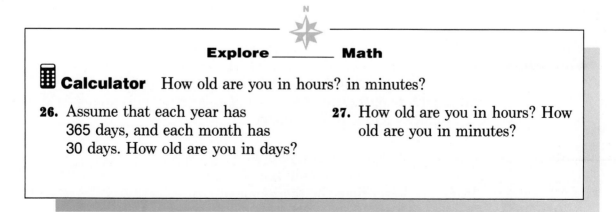

Explore ———— Math

Calculator   How old are you in hours? in minutes?

26. Assume that each year has 365 days, and each month has 30 days. How old are you in days?

27. How old are you in hours? How old are you in minutes?

Use Data from a Table

PROBLEM SOLVING
GUIDE

Build Understanding

Do you feel colder on windy days? Your skin cools faster in a high wind than when it is exposed to the same temperature on a calm day.

The wind chill temperature is the temperature it seems to be because of the speed of the wind. What does the temperature seem to be when the air temperature is 20°F and the wind speed is 10 miles per hour?

⮕ Understand
QUESTION
FACTS
KEY IDEA

Plan and Solve
STRATEGY
ANSWER

Look Back
SENSIBLE ANSWER
ALTERNATE APPROACH

Wind Chill Table

Wind (mi per h)	Air Temperature (Fahrenheit)							
	25	20	15	10	5	0	−5	−10
5	21	19	12	7	0	−5	−10	−15
10	10	3	−3	−9	−15	−22	−27	−34
15	2	−5	−11	−18	−25	−31	−38	−45
20	−3	−10	−17	−24	−31	−39	−46	−53
25	−7	−15	−22	−29	−36	−44	−51	−59

Wind chill measurements were developed from experiments performed in Antarctica in 1939.

⮕ Understand

QUESTION   What temperature does it seem to be when both the air temperature and wind speed are taken into account?

FACTS   The air temperature is 20°F. The wind speed is 10 miles per hour.

KEY IDEA   Use the data from the wind chill table.

Plan and Solve

Find the column for 20°F and the row for 10 miles per hour in the table. The point where the column and row meet gives the wind chill temperature. The wind chill is 3°F. It feels like it is 3°F outside.

Look Back

The wind blowing against your skin makes you colder, so the wind chill temperature should be lower than the thermometer reading. A wind chill of 3°F is lower than an air temperature of 20°F.

■ **Talk About Math**   Which would feel colder: 20°F with a 25-mile-per-hour wind or 15°F with a 15-mile-per-hour wind?

Check Understanding

Find the wind chill temperature.

1. 10°F with a 25-mile-per-hour wind

2. −5°F with a 15-mile-per-hour wind

3. −10°F with a 20-mile-per-hour wind

4. 0°F with a 25-mile-per-hour wind

Practice

If the wind is blowing at 20 miles per hour, what would the actual temperature be if the wind chill temperature is

5. −17°F?   **6.** −53°F?   **7.** −10°F?   **8.** −39°F?

What would the wind speed be if the actual temperature is 0°F and the wind chill temperature is

9. −22°F?   **10.** −44°F?   **11.** −5°F?   **12.** −39°F?

Choose a ⬛ Strategy

It's Cold Enough   The air temperature was 25°F when a cold front moved in at noon. The air temperature dropped 5 degrees each hour. The wind speed was steady at 15 miles per hour. What was the wind chill temperature at 4 P.M.?

13. How many hours are there between noon and 4 P.M.?

14. How many degrees did the air temperature drop by 4 P.M.?

15. What was the air temperature at 4 P.M.?

16. Use the table on page 202 to find the wind chill temperature at 4 P.M.

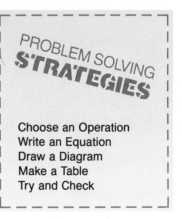

PROBLEM SOLVING
STRATEGIES

Choose an Operation
Write an Equation
Draw a Diagram
Make a Table
Try and Check

Skills Review

Tell whether each figure is a cube, rectangular prism, both or neither.

1.   **2.**

If each small cube represents 1 cubic centimeter, find the volume of the figure in

3. Exercise 1.   **4.** Exercise 2.

Find the volume of each figure.

5.   **6.**

5 m   3 m   5 m   6 ft   4 ft

Tell which measure is larger.

7. 7 c or 3 pt

8. 250 mL or 2 L

9. 30 oz or 2 lb

10. 5,000 g or 50 kg

Complete.

11. 8 qt = ▦ gal

12. 4000 mL = ▦ L

13. 42 oz = ▦ lb ▦ oz

14. 8 kg = ▦ g

Find each answer.

15.   6 ft 8 in.
       − 2 ft 9 in.

16.   2 hr 30 min
       ×   3

17.   1 gal 3 qt
       + 4 gal 3 qt

18. 3 yd 1 ft ÷ 5

Problem-Solving Review

Solve each problem.

19. Josh has 750 centimeter cubes. Can he store all of them in a box 10 cm wide, 8 cm deep, and 12 cm long?

20. Can Jenny ship two photo cubes in the box?

3 in.   4 in.   3 in.   3 in.   10 in.   5 in.

21. A recipe calls for 3 cups of milk. Alberto has 2 pints of milk. Does he have enough?

22. Iris has four 1-liter bottles of juice. Can she give each of 12 people 250 mL of juice?

23. Kim made 48 turkey sandwiches. If she used 5 oz of turkey for each sandwich, how many pounds of turkey did she use?

24. A box has a volume of 105 cubic centimeters. The length of each side is a whole number. What are the dimensions of the box?

25. Data File How many different size rectangular prisms can hold one million $1 bills? Use the information on pages 244–245 to help you decide.

26. Make a Data File Which United States President's portrait is on each denomination of United States Savings Bonds?

Tell which measure is larger.

1. 4 ft or 50 in.   **2.** 2 gal or 10 qt   **3.** 4,500 lb or 2 T

4. 655 mm or 65 cm   **5.** 3,500 mL or 5 L   **6.** 4 kg or 3,500 g

Use mental math to find each quotient.

7. 90 ÷ 6   **8.** 800 ÷ 80   **9.** 240 ÷ 60   **10.** 10,000 ÷ 50

Use Figures a–d for Exercises 11–14.

a. 12 ft   3 ft   5 ft   11 ft   **b.** 4 cm   7 cm   **c.** 3 m   4 m   5 m   **d.** 3 yd   6 yd

11. Find the perimeter of Figure a.   **12.** Find the area of Figure b.

13. Find the volume of Figure c.   **14.** Find the area of Figure d.

Write in standard form. Remember to use commas where needed.

15. 6 million, 147 thousand, two   **16.** 10 billion, 450 million

17. 4,000,000 + 7,000 + 600 + 1   **18.** 800,000 + 5,000 + 70 + 5

Write the missing number.

19. 3 ft = ▒ in.   **20.** 5 pt = ▒ c   **21.** 2 lb 6 oz = ▒ oz

Find the least common multiple for each pair of numbers.

22. 8 and 12   **23.** 15 and 45   **24.** 5 and 7   **25.** 10 and 20

Estimate. Then compute.

26. 65
  × 55

27. 4,098
  − 2,100

28. 168
  × 27

29. 54,390
  + 20,568

30. 152
  × 214

31. 8)64   **32.** 4)340   **33.** 5)543   **34.** 7)3,520

35. 30)270   **36.** 38)84   **37.** 19)47   **38.** 73)4,462

Find each answer.

39. 6 ft 4 in.
  − 2 ft 6 in.

40. 5 h 25 min
  + 2 h 45 min

41. 1 gal 3 qt
  ×   2

Reteaching

Set A pages 182–183

Each of the six faces of a cube is a square.

Each of the six faces of a rectangular prism is a rectangle.

Remember that a cube is a special rectangular prism.

Tell whether each object is like a cube, a rectangular prism, both a cube and a rectangular prism, or neither.

1.   **2.**

Set B pages 184–185

Each cube represents 1 cubic inch. What is the volume of this figure?

Each layer has 4 rows. Each row has 4 cubes. 4 × 4 = 16

There are 3 layers. 3 × 16 = 48

The volume is **48** cubic inches.

Remember that volume is the measure of the amount of space inside a solid figure.

Each small cube represents 1 cubic inch. Find the volume of each figure.

1.   **2.**

Set C pages 186–187

Find the volume of this figure.

Multiply the length, the width, and the height.

Length   Width   Height   Volume
4 cm × 3 cm × 3 cm = **36 cm³**

Remember to write the unit of measure.

Find the volume of each figure.

1.   **2.**

Set D pages 188–189

Write 3 gallons in

a. quarts.   **b.** pints.

a. Since 1 gallon equals 4 quarts, 3 gallons equals 3 × 4 quarts, or 12 quarts.

b. Since 1 quart equals 2 pints, 12 quarts equals 12 × 2 pints, or 24 pints.

Remember that you multiply to change a larger unit of measure to a smaller unit of measure. Write each measure in quarts.

1. 4 gal   **2.** 5 gal

Write each measure in pints.

3. 6 qt   **4.** 6 gal

Set E   pages 190–191

Write 19 liters in milliliters.

Since 1 liter = 1,000 milliliters, 19 liters is 19 × 1,000 mL, or 19,000 mL.

Remember that 1 L = 1,000 mL.

Mental Math   Use mental math to write each measure in milliliters.

1. 4 L   **2.** 17 L

Set F   pages 194–195

Write 4 tons in

a. pounds.   **b.** ounces.

a. Since 1 ton is 2,000 pounds, 4 tons is 4 × 2,000 lb, or 8,000 lb.

b. Since 1 pound is 16 ounces, 8,000 lb is 8,000 × 16 oz, or 128,000 oz.

Remember that the abbreviation for pound is lb, ounce is oz, and ton is T.

Write each measure in ounces.

1. 36 lb   **2.** 2 T

Write each measure in pounds.
3. 12 T   **4.** 30 T

Set G   pages 196–197

How many kilograms is 21,000 grams? Since 1 kilogram is 1,000 grams, divide the number of grams by 1,000 to find the number of kilograms.

$$
\begin{array}{r}
2\,1 \\
1{,}0\,0\,0\,\overline{)2\,1\,0{,}0\,0\,0} \\
2\,1{,}0\,0\,0 \\
\hline
0
\end{array}
$$
   21,000 g = 21 kg

Remember that you divide to change a smaller unit of measure to a larger unit of measure.

Write each measure in kilograms.

1. 6,000 g   **2.** 10,000 g

3. 18,000 g   **4.** 13,000 g

Set H   pages 200–201

Find 14 lb 6 oz − 7 lb 10 oz.

$$
\begin{array}{r}
14\ \text{lb}\ \ 6\ \text{oz} \\
-\ \ 7\ \text{lb}\ 10\ \text{oz} \\
\hline
\end{array}
$$

You cannot subtract 10 oz from 6 oz. Rename 14 lb 6 oz.

$$
\begin{array}{r}
13\ \text{lb}\ 22\ \text{oz} \\
-\ \ 7\ \text{lb}\ 10\ \text{oz} \\
\hline
6\ \text{lb}\ 12\ \text{oz}
\end{array}
$$
   14 lb = 13 lb 16 oz
   So, 14 lb 6 oz = 13 lb 22 oz

Remember that when you subtract measures, you may have to rename the minuend.

Subtract.

1.   11 lb 7 oz
      − 9 lb 12 oz

2.   9 ft 3 in.
      − 5 ft 9 in.

3.   6 gal 1 qt
      − 2 gal 3 qt

4.   14 yd 1 ft
      − 3 yd 2 ft

More Practice

Set A   pages 182–183

Tell whether each object is like a cube, like a rectangular prism, like both a cube and a rectangular prism, or like neither.

1.

2.

3.

Set B   pages 184–185

Each small cube in Exercises 1–4 represents 1 cubic centimeter. Find the volume of each figure. **Remember** to write the unit of measure.

1.   2.   3.   4.

Set C   pages 186–187

For Exercises 1–3, tell whether you would use paper and pencil, mental math, or a calculator to find the volume of each figure. Then find the volume.

1.   6 cm
8 cm
6 cm

2.   1 in.
10 in.
10 in.

3.

Set D   pages 188–189

Estimation   Choose the most sensible measure.

1. Gas tank of a car
   20 c   20 qt   20 gal

2. Teapot
   6 c   6 qt   6 gal

Write each measure in pints.

3. 3 gal   4. 4 qt   5. 7 gal   6. 5 qt

Write each measure in quarts.

7. 16 c   8. 4 gal   9. 8 pt   10. 32 c

Write each measure in quarts and pints.

11. 17 pt   12. 24 pt   13. 11 pt   14. 10 c

Set E   pages 190–191

Estimation   Choose the most sensible measure.

1. Tablespoon
   5 mL   15 mL   150 mL

2. Pail of water
   10 L   100 L   1,000 L

Mental Math   Use mental math for Exercises 3–6.
Write each measure in milliliters.

3. 5 L

4. 10 L

5. 13 L

6. 22 L

Set F   pages 194–195

Write each measure in Exercises 1 and 2 in ounces and in
Exercises 3 and 4 in pounds.

1. 30 lb

2. 3 T

3. 5 T

4. 160 oz

Write each measure in pounds and ounces.

5. 20 oz

6. 42 oz

7. 88 oz

8. 164 oz

9. Write 4 qt 2 c in cups.

10. Write 4 lb 7 oz in ounces.

Set G   pages 196–197

Choose the most sensible measure.

1. Couch
   100 g or 100 kg

2. Cat
   4 g or 4 kg

3. Shoelace
   1 g or 1 kg

Write each measure in Exercises 4 and 5 in grams and in
Exercises 6 and 7 in kilograms.

4. 3 kg

5. 10 kg

6. 8,000 g

7. 10,000 g

Set H   pages 200–201

Mental Math   Use mental math for Exercises 1 and 2.
Find the missing number.

1. 5 qt 1 pt = 4 qt ▦ pt

2. 9 ft 17 in. = 10 ft ▦ in.

Add, subtract, or multiply.

3. $\begin{array}{r} 3 \text{ ft } 9 \text{ in.} \\ + 4 \text{ ft } 6 \text{ in.} \end{array}$

4. $\begin{array}{r} 6 \text{ gal } 1 \text{ qt} \\ - 2 \text{ gal } 3 \text{ qt} \end{array}$

5. $\begin{array}{r} 7 \text{ h } 25 \text{ min} \\ + 4 \text{ h } 45 \text{ min} \end{array}$

6. 3 × 6 qt 1 pt

7. 5 × 3 yd 2 ft 9 in.

8. 6 ft 5 in. − 2 ft 8 in.

Enrichment

Polyominoes

What do you notice about these figures?

In each figure, all the squares are the
same size. Each square shares at least
one of its sides with another square.

All the figures shown above are *polyominoes*.

1. These figures are not polyominoes. Why not?

2. These figures are not considered different polyominoes. Why not?

3. How many different polyominoes are
there for 4 squares? Draw each
polyomino on grid paper.

4. How many different polyominoes are
there for 5 squares? Draw each
polyomino on grid paper.

Chapter 6 Review/Test

Tell whether each figure is a cube, a rectangular prism, both, or neither.

1.   **2.**

If each small cube represents 1 cm³, find the volume of the figure in

3. Item 1.   **4.** Item 2.

Find the volume of each figure.

5. 6 cm, 6 cm, 6 cm   **6.** 3 in., 5 in., 10 in.

Choose the most sensible measure.

7. Capacity of a soup bowl

2 c   2 qt   2 gal

8. Weight of a 10-year-old boy

30 g   3 kg   30 kg

Complete.

9. 12 qt = ▦ gal

10. 6 L = ▦ mL

11. 16 lb = ▦ oz

12. 4,000 g = ▦ kg

Add or subtract.

13.   2 gal 2 qt
        + 3 gal 3 qt

14.   6 ft 2 in.
        − 4 ft 5 in.

Use the table with the problem given below to answer Items 15 and 16.

Wind Chill Table

Wind (mi per h)	Temperature (Fahrenheit)							
	25	20	15	10	5	0	−5	−10
5	21	19	12	7	0	−5	−10	−15
10	10	3	−3	−9	−15	−22	−27	−34
15	2	−5	−11	−18	−25	−31	−38	−45
20	−3	−10	−17	−24	−31	−39	−46	−53
25	−7	−15	−22	−29	−36	−44	−51	−59

The wind is blowing at 25 miles per hour. If the wind-chill temperature is −15°F, what is the actual temperature?

15. To solve the problem, which would you look for in the table?

   a. −15 in the column for an actual temperature of −10°F

   b. −15 in the row for a wind of 25 mi per h

   c. −15 in the column for an actual temperature of 5°F

   d. −25 in the row for a wind of 15 mi per h

16. Solve the problem.

17. The table below shows how many cans of each kind of food Alice has. She wants to make three 10-pound packages. What should she put in each package?

Items	Number of Cans	Weight of Each Can
Peanuts	1	1 lb
Fruit	4	3 lb
Trail mix	4	2 lb
Ham	1	9 lb

18. Write About Math What makes a cube a special kind of rectangular prism?

211

Addition and Subtraction of Decimals

7

Did You Know: The fingers of pianist Sergei Rachmaninoff could span 12 white keys of the piano, about 26 centimeters.

Number-Sense Project

Estimate
Do taller people have wider hand spans? What do you predict?

Gather Data
Ask someone to help you measure your height and the span of one of your hands in centimeters. Do the same with 3 other people.

Analyze and Report
Plot the data you collected on a graph. Compare your results with those of other students.

213

Tenths and Hundredths

For sale
0.7 acre

Build Understanding

Numbers with decimal points are all around us. They are called **decimals.**

Decimals are used to name a fractional part. For 10 or 100 equal parts, the numbers can be written using our place-value system instead of fractions.

A. Some decimals name numbers less than 1. The For Sale sign names 0.7 acre. An acre is a measure of land area.

Think of 1 acre divided into 10 equal parts. Each part is one **tenth** of an acre.

Read: seven tenths

$\frac{7}{10}$ or 0.7

B. Some decimals name numbers greater than 1. A larger parcel of land could be 2.93 acres.

If each tenth is divided into 10 equal parts, then the whole square is divided into 100 equal parts. Each part is one **hundredth.**

2 wholes $\frac{93}{100}$ or 0.93

Read: two and ninety-three hundredths

$2\frac{93}{100}$ or 2.93

C. Our place-value system is based on 10. The chart shows the value of each digit in a decimal.

The decimal 0.7 means 7 of 10 equal parts.

The decimal 2.93 means 2 wholes and 93 of 100 equal parts of another whole.

	Tens	Ones	Tenths	Hundredths
0.7		0	7	
2.93		2	9	3

■ **Write About Math** Use the hundredths model and the tenths model to show that 0.10 and 0.1 are equal.

Check Understanding

For another example, see Set A, pages 238–239.

Write a fraction and a decimal for each exercise.

1. **2.** **3.** **4.**

5. Seventeen and one tenth

6. Thirty and forty-five hundredths

Practice

For More Practice, see Set A, pages 240–241.

Write a fraction and a decimal for each exercise.

7. **8.** **9.** **10.**

11. Thirty-five hundredths

12. Two tenths

13. Four and one tenth

14. Six and one hundredth

15. Ten and one tenth

16. Eleven hundredths

17. Eight and two tenths

18. Five hundredths

19. One and six tenths

20. Eleven and six hundredths

21. Six and one tenth

22. Sixty-four hundredths

Write each number in words.

23. 0.7   **24.** 0.03   **25.** 6.8   **26.** 4.39   **27.** 5.02

28. 47   **29.** 10.4   **30.** 0.43   **31.** 4.03   **32.** 40.3

33. 53.6   **34.** 8.72   **35.** 29.7   **36.** 15.06   **37.** 20.47

Problem Solving

38. Write each amount with a dollar sign and decimal point: paper for 60¢, a book for five dollars and five cents, pens for 98¢, and a magazine for one dollar and forty-seven cents.

39. **Critical Thinking** Use each of the digits 2, 4, and 6 only once. Write a decimal number between 3 and 5 in which the tenths digit is greater than the hundredths digit.

Thousandths

Build Understanding

Linda was designing letters using the squares on a grid.
She used a rectangle 50 squares long and 20 squares wide.
Can she fit the entire alphabet on the grid?

A. Designing Decimals
Materials: Grid paper, ruler, colored pencil

a. Make a rectangle 50 squares long and 20 squares wide.

b. Draw vowels on the grid. Remember to color only whole squares. Make the letters about the same size as the G.

B. What part of the rectangle is shaded to make the G?

The whole rectangle has 1,000 squares. Each square is *one thousandth* of the rectangle, or:

$$\frac{1}{1,000} \longleftarrow \text{1 of 1,000 equal parts}$$

Seventeen squares are shaded to make the G. The G uses *seventeen thousandths* of the rectangle, or:

$$\frac{17}{1,000} \longleftarrow \text{17 of 1,000 equal parts}$$

c. Remember that one decimal place shows tenths and two decimal places show hundredths. Three decimal places show thousandths.

Tens	Ones	Tenths	Hundredths	Thousandths		
	0	0	0	1	0.001	one thousandth
	0	0	1	7	0.017	seventeen thousandths

216

■ **Talk About Math** If the rectangle in Example A represents one whole, how many squares are in one tenth of the rectangle? How many squares are in one hundredth of the rectangle?

Check Understanding

For another example, see Set B, pages 238–239.

Write a decimal to name the part of your rectangle you would shade to make

1. A. **2.** E. **3.** I. **4.** O. **5.** U. **6.** I and O. **7.** E and U.

Write a fraction and a decimal for each exercise.

8. Two thousandths

9. Fifty-four thousandths

Practice

For More Practice, see Set B, pages 240–241.

Write each number in words. **Remember** to use "and" for decimals greater than 1.

10. 0.008   **11.** 0.071   **12.** 0.378   **13.** 5.046   **14.** 93.607

15. 10.093   **16.** 300.006 **17.** 5.812   **18.** 4.340   **19.** 0.902

20. 24.107   **21.** 54.018   **22.** 40.657   **23.** 15.206   **24.** 31.408

Write a fraction and a decimal for each exercise.

25. Three thousandths

26. Thirty-two thousandths

27. Nine hundred fifty-seven thousandths

28. Six hundred forty thousandths

29. Ten and three hundred five thousandths

30. Forty-two and sixty-five thousandths

31. Fifty-one and thirty-two thousandths

32. Seven and four hundred one thousandths

Problem Solving

33. One centimeter is what part of a meter? One millimeter is what part of a meter?

34. A liter contains 1.000 milliliters. A quart is 946 milliliters. What part of a liter is a quart?

35. Critical Thinking How many thousandths are in one tenth? How many thousandths are in one hundredth?

Place Value

Build Understanding

Throughout history, different cultures have used different symbols to represent numbers. In ancient times, Babylonian mathematicians used only two different symbols to write all their numbers.

The system of writing numbers used today in the U.S. originated in India and spread throughout the world.

A. What do the 2s mean in the number 2,017.267?

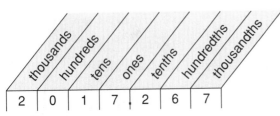

thousands	hundreds	tens	ones	tenths	hundredths	thousandths
2	0	1	7	2	6	7

2,017.267
two thousand, seventeen and two hundred sixty-seven thousandths

The Babylonians used a wedge-shaped tool to press marks into clay to represent numbers. These symbols are shown at the left of each column in the Babylonian calendar above.

The 2 at the left means
2 thousands and the 2 to
the right means 2 tenths.

B. What part of the rectangle is shaded?

Ones	Tenths	Hundredths	Thousandths
0	**1**	**3**	**8**

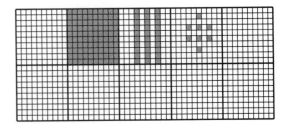

1 tenth, 3 hundredths, 8 thousandths
138 thousandths = 0.138

■ **Talk About Math** In the amount of money $34.53, the 3 in the tens place is how many times as large as the 3 in the hundredths place? Explain.

Check Understanding

For another example, see Set C, pages 238–239.

Use the number in Example A to answer the following questions.

1. What does the 6 mean? the 0? the 1?   **2.** In the number 3.275, what number is in the tenths place?

Practice

For More Practice, see Set C, pages 240–241.

Tell what 7 means in each number.

3. 71.3   **4.** 21.07   **5.** 9.703   **6.** 7,031.5   **7.** 3.027   **8.** 2,783

Tell what the 2 means in each number.

9. 32.5   **10.** 40.52   **11.** 0.207   **12.** 8,295   **13.** 5.429   **14.** 7.032

Which decimals have

15. 4 in the tenths place?
  a. 40.12   **b.** 26.43   **c.** 13.146

16. 7 in the thousandths place?
  a. 413.57   **b.** 7,104.5   **c.** 2.357

17. 9 in the hundredths place?
  a. 123.49   **b.** 951.92   **c.** 23.509

18. 3 in the hundreds place?
  a. 5.035   **b.** 6,361.38   **c.** 37.36

Problem Solving

19. The ancient Egyptians needed 31 symbols to write the number 7,897. How many times greater is the 7 on the left than the 7 on the right?

20. **Visual Thinking**   To the right are the Mayan symbols for 3, 7, 9, and 18. Write the Mayan symbol for 12.

3

7

9

18

The Mayans recorded important events by carving numbers like the ones above on tall stones called *stelas*.

Explore ———— Math

Look for a pattern in the place-value chart in Example A.

21. How are the names of the places similar? How are they different?

22. What name is used for the fourth decimal place? the fifth? the sixth?

Comparing and Ordering Decimals

Build Understanding

A. Two trails lead up Sugarloaf Mountain. Which distance is shorter?

Compare 0.5 and 0.75.

0.5 < 0.75

5 tenths is less than 75 hundredths. The shorter distance is 0.5 miles.

B. Compare 0.3 and 0.30.

$0.3 = 0.30$
0.3 and 0.30 are
equal decimals.

C. Compare 0.385 and 0.38.

0.385 ⠿ 0.38   The ones are the same.
The tenths are the same.
The hundredths are the same.

0.385 ⠿ 0.380   Think: 0.38 = 0.380
Compare the thousandths.
5 thousandths is greater than

0.385 > 0.38   0 thousandths.

D. Decimals can be shown on a number line in order from least to greatest.

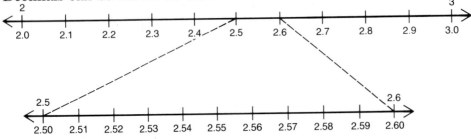

■ **Talk About Math**   Explain how to write a decimal in thousandths equal to 3 tenths.

220

Check Understanding

For another example, see Set D, pages 238–239.

Compare the numbers. Use <, >, or =.

1. 0.8 ⬚ 0.3   **2.** 0.50 ⬚ 0.49   **3.** 0.316 ⬚ 0.314   **4.** 6.7 ⬚ 6.70

Practice

For More Practice, see Set D, pages 240–241.

Compare the numbers. Use <, >, or =. Draw a diagram if needed.

5. 0.4 ⬚ 0.6   **6.** 2.46 ⬚ 2.41   **7.** 0.5 ⬚ 0.416   **8.** 9.831 ⬚ 9.83

9. 6.8 ⬚ 0.68   **10.** 0.3 ⬚ 0.30   **11.** 0.90 ⬚ 0.09   **12.** 12.8 ⬚ 1.28

13. 7.2 ⬚ 2.97   **14.** 4.5 ⬚ 0.45   **15.** 3.2 ⬚ 3.20   **16.** 4.16 ⬚ 4.61

List the numbers in order from least to greatest.
Use a number line if needed.

17. 0.4   0.7   0.3   **18.** 5.68   5.73   5.51   **19.** 0.483   0.481   0.486

20. 7.7   7.0   7.5   **21.** 27.3   27.31   27.03   **22.** 1.001   1.101   1.01

23. 0.56   0.506   0.5   **24.** 8.9   9.08   10.1   **25.** 2.03   3.2   2.32

Problem Solving

26. Red Trail is 1 mile long. There is a red flag at each end of the trail. A yellow flag is at each 0.1 mile. How many yellow flags are there?

27. Number Sense Write the greatest possible decimal having four different digits and a 3 in the hundredths place.

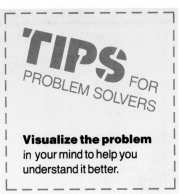

Visualize the problem in your mind to help you understand it better.

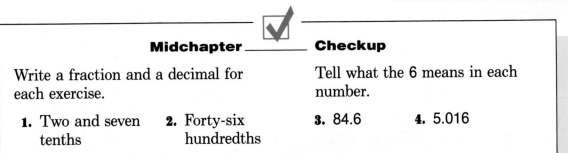

Midchapter ✓ Checkup

Write a fraction and a decimal for each exercise.

1. Two and seven tenths

2. Forty-six hundredths

Tell what the 6 means in each number.

3. 84.6

4. 5.016

Problem-Solving Workshop

Explore as a Team

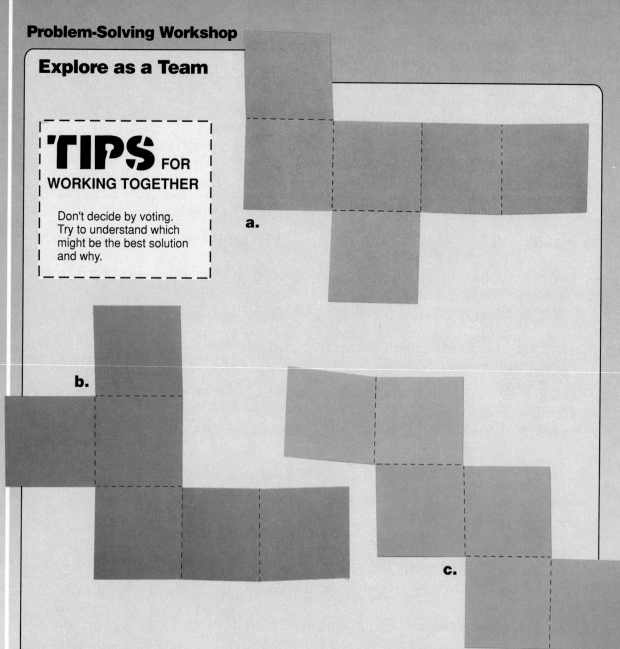

a.

b.

c.

1. Which of the diagrams form cubes when folded along the dotted lines?

2. Use 1-inch or larger grid paper. Cut out different diagrams of 6 squares.

3. Fold the diagrams you made to see which ones can form cubes. Draw your diagrams on grid paper. Show which diagrams do and which do not form cubes.

222

Explore with a Computer

Use the *Spreadsheet Workshop Project* for this activity.
At the School Olympic Days, five students entered the softball throw event. Each student threw the ball three times. The distances were recorded in the spreadsheet.

1. At the computer, type the greatest distance each student threw the ball in the "Best" column. Use the **Sort** option to list the students in order by best throw. Find the student who is the overall winner.

Student	1st throw	2nd throw	3rd throw	Best
Carrie	25.73 m	26.35 m	26.4 m	
Roy	15.7 m	15.47 m	15.28 m	
Kyle	20.2 m	21.18 m	18.2 m	
Ingrid	15.07 m	13.07 m	14.9 m	
Edwardo	23.7 m	26.34 m	26.24 m	

2. The school record for the softball throw is 39.68 m. Estimate how much farther a student would have to throw the ball to break or tie the record.

Number-Sense Project

Look back at pages 212-213.
A number of centimeters can be written as a part of a meter.
Since there are 100 cm in 1 m, 1 cm is the same as 0.01 m.

Byron's hand span measured 9 cm or 0.09 m. His height measured 154 cm or 1.54 m.

Measure the width of each of the tracks. Write each measurement in centimeters and meters.

1.

2.

3.

223

Use Logical Reasoning

Build Understanding

West School has teams only in volleyball, swimming, soccer, and basketball. Erica, Justin, Molly, and Dave each play a different sport. Justin's sport does not use a ball. Molly is older than the volleyball player. Neither Molly nor Dave plays soccer. Who plays volleyball?

PROBLEM SOLVING
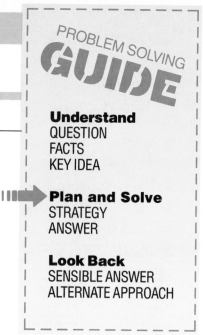
GUIDE

Understand
QUESTION
FACTS
KEY IDEA

▶ **Plan and Solve**
STRATEGY
ANSWER

Look Back
SENSIBLE ANSWER
ALTERNATE APPROACH

Understand   Only one student plays volleyball. You know a ball is not used in swimming and people cannot be older than themselves.

▶ **Plan and Solve**   STRATEGY   Logical reasoning is thinking in a sensible and orderly way to draw conclusions using known facts. Putting the facts in a chart can help.

Justin is the swimmer since his sport does not use a ball. Write yes for swimming and no for the other sports. Also, write no for swimming for the other students. Molly is not older than herself. Write no for

	Volleyball	Basketball	Swimming	Soccer
Erica			no	
Justin	no	no	yes	no
Molly	no		no	no
Dave			no	no

her for volleyball. Since neither Molly nor Dave plays soccer, write no for them for soccer. The chart shows only Erica can play soccer. So she does not play volleyball.

ANSWER   Dave plays volleyball.

Look Back   Check that the answer fits all the facts.

■ **Talk About Math**   Who plays basketball? How does using facts together help you learn new facts?

Check Understanding

Organize the facts in a chart to answer each question.

Mr. Smythe, Mr. McCarthy, and Mrs. Roberts teach at West school. One of them teaches math, one teaches science, and one teaches reading. No one teaches a subject with the same first letter as his or her name. Mr. Smythe does not teach math.

1. Who teaches reading?
2. Who teaches science?
3. Who teaches math?

Practice

Solve each problem. **Remember** to make a chart to help you.

4. Harold, Mary Ann, and Jorge each have a pet. One person has a dog, one a cat, and one a goldfish. One of the boys has a dog. The owner of the goldfish lives next to Mary Ann. Jorge does not have a dog. Which pet does each person own?

5. In the last basketball game, Melissa scored twice as many points as Debbie, and Debbie scored 4 more points than Rachel. Rachel scored 4 points. How many points did Debbie and Melissa score?

6. Jenni, Kevin, Susan, and Maria each bought food for lunch. The menu choices were pizza, salad, hamburger, and fish sandwich. None of the girls ate salad. Susan and the girl who had pizza are in different grades. Maria had pickles on her hamburger. What did each person buy for lunch?

7. The soccer game begins at 4:15 P.M. It takes Kim 20 minutes to ride her bike from home to the soccer field. What time should she leave home if she wants to arrive at the field 30 minutes before the game?

8. Raul bought a flea collar for $5.99, fish food for $4.99, and a cat toy for $1.99. How much did he spend?

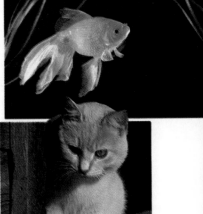

Rounding Decimals

Build Understanding

A. The average January temperatures for three cities are given in degrees Fahrenheit. Round each temperature to the nearest whole number.

City	Average January Temperature
Berlin, Germany	31.5° F
Albuquerque, NM	35.2° F
London, England	38.9° F

Showing these temperatures on a number line will help.

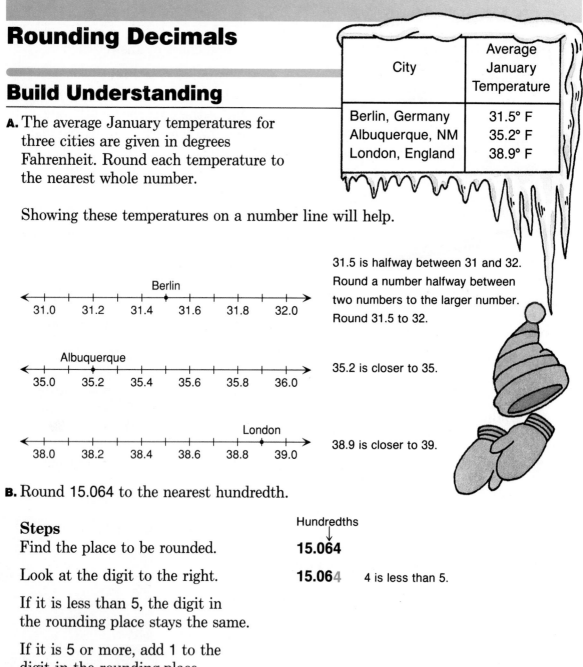

31.5 is halfway between 31 and 32. Round a number halfway between two numbers to the larger number. Round 31.5 to 32.

35.2 is closer to 35.

38.9 is closer to 39.

B. Round 15.064 to the nearest hundredth.

Steps

Find the place to be rounded.

Look at the digit to the right.

If it is less than 5, the digit in the rounding place stays the same.

If it is 5 or more, add 1 to the digit in the rounding place.

Write the rounded decimal.

Hundredths
↓
15.064

15.064   4 is less than 5.

15.06   Drop digits to the right of the rounding place.

■ **Talk About Math** Explain how to round 6.21, 6.25, and 6.28 to the nearest tenth using the number line.

Check Understanding

For another example, see Set E, pages 238–239.

Round 6.28 to the nearest tenth.

1. What digit is in the rounding place?

2. What is 6.28 rounded to the nearest tenth?

Nick used the calculator to see if **9,887** was divisible by **439**. The display showed *22.52164*. Round this to the nearest

3. ten.   **4.** one.   **5.** tenth.   **6.** hundredth.   **7.** thousandth.

Practice

For More Practice, see Set E, pages 240–241.

Round to the nearest whole number.

8. 1.3   **9.** 58.7   **10.** 22.5   **11.** 0.6   **12.** 9.61

13. 5.05   **14.** 7.49   **15.** 29.5   **16.** 1.632   **17.** 0.980

Round to the nearest tenth.

18. 0.41   **19.** 1.75   **20.** 12.37   **21.** 8.03   **22.** 8.409

23. 14.07   **24.** 3.18   **25.** 17.56   **26.** 92.42   **27.** 18.99

28. 8.591   **29.** 2.864   **30.** 43.927   **31.** 5.082   **32.** 7.983

Round to the nearest hundredth.

33. 0.675   **34.** 2.344   **35.** 74.009   **36.** 0.399   **37.** 0.595

38. 0.998   **39.** 5.972   **40.** 38.017   **41.** 17.003   **42.** 0.909

43. 4.229   **44.** 6.815   **45.** 57.183   **46.** 84.029   **47.** 72.468

Problem Solving

48. Mental Math Luis collected rainfall for a science project. He collected 0.325 inch one week and 0.335 the next week. In which week did it rain more?

49. Rosita hoped to collect 1.5 inches of rain for her project. She collected 1.46 inches. Did she have enough for her project?

50. The temperature in St. Louis is 78.9°F, Nashville is 79.4°F, and Charlotte is 78.5°F. List the cities in order from coolest to warmest.

Estimating Sums and Differences

Build Understanding

This table shows the average monthly rainfall in inches for Seattle, Washington.

A. About how many inches of rain will fall during the first three months of the year?

Use addition to find the total amount. Estimate the answer first.
Estimate: 6.04 + 4.22 + 3.59.

Month	Inches	Month	Inches
Jan.	6.04	July	0.74
Feb.	4.22	Aug.	1.27
Mar.	3.59	Sept.	2.02
Apr.	2.40	Oct.	3.43
May	1.58	Nov.	5.60
June	1.38	Dec.	6.33

You can estimate with decimals the same way you estimate with whole numbers.

Round to the nearest whole number.   Use front-end digits.

$$6.04 \rightarrow 6$$
$$4.22 \rightarrow 4$$
$$+3.59 \rightarrow \underline{4}$$
$$14$$

$$6.04 \rightarrow 6$$
$$4.22 \rightarrow 4$$
$$+3.59 \rightarrow \underline{3}$$
$$13$$

About 13 or 14 inches of rain can be expected during January, February, and March.

B. How much more rain fell in December than in June?

Use front-end digits.   Round to the nearest whole number.

$$6.33 \rightarrow 6$$
$$-\ 1.38 \rightarrow \underline{1}$$
$$5$$

$$6.33 \rightarrow 6$$
$$-\ 1.38 \rightarrow \underline{1}$$
$$5$$

About 5 more inches of rain fell in December than in June.

■ **Talk About Math** When both methods for estimating sums are used and the estimates are different, which method will always give the smaller sum? Explain.

Check Understanding

For another example, see Set F, pages 238–239.

For each exercise, estimate each sum or difference. Use both methods of estimating sums.

1. 3.9 + 6.7 + 9.2   **2.** 7.8 + 1.1 + 5.2   **3.** 12.19 − 6.82   **4.** 18.57 − 10.48

Practice

For More Practice, see Set F, pages 240–241.

Estimate each sum or difference. Round to the nearest whole number.

5.	30.2 + 15.5	**6.**	99.7 + 60.2	**7.**	4.216 + 8.190	**8.**	59.1 − 19.8	**9.**	19.5 − 4.6	**10.**	20.350 − 14.627
11.	50.3 + 18.2	**12.**	89.8 − 19.3	**13.**	38.7 + 32.9	**14.**	3.228 − 1.917	**15.**	47.3 − 36.2	**16.**	71.259 − 29.815

Estimate each sum or difference. Use front-end digits.

17. 3.9 + 35.4   **18.** 48.3 − 6.1   **19.** 52.62 + 9.75   **20.** 78.03 − 10.48

21. 65.006 − 2.980   **22.** 88.4 + 5.2 + 6.7   **23.** 47.3 + 8.9 + 2.6

24. 71.94 − 3.28   **25.** 81.73 − 9.48   **26.** 27.953 + 1.276

27. 9.2 + 8.6 + 10.1   **28.** 73.42 − 4.85   **29.** 23.71 + 9.6 + 3.91

30. 59.89 − 3.41   **31.** 60.2 + 3.2 + 7.9   **32.** 17.81 + 39.52

33. 57.8 − 2.8   **34.** 46.9 − 3.9   **35.** 82.3 + 3.8 + 4.9

36. **Calculator**   Estimate 8.27 + 11.94 + 6.458 + 3.91 first using front-end digits, then by rounding to the nearest whole number. Find the exact sum with a calculator. Which method of estimating is more accurate?

Problem Solving

37. About how many inches of rain will fall in Seattle during April, May, and June?

38. About how many more inches of rain fell during the wettest month than during the driest month?

39. **Use Data**   Use the table on page 233. Julio and Wally were how much faster than Clyde and Tai on the first 200 meters?

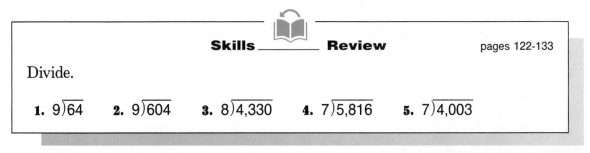

Skills _____ Review   pages 122-133

Divide.

1. 9)64   **2.** 9)604   **3.** 8)4,330   **4.** 7)5,816   **5.** 7)4,003

Too Much or Too Little Information

Understand
QUESTION
FACTS
KEY IDEA

Plan and Solve
STRATEGY
ANSWER

Look Back
SENSIBLE ANSWER
ALTERNATE APPROACH

Build Understanding

Cory bought a pair of blue cycling pants for $25.75, a pair of black ones for $28.88, and a touring helmet for $39.99. How much did he pay for the two pairs of cycling pants?

Understand   QUESTION   What was the cost of the two pairs of pants?

FACTS   Blue pants: $25.75; black pants: $28.88; helmet: $39.99

KEY IDEA   Find the total cost for pants only. The cost of the helmet is extra information.

Plan and Solve   To find the total cost of the pants, add the prices. First estimate. Then find the exact amount.

		Estimate	Exact Amount
$ 2 5.7 5	rounds to	$ 2 6	$ 2 5.7 5
+ 2 8.8 8	rounds to	+ 2 9	+ 2 8.8 8
		$ 5 5	$ 5 4.6 3

Cory paid $54.63 for the two pairs of pants.

Look Back   Since $54.63 is close to $55, the answer is sensible.

■ **Talk About Math**   Why can't you tell how much change Cory received?

Check Understanding

Cory bought a pair of meshback gloves for $24.95. How much money does he have left?

1. What facts are given in the problem?

2. To find how much money is left, do you add, subtract, or multiply?

3. Can you solve this problem with the facts that are given? Why?

Practice

Solve each problem. If there is not enough information given to do so, write *too little information*.

4. Cory and his friends biked 3 hours in the morning. Then they stopped for 1 hour for lunch. They biked for 3 more hours after lunch. How many hours did they bike that day?

5. Cory had $15 with him, Al had $11, and Floyd had $9.60. How much money did they have in all?

6. Cory's 12-speed bike weighs 37 pounds. To it he added a seat pack of 215 cubic inches. What is the total weight of his bike, including the pack?

7. A 6-foot vinyl-covered steel cable with a combination barrel lock costs $14.99. A 2-pound steel U-lock with bracket and keys is $24.99. How much more is the U-lock than the barrel lock?

8. A seat pack cost $12.99. How much change did Cory get back?

9. Before lunch, the boys had spent only $7.00. How much money did they have after lunch?

10. Gumwall tires cost $12.99 and blackwall tires cost $12.49. Tire tubes cost $6.49 for standard tubes and $10.49 for puncture-resistant tubes. How much did Cory pay for new tires and tubes?

11. At the Rest Stop, hamburgers cost $1.59 each. A chicken sandwich costs $1.85. Cory and Hank each ordered a chicken sandwich. How much did they spend together for sandwiches?

Choose a Strategy

Color Combos

12. Cory has 3 shirts: white, red, and yellow, and 2 pairs of biking pants: blue and black. How many different biking outfits could he have?

13. Cory also has 2 helmets: gold and silver. How many different biking outfits could he have?

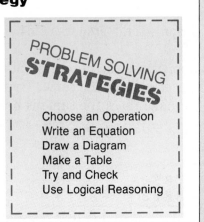

PROBLEM SOLVING
STRATEGIES

Choose an Operation
Write an Equation
Draw a Diagram
Make a Table
Try and Check
Use Logical Reasoning

Adding Decimals

Build Understanding

A. To make the swim team, Jason must swim 400 meters in less than 7 minutes. Jason swam the first 200 meters in 2.86 minutes. He swam the second 200 meters in 3.95 minutes. Did he make the team?

Use addition to find the *total* amount of time he took to swim 400 meters. Find 2.86 + 3.95.

Estimate using rounding. 3 + 4 = 7

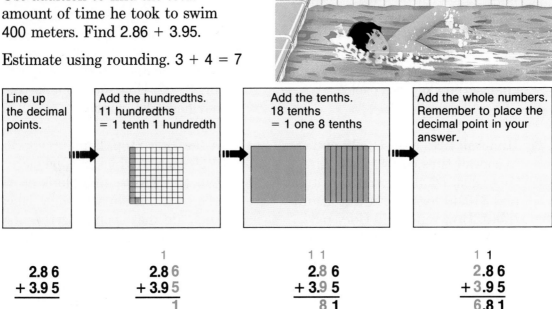

Line up the decimal points.	Add the hundredths. 11 hundredths = 1 tenth 1 hundredth	Add the tenths. 18 tenths = 1 one 8 tenths	Add the whole numbers. Remember to place the decimal point in your answer.

```
                    1              1 1            1 1
  2.8 6           2.8 6          2.8 6          2.8 6
+ 3.9 5         + 3.9 5        + 3.9 5        + 3.9 5
                      1            8 1          6.8 1
```

Jason's total time was 6.81 minutes. He made the team.

B. Sometimes the numbers of decimal places are not the same. Writing zeros to make them the same is helpful.

Find 7.85 + 8.673.

```
                  1 1
  7.8 5         7.8 5 0
+ 8.6 7 3     + 8.6 7 3
              1 6.5 2 3
```

C. Estimation   Use *clustering* when the addends are close to each other.

```
  $ 2 2.3 9
    2 8.4 0
    2 4.1 7
+   2 6.2 5
```

The numbers cluster around $25. Estimate: 25 + 25 + 25 + 25 = $100.

■ **Talk About Math** The work at the right shows how one student found 16.05 + 21.834. What did the student do wrong?

$$
\begin{array}{r}
16.005 \\
+\ 21.834 \\
\hline
37.839
\end{array}
$$

Check Understanding

For another example, see Set G, pages 238–239.

Add. **Remember** to estimate to be sure your answer makes sense.

1.
$$
\begin{array}{r}
0.7 \\
+\ 0.8 \\
\hline
\end{array}
$$

2.
$$
\begin{array}{r}
\$7.63 \\
+\ \$2.07 \\
\hline
\end{array}
$$

3.
$$
\begin{array}{r}
\$86.75 \\
+\ \$26.58 \\
\hline
\end{array}
$$

4.
$$
\begin{array}{r}
3.20 \\
+\ 5.292 \\
\hline
\end{array}
$$

5.
$$
\begin{array}{r}
42.881 \\
+\ 8.95 \\
\hline
\end{array}
$$

6. 6 + 8.2   7. 19.3 + 21.68 + 20.4   8. 14.62 + 917.1 + 0.629

Practice

For More Practice, see Set G, pages 240–241.

Add. **Remember** to estimate to be sure your answer makes sense.

9.
$$
\begin{array}{r}
6.4 \\
+\ 9.8 \\
\hline
\end{array}
$$

10.
$$
\begin{array}{r}
82.7 \\
+\ 3.2 \\
\hline
\end{array}
$$

11.
$$
\begin{array}{r}
\$6.37 \\
+\ \$10.45 \\
\hline
\end{array}
$$

12.
$$
\begin{array}{r}
42.9 \\
+\ 7.463 \\
\hline
\end{array}
$$

13.
$$
\begin{array}{r}
1.806 \\
+\ 4.29 \\
\hline
\end{array}
$$

14. 10.8 + 12

15. $861.20 + $43.39

16. 8.91 + 11.4 + 0.006

17. 0.6 + 9.75 + 11

18. 13.9 + 236.7

19. $75.76 + $3.80

20. 0.4 + 90

21. $95.70 + $8.50

22. $20.10 + $12.80

23. 0.7 + 87.8

24. 50.5 + 8.176

25. 51.25 + 4.086

26. 13.8 + 8.62

27. 75.452 + 82.1

28. 15.84 + 9.216

29. 6.1 + 2.3 + 5.0

30. 28.7 + 30.1 + 32.4

31. 3.618 + 4.021 + 9.0

Problem Solving

Julio and Wally were one team, and Clyde and Tai were the other team in a two person 400-meter freestyle relay. Their times are shown in the table.

32. What was the total time for Julio and Wally?

33. What was the total time for Clyde and Tai?

34. Who won the relay?

400-Meter Relay

Names	1st 200 m	2nd 200 m
Julio/Wally	2.92 min	4.01 min
Clyde/Tai	3.00 min	3.95 min

Subtracting Decimals

Build Understanding

A. The school record for the 400-meter relay race was 65.5 seconds. This year's Whiz Kids would like to tie or break the record. It took them 53.96 seconds to run 300 meters. In how much time must they run the last 100 meters to tie the record?

Use subtraction to find how much time is left. Find 65.5 − 53.96.

Estimate using front-end digits. 65 − 53 = 12

Each person in a 400-meter relay runs 100 meters.

| Line up the decimal points. Write 65.5 as 65.50. Rename to get 10 more hundredths. 1 tenth = 10 hundredths Subtract the hundredths. | Rename to get 10 more tenths. 5 ones 4 tenths = 4 ones 14 tenths Subtract the tenths. | Subtract the ones. Subtract the tens. |

$$
\begin{array}{r}
^{4\,10} \\
6\,5.\cancel{5}\,\cancel{0} \\
-\,5\,3.9\,6 \\
\hline
4
\end{array}
\qquad
\begin{array}{r}
^{14} \\
^{4\,\cancel{4}\,10} \\
6\,\cancel{5}.\cancel{5}\,\cancel{0} \\
-\,5\,3.9\,6 \\
\hline
.5\,4
\end{array}
\qquad
\begin{array}{r}
^{14} \\
^{4\,\cancel{4}\,10} \\
6\,\cancel{5}.\cancel{5}\,\cancel{0} \\
-\,5\,3.9\,6 \\
\hline
1\,1.5\,4
\end{array}
$$

The Whiz Kids have to run the last 100 meters in 11.54 seconds to tie the record.

B. Find 36.8 − 32.476.
Write 36.8 as 36.800.

$$
\begin{array}{r}
^{9} \\
^{7\,\cancel{10}\,10} \\
3\,6.\cancel{8}\,\cancel{0}\,\cancel{0} \\
-\,3\,2.4\,7\,6 \\
\hline
4.3\,2\,4
\end{array}
$$

■ **Talk About Math**   Why is lining up the decimal points so important when adding and subtracting decimals?

Check Understanding

For another example, see Set H, pages 238–239.

Subtract.

.1. $5.65 − $4.34	**2.** 6.27 − 0.94	**3.** $18.63 − $12.69	**4.** 9.61 − 3.582	**5.** 85.089 − 54.12

6. 7 − 4.5   **7.** 5.17 − 3.5   **8.** 50.87 − 4.271

234

Practice

Subtract. **Remember** to estimate to be sure your answer makes sense.

9. 7.8
  − 3.2

10. $8.25
  − $4.62

11. $16.35
  − $ 6.50

12. 9.2
  − 4.546

13. 15.406
  − 8.73

14. $37.64
  − $33.95

15. 85.04
  − 65.9

16. 98.1
  − 61.574

17. 49.75
  − 1.843

18. 52.007
  − 6.2

19. 21 − 3.183

20. 85.22 − 41.6

21. 37.49 − 33.392

22. $91.96 − $90.97

23. 17.78 − 4.7

24. 72.008 − 51.992

25. 10.6 − 9.87

26. 32.47 − 17.098

27. 560 − 8.651

Mixed Practice Tell whether you would use paper and pencil or mental math. Then find each answer.

28. 5.03 + 4.387

29. 16 − 15.86

30. 18.932 + 6.6068

31. 403 + 27

32. 176 − 16

33. 49.071 + 20

34. 87.094 + 983

35. 874 − 15.473

36. $24.00 − $16.98

A
L
G
E
B
R
A ▶ Solve these equations.

37. $41.85 + x = 45.35$

38. $y − 0.409 = 3.421$

39. $n − 37.74 = 377.76$

40. $m + 12.6 = 16.92$

41. $20.91 − w = 13.762$

42. $31.07 − 9.402 = t$

Problem Solving

43. The Green Team ran the 400-meter relay race in 47.35 seconds. Their time for the first 300 meters was 35.58 seconds. What was their time for the last 100 meters?

44. At the age of 92, Duncan McLean ran a 100-meter race in 21.7 seconds. This is 11.8 seconds slower than the 100-meter race he ran in 1904. What was his time for the race in 1904?

45. Estimation Sarah said that the sum of 8.946 and 7,692 is more than 16. Do you agree? Explain why or why not?

Skills Review

Write a fraction and a decimal for each exercise.

1.   **2.**

3. Six tenths   **4.** Two hundredths

5. Four and twenty-five hundredths

6. Eleven and nineteen thousandths

Tell what the 5 means in each number.

7. 6,512.6   **8.** 1.95   **9.** 430.59

Compare the numbers. Use <, >, or =.

10. 0.8 ▦ 0.08   **11.** 2.6 ▦ 2.38

Round 23.705 to the nearest

12. hundredth.   **13.** tenth.

Round 45.572 to the nearest

14. hundredth.   **15.** tenth.

Estimate each sum or difference.

16.　　9.6　　**17.**　　22.4　　**18.**　　5.32
　　　　+ 12.2　　　　　− 19.6　　　　　+ 2.98

19. 5.8 + 6.4   **20.** 82.6 − 71.9

Add or subtract. Then estimate to check your answer.

21.　　5.3　　**22.**　　62.8　　**23.**　　9.6
　　　　+ 9.8　　　　　+ 4.4　　　　　− 4.75

24. 8.5 + 2.75   **25.** 78.425 + 6.8

26. 12 − 2.45   **27.** 45.68 − 3.75

Problem-Solving Review

Solve each problem.

28. A kilogram is 1,000 grams. A quarter weighs 6 grams. What part of a kilogram is that?

29. A cubit is an ancient unit of measure. In ancient China, the cubit was 20.9 inches. In ancient Greece, the cubit was 18.2 inches. How much longer was the cubit in ancient China?

30. Janice ran 100 meters in 14.1 seconds. Beth's time was 14.01 seconds. Who won the race?

31. Monty, Ned, and Tony play different sports. The sports are basketball, golf, and swimming. Monty is not as tall as the basketball player. Ned does not use a ball in his sport. Which sport does each person play?

32. Wendy started work at 9:00 A.M. She took a 1-hour lunch break and two 15-minute breaks. She left work at 4:30 P.M. How many hours did she work?

33. **Data File** Order the batting averages from the highest to lowest given in the chart on pages 244–245. Whose average was highest?

34. **Make a Data File** Make a chart to show the average monthly rainfall where you live for one year. What is the difference in the amount of rainfall between the wettest and the driest months?

Round 53,802.547 to the nearest

1. thousand.　　　　**2.** one.

3. tenth.　　　　**4.** hundredth.

Use mental math to compute.

5. 375 + 400　　　**6.** 780 − 99

7. 30 × 40　　　**8.** 203 × 3

9. 900 ÷ 3　　　**10.** 164 ÷ 4

11. 180 ÷ 20　　　**12.** 7,700 ÷ 70

Find the least common multiple of the following.

13. 4 and 6　　　**14.** 7 and 9

Use a ruler to draw a line of each length.

15. $4\frac{1}{2}$ inches　　　**16.** 58 mm

17. Measure the length of each side in centimeters. Then find the perimeter.

What is the length of time from

18. 8:45 A.M. to 11:40 A.M.?

19. 10:30 A.M. to 3:45 P.M.?

Write each number in words.

20. 5,430,015　　　**21.** 5.6

22. 37.34　　　**23.** 40.071

Estimate each quotient. Tell what compatible numbers you used.

24. 317 ÷ 29　　　**25.** 639 ÷ 81

26. 8,104 ÷ 92　　　**27.** 2,445 ÷ 58

Choose the more sensible measure.

28. Glass of milk　　　**29.** Eyedropper
　　1 c　　1 qt　　　　1 mL　　1L

30. Dog　　　**31.** Grape
　　20 oz　　20 lb　　　10 g　　10 kg

Each small cube represents 1 cubic centimeter. Find the volume.

32. 　　　**33.**

Estimate. Then compute.

34. 　2,649　**35.** 　530　**36.** 　6,000
　　+ 　725　　　× 　7　　　− 　943

37. 　433　**38.** 　506　**39.** 　293
　　× 　80　　　× 　42　　　× 405

40. 　0.6　**41.** 　6.5　**42.** 　8.4
　　+ 4.5　　　− 2.3　　　− 3.925

43. 3)‾21　　**44.** 5)‾635　　**45.** 2)‾481

46. 44)‾890　　　　　**47.** 35)‾8,452

48. 5.1 + 3.47　　　**49.** 6.2 − 0.75

Tell which measure is larger.

50. 5 gal or 18 qt

51. 350 mL or 2 L

52. 2 T or 1,500 lb

Reteaching

Set A   pages 214–215

The decimal 0.5 means 5 of 10 equal parts. The decimal 4.86 means 4 wholes and 86 of 100 equal parts of another whole.

Tens	Ones	Tenths	Hundredths
	0	5	
	4	8	6

Remember that a fraction whose denominator is 10 or 100 can be written as a decimal.

Write a fraction and a decimal for each.

1.

2. Three hundredths

3. Eight and five tenths

Set B   pages 216–217

The fraction $\frac{22}{1,000}$ means 22 of 1,000 equal parts. Three decimal places show thousandths.

Ones	Tenths	Hundredths	Thousandths
0	0	2	2

0.022 is read twenty-two thousandths.

Remember that one decimal place shows tenths and two decimal places show hundredths.

Write a fraction and a decimal for each.

1. Twenty-five thousandths

2. Four hundred thirty-seven thousandths

Set C   pages 218–219

This chart shows the value of each digit in 0.245.

Ones	Tenths	Hundredths	Thousandths
0	2	4	5

2 tenths, 4 hundredths, 5 thousandths
245 thousandths.

Remember that the value of each place in a decimal is 10 times as large as the value of the place to its right.

1. Tell what 4 means in 52.045.

2. Which decimals have 6 in the hundredths place?

   a. 32.006   b. 48.162   c. 51.069

Set D   pages 220–221

Compare 0.526 and 0.527.

Start at the left.   **0.526**
Compare digits in   **0.527**
the same place.

The ones, tenths, and
hundredths are the same.

6 thousandths is less than
7 thousandths.

0.526 < 0.527

Remember that writing zeros to the right of a decimal does not change its value.

Compare the numbers. Use <, >, or =.

1. 6.4 ▦ 6.40   2. 6.947 ▦ 6.946

List the numbers in order from least to greatest.

3. 3.28   3.82   3.58

Set E pages 226–227

Round 3.185 to the nearest hundredth.

The digit 8 is in the hundredths place.

The digit to the right of 8 is 5.

When the digit to the right is 5 or more, add 1 to the digit in the place to be rounded.

The answer is 3.19.

Remember that the digit in the place to be rounded stays the same if the digit to its right is less than 5.

Round to the nearest

1. whole number: 28.72

2. tenth: 16.04

3. hundredth: 42.015

Set F pages 228–229

Estimate 7.21 + 8.61 + 4.08.

Round to the nearest whole number.	Add the front-end digits.
7.21 ---> 7	7.21 ---> 7
8.61 ---> 9	8.61 ---> 8
+ 4.08 ---> 4	+ 4.08 ---> 4
20	19

The exact sum is about 19 or 20.

Remember that adding front-end digits will always give an estimate that is less than the actual sum.

Estimate each sum or difference. Round to the nearest whole number.

1. 6.84 + 9.32   2. 72.9 − 41.7

Estimate using front-end digits.

3. 49.81 − 3.75   4. 37.94 + 26.41

Set G pages 232–233

Find 8.97 + 9.339.

Estimate using rounding: 9 + 9 = 18.

Write 8.970 for 8.97 to make the number of decimal places the same.

```
                1          1 1        1 1
  8.970      8.970      8.970      8.970
+ 9.339    + 9.339    + 9.339    + 9.339
      9         09        309     18.309
```

Remember to estimate the sum to be sure your answer makes sense.

Add.

1.	5.9	2.	43.8	3.	81.09
	+ 4.3		+ 16.1		+ 9.118

4. 12.9 + 8.3   5. 42.4 + 39.2 + 41.8

Set H pages 234–235

Find 36.07 − 29.481.

Estimate using front-end digits: 36 − 29 = 7

```
   15 916
  2 5 10 6 10
  36.070   <- Write 36.070 for 36.07.
- 29.481
   6.589
```

Remember to line up the decimal points, and write zeros so that each decimal will have the same number of decimal places. Subtract.

1.	6.5	2.	$7.46	3.	4.8
	− 2.4		− 4.52		− 2.902

4. 19 − 5.281   5. 13.89 − 8.8

More Practice

Set A   pages 214–215

Write a fraction and a decimal for each exercise.

1. Six tenths

2. Forty-six hundredths

3. Two and eight hundredths

4. Twelve and three tenths

Write each decimal in words.

5. 0.8   **6.** 0.06   **7.** 7.3   **8.** 9.26   **9.** 3.04   **10.** 31.01

Set B   pages 216–217

Write each number in words.

1. 0.005   **2.** 0.084   **3.** 0.647   **4.** 3.028   **5.** 93.109

Write a fraction and a decimal for each exercise.

6. Forty-one thousandths

7. Seven thousandths

8. Five hundred thirty-two thousandths

9. Fifty-four and forty-nine thousandths

Set C   pages 218–219

Write what 3 means in each number.

1. 17.3   **2.** 62.023   **3.** 19.03   **4.** 9,305.6   **5.** 13.205

Which decimals have

6. 9 in the tenths place?
   a. 34.09   **b.** 19.02   **c.** 1.941

7. 5 in the thousandths place?
   a. 103.205   **b.** 82.254   **c.** 5,180.49

8. 2 in the hundredths place?
   a. 901.48   **b.** 851.021   **c.** 44.172

9. 6 in the hundredths place?
   a. 2.86   **b.** 684.13   **c.** 13.026

Set D   pages 220–221

Compare the numbers. Use <, >, or =. Draw a diagram if needed.

1. 9.74 ⁒ 9.72   **2.** 0.8 ⁒ 0.7   **3.** 3.8 ⁒ 3.80

4. 2.842 ⁒ 2.843   **5.** 6.242 ⁒ 6.42   **6.** 0.4 ⁒ 0.395

List the numbers in order from least to greatest. Use a number line if needed.

7. 0.4   0.9   0.5   **8.** 3.48   7.06   3.19   **9.** 0.274   0.272   0.277

10. 5.1   1.5   1.7   **11.** 0.42   0.35   0.53   **12.** 2.896   8.629   6.928

Set E pages 226–227

Round to the nearest whole number.

1. 4.6 **2.** 38.4 **3.** 0.738 **4.** 43.5 **5.** 8.04

Round to the nearest tenth.

6. 1.82 **7.** 0.86 **8.** 8.14 **9.** 6.305 **10.** 5.06

Round to the nearest hundredth.

11. 2.433 **12.** 8.049 **13.** 46.481 **14.** 11.006 **15.** 0.825

Set F pages 228–229

Estimate each sum or difference. Round to the nearest whole number.

1. 41.4 **2.** 87.4 **3.** 6.256 **4.** 64.8 **5.** 49.6 **6.** 31.409
$+ 19.6$ $+ 62.2$ $+ 1.498$ $- 32.4$ $- 10.8$ $- 13.811$

Estimate each sum or difference. Use front-end digits.

7. 4.82 + 20.06 **8.** 39.4 − 9.8 **9.** 87.33 − 20.48 **10.** 43.56 + 10.84

11. 83.106 − 4.612 **12.** 26.5 + 6.4 + 4.8 **13.** 66.6 + 7.8 + 9.3

Set G pages 232–233

Add. **Remember** to line up the decimal points.

1. 7.6 **2.** 45.8 **3.** $12.18 **4.** 91.4 **5.** 5.924
$+ 8.5$ $+ 6.1$ $+ 5.61$ $+ 8.815$ $+ 3.47$

6. 12.1 + 20 **7.** 4.62 + 10.2 + 0.101 **8.** $731.40 + $42.59

9. 7.82 + 0.8 + 12 **10.** 15.8 + 147.7 **11.** 0.8 + 36.5

12. $26.84 + $4.60 **13.** 19.8 + 18.9 + 21.7 **14.** 4.183 + 1.204 + 6.0

Set H pages 234–235

Subtract.

1. 9.7 **2.** $6.48 **3.** $25.66 **4.** 14.3 **5.** 18.204
$- 4.5$ $- 3.86$ $- 4.71$ $- 3.429$ $- 9.54$

6. 42 − 6.091 **7.** 63.48 − 53.7 **8.** 26.004 − 14.873

9. 29.46 − 8.4 **10.** $42.34 − $41.33 **11.** 48.26 − 36.168

12. 17.6 − 9.8 **13.** $9.00 − $5.49 **14.** 62.04 − 29.004

Enrichment

Prime and Composite Numbers

Mathematicians put numbers into two categories. They say a number is either prime or composite.

A whole number greater than 1 that has exactly two whole-number divisors is a *prime number*.

A whole number greater than 1 that is not a prime number, such as 12, is a *composite number*. A composite number has more than two whole-number divisors.

The number 2 has only two divisors: itself and 1. The number 2 is prime.

The number 12 has six divisors: 1, 2, 3, 4, 6, 12. When 12 is divided by each of these numbers, the remainder is 0. The number 12 is composite.

The number 1 has only one divisor: itself. The number 1 is neither prime nor composite.

The Sieve of Eratosthenes can be used to find prime numbers.

1. Copy the table of numbers from 1 to 50.
2. Cross out 1. 1 is not prime.
3. Circle 2. 2 is prime. Why?
4. Cross out all the numbers divisible by 2. Why are they not prime?
5. Circle 3. 3 is prime. Why?
6. Cross out all the numbers divisible by 3. Why are they not prime?
7. Circle 5. 5 is prime. Why?
8. Cross out all the numbers divisible by 5.
9. Circle 7. Why is 7 prime?
10. Cross out all the numbers divisible by 7.
11. The numbers left are prime. Circle them.
12. Extend the table of numbers to 100.
13. Repeat Steps 4, 6, 8, and 10.
14. List all the prime numbers to 100.

1	2	3	4	5	6	7	8	9	10
11	12	13	14	15	16	17	18	19	20
21	22	23	24	25	26	27	28	29	30
31	32	33	34	35	36	37	38	39	40
41	42	43	44	45	46	47	48	49	50

Chapter 7 Review/Test

Write a fraction and a decimal for each exercise.

1.

2. Sixteen and five hundredths

3. Six thousandths

Write each number in words.

4. 0.007   **5.** 6.021

Which decimal has

6. a 7 in the tenths place?

    a. 7.13   **b.** 1.73   **c.** 2.074

7. a 2 in the thousandths place?

    a. 0.203   **b.** 0.023   **c.** 0.302

8. Find a pattern. Write the missing decimals.

    17.02, 17.05, 17.08, ▦, ▦

Compare the numbers. Use <, >, or =.

9. 0.7 ▦ 0.53   **10.** 4.4 ▦ 4.40

11. Joel, Jill, and Janelle each are on a different team. One plays baseball, one plays volleyball, and one plays tennis. The sport that Jill plays does not use a net. Janelle does not play tennis. Who plays volleyball?

Round to the nearest tenth.

12. 0.73   **13.** 7.89

Round to the nearest hundredth.

14. 0.083   **15.** 19.729

Estimate each sum or difference. Round to the nearest whole number.

16. $\begin{array}{r} 40.1 \\ + \ 6.5 \end{array}$ **17.** $\begin{array}{r} 29.5 \\ -19.9 \end{array}$

Estimate each sum or difference. Use front-end digits.

18. 5.8 + 17.9   **19.** 58.7 − 10.9

Add.

20. $\begin{array}{r} 0.8 \\ +0.9 \end{array}$ **21.** $\begin{array}{r} 1.73 \\ +2.789 \end{array}$

22. 1.6 + 2.79   **23.** 17.8 + 0.9

Subtract.

24. 15.7 − 6.8   **25.** 32 − 1.63

26. The school record in relay race was 46.8 seconds. This year the record was broken by 1.9 seconds. What was the time this year?

Read the problem below. Then answer the questions.

Erin saved $12.75 toward the cost of a cassette player. How much more money does she need?

27. What additional data, if any, do you need to solve the problem?

28. **Write About Math** How would you write a decimal in the thousandths equal to 0.1?

1. Round-Trip Fares
From Chicago

1. Airfares
Round-trip means to go to
a place and back again.

2. List
The list tells how many
years would pass before the
given population doubles.

3. Picture
One million $1 bills would
fill two average size
refrigerators.

4. Table
A meteor is a mass of
rock that enters earth's
atmosphere.

5. Chart
The chart shows the
averages of leading hitters
on August 18, 1989.

2. When Populations Will Double

U.S.A.	India	Japan
222.5 million	576.2 million	116.8 million
99 Years	36 Years	79 Years
Mexico	Poland	Australia
68.2 million	35.5 million	14.6 million
22 Years	71 Years	86 Years
Brazil	Iraq	Kenya
122 million	13.2 million	19.9 million
25 Years	20 Years	18 Years
France	U.S.S.R.	Sweden
53.6 million	266 million	8.3 million
198 Years	82 Years	1,386 Years
Egypt	China	
42.1 million	975 million	
26 Years	58 Years	

DATA FILE

To New York $178
To Denver $198
To Miami $218
To Boston $198
To Los Angeles $298

4. Meteor Showers

NAME	MONTH VISIBLE	METEORS PER HOUR	NIGHTS VISIBLE
Quadrantids	January	40	1
Lyrids	April	15	2
N. Aquarids	May	20	3
S. Aquarids	July	20	7
Perseids	August	50	4
Orionids	October	25	2
S. Taurids	November	15	1
Leonids	November	15	1
Geminids	December	50	2
Ursids	December	15	2

3. Weight and Volume of a Million Dollars

Volume — 42 cubic ft
Weight — more than 1 ton

5. Batting Average

Player	Batting Average
Baines, Harold	.315
Boggs, Wade	.338
Browne, Jerry	.309
Davis, Alvin	.332
Greenwell, Mike	.308
Lansford, Carney	.333
Puckett, Kirby	.339
Sax, Steve	.322
Sierra, Ruben	.312
Steinbach, Terry	.308
Yount, Robin	.326

1. List these numbers in order from least to greatest.

486   456   449

a. 486 456 449   **c.** 449 456 486
b. 486 449 456   **d.** 449 486 459

2. Multiply.

412×80

a. 32,096
b. 32,860
c. 32,960
d. 3,286

3. Subtract.

$$\begin{array}{r} 12,000 \\ -3,278 \\ \hline \end{array}$$

a. 9,278
b. 8,278
c. 8,722
d. 9,722

4. Find the average of these numbers.

18   18   22   30   37

a. 18   **b.** 125   **c.** 25   **d.** 22

5. Divide.

$5\overline{)1,795}$

a. 35
b. 360
c. 358
d. 359

6. Find the missing factor.

$9 \times n = 261$

a. 29   **c.** 2,349
b. 252   **d.** 28

7. Find the quotient.

$7,200 \div 90$

a. 80   **c.** 800
b. 8   **d.** 8,000

8. Use compatible numbers to estimate.

$6,310 \div 71$

a. 9   **b.** 90   **c.** 80   **d.** 900

9. Divide.

$16\overline{)3,201}$

a. 2 R1
b. 20 R1
c. 200 R1
d. 20

10. Find the volume.

7 cm
7 cm
7 cm

a. 21 cm³   **c.** 343 cm³
b. 49 cm³   **d.** 98 cm³

11. Complete.

16 qt = ▦ gal

a. 8
b. 4
c. 32
d. 64

12. Complete.

9 L = ▦ mL

a. 90
b. 900
c. 9,000
d. 90,000

Choose the most sensible measure.

13. Milk in a bowl of cereal

a. 1 c   **b.** 1 pt   **c.** 1 qt   **d.** 1 gal

14. A grapefruit

a. 7 lb   **b.** 70 lb   **c.** 7 T   **d.** 7 oz

15. When you convert from kg to g, you

a. multiply by 1,000.
b. divide by 1,000.
c. multiply by 100.
d. divide by 100.

16. Subtract.

    7 ft 5 in.
    − 4 ft 9 in.

a. 3 ft 4 in.   **c.** 2 ft 8 in.
b. 3 ft 8 in.   **d.** 2 ft 6 in.

17. Which digit in 0.715 is in the hundredths place?

a. 7   **c.** 5
b. 1   **d.** 0

18. Which decimal represents seven thousandths?

a. 0.700   **c.** 0.007
b. 0.070   **d.** 7000

19. Add.

    2.9 + 3.78

a. 4.07   **c.** 5.68
b. 6.68   **d.** 5.87

20. Tell whether you would *add, subtract, multiply,* or *divide.* Then solve the problem.

An office supply store has 36 boxes of pencils. Each box holds 144 pencils. How many pencils are there in all?

a. Add; 180 boxes
b. Subtract; 108 boxes
c. Divide; 4 boxes
d. Multiply; 5,184 pencils

21. Plates are being packed 8 per box. There are 300 plates to be packed. How many boxes are needed?

a. 37 boxes   **c.** 4 boxes
b. 38 boxes   **d.** none of these

22. A relay team ran a race in 48.8 seconds. This was 1.9 seconds slower than the school record. What was the school record?

a. 50.7 sec   **c.** 47.1 sec
b. 46.9 sec   **d.** 36.9 sec

23. Jack is making a rectangular pen with 40 feet of fencing. What is the area of the largest pen he can make with the fencing?

a. 40 sq ft   **c.** 100 sq ft
b. 400 sq ft   **d.** 80 sq ft

Read the problem below. Then answer the question.

Alice has worked part-time as a cashier at Smith's Restaurant for 14 weeks. She earns $30 on Friday evenings and $45 working on Saturdays. How much does she earn each week?

24. Which information is not needed to solve the problem?

a. Alice's pay for Friday evening is $30.
b. Alice works only 2 days per week.
c. Alice has worked for 14 weeks.
d. She is paid $45 for working on Saturdays.

Multiplication of Decimals

8

OREGON

Astoria

IDAHO

Did You Know:
In 8 hours, a typical pack horse, or mule, can travel approximately 20 miles. A horse-drawn carriage can travel approximately 40 miles in 8 hours.

Number-Sense Project

Estimate
What is the approximate distance around your school's playground?

Gather Data
Develop a method for estimating the distance. Then use the method to estimate the perimeter of the playground.

Analyze and Report
Describe how you estimated the distance around the playground. Compare estimates with other students.

THE OREGON TRAIL

WYOMING

NEBRASKA

KANSAS

MISSOURI

Independence

Extending Place Value

Build Understanding

A. Carla was trying out different keys on her calculator. She entered the number 37.150. The display looked like this:

$$37.150$$

There are three places to the right of the decimal point.

Read: Thirty-seven and one hundred fifty thousandths

B. Next, Carla entered a 4. The display looked like this:

$$37.1504$$

There are four places to the right of the decimal point.

Read: Thirty-seven and one thousand five hundred four ten-thousandths

Electronic calculators perform calculations automatically by the use of miniature electronic circuits.

C. Carla then entered an 8. The display looked like this:

$$37.15048$$

There are five places to the right of the decimal point.

Read: Thirty-seven and fifteen thousand forty-eight hundred-thousandths

A place-value chart can be extended to show these decimal places.

■ Talk About Math

What two places are just to the right of the hundred-thousandths place?

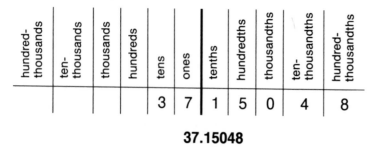

hundred-thousands	ten-thousands	thousands	hundreds	tens	ones	tenths	hundredths	thousandths	ten-thousandths	hundred-thousandths
				3	7	1	5	0	4	8

37.15048

Check Understanding

For another example, see Set A, pages 274–275.

For each number, name the value of the place that contains a 4.

1. 6.24   **2.** 19.65341   **3.** 0.63204   **4.** 42.693

Practice

For More Practice, see Set A, pages 276–277.

Tell how many decimal places are in each number. Write each decimal in words.

5. 91.34   **6.** 3.7602   **7.** 192.64391   **8.** 2.0003   **9.** 30.04017

10. How many zeros are between the decimal point and the one in the decimal for one hundred-thousandth?

11. If one ten-thousandth is written as a fraction, what number would be in the denominator?

For each number, name the digit in the ten-thousandths place.

12. 4.70892   **13.** 15.0036   **14.** 2.347254   **15.** 512.8900

For each number, name the digit in the hundred-thousandths place.

16. 8.96671   **17.** 0.552668   **18.** 91.060008   **19.** 2.2140825

Look at each calculator display. Name the value of the last decimal place.

20. 4812.67   **21.** 201.7802   **22.** 0.1823

23. 0.00491   **24.** 1900.1027   **25.** 81.20782

For each number, name the place that contains an 8.

26. 5.008   **27.** 27.1811   **28.** 3.00087   **29.** 198.074

30. 817.473   **31.** 47.17468   **32.** 89.0631   **33.** 176.4832

34. 28,763.02   **35.** 36.0984   **36.** 349,307.8   **37.** 74.30798

Problem Solving

Solve each problem.

38. **Calculator** Enter 12.34567 into a calculator. What number must you add so that the 6 in the display becomes a 9?

39. **Number Sense** Is a number with five decimal places always less than a number with one decimal place? Explain.

40. **Critical Thinking** In the number 546,237,641.024746751, the 5 at the left means 5 hundred-millions. What does the 5 at the right mean? the 1 at the right?

Multiplying a Decimal by a Whole Number

Build Understanding

A. Payday
Materials: Play money ($10 bills,
$1 bills, dimes, pennies)
Groups: Small groups

José works at the Great Movies Video Store
after school and on weekends. He earns $4.17
an hour.

On Thursday, he worked from 3:00 P.M. until
6:00 P.M. How much did José earn?

José worked for 3 hours. He earned $4.17
each hour.

Estimate: $4.17 is a little more than $4.00,
so José earned a little more than 3 × $4, or $12.

You can use play money to help solve problems
in which you need to multiply a decimal
by a whole number. Remember:

1 dollar	1 dime	1 penny
1 one	1 tenth	1 hundredth
1	0.1	0.01

a. Make 3 groups of $4.17.

b. Combine all of the similar coins and bills.
How many dollars do you have? How many
dimes? How many pennies?

c. How many pennies can you trade for dimes?
How many dimes can you trade for $1 bills?
How many dollars can you trade for $10 bills?

Add the value of all the bills and coins. How much
money do you have in all? How much did José earn?

B. Find 3×2.4.

You could use play money to model 3 groups of 2.4. Or you could use multiplication to find the total since you are combining groups of equal size.

Multiply the tenths.	Multiply the ones.
3×4 tenths = 12 tenths	3×2 ones = 6 ones
Rename as 1 one 2 tenths.	6 ones + 1 one = 7 ones

$$\begin{array}{r} 1 \\ 2.4 \\ \times \quad 3 \\ \hline 2 \end{array} \qquad \begin{array}{r} 1 \\ 2.4 \\ \times \quad 3 \\ \hline 7.2 \end{array}$$

What do you do with play money that is the same as renaming?

c. Find 45×0.217.

$$\begin{array}{r} 0.217 \\ \times \quad 45 \\ \hline 1085 \\ 8680 \\ \hline 9.765 \end{array}$$

0.217 — 3 decimal places
45 — 0 decimal places

9.765 — 3 decimal places

■ **Write About Math**   Find the products.

3×417 3×24 45×217

What can you say about these products and the products in Examples A, B, and C? Describe how to multiply a decimal by a whole number.

Great Movies Video

Check Understanding

For another example, see Set B, pages 274–275.

Copy each exercise. Place the decimal point in the product.

1. $3 \times 53.7 = 1611$ **2.** $8 \times 5.27 = 4216$

Solve each problem. Use play money if you need to.

3. Find 6×2.37 **4.** Find 3×2.24

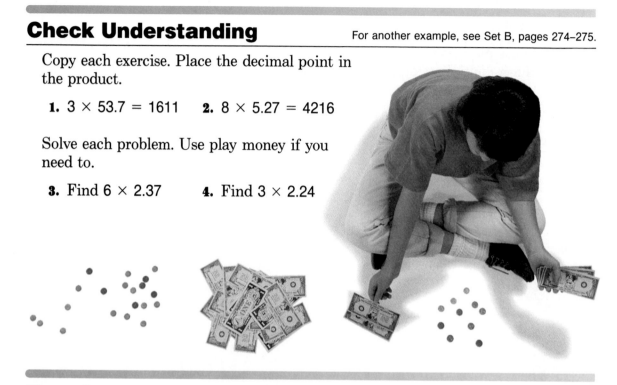

Practice

For More Practice, see Set B, pages 276–277.

Multiply. **Remember** to place the decimal point in the product.

5. $\begin{array}{r} 0.4 \\ \times\ 6 \\ \hline \end{array}$	**6.** $\begin{array}{r} 0.09 \\ \times\ 3 \\ \hline \end{array}$	**7.** $\begin{array}{r} 0.12 \\ \times\ 7 \\ \hline \end{array}$	**8.** $\begin{array}{r} 8.3 \\ \times\ 6 \\ \hline \end{array}$	**9.** $\begin{array}{r} 4.5 \\ \times\ 3 \\ \hline \end{array}$
10. $\begin{array}{r} 2.81 \\ \times\ 4 \\ \hline \end{array}$	**11.** $\begin{array}{r} 1.76 \\ \times\ 5 \\ \hline \end{array}$	**12.** $\begin{array}{r} 3.03 \\ \times\ 6 \\ \hline \end{array}$	**13.** $\begin{array}{r} 2.8 \\ \times\ 34 \\ \hline \end{array}$	**14.** $\begin{array}{r} 6.2 \\ \times\ 13 \\ \hline \end{array}$
15. $\begin{array}{r} 3.7 \\ \times\ 65 \\ \hline \end{array}$	**16.** $\begin{array}{r} 0.17 \\ \times\ 14 \\ \hline \end{array}$	**17.** $\begin{array}{r} 0.52 \\ \times\ 26 \\ \hline \end{array}$	**18.** $\begin{array}{r} 0.208 \\ \times\ 21 \\ \hline \end{array}$	**19.** $\begin{array}{r} 0.836 \\ \times\ 52 \\ \hline \end{array}$
20. $\begin{array}{r} 0.92 \\ \times\ 27 \\ \hline \end{array}$	**21.** $\begin{array}{r} 9.909 \\ \times\ 54 \\ \hline \end{array}$	**22.** $\begin{array}{r} 302.6 \\ \times\ 83 \\ \hline \end{array}$	**23.** $\begin{array}{r} 3.208 \\ \times\ 91 \\ \hline \end{array}$	**24.** $\begin{array}{r} 5.634 \\ \times\ 49 \\ \hline \end{array}$

25. 7×2.3 **26.** 3×2.54 **27.** 4×0.205

28. 6×0.0513 **29.** 8×0.5149 **30.** 27×0.035

31. 38×0.22 **32.** 17×8.15 **33.** 54×6.02

34. 48×3.806 **35.** 9×0.328 **36.** 3×0.789

37. 5×0.495 **38.** 7×1.208 **39.** 7×0.9081

Mixed Practice Multiply.

40. 32×0.907　　　　**41.** 81×654　　　　**42.** 5×8.07

43. 82×0.305　　　　**44.** 477×604　　　　**45.** 73×8.05

46. 52×606　　　　**47.** 45×0.702　　　　**48.** 84×0.1212

Problem Solving

49. Mental Math On Friday José got paid $87.50 for the whole week. The week before, he earned $79.00. How much more did he earn this week than last?

50. On Saturday, José worked from 8:30 A.M. until 1:30 P.M. He did not get paid for the one hour he took off for lunch. At $4.17 an hour, how much did he earn?

51. Write a question for these data. A quarter is 1.8 millimeters thick. Tom has $12 in quarters.

52. Tom's Videos rents videos for $1.00 the first night. Each additional night costs $2.50. Prices include tax. How much would it cost to keep a video for 3 nights?

TIPS FOR PROBLEM SOLVERS

Organize your work to help you think clearly.

Skills _____ Review　　　pages 150–169

Divide.

1. $57\overline{)90}$　　　**2.** $50\overline{)212}$　　　**3.** $49\overline{)155}$　　　**4.** $89\overline{)356}$

5. $42\overline{)849}$　　　**6.** $50\overline{)4,745}$　　　**7.** $22\overline{)748}$　　　**8.** $46\overline{)2,391}$

9. $30\overline{)4,589}$　　　**10.** $48\overline{)6,796}$　　　**11.** $52\overline{)7,996}$　　　**12.** $74\overline{)9,546}$

13. $98\overline{)2,962}$　　　**14.** $51\overline{)6,656}$　　　**15.** $24\overline{)7,236}$　　　**16.** $61\overline{)199}$

17. $3,653 \div 41$　　　**18.** $8,001 \div 32$　　　**19.** $7,654 \div 76$

Choose an Operation

Build Understanding

The 5th-grade class at Elkins School was having a party to celebrate the upcoming wedding of its teacher, Miss Wolfe. Choy's mother bought four cheese and cracker trays for the party. Each tray cost $12.65. How much did Choy's mother pay for the four trays?

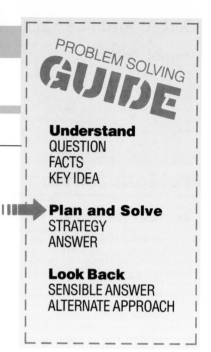

PROBLEM SOLVING GUIDE

Understand
QUESTION
FACTS
KEY IDEA

Plan and Solve
STRATEGY
ANSWER

Look Back
SENSIBLE ANSWER
ALTERNATE APPROACH

Understand   What was the total cost of the four cheese and cracker trays? Choy's mother bought 4 trays and each tray was the same price. Each tray cost $12.65.

Plan and Solve   STRATEGY   Since each tray was the same price, use multiplication to find the total cost.
Find 4 × $12.65.
Estimate: $12.65 is about $13.   4 × 13 = 52

Paper and Pencil

$$\begin{array}{r} \$12.65 \\ \times \quad 4 \\ \hline \$50.60 \end{array}$$

Calculator

Press: 12 ⬚.⬚ 65 ⬚×⬚ 4 ⬚=⬚

Display: *50.6*

ANSWER   Choy's mother paid $50.60 for the four cheese and cracker trays.

Look Back   Check the answer using addition.

$12.65 + $12.65 + $12.65 + $12.65 = $50.60
The answer of $50.60 is close to the estimate of $52.
The answer is reasonable.

■ **Talk About Math**   Which computation method—paper and pencil, calculator, or mental math—would you prefer for working a problem in which you need to multiply an amount of money?

Check Understanding

To answer these questions, use the problem at the right.

1. What is the question?

2. What are the facts?

3. What operations would you use?

4. How will you know if your answer is reasonable?

> Brett's mother bought three rolls of crepe paper at $7.75 each and a box of balloons for $4.85. How much did she spend in all?

Practice

Tell which operation to use. Then solve the problem.

5. Three parents donated a meat tray. The tray cost $36. If they shared the cost equally, how much did each parent spend?

6. Mrs. Gallo, the principal, bought 5 cases of fruit drinks. Each case cost $8.79. How much did she spend?

7. If 28 students shared the cost of a gift for $112, how much did each contribute?

8. If 15 teachers gave a total of $178 for a gift that cost $169.75, how much money was left over?

Choose a ———— Strategy

Paper Routes   Meg and Suzie deliver different newspapers on Monday through Saturday. Meg earns $0.06 for every paper she delivers. Suzie makes $13.00 a month plus $0.05 for every paper delivered. Use the calendar to help you answer the questions.

9. How much would each girl earn in September if each delivered 20 papers each day?

10. How much would each girl earn if she delivered 30 papers each day? 40 papers? 60 papers?

11. One September the girls earned the same salary and delivered the same number of papers. How much did each earn? How many newspapers were delivered each day?

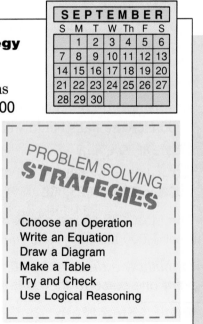

SEPTEMBER						
S	M	T	W	Th	F	S
		1	2	3	4	5	6
7	8	9	10	11	12	13
14	15	16	17	18	19	20
21	22	23	24	25	26	27
28	29	30				

PROBLEM SOLVING
STRATEGIES

Choose an Operation
Write an Equation
Draw a Diagram
Make a Table
Try and Check
Use Logical Reasoning

Mental Math for Multiplying by 10, 100, or 1,000

Build Understanding

Ball games are popular in all countries of the world. Lacrosse developed from a game called *baggataway*. Baggataway was first played by members of the Iroquois Confederation, whose members lived and live in what is now called New York and southeastern Ontario. Lacrosse is played on a field with two teams. Each team tries to score by throwing, scooping, or kicking a rubber ball into the other team's goal. The ball weighs between 5 and 5.25 ounces.

Lacrosse is the national game of Canada.
Crosse means *stick* in French.

A. What is the most 10 lacrosse balls could weigh?

If each ball weighs 5.25 ounces, the total weight is 10 × 5.25 ounces. You know 10 × 525 = 5,250. So 10 × 5.25 will have the same digits, but two digits will be to the right of the decimal point.

$$10 \times 5.25 = 52.50$$

The most 10 lacrosse balls could weigh is 52.50 ounces.

B. What would be the most 100 lacrosse balls or 1,000 lacrosse balls could weigh?

10 × 525 = 5,250	10 × 5.25 = 52.50
100 × 525 = 52,500	100 × 5.25 = 525.00
1,000 × 525 = 525,000	1,000 × 5.25 = 5,250.00

Use what you know about multiplying by 10, 100, or 1,000 and multiplying decimals by whole numbers. Notice how the decimal point moves.

The most 100 lacrosse balls could weigh is 525 ounces. The most 1,000 lacrosse balls could weigh is 5,250 ounces.

To multiply a decimal by 10, 100, or 1,000, move the decimal point one place to the right for each zero in 10, 100, or 1,000.

■ **Write About Math** In the products in Example B, which zeros do not need to be written? Why can they be left off? Which zeros must be written? Why?

Check Understanding

For another example, see Set C, pages 274–275.

Match the product with the letter of the correct answer.

1. 1,000 × 2.7 **a.** 27 **b.** 2,700   **2.** 10 × 0.027 **a.** 2.7 **b.** 0.27

Practice

For More Practice, see Set C, pages 276–277.

Find each product. Use mental math.

3. 10 × 0.6   **4.** 100 × 0.06   **5.** 1,000 × 0.06   **6.** 10 × 4.3

7. 100 × 4.3   **8.** 1,000 × 4.3   **9.** 10 × 0.17   **10.** 0.4 × 100

11. 0.653 × 1,000   **12.** 1.09 × 10   **13.** 21.3 × 10   **14.** 10 × 0.007

15. 1,000 × 0.004   **16.** 0.46 × 1,000   **17.** 0.46 × 10,000   **18.** 0.46 × 100,000

19. 10,000 × 3.9   **20.** 0.0045 × 10   **21.** 100 × 0.03   **22.** 12.6 × 1,000

23. 1.234 × 100   **24.** 1.1 × 10,000   **25.** 34.6 × 1,000   **26.** 100,000 × 9.8

Problem Solving

Solve each problem.

27. *Jai alai* is a popular game in Cuba, Mexico, Spain, and the United States. It is played with a ball, called a *pelota,* that weighs 4.5 ounces. What is the weight of 100 jai alai balls?

28. Many table tennis tournaments are held in China. Chiang bought 6 table tennis balls for $2.27 and 4 paddles for $14.88. What was the total price of the equipment?

29. Modern bowling was brought to the United States by the Dutch. Bowling balls used in leagues weigh between 4.5 and 7.3 kilograms. In the metric system, 1 kilogram equals 1,000 grams. Give the lightest and heaviest weights of bowling balls in grams.

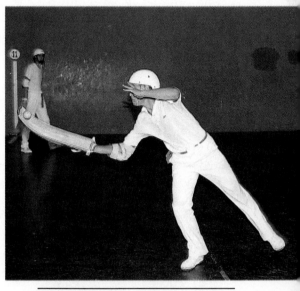

Jai alai has been called the fastest game in the world. The ball has been clocked at more than 150 miles per hour. It is similar to handball.

Estimating Products

Build Understanding

How tall will you be when you are an adult?

Growth Factor		
Age	Girls	Boys
8	1.29	1.39
9	1.24	1.33
10	1.18	1.28
11	1.13	1.23
12	1.08	1.19
13	1.04	1.15

A. In her science book, Lisa found a growth factor table for predicting adult height. To use the table, multiply the person's height in centimeters by the growth factor for the person's age.

Lisa is 10 years old and her height is 159 centimeters. The growth factor for a 10-year-old girl is 1.18. To estimate her adult height, she rounded each number.

1.18 × 159 → 1 × 200 = 200   1.18 rounds to 1.
159 rounds to 200.

Her adult height will be about 200 centimeters.

B. Estimate the product of 94.8 and 5.82. Substitute a compatible number to multiply mentally.

94.8 × 5.82 → 100 × 5.82 = 582

The product of 94.8 and 5.82 is about 582.

■ **Talk About Math** Will the actual product in Example B be more than 582 or less? Why?

Check Understanding

For another example, see Set D, pages 274-275.

Match each with the most reasonable estimate.

1. 6.42 × 2.87   **2.** 9.75 × 2.2   **3.** 3.02 × 9.18   **4.** 42.3 × 7.04

  a. 280   **b.** 27   **c.** 18   **d.** 22

Estimate each product. Use your estimate to put the decimal point in each product.

5. 3.83 × 3.1 = 11873   **6.** 12.34 × 9.5 = 11723   **7.** 102.4 × 4.71 = 482304

Practice

For More Practice, see Set D, pages 276–277.

Estimate the products.

8. 3.22×5.7 **9.** 4.09×1.34 **10.** 23.7×8.5 **11.** 6.554×2.3

12. 63.5×4.9 **13.** 81.2×8.7 **14.** 92.5×1.07 **15.** 100.2×24.6

16. 0.34×0.99 **17.** 89.32×11.03 **18.** 123.4×10.8 **19.** 54.37×0.83

20. 51.6×5.2 **21.** 151.1×2.2 **22.** 64.8×0.93 **23.** 100.6×11.2

24. 96.6×1.08 **25.** 6.02×1.24 **26.** 3.11×5.2 **27.** 75.29×0.899

28. $1{,}034.25 \times 7.17$ **29.** $0.06 \times \$25$ **30.** $1.25 \times \$150$

Mixed Practice   Complete only those exercises with products less than 20.

31. 20×0.9 **32.** 20×0.09 **33.** 20×1.2 **34.** 20×2.4

35. 6×0.3 **36.** 6×3.9 **37.** 6×0.03 **38.** 6×3.1

Problem Solving

39. Number Sense   Adam told Lisa the product of 23.2 and 1.5 is 3.48. Was he correct? Explain.

40. Lisa said the product of 9.23 and 8.76 is less than 90. Explain her thinking.

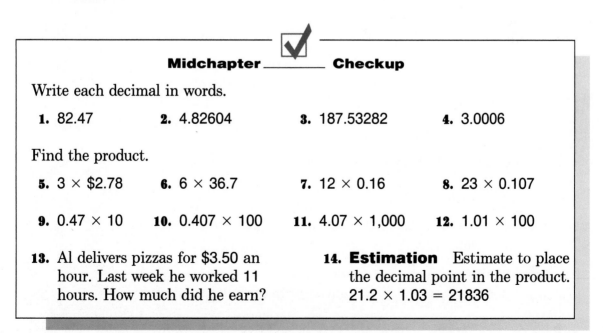

Midchapter ✓ Checkup

Write each decimal in words.

1. 82.47   **2.** 4.82604   **3.** 187.53282   **4.** 3.0006

Find the product.

5. $3 \times \$2.78$ **6.** 6×36.7 **7.** 12×0.16 **8.** 23×0.107

9. 0.47×10 **10.** 0.407×100 **11.** $4.07 \times 1{,}000$ **12.** 1.01×100

13. Al delivers pizzas for $3.50 an hour. Last week he worked 11 hours. How much did he earn?

14. Estimation   Estimate to place the decimal point in the product. $21.2 \times 1.03 = 21836$

Problem-Solving Workshop

Real-Life Decision Making

You and 5 friends have $5 each to play miniature golf and buy pizza at the Pizza Shack. Two people want pepperoni, 2 people want sausage, and 2 people like all the toppings.

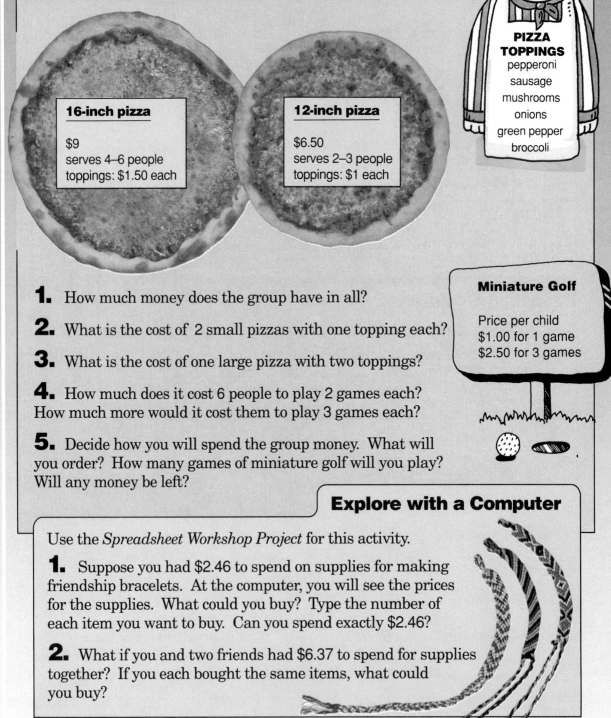

16-inch pizza

$9
serves 4–6 people
toppings: $1.50 each

12-inch pizza

$6.50
serves 2–3 people
toppings: $1 each

PIZZA TOPPINGS
pepperoni
sausage
mushrooms
onions
green pepper
broccoli

Miniature Golf

Price per child
$1.00 for 1 game
$2.50 for 3 games

1. How much money does the group have in all?

2. What is the cost of 2 small pizzas with one topping each?

3. What is the cost of one large pizza with two toppings?

4. How much does it cost 6 people to play 2 games each? How much more would it cost them to play 3 games each?

5. Decide how you will spend the group money. What will you order? How many games of miniature golf will you play? Will any money be left?

Explore with a Computer

Use the *Spreadsheet Workshop Project* for this activity.

1. Suppose you had $2.46 to spend on supplies for making friendship bracelets. At the computer, you will see the prices for the supplies. What could you buy? Type the number of each item you want to buy. Can you spend exactly $2.46?

2. What if you and two friends had $6.37 to spend for supplies together? If you each bought the same items, what could you buy?

Number-Sense Project

Look back at pages 248-249.
Mr. Hill's class estimated the perimeter of the school's
playground is about 1,300 feet, or 0.25 miles.

The class planned a route across the United States. For each
lap a student walked around the playground, he or she moved
a marker 0.25 miles along the route. If each of the 30 students
in the class walked 1 lap, Mr. Hill moved the marker
30×0.25, or 7.5 miles.

1. In all, how many miles did the class walk on
Tuesday, the 6th?

2. How many laps were logged on Wednesday, the 7th?
What is a possible explanation for this number?

3. What was the greatest distance in miles covered by
Mr. Hill's class in one day?

4. Write a statement comparing the perimeter of your
playground to the one at Mr. Hill's school.

Log of the laps
Mr. Hill's class
walked in
12 days

Date	Day	Laps
1	Thursday	97
2	Friday	112
5	Monday	65
6	Tuesday	40
7	Wednesday	0
8	Thursday	101
9	Friday	135
12	Monday	150
13	Tuesday	90
14	Wednesday	148
15	Thursday	67
16	Friday	125

Multiplying by a Decimal

Build Understanding

A. On his last sales trip, Mr. McCall averaged 55 miles per hour driving on the interstate highway. How far did he travel in 3.5 hours?

He traveled the same distance each hour, so multiply to find the total distance.

Estimate: 4 × 55 = 220

$$
\begin{array}{r}
55 \\
\times\, 3.5 \leftarrow \text{1 decimal place} \\
\hline
275 \\
1650 \\
\hline
192.5 \leftarrow \text{1 decimal place}
\end{array}
$$

Mr. McCall covered a distance of 192.5 miles.

East-west interstate highways have even numbers. Odd numbers are used for north-south highways.

B. Find 0.7 of 0.5. Use models to show how to place the decimal point.

Shade 0.5 of a square yellow.

Separate each tenth into 10 equal parts. Shade 7 of the 10 equal parts red.

Name the number of parts of the square that are orange.

$$
\begin{array}{r}
0.5 \;\; \text{1 decimal place} \\
\times\, 0.7 \;\; \text{1 decimal place} \\
\hline
0.35 \;\; \text{2 decimal places}
\end{array}
$$

C. Find 4.12 × 6.89.

Estimate: 4 × 7 = 28

Step 1
Multiply as with whole numbers.

$$
\begin{array}{r}
689 \\
\times\, 412 \\
\hline
1378 \\
6890 \\
275600 \\
\hline
283868
\end{array}
$$

Step 2
Count the number of decimal places in both factors.

$$
\begin{array}{r}
6.89 \leftarrow \text{2 decimal places} \\
\times\, 4.12 \leftarrow \text{2 decimal places} \\
\hline
1378 \\
6890 \\
275600 \\
\hline
283868
\end{array}
$$

Step 3
The number of decimal places in the product is the total number of decimal places in the factors.

$$
\begin{array}{r}
6.89 \leftarrow \text{2 decimal places} \\
\times\, 4.12 \leftarrow \text{2 decimal places} \\
\hline
1378 \\
6890 \\
275600 \\
\hline
28.3868 \leftarrow \text{4 decimal places}
\end{array}
$$

■ **Write About Math** What coin is one tenth of a dollar? Write its value as a decimal. What coin is one tenth of a tenth of a dollar? Write its value as a decimal.

Check Understanding

For another example, see Set E, pages 274-275.

Tell how many decimal places should be shown in each product.

1. 23 × 5.7   **2.** 2.3 × 5.7   **3.** 0.23 × 5.7   **4.** 0.23 × 0.57

5. 1.34 × 4.96   **6.** 0.46 × 1.56   **7.** 345 × 0.5   **8.** 1.25 × 1.25

Practice

For More Practice, see Set E, pages 276-277.

Multiply.

9.   0.7
     × 0.4

10.   0.3
      × 0.5

11.   7
      × 0.6

12.   0.54
      × 0.7

13.   2.9
      × 5.4

14.   8.4
      × 0.6

15.   23.7
      × 0.12

16.   23.9
      × 0.2

17.   9.12
      × 0.22

18.   2.126
      ×   8

19. 721 × 0.3   **20.** 56.1 × 2.1   **21.** 3.16 × 0.9   **22.** 1.02 × 0.6

23. 0.9 × 5   **24.** 0.7 × 6   **25.** 0.4 × 0.87   **26.** 56 × 2.7

27. 0.04 × 5.7   **28.** 4.9 × 0.3   **29.** 0.2 × 78   **30.** 0.33 × 4.6

31. 34.1 × 0.3   **32.** 9.1 × 4.3   **33.** 0.25 × 65.1   **34.** 5.01 × 3.047

Problem Solving

Read for the facts to solve the problems.

35. On a previous trip, Mr. McCall averaged 54.5 miles per hour. If he traveled 7.5 hours, how many miles did he travel?

36. When Mr. McCall began his last trip, the odometer on his car read 34,512.9. The reading when he returned home was 35,389.2. How many miles did he travel?

37. If gas costs $1.18 a gallon and Mr. McCall bought 9 gallons, how much did he pay?

38. ▦ **Calculator** The price of gas is $1.349 per gallon as shown on a pump. Mr. McCall bought 5.947 gallons. What total cost did the pump show?

Multiplying Decimals: Zeros in the Product

Build Understanding

A. At Val's Variety Store, Maria bought a notebook for $1.50. A state sales tax of 6 cents on each dollar is added to the cost of any purchase. How much tax did Maria pay?

To find the amount of the sales tax, multiply the cost by 0.06. Find 0.06 × 1.50.

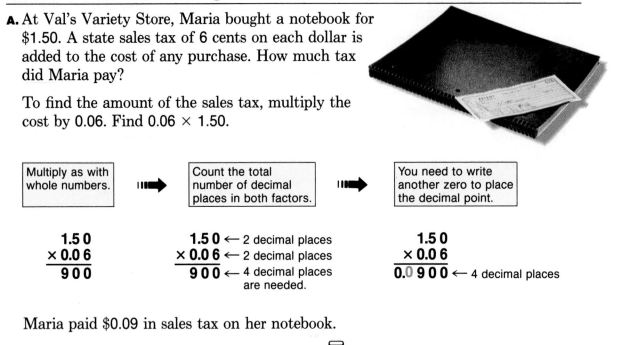

| Multiply as with whole numbers. | ➡ | Count the total number of decimal places in both factors. | ➡ | You need to write another zero to place the decimal point. |

$$\begin{array}{r} 1.5\,0 \\ \times\,0.0\,6 \\ \hline 9\,0\,0 \end{array}$$

$$\begin{array}{r} 1.5\,0 \leftarrow \text{2 decimal places} \\ \times\,0.0\,6 \leftarrow \text{2 decimal places} \\ \hline 9\,0\,0 \leftarrow \text{4 decimal places} \\ \text{are needed.} \end{array}$$

$$\begin{array}{r} 1.5\,0 \\ \times\,0.0\,6 \\ \hline 0.0\,9\,0\,0 \leftarrow \text{4 decimal places} \end{array}$$

Maria paid $0.09 in sales tax on her notebook.

B. Find 0.08 × 0.012.

$$\begin{array}{r} 0.0\,1\,2 \leftarrow \text{3 decimal places} \\ \times\quad 0.0\,8 \leftarrow \text{2 decimal places} \\ \hline 0.0\,0\,0\,9\,6 \leftarrow \text{5 decimal places} \end{array}$$

↑ Need to write 3 extra zeros in product.

c. 🖩 **Calculator**   Find 0.215 × 0.174.

Press: ⎡.⎤ 215 ⎡×⎤ ⎡.⎤ 174 ⎡=⎤

Display: *0.03741*

■ **Talk About Math**   In Example C, why are there only 5 decimal places in the product but 6 decimal places in the 2 factors?

Check Understanding

For another example, see Set F, pages 274–275.

Copy each exercise. Place the decimal point in the product. Write extra zeros when necessary.

1.	**2.**	**3.**	**4.**	**5.**
0.07	6.4	0.18	1.25	0.09
× 0.3	×0.2	× 0.4	×0.07	×0.06
21	128	72	875	54

Practice

For More Practice, see Set F, pages 276–277.

Multiply. **Remember** to write extra zeros when necessary.

6. 0.09×0.02 **7.** 0.004×9 **8.** 0.007×0.07 **9.** 0.025×0.04

10. 33×0.003 **11.** 1.4×0.004 **12.** 2.05×0.01 **13.** 45×0.002

14. 0.01×0.01 **15.** 0.125×0.08 **16.** 2.7×0.002 **17.** 0.025×2

18. 36×0.002 **19.** 0.005×0.006 **20.** 0.041×3 **21.** 0.12×0.06

Tell whether you would use paper and pencil, a calculator, or mental math. Then find each product.

22. 2.2×0.007 **23.** 0.22×0.007 **24.** 0.022×0.007

25. $0.2 \times 0.2 \times 0.2$ **26.** $0.3 \times 0.4 \times 0.5$ **27.** $1 \times 0.03 \times 0.05$

Problem Solving

Use Data   Study the table of telephone rates on page 271. Find the cost of a call lasting 0.5 minutes at the following times.

28. 11:00 A.M.   **29.** 6:00 P.M.   **30.** 6:00 A.M.

For each problem, multiply by 0.06 to find the sales tax.

31. Akato bought a felt-tipped pen at Val's for $1.00. How much was the sales tax?

32. What is the sales tax on a box of paper clips for 89 cents and a tablet for 46 cents?

A
L
G
E
B
R
A

Explore ———— Math

Easy Products   Find the value of each variable using paper and pencil or a calculator.

33. a. $0.1 \times 7.52 = n$
  b. $0.1 \times 69.08 = a$
  c. $0.1 \times 547.6 = t$
  d. $0.1 \times 0.03 = h$

34. a. $0.01 \times 7.52 = x$
  b. $0.01 \times 69.08 = y$
  c. $0.01 \times 547.6 = w$
  d. $0.01 \times 0.03 = c$

35. Describe an easy way to find the product of a decimal and 0.1.

36. Describe an easy way to find the product of a decimal and 0.01.

Exploring Division of Decimals

Build Understanding

Be Fair

Materials: Play money ($10 bills, $1 bills, dimes, and pennies)

Groups: Small groups

Daniel, RJ, and Scott have a lawn-raking business in the fall. One day they earned $17.25. How much was each boy's share of their earnings?

Find $17.25 ÷ 3.

a. Use play money to divide $17.25 into 3 equal shares.

b. First trade $10 for 10 $1 bills. How many dollars do you have in all?

c. Divide the dollars into 3 equal groups. How many dollars can each boy have? How many dollars are left over?

d. Trade the remaining dollars for dimes. How many dimes do you have in all? How many dimes can each boy have?

e. How many dimes are left over? Trade the extra dime for pennies. How many pennies do you have in all? How many can each boy have?

f. What is each boy's share?

■ **Talk About Math** Find 1,725 ÷ 3. What can you say about this quotient and your answer to the problem above?

Check Understanding

For another example, see Set G, pages 274–275.

1. If you were dividing $18.40 among 4 girls, how many dollar bills would each girl get?

2. What would you do with the dollar bills that were left? What coins would each girl get?

3. How much money would each girl get?

4. What is the quotient for 18.4 ÷ 4?

Practice

For More Practice, see Set G, pages 276–277.

Divide. **Remember** to put the decimal point in the quotient.

5. 8.6 ÷ 2 **6.** 7.2 ÷ 3 **7.** 3.69 ÷ 3 **8.** 6.08 ÷ 4 **9.** 14.94 ÷ 6

10. 23.25 ÷ 5 **11.** 20.4 ÷ 3 **12.** 16.8 ÷ 7 **13.** 13.8 ÷ 6 **14.** 27.2 ÷ 8

15. 41.5 ÷ 5 **16.** 2.43 ÷ 9 **17.** 40.6 ÷ 7 **18.** 11.55 ÷ 5 **19.** 8.52 ÷ 4

20. 71.4 ÷ 3 **21.** 56.28 ÷ 6 **22.** 0.847 ÷ 7 **23.** 1.338 ÷ 2 **24.** 310.5 ÷ 9

25. 0.448 ÷ 4 **26.** 7.36 ÷ 8 **27.** 3.110 ÷ 5 **28.** 0.948 ÷ 3 **29.** 25.26 ÷ 6

Problem Solving

Use play money, if you need to, to solve these problems.

30. If you and two of your friends earned $8.43 together, what would your share be?

31. RJ worked for 2 hours, and Scott and Daniel each worked 1 hour. They were paid $21.60. How could the money be split fairly?

32. One day Scott worked for 2 hours raking a lawn, but Daniel worked for only 1 hour. The two boys earned $10.35. What would be a fair way to share the money? Why?

33. Visual Thinking You have quarters, nickels, pennies, and dimes in your pocket. There are 12 coins all together. There are 2 large silver coins, 3 small silver coins, and 3 medium silver coins. The rest are copper coins. What is the total?

Multiple-Step Problems

PROBLEM SOLVING
GUIDE

Build Understanding

Floyd's father bought a fishing vest for his son's birthday. It was gray with 17 pockets and cost $26.60. A state sales tax of 5 cents on each dollar is added to the cost of every purchase. What was the total cost of the fishing vest, including tax?

Understand

QUESTION   What was the total cost including tax?

FACTS   The vest cost $26.60. The sales tax is 5 cents on every dollar.

KEY IDEA   You need to find the amount of sales tax on $26.60. The sales tax then must be added to the cost of the vest to find the total cost.

Plan and Solve

First, compute the sales tax. The tax is 5 cents on each dollar, so multiply $26.60 by 0.05. To find the total cost, add sales tax to the cost of the vest.

Find 0.05 × $26.60.
Estimate:
0.05 × 30 = 1.50

$$\begin{array}{r} 26.60 \\ \times\ 0.05 \\ \hline 1.3300 \end{array}$$

The sales tax is $1.33.

Find $26.60 + $1.33.
Estimate:
27.00 + 1.00 = 28.00

$$\begin{array}{r} 26.60 \\ +\ 1.33 \\ \hline 27.93 \end{array}$$

The total cost, including tax, was $27.93.

Look Back   The computed sales tax and total cost are close to the estimates. The answer is reasonable.

■ **Talk About Math**   If an item is on sale, do you pay tax on the original price or on the sale price?

Problem Solving Guide sidebar

Understand
QUESTION
FACTS
KEY IDEA

Plan and Solve
STRATEGY
ANSWER

Look Back
SENSIBLE ANSWER
ALTERNATE APPROACH

Check Understanding

Use the problem at the right to answer these questions.

1. What is the question?

2. What are the facts?

3. How would you solve the problem?

> Floyd's father bought a canvas creel that cost $20.25. What is the total cost of this purchase if the sales tax is the same as in the example?

Practice

Solve each problem. Use a sales tax of 5 cents on the dollar.

4. A customer bought a landing net for $16. What is the total cost of the net, including sales tax?

5. Mr. Cardona bought 2 fly fishing videotapes at $45 each. What was his total cost, including tax?

6. Mrs. Torres bought a graphite rod for $57.55 and a reel for $49.05. What is the total cost, including sales tax?

7. Tom's Tackle Shop donates 1 cent of every dollar in sales to a conservation fund. How much would be donated for $110 in sales?

8. ▦ **Calculator** Explain how to do this problem with your calculator: $26.60 × 1.05.

9. Critical Thinking Why is the answer in Problem 8 the same as the answer in the example?

Choose a ▬▬▬▬ Strategy

Timed Talk The cost of a long distance call depends on the distance and the time of day the call is made. Here is a table of rates for telephone calls.

Time of day	Cost of first minute	Cost for each additional minute
11:00 P.M. to 8:00 A.M.	$0.25	$0.18
8:00 A.M. to 5:00 P.M.	$0.62	$0.43
5:00 P.M. to 11:00 P.M.	$0.38	$0.26

10. How much would it cost to make a 3-minute call at noon? at 8:00 P.M.? at 6:00 A.M.?

11. How much would it cost to make a 20-minute call at noon? at 8:00 P.M.? at 6:00 A.M.?

12. The cost of a 7:30 A.M. call was $2.05. How long was the call?

Skills Review

For each number, name the place that contains a 2.

1. 6.028   **2.** 25.10   **3.** 0.0052

4. 65.249   **5.** 1,562   **6.** 34.002

Tell how many decimal places should be shown in each product.

7. 45×3.9 **8.** 0.85×4.5

Multiply.

9.   0.3
      $\times$ 8

10.   0.15
       $\times$ 9

11.   0.378
       $\times$ 42

12.   0.8
       $\times 0.4$

13.   2
       $\times 0.9$

14.   5.96
       $\times 0.44$

15. 5×0.074 **16.** 19×1.37

17. 3.6×0.21 **18.** 2.54×0.7

19. 0.08×0.03 **20.** 0.005×6

21. 2.03×0.02 **22.** 75×0.0004

Use mental math to find each product.

23. 100×0.25 **24.** $1,000 \times 6.81$

25. 10×0.13 **26.** $7.5 \times 1,000$

Estimate the products.

27. 1.22×6.8 **28.** 9.74×3.25

29. 94.6×23.8 **30.** 11.1×58

Divide.

31. $4.68 \div 2$ **32.** $6.09 \div 3$

33. $16.73 \div 7$ **34.** $31.555 \div 5$

Problem-Solving Review

Solve each problem.

35. Find the cost of 3 rolls of film if each roll costs $2.49.

36. Parking at Ace Garage costs $2.75 for the first hour and $0.75 for each additional hour. How much would it cost to park for 4 hours?

37. Mr. Wilkinson wants to plant 5 rows of raspberries. Each row is 20 feet long. If he places a plant every 2 feet, how many raspberry plants does he need?

38. If sales tax is 6%, find the total cost of an $18 football.

39. Each of the 15 members of a soccer team gave $3 for a $42.80 gift for the coach. How much money was left?

40. A dime weighs 2 grams. How much does $10 worth of dimes weigh?

41. **Data File** Ron and his two brothers want to buy season concert tickets. The most they can spend as a family for tickets is $300. Use the price chart on pages 380–381. Which tickets can they buy? Which ones would you buy? Why?

42. **Make a Data File** Find the current rates for mailing envelopes by first-class that range in weight from 1 ounce to 1 pound. Show data on a chart.

Estimate each answer.

1. 86 + 88

2. 5,842 + 7,489

3. 785 − 234

4. 9,521 − 496

5. 7 × 62

6. 4 × 49 × 6

7. 638 ÷ 81

8. 5,631 ÷ 72

9. 4.8 + 5.33

10. 82.41 + 6.62

11. 65.2 − 9.6

12. 92.15 − 13.6

Use a ruler to measure the line below to the nearest

13. $\frac{1}{8}$ inch.

14. millimeter.

Find the area of each figure.

15.

16.

3 ft

3 ft

15 cm

30 cm

Write each number in standard form.

17. 57 billion, 205 thousand, 350

18. 20,000,000 + 600,000 + 200 + 5

Choose the more sensible temperature for

19. snow skiing.   30°F or 80°F

20. water-skiing.   35°C or 5°C

Find each answer.

21. 4 ft 8 in.
      + 2 ft 9 in.

22. 5 gal
      − 2 gal 2 qt

List the numbers in order from least to greatest.

23. 4,065   4,650   4,605

24. 0.63   0.36   0.33

25. 0.459   0.453   0.455

Find the volume of each figure.

26.

4 cm

4 cm

4 cm

27.

5 in.

7 in.

10 in.

Multiply or divide.

28.   473
       ×   6

29.   78
       × 40

30.   275
       × 91

31.   23.7
       ×   5

32   0.63
       × 8.7

33.   2.874
       × 0.32

34. 9)836

35. 4)3,255

36. 285 ÷ 34

37. 998 ÷ 44

38. 6.09 ÷ 3

39. 2.45 ÷ 7

For each decimal, name the place that contains a 5.

40. 2.50789

41. 39.7865

42. 0.45678

43. 185.976

Tell whether you would use paper and pencil, a calculator, or mental math. Then find each product.

44. 0.7 × 0.6

45. 0.235 × 0.09

46. 0.01 × 35.2

47. 0.033 × 0.002

Reteaching

Set A   pages 250–251

This chart shows the value of each digit in 3.04263, which is read as: three and four thousand two hundred sixty-three hundred-thousandths.

hundred-thousands	ten-thousands	thousands	hundreds	tens	ones	tenths	hundredths	thousandths	ten-thousandths	hundred-thousandths
					3	0	4	2	6	3

Remember that the decimal point separates the ones place from the tenths place.

Name the value of the last decimal place.

1. 364.825   **2.** 247.6837

For each number, name the place that contains a 6.

3. 5.206   **4.** 14.39763

Set B   pages 252–255

Find 32 × 0.366.

Multiply as with whole numbers	0.3 6 6	3 decimal places
	× 3 2	0 decimal places
	7 3 2	
	1 0 9 8	
	1 1.7 1 2	3 decimal places

Remember to place the decimal point in the product.

Multiply.

1. 0.7   **2.** 0.04   **3.** 0.16
   × 7   × 9   × 4

4. 5 × 3.47   **5.** 8 × 0.314

Set C   pages 258–259

To multiply a decimal by 10, 100, or 1,000, move the decimal point one place to the right for each zero in 10, 100, or 1,000.

Find 100 × 0.3.

Since there are two zeros in 100, move the decimal point two places to the right.

100 × 0.3 = 30

Remember that you may have to write zeros in the product when multiplying a number by 10, 100, or 1,000.

Find each product. Use mental math.

1. 10 × 0.8   **2.** 100 × 0.08

3. 1,000 × 0.49   **4.** 32.5 × 100

Set D   pages 260–261

Estimate the product 48.3 × 102.6. Use a compatible number, a number that is easy to multiply, for 102.6.

100 × 48.3 = 4830

Notice that a zero was written after 3 in the product.

Remember that an estimated product will be larger than the actual product if you substitute a larger number for one of the factors.

Estimate the product.

1. 4.45 × 3.7   **2.** 8.04 × 2.52

3. 94.1 × 1.12   **4.** 48.6 × 9.47

Set E pages 264–265

Find 7.43×3.79.
Estimate: $7 \times 4 = 28$

Multiply as with whole numbers.

$$
\begin{array}{r}
7.4\,3 \\
\times\,3.7\,9 \\
\hline
6\,6\,8\,7 \\
5\,2\,0\,1 \\
2\,2\,2\,9 \\
\hline
2\,8\,1\,5\,9\,7
\end{array}
$$

Count the number of decimal places in both factors.
7.43: 2 places; 3.79; 2 places; total 4

Write the product with 4 decimal places:
28.1597

Remember that the number of decimal places in the product is the total number of decimal places in the factors.

Multiply.

1. $\begin{array}{r} 0.6 \\ \times\,0.3 \\ \hline \end{array}$
2. $\begin{array}{r} 0.9 \\ \times\,0.4 \\ \hline \end{array}$

3. $\begin{array}{r} 8 \\ \times\,0.7 \\ \hline \end{array}$
4. $\begin{array}{r} 0.49 \\ \times\,0.5 \\ \hline \end{array}$

5. $\begin{array}{r} 24.2 \\ \times\,0.06 \\ \hline \end{array}$
6. $\begin{array}{r} 8.32 \\ \times\,0.33 \\ \hline \end{array}$

Set F pages 266–267

Find 3.72×0.007.
Multiply as with whole numbers.

$$
\begin{array}{rl}
3.7\,2 & \text{2 decimal places} \\
\times\,0.0\,0\,7 & \text{3 decimal places} \\
\hline
2\,6\,0\,4 &
\end{array}
$$

The total number of decimal places needed is 5. Write an extra zero to show the fifth place.

$$3.72 \times 0.007 = 0.02604$$

Remember that you may have to have to write zeros when you place the decimal point in the product.

Multiply.

1. 0.08×0.03
2. 0.006×8

3. 3.09×0.01
4. 55×0.005

5. $\begin{array}{r} 0.007 \\ \times\,3.8 \\ \hline \end{array}$
6. $\begin{array}{r} 0.075 \\ \times\,4 \\ \hline \end{array}$

Set G pages 268–269

Find $\$17.45 \div 5$.

Think: Divide $17 among 5 people. Each would receive $3 from the $17.

Trade the remaining dollars for dimes.
$2 = 20 dimes   Divide 20 dimes among the 5 people. Each would get 4 dimes.

Now divide the 45¢ among the 5 people. Each will get 9¢.
So each person receives:
three $1 bills + 4 dimes + 9 cents

$\$3.00 + 0.40 + 0.09 = \$3.49$

So $\$17.45 \div 5 = \$3.49$.

Remember to place the decimal point in the quotient directly above the decimal point in the dividend. Then divide as with whole numbers.

Divide.

1. $16.8 \div 4$
2. $42.6 \div 3$

3. $20.55 \div 5$
4. $54.6 \div 6$

5. $3.28 \div 8$
6. $38.5 \div 7$

7. $6.03 \div 9$
8. $2.52 \div 6$

More Practice

Set A pages 250–251

Look at each calculator display. Name the value of the
last decimal place.

1. *3678.582*   **2.** *456.89*   **3.** *80.43052*   **4.** *527.0745*

For each number, name the place that contains a 7.

5. 16.071   **6.** 36.287   **7.** 5.03087   **8.** 701.342

9. 827.133   **10.** 472.0912   **11.** 320.744   **12.** 58.18307

Set B pages 252–255

Multiply. **Remember** to place the decimal point in the
product.

1.   0.8   **2.**   0.34   **3.**   0.05   **4.**   7.4   **5.**   6.5
    $\times$ 9 $\times$ 6 $\times$ 7 $\times$ 4 $\times$ 5

6.   4.32   **7.**   3.87   **8.**   3.2   **9.**   7.07   **10.**   0.504
    $\times$ 3 $\times$ 6 $\times$ 44 $\times$ 9 $\times$ 32

11. 6 $\times$ 4.7   **12.** 4 $\times$ 5.63   **13.** 9 $\times$ 0.802   **14.** 48 $\times$ 0.66   **15.** 68 $\times$ 4.07

Set C pages 258–259

Find each product. Use mental math.

1. 10 $\times$ 0.9   **2.** 100 $\times$ 0.09   **3.** 1,000 $\times$ 0.09   **4.** 10 $\times$ 6.7

5. 100 $\times$ 6.7   **6.** 1,000 $\times$ 6.7   **7.** 10 $\times$ 0.28   **8.** 0.6 $\times$ 100

Mixed Practice Find the product.

9. 0.83 $\times$ 6   **10.** 7.9 $\times$ 5   **11.** 1.62 $\times$ 8   **12.** 474 $\times$ 12

Set D pages 260–261

Estimate the product.

1. 6.43 $\times$ 8.7   **2.** 34.5 $\times$ 6.6   **3.** 3.07 $\times$ 1.85   **4.** 24.5 $\times$ 3.91

5. 73.9 $\times$ 2.4   **6.** 490 $\times$ 5.33   **7.** 106.9 $\times$ 11.1   **8.** 0.48 $\times$ 1.09

Mixed Practice Complete only those exercises with
products less than 30.

9. 30 $\times$ 1.1   **10.** 30 $\times$ 0.99   **11.** 8.4 $\times$ 3.7   **12.** 7.03 $\times$ 4.8

13. 0.8 $\times$ 32   **14.** 5.4 $\times$ 5.9   **15.** 30 $\times$ 1.4   **16.** 7 $\times$ 4.9

Set E   pages 264–265

Multiply.

1.   0.8
       $\times\,0.4$

2.   0.6
       $\times\,0.7$

3.   9
       $\times\,0.5$

4.   0.83
       $\times\,\;0.6$

5.   3.7
       $\times\,8.2$

6.   6.8
       $\times\,0.4$

7.   41.5
       $\times\,0.17$

8.   35.9
       $\times\,\;0.3$

9.   8.13
       $\times\,0.33$

10.   2.385
       $\times\,\quad 6$

11.   682
       $\times\,\;0.9$

12.   65.4
       $\times\,\;7.1$

13.   4.18
       $\times\,\;0.6$

14.   1.08
       $\times\,\;0.4$

15.   68.5
       $\times\,\quad 4$

16. 0.7×9

17. 0.4×5

18. 5.6×0.5

19. 0.2×46

20. 44.2×0.6

21. 8.2×6.7

22. 0.35×85.2

23. 0.44×6.7

Set F   pages 266–267

Multiply. **Remember** to write extra zeros if necessary.

1.   0.07
       $\times\,0.06$

2.   0.008
       $\times\,\quad 7$

3.   0.009
       $\times\,\;0.09$

4.   0.048
       $\times\,\;0.05$

5. 1.6×0.006

6. 55×0.005

7. 35×0.003

8. 4.06×0.01

9. 0.145×0.06

10. 0.001×0.01

11. 0.075×4

12. 3.8×0.004

For Exercises 13–19, tell whether you would use paper and pencil, a calculator, or mental math. Then find each product.

13. 4.4×0.006

14. 0.44×0.006

15. 0.044×0.006

16.   832.4
       $\times\,\;0.01$

17.   940.11
       $\times\,\quad 100$

18.   76.2
       $\times\,\quad 5$

19.   16.94
       $\times\,\;0.02$

Set G   pages 268–269

Divide.

1. $24.3 \div 3$

2. $81.9 \div 9$

3. $16.35 \div 5$

4. $34.32 \div 8$

5. $192.6 \div 6$

6. $30.8 \div 4$

7. $26.6 \div 7$

8. $410.4 \div 8$

9. $3.304 \div 4$

10. $0.714 \div 6$

11. $4.401 \div 9$

12. $3.864 \div 7$

13. $59.6 \div 2$

14. $19.16 \div 4$

15. $31.8 \div 3$

16. $25.25 \div 5$

Enrichment

Equal Metric Measures

When you know the measure of an object, you can find its measure in a smaller unit by *multiplying*.

The Statue of Liberty is 0.04605 kilometer tall. How many meters tall is it?

Since 1 kilometer equals 1,000 meters, you need to multiply. Find 0.04605 × 1,000.

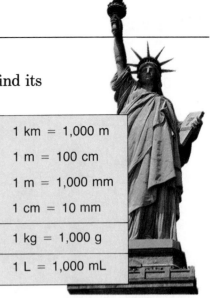

1 km	=	1,000 m
1 m	=	100 cm
1 m	=	1,000 mm
1 cm	=	10 mm
1 kg	=	1,000 g
1 L	=	1,000 mL

$$0.04605 \times 1{,}000 = 46.05$$

The Statue of Liberty is 46.05 meters tall.

Multiply to find the missing measure.

1. Height of a giraffe
   0.00599 km = ▦ m

2. Anaconda snake
   11.2 m = ▦ cm

3. Fork length
   14.3 cm = ▦ mm

4. Length of ribbon
   2.56 m = ▦ mm

5. Length of a trail
   3.4 km = ▦ m

6. Bottle of juice
   0.496 L = ▦ mL

When you know the measure of an object, you can find its measure in a larger unit by *dividing*.

The Statue of Liberty has a mass of 204,000,000 grams. How many kilograms is it?

Since 1,000 grams equals 1 kilogram, you need to divide. Find 204,000,000 ÷ 1,000.

$$204{,}000{,}000 \div 1{,}000 = 204{,}000$$

The mass of the Statue of Liberty is 204,000 kilograms.

Divide to find the missing measure.

7. Fishing rod
   165 cm = ▦ m

8. Mass of a melon
   2,482 g = ▦ kg

9. Watch
   20.5 g = ▦ kg

10. Capacity of a glass
    265 mL = ▦ L

11. Length of a field
    827 m = ▦ km

12. Capacity of a jar
    869 mL = ▦ L

Which measure is greater?

13. 4,775 g or 5.2 kg

14. 0.235 m or 25 cm

15. 6.1 cm or 64.2 mm

Chapter 8 Review/Test

For each number, name the place that contains a 5.

1. 3.075   **2.** 52.138

Tell how many decimal places should be shown in each product.

3. 8.2 × 3.6   **4.** 1.75 × 1.75

Multiply.

5. 0.0 7
   × 1 8

6. 0.7 2 9
   ×   6 4

7. 0.8
   × 0.4

8. 3.1 4
   × 1.8 6

9. 0.07 × 0.9   **10.** 0.075 × 0.3

Estimate each product.

11. 2.87 × 5.43   **12.** 92.6 × 9.92

Find each product. Use mental math.

13. 10 × 0.9   **14.** 0.46 × 100

15. 1,000 × 68.5   **16.** 0.82 × 10,000

Divide.

17. 1.95 ÷ 5   **18.** 18.9 ÷ 9

Tell what operation you would use to solve Items 19 and 20. Then solve.

19. Four friends shared the cost of a $56 gift equally. How much did each friend pay?

20. A machine part weighs 1.34 ounces. How much do 100 parts weigh?

Read this problem. Then answer the questions below.

The Langer family bought a new chair for $195 and a table for $152. The sales tax is 6 cents on each dollar. What is the total cost?

21. Which could you use as the *first steps* in solving this problem?

   a. 195 − 152 = 43
      0.06 × 43 = 2.58
   b. 195 + 152 = 347
      0.06 × 347 = 20.82
   c. 195 × 0.06 = 11.70
      195 − 11.70 = 183.30
   d. 195 + 152 = 347
      347 + 6 = 353

22. Solve the problem.

23. **Write About Math** Explain how to multiply a decimal by 100 mentally.

Patterns and Coordinate Graphing

9

Did You Know: The most common street name in the United States is Park. Washington is the second most common. Maple is third in popularity.

Number-Sense Project

Estimate
What different plans do you think people would suggest for naming streets on a city map?

Gather Data
Interview three older people. Have each person look at a layout of streets around a central square. Ask them what plan they would use to name the streets.

Analyze and Report
Make a list of the different plans that were suggested. Compare your results with those of other students.

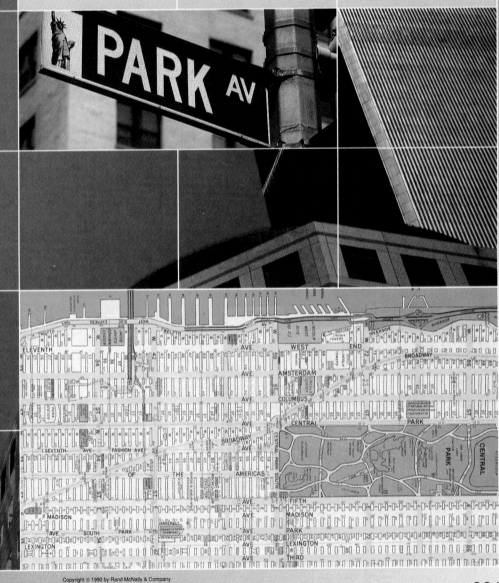

Patterns

Build Understanding

The hands on this Osage blanket are a symbol of friendship.

Blankets, like the one shown above, are called *wearing blankets.* They were worn by the Osage Indians. The Osage Indians originally lived in what is now Missouri.

The shapes and colors on the blanket form a **pattern.** A pattern is an organized way things can be arranged. If another row of diamonds were added across the bottom of the blanket, what color would the row of diamonds be?

The pattern of colors in the rows of diamonds is: yellow, white, tan, yellow, white, tan.

The next row of diamonds would be white.

■ **Write About Math**   Make a list of five places where you see patterns each day. Describe each pattern.

Check Understanding

For another example, see Set A, pages 300–301.

Tell what would be the next color in each pattern.

1. ◆◇◆◇◆◇◆◆

2. ◆◇◆◇◆◆◇◆◆

Draw the next figure in each pattern.

3. □ ▭ □ ▭

4. □ □ △ □ □

Practice

For More Practice, see Set A, pages 302–303.

Draw the next three figures in each pattern.

5.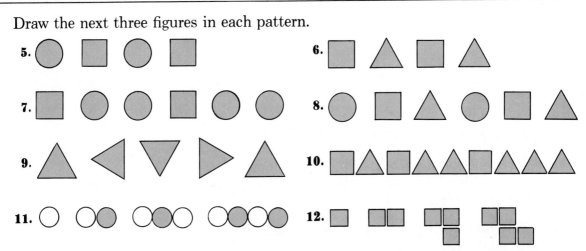

6.

7.

8.

9.

10.

11.

12.

Problem Solving

13. The traditional costume of Japan is the *kimono,* a long robe that is sometimes tied at the waist with a large sash called an *obi.* Part of an obi is shown at the right. Describe the next three cranes going down the pattern.

14. The design below is taken from a piece of cloth woven on a hand loom by a Guatemalan Indian woman. Each village produces its own unique pattern. Draw the next two figures in this pattern.

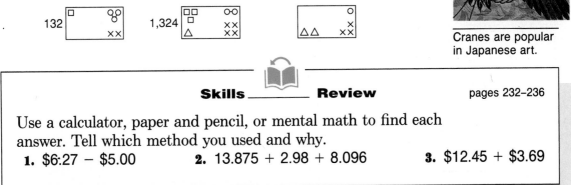

15. Number Sense Look for a pattern on the cards. What number does the third card show?

132   1,324

Cranes are popular in Japanese art.

Skills _____ Review   pages 232–236

Use a calculator, paper and pencil, or mental math to find each answer. Tell which method you used and why.

1. $6.27 - $5.00   **2.** 13.875 + 2.98 + 8.096   **3.** $12.45 + $3.69

Number Patterns

Build Understanding

Into how many sections can you fold a piece of paper?

Forever Folding
Materials: A sheet of paper

a. Fold a sheet of paper in half by putting opposite sides together. Then unfold the paper. How many sections are there?

b. Refold the paper. Then fold it in half again. Undo both folds. How many sections are there?

c. Make a table like the one shown to record the results of each fold.

Number of folds	0	1	2	3		
Number of sections	1	2				

d. Redo the first and second folds. Then fold the paper again. Undo the folds to find the number of sections. Record the number in the table.

e. The pattern in the table tells you what number of sections the paper can be folded into.

■ **Talk About Math** Describe the pattern in the table. Show the pattern is correct by folding the paper five times. Did you get the right number of sections?

Check Understanding

For another example, see Set B, pages 300–301.

1. How many sections would you have after six folds?

2. To get 128 sections, how many folds would you make?

3. Continue the toothpick pattern to make 3 more squares.

4. Complete the table.

Number of

Squares	1	2	3	4	5	6
Toothpicks	4	7	10			

Draw the next three figures in each pattern. Copy and complete each table.

5.

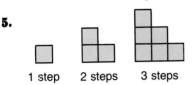

1 step   2 steps   3 steps

6. Number of

Steps	1	2	3	4	5	6
Squares	1	3	6			

7. How many squares are in 10 steps?

8.

1 row   2 rows   3 rows

9. Number of

Rows	1	2	3	4	5	6
Squares	1	4	9			

10. How many squares are in 10 rows?

11.

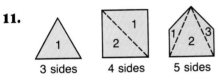

3 sides   4 sides   5 sides

12. Number of

Sides	3	4	5	6	7	8
Triangles	1	2	3			

13. How many triangles are in a figure with 10 sides?

14.

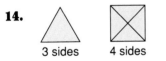

3 sides   4 sides   5 sides

15. Number of

Sides	3	4	5	6	7	8
Diagonals	0	2	5			

16. How many diagonals are in a figure with 10 sides?

Problem Solving

In the school cafeteria, 4 people can sit together at 1 table. If 2 tables are placed together, 6 people can sit together.

How many tables must be placed together in a row to seat
17. 10 people?   **18.** 20 people?   **19.** 30 people?

If the tables are placed together in a row, how many people can be seated using
20. 10 tables?   **21.** 15 tables?   **22.** 20 tables?

Number Relationships

Build Understanding

You can find interesting patterns in many wallpapers and fabrics. You also can find patterns involving the counting numbers when they are written in an array. Look at the 8-by-8 array. Do you see any patterns?

1	2	3	4	5	6	7	8
9	10	11	12	13	14	15	16
17	18	19	20	21	22	23	24
25	26	27	28	29	30	31	32
33	34	35	36	37	38	39	40
41	42	43	44	45	46	47	48
49	50	51	52	53	54	55	56
57	58	59	60	61	62	63	64

A. A *diagonal* has one pattern. The numbers are: 1, 10, 19, 28, 37, 46, 55, 64.

The pattern is add 9 to get the next number.

$$+9 \quad +9 \quad +9 \quad +9 \quad +9 \quad +9 \quad +9$$
1, 10, 19, 28, 37, 46, 55, 64

B. A sequence is a set of numbers formed by a pattern.

Describe the pattern in this sequence. Then write the next four numbers.

3, 7, 5, 9, 7, 11, . . .   The three dots tell you the pattern continues in the same way.

To find a pattern, compare each number with the number before it. The second number is 4 more than the first. The third number is 2 less than the second number, and so on.

$$+4 \quad -2 \quad +4 \quad -2 \quad +4 \quad -2 \quad +4 \quad -2 \quad +4$$
3, 7, 5, 9, 7, 11, 9, 13, 11, 15, . . .

■ **Talk About Math** What operation can be used to get the next number in a sequence?

Check Understanding

For another example, see Set C, pages 300–301.

1. Write the sequence of numbers in the other diagonal for the array above. Describe the pattern.

2. Where are the even numbers in the array above? the odd numbers?

Describe the pattern in each sequence. Then write the next four numbers.

3. 6, 13, 20, 27, 34

4. 2, 7, 4, 9, 6, 11

Practice

For More Practice, see Set C, pages 302–303.

Describe the pattern in each sequence. Then write the next four numbers.

5. 5, 9, 13, 17, . . .

6. 36, 31, 26, 21, . . .

7. 7, 9, 5, 7, . . .

8. 1, 2, 4, 8, 16, . . .

9. 2, 8, 7, 28, . . .

10. 5, 10, 7, 14, 11, . . .

11. 9, 11, 8, 10, 7, . . .

12. 0.05, 0.1, 0.15, . . .

13. 1, 3, 9, 27, . . .

14. 58, 55, 51, 46, . . .

15. 20, 30, 29, 39, . . .

16. $1.00, $1.25, $1.50, . . .

17. 4, 2, 1, 0.5, 0.25, . . .

18. 1.2, 2.7, 4.2, . . .

19. 3, 7, 5, 10, 14, . . .

Problem Solving

Solve each problem.

20. Critical Thinking To conserve water, people with even-numbered addresses water their lawn on even-numbered dates. People with odd-numbered addresses water on odd-numbered dates. Which kind of address allows more days to water? Why?

21. In the sequence below, pick any number for n. Write the first four numbers. Describe the pattern. Write the next four numbers. Repeat with another value for n. Describe the pattern using the variable n.
$3 \times n, 4 \times n, 5 \times n, 6 \times n, . . .$

22. 📟 **Calculator** Find this product: your age $\times$ 37 $\times$ 21 $\times$ 13. Find the product for other ages. Describe the pattern.

Explore ———— Math

Make a 10-by-10 array, a 6-by-6 array, and a 4-by-4 array of the counting numbers. For each array start with the number 1.

23. Describe the patterns in both diagonals for each array. List these patterns and that of an 8-by-8 array in a table.

24. Predict the patterns in the diagonals for other arrays of counting numbers. Check your predictions by making the arrays.

Find a Pattern

Build Understanding

Six teams are playing in the first round of a volleyball tournament. Each team will play one match against each of the other teams. How many matches will there be?

Understand   What is the total number of matches among the six teams? Each team is to play each other team only once.

▥▥▶ **Plan and Solve**   STRATEGY   Find the number of matches with 2 teams, 3 teams, and 4 teams. Try to find a pattern in the number of matches as the number of teams increases.

Number of teams	2	3	4	5	6
Number of matches	1	3	6		

According to this pattern, add 4 to find the number of matches among 5 teams. Then add 5 to find the number of matches among 6 teams.

ANSWER   There will be **15** matches.

Look Back   List the matches or draw diagrams to check that the pattern works.

■ **Talk About Math**   In the diagrams above, what does each line segment show?

Check Understanding

1. How many matches would be played among eight teams?

2. How many tennis matches would be needed for nine players to play each other once?

Practice

Solve each problem.

3. Each team has 12 players. If each Tiger shakes hands with each Eagle, how many handshakes are there in all?

4. There are 32 teams in an elimination tournament. In the first round, every team plays one game. Only the winners play another game in the second round. How many games would be played until one team won the tournament?

5. If 16 teams played in an elimination tournament, how many rounds would be played until one team won?

Share your thinking with others. Explaining your ideas helps you think better.

Mandy is saving for volleyball equipment. On the first day she deposited $1 in the bank. On the second day, she deposited $2 more than on the first day. On the third day, she deposited $2 more than on the second day. She continued in this way, each day depositing $2 more than on the previous day.

6. How much had Mandy saved after 4 days?

7. How much had Mandy saved after 7 days?

8. After which day will Mandy have more than $120 saved?

9. How much had Mandy saved after 23 days?

Volleyball became an official sport of the Olympic Games in 1964.

✓ Midchapter ——— Checkup

1. Draw the next figure.

   □ ○ □ ○

2. Use this pattern to complete the table.

Number of Squares	1	2	3	4	5	6
Number of Dots	4	6	8			

3. Write the next three numbers.
   3, 5, 7, 9, . . .

4. Each of the 5 players on the Lions says hello to each of the 5 Bears, and each Bear answers. How many hellos are spoken?

Number-Sense Project

Look back at pages 280-281.
Tell if you think these statements
are *seldom true, sometimes true,* or
always true. Consult an atlas or
maps to help you decide.

1. Interstate highways which run
north and south have odd numbers,
and interstate highways which run
east and west have even numbers.

2. An organized plan was used to
name the streets in your school's
neighborhood.

3. Streets in the center of large
cities are named according to a
plan of some type.

Math-at-Home Activity

Play *Find the
Spaceship* with
someone at home.

Each player labels
a five-by-five grid.

Each player secretly marks 3 points
in a row, column, or diagonal to
show where the other player's lost
spaceship is. Do not let the other
player see your grid.

Players take turns trying to find each
point of their spaceship. To guess,
name the number and letter of a
point. The other player marks the
point named with an **X** and tells if
the point is in the spaceship. The
first player to get an **X** on each
spaceship point wins.

What plan would you
use if you were the
city planner and could
name the streets in
this town?

Problem Solving WORKSHOP

Explore as a Team

1. Draw the next figure in each pattern.

2. Find the perimeter for each figure. What pattern does your team see in the perimeters?

3. Predict the perimeter of the fifth figure in each pattern.

4. Draw the fifth figures. Were your predictions correct?

5. Draw other figures that have a perimeter of 12 cm.

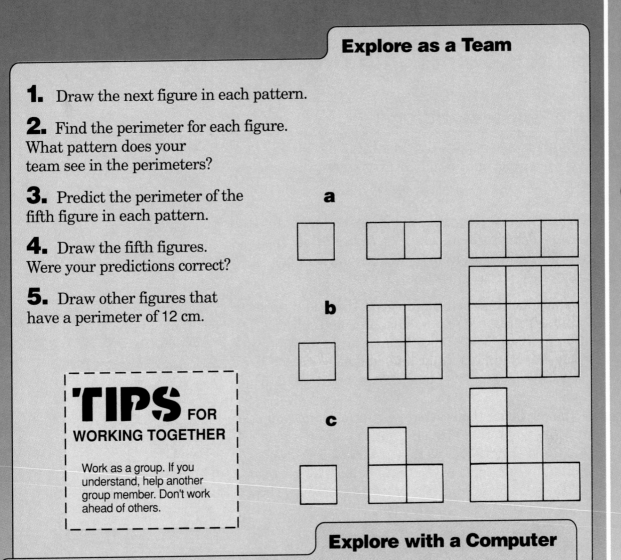

a

b

c

TIPS FOR
WORKING TOGETHER

Work as a group. If you
understand, help another
group member. Don't work
ahead of others.

Explore with a Computer

Use the *Graphing and Probability Workshop Project* for this activity.

1. You can plan your own city on a grid of ordered pairs. On the screen you will see a grid with one location marked A at the center. Suppose this spot marks a statue in the center of the city.

2. Plan other points on the map. You may add houses, apartment buildings, stores, parks, or other important features of a city.

3. Plot the points on the map by entering an ordered pair in the table. Label the points with letters.

4. When you are finished marking your map, use the **Print** option to make a printout of the graph. On the printout write what each letter on the map represents.

A
L
G
E
B
R
A

Locating Points with Ordered Pairs

Build Understanding

A forest ranger maps where lightning has struck. To show the exact spot of a lightning strike, the ranger uses a grid.

A. Each point on this grid can be matched with an *ordered pair* of numbers. The first number shows how far right to go from 0. The second number shows how far up to go from 0.

The distance between the lines on the grid represents 2 units. To reach point A, start at 0 and move 12 units right. Then move 5 units up on that line. Point A is 5 units up that line, halfway between the lines for 4 and 6. The ordered pair for A is (12, 5).

B. If you are given the ordered pair for a point, you can *plot* the point on a grid. To plot the ordered pair (7, 10) on the grid at the right, start at 0. Move 7 units to the right. Seven units is halfway between the lines for 6 and 8. Then move 10 units up. Draw a dot and label the point (7, 10).

■ **Talk About Math** Find Point G and Point E. How are the ordered pairs for these points alike? How are they different?

Check Understanding

For another example, see Set D, pages 300–301.

Use the grid in Example A.

1. Point B is _____ units to the right of 0 and _____ units up.

2. Write the ordered pairs for Point B and for Point C.

3. Name two points on the grid that are 4 units up from 0.

4. What point is at (11, 8)?

5. Write the ordered pair for Point X.

Practice

For More Practice, see Set D, pages 302–303.

Use the grid at the right. Write the
letter that names the point located by
each ordered pair.

6. (2, 6)　　　**7.** (16, 2)　　　**8.** (18, 18)

9. (8, 20)　　　**10.** (0, 4)　　　**11.** (6, 2)

Write the ordered pair for each point.
Remember to use parentheses and a comma.

12. N　　　**13.** Q　　　**14.** Y　　　**15.** T

16. U　　　**17.** M　　　**18.** S　　　**19.** P

Make a grid in which each unit on the grid
represents 2 units. Label your grid from
0 to 20 in both directions. Then plot and
label each point.

20. A (8, 2)　　　**21.** B (6, 12)　　　**22.** C (20, 4)　　　**23.** D (10, 10)

24. E (7, 6)　　　**25.** F (2, 9)　　　**26.** G (14, 11)　　　**27.** J (11, 13)

28. Mixed Practice　Make a grid. Plot and connect the points
in order. Continue the pattern.

(0, 2) (0, 1) (1, 1) (1, 2) (2, 2) (2, ▦) (▦, 1) (▦, ▦)

Problem Solving

An archaeologist uses a grid to map the location of artifacts.
The corners of each room are given by the ordered pairs below.
Plot the points for each room on the same grid, and connect
them to show the floor plan.

29. Main Hall: (1, 6); (1, 1); (9, 1);
(9, 6)

30. Kitchen: (1, 6); (4, 6); (4, 9); (1, 9)

31. Bedroom: (4, 6); (9, 6); (9, 9); (4, 9)

32. Treasury: (1, 9); (4, 9); (4, 11);
(1, 11)

33. List the ordered pairs for some artifacts found in
each room. Ask a classmate to find the location of
the items.

293

Use Data from a Graph

Build Understanding

You are planning to buy a basket of fruit. How many pounds of fruit will you get for $10?

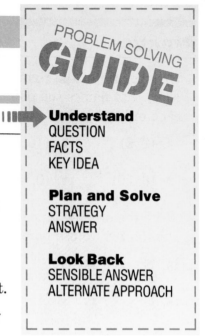

▶ Understand   QUESTION   How many pounds of fruit in a basket can you buy for $10?

FACTS   You want to spend $10. The graph shows the cost of fruit in a basket for 0 through 5 pounds of fruit.

KEY IDEA   You need to find how many pounds of fruit you can buy for $10 by reading the graph.

Fruit in a Basket

Cost (dollars)

Pounds

Plan and Solve   Find $10 on the left side of the graph. Move across to the graph line. Then move straight down to find the number of pounds.

The number of pounds is halfway between 3 and 4. You can buy about $3\frac{1}{2}$ pounds for $10.

Look Back   The answer is reasonable because a $3\frac{1}{2}$-pound basket costs more than a 3-pound basket and less than a 4-pound basket.

How much of the $10 is the cost for the fruit? Each cost includes $3 for the basket. If you did not have the graph, what other information would you need to find the number of pounds of fruit?

■ **Talk About Math**   Explain how you could use data from the graph to find amounts or costs that are not on the graph. For example, how could you find how many pounds you can buy for $20?

Check Understanding

1. How much would 2 pounds of fruit in a basket cost?

2. How much would $4\frac{1}{2}$ pounds of fruit in a basket cost?

3. What size basket of fruit could you buy for $12?

4. What does the point (0, 3) tell you?

Practice

Use the graph at the right.

5. How many pounds of dried fruit could you buy for $8? for $12?

6. How much would 4 pounds cost?

7. How much does the basket cost?

8. How much does 1 pound of dried fruit without a basket cost?

9. **Mental Math** How many pounds with a basket could you buy for $14? $20?

10. How much does $2\frac{1}{2}$ pounds without a basket cost?

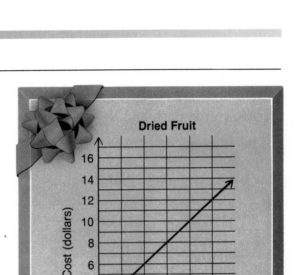

Dried Fruit

Cost (dollars) / Pounds

Choose a ——— Strategy

Basket Bonanza On Sports Day, Bob, Rhoda, and Sue played on the winning basketball team.

11. Bob made 3 more baskets than Sue. Sue made 2 fewer baskets than Rhoda. Altogether they scored 26 baskets. How many baskets did each of them make?

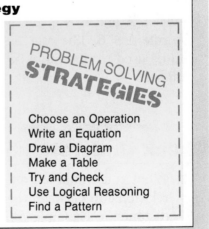

PROBLEM SOLVING STRATEGIES

Choose an Operation
Write an Equation
Draw a Diagram
Make a Table
Try and Check
Use Logical Reasoning
Find a Pattern

A flash of lightning between a cloud and the ground may be up to 9 miles long.

Number Relationships and Ordered Pairs

Build Understanding

A. The distance in feet between you and a lightning strike can be computed if you count the seconds between the flash and the thunder. Then multiply the number of seconds by 1,100.

How far away was a lightning strike if the time between the flash and thunder was 4 seconds?

The relationship between the time and distance can be shown in a table and as ordered pairs plotted on a graph.

Time (seconds)	Distance (feet)	Ordered Pair
1	1,100	(1, 1,100)
2	2,200	(2, 2,200)
3	3,300	(3, 3,300)
4	4,400	(4, 4,400)

The lightning strike was 4,400 feet away.

B. The relationship between numbers can be stated using a rule. In the table at the right, the relationship between A and B is given by the rule A + 5. The rule can be used to find more numbers.

Rule: A + 5

A	B	A + 5
7	12	
18	23	
26		26 + 5
	41	$n + 5$

Talk About Math Can the graph in Example A be extended to show longer amounts of time? Why or why not?

Check Understanding

For another example, see Set E, pages 300–301.

1. What rule would state the relationship between the time and distance in Example A?

2. Write a rule for the relationship between A and B in Example B using subtraction.

Practice

Find the rule.

3.

A	B
8	18
11	21
0	10
3	13

4.

A	B
19	13
22	16
9	3
11	5

5.

A	B
2	14
12	84
6	42
4	28

6.

A	B
48	12
60	15
36	9
0	0

7.

A	B
8	64
3	24
5	40
9	72

Find the missing numbers. Write the rule.

8.

A	B
16	42
15	
9	
4	30

9.

A	B
3	9
6	18
10	
	27

10.

A	B
15	8
21	
14	
13	6

11.

A	B
	16
	8
16	21
69	74

12.

A	B
21	7
	9
9	3
15	

13.

A	B
	35
8	
11	26
4	19

14.

A	B
17	9
20	
23	15
	10

15.

A	B
	60
5	25
	45
8	40

16.

A	B
6	13
2	
	21
9	19

17.

A	B
7.2	8.6
3.9	5.3
4.6	
	9.1

Problem Solving

Make a table to show the relationship between time and distance for a car traveling at

18. 35 miles per hour.

19. 55 miles per hour.

20. 65 miles per hour.

21. On one grid, graph the ordered pairs in Problems 18–20.

22. Use Data Use the graph on page 293. Write the ordered pair for Point R.

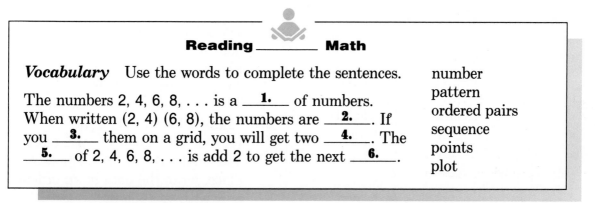

Reading ———— Math

Vocabulary Use the words to complete the sentences.

The numbers 2, 4, 6, 8, . . . is a __1.__ of numbers.
When written (2, 4) (6, 8), the numbers are __2.__ If
you __3.__ them on a grid, you will get two __4.__ . The
__5.__ of 2, 4, 6, 8, . . . is add 2 to get the next __6.__ .

number
pattern
ordered pairs
sequence
points
plot

Skills Review

Draw the next three figures in each pattern.

1. ◯ △ △ ◯ △ △

2.

Draw the next three figures. Then complete the table.

3.

1 row   2 rows   3 rows

4. Number of

Rows	1	2	3	4	5	6
Squares	1	3	6			

Describe each pattern. Then write the next four numbers.

5. 7, 11, 8, 12, . . .

6. 3, 4, 8, 9, . . .

Write the letter that names the point located by each ordered pair.

7. (4, 2)   **8.** (3, 4)

Write the ordered pair for each point.

9. D   **10.** F   **11.** G

Write the rule.

12.

A	B
5	25
1	5
8	40
10	50

13.

A	B
2	9
15	22
4	11
10	17

Problem-Solving Review

Solve each problem.

14. Ellen arranged 12 coins in the pattern shown. What is the total value of the coins?

15. A train made 12 stops before arriving at Ridersville. One passenger got on at the first stop, three at the second stop, five at the third stop, and so on. If no one got off the train, how many passengers arrived at Ridersville?

16. How much fence will Lee need to enclose a vegetable garden 12 feet wide and 24 feet long?

17. How many fence posts will Lee need if he puts one every 4 ft?

18. Bob made this "bow tie" pattern with 36 toothpicks. How many "bow ties" did he make?

19. **Data File** Use the data on pages 380–381. Estimate the number of nights vacationers spent away from home per trip in 1986.

20. **Make a Data File** Find the latitude and longitude of 5 places you would like to visit. For each place, write the data in an ordered pair with latitude first.

Tell what the 9 in each number means.

1. 790,500   **2.** 19,432,600

3. 42.95   **4.** 1.059

5. 0.57609   **6.** 2.00095

Find the missing addend or product.

7. $n + 57 = 95$ **8.** $25 + n = 403$

9. $5 \times n = 625$ **10.** $n \times 9 = 387$

Write the missing number.

11. 10 yd = ▦ ft

12. 4 m = ▦ cm

13. 12 c = ▦ pt

14. 2,000 mL = ▦ L

15. 3 lb = ▦ oz

16. 5 kg = ▦ g

Use mental math to find each product.

17. 100×5.65 **18.** 0.8×100

19. 2.06×10 **20.** $1,000 \times 3.2$

21. Measure the length and width in centimeters. Then find the area.

Draw the next three figures.

22. ⊤ ⊣ ⊥ ⊢ ⊤ ⊣

Estimate. Then compute.

23. $\begin{array}{r} 325 \\ \times\, 400 \\ \hline \end{array}$ **24.** $\begin{array}{r} 874 \\ \times\, 68 \\ \hline \end{array}$ **25.** $\begin{array}{r} 125 \\ \times\, 290 \\ \hline \end{array}$

26. $455 \div 3$ **27.** $5,760 \div 9$

28. $24\overline{)238}$ **29.** $54\overline{)9,524}$

30. $2.45 + 32.6$ **31.** $4.005 - 1.25$

32. 0.76×2.5 **33.** 2.357×5.76

34. $45.9 \div 9$ **35.** $30.4 \div 4$

Write the letter that names the point located by each ordered pair.

36. (2, 4)   **37.** (4, 3)

Write the ordered pair for each point.

38. A   **39.** B   **40.** C

Find the average of each group of numbers.

41. 25   27   16   28

42. 315   265   326

Describe each pattern. Then write the next four numbers.

43. 8, 11, 14, 17, . . .

44. 3, 6, 12, 24, . . .

45. 4, 9, 7, 12, 10, . . .

Reteaching

Set A   pages 282–283

A pattern is a general idea by which things can be arranged or events can happen in an organized way. Draw the next three figures in this pattern.

To do this, describe the pattern: triangle, square, circle, triangle, square.
The pattern repeats after three figures. So the next three figures are:

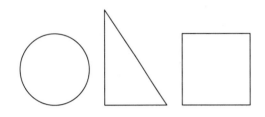

Remember that the description of a pattern of geometric figures can involve different types of changes, such as color, size, position, and shape.

Draw the next three figures in each pattern.

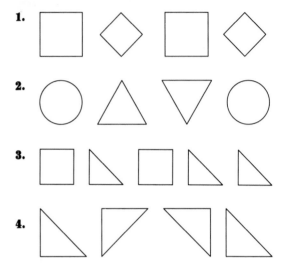

Set B   pages 284–285

Draw the next two figures in this pattern.

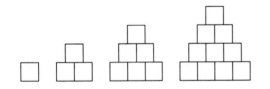

First, describe the pattern: To get the next figure, add a row to the previous figure. The new row has 1 more square than the bottom row of the previous figure.

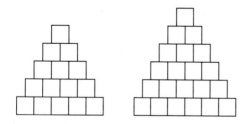

Remember that a pattern is a general idea by which things, such as geometric figures or numbers, can be arranged in an organized manner.

Draw the next three figures in the pattern.

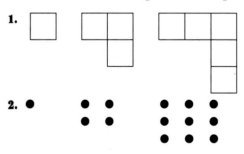

Set C pages 286–287

A sequence is a set of numbers formed by a pattern.

Describe the pattern in this sequence. Then write the next three numbers.

3, 6, 9, 12, 15, . . .

The pattern is to add 3 to get the next number.

Remember that to find a pattern, compare each number with the number before it.

Describe the pattern in each sequence. Then write the next four numbers.

1. 5, 10, 15, 20, . . .

2. 49, 43, 37, 31, . . .

3. 1, 10, 19, 28, . . .

Set D pages 292–293

Each point on this grid can be matched with an ordered pair of numbers.

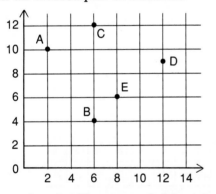

To reach point E, start at 0. Move 8 units to the right. Then move 6 units up that line. The ordered pair for E is (8, 6).

Remember that the first number in an ordered pair tells how many units to move to the right. The second number tells how many units to move up.

Use the grid at the left. Write the ordered pair for each point.

1. A **2.** B **3.** C **4.** D

Make a grid in which units on the grid represent 2 units. Label your grid 0 to 12 in both directions. Then plot and label each point.

5. E (6, 4) **6.** F (4, 6)
7. G (8, 12) **8.** H (12, 9)

Set E pages 296–297

Write a rule for the numbers on the table at the right.

Each number in the B column is 2 times the number in the A column. The missing number in B is 2 × 5, or 10.

A	B
1	2
2	4
4	8
5	

Remember that if the rule for finding the numbers in column B uses addition, then you find the numbers in column A by using subtraction.

Find the missing numbers. Write the rule.

1.

A	B
4	16
8	20
12	
16	

2.

A	B
3	8
4	9
	10
	11

More Practice
Set A   pages 282–283

Draw the next three figures in each pattern.

1. △ □ △ □

2. ○ △ ▽ ○

3. ▽ ▽ □ ▽ ▽ □

4. □ □ ○ ○ △ □ □

5. △ ▷ ▽ ◁ △

6. □ ◣ □ □ ◣ ◣ □ □ □

7. □ ○□ □○□ □○□○□

8. □ ◪ ⊠ ⊠ ⊠

Set B   pages 284–285

Draw the next three figures in each problem. Copy and complete each table.

1.

2. Number of

Rows	1	2	3	4	5	6
Squares	1	4	9	▦	▦	▦

3. How many squares in 10 rows?

4.

5. Number of

Rows	1	2	3	4	5	6
Squares	1	4	7	▦	▦	▦

6. How many squares in 10 rows?

Set C   pages 286–287

Describe the pattern in each sequence. Then write the next four numbers.

1. 3, 9, 15, 21, . . .

2. 44, 41, 38, 35, . . .

3. 10, 20, 30, 40, . . .

4. 1, 3, 9, 27, . . .

5. 2, 6, 4, 12, . . .

6. 4, 9, 8, 13, . . .

7. 3, 9, 8, 24, . . .

8. 1, 3, 2, 4, . . .

Set D   pages 292–293

Use the grid at the right. Write the letter that names the point located by each ordered pair.

1. (4, 6)   **2.** (18, 8)   **3.** (14, 14)

4. (10, 6)   **5.** (6, 0)   **6.** (12, 18)

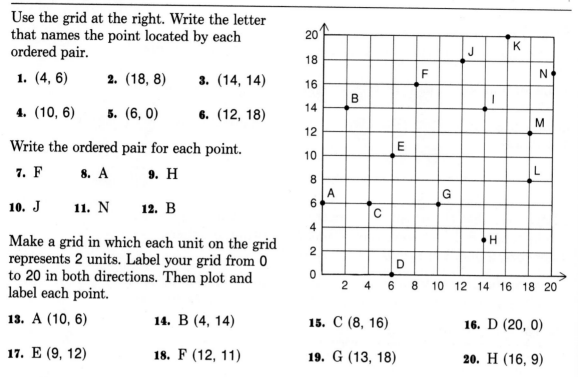

Write the ordered pair for each point.

7. F   **8.** A   **9.** H

10. J   **11.** N   **12.** B

Make a grid in which each unit on the grid represents 2 units. Label your grid from 0 to 20 in both directions. Then plot and label each point.

13. A (10, 6)   **14.** B (4, 14)   **15.** C (8, 16)   **16.** D (20, 0)

17. E (9, 12)   **18.** F (12, 11)   **19.** G (13, 18)   **20.** H (16, 9)

21. Mixed Practice   Make a grid. Plot and connect the points in order. Continue the pattern.
(0, 0) (1, 2) (2, 1) (3, 4) (4, 3) (5, ▒) (▒, 5) (▒, ▒)

Set E   pages 296–297

Find the missing numbers. Write the rule.

1.

A	B
13	28
12	▒
8	▒
3	18

2.

A	B
2	10
4	20
8	▒
▒	60

3.

A	B
20	14
30	▒
25	▒
8	2

4.

A	B
▒	20
▒	15
20	28
34	42

Find the rule.

5.

A	B
3	15
9	45
4	20
8	40

6.

A	B
12	8
26	22
8	4
16	12

7.

A	B
3	27
10	90
6	54
1	9

8.

A	B
5	14
17	26
39	48
21	30

Enrichment

Prime Factorization

Mattie has 6 new mugs. How can she arrange them in even rows?

1 row of 6 mugs $1 \times 6 = 6$

2 rows of 3 mugs
$2 \times 3 = 6$

3 rows of 2 mugs
$3 \times 2 = 6$

Mattie sees that the possible arrangements for the mugs give her the factors of 6. She knows that 2 and 3 are prime numbers. Therefore, 2 and 3 are **prime factors** of 6.

To write the prime factors of a composite number, divide by prime numbers until all the factors are prime. You can use a factor tree.

$$18 = \underset{\text{prime}}{2} \times \underset{\text{composite}}{9}$$

$$9 = \underset{\text{prime}}{3} \times \underset{\text{prime}}{3}$$

The prime factorization of 18 is $2 \times 3 \times 3$.

Find the missing numbers.

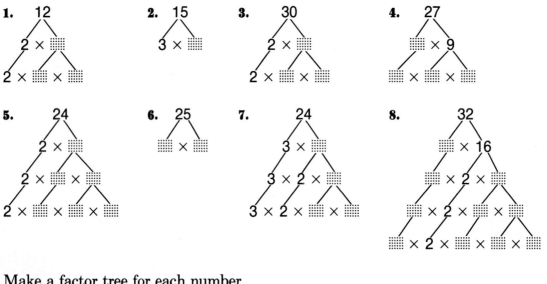

1. 12

2. 15

3. 30

4. 27

5. 24

6. 25

7. 24

8. 32

Make a factor tree for each number.

9. 54   **10.** 48   **11.** 16   **12.** 22   **13.** 30   **14.** 49

Chapter 9 Review/Test

1. Draw the next three figures in the pattern.

2. Draw the next three figures in the pattern. Then copy and complete the table below.

1 row   2 rows   3 rows

Number of

Rows	1	2	3	4	5	6
Squares	1	3	5			

Describe the pattern in each sequence. Then write the next four numbers.

3. 7, 12, 17, 22, . . .

4. 8, 12, 10, 14, 12, . . .

Use the grid at the right for Items 5–8.

Write the letter that names the point located by the ordered pair.

5. (3, 2)   **6.** (1, 4)

Write the ordered pair for each point.

7. A   **8.** B

Use the graph below to answer Items 9 and 10.

Cashews

9. Which information from the graph could you use to find how many pounds you can buy for $3?

a. 3 pounds of cashews cost $2.

b. $3 is halfway between the cost of 3 pounds and the cost of 6 pounds.

c. 6 pounds cost $4.

10. How many pounds of cashews can you buy for $3?

11. Five brothers will each play 1 game of chess with every other brother. How many games will they play?

Find the rule.

12.

A	B
5	30
3	18
7	42
10	60

13.

A	B
20	15
10	5
6	1
12	7

14. **Write About Math** Explain in your own words how you found the rule in Item 13.

305

Fraction Concepts

10

Number-Sense Project

Estimate
Estimate how many minutes of each $\frac{1}{2}$ hour of your favorite TV program is commercial time.

Gather Data
Record the starting and stopping time of each commercial break during $\frac{1}{2}$ hour of your favorite TV program.

Analyze and Report
Make a graph to show the number of minutes used for commercials and for the program during your $\frac{1}{2}$ hour program. Compare your results with other students.

Fractions

Build Understanding

A. Paula Sanchez is a flag maker. She makes all the flags of the world using shades of 8 different colors: red, blue, yellow, green, orange, brown, black, and white. For the flag of Western Samoa, she uses white, blue, and red.

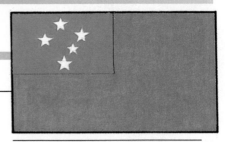

The main element in the flag of Western Samoa is the constellation of the Southern Cross. The white stands for purity, the blue for freedom, and the red for courage.

A fraction can name a part of a set. For the flag of Western Samoa, 3 of the 8 colors are used.

Number of colors used → $\dfrac{3}{8}$ ← **Numerator**
Number of possible colors → ← **Denominator**

three eighths

Ms. Sanchez uses $\frac{3}{8}$ of the colors to make the flag of Western Samoa.

The blue stripes on the Guatemalan flag represent the Atlantic and Pacific oceans which border the country.

B. The flag of Guatemala is divided into 3 equal parts, and 2 of the 3 parts of the flag are blue.

A fraction can name a part of a whole.

Number of blue parts → $\dfrac{2}{3}$
Number of equal parts →

So $\frac{2}{3}$ of the flag of Guatemala is blue.

C. Fractions can be used to identify points on a number line.

The fraction $\frac{5}{8}$ identifies point A.

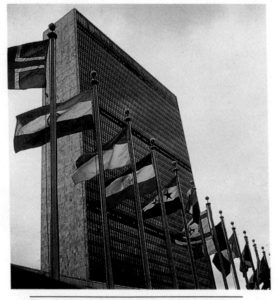

The flags of the countries in the United Nations are flown in front of the General Assembly Building in New York.

■ **Talk About Math** What different ways can fractions be used?

308

Check Understanding

For another example, see Set A, pages 334–335.

1. Complete this sentence: When the ___?___ of a fraction names the number of equal parts in a whole amount, the ___?___ names the number of parts you are talking about.

2. On the flag of Western Samoa, what fraction of the stars are the same size?

3. Use the number line in Example C. What fraction identifies point B? point C?

Practice

For More Practice, see Set A, pages 336–337.

Write the fraction to name the part that is shaded.

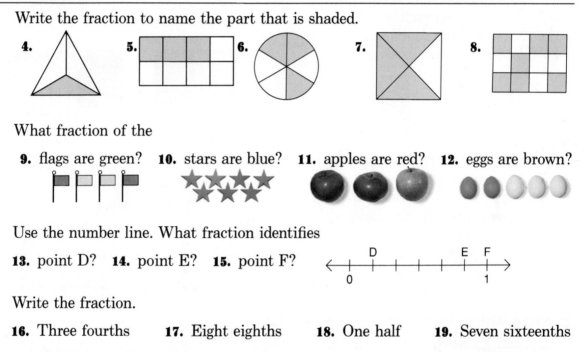

4.   5.   6.   7.   8.

What fraction of the

9. flags are green?   10. stars are blue?   11. apples are red?   12. eggs are brown?

Use the number line. What fraction identifies

13. point D?   14. point E?   15. point F?

Write the fraction.

16. Three fourths   17. Eight eighths   18. One half   19. Seven sixteenths

Problem Solving

For each flag, write a fraction to show how many of the 8 possible colors are used.

20. Syria   21. Israel   22. Zimbabwe   23. Philippines

Critical Thinking   Write the next two fractions in each pattern.

24. $\frac{1}{12}, \frac{3}{12}, \frac{5}{12}, \frac{7}{12}$, ▦, ▦

25. $\frac{1}{2}, \frac{2}{3}, \frac{3}{4}, \frac{4}{5}$, ▦, ▦

Equal Fractions

Build Understanding

Each pitcher has the same amount of cranberry juice.

Fractions that name the same amount are called *equal fractions.*

To find a fraction that is equal to a fraction, you can multiply the numerator and the denominator by the same number (not zero).

$\frac{1}{2}$ $\frac{2}{4}$

$$\frac{1}{2} \xrightarrow[2 \times 6]{1 \times 6} = \frac{6}{12}$$

To find a fraction that is equal to a fraction, you can divide the numerator and the denominator by the same number (not zero).

$\frac{1}{2}$ $\frac{6}{12}$

$$\frac{4}{16} \xrightarrow[16 \div 2]{4 \div 2} = \frac{2}{8}$$

■ **Write About Math** If a fraction is equal to $\frac{1}{2}$, can its denominator be an odd number? Can its numerator be an odd number? Why?

Check Understanding

For another example, see Set B, pages 334–335.

1. Write equal fractions for the shaded part.

2. Multiply to find equal fractions.

$$\frac{2}{5} = \frac{8}{}$$

3. Divide to find equal fractions.

$$\frac{4}{6} = \frac{}{3}$$

4. Tell whether $\frac{1}{2}$ and $\frac{5}{11}$ are equal. Explain why or why not.

310

Practice

For More Practice, see Set B, pages 336–337.

Multiply to find equal fractions.

5. $\frac{1}{3} = \frac{3}{\square}$
6. $\frac{3}{8} = \frac{6}{\square}$
7. $\frac{2}{3} = \frac{\square}{15}$
8. $\frac{5}{5} = \frac{\square}{10}$
9. $\frac{4}{9} = \frac{\square}{36}$

10. $\frac{3}{4} = \frac{\square}{20}$
11. $\frac{9}{12} = \frac{36}{\square}$
12. $\frac{3}{10} = \frac{21}{\square}$
13. $\frac{8}{11} = \frac{\square}{187}$
14. $\frac{7}{15} = \frac{56}{\square}$

Divide to find equal fractions.

15. $\frac{8}{12} = \frac{2}{\square}$
16. $\frac{6}{9} = \frac{\square}{3}$
17. $\frac{10}{25} = \frac{2}{\square}$
18. $\frac{16}{32} = \frac{\square}{8}$
19. $\frac{40}{45} = \frac{8}{\square}$

20. $\frac{20}{40} = \frac{\square}{2}$
21. $\frac{16}{48} = \frac{1}{\square}$
22. $\frac{20}{36} = \frac{\square}{9}$
23. $\frac{217}{420} = \frac{31}{\square}$
24. $\frac{54}{81} = \frac{\square}{3}$

Mixed Practice Multiply or divide to find equal fractions.

25. $\frac{5}{8} = \frac{\square}{16}$
26. $\frac{9}{12} = \frac{3}{\square}$
27. $\frac{3}{14} = \frac{6}{\square}$
28. $\frac{4}{6} = \frac{\square}{24}$
29. $\frac{60}{120} = \frac{\square}{10}$

ALGEBRA ▶ Find the value of each variable.

30. $\frac{3}{8} = \frac{x}{24}$
31. $\frac{25}{30} = \frac{5}{a}$
32. $\frac{11}{12} = \frac{44}{y}$
33. $\frac{7}{10} = \frac{56}{w}$
34. $\frac{115}{207} = \frac{n}{9}$

Tell whether the fractions are equal. Explain why or why not.

35. $\frac{3}{5}$ $\frac{12}{20}$
36. $\frac{20}{28}$ $\frac{3}{4}$
37. $\frac{7}{8}$ $\frac{28}{36}$
38. $\frac{14}{20}$ $\frac{7}{10}$
39. $\frac{5}{12}$ $\frac{30}{72}$

Problem Solving

Solve each problem.

40. Judy used 8 of 12 boxes of raisins for school lunches. Write this as a fraction. Write two equal fractions.

41. Critical Thinking How is the denominator related to the numerator in all fractions equal to $\frac{1}{4}$?

311

Fractions in Lowest Terms

Build Understanding

In the United States, 10 out of the 50 states, or $\frac{10}{50}$ of the states, have names consisting of two words. South Dakota is one example.

To show this number more simply, you can write the fraction $\frac{10}{50}$ in *lowest terms*.

The numerator and denominator are the **terms** of a fraction. A fraction is in lowest terms when the only number that both terms can be divided by evenly is 1.

A. One way to write $\frac{10}{50}$ in lowest terms is to divide both terms by any common factor. Then divide the resulting terms, and repeat until 1 is the only number that can be divided evenly into both terms.

$$\frac{10}{50} \xrightarrow[50 \div 2]{10 \div 2} = \frac{5}{25} \xrightarrow[25 \div 5]{5 \div 5} = \frac{1}{5}$$

The fraction $\frac{1}{5}$ is in lowest terms because 1 and 5 can be divided only by 1.

B. Another way to write $\frac{10}{50}$ in lowest terms is to divide the terms by the **greatest common factor.** The greatest common factor is the greatest number that is a factor of both terms.

Factors of 10: **1, 2, 5, 10**
Factors of 50: **1, 2, 5, 10, 25, 50**

The greatest common factor is 10.

$$\frac{10}{50} \xrightarrow[50 \div 10]{10 \div 10} = \frac{1}{5}$$

A fraction is in lowest terms when the greatest common factor of both terms is 1.

■ **Talk About Math** What number is a common factor of every number?

Check Understanding

For another example, see Set C, pages 334–335.

Write the common factors of the numerator and denominator.
Then write each fraction in lowest terms.

1. $\frac{6}{15}$ **2.** $\frac{3}{4}$ **3.** $\frac{8}{10}$ **4.** $\frac{5}{12}$ **5.** $\frac{12}{16}$ **6.** $\frac{5}{10}$ **7.** $\frac{12}{18}$ **8.** $\frac{8}{48}$

Practice

For More Practice, see Set C, pages 336–337.

Write the greatest common factor of the numerator and denominator.

9. $\frac{8}{12}$ **10.** $\frac{9}{12}$ **11.** $\frac{13}{20}$ **12.** $\frac{5}{25}$ **13.** $\frac{16}{20}$ **14.** $\frac{6}{9}$ **15.** $\frac{11}{15}$

16. $\frac{18}{27}$ **17.** $\frac{9}{72}$ **18.** $\frac{7}{35}$ **19.** $\frac{12}{21}$ **20.** $\frac{9}{14}$ **21.** $\frac{16}{100}$ **22.** $\frac{50}{75}$

Write each fraction in lowest terms.

23. $\frac{3}{6}$ **24.** $\frac{4}{12}$ **25.** $\frac{10}{15}$ **26.** $\frac{8}{18}$ **27.** $\frac{6}{9}$ **28.** $\frac{18}{20}$ **29.** $\frac{20}{50}$

30. $\frac{15}{30}$ **31.** $\frac{16}{24}$ **32.** $\frac{14}{21}$ **33.** $\frac{3}{10}$ **34.** $\frac{18}{45}$ **35.** $\frac{8}{64}$ **36.** $\frac{21}{42}$

37. $\frac{32}{40}$ **38.** $\frac{16}{28}$ **39.** $\frac{30}{36}$ **40.** $\frac{24}{32}$ **41.** $\frac{12}{25}$ **42.** $\frac{60}{100}$ **43.** $\frac{100}{300}$

44. $\frac{15}{40}$ **45.** $\frac{16}{72}$ **46.** $\frac{30}{80}$ **47.** $\frac{75}{100}$ **48.** $\frac{62}{75}$ **49.** $\frac{133}{203}$ **50.** $\frac{216}{279}$

51. Number Sense Can a fraction be in lowest terms if both terms are even? Explain your answer.

Problem Solving

Write each answer in lowest terms.

52. Five out of 50 states have land borders on the Pacific Ocean. What fraction of the states border the Pacific Ocean?

53. Fourteen out of 50 states border the Atlantic Ocean. What fraction of the states border the Atlantic Ocean?

Explore ———— Math

54. Start with the fraction $\frac{1}{2}$. Add 1 to each term of the fraction. Is the resulting fraction equal to $\frac{1}{2}$?

55. Pick 2 other fractions. Add the same number to both terms of the fractions. Are the resulting fractions equal to the original fractions?

56. Does adding the same number to both the numerator and the denominator of a fraction give an equal fraction?

Mixed Numbers

Build Understanding

Carpenters often make measurements longer than one inch. The nail in the picture is $2\frac{1}{4}$ inches long.

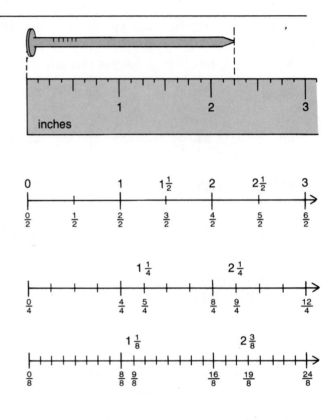

The number $2\frac{1}{4}$ is a ***mixed number***. Every mixed number is made up of a whole number and a fraction.

whole number ⎯ ↑ ↑ ⎯⎯⎯ fraction

two and one fourth

Think of a ruler as a combination of number lines. These number lines show that mixed numbers and improper fractions can name the same point. A fraction equal to or greater than 1 is an ***improper*** fraction. A fraction less than 1 is a ***proper*** fraction.

■ **Talk About Math** Is $\frac{4}{4}$ proper or improper?

Check Understanding

For another example, see Set D, page 334–335.

Write a mixed number for each picture.

1. How many melons?

2. How many cups of punch?

Use the number lines above to answer these questions.

3. What mixed number is equal to $\frac{9}{4}$?

4. What whole number is equal to $\frac{8}{8}$?

Practice

For More Practice, see Set D, pages 336–337.

Write a mixed number.

5. One and two fifths   **6.** Four and three tenths   **7.** Two and five eighths

Use these number lines for Exercises 8–13.

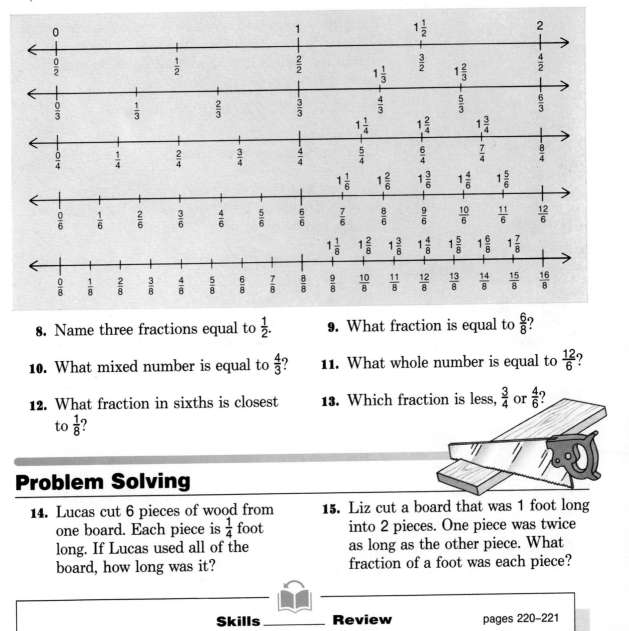

8. Name three fractions equal to $\frac{1}{2}$.

9. What fraction is equal to $\frac{6}{8}$?

10. What mixed number is equal to $\frac{4}{3}$?

11. What whole number is equal to $\frac{12}{6}$?

12. What fraction in sixths is closest to $\frac{1}{8}$?

13. Which fraction is less, $\frac{3}{4}$ or $\frac{4}{6}$?

Problem Solving

14. Lucas cut 6 pieces of wood from one board. Each piece is $\frac{1}{4}$ foot long. If Lucas used all of the board, how long was it?

15. Liz cut a board that was 1 foot long into 2 pieces. One piece was twice as long as the other piece. What fraction of a foot was each piece?

Skills ———— Review   pages 220–221

Use >, <, or = to compare.
1. 7.2 ▦ 0.72   **2.** 4.5 ▦ 4.50   **3.** 9.07 ▦ 9.7   **4.** 7.463 ▦ 7.467

Improper Fractions, Quotients, and Mixed Numbers

Build Understanding

Bill Stahm owns and operates a farm where he raises chickens for eggs. Bill ships the eggs in boxes containing flats of eggs. Each flat holds 30 eggs. How many dozen eggs are in a flat?

You could think of an improper fraction.

$\dfrac{30}{12}$ ← Number of eggs in all
← Number of eggs in one dozen

The improper fraction can be simplified using division. Divide 30 by 12 to find how many groups of 12 eggs can be made using 30 eggs.

$$30 \div 12 \qquad 12\overline{)30}\;\;2\tfrac{6}{12} \begin{array}{l} \leftarrow \text{Remainder} \\ \leftarrow \text{Divisor} \end{array}$$

There are 2 dozen eggs with 6 eggs left over. Show those eggs as part of a dozen by writing the fraction $\frac{6}{12}$. The fraction $\frac{6}{12}$ can be written in lowest terms.

$$\frac{30}{12} = 2\frac{6}{12} = 2\frac{1}{2}$$

A flat is $2\frac{1}{2}$ dozen eggs.

■ **Write About Math** Is any improper fraction equal to $\frac{2}{3}$? Why or why not?

Check Understanding

For another example, see Set E, pages 334–335.

1. Write $16 \div 5$ as an improper fraction.

2. Write $3\overline{)5}$ as an improper fraction.

3. Write $7 \div 8$ as a fraction.

Refer to the example at the right.

4. What is the divisor?

5. What is the remainder?

$$73 \div 5 \qquad \frac{73}{5} \qquad 5\overline{)73}$$

6. Express the quotient as a mixed number.

Practice

For More Practice, see Set E, pages 336–337.

Write a whole number or a mixed number for each improper fraction. **Remember** to write each fraction in lowest terms.

7. $\frac{34}{10}$ 8. $\frac{27}{6}$ 9. $\frac{48}{9}$ 10. $\frac{54}{4}$ 11. $\frac{51}{18}$ 12. $\frac{75}{20}$ 13. $\frac{16}{12}$

14. $\frac{24}{14}$ 15. $\frac{60}{3}$ 16. $\frac{58}{8}$ 17. $\frac{288}{9}$ 18. $\frac{264}{18}$ 19. $\frac{81}{25}$ 20. $\frac{244}{10}$

Tell whether you would use paper and pencil or mental math. Write each quotient as a whole number, mixed number, or proper fraction.

21. $3\overline{)17}$ 22. $6\overline{)25}$ 23. $9\overline{)147}$ 24. $5\overline{)65}$ 25. $24\overline{)60}$

26. $12\overline{)147}$ 27. $30\overline{)303}$ 28. $26\overline{)260}$ 29. $15\overline{)5}$ 30. $76\overline{)1,349}$

Problem Solving

Use the information on page 316 to solve each problem. If the answer is a mixed number, write the fraction in lowest terms.

31. **Mental Math**   If Bill ships 100 flats, how many eggs does he ship?

32. Bill worked 57 hours in 6 days. What was the average number of hours he worked per day?

Midchapter ✓ Checkup

1. Write a fraction to name the shaded part.

2. Write a fraction to name the fraction of glasses that are full.

3. Multiply to find an equal fraction. $\frac{5}{12} = \frac{}{24}$

4. Write $\frac{12}{18}$ as a fraction in lowest terms.

5. Write a mixed number to show how much is shaded.

6. What mixed number equals $\frac{8}{3}$?

7. Write a mixed number for $\frac{37}{9}$.

8. Write $50 \div 12$ as a mixed number.

Explore as a Team

1. How many different ways can you cut a 3-inch by 5-inch card into 8 equal pieces? All pieces have to be the same size and shape.

TIPS FOR **WORKING TOGETHER**

Help keep your group on task.

Real-Life Decision Making

Your neighbor hired you and your friend to shovel the snow off her sidewalks. Her front sidewalk and back sidewalk are the same size.

Your friend forgot to show up, so you did the front sidewalk alone. When your friend came, you were ready to start shoveling the back sidewalk. The two of you shoveled the back sidewalk together.

How should you split the money?

Problem Solving WORKSHOP

Explore with a Computer

Use the *Fractions Workshop Project* for this activity.

1. Divide the first unit into 3 equal parts. Shade $\frac{1}{3}$ of the unit.

2. Divide the second unit into six equal parts. Divide the third unit into twelve equal parts. Shade parts of these units to equal $\frac{1}{3}$. How many parts did you shade?

3. Shade parts of all the units to show $\frac{2}{3}$. How many parts did you shade?

```
File  Edit  Model  Change  Extras  Help
┌─────┬─────┬─────┐
│     │     │     │
└─────┴─────┴─────┘
┌─────────────────┐
│                 │
└─────────────────┘
┌─────────────────┐
│                 │
└─────────────────┘

Use the arrows to move cursor.
Press Return to shade.
```

Number-Sense Project

Look back at pages 306-307.

A student made the chart below showing how time was used during $\frac{1}{2}$ hour of her favorite program.

| Time | | Type of Program/Elapsed Time | | |
Start	Stop	Commercial	Program	Other
7:30	7:33	3 min		
7:33	7:40		7 min	
7:40	7:42	2 min		
7:42	7:48		6 min	
7:48	7:51	3 min		
7:51	7:52			1 min
7:52	7:58		6 min	
7:58	8:00	2 min		

a. How many minutes of the program were used for commercials?

b. What fraction of the program was used for commercials?

c. One minute was classified as other. What could this minute have been used for?

d. What patterns do you notice in the amount of time used for commercials in the TV programs you watch?

319

Fractions and Estimation

Build Understanding

To estimate with fractions and mixed numbers, it is helpful to compare the fractions to $\frac{1}{2}$.

A. Half Is for You
Materials: Fraction pieces
Groups: Groups of 4

a. For reference, place the piece that shows one whole on your desk and below it, the piece that shows $\frac{1}{2}$.

b. To compare $\frac{1}{3}$ to $\frac{1}{2}$, place the piece for $\frac{1}{3}$ below the piece for $\frac{1}{2}$. Is $\frac{1}{3}$ less than $\frac{1}{2}$, equal to $\frac{1}{2}$, or greater than $\frac{1}{2}$? Use two pieces for $\frac{1}{3}$ to compare $\frac{2}{3}$ to $\frac{1}{2}$. How does $\frac{2}{3}$ compare to $\frac{1}{2}$?

c. Use fraction pieces to tell if each fraction is less than $\frac{1}{2}$, equal to $\frac{1}{2}$, or greater than $\frac{1}{2}$.
$\frac{1}{4}$ $\frac{2}{4}$ $\frac{3}{4}$ $\frac{3}{6}$ $\frac{5}{6}$ $\frac{3}{8}$ $\frac{7}{8}$

B. Estimate $\frac{3}{8} + \frac{1}{4}$.

$\frac{3}{8} < \frac{1}{2}$ and $\frac{1}{4} < \frac{1}{2}$

The sum is less than 1 since each addend is less than $\frac{1}{2}$.

C. Estimate $\frac{5}{6} + \frac{3}{4}$.

$\frac{5}{6} > \frac{1}{2}$ and $\frac{3}{4} > \frac{1}{2}$

The sum is greater than 1 since each addend is greater than $\frac{1}{2}$.

D. Estimate $\frac{1}{8} + \frac{7}{12}$.

$\frac{1}{8} < \frac{1}{2}$ and $\frac{7}{12} > \frac{1}{2}$

You cannot tell how the sum compares to 1. The sum must be larger than the larger fraction, $\frac{7}{12}$.

■ **Talk About Math** Explain how you can compare a fraction to $\frac{1}{2}$ by looking at its numerator and denominator.

Check Understanding

For another example, see Set F, pages 334–335.

Estimate by using the method in Examples B–D.

1. $\frac{1}{4} + \frac{1}{6}$ **2.** $\frac{1}{3} + \frac{7}{8}$ **3.** $\frac{2}{5} + \frac{1}{2}$ **4.** $\frac{5}{9} + \frac{2}{3}$

Practice

For More Practice, see Set F, pages 336–337.

Tell if the fraction is less than $\frac{1}{2}$, equal to $\frac{1}{2}$, or greater than $\frac{1}{2}$.

5. $\frac{1}{6}$ **6.** $\frac{5}{8}$ **7.** $\frac{1}{8}$ **8.** $\frac{9}{10}$ **9.** $\frac{5}{10}$ **10.** $\frac{3}{12}$ **11.** $\frac{4}{8}$

12. $\frac{1}{20}$ **13.** $\frac{4}{5}$ **14.** $\frac{1}{7}$ **15.** $\frac{5}{9}$ **16.** $\frac{9}{18}$ **17.** $\frac{3}{5}$ **18.** $\frac{6}{12}$

19. $\frac{2}{25}$ **20.** $\frac{7}{16}$ **21.** $\frac{7}{12}$ **22.** $\frac{29}{32}$ **23.** $\frac{16}{32}$ **24.** $\frac{3}{7}$ **25.** $\frac{11}{12}$

Estimate whether each sum is (a) less than 1, (b) greater than 1, or (c) greater than the larger fraction.

26. $\frac{2}{5} + \frac{1}{6}$ **27.** $\frac{5}{12} + \frac{1}{4}$ **28.** $\frac{2}{3} + \frac{3}{5}$ **29.** $\frac{7}{8} + \frac{7}{10}$ **30.** $\frac{3}{4} + \frac{4}{9}$

31. $\frac{4}{15} + \frac{5}{8}$ **32.** $\frac{3}{10} + \frac{9}{20}$ **33.** $\frac{3}{8} + \frac{3}{16}$ **34.** $\frac{11}{24} + \frac{1}{3}$ **35.** $\frac{5}{6} + \frac{8}{9}$

36. $\frac{3}{8} + \frac{2}{3}$ **37.** $\frac{1}{4} + \frac{2}{9}$ **38.** $\frac{1}{6} + \frac{8}{9}$ **39.** $\frac{5}{6} + \frac{7}{9}$ **40.** $\frac{1}{5} + \frac{3}{10}$

Problem Solving

Solve each problem.

41. Celia bought $\frac{7}{8}$ yard of fabric to make a skirt and $\frac{3}{4}$ yard of fabric to make a top. Did she buy more or less than 1 yard of fabric in all?

42. Eleanor bought $\frac{1}{4}$ dozen walnut muffins and $\frac{1}{3}$ dozen cranberry muffins. In all, did she buy more or less than 1 dozen muffins?

43. When $a < b$, is the fraction $\frac{a}{b}$ a proper fraction or an improper fraction? When $a > b$?

44. Oscar Ventura planted $\frac{3}{4}$ acre of sweet corn and $\frac{2}{3}$ acre of cabbage for the farmers' market. Did he plant more or less than 1 acre in all?

A
L
G
E
B
R
A

Reading ———— Math

Numbers and Symbols   Write each expression in words.

1. $\frac{16}{3}$ **2.** $8\overline{)27}$ **3.** $11 \div 2$ **4.** 14×12 **5.** $19 - 14$

Work Backward

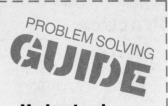

Build Understanding

Brian is raising gerbils that other students will use in a science project. Some gerbils will be fed vitamins to see if they grow faster than gerbils that are not fed vitamins.

Brian gives $\frac{1}{2}$ of the gerbils he has to Susan. Then Susan gives $\frac{1}{2}$ of these gerbils to Yolanda. Yolanda then gives $\frac{1}{2}$ of her gerbils to Chen. Chen has 4 gerbils.

How many gerbils did Brian have before he gave any away?

Understand
QUESTION
FACTS
KEY IDEA

▶ **Plan and Solve**
STRATEGY
ANSWER

Look Back
SENSIBLE ANSWER
ALTERNATE APPROACH

Understand   How many gerbils did Brian have when he started the project? Brian gives $\frac{1}{2}$ of the gerbils to Susan. She gives $\frac{1}{2}$ of those gerbils to Yolanda. Yolanda gives $\frac{1}{2}$ of those gerbils to Chen. Chen has 4 gerbils. Chen has the fewest gerbils.

▶ **Plan and Solve**   STRATEGY   Start with the number of gerbils Chen has and work backward to find the original number.

Chen has 4 gerbils. This is half the gerbils that Yolanda had. So Yolanda had 8 gerbils.

Since 8 gerbils is half the number that Susan had, Susan had 16 gerbils.

Since 16 is half the number of gerbils that Brian had, then Brian had 32 gerbils.

ANSWER   Brian started with 32 gerbils.

Look Back   Check your work by starting with 32 gerbils. Go through the steps in the problem and see if the result is 4.

■ **Talk About Math** How do you "undo" the result of adding 10? subtracting 5? multiplying by 2? dividing by 3?

Check Understanding

One gerbil gained 2 ounces in week 1, 1 ounce in week 2, and 3 ounces in week 3. The gerbil weighed 15 ounces at the end of week 3. How much did the gerbil weigh

1. at the end of week 2?   **2.** at the end of week 1?

3. What was the original weight of the gerbil at the beginning of the project?

Practice

4. One gerbil lost 1 ounce in week 1, gained 2 ounces in week 2, and then gained 3 ounces in week 3. What was the original weight of the gerbil if it weighed 14 ounces at the end of week 3?

5. Brian also raises guinea pigs. One time he gave $\frac{1}{3}$ of his guinea pigs to Lila. Lila gave 5 away and had 2 left. How many guinea pigs did Brian originally have?

6. For a science project, the teacher divided the class into 3 groups. There were 7 students in each group. The two students who were not in any group kept records of the class's project. How many students were there in the class?

7. Brian, Susan, Yolanda, and Chen helped raise money for the Science Fair. Brian raised $\frac{1}{3}$ as much as Susan. Yolanda raised $\frac{1}{2}$ as much as Susan but $3 less than Chen. Chen raised $15. How much money did each student raise?

Choose a ⸺ Strategy

Zoo-onomics On a science field trip, each student paid $3 for admission to the zoo. Half of the students also spent $4 each in the gift shop for books on animal care.

8. If 10 students had gone on the trip, how much would they have spent in all?

9. If the students spent $80 in all at the zoo, how many students went on the trip?

Finding the Least Common Denominator

Build Understanding

Sometimes estimation is not exact enough to compare fractions. Comparing, adding, and subtracting fractions are easier when they have the same denominator.

A. Denominator Detectives
Materials: Fraction pieces
Groups: Groups of 4

a. With another member of your group, use your fraction pieces to find fractions equal to $\frac{1}{2}$. Try to cover exactly the piece for $\frac{1}{2}$ using the pieces for thirds, then fourths, and so on. Make a list of the fractions equal to $\frac{1}{2}$.

b. The other two members of the group should find fractions equal to $\frac{2}{3}$ in the same way. Remember that the piece for $\frac{2}{3}$ must be covered exactly. Make a list of fractions equal to $\frac{2}{3}$.

c. Compare the lists. What fractions on both lists have denominators in common? Which common denominator is the least?

d. Write fractions equal to $\frac{1}{2}$ and $\frac{2}{3}$ using the *least common denominator.*

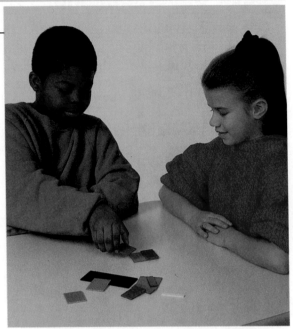

B. Write $\frac{3}{4}$ and $\frac{5}{6}$ with the least common denominator. Here is another way to find the least common denominator.

List the multiples of both 4 and 6.

Multiples of **4: 4, 8, 12, 16, 20, 24, 28**
Multiples of **6: 6, 12, 18, 24, 30, 36, 42**

Common multiples are 12 and 24. The least common multiple is 12. Use 12 for the least common denominator.

■ **Write About Math** Why is it an advantage to use the least common denominator when writing two fractions with a common denominator?

Check Understanding

For another example, see Set G, pages 334–335.

1. Use fraction pieces to find the least common denominator for $\frac{1}{3}$ and $\frac{1}{4}$. Draw the pieces to show your answer.

2. List multiples to find the least common denominator for $\frac{1}{3}$ and $\frac{1}{4}$.

3. Write fractions with the least common denominator for $\frac{1}{3}$ and $\frac{1}{4}$.

4. What is the least common denominator for $\frac{4}{5}$ and $\frac{3}{5}$?

Practice

For More Practice, see Set G, pages 336–337.

Write the fractions with the least common denominator.

5. $\frac{3}{8}, \frac{3}{4}$
6. $\frac{2}{5}, \frac{3}{10}$
7. $\frac{1}{3}, \frac{1}{12}$
8. $\frac{1}{2}, \frac{3}{4}$
9. $\frac{1}{6}, \frac{1}{2}$
10. $\frac{7}{10}, \frac{1}{4}$

11. $\frac{5}{6}, \frac{2}{3}$
12. $\frac{1}{2}, \frac{3}{5}$
13. $\frac{3}{4}, \frac{2}{5}$
14. $\frac{1}{6}, \frac{2}{9}$
15. $\frac{1}{3}, \frac{3}{4}$
16. $\frac{1}{3}, \frac{1}{2}$

17. $\frac{3}{5}, \frac{3}{7}$
18. $\frac{2}{3}, \frac{2}{5}$
19. $\frac{1}{2}, \frac{4}{9}$
20. $\frac{3}{16}, \frac{7}{8}$
21. $\frac{1}{10}, \frac{5}{6}$
22. $\frac{2}{3}, \frac{5}{8}$

23. $\frac{4}{9}, \frac{11}{12}$
24. $\frac{1}{2}, \frac{3}{10}$
25. $\frac{7}{8}, \frac{5}{12}$
26. $\frac{1}{6}, \frac{1}{8}$
27. $\frac{1}{3}, \frac{9}{10}$
28. $\frac{2}{25}, \frac{77}{100}$

29. $\frac{3}{4}, \frac{9}{16}$
30. $\frac{4}{5}, \frac{5}{12}$
31. $\frac{2}{3}, \frac{7}{15}$
32. $\frac{9}{50}, \frac{1}{2}$
33. $\frac{1}{5}, \frac{7}{25}$
34. $\frac{7}{10}, \frac{81}{100}$

35. $\frac{1}{2}, \frac{3}{4}, \frac{5}{6}$
36. $\frac{2}{3}, \frac{1}{6}, \frac{3}{8}$
37. $\frac{3}{10}, \frac{7}{12}, \frac{11}{15}$
38. $\frac{5}{12}, \frac{1}{4}, \frac{7}{8}$
39. $\frac{3}{4}, \frac{8}{9}, \frac{1}{12}$

Problem Solving

Critical Thinking   Solve each problem.

40. For each of Exercises 5–9, compare the denominators of the fractions and the least common denominator. What do you notice? Does this always happen?

41. For each of Exercises 15–19, compare the denominators of the fractions and the least common denominator. What do you notice? Does this always happen?

42. What number is always a common denominator of two fractions? Is it always the least common denominator? Use examples to explain your answer.

43. Select any two fractions with different denominators. How many common denominators can you find? How many least common denominators are there?

Comparing and Ordering Fractions

Build Understanding

A. Martha's recipe for pumpkin bread calls for $\frac{2}{3}$ cup of milk. She has $\frac{3}{4}$ of a cup. Does she have enough milk?

Compare $\frac{2}{3}$ and $\frac{3}{4}$.

$\frac{2}{3}$ ⬚ $\frac{3}{4}$ The denominators are not the same.

↓   ↓

$\frac{8}{12}$ ⬚ $\frac{9}{12}$ Write the fractions with the least common denominator.

$\frac{8}{12} < \frac{9}{12}$ Compare the numerators. $8 < 9$, so $\frac{8}{12} < \frac{9}{12}$.

↓   ↓

$\frac{2}{3} < \frac{3}{4}$ $\frac{2}{3}$ is less than $\frac{3}{4}$.

Martha has enough milk.

B. Compare $2\frac{1}{5}$ and $2\frac{2}{3}$.

$2\frac{1}{5}$ ⬚ $2\frac{2}{3}$ The whole numbers are the same.

↓   ↓

$2\frac{3}{15}$ ⬚ $2\frac{10}{15}$ Compare the fractions. First write the fractions with the least common denominator.

$2\frac{3}{15} < 2\frac{10}{15}$ $\frac{3}{15}$ is less than $\frac{10}{15}$.

↓   ↓

$2\frac{1}{5} < 2\frac{2}{3}$ $2\frac{1}{5}$ is less than $2\frac{2}{3}$.

C. Write $\frac{1}{3}$, $\frac{5}{18}$, and $\frac{4}{9}$ in order from least to greatest.

$\frac{1}{3}$ $\frac{5}{18}$ $\frac{4}{9}$

$\frac{6}{18}$ $\frac{5}{18}$ $\frac{8}{18}$ Write the fractions with the least common denominator.

$\frac{5}{18}$ $\frac{6}{18}$ $\frac{8}{18}$ Compare the numerators.

↓   ↓   ↓

$\frac{5}{18}$ $\frac{1}{3}$ $\frac{4}{9}$ Write the fractions in order.

■ **Talk About Math** If two fractions have the same numerator, how can you tell which fraction is larger without finding a common denominator?

Check Understanding

For another example, see Set H, pages 334–335.

Compare the fractions or mixed numbers. Use $<$, $>$, or $=$.

1. $\frac{3}{4}$ ⬚ $\frac{9}{16}$ **2.** $\frac{1}{3}$ ⬚ $\frac{5}{9}$ **3.** $3\frac{1}{2}$ ⬚ $3\frac{4}{8}$

Order the fractions or mixed numbers from least to greatest.

4. $\frac{3}{4}$ $1\frac{1}{4}$ $\frac{5}{8}$ **5.** $\frac{2}{5}$ $\frac{7}{10}$ $\frac{3}{10}$

Practice

For More Practice, see Set H, pages 336–337.

Compare the fractions, whole numbers, and mixed numbers.
Use <, >, or =. **Remember** to find the least common denominator.

6. $\frac{1}{2}$ ▦ $\frac{2}{3}$ **7.** $\frac{1}{3}$ ▦ $\frac{4}{9}$ **8.** $\frac{2}{5}$ ▦ $\frac{1}{2}$ **9.** $\frac{3}{4}$ ▦ $\frac{2}{5}$

10. $\frac{5}{8}$ ▦ $\frac{2}{3}$ **11.** $\frac{1}{3}$ ▦ $\frac{5}{9}$ **12.** $\frac{3}{16}$ ▦ $\frac{1}{4}$ **13.** $\frac{29}{100}$ ▦ $\frac{13}{50}$

14. $\frac{2}{3}$ ▦ $\frac{4}{6}$ **15.** $\frac{5}{6}$ ▦ $\frac{3}{4}$ **16.** 1 ▦ $\frac{3}{8}$ **17.** $\frac{3}{4}$ ▦ $\frac{6}{8}$

18. $1\frac{3}{5}$ ▦ $2\frac{1}{5}$ **19.** $5\frac{1}{2}$ ▦ $3\frac{3}{4}$ **20.** 3 ▦ $5\frac{5}{16}$ **21.** $7\frac{5}{12}$ ▦ $6\frac{2}{3}$

22. $3\frac{1}{2}$ ▦ $3\frac{5}{8}$ **23.** $8\frac{5}{6}$ ▦ $8\frac{2}{3}$ **24.** $6\frac{3}{10}$ ▦ $6\frac{5}{12}$ **25.** $9\frac{7}{8}$ ▦ 9

26. $5\frac{1}{3}$ ▦ $5\frac{1}{5}$ **27.** $6\frac{7}{10}$ ▦ $6\frac{1}{15}$ **28.** $4\frac{7}{16}$ ▦ $4\frac{1}{2}$ **29.** $\frac{311}{200}$ ▦ $1\frac{1}{2}$

Write the fractions, whole numbers, and mixed
numbers in order from least to greatest.

30. $\frac{2}{3}$ $\frac{1}{2}$ $\frac{1}{3}$ **31.** $1\frac{3}{4}$ $1\frac{1}{8}$ $1\frac{3}{8}$ **32.** $1\frac{1}{2}$ 2 $\frac{3}{8}$ **33.** $\frac{3}{8}$ $\frac{1}{4}$ $\frac{9}{16}$

34. $2\frac{7}{8}$ $2\frac{1}{2}$ $2\frac{1}{3}$ **35.** $4\frac{1}{6}$ $4\frac{2}{5}$ $4\frac{1}{3}$ **36.** $\frac{3}{4}$ $\frac{7}{12}$ $\frac{5}{6}$ **37.** $\frac{1}{8}$ $\frac{1}{3}$ $\frac{1}{6}$

38. $3\frac{1}{2}$ 4 $3\frac{5}{8}$ **39.** $\frac{1}{2}$ $\frac{1}{3}$ $\frac{1}{4}$ **40.** $5\frac{1}{4}$ $5\frac{1}{8}$ $5\frac{3}{8}$ **41.** $1\frac{2}{3}$ $1\frac{4}{5}$ $1\frac{8}{15}$

42. $\frac{3}{20}$ $\frac{3}{5}$ $\frac{3}{10}$ **43.** $1\frac{1}{4}$ $\frac{3}{4}$ $\frac{7}{8}$ **44.** $3\frac{2}{3}$ $3\frac{5}{6}$ $3\frac{3}{8}$ **45.** $8\frac{4}{5}$ $8\frac{1}{2}$ $8\frac{7}{10}$

Problem Solving

Read for the facts to solve the problems.

46. The pumpkin bread recipe calls for $\frac{3}{4}$ cup of shortening. Martha has $\frac{5}{8}$ of a cup. Does she have enough shortening?

47. Martha made two loaves of pumpkin bread the same size. She cut one into 12 equal slices and the other into 16 equal slices. Which slices were larger?

48. Use Data Refer to the fractions in Example A and Example B on page 308. Which fraction is larger?

Fractions and Decimals

Build Understanding

A. Scientists have estimated that less than three tenths of the earth's surface is land. The number *three tenths* can be written either as a decimal or as a fraction.

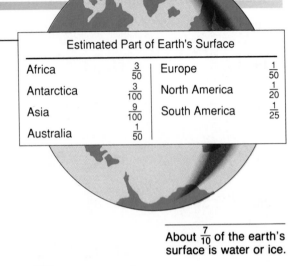

Estimated Part of Earth's Surface			
Africa	$\frac{3}{50}$	Europe	$\frac{1}{50}$
Antarctica	$\frac{3}{100}$	North America	$\frac{1}{20}$
Asia	$\frac{9}{100}$	South America	$\frac{1}{25}$
Australia	$\frac{1}{50}$		

$$0.3 = \frac{3}{10}$$

About $\frac{7}{10}$ of the earth's surface is water or ice.

B. South America covers about $\frac{1}{25}$ of the earth's surface. Rename $\frac{1}{25}$ as a fraction with a denominator of 100. Then write it as a decimal.

$$\overset{\overset{1 \times 4}{\curvearrowright}}{\underset{\underset{25 \times 4}{\curvearrowright}}{\frac{1}{25}}} = \frac{4}{100} = 0.04$$

C. 📱 **Calculator** Write $\frac{7}{50}$ as a decimal. Use your calculator to divide the numerator by the denominator.

Press: 7 ÷ 50 =

Display: *0.14*

■ **Talk About Math** What is $6\frac{2}{5}$ as a decimal? If you used a calculator, what keys would you press to get the correct display of 6.4? Remember that $6\frac{2}{5}$ means $6 + \frac{2}{5}$.

Check Understanding

For another example, see Set I, pages 334–335.

1. Write 0.8 as a fraction. Then write it in lowest terms.

2. Write 0.25 as a fraction in lowest terms.

3. Write 0.325 as a fraction in lowest terms.

4. Write 2.35 in lowest terms.

5. Write $\frac{7}{5}$ as a fraction with denominator 10. Then write it as a decimal.

6. Write $\frac{9}{20}$ as a fraction with denominator 100. Then write it as a decimal.

Practice

For More Practice, see Set I, pages 336–337.

Write each decimal as a fraction or a mixed number. **Remember** to write all fractions in lowest terms.

7. 0.7   **8.** 0.4   **9.** 0.6   **10.** 0.9

11. 0.24   **12.** 0.36   **13.** 1.24   **14.** 3.48

15. 0.025   **16.** 0.175   **17.** 2.144   **18.** 12.056

Mental Math Write each fraction with a denominator of 10, 100, or 1,000. Then write it as a decimal.

19. $\frac{1}{4}$ **20.** $\frac{3}{20}$ **21.** $\frac{1}{2}$ **22.** $\frac{9}{50}$

23. $\frac{7}{25}$ **24.** $\frac{9}{250}$ **25.** $\frac{9}{125}$ **26.** $\frac{7}{500}$

▦ Calculator Write each fraction as a decimal.

27. $\frac{3}{4}$ **28.** $\frac{1}{8}$ **29.** $\frac{1}{5}$ **30.** $\frac{3}{8}$

31. $\frac{3}{16}$ **32.** $\frac{27}{50}$ **33.** $\frac{1}{50}$ **34.** $\frac{3}{40}$

Estimation Tell if the fraction is less than $\frac{1}{2}$, equal to $\frac{1}{2}$, or greater than $\frac{1}{2}$.

35. $\frac{49}{100}$ **36.** $\frac{3}{100}$ **37.** $\frac{887}{1,000}$ **38.** $\frac{250}{500}$

For Exercises 39–42, tell whether you would use paper and pencil, mental math, or a calculator. Then change each fraction to a decimal.

39. $\frac{9}{25}$ **40.** $\frac{19}{95}$ **41.** $\frac{7}{20}$ **42.** $\frac{12}{25}$

Problem Solving

43. Compare the fractional parts of the earth's surface taken up by Africa and South America. Which is greater?

44. Order the fractional parts of the earth's surface taken up by the continents from least to greatest.

TIPS FOR PROBLEM SOLVERS

Share your thinking with others. Explaining your ideas helps you think better.

Interpret the Remainder

Build Understanding

Rita sells office equipment. Each day, she reports the orders she takes.

DAILY REPORT

Sales Agent: _Rita Landry_   DATE: _July 17_

CUSTOMER	ORDER NO.	AMOUNT	SHIPPING DATE
1. Star Co.	4123	$1342.20	Oct. 24
2. Star Co.	4124	238.17	Sept. 11
3. Compco	4125	2841.32	Sept. 18
4. Action Co.	4126	137.50	Oct. 15

PROBLEM SOLVING GUIDE

Understand
QUESTION
FACTS
KEY IDEA

➤ **Plan and Solve**
STRATEGY
ANSWER

Look Back
SENSIBLE ANSWER
ALTERNATE APPROACH

Each daily report sheet has **9** lines. How many sheets did Rita need to report **67** orders?

Understand   How many daily report sheets did Rita use for 67 orders? Each sheet is a list for 9 orders. She must use enough sheets to list all the orders.

➤ **Plan and Solve**   STRATEGY   Find how many groups of 9 are in 67, and how many are left over. Divide 67 by 9.

$$9)\overline{67} \quad 7\frac{4}{9}$$
$$\underline{63}$$
$$4$$

The quotient is 7, and the remainder is 4. There are 7 groups of 9, and 4 are left over.

ANSWER   Rita had to use **8** sheets of report paper: 7 full sheets and 1 sheet with 4 orders. Even though she would only use a fraction of the page, Rita would still need 8 sheets.

Look Back   Check the answer. Since 7 × 9 = 63, 7 full sheets can list 63 names. The eighth sheet lists 4 names. All the names are listed.

■ **Talk About Math**   When division is used to solve a problem, in what three ways might the answer be used?

Check Understanding

Nova Computers are shipped in crates. Each crate holds 12 computers.

1. If 150 computers are shipped, how many crates can be completely filled?

2. How many computers will be left over?

3. How many crates are needed in all?

4. Each full crate weighs 260 pounds. What is the average weight of each computer?

Practice

5. Each page of Rita's checkbook has 4 checks. She wrote 58 checks. How many full pages did she use? How many checks on the next page did she use?

6. Calculators are packed 8 to a box. Rita can order only full boxes. A customer wants to buy 100 calculators. How many boxes are needed to complete the order?

7. Packages of computer paper are shipped in cartons of 24 packages. If a full carton weighs 36 pounds, what is the weight of each package of computer paper?

Choose a _____ Strategy

Yoshi has 9 coins. He spends a quarter in the bakery and 5 cents in the grocery store. Now he has only 23 cents left. What coins did he have before shopping?

8. If he has 23 cents left, how much money did he have before spending the quarter and 5 cents?

9. How many coins could he use to spend 5 cents?

10. What coins did Yoshi have before shopping?

PROBLEM SOLVING STRATEGIES

Choose an Operation
Write an Equation
Draw a Diagram
Make a Table
Try and Check
Use Logical Reasoning
Find a Pattern
Work Backward

Skills Review

Write a fraction to name the shaded part.

1.   **2.**

Multiply or divide to find equal fractions.

3. $\frac{1}{4} = \frac{}{12}$ **4.** $\frac{15}{25} = \frac{}{5}$ **5.** $\frac{5}{8} = \frac{25}{}$

Write each fraction in lowest terms.

6. $\frac{12}{18}$ **7.** $\frac{8}{16}$ **8.** $\frac{10}{12}$

9. Write a mixed number for six and three tenths.

Write a whole number or a mixed number for each improper fraction.

10. $\frac{25}{4}$ **11.** $\frac{36}{12}$ **12.** $\frac{52}{15}$

Is each fraction greater than $\frac{1}{2}$, less than $\frac{1}{2}$, or equal to $\frac{1}{2}$?

13. $\frac{1}{15}$ **14.** $\frac{13}{15}$ **15.** $\frac{10}{20}$

Write the fractions with the least common denominator.

16. $\frac{1}{2}, \frac{5}{6}$ **17.** $\frac{1}{4}, \frac{3}{5}$ **18.** $\frac{2}{9}, \frac{1}{6}$

Write the numbers in order from least to greatest.

19. $\frac{2}{3}, \frac{5}{6}, \frac{3}{4}$ **20.** $2\frac{3}{4}, 2\frac{5}{8}, 2\frac{3}{8}$

Write each decimal as a fraction or a mixed number.

21. 0.9   **22.** 0.12   **23.** 5.02

Problem-Solving Review

Solve each problem.

24. What fraction of the stripes on the American flag are red?

25. Of the 50 United States, 8 have names that begin with the letter M. What fraction of the states have names that do not begin with the letter M? Give your answer in lowest terms.

26. Of Vince's shirts, $\frac{1}{3}$ are blue. Of the remaining shirts, $\frac{1}{2}$ are striped. The other 3 shirts are yellow. How many shirts does Vince have?

27. Stunt kites cost $27. How many kites can Mike buy with $150?

28. Use the bar graph below. What fraction of the people surveyed chose a cruise as a favorite vacation?

Favorite Vacation

29. **Data File** Using the map on pages 380–381, find the number of cities with a high temperature of 83°. What fraction of the cities shown had that temperature?

30. **Make a Data File** Find pictures of flags of different countries. List 5 countries whose flags are divided into thirds. Draw the flags.

Compare the numbers. Use >, <, or =.

1. 5,890 ⬚ 5,908

2. 35,452 ⬚ 35,425

3. 9.5 ⬚ 9.50   **4.** 0.472 ⬚ 1.3

5. $\frac{1}{3}$ ⬚ $\frac{1}{2}$ **6.** $2\frac{3}{4}$ ⬚ $2\frac{2}{3}$

Use mental math to compute.

7. 7×30 **8.** 50×400

9. $20 \times 1,000$ **10.** $1,200 \div 30$

11. $189 \div 9$ **12.** $7,200 \div 80$

Use a ruler to draw a line of each length.

13. $5\frac{1}{4}$ in.   **14.** 76 mm

Find the volume of each prism.

15. 10 mm, 10 mm, 5 mm

16. 10 ft, 14 ft, 16 ft

Find each answer.

17. 8 ft 2 in.
       − 2 ft 8 in.

18. 3 gal 3 qt
       + 4 gal 3 qt

19. 5 lb 10 oz × 3

20. 2 hr 20 min ÷ 7

Write each fraction in lowest terms.

21. $\frac{6}{8}$ **22.** $\frac{6}{12}$ **23.** $\frac{16}{20}$

Compute. Remember to estimate to be sure your answer makes sense.

24. $31.6 + 0.28$

25. $88.9 + 16.375$

26. $37.45 - 21.755$

27. 45×6.76 **28.** 0.25×6.93

29. 0.003×7 **30.** 4.03×0.02

31. $6.93 \div 3$ **32.** $0.725 \div 5$

Describe the pattern. Then write the next four numbers.

33. 2, 6, 10, 14, . . .

34. 3, 9, 27, 81, . . .

35. 5, 10, 9, 18, . . .

Write the letter that names the point located by each ordered pair.

36. (3, 0)   **37.** (2, 4)

Write the ordered pair for each point.

38. A   **39.** B   **40.** C

Write the fractions with the least common denominator.

41. $\frac{3}{4}, \frac{1}{8}$ **42.** $\frac{2}{3}, \frac{1}{2}$

Write each decimal as a fraction or a mixed number.

43. 0.3   **44.** 0.56   **45.** 3.45

Reteaching

Set A   pages 308–309

A fraction can be used to name part of a set.

Three of 7 coins are dimes. Write this as a fraction.

3 ← Number of dimes
$\overline{7}$ ← Total number of coins

Remember that the denominator is the number of objects in the set.

What fraction of the

1. glasses have straws?   2. candles are lit?

Set B   pages 310–311

Find equal fractions: $\frac{3}{8} = \frac{9}{}$

To find equal fractions, you can multiply both the numerator and the denominator by the same number (not zero).

So $\frac{3}{8} \overset{3\times 3}{\underset{8\times 3}{\frown}} \frac{9}{24}$

Remember that you can divide the numerator and denominator by the same number (not zero) to find equal fractions. Multiply or divide to find equal fractions.

1. $\frac{3}{5} = \frac{12}{}$ 2. $\frac{6}{12} = \frac{1}{}$ 3. $\frac{5}{8} = \frac{10}{}$

4. $\frac{14}{16} = \frac{}{8}$ 5. $\frac{16}{18} = \frac{}{9}$ 6. $\frac{3}{4} = \frac{}{12}$

Set C   pages 312–313

Write $\frac{8}{12}$ in lowest terms.

You can divide both 8 and 12 by 2.

$\frac{8}{12} \overset{8\div 2}{\underset{12\div 2}{=}} \frac{4}{6}$

You can divide both 4 and 6 by 2.

$\frac{4}{6} \overset{4\div 2}{\underset{6\div 2}{=}} \frac{2}{3}$ Lowest terms

Remember that the greatest common factor can be used to write a fraction in lowest terms.

Write each fraction in lowest terms.

1. $\frac{5}{15}$ 2. $\frac{16}{28}$ 3. $\frac{4}{16}$

4. $\frac{3}{9}$ 5. $\frac{12}{16}$ 6. $\frac{14}{35}$

Set D   pages 314–315

You can use the number lines on page 315 to find equal fractions, mixed numbers, and improper fractions. What mixed number is equal to $\frac{5}{3}$?

Look at the number line for thirds.

$\frac{5}{3} = 1\frac{2}{3}$

Remember that a point on a number line can have more than one name. Use the number lines on page 315 to answer these questions.

1. What mixed number is equal to $\frac{11}{8}$?

2. What fraction is equal to $\frac{2}{8}$?

Set E pages 316–317

Write a whole number or a mixed number for $\frac{26}{4}$.

$$6\frac{2}{4} \leftarrow \text{Remainder}$$
$$4\overline{)2\,6}$$

Divide.

The fraction $\frac{2}{4}$ can be written in lowest terms. So $\frac{26}{4} = 6\frac{2}{4} = 6\frac{1}{2}$.

Remember that an improper fraction names a number greater than or equal to 1.

Write a whole number or a mixed number for each improper fraction. Write each fraction in lowest terms.

1. $\frac{20}{6}$ **2.** $\frac{36}{12}$ **3.** $\frac{36}{8}$

Set F pages 320–321

Estimate $\frac{1}{3} + \frac{6}{7}$.

Think: $\frac{1}{3}$ is less than $\frac{1}{2}$, and $\frac{6}{7}$ is greater than $\frac{1}{2}$.

The sum is greater than the larger fraction.

Remember that the sum is less than 1 if each addend is less than $\frac{1}{2}$, and greater than 1 if each addend is greater than $\frac{1}{2}$. Estimate each sum.

1. $\frac{3}{4} + \frac{5}{6}$ **2.** $\frac{1}{5} + \frac{3}{8}$ **3.** $\frac{1}{3} + \frac{1}{4}$

Set G pages 324–325

Write $\frac{7}{8}$ and $\frac{1}{12}$ with the least common denominator.

List multiples of each denominator.
Multiples of 8: 8, 16, 24, 32, 40
Multiples of 12: 12, 24, 36, 48
The least common multiple of 8 and 12 is 24.

$$\frac{7}{8} = \frac{21}{24} \leftarrow 7 \times 3 \atop \leftarrow 8 \times 3 \qquad \frac{1}{12} = \frac{2}{24} \leftarrow 1 \times 2 \atop \leftarrow 12 \times 2$$

Remember that multiplying the numerator and denominator by the same number does not change the value of the fraction.

Write the fractions with the least common denominator.

1. $\frac{2}{5}, \frac{1}{6}$ **2.** $\frac{1}{3}, \frac{2}{9}$ **3.** $\frac{5}{6}, \frac{4}{9}$

Set H pages 326–327

Compare $2\frac{5}{6}$ and $2\frac{7}{8}$.

Write the fractions with the least common denominator, 24.

$$2\frac{5}{6} = 2\frac{20}{24} \qquad 2\frac{7}{8} = 2\frac{21}{24}$$

Since $2\frac{20}{24} < 2\frac{21}{24}$, then $2\frac{5}{6} < 2\frac{7}{8}$.

Remember that the inequality symbol always points to the smaller number.

Compare the fractions, whole numbers, and mixed numbers. Use $<$, $>$, or $=$.

1. $\frac{3}{4} ⬚ \frac{1}{2}$ **2.** $\frac{3}{8} ⬚ \frac{5}{12}$ **3.** $1\frac{3}{4} ⬚ 1\frac{9}{12}$

Set I pages 328–329

The number nine tenths can be written as a decimal or as a fraction.

$$0.9 = \frac{9}{10}$$

Remember that the first place to the right of the decimal point is the tenths place.

Write each decimal as a fraction. Write all fractions in lowest terms.

1. 0.8   **2.** 0.32   **3.** 0.202

More Practice

Set A pages 308–309

What fraction of the

1. letters are Es?   **2.** symbols are dollar signs?   **3.** punctuation marks are commas?

   E E G T E   % $ #   ? , , ? ! !

4. Write a fraction to name the point labeled B.

    0   B   1

Write the fraction.

5. Three fifths   **6.** Five sixths   **7.** One fourth   **8.** Seven sixteenths

Set B pages 310–311

Multiply to find each fraction.

1. $\frac{1}{4} = \frac{4}{}$ **2.** $\frac{5}{8} = \frac{15}{}$ **3.** $\frac{5}{6} = \frac{}{24}$ **4.** $\frac{7}{7} = \frac{}{14}$

Divide to find each fraction.

5. $\frac{24}{32} = \frac{}{4}$ **6.** $\frac{9}{24} = \frac{}{8}$ **7.** $\frac{30}{36} = \frac{5}{}$ **8.** $\frac{10}{12} = \frac{5}{}$

Set C pages 312–313

Write the greatest common factor of the numerator and denominator.

1. $\frac{6}{15}$ **2.** $\frac{11}{19}$ **3.** $\frac{18}{24}$ **4.** $\frac{16}{36}$ **5.** $\frac{15}{35}$

Write each fraction in lowest terms.

6. $\frac{4}{8}$ **7.** $\frac{6}{18}$ **8.** $\frac{10}{45}$ **9.** $\frac{15}{60}$ **10.** $\frac{9}{24}$

Set D pages 314–315

Write a mixed number.

1. One and three fourths   **2.** Two and five sixths   **3.** Five and two fifths

Use the number lines on page 315 to answer the questions.

4. What fraction is equal to $\frac{4}{6}$?   **5.** What whole number is equal to $\frac{8}{4}$?

6. What mixed number is equal to $\frac{5}{4}$?   **7.** What improper fraction is equal to $1\frac{5}{6}$?

8. Which fraction is less, $\frac{2}{3}$ or $\frac{4}{8}$?   **9.** Which number is greater, $1\frac{3}{8}$ or $\frac{7}{4}$?

Set E pages 316–317

Write a whole number or a mixed number for each improper fraction. **Remember** to write each fraction in lowest terms.

1. $\frac{21}{4}$　　　　**2.** $\frac{26}{6}$　　　　**3.** $\frac{48}{15}$　　　　**4.** $\frac{68}{17}$　　　　**5.** $\frac{34}{16}$

Tell whether you would use paper and pencil or mental math. Write each quotient as a whole number, a mixed number, or a proper fraction.

6. $4\overline{)19}$　　　**7.** $8\overline{)33}$　　　**8.** $9\overline{)263}$　　　**9.** $12\overline{)136}$　　　**10.** $20\overline{)4}$

Set F pages 320–321

Tell if the fraction is less than $\frac{1}{2}$, equal to $\frac{1}{2}$, or greater than $\frac{1}{2}$.

1. $\frac{2}{3}$　　**2.** $\frac{1}{4}$　　**3.** $\frac{9}{12}$　　**4.** $\frac{2}{7}$　　**5.** $\frac{8}{16}$　　**6.** $\frac{39}{41}$　　**7.** $\frac{50}{100}$

Estimate whether each sum is (a) less than 1, (b) greater than 1, or (c) greater than the larger fraction.

8. $\frac{1}{4} + \frac{5}{8}$　　　**9.** $\frac{5}{9} + \frac{7}{12}$　　　**10.** $\frac{7}{15} + \frac{2}{5}$　　　**11.** $\frac{7}{8} + \frac{5}{16}$　　　**12.** $\frac{1}{2} + \frac{4}{5}$

Set G pages 324–325

Write the fractions with the least common denominator.

1. $\frac{1}{6}, \frac{3}{4}$　　　**2.** $\frac{1}{3}, \frac{1}{15}$　　　**3.** $\frac{3}{10}, \frac{1}{5}$　　　**4.** $\frac{5}{6}, \frac{3}{8}$　　　**5.** $\frac{1}{4}, \frac{2}{5}$

Set H pages 326–327

Compare the fractions, whole numbers, and mixed numbers. Use $<$, $>$, or $=$. **Remember** to find the least common denominator.

1. $\frac{5}{8} \,\blacksquare\, \frac{3}{4}$　　　　**2.** $\frac{2}{3} \,\blacksquare\, \frac{3}{5}$　　　　**3.** $1 \,\blacksquare\, \frac{7}{8}$　　　　**4.** $4\frac{1}{4} \,\blacksquare\, 4\frac{1}{5}$

Write the fractions, whole numbers, and mixed numbers in order from least to greatest.

5. $\frac{7}{8}, \frac{3}{4}, \frac{5}{6}$　　　**6.** $1\frac{2}{3}, 1\frac{3}{8}, 1\frac{1}{4}$　　　**7.** $\frac{1}{3}, \frac{2}{5}, \frac{1}{6}$

Set I pages 328–329

Write each decimal as a fraction or a mixed number. **Remember** to write all fractions in lowest terms.

1. 0.3　　　　**2.** 0.46　　　　**3.** 2.38　　　　**4.** 0.275

Mental Math Write each fraction with a denominator of 10, 100, or 1,000. Then write it as a decimal.

5. $\frac{1}{5}$　　　　**6.** $\frac{4}{25}$　　　　**7.** $\frac{9}{500}$　　　　**8.** $\frac{3}{4}$

Enrichment

Terminating and Repeating Decimals

Byron was using his calculator to change the fractions on page 329 to decimals. After he finished with those fractions, he thought he would try some others. Here are the fractions he tried, along with the results:

$\frac{5}{12}$ **Press:** 5 $\div$ 12 $=$ **Display:** *0.4166666*

$\frac{6}{11}$ **Press:** 6 $\div$ 11 $=$ **Display:** *0.5454545*

$\frac{7}{32}$ **Press:** 7 $\div$ 32 $=$ **Display:** *0.21875*

The decimals for $\frac{5}{12}$ and $\frac{6}{11}$ are **repeating decimals**. A repeating decimal has a digit or pattern of digits that repeats endlessly. To write a repeating decimal, put a bar over the digit or digits that repeat.

$0.4166666\ldots = 0.41\overline{6}$ $0.5454545\ldots = 0.\overline{54}$

The decimal for $\frac{7}{32}$ is a **terminating decimal**. Terminating decimals have digits in an exact number of decimal places.

Calculator Use your calculator to change these fractions to decimals.

1. $\frac{3}{4}$ 2. $\frac{5}{8}$ 3. $\frac{4}{9}$ 4. $\frac{5}{6}$ 5. $\frac{17}{20}$ 6. $\frac{5}{24}$

7. $\frac{11}{32}$ 8. $\frac{8}{15}$ 9. $\frac{13}{16}$ 10. $\frac{29}{40}$ 11. $\frac{9}{11}$ 12. $\frac{7}{18}$

13. For each fraction, write the prime factorization of the denominator.

14. What are the prime factors of denominators in fractions that become terminating decimals?

15. What are the prime factors of denominators in fractions that become repeating decimals?

16. How can you tell if a fraction will be a terminating or a repeating decimal by looking at the denominator?

Chapter 10 Review/Test

Write a fraction to name the shaded part.

1.   **2.**

Multiply or divide to find equal fractions.

3. $\frac{7}{8} = \frac{14}{\ \ }$ **4.** $\frac{10}{20} = \frac{\ \ }{2}$

Write each fraction in lowest terms.

5. $\frac{10}{16}$ **6.** $\frac{12}{20}$

7. What mixed number equals $\frac{5}{4}$?

Write a whole number or a fraction for each improper fraction.

8. $\frac{19}{8}$ **9.** $\frac{30}{10}$

Tell if the fraction is less than $\frac{1}{2}$, equal to $\frac{1}{2}$, or greater than $\frac{1}{2}$.

10. $\frac{1}{12}$ **11.** $\frac{29}{32}$

Write the fractions with the least common denominator.

12. $\frac{7}{16}$ $\frac{3}{8}$ **13.** $\frac{2}{3}$ $\frac{1}{4}$

Compare the fractions, whole numbers, and mixed numbers.

14. $\frac{5}{8}$ ▦ $\frac{1}{2}$ **15.** 7 ▦ $6\frac{2}{3}$

Write each decimal as a fraction or a mixed number.

16. 0.8   **17.** 2.19

18. Hal picked some tomatoes and gave $\frac{1}{2}$ of them to Melissa. She gave 4 away and had 3 left. How many tomatoes did Hal pick?

Read this problem. Then answer the questions below.

Arturo is packing glasses in boxes that hold 8 glasses each. If he has 50 glasses to pack, how many boxes will he need?

19. Which statement describes a method for getting a reasonable answer?

a. Divide. Use the whole-number part of the quotient.

b. Divide. Use the remainder.

c. Divide. Write the quotient as a mixed number.

d. Divide. Add 1 to the whole-number part of the quotient, if the remainder is not zero.

20. Solve the problem.

21. **Write About Math**   Write a sentence in which a fraction is used to name part of a set.

Exploring Addition and Subtraction of Fractions

Did You Know: Fractions are used in different measurements:

- Fingernails grow about $\frac{1}{25}$ of an inch a week. They grow faster on the hand you use the most.
- On the average, human hair grows an average of $\frac{1}{2}$ inch a month. It grows slower as you age.
- You are about $\frac{1}{4}$ inch taller when you get up in the morning than when you go to bed at night. The cartilage between the vertebrae of your spine is compressed as you stand and move during the day. It recovers as you sleep.

Number-Sense Project

Estimate
Who can estimate the length of short lines more accurately: adults or students your age?

Gather Data
Draw 5 lines on a sheet of paper from 1 to 8 inches long. Have 2 adults and 2 classmates estimate the length of your lines to the nearest $\frac{1}{4}$ inch.

Analyze and Report
Compute the accuracy of the different estimates. Share your results with other students. Who was more accurate in estimating?

341

Adding Fractions: Same Denominator

Build Understanding

Cheese, one of the world's most important foods, is made from the milk of many different animals. For example, in Europe and Asia, cheese is made from the milk of buffaloes, goats, and sheep. Reindeer milk is used to make cheese in Lapland, while milk from yaks is used in Tibet.

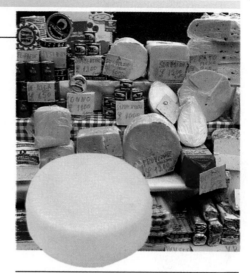

Cheese is frequently used in such recipes as pizza, eggplant parmigiana, and enchiladas.

A. Many cheeses are molded into cylindrical shapes called wheels. Last week, Chef Angelo used $\frac{2}{6}$ of a wheel of *Parmesan,* a popular Italian cheese. This week he used $\frac{3}{6}$ of a wheel. How much did he use in all?

Use addition to find the total. Add $\frac{2}{6} + \frac{3}{6}$.

2 sixths + 3 sixths = 5 sixths

$$\frac{2}{6}$$
$$+\frac{3}{6}$$
$$\overline{\frac{5}{6}}$$

To add two fractions with the same denominator, add the numerators. Write their sum over the common denominator.

$$\frac{2}{6} + \frac{3}{6} = \frac{2+3}{6} = \frac{5}{6}$$

Chef Angelo used $\frac{5}{6}$ of a wheel of cheese.

B. Find the sum of $\frac{3}{4}$ and $\frac{3}{4}$.

$$\frac{3}{4}$$
$$+\frac{3}{4}$$
$$\overline{\frac{6}{4}} = 1\frac{2}{4} = 1\frac{1}{2}$$

Always write the answer in simplest form. Change improper fractions to mixed numbers and write fractions in lowest terms.

■ **Talk About Math** In Example A, if Chef Angelo uses another $\frac{1}{6}$ of a wheel, what will be the total amount used? Explain.

Check Understanding

For another example, see Set A, pages 374–375.

Add these fractions. **Remember** to simplify the answer if necessary.

1.   3 fifths
   + 1 fifth

2.
$$\frac{3}{8} + \frac{1}{8}$$

3. $\frac{2}{7}$
$+\frac{2}{7}$

4. $\frac{3}{5}$
$+\frac{4}{5}$

Practice

For More Practice, see Set A, pages 376–377.

Add the fractions. **Remember** to simplify the answer if necessary.

5. $\dfrac{1}{5}$
$+\dfrac{1}{5}$

6. $\dfrac{4}{10}$
$+\dfrac{5}{10}$

7. $\dfrac{2}{8}$
$+\dfrac{3}{8}$

8. $\dfrac{2}{8}$
$+\dfrac{4}{8}$

9. $\dfrac{6}{12}$
$+\dfrac{3}{12}$

10. $\dfrac{7}{9}$
$+\dfrac{4}{9}$

11. $\dfrac{7}{10}$
$+\dfrac{9}{10}$

12. $\dfrac{7}{11} + \dfrac{4}{11}$

13. $\dfrac{3}{9} + \dfrac{7}{9}$

14. $\dfrac{4}{5} + \dfrac{3}{5} + \dfrac{1}{5}$

15. $\dfrac{5}{12} + \dfrac{7}{12} + \dfrac{6}{12}$

16. $\dfrac{3}{10} + \dfrac{4}{10} + \dfrac{5}{10}$

17. $\dfrac{2}{5} + \dfrac{4}{5} + \dfrac{1}{5}$

18. $\dfrac{5}{6} + \dfrac{2}{6} + \dfrac{5}{6}$

19. $\dfrac{5}{16} + \dfrac{7}{16} + \dfrac{6}{16}$

20.　　3 sevenths
　　+ 2 sevenths

21.　　1 fourth
　　+ 2 fourths

22.　　2 eighths
　　+ 3 eighths

23.　　5 tenths
　　+ 2 tenths

Problem Solving

Solve each problem.

24. Jessie bought two pieces of *Kasseri,* a Greek cheese made from sheep's milk. One piece weighed $\frac{5}{8}$ pound and the other weighed $\frac{4}{8}$ pound. Find the total weight of the cheese.

25. The Old World Room serves *fondue,* a Swiss recipe for warm cheese sauce. They used 11 pounds of *Gruyère* one evening. What fraction of a 77-pound wheel is this?

26. *Roquefort* is a French cheese made from sheep's milk. It is aged in caves in France. Rial's Cafe charges $1.75 for a salad and an additional $0.75 for Roquefort salad dressing. What is the total price of a salad and Roquefort dressing?

27. In Mexico, people enjoy *Guajaqueno,* a cheese made from goat's milk. It is formed into long, stringy fibers and then rolled up like yarn. Kent ate a strand of Guajaqueno that was 2 feet long. Write 2 feet in inches.

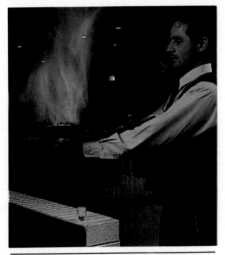

Saganaki is a flaming Greek dish made with *Kasseri* cheese.

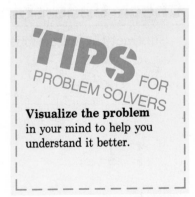

TIPS FOR PROBLEM SOLVERS

Visualize the problem in your mind to help you understand it better.

Subtracting Fractions: Same Denominator

Build Understanding

Greta's house is $\frac{1}{8}$ of a mile from the Twin Oaks shopping mall. Flora's house is $\frac{5}{8}$ of a mile from the mall. How much farther is Flora's house from the mall than Greta's house?

Use subtraction to compare the distances. Subtract $\frac{5}{8} - \frac{1}{8}$.

$$
\begin{array}{r}
5 \ \text{eighths} \\
- 1 \ \text{eighth} \\
\hline
4 \ \text{eighths}
\end{array}
$$

Twin Oaks
Shopping Mall

Greta's
House

Flora's
House

Notice how each method below gives the same answer. The answer is written in lowest terms to give the difference a simpler name.

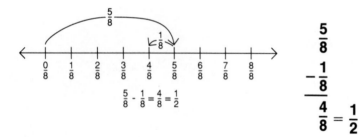

$$\frac{5}{8} - \frac{1}{8} = \frac{4}{8} = \frac{1}{2}$$

$$
\begin{array}{r}
\dfrac{5}{8} \\
- \dfrac{1}{8} \\
\hline
\dfrac{4}{8} = \dfrac{1}{2}
\end{array}
$$

To subtract two fractions with the same denominator, subtract the numerators. Write their difference over the common denominator.

$$\frac{5}{8} - \frac{1}{8} = \frac{5-1}{8} = \frac{4}{8}$$

Write the answer in lowest terms.

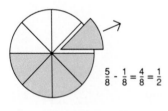

$$\frac{5}{8} - \frac{1}{8} = \frac{4}{8} = \frac{1}{2}$$

Flora's house is $\frac{1}{2}$ mile farther from the mall than is Greta's house.

■ **Talk About Math**
Explain how to check the subtraction in the example.

Check Understanding

For another example, see Set B, pages 374–375.

Subtract these fractions. Write the answer in simplest form.

1.

$$\frac{4}{5} - \frac{1}{5}$$

2.

$$\frac{5}{6} - \frac{1}{6}$$

3.
$$
\begin{array}{r}
5 \ \text{sevenths} \\
- 2 \ \text{sevenths}
\end{array}
$$

Practice

For More Practice, see Set B, pages 376–377.

Subtract the fractions. **Remember** to simplify the answers if necessary.

4. $\frac{2}{3} - \frac{1}{3}$

5. $\frac{4}{5} - \frac{2}{5}$

6. $\frac{7}{8} - \frac{1}{8}$

7. $\frac{5}{6} - \frac{3}{6}$

8. $\frac{6}{7} - \frac{3}{7}$

9. $\frac{11}{12} - \frac{5}{12}$

10. $\frac{8}{15} - \frac{2}{15}$

11. $\frac{8}{8} - \frac{3}{8}$

12. $\frac{2}{4} - \frac{1}{4}$

13. $\frac{5}{6} - \frac{2}{6}$

14. $\frac{7}{9} - \frac{5}{9}$

15. $\frac{12}{13} - \frac{10}{13}$

16. $\frac{5}{5} - \frac{1}{5}$

17. $\frac{9}{10} - \frac{7}{10}$

18. $\frac{20}{24} - \frac{12}{24}$

19. $\frac{13}{17} - \frac{3}{17}$

20. $\frac{8}{9} - \frac{3}{9}$

21. $\frac{12}{10} - \frac{2}{10}$

22. $\frac{3}{8} - \frac{3}{8}$

23. $\frac{9}{6} - \frac{3}{6}$

24. 4 sixths − 3 sixths

25. 8 tenths − 1 tenth

26. 8 ninths − 3 ninths

27. 4 fourths − 1 fourth

Mixed Practice   Add or subtract these fractions. Write your answers in simplest form. Check your work.

28. $\frac{3}{4} + \frac{5}{4}$

29. $\frac{11}{28} + \frac{13}{28}$

30. $\frac{7}{21} + \frac{7}{21}$

31. $\frac{5}{9} + \frac{4}{9}$

32. $\frac{17}{10} - \frac{7}{10}$

33. $\frac{15}{22} - \frac{4}{22}$

34. $\frac{6}{14} - \frac{4}{14}$

35. $\frac{21}{13} - \frac{17}{13}$

36. $\frac{9}{10} - \frac{5}{10}$

37. $\frac{11}{16} - \frac{7}{16}$

38. $\frac{7}{8} + \frac{3}{8}$

39. $\frac{4}{5} + \frac{4}{5}$

40. $\frac{7}{6} - \frac{3}{6}$

41. $\frac{1}{4} + \frac{1}{4} + \frac{3}{4}$

42. $\frac{5}{12} - \frac{1}{12}$

43. $\frac{7}{10} + \frac{3}{10} + \frac{5}{10}$

44. $\frac{1}{6} + \frac{5}{6} + \frac{5}{6}$

45. $\frac{11}{15} - \frac{6}{15}$

46. $\frac{7}{9} + \frac{3}{9} + \frac{5}{9}$

47. $\frac{17}{20} - \frac{7}{20}$

Problem Solving

Read for the facts to solve the problems.

48. Franco takes 18 minutes to walk to the mall. William can walk there in only 8 minutes. By what fraction of an hour longer does it take Franco to walk to the mall?

49. Franco spent 23 minutes shopping for school supplies. He spent another 18 minutes shopping for gym equipment. How many minutes did he spend in all?

Adding and Subtracting Mixed Numbers: Same Denominator

Build Understanding

A. Lou and Gina were helping their father make a carrot salad for a party. They used $8\frac{1}{3}$ cups of shredded carrots and $4\frac{1}{3}$ cups of raisins. How many cups would the mixing bowl need to hold for just these two ingredients?

Use addition to find a total. Find $8\frac{1}{3} + 4\frac{1}{3}$.

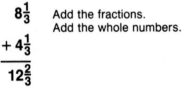

$$\begin{array}{r} 8\frac{1}{3} \\ +\ 4\frac{1}{3} \\ \hline 12\frac{2}{3} \end{array}$$

Add the fractions.
Add the whole numbers.

The bowl must hold at least $12\frac{2}{3}$ cups.

B. Estimation Estimate to find the sum of $10\frac{2}{5}$ and $6\frac{3}{7}$.

$$\begin{array}{r} 10\frac{2}{5} \\ +\ 6\frac{3}{7} \\ \hline \end{array}$$

Use only the whole number parts.

$$10 + 6 = 16$$

$10\frac{2}{5} + 6\frac{3}{7}$ is about 16.

C. Find $19\frac{3}{4} - 17\frac{1}{4}$.

Estimate by using whole number parts: $19 - 17 = 2$.

$$\begin{array}{r} 19\frac{3}{4} \\ -\ 17\frac{1}{4} \\ \hline 2\frac{2}{4} = 2\frac{1}{2} \end{array}$$

First, subtract the fractions. Then subtract the whole numbers.

Write the answer in simplest form.

■ **Talk About Math** When you estimate using whole number parts, what can you say about how your estimate compares to the sum?

Check Understanding

For another example, see Set C, pages 374–375.

Choose the correct answer.

1. $\begin{array}{r} 1\frac{1}{6} \\ +\ 4\frac{4}{6} \end{array}$ **a.** $5\frac{5}{12}$ **b.** $5\frac{5}{6}$ **c.** $6\frac{5}{6}$

2. $\begin{array}{r} 5\frac{4}{5} \\ -\ 3\frac{1}{5} \end{array}$ **a.** $2\frac{1}{5}$ **b.** $1\frac{5}{5}$ **c.** $2\frac{3}{5}$

Practice

For More Practice, see Set C, pages 376–377.

Add. **Remember** to write your answers in simplest form.

3. $\quad 3\frac{3}{5}$ $\qquad$ **4.** $\quad 1\frac{5}{9}$ $\qquad$ **5.** $\quad 8\frac{1}{12}$ $\qquad$ **6.** $\quad 3\frac{2}{8}$ $\qquad$ **7.** $\quad 14\frac{3}{15}$ $\qquad$ **8.** $\quad 21\frac{4}{17}$

$\quad +2\frac{1}{5}$ $\qquad$ $\quad +4\frac{3}{9}$ $\qquad$ $\quad +\frac{10}{12}$ $\qquad$ $\quad +7\frac{3}{8}$ $\qquad$ $\quad +12\frac{3}{15}$ $\qquad$ $\quad +\ 9\frac{3}{17}$

9. $6\frac{3}{10} + 2\frac{5}{10}$ $\qquad$ **10.** $9\frac{1}{4} + 5\frac{1}{4}$ $\qquad$ **11.** $2\frac{5}{8} + 6\frac{1}{8}$ $\qquad$ **12.** $8\frac{1}{2} + 8$

13. $1\frac{3}{16} + 5\frac{7}{16}$ $\qquad$ **14.** $7\frac{1}{6} + 3\frac{4}{6}$ $\qquad$ **15.** $2\frac{1}{3} + 12\frac{1}{3}$ $\qquad$ **16.** $\frac{5}{9} + 6\frac{1}{9}$

17. $8\frac{1}{4} + 10\frac{1}{4} + 6\frac{1}{4}$ $\qquad$ **18.** $7\frac{1}{16} + \frac{3}{16} + 4\frac{1}{16}$ $\qquad$ **19.** $5\frac{1}{5} + 10\frac{2}{5} + \frac{1}{5}$

Subtract. **Remember** to write your answers in simplest form.

20. $\quad 2\frac{8}{14}$ $\qquad$ **21.** $\quad 6\frac{8}{9}$ $\qquad$ **22.** $\quad 8\frac{8}{12}$ $\qquad$ **23.** $\quad 11\frac{13}{15}$ $\qquad$ **24.** $\quad 21\frac{19}{24}$ $\qquad$ **25.** $\quad 13\frac{7}{8}$

$\quad -1\frac{5}{14}$ $\qquad$ $\quad -3\frac{3}{9}$ $\qquad$ $\quad -7\frac{1}{12}$ $\qquad$ $\quad -\ 5\frac{9}{15}$ $\qquad$ $\quad -\ 8\frac{16}{24}$ $\qquad$ $\quad -\ \frac{3}{8}$

26. $5\frac{3}{9} - 2\frac{1}{9}$ $\qquad$ **27.** $7\frac{3}{4} - 5\frac{1}{4}$ $\qquad$ **28.** $2\frac{5}{6} - \frac{1}{6}$ $\qquad$ **29.** $18\frac{1}{3} - 13$

30. $15\frac{7}{10} - 7\frac{2}{10}$ $\qquad$ **31.** $11\frac{8}{16} - 2\frac{3}{16}$ $\qquad$ **32.** $7\frac{9}{12} - 7\frac{5}{12}$ $\qquad$ **33.** $19\frac{17}{20} - 16\frac{5}{20}$

34. $14\frac{3}{4} - 14$ $\qquad$ **35.** $22\frac{13}{18} - 10\frac{3}{18}$ $\qquad$ **36.** $4\frac{7}{8} - 4\frac{1}{8}$ $\qquad$ **37.** $10\frac{5}{6} - 4\frac{5}{6}$

Estimation Estimate using whole number parts.

38. $7\frac{1}{5} + 8\frac{3}{5}$ $\qquad$ **39.** $3\frac{2}{4} + 2\frac{1}{4}$ $\qquad$ **40.** $15\frac{3}{8} - 5\frac{2}{8}$

41. $15\frac{1}{2} - 3\frac{1}{3}$ $\qquad$ **42.** $23\frac{2}{3} - 14\frac{5}{8}$ $\qquad$ **43.** $26\frac{3}{8} + 9\frac{1}{4}$

Problem Solving

44. Write a problem using this information: Mrs. Russo made $11\frac{1}{3}$ quarts of lemonade. Then she made $14\frac{2}{3}$ quarts of orangeade.

45. Amy has a pint container of yogurt. A recipe for onion dip calls for $\frac{3}{4}$ cup of yogurt. Does Amy have enough yogurt to make the recipe three times?

Adding Mixed Numbers: Renaming Sums

Build Understanding

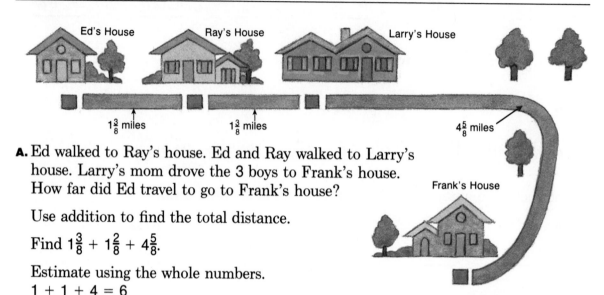

Ed's House   Ray's House   Larry's House

$1\frac{3}{8}$ miles $1\frac{3}{8}$ miles $4\frac{5}{8}$ miles

Frank's House

A. Ed walked to Ray's house. Ed and Ray walked to Larry's house. Larry's mom drove the 3 boys to Frank's house. How far did Ed travel to go to Frank's house?

Use addition to find the total distance.

Find $1\frac{3}{8} + 1\frac{2}{8} + 4\frac{5}{8}$.

Estimate using the whole numbers.
$1 + 1 + 4 = 6$

Add the fractions.
Add the whole numbers.

$$1\frac{3}{8}$$

$$1\frac{2}{8}$$

$$+4\frac{5}{8}$$

$$\overline{6\frac{10}{8}} = 7\frac{1}{4}$$

Rename the sum.

$6\frac{10}{8} = 6 + \frac{10}{8}$

$= 6 + 1\frac{2}{8}$

$= 7\frac{2}{8} = 7\frac{1}{4}$

Ed traveled $7\frac{1}{4}$ miles.

B. Mental Math   Sometimes you can add mixed numbers mentally. Look for fractions whose sum will equal 1.

Find $1\frac{4}{5} + 1\frac{3}{5} + 2\frac{1}{5}$.

$1\frac{4}{5} + 1\frac{3}{5} + 2\frac{1}{5}$ $\frac{4}{5} + \frac{1}{5} = \frac{5}{5} = 1$

$1 + 1 + 1\frac{3}{5} + 2 = 5\frac{3}{5}$

■ **Talk About Math**   How would you use the fraction part of the mixed numbers in Example A to find an estimate closer to the actual sum?

Check Understanding

For another example, see Set D, pages 374–375.

For Exercises 1 and 2, tell which is the correct answer.

1. $2\frac{3}{8} + \frac{3}{8} + 5\frac{4}{8}$

   a. $8\frac{1}{2}$ **b.** $8\frac{1}{4}$ **c.** 8

2. $17\frac{5}{6} + 7\frac{2}{6}$

   a. $24\frac{5}{6}$ **b.** $25\frac{1}{6}$ **c.** $25\frac{7}{6}$

Practice

For More Practice, see Set D, pages 376–377.

Add. **Remember** to write your answers in simplest form.

3. $\frac{3}{6}$
$+1\frac{5}{6}$

4. $\frac{1}{2}$
$+1\frac{1}{2}$

5. $1\frac{3}{4}$
$+5\frac{1}{4}$

6. $7\frac{14}{15}$
$+8\frac{8}{15}$

7. $16\frac{1}{13}$
$+16\frac{12}{13}$

8. $21\frac{5}{10}$
$+13\frac{9}{10}$

9. $15\frac{2}{5} + 8\frac{4}{5}$

10. $2\frac{13}{16} + 10\frac{9}{16}$

11. $5\frac{5}{6} + 5\frac{1}{6}$

12. $13\frac{8}{9} + 1\frac{5}{9}$

13. $11\frac{2}{8} + 5\frac{7}{8}$

14. $4\frac{13}{20} + 7\frac{11}{20}$

15. $9\frac{7}{10} + 9\frac{3}{10}$

16. $6\frac{5}{6} + \frac{4}{6}$

17. $3\frac{2}{3} + 5\frac{2}{3}$

18. $\frac{11}{18} + 9\frac{15}{18}$

19. $5\frac{1}{2} + 5\frac{1}{2}$

20. $2\frac{3}{4} + 7\frac{2}{4}$

21. $15\frac{2}{8} + 10\frac{3}{8} + 4\frac{5}{8}$

22. $2\frac{11}{12} + 10\frac{2}{12} + \frac{3}{12}$

23. $11\frac{5}{6} + 4 + 8\frac{1}{6}$

24. $7 + 21\frac{2}{3} + 6\frac{2}{3}$

25. $10\frac{1}{4} + 10\frac{3}{4} + 6\frac{1}{4}$

26. $4\frac{2}{3} + 14\frac{2}{3} + 2\frac{1}{3}$

Mental Math   Use mental math to add these fractions.

27. $1\frac{5}{8} + 1\frac{3}{8} + 2\frac{1}{8}$

28. $6\frac{1}{3} + 2\frac{1}{3} + 1\frac{2}{3}$

29. $5\frac{3}{5} + 5\frac{3}{5} + \frac{2}{5}$

30. $5\frac{1}{4} + 2\frac{3}{4} + 4\frac{3}{4}$

31. $4\frac{5}{12} + 1\frac{9}{12} + \frac{3}{12}$

32. $3\frac{3}{10} + 2 + 8\frac{7}{10}$

Problem Solving

Use the map to help you solve the problems.

33. How far is it from Anna's house to Fred's house?

34. How much farther is it from school to Fred's house than from Lou's house to Fred's house?

35. How much farther is it from the school to Lou's house than from Lou's house to Anna's house?

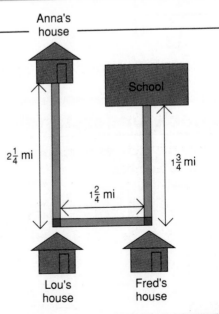

349

Subtracting from a Whole Number

Build Understanding

A. Manuel is a pianist. He is preparing for a concert. He has practiced $3\frac{1}{4}$ hours so far today. He practices 7 hours every day. How much longer must he practice?

Since you want to know how much time is left, subtract.

Find $7 - 3\frac{1}{4}$.

To subtract fourths from 7, rename 7 as a mixed number with the fraction part in fourths.

The standard piano keyboard has 88 keys that are arranged according to pitch.

$$
\begin{array}{ll}
7 & 7 = 6 + 1 \\
-3\frac{1}{4} & = 6 + \frac{4}{4}
\end{array}
$$

$$
\begin{aligned}
7 &= 6\frac{4}{4} \\
-3\frac{1}{4} &= 3\frac{1}{4} \\
\hline
& 3\frac{3}{4}
\end{aligned}
$$

Manuel must practice for $3\frac{3}{4}$ hours longer.

B. Find $1 - \frac{7}{12}$.

$$
\begin{aligned}
1 &= \frac{12}{12} \qquad \text{Rename 1 as } \frac{12}{12}. \\
&\phantom{= \frac{12}{12} \qquad} \text{Subtract the fractions.} \\
-\frac{7}{12} &= \frac{7}{12} \\
\hline
& \frac{5}{12}
\end{aligned}
$$

■ **Talk About Math** In Example B, why is 1 renamed as $\frac{12}{12}$? Could 1 be renamed as $\frac{4}{4}$? Why or why not?

Check Understanding

For another example, see Set E, pages 374–375.

Use the pictures to rename each whole number.

1.

$3 = 2\frac{}{8}$

2.

$4 = 3\frac{}{}$

Copy and complete each subtraction exercise.

3.
$$
\begin{aligned}
5 &= 4\frac{}{8} \\
-2\frac{3}{8} &= 2\frac{3}{8} \\
\hline
\end{aligned}
$$

4.
$$
\begin{aligned}
1 &= \frac{}{} \\
-\frac{2}{5} &= \frac{2}{} \\
\hline
\end{aligned}
$$

Practice

For More Practice, see Set E, pages 376–377.

Rename each whole number.

5. $1 = \frac{}{8}$ **6.** $3 = 2\frac{}{6}$ **7.** $6 = 5\frac{}{12}$ **8.** $15 = 14\frac{}{10}$

Subtract. **Remember** to write your answers in simplest form.

9. $\begin{array}{r} 1 \\ -\frac{7}{10} \\ \hline \end{array}$ **10.** $\begin{array}{r} 2 \\ -1\frac{6}{11} \\ \hline \end{array}$ **11.** $\begin{array}{r} 4 \\ -2\frac{1}{2} \\ \hline \end{array}$ **12.** $\begin{array}{r} 7 \\ -3\frac{14}{15} \\ \hline \end{array}$ **13.** $\begin{array}{r} 5 \\ -2\frac{9}{10} \\ \hline \end{array}$

14. $\begin{array}{r} 6 \\ -1\frac{1}{6} \\ \hline \end{array}$ **15.** $\begin{array}{r} 12 \\ -8\frac{7}{9} \\ \hline \end{array}$ **16.** $\begin{array}{r} 20 \\ -3\frac{1}{4} \\ \hline \end{array}$ **17.** $\begin{array}{r} 25 \\ -13\frac{5}{7} \\ \hline \end{array}$ **18.** $\begin{array}{r} 32 \\ -30\frac{4}{5} \\ \hline \end{array}$

19. $1 - \frac{7}{16}$ **20.** $3 - 1\frac{17}{20}$ **21.** $32 - 17\frac{9}{11}$ **22.** $46 - 1\frac{14}{17}$ **23.** $42 - 41\frac{12}{13}$

24. $5 - 2\frac{1}{3}$ **25.** $6 - 3\frac{7}{8}$ **26.** $10 - 8\frac{4}{5}$ **27.** $3 - 2\frac{3}{10}$ **28.** $7 - \frac{4}{9}$

29. $9 - 8\frac{13}{20}$ **30.** $27 - \frac{7}{12}$ **31.** $14 - 11\frac{5}{24}$ **32.** $38 - 31\frac{1}{4}$ **33.** $16 - \frac{2}{5}$

Mixed Practice Add or subtract. **Remember** to write your answers in simplest form.

34. $6\frac{4}{9} + 2\frac{1}{9}$ **35.** $4\frac{1}{5} + 5\frac{4}{5}$ **36.** $7\frac{2}{3} - 5\frac{1}{3}$ **37.** $9\frac{5}{8} + 3\frac{5}{8}$ **38.** $17 - 4\frac{5}{11}$

39. $5\frac{5}{6} + 2\frac{1}{6}$ **40.** $12 - 4\frac{5}{16}$ **41.** $5\frac{11}{12} - \frac{7}{12}$ **42.** $10\frac{9}{10} + 6\frac{3}{10}$ **43.** $5 + 9\frac{3}{4} + 1\frac{3}{4}$

Problem Solving

44. Manuel spends $2\frac{1}{2}$ hours practicing exercises during his 7 hours of daily practice. How much of his practice time is left to practice the pieces he will play?

45. Manuel's last concert was $2\frac{3}{4}$ hours long. Before the concert, he practiced for $3\frac{3}{4}$ hours. How many hours did Manuel play the piano that day?

46. **Critical Thinking** Explain two different ways to solve this problem. Then give the answer. On the standard piano keyboard, 36 of the 88 keys are black. What fraction of the keys are white?

Subtracting Mixed Numbers with Renaming

Build Understanding

The first time Shaun tried an experiment in science class, he used $7\frac{3}{8}$ inches of wire. The second time he did the experiment, he needed only $5\frac{7}{8}$ inches. How many inches more did he use in the first experiment than in the second experiment?

You want to find how many more inches. You can subtract. Find $7\frac{3}{8} - 5\frac{7}{8}$.

You cannot subtract the fractions because $\frac{7}{8}$ is greater than $\frac{3}{8}$. Rename $7\frac{3}{8}$.

$$\begin{array}{l} 7\frac{3}{8} \\ -5\frac{7}{8} \\ \hline \end{array}$$

Think: $7\frac{3}{8} = 7 + \frac{3}{8}$
$= 6 + 1 + \frac{3}{8}$
$= 6 + \frac{8}{8} + \frac{3}{8}$
$= 6 + \frac{11}{8} = 6\frac{11}{8}$

$$\begin{array}{l} 7\frac{3}{8} = 6\frac{11}{8} \\ -5\frac{7}{8} = 5\frac{7}{8} \\ \hline 1\frac{4}{8} = 1\frac{1}{2} \end{array}$$

Subtract the fractions. Subtract the whole numbers.

Write the answer in simplest form.

Shaun used $1\frac{1}{2}$ inches more wire in the first experiment.

■ **Talk About Math** In the example, why is 1 renamed as $\frac{8}{8}$ and not $\frac{7}{7}$ or $\frac{6}{6}$?

Check Understanding

For another example, see Set F, pages 374–375.

Use the pictures to help you rename the mixed numbers.

1. $2\frac{5}{6} = 1\frac{\square}{6}$

2. $1\frac{2}{3} = \frac{\square}{3}$

Copy and complete each subtraction exercise.

3. $6\frac{1}{3} = 5\frac{\square}{3}$
$-3\frac{2}{3} = 3\frac{2}{3}$
$\overline{}$

4. $4\frac{1}{6} = 3\frac{\square}{6}$
$-2\frac{5}{6} = 2\frac{5}{6}$
$\overline{}$

5. $11\frac{3}{5} = \square\frac{\square}{5}$
$-9\frac{4}{5} = 9\frac{4}{5}$
$\overline{}$

Practice

For More Practice, see Set F, pages 376–377.

Copy and complete the renaming of each mixed number.

6. $7\frac{3}{4} = 6\frac{\square}{4}$　　**7.** $2\frac{2}{9} = 1\frac{\square}{9}$　　**8.** $12\frac{3}{10} = 11\frac{\square}{10}$　　**9.** $25\frac{7}{12} = 24\frac{\square}{12}$

Subtract. **Remember** to write the answer in simplest form.

10. $4\frac{1}{4}$ 　 **11.** $9\frac{3}{8}$ 　 **12.** $7\frac{2}{5}$ 　 **13.** $6\frac{1}{6}$ 　 **14.** $4\frac{5}{8}$ 　 **15.** $3\frac{1}{5}$

$\underline{\ -1\frac{3}{4}\ }$ 　 $\underline{\ -5\frac{5}{8}\ }$ 　 $\underline{\ -2\frac{4}{5}\ }$ 　 $\underline{\ -2\frac{5}{6}\ }$ 　 $\underline{\ -1\frac{7}{8}\ }$ 　 $\underline{\ -1\frac{3}{5}\ }$

16. $13\frac{3}{5} - 4\frac{4}{5}$　　**17.** $12\frac{7}{16} - 10\frac{11}{16}$　　**18.** $8\frac{5}{9} - \frac{8}{9}$　　**19.** $14\frac{1}{12} - 1\frac{7}{12}$

20. $24 - 8\frac{1}{2}$　　**21.** $36 - 28\frac{2}{3}$　　**22.** $16 - 2\frac{3}{4}$　　**23.** $12 - 4\frac{5}{12}$

24. $12\frac{2}{10} - 11\frac{7}{10}$　　**25.** $8\frac{13}{24} - 2\frac{17}{24}$　　**26.** $9\frac{3}{20} - \frac{8}{20}$　　**27.** $11\frac{2}{8} - 5\frac{7}{8}$

28. $13 - 5\frac{2}{3}$　　**29.** $5\frac{1}{5} - 1\frac{3}{5}$　　**30.** $6\frac{7}{10} - 5\frac{8}{10}$　　**31.** $20\frac{1}{4} - 7\frac{3}{4}$

Problem Solving

Read for the facts to solve the problems.

32. For an experiment on the eating habits of gerbils, Ruth put $3\frac{1}{5}$ cups of feed in the gerbils' cage. After 3 days, only $1\frac{4}{5}$ cups were left. How much feed did the gerbils eat?

33. Connie's corn plant was $9\frac{3}{8}$ inches tall on Monday. The plant grew $2\frac{5}{8}$ inches during the week. How tall was the corn plant on Friday?

✓

Midchapter ——— Checkup

Add or subtract. Write your answers in simplest form.

1. $\frac{5}{8} + \frac{3}{8}$　　**2.** $7\frac{10}{14} + 2\frac{3}{14}$　　**3.** $\frac{3}{5} - \frac{2}{5}$　　**4.** $3\frac{7}{12} - 1\frac{5}{12}$

5. $12 + 1\frac{2}{3} + 5\frac{2}{3}$　　**6.** $16\frac{7}{18} - 3\frac{11}{18}$　　**7.** $20 - 4\frac{1}{5}$　　**8.** $4\frac{2}{12} + 3\frac{5}{12} + 7\frac{9}{12}$

Explore as a Team

1. Play *Multiples and Factors* with another player. You will need a new game mat for each game you play. To make a game mat, write the numbers from 1 to 30 on a piece of paper.

• Players take turns. Player A marks an **X** on a *multiple*. Player B marks an **O** on each of the *factors* of Player A's multiple.

• Then Player B marks an **O** on a new multiple. Player A marks **X**s on all of the unmarked factors of Player B's multiple. (Never mark numbers already marked.)

• You may only mark a multiple that still has some factors left for the other player to mark.

• When no more moves are left on the mat, count your points (numbers you marked).

• The player with the greatest number of points is the winner.

2. Discuss with your team.

a. 9 has 3 factors: 1, 9, and 3. Find other numbers with exactly 3 factors.

b. What is the largest factor the other player can get when you mark 30? 29? 28?

c. Which first moves give the other player exactly 1 point?

d. What are the best moves? What are the worst moves?

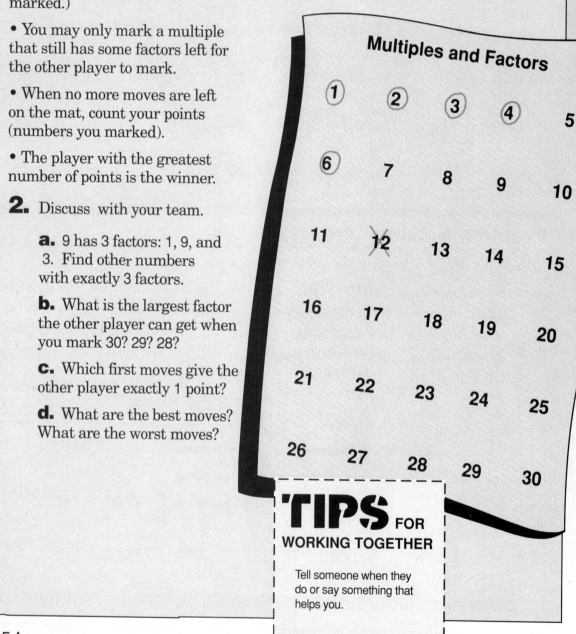

Multiples and Factors

① ② ③ ④ 5
⑥ 7 8 9 10
11 X̶1̶2̶ 13 14 15
16 17 18 19 20
21 22 23 24 25
26 27 28 29 30

TIPS FOR **WORKING TOGETHER**

Tell someone when they do or say something that helps you.

Explore with a Computer

Use the *Fractions Workshop Project* for this activity.

Maria is planning a dinner. A recipe calls for $4\frac{3}{8}$ cups of rice. Maria has $1\frac{1}{2}$ cups of rice. Find how much more rice she needs to buy.

1. At the computer, use the **Mark** option to divide the circles to have equal parts.

2. Use the **Shade** option to fill $4\frac{3}{8}$.

3. Using the **Erase** option, take away $1\frac{1}{2}$ of the shaded parts. How much is left?

Number-Sense Project

Look back at pages 340-341.
A student collected these estimates.

Line	Estimates in inches				Actual length
	Adult 1	Adult 2	Classmate 1	Classmate 2	
1	3	$3\frac{3}{4}$	4	$3\frac{1}{4}$	$3\frac{1}{4}$
2	6	6	6	6	$6\frac{1}{4}$
3	7	$6\frac{1}{2}$	$6\frac{1}{2}$	7	$7\frac{1}{2}$
4	1	$1\frac{1}{4}$	1	$1\frac{3}{4}$	$1\frac{1}{4}$
5	$5\frac{1}{4}$	6	$5\frac{3}{4}$	$5\frac{3}{4}$	$5\frac{3}{4}$

a. How far off was Adult 1 in estimating Line 3?

b. Find the total amount Classmate 1 was off in estimating all 5 lines.

c. Who was the most accurate in their estimates?

d. Write a statement comparing the accuracy of the two adults to the accuracy of the two classmates.

355

Adding and Subtracting Fractions: Related Denominators

Build Understanding

A. Mr. Nochim is building a fence. He wants to bolt two boards together. One board is $\frac{3}{4}$ inch thick and the other is $\frac{1}{2}$ inch thick. To decide on a length of bolt to use, he must find the total thickness of the two boards.

You can see from the rulers that

$$
\begin{array}{rl}
3 \text{ fourths} &= 3 \text{ fourths} \\
+ 1 \text{ half} &= 2 \text{ fourths} \\
\hline
5 \text{ fourths} &= 1\frac{1}{4}
\end{array}
$$

Mr. Nochim needs a bolt longer than $1\frac{1}{4}$ inches.

When you add or subtract fractions, think of the denominators as units. To name the sum or difference, you must use the same size units.

B. Find $\frac{1}{4} + \frac{7}{12}$.

$$\frac{1}{4} = \frac{3}{12} \quad \overset{\times 3}{\underset{\times 3}{}}$$

Find a common denominator. 12 is the least common denominator.

$$+\frac{7}{12} = \frac{7}{12}$$

Write equal fractions with the least common denominator. Add the fractions.

$$\frac{10}{12} = \frac{5}{6}$$

Write the answer in simplest form.

C. Find $\frac{2}{3} - \frac{1}{6}$.

$$\frac{2}{3} = \frac{4}{6} \quad \overset{\times 2}{\underset{\times 2}{}}$$

Find a common denominator. 6 is the least common denominator.

$$-\frac{1}{6} = \frac{1}{6}$$

Write equal fractions with the least common denominator. Subtract the fractions.

$$\frac{3}{6} = \frac{1}{2}$$

Write the answer in simplest form.

■ **Talk About Math** In Example A, why is 4 better than 8 or 16 for a common denominator? Could you use 2 as a common denominator?

Check Understanding

Copy and complete to find equal fractions.

1. $\frac{1}{6} = \frac{}{12}$ **2.** $\frac{1}{4} = \frac{}{16}$ **3.** $\frac{2}{3} = \frac{}{9}$

Copy and complete each exercise.

4. $\frac{1}{3} = \frac{}{}$

$$+\frac{8}{9} = \frac{8}{}$$

5. $\frac{7}{16} = \frac{}{}$

$$-\frac{1}{8} = \frac{}{}$$

356

Practice

Add or subtract by finding a common denominator.
Remember to write your answers in simplest form.

6. $\frac{1}{5}$
  $+\frac{7}{10}$

7. $\frac{1}{6}$
  $+\frac{7}{12}$

8. $\frac{1}{4}$
  $-\frac{1}{8}$

9. $\frac{4}{5}$
  $-\frac{3}{10}$

10. $\frac{1}{2}$
  $+\frac{3}{8}$

11. $\frac{5}{6}$
  $-\frac{2}{3}$

12. $\frac{1}{8} + \frac{3}{4}$ **13.** $\frac{5}{8} - \frac{1}{2}$ **14.** $\frac{1}{6} + \frac{1}{2}$ **15.** $\frac{1}{4} + \frac{5}{8}$ **16.** $\frac{2}{5} - \frac{1}{10}$ **17.** $\frac{2}{9} + \frac{1}{3}$

18. $\frac{3}{4} + \frac{11}{12}$ **19.** $\frac{3}{5} - \frac{4}{15}$ **20.** $\frac{5}{8} + \frac{3}{4}$ **21.** $\frac{7}{15} + \frac{1}{5}$ **22.** $\frac{5}{6} - \frac{1}{12}$ **23.** $\frac{4}{5} - \frac{2}{15}$

24. $\frac{1}{3} - \frac{1}{6}$ **25.** $\frac{5}{18} + \frac{2}{9}$ **26.** $\frac{7}{10} - \frac{1}{2}$ **27.** $\frac{3}{16} + \frac{3}{4}$ **28.** $\frac{3}{20} + \frac{3}{4}$ **29.** $\frac{3}{4} - \frac{1}{12}$

30. $\frac{1}{3} - \frac{2}{15}$ **31.** $\frac{1}{2} - \frac{3}{14}$ **32.** $\frac{1}{6} + \frac{3}{24}$ **33.** $\frac{7}{24} + \frac{7}{12}$ **34.** $\frac{5}{8} - \frac{3}{16}$ **35.** $\frac{1}{20} + \frac{1}{10}$

Number Sense   Name the least common
denominator for the following fractions of an inch.

36. Fourths and eighths

37. Eighths and halves

Mixed Practice   Add or subtract. **Remember** to
write your answers in simplest form.

38. $2\frac{1}{5} + 3\frac{2}{5}$ **39.** $1\frac{5}{8} + 2\frac{3}{8}$ **40.** $3\frac{5}{6} - 2\frac{1}{6}$ **41.** $5\frac{3}{4} - 1\frac{1}{4}$

42. $5\frac{1}{3} - 2\frac{2}{3}$ **43.** $\frac{9}{16} + \frac{1}{4}$ **44.** $7\frac{4}{9} - \frac{7}{9}$ **45.** $\frac{1}{3} + 4\frac{2}{3} + 7\frac{2}{3}$

46. $4 - 1\frac{2}{3}$ **47.** $8 - 3\frac{1}{5}$ **48.** $1\frac{3}{4} + 2\frac{1}{2} + 2\frac{1}{4}$ **49.** $3\frac{3}{5} + 2\frac{9}{10} + 1\frac{4}{5}$

Problem Solving

Solve each problem.

50. Mr. Nochim attached the gate to
the fence in $\frac{3}{4}$ hour. He took
$\frac{2}{12}$ hour to put the handle on
the gate. How much time in all did
he work on the gate?

51. Jackie is nailing two boards
together. Both boards are $\frac{1}{4}$ inch
thick. Will a nail $\frac{3}{8}$ of an inch long
go through both boards?

Use Alternate Strategies

Build Understanding

Mr. Alfano plans to put a chef's work table in the middle of his restaurant kitchen. The kitchen is $12\frac{1}{2}$ feet wide and 18 feet long. The table is 6 feet long and $3\frac{1}{2}$ feet wide. He plans 3 feet of walking space on each side of the table. How much space will be left for cabinets along each end of the room?

Understand Find how much space will not be used for the table or for walking. The kitchen is $12\frac{1}{2}$ feet by 18 feet. The table is 6 feet by $3\frac{1}{2}$ feet. Allow 3 feet on each side of the table.

Plan and Solve Make a drawing on grid paper. Let the side of each square represent one foot. Draw the table and show the walking space. Count the squares to find the space left.

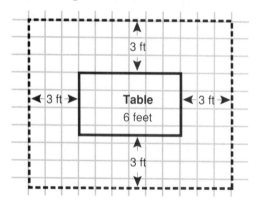

By counting squares, you can see that 12 feet of the 18-foot length are used. Since 6 feet are left, this leaves 3 feet along each end of the room for cabinets.

Look Back ALTERNATE APPROACH You can find the amount of space along each end by first subtracting the used space from the length.

Room	18
Table	− 6
	12
Walking space (2 × 3)	− 6
	6

Then divide by 2 to allow equal space at each end. 6 ÷ 2 = 3

Problem Solving GUIDE

Understand
QUESTION
FACTS
KEY IDEA

Plan and Solve
STRATEGY
ANSWER

Look Back
SENSIBLE ANSWER
ALTERNATE APPROACH

■ **Talk About Math** Could you choose a different operation to solve this problem? Explain.

Check Understanding

Use information in the Example to answer these questions.

1. How much space will be left for cabinets along the other two sides of the room?

2. In the Look Back step, why must you subtract twice the measure of the walking space?

Practice

3. Mr. Alfano wants to install a window in the front wall. The wall is 12 feet tall and 30 feet wide. The window will be 5 feet by 20 feet. If the window is centered in the wall, how much wall space will be left on each side?

4. Mr. Alfano's kitchen is 9 feet high. He plans to install floor cabinets with countertops that are $3\frac{3}{4}$ feet high and wall cabinets that are $2\frac{1}{4}$ feet high. How much wall space will be left above the countertops?

5. In the back of Mr. Alfano's restaurant is a patio that is 26 feet by $22\frac{1}{2}$ feet. He wants to plant a rectangular garden in the center. If he wants to leave $8\frac{1}{2}$ feet on each side for seating, how big can the garden be?

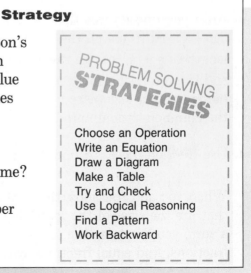

Choose a ———— Strategy

A Fraction of the Value Mr. Gary Johnson's fifth-grade class gave a fraction value to each letter of the alphabet. Students found the value of their first names by adding the letter values together.

$A = \frac{1}{24}$, $B = \frac{2}{24}$, $C = \frac{3}{24}$, $D = \frac{4}{24}$, and so on.

6. What is the value of the teacher's first name?

7. Which day of the week has a whole-number value?

PROBLEM SOLVING STRATEGIES

Choose an Operation
Write an Equation
Draw a Diagram
Make a Table
Try and Check
Use Logical Reasoning
Find a Pattern
Work Backward

Adding Fractions: Different Denominators

Build Understanding

You know how to find the sum of fractions with the same denominator. How do you think you can find the sum of fractions with different denominators?

 A. Fraction Match
Materials: Fraction pieces
Groups: 4 students

a. Find $\frac{1}{2} + \frac{1}{3}$ using fraction pieces.

b. Place the piece that shows one whole on your desk as a reference. Below it, place the pieces that show $\frac{1}{2} + \frac{1}{3}$ end to end.

c. To find the fraction that names the sum, place fraction pieces below them. Try halves. Is the sum equal to a number of halves?

d. Try thirds. Is the sum equal to a number of thirds? Continue using different size pieces for other fractions until you find a size that matches the length of $\frac{1}{2} + \frac{1}{3}$.

e. After you find a piece that can be used to match the length of $\frac{1}{2} + \frac{1}{3}$, rewrite the addition exercise using the name for that size piece as the common denominator.

$$\frac{1}{2} = \frac{}{}$$
$$+\frac{1}{3} = \frac{}{}$$

f. Use fraction pieces to find $\frac{2}{3} + \frac{1}{4}$.

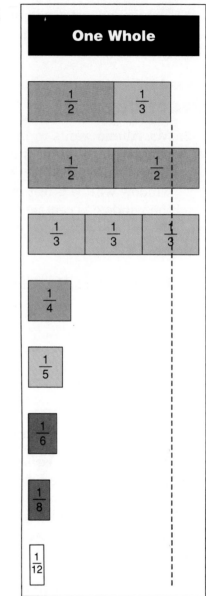

When you add fractions, think of the denominators as units that are the sizes of the matching fraction pieces. To name a sum, you must use the same size units. So before adding fractions, find equal fractions with a common denominator.

B. Find $\frac{1}{6} + \frac{3}{10}$.

The denominators are different.
Find a common denominator.

$$\frac{1}{6}$$
$$+\frac{3}{10}$$

Think:
Multiples of 6: 6, 12, 18, 24, $\boxed{30}$, 36, . . .
Multiples of 10: 10, 20, $\boxed{30}$, . . .

Write equal fractions.
Add the fractions.

$$\frac{1}{6} = \frac{5}{30}$$
$$+\frac{3}{10} = \frac{9}{30}$$
$$\frac{14}{30} = \frac{7}{15}$$

C. Find $\frac{3}{8} + \frac{1}{6} + \frac{1}{4}$.

The denominators are different.
Find a common denominator.

$$\frac{3}{8}$$
$$\frac{1}{6}$$
$$+\frac{1}{4}$$

Think:
Multiples of 8: 8, 16, 24, 32, . . .
8 is a multiple of 4 but not a multiple of 6.
16 is a multiple of 4 but not a multiple of 6.
24 is a multiple of 4 and 6.

Write equal fractions.
Add the fractions.

$$\frac{3}{8} = \frac{9}{24}$$
$$\frac{1}{6} = \frac{4}{24}$$
$$+\frac{1}{4} = \frac{6}{24}$$
$$\frac{19}{24}$$

D. Mental Math When adding three or more fractions, look for sums of 1 to help you add mentally.

Find $\frac{2}{3} + \frac{1}{8} + \frac{1}{3}$.

$\frac{2}{3} + \frac{1}{8} + \frac{1}{3}$ $\frac{2}{3} + \frac{1}{3} = \frac{3}{3} = 1$

$1 + \frac{1}{8} = 1\frac{1}{8}$

■ **Talk About Math**
Can you use a common denominator greater than the least common denominator? Explain why or why not.

Check Understanding

For another example, see Set G, pages 374–375.

1. If you were adding $\frac{1}{3}$ and $\frac{1}{4}$, name two of the common denominators that could be used.

2. What is the least common denominator of $\frac{1}{3}$ and $\frac{1}{4}$?

Copy and complete each exercise.

3. $\frac{1}{6} = \frac{}{12}$
$+\frac{1}{4} = \frac{}{12}$

4. $\frac{3}{8} = \frac{}{}$
$+\frac{5}{12} = \frac{}{24}$

5. $\frac{7}{10} = \frac{}{}$
$+\frac{1}{4} = \frac{}{}$

6. $\frac{5}{9} = \frac{}{}$
$+\frac{5}{6} = \frac{}{}$

Practice

For More Practice, see Set G, pages 376–377.

In each exercise, give the least common denominator.

7. $\frac{1}{5}$ $\frac{2}{3}$ **8.** $\frac{3}{8}$ $\frac{5}{6}$ **9.** $\frac{1}{4}$ $\frac{5}{16}$ **10.** $\frac{1}{4}$ $\frac{1}{6}$ **11.** $\frac{5}{6}$ $\frac{1}{5}$ **12.** $\frac{7}{10}$ $\frac{7}{8}$

Find each sum. **Remember** to write your answer in simplest form.

13. $\frac{4}{9}$ **14.** $\frac{5}{8}$ **15.** $\frac{11}{15}$ **16.** $\frac{9}{10}$ **17.** $\frac{5}{12}$ **18.** $\frac{4}{9}$
$+\frac{5}{6}$ $+\frac{7}{12}$ $+\frac{7}{10}$ $+\frac{1}{6}$ $+\frac{7}{8}$ $+\frac{7}{15}$

19. $\frac{3}{8} + \frac{1}{6}$ **20.** $\frac{5}{12} + \frac{2}{3}$ **21.** $\frac{1}{3} + \frac{5}{6}$ **22.** $\frac{3}{4} + \frac{1}{5}$

23. $\frac{1}{2} + \frac{9}{11}$ **24.** $\frac{3}{5} + \frac{3}{4}$ **25.** $\frac{4}{5} + \frac{1}{2}$ **26.** $\frac{5}{6} + \frac{4}{7}$

27. $\frac{1}{6}$ **28.** $\frac{3}{8}$ **29.** $\frac{5}{9}$ **30.** $\frac{3}{4}$ **31.** $\frac{5}{12}$ **32.** $\frac{1}{6}$
$\frac{3}{4}$ $\frac{5}{6}$ $\frac{1}{6}$ $\frac{5}{6}$ $\frac{2}{3}$ $\frac{3}{8}$
$+\frac{1}{2}$ $+\frac{1}{3}$ $+\frac{2}{3}$ $+\frac{2}{3}$ $+\frac{1}{8}$ $+\frac{7}{12}$

Mental Math   Use mental math to find each sum.

33. $\frac{1}{4} + \frac{3}{5} + \frac{3}{4}$ **34.** $\frac{2}{5} + \frac{1}{2} + \frac{3}{5}$ **35.** $\frac{5}{8} + \frac{3}{8} + \frac{4}{5}$ **36.** $\frac{4}{7} + \frac{1}{6} + \frac{5}{6}$

37. $\frac{1}{8} + \frac{2}{3} + \frac{7}{8}$ **38.** $\frac{3}{4} + \frac{2}{7} + \frac{5}{7}$ **39.** $\frac{4}{5} + \frac{1}{3} + \frac{1}{5}$ **40.** $\frac{7}{9} + \frac{2}{9} + \frac{4}{5}$

Mixed Practice   Add or subtract. **Remember** to write your answers in simplest form.

41. $\frac{7}{8} - \frac{5}{8}$ **42.** $\frac{5}{6} + \frac{5}{12}$ **43.** $4\frac{1}{3} - 1\frac{2}{3}$ **44.** $5 - \frac{7}{20}$

45. $6\frac{4}{5} + 10\frac{3}{5}$ **46.** $12\frac{7}{9} - 3\frac{1}{9}$ **47.** $7\frac{7}{8} + \frac{3}{8} + 4\frac{1}{8}$ **48.** $\frac{1}{2} + \frac{4}{5} + \frac{3}{4}$

49. $3\frac{5}{12} + 6\frac{7}{12} + 4\frac{1}{12}$ **50.** $7 - 4\frac{1}{2}$ **51.** $\frac{1}{6} + \frac{7}{10} + \frac{3}{10}$ **52.** $9\frac{1}{2} - \frac{1}{2}$

Problem Solving

Use the information on Mrs. Briggman's shopping list at the right.

53. How many pounds of cheese did Mrs. Briggman buy?

54. How many pounds of meat did Mrs. Briggman buy?

55. Did she buy more cheese or more meat?

Critical Thinking Use the digits in the box below to solve these problems. Use each digit only once in a solution.

1	2	3	4	6	8

56. Write two fractions that have a sum of 1.

57. Write two fractions that have a sum less than 1.

58. Write two fractions that have a sum between 1 and 2.

Shopping List

$\frac{2}{3}$ pound–Colby cheese

$\frac{3}{4}$ pound–bologna

$\frac{1}{2}$ pound–turkey

$\frac{1}{3}$ pound–corned beef

$\frac{7}{8}$ pound–American cheese

$\frac{1}{4}$ pound–Swiss cheese

3 pounds–apples

Explore ——— Math

An ancient Egyptian papyrus shows only unit fractions. A ***unit fraction*** has 1 as the numerator. Some examples of unit fractions are:

$\frac{1}{2}, \frac{1}{3}, \frac{1}{4}, \frac{1}{5}, \frac{1}{8}, \frac{1}{12}$

The Egyptians wrote other fractions as the sum of unit fractions. For example:

$\frac{3}{4} = \frac{1}{4} + \frac{2}{4}$

        Reduce $\frac{2}{4}$ to lowest terms.

$\frac{3}{4} = \frac{1}{4} + \frac{1}{2}$

Write each fraction as the sum of two unit fractions.

59. $\frac{2}{7}$ **60.** $\frac{3}{10}$ **61.** $\frac{5}{12}$ **62.** $\frac{8}{15}$ **63.** $\frac{5}{8}$

Subtracting Fractions: Different Denominators

Build Understanding

Brett and Donna were making oatmeal cookies for their school fun fair. Their recipe calls for $\frac{3}{4}$ cup of oatmeal and $\frac{2}{3}$ cup of flour. How much more oatmeal than flour is called for in this recipe?

You want to compare the amount of flour with the amount of oatmeal. You can subtract. Find $\frac{3}{4} - \frac{2}{3}$.

If you try to use fraction models for this subtraction, you see that a common denominator is needed to tell how much larger $\frac{3}{4}$ is than $\frac{2}{3}$.

The denominators are different. Find a common denominator.

$$\begin{array}{l} \frac{3}{4} \\ -\frac{2}{3} \end{array}$$

Think:
Multiples of 4: 4, 8, 12, 16, . . .
Multiples of 3: 3, 6, 9, 12, . . .

Write equal fractions. Subtract the fractions.

$$\frac{3}{4} = \frac{9}{12}$$
$$-\frac{2}{3} = \frac{8}{12}$$
$$\frac{1}{12}$$

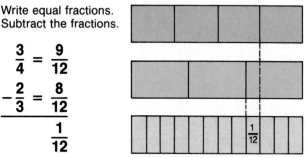

The recipe calls for $\frac{1}{12}$ cup more oatmeal than flour.

■ **Talk About Math** What can you do to always find a common denominator for two fractions with different denominators?

Check Understanding

For another example, see Set H, pages 374–375.

Copy and complete each exercise.

1. $\frac{5}{6} = \frac{}{12}$

   $-\frac{1}{4} = \frac{}{12}$

2. $\frac{4}{5} = \frac{}{}$

   $-\frac{1}{2} = \frac{}{10}$

3. $\frac{3}{4} = \frac{}{}$

   $-\frac{3}{8} = \frac{}{}$

4. $\frac{5}{8} = \frac{}{}$

   $-\frac{1}{6} = \frac{}{}$

Practice

For More Practice, see Set H, pages 376–377.

Find each difference. **Remember** to write your
answer in simplest form.

5. $\dfrac{3}{4}$ $-\dfrac{1}{10}$ **6.** $\dfrac{5}{8}$ $-\dfrac{1}{12}$ **7.** $\dfrac{17}{20}$ $-\dfrac{3}{8}$ **8.** $\dfrac{9}{10}$ $-\dfrac{5}{6}$ **9.** $\dfrac{4}{15}$ $-\dfrac{1}{10}$ **10.** $\dfrac{1}{2}$ $-\dfrac{1}{9}$

11. $\dfrac{4}{5} - \dfrac{2}{3}$ **12.** $\dfrac{3}{4} - \dfrac{1}{3}$ **13.** $\dfrac{2}{5} - \dfrac{1}{6}$ **14.** $\dfrac{7}{8} - \dfrac{2}{5}$ **15.** $\dfrac{3}{4} - \dfrac{1}{5}$

16. $\dfrac{7}{9} - \dfrac{7}{12}$ **17.** $\dfrac{3}{4} - \dfrac{3}{20}$ **18.** $\dfrac{5}{9} - \dfrac{1}{4}$ **19.** $\dfrac{3}{8} - \dfrac{1}{10}$ **20.** $\dfrac{5}{6} - \dfrac{1}{4}$

21. $\dfrac{2}{3} - \dfrac{2}{7}$ **22.** $\dfrac{7}{8} - \dfrac{5}{12}$ **23.** $\dfrac{3}{4} - \dfrac{5}{16}$ **24.** $\dfrac{1}{2} - \dfrac{2}{5}$ **25.** $\dfrac{3}{8} - \dfrac{1}{3}$

26. $\dfrac{9}{10} - \dfrac{5}{6}$ **27.** $\dfrac{5}{8} - \dfrac{1}{10}$ **28.** $\dfrac{17}{25} - \dfrac{2}{5}$ **29.** $\dfrac{5}{7} - \dfrac{1}{2}$ **30.** $\dfrac{2}{3} - \dfrac{7}{20}$

31. $\dfrac{2}{3} - \dfrac{1}{4}$ **32.** $\dfrac{5}{6} - \dfrac{3}{8}$ **33.** $\dfrac{6}{7} - \dfrac{1}{4}$ **34.** $\dfrac{5}{6} - \dfrac{3}{10}$ **35.** $\dfrac{4}{5} - \dfrac{1}{6}$

Problem Solving

Solve each problem.

36. A fruit salad recipe calls for $\dfrac{5}{8}$ cup
of raisins. Brett has only $\dfrac{1}{6}$ cup of
raisins. How many more cups of
raisins does he need?

37. The recipe calls for $\dfrac{7}{8}$ cup of
chopped watermelon and $\dfrac{2}{3}$ cup of
chopped honeydew melon. How
many cups of melon is this?

Skills ———— **Review**   pages 312–313,
316–317, 328–329

Write each fraction in lowest terms.

1. $\dfrac{9}{12}$ **2.** $\dfrac{15}{30}$ **3.** $\dfrac{6}{18}$ **4.** $\dfrac{3}{9}$ **5.** $\dfrac{18}{30}$ **6.** $\dfrac{36}{84}$

Tell whether you would use pencil and
paper, mental math, or a calculator.
Change each fraction to a decimal.

Write each improper fraction as a
whole number or mixed number.
Write each fraction in lowest terms.

7. $\dfrac{3}{4}$ **8.** $\dfrac{13}{20}$ **9.** $\dfrac{48}{25}$ **10.** $\dfrac{188}{50}$ **11.** $\dfrac{24}{10}$ **12.** $\dfrac{46}{7}$ **13.** $\dfrac{65}{13}$ **14.** $\dfrac{146}{8}$

Adding Mixed Numbers: Different Denominators

Build Understanding

A. Mr. Bosnak is a butcher at the Harvest Faire supermarket. A customer ordered meat for chop suey. To fill the order, Mr. Bosnak chopped $3\frac{5}{8}$ pounds of beef and $2\frac{3}{4}$ pounds of pork. What is the total weight of the meat?

The denominators are different. Find a common denominator.

$$3\frac{5}{8}$$
$$+2\frac{3}{4}$$

Write equal fractions. Add the mixed numbers.

$$3\frac{5}{8} = 3\frac{5}{8}$$
$$+2\frac{3}{4} = 2\frac{6}{8}$$

Write the answer in simplest form.

$$5\frac{11}{8} = 5 + 1\frac{3}{8} = 6\frac{3}{8}$$

Mr. Bosnak chopped $6\frac{3}{8}$ pounds of meat to fill the order.

B. Mental Math When adding mixed numbers, look for fractions whose sum will equal 1 to help you add mentally.

Find $4\frac{1}{4} + 2\frac{2}{3} + 1\frac{3}{4}$.

$4\frac{1}{4} + 2\frac{2}{3} + 1\frac{3}{4}$ $\frac{1}{4} + \frac{3}{4} = \frac{4}{4} = 1$

$1 + 4 + 2\frac{2}{3} + 1 = 8\frac{2}{3}$

C. Estimation Estimate this sum.

$$4\frac{5}{8}$$ Since $\frac{5}{8}$ is $> \frac{1}{2}$, round $4\frac{5}{8}$ to 5.

$$+2\frac{1}{3}$$ Since $\frac{1}{3} < \frac{1}{2}$, round $2\frac{1}{3}$ to 2.

$5 + 2 = 7$ $4\frac{5}{8} + 2\frac{1}{3}$ is about 7.

■ **Talk About Math** Explain how you could find a range to estimate the total weight in Example A.

Check Understanding

For another example, see Set I, pages 374–375.

Find each sum.

1. $3\frac{5}{8}$ $+2\frac{1}{6}$

2. $4\frac{5}{6}$ $+1\frac{1}{9}$

3. $6\frac{7}{10}$ $+3\frac{3}{4}$

4. $5\frac{5}{6}$ $+5\frac{9}{10}$

5. $3\frac{8}{9}$ $+12\frac{5}{6}$

Practice

For More Practice, see Set I, pages 376–377.

Add. **Remember** to write your answers in simplest form.

6. $12\frac{1}{2}$
$+\ 3\frac{2}{3}$

7. $13\frac{5}{8}$
$+12\frac{7}{12}$

8. $6\frac{9}{10}$
$+3\frac{5}{8}$

9. $4\frac{3}{4}$
$+2\frac{2}{3}$

10. $42\frac{3}{10}$
$+15\frac{1}{3}$

11. $13\frac{1}{4}$
$2\frac{5}{6}$
$+\ 1\frac{2}{3}$

12. $2\frac{3}{8}$
$5\frac{1}{2}$
$+14\frac{1}{6}$

13. $12\frac{7}{12}$
$3\frac{3}{4}$
$+\ 2\frac{5}{8}$

14. $4\frac{7}{15}$
$10\frac{4}{9}$
$+\ 2\frac{1}{5}$

15. $17\frac{13}{18}$
$15\frac{5}{12}$
$+\ 3\frac{4}{9}$

16. $10\frac{3}{4} + 13\frac{2}{5}$

17. $4\frac{7}{9} + 20\frac{7}{18}$

18. $19\frac{3}{4} + 5\frac{5}{6}$

19. $35\frac{1}{4} + 12\frac{7}{12}$

20. $5\frac{5}{8} + 3\frac{5}{6}$

21. $17\frac{1}{10} + 4\frac{2}{3}$

22. $7\frac{1}{3} + \frac{3}{4}$

23. $5\frac{4}{9} + 10\frac{1}{4}$

24. $6\frac{7}{20} + 8\frac{4}{5}$

25. $11\frac{1}{8} + 2\frac{5}{16}$

26. $9\frac{1}{2} + 2\frac{4}{5}$

27. $8\frac{1}{12} + 8\frac{1}{8}$

Estimation Estimate these sums by rounding.

28. $1\frac{2}{3} + 7\frac{7}{12}$

29. $6\frac{1}{6} + 7\frac{2}{15}$

30. $14\frac{7}{20} + 7\frac{2}{5}$

31. $6\frac{2}{3} + 23\frac{3}{10}$

Mental Math Find each sum mentally.

32. $3\frac{1}{3} + 1\frac{4}{5} + 2\frac{2}{3}$

33. $4\frac{5}{8} + 1\frac{1}{2} + 2\frac{3}{8}$

34. $2\frac{3}{7} + 1\frac{4}{7} + 4\frac{3}{4}$

35. $13\frac{11}{12} + 4\frac{1}{12} + 1\frac{2}{3}$

36. $2\frac{3}{4} + 12\frac{5}{6} + 1\frac{1}{4}$

37. $13\frac{5}{8} + 2\frac{4}{5} + 1\frac{6}{5}$

Problem Solving

Read for the facts to solve each problem.

38. A shipment of fruit included two crates of apples, each weighing $45\frac{5}{8}$ pounds, and a crate of pears weighing $17\frac{7}{10}$ pounds. How many pounds did the three crates weigh?

39. A customer ordered 8 pounds of chicken. Mr. Bosnak filled the order with three chickens. One chicken weighed $2\frac{3}{4}$ pounds and another weighed $3\frac{1}{2}$ pounds. How much did the third chicken weigh?

Subtracting Mixed Numbers: Different Denominators

Build Understanding

How much longer was the triple jump that won the gold medal in 1980 than the winning triple jump in 1984?

Use subtraction to compare the distances. Since the number of feet are the same, find $11\frac{1}{8} - 7\frac{1}{2}$.

Estimate: Round to the nearest whole number. $11 - 8 = 3$

Olympic Gold Medals Triple Jump		
1976	Viktor Saneyev USSR	56 ft $8\frac{3}{4}$ in.
1980	Jaak Uudmare USSR	56 ft $11\frac{1}{8}$ in.
1984	Al Joyner USA	56 ft $7\frac{1}{2}$ in.
1988	Histo Markov Bulgaria	57 ft $9\frac{1}{4}$ in.

A first-place Olympic medal is made of silver with a gold coating.

Find a common denominator.	Write equal fractions. Try to subtract.	Rename, if necessary. Subtract.
$\begin{array}{r} 11\frac{1}{8} \\ -\ 7\frac{1}{2} \\ \hline \end{array}$	$11\frac{1}{8} = 11\frac{1}{8}$ $-\ 7\frac{1}{2} = 7\frac{4}{8}$	$= 10\frac{9}{8}$ $= 7\frac{4}{8}$ $\overline{\ 3\frac{5}{8}}$

The triple jump that won in the 1980 Olympics was $3\frac{5}{8}$ inches longer.

■ **Talk About Math** What other numbers could have been used as a common denominator?

Check Understanding

For another example, see Set J, pages 374–375.

Find each difference.

1. $\begin{array}{r} 7\frac{1}{4} \\ -\ 4\frac{1}{6} \\ \hline \end{array}$

2. $\begin{array}{r} 5\frac{1}{4} \\ -\ 1\frac{1}{3} \\ \hline \end{array}$

3. $\begin{array}{r} 4\frac{5}{8} \\ -\ 3\frac{1}{6} \\ \hline \end{array}$

4. $\begin{array}{r} 9\frac{8}{9} \\ -\ 2\frac{5}{6} \\ \hline \end{array}$

5. $12\frac{1}{4} - 3\frac{3}{10}$

Number Sense Answer each question.

6. Can a common denominator of a pair of fractions ever be smaller than either of the denominators?

7. Do the subtraction in the example two more times, each time with a different common denominator. Do you get the same answer? Why or why not?

Practice

For More Practice, see Set J, pages 376–377.

Subtract. **Remember** to write your answers in simplest form.

8. $11\frac{7}{8}$
$\quad - 4\frac{5}{6}$

9. $17\frac{8}{9}$
$\quad - 9\frac{1}{2}$

10. $24\frac{7}{12}$
$\quad - 19\frac{7}{8}$

11. $34\frac{5}{6}$
$\quad - 17\frac{5}{8}$

12. $40\frac{1}{3}$
$\quad - 13\frac{7}{10}$

13. $26\frac{3}{8}$
$\quad - 8\frac{7}{12}$

14. $14\frac{8}{9}$
$\quad - 1\frac{3}{4}$

15. $32\frac{1}{3}$
$\quad - 23\frac{5}{8}$

16. $56\frac{5}{12}$
$\quad - 8\frac{2}{9}$

17. $33\frac{4}{5}$
$\quad - 6\frac{5}{6}$

18. $6\frac{3}{10} - 2\frac{1}{4}$

19. $7\frac{2}{5} - 3\frac{1}{2}$

20. $5\frac{7}{10} - 5\frac{5}{16}$

21. $12\frac{1}{9} - 11\frac{2}{7}$

22. $8\frac{2}{3} - 5\frac{1}{2}$

23. $7\frac{1}{5} - 5\frac{1}{4}$

24. $14\frac{1}{6} - 8\frac{1}{4}$

25. $21\frac{1}{2} - 9\frac{2}{3}$

Mixed Practice Add or subtract. **Remember** to write your answers in simplest form.

26. $3\frac{4}{5} + 11\frac{3}{10}$

27. $48\frac{2}{9} - 21\frac{5}{12}$

28. $5\frac{5}{8} + 2\frac{3}{4}$

29. $28\frac{4}{5} + 14\frac{2}{15}$

30. $16\frac{1}{2} + 8\frac{3}{8}$

31. $34\frac{3}{5} - 2\frac{7}{10}$

32. $40\frac{2}{3} + 4\frac{3}{4}$

33. $8\frac{1}{2} - 1\frac{5}{6}$

Problem Solving

34. The world record for the pole vault was set by the Russian Sergey Bubka in 1988 at 19 feet $10\frac{1}{2}$ inches. The American record was set in 1987 by Joe Dial at 19 feet $10\frac{1}{4}$ inches. How much higher is the world record?

35. American Jackie Joyner-Kersee won the 1988 gold medal for the long jump with a jump of 24 feet $3\frac{1}{2}$ inches. She set an American record in 1987 with a jump that was $1\frac{3}{4}$ inches longer than her gold-medal jump. How long was her record jump in 1987?

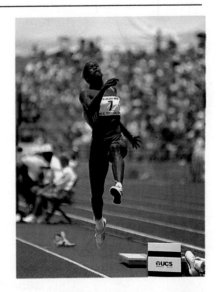

Solve a Simpler Problem

PROBLEM SOLVING
GUIDE

Understand
QUESTION
FACTS
KEY IDEA

➤ **Plan and Solve**
STRATEGY
ANSWER

Look Back
SENSIBLE ANSWER
ALTERNATE APPROACH

Build Understanding

The Cloth Company sells material and other sewing needs. As material is cut from a bolt, the clerk marks how much material is left. Mrs. Trygar bought material to make 2 skirts for each of her daughters. She needed $1\frac{7}{8}$ yards for one size skirt and $2\frac{1}{4}$ yards for the other. The material was cut from a bolt with $31\frac{1}{3}$ yards. How much material was left on the bolt?

Understand   How many yards of material are left? The bolt had $31\frac{1}{3}$ yards. The clerk cut 2 pieces $1\frac{7}{8}$ yards long and 2 pieces $2\frac{1}{4}$ yards long.

➤ **Plan and Solve**   STRATEGY   Sometimes the numbers make a problem look difficult. Replace them with simpler numbers to help you decide how to solve the problem. Then use the actual numbers.

	Simpler Problem	Actual Problem
Find the total amount cut from the bolt.	1	$1\frac{7}{8} = 1\frac{7}{8}$
	1	$1\frac{7}{8} = 1\frac{7}{8}$
	2	$2\frac{1}{4} = 2\frac{2}{8}$
	$+\,2$	$+\,2\frac{1}{4} = 2\frac{2}{8}$
	6	$6\frac{18}{8} = 8\frac{1}{4}$
Find the amount left on the bolt.	30	$31\frac{1}{3} = 31\frac{4}{12}$
	$-\,6$	$-\,8\frac{1}{4} = 8\frac{3}{12}$
	24	$23\frac{1}{12}$

ANSWER   The bolt has $23\frac{1}{12}$ yards of material left.

Look Back   Be sure you subtracted the lengths of all the pieces of material that were cut from the bolt. Check your computation.

■ **Talk About Math** Explain how you could solve
the problem using another method.

Check Understanding

1. What numbers would you use to
   make the problem simpler?

2. Solve the problem.

> The first three sales from a new
> $45\frac{1}{2}$-yard bolt were $2\frac{5}{8}$ yards, $5\frac{2}{3}$ yards,
> and $4\frac{1}{4}$ yards. How many yards were left
> on the bolt?

Practice

3. A pattern for the front of a penguin puppet is a square
   measuring $4\frac{1}{2}$ inches on each side. Judy has a piece of
   white material that is 15 inches wide and 20 inches long.
   How many patterns can she cut out?

4. **Use Data** Use the information in the table on page 368.
   In 1985, Willie Banks set a world record with a triple
   jump of 58 feet $11\frac{1}{2}$ inches. How much longer was
   this jump than the gold medal jump in 1976?

5. ▦ **Calculator** Linda worked $7\frac{3}{4}$ hours each of 6 days
   last week at The Cloth Company. If she is paid $7.20
   per hour, how much did she earn last week?

6. Jane wants to sew a ruffle around the 4 sides of a bedspread
   that is $2\frac{1}{3}$ yards long and $1\frac{5}{6}$ yards wide. To make
   the ruffle, she needs twice the length and twice the width.
   How much material does she need?

Choose a _____ Strategy

Follow the Leader
7. On a long hike, Joseph, Rhonda, Bob, and Steve took turns
   leading. Joseph led for $4\frac{1}{2}$ miles. This was $1\frac{1}{2}$ miles
   less than Rhonda led. Rhonda led twice as far as Bob. Steve
   led 2 miles less than Bob. How long was the hike?

Skills Review

Add or subtract. Write the answer in simplest form.

1. $\frac{5}{12} + \frac{1}{12}$ **2.** $\frac{3}{8} + \frac{1}{8} + \frac{5}{8}$

3. $\frac{7}{10} - \frac{4}{10}$ **4.** $\frac{11}{6} - \frac{5}{6}$

5. $4\frac{3}{8} + 2\frac{1}{8}$ **6.** $8\frac{9}{12} - 3\frac{5}{12}$

7. $3\frac{3}{5} + 6\frac{2}{5}$ **8.** $2\frac{3}{4} + 2\frac{3}{4}$

9. $3 - \frac{8}{9}$ **10.** $10 - 4\frac{3}{7}$

11. $5\frac{4}{9} - 2\frac{5}{9}$ **12.** $12\frac{3}{10} - 4\frac{7}{10}$

13. $\frac{5}{12} + \frac{1}{6}$ **14.** $\frac{3}{4} - \frac{3}{8}$

15. $\frac{7}{8} + \frac{5}{6}$ **16.** $\frac{3}{4} + \frac{2}{5}$

17. $\frac{2}{3} - \frac{1}{4}$ **18.** $\frac{9}{10} - \frac{3}{6}$

19. $3\frac{2}{3} + 5\frac{2}{5}$ **20.** $14\frac{3}{4} + 6\frac{1}{8}$

21. $5\frac{5}{6} - 1\frac{1}{4}$ **22.** $10\frac{2}{5} - 3\frac{1}{2}$

Use mental math to find each sum or difference.

23. $1\frac{1}{12} + 5\frac{7}{12} + 2\frac{5}{12}$

24. $2\frac{3}{8} + 4\frac{1}{2} + 3\frac{5}{8}$

25. $6\frac{3}{10} + 4\frac{7}{15} + 2\frac{7}{10}$

Problem-Solving Review

Solve each problem.

26. Jake had 15 minutes to finish a test. He spent 7 minutes on the true-false questions and 5 minutes on the essay question. What fraction of the time was left to check his work?

27. Leroy is $55\frac{1}{2}$ inches tall. LuAnne is $1\frac{3}{4}$ inches taller than Linda. Linda is $3\frac{1}{8}$ inches shorter than Leroy. How tall are Linda and LuAnne?

28. Ms. McRae wants to fence in an area $24\frac{1}{2}$ feet wide and $29\frac{1}{4}$ feet long. How much wire does she need for the fence?

29. Use the circle graph below. What fraction of the people surveyed took

a. only the elephant ride?

b. the elephant ride?

30. **Data File** Using the chart of heights on pages 380–381, find the difference in height between Manute Bol and the top of a telephone booth.

31. **Make a Data File** Make a chart to show data about types of programs on TV during the evening hours for 1 week. Include the number of hours of news, comedy, and drama.

Tell what the 5 in each number means.

1. 45,887,200   **2.** 132,450,000

3. 123.05   **4.** 4.9752

5. 90.6425   **6.** 0.12345

Estimate each product or quotient.

7. 481×32 **8.** $2 \times 697 \times 5$

9. $815 \div 88$ **10.** $3,427 \div 68$

11. 5.3×7.8 **12.** 84.5×10.4

13. Find the perimeter. Measure each
side in centimeters.

Choose the larger measure.

14. 30 inches or 3 feet

15. 16 cups or 3 quarts

16. 25 ounces or 2 pounds

Find the missing addend or factor.

17. $85 = n + 17$ **18.** $n + 456 = 921$

19. $4 \times n = 56$ **20.** $n \times 9 = 9,225$

Each cube represents 1 cubic inch.
Find the volume of each figure.

21.   **22.**

Draw the next three figures in each
pattern.

23.

24. □○□○○□○○○

Write the rule.

25.

A	B
2	6
5	15
3	9
9	29

26.

A	B
10	4
6	0
15	9
20	14

Write a whole number or a mixed
number for each improper fraction.

27. $\frac{12}{8}$ **28.** $\frac{25}{20}$ **29.** $\frac{60}{15}$

Estimate if the fraction is greater than
$\frac{1}{2}$, less than $\frac{1}{2}$, or equal to $\frac{1}{2}$.

30. $\frac{15}{17}$ **31.** $\frac{2}{15}$ **32.** $\frac{13}{26}$

Write each fraction as a decimal.

33. $\frac{1}{2}$ **34.** $\frac{3}{4}$ **35.** $\frac{7}{50}$ **36.** $\frac{3}{25}$

Add or subtract.

37. $\frac{3}{5} + \frac{4}{5}$ **38.** $\frac{7}{9} - \frac{3}{9}$

39. $3\frac{3}{4} + 1\frac{2}{4}$ **40.** $6\frac{3}{10} - 2\frac{7}{10}$

41. $\frac{5}{8} + \frac{3}{4}$ **42.** $4\frac{7}{12} - 2\frac{1}{3}$

43. $\frac{7}{8} + \frac{2}{3}$ **44.** $\frac{5}{12} - \frac{1}{8}$

45. $5\frac{1}{4} + 2\frac{1}{3}$ **46.** $7\frac{3}{4} - 2\frac{2}{5}$

Reteaching

Find the sum of $\frac{3}{8}$ and $\frac{7}{8}$.

Add the numerators.

Write the sum over the common denominator.

$$\begin{array}{r} \frac{3}{8} \\ +\frac{7}{8} \\ \hline \frac{10}{8} = 1\frac{2}{8} = 1\frac{1}{4} \end{array}$$

Remember to change improper fractions to mixed numbers and write fractions in lowest terms. Add the fractions.

1. $\begin{array}{r} \frac{5}{6} \\ +\frac{3}{6} \\ \hline \end{array}$ 2. $\begin{array}{r} \frac{3}{5} \\ +\frac{1}{5} \\ \hline \end{array}$ 3. $\begin{array}{r} \frac{1}{4} \\ +\frac{2}{4} \\ \hline \end{array}$

Subtract: $\frac{5}{8} - \frac{1}{8}$.

Subtract the numerators.

Write the difference over the common denominator.

$$\begin{array}{r} \frac{5}{8} \\ -\frac{1}{8} \\ \hline \frac{4}{8} = \frac{1}{2} \end{array}$$

Remember to simplify the answers if necessary. Subtract the fractions.

1. $\frac{4}{6} - \frac{1}{6}$ 2. $\frac{11}{12} - \frac{5}{12}$

3. $\frac{7}{10} - \frac{3}{10}$ 4. $\frac{19}{20} - \frac{7}{20}$

Find the sum of $6\frac{1}{5}$ and $8\frac{3}{5}$.

Add the fractions.

$$\begin{array}{r} 6\frac{1}{5} \\ +8\frac{3}{5} \\ \hline \frac{4}{5} \end{array}$$

Add the whole numbers.

$$\begin{array}{r} 6\frac{1}{5} \\ +8\frac{3}{5} \\ \hline 14\frac{4}{5} \end{array}$$

Remember to write fractions in lowest terms. Add or subtract.

1. $\begin{array}{r} 2\frac{1}{3} \\ +7\frac{1}{3} \\ \hline \end{array}$ 2. $\begin{array}{r} 15\frac{7}{8} \\ -8\frac{3}{8} \\ \hline \end{array}$ 3. $\begin{array}{r} 25\frac{1}{6} \\ +4\frac{1}{6} \\ \hline \end{array}$

Find $2\frac{1}{4} + 3\frac{3}{4} + 3\frac{2}{4}$.

$2\frac{1}{4} + 3\frac{3}{4} + 3\frac{2}{4} = 8\frac{6}{4}$

Rename: $8\frac{6}{4} = 8 + \frac{6}{4}$

$= 8 + \frac{4}{4} + \frac{2}{4}$

$= 8 + 1 + \frac{2}{4} = 9\frac{2}{4} = 9\frac{1}{2}$

Remember to rename a sum if it contains an improper fraction. Add.

1. $4\frac{1}{4} + 6\frac{3}{4}$ 2. $3\frac{5}{6} + 9\frac{5}{6}$

3. $3\frac{3}{8} + 2\frac{5}{8} + 5\frac{3}{8}$ 4. $4\frac{2}{5} + 5\frac{4}{5} + 4\frac{3}{5}$

Find $4 - 2\frac{3}{8}$.

Rename 4:

$$\begin{array}{r} 4 = 3\frac{8}{8} \\ -2\frac{3}{8} = 2\frac{3}{8} \\ \hline 1\frac{5}{8} \end{array}$$

Think:
$4 = 3 + 1$
$= 3 + \frac{8}{8}$

Remember that a whole number can be renamed as a mixed number. Subtract.

1. $5 - 2\frac{4}{5}$ 2. $9 - 4\frac{1}{6}$

3. $2 - 1\frac{3}{4}$ 4. $6 - 3\frac{3}{7}$

Set F pages 352–353

Find $8\frac{1}{6} - 4\frac{5}{6}$.

Rename $8\frac{1}{6}$:

$$8\frac{1}{6} = 7\frac{7}{6}$$
$$-4\frac{5}{6} = 4\frac{5}{6}$$
$$\overline{3\frac{2}{6}} = 3\frac{1}{3}$$

Think:
$$8\frac{1}{6} = 7 + 1 + \frac{1}{6}$$
$$= 7 + \frac{6}{6} + \frac{1}{6}$$
$$= 7\frac{7}{6}$$

Remember that renaming a mixed number is sometimes necessary when subtracting mixed numbers. Subtract.

1. $6\frac{1}{5} - 3\frac{2}{5}$ 2. $3\frac{1}{8} - 1\frac{3}{8}$

Set G pages 360–363

Find $\frac{4}{5} + \frac{2}{3}$.

Write equal fractions with a common denominator of 15.

$$\frac{4}{5} = \frac{12}{15}$$
$$+\frac{2}{3} = \frac{10}{15}$$
$$\overline{\frac{22}{15}} = 1\frac{7}{15}$$

Remember to make a list of multiples for each denominator to find a common denominator. Find each sum.

1. $\frac{3}{4}$ 2. $\frac{5}{6}$ 3. $\frac{3}{8}$
 $+\frac{1}{8}$ $+\frac{1}{10}$ $+\frac{5}{6}$

Set H pages 364–365

Find $\frac{5}{6} - \frac{3}{8}$.

A common denominator is 24.

$$\frac{5}{6} = \frac{20}{24}$$
$$-\frac{3}{8} = \frac{9}{24}$$
$$\overline{\frac{11}{24}}$$

Remember that you can always find a common denominator by multiplying the denominators. Find each difference.

1. $\frac{4}{5}$ 2. $\frac{2}{3}$ 3. $\frac{7}{8}$
 $-\frac{1}{4}$ $-\frac{3}{5}$ $-\frac{1}{12}$

Set I pages 366–367

Find $4\frac{7}{10} + 2\frac{5}{6}$.

$$4\frac{7}{10} = 4\frac{21}{30}$$
$$+2\frac{5}{6} = 2\frac{25}{30}$$
$$\overline{6\frac{46}{30}} = 6 + 1\frac{16}{30} = 7\frac{16}{30} = 7\frac{8}{15}$$

Remember that fractions must have the same denominator before you can add them.

Add.

1. $5\frac{2}{3}$ 2. $2\frac{3}{10}$ 3. $9\frac{4}{7}$
 $+6\frac{1}{4}$ $+2\frac{1}{5}$ $+3\frac{1}{2}$

Set J pages 368–369

Find $8\frac{3}{4} - 3\frac{4}{5}$.

$$8\frac{3}{4} = 8\frac{15}{20} = 7\frac{35}{20}$$
$$-3\frac{4}{5} = 3\frac{16}{20} = 3\frac{16}{20}$$
$$\overline{4\frac{19}{20}}$$

Remember that there is more than one number that you can use as a common denominator.

Subtract.

1. $10\frac{2}{3}$ 2. $7\frac{1}{2}$ 3. $12\frac{1}{10}$
 $-8\frac{5}{6}$ $-3\frac{3}{5}$ $-6\frac{1}{4}$

More Practice

Set A pages 342–343

Add the fractions. **Remember** to simplify the answer if necessary.

1. $\frac{5}{8} + \frac{2}{8}$ **2.** $\frac{2}{6} + \frac{1}{6}$ **3.** $\frac{4}{7} + \frac{2}{7}$ **4.** $\frac{1}{5} + \frac{3}{5}$

5. $\frac{3}{13} + \frac{7}{13}$ **6.** $\frac{3}{8} + \frac{7}{8}$ **7.** $\frac{2}{7} + \frac{4}{7} + \frac{3}{7}$ **8.** $\frac{4}{9} + \frac{5}{9} + \frac{7}{9}$

Set B pages 344–345

Subtract the fractions. **Remember** to simplify the answer if necessary.

1. $\frac{7}{8} - \frac{3}{8}$ **2.** $\frac{7}{10} - \frac{3}{10}$ **3.** $\frac{5}{6} - \frac{1}{6}$ **4.** $\frac{4}{5} - \frac{2}{5}$

5. $\frac{5}{9} - \frac{2}{9}$ **6.** $\frac{5}{8} - \frac{1}{8}$ **7.** $\frac{9}{13} - \frac{6}{13}$ **8.** $\frac{9}{10} - \frac{3}{10}$

Set C pages 346–347

Add. **Remember** to write your answers in simplest form.

1. $3\frac{1}{5} + 6\frac{2}{5}$ **2.** $6\frac{7}{10} + 1\frac{1}{10}$ **3.** $8\frac{3}{10} + 2\frac{3}{10}$ **4.** $7\frac{5}{12} + 3\frac{1}{12}$

Subtract. **Remember** to write your answers in simplest form.

5. $11\frac{9}{10} - 6\frac{3}{10}$ **6.** $9\frac{7}{12} - 1\frac{5}{12}$ **7.** $6\frac{11}{16} - 2\frac{3}{16}$ **8.** $15\frac{17}{20} - 8\frac{11}{20}$

Set D pages 348–349

Add. **Remember** to write your answers in simplest form.

1. $2\frac{4}{5} + 3\frac{3}{5}$ **2.** $5\frac{5}{12} + 6\frac{11}{12}$ **3.** $8\frac{7}{10} + 9\frac{9}{10}$ **4.** $9\frac{3}{4} + 6\frac{1}{4}$

5. $13 + 9\frac{3}{4} + 5\frac{3}{4}$ **6.** $4\frac{7}{13} + 2\frac{9}{13} + 6\frac{1}{13}$ **7.** $8\frac{3}{7} + 1\frac{4}{7} + 6\frac{5}{7}$

Set E pages 350–351

Subtract. **Remember** to write your answers in simplest form.

1. $\begin{array}{r} 3 \\ -\ \frac{3}{10} \\ \hline \end{array}$ **2.** $\begin{array}{r} 7 \\ -\ 2\frac{2}{5} \\ \hline \end{array}$ **3.** $\begin{array}{r} 6 \\ -\ 3\frac{4}{7} \\ \hline \end{array}$ **4.** $\begin{array}{r} 11 \\ -\ 4\frac{5}{9} \\ \hline \end{array}$ **5.** $\begin{array}{r} 13 \\ -\ 8\frac{5}{8} \\ \hline \end{array}$

6. $2 - \frac{9}{14}$ **7.** $36 - 21\frac{7}{12}$ **8.** $29 - 18\frac{5}{6}$ **9.** $18 - 12\frac{7}{10}$

Set F   pages 352–353

Subtract. **Remember** to write the answer in simplest form.

1. $8\frac{2}{5}$
   $-3\frac{3}{5}$

2. $8\frac{3}{8}$
   $-6\frac{7}{8}$

3. $10\frac{5}{9}$
   $-4\frac{7}{9}$

4. $12\frac{2}{5}$
   $-3\frac{4}{5}$

5. $16\frac{5}{12}$
   $-9\frac{11}{12}$

6. $14\frac{1}{6}$
   $-10\frac{5}{6}$

Set G   pages 360–363

Find each sum. **Remember** to write your answer in simplest form.

1. $\frac{3}{8}$
   $+\frac{5}{6}$

2. $\frac{7}{10}$
   $+\frac{3}{4}$

3. $\frac{3}{4}$
   $+\frac{6}{7}$

4. $\frac{5}{9}$
   $+\frac{1}{6}$

5. $\frac{2}{3}$
   $+\frac{5}{9}$

6. $\frac{11}{12}$
   $+\frac{1}{8}$

7. $\frac{1}{5} + \frac{3}{4} + \frac{1}{2}$

8. $\frac{5}{6} + \frac{4}{9} + \frac{1}{3}$

9. $\frac{3}{4} + \frac{7}{12} + \frac{5}{8}$

Set H   pages 364–365

Find each difference. **Remember** to write your answer in simplest form.

1. $\frac{3}{4}$
   $-\frac{2}{5}$

2. $\frac{11}{12}$
   $-\frac{3}{8}$

3. $\frac{7}{10}$
   $-\frac{1}{4}$

4. $\frac{5}{9}$
   $-\frac{1}{2}$

5. $\frac{3}{5}$
   $-\frac{1}{6}$

6. $\frac{5}{9}$
   $-\frac{5}{12}$

7. $\frac{3}{10} - \frac{1}{5}$

8. $\frac{2}{3} - \frac{1}{6}$

9. $\frac{5}{6} - \frac{1}{4}$

10. $\frac{5}{6} - \frac{7}{9}$

Set I   pages 366–367

Add. **Remember** to write your answer in simplest form.

1. $6\frac{3}{4} + 8\frac{1}{3}$

2. $5\frac{4}{5} + 9\frac{1}{6}$

3. $3\frac{1}{9} + 7\frac{5}{6}$

4. $4\frac{11}{12} + 8\frac{5}{6}$

5. $16\frac{2}{5} + 17\frac{1}{3}$

6. $19\frac{5}{6} + 17\frac{1}{2}$

7. $8\frac{2}{5} + 10\frac{3}{4}$

8. $25\frac{3}{10} + 21\frac{1}{6}$

Set J   pages 368–369

Subtract. **Remember** to write your answer in simplest form.

1. $5\frac{3}{10}$
   $-2\frac{4}{5}$

2. $8\frac{1}{5}$
   $-6\frac{3}{8}$

3. $10\frac{1}{9}$
   $-8\frac{3}{4}$

4. $16\frac{5}{12}$
   $-9\frac{7}{8}$

5. $21\frac{2}{7}$
   $-18\frac{3}{5}$

6. $8\frac{3}{10} - 5\frac{5}{8}$

7. $4\frac{1}{2} - 2\frac{3}{5}$

8. $9\frac{1}{4} - 6\frac{7}{10}$

9. $14\frac{2}{9} - 11\frac{7}{12}$

Enrichment

Betweenness for Fractions

A. You know there is no whole number between 3 and 4. Between any two fractions, however, there is another fraction. To find a fraction between $\frac{3}{8}$ and $\frac{4}{8}$, think of dividing the number line from 0 to 1 into 16 equal parts instead of 8 equal parts. What fraction appears between $\frac{3}{8}$ and $\frac{4}{8}$ on the number line?

A fraction between $\frac{3}{8}$ and $\frac{4}{8}$ is $\frac{7}{16}$.

B. You can also use a common denominator to find a fraction between two fractions. Find a fraction between $\frac{5}{6}$ and $\frac{7}{8}$.

First, rename the fractions using a common denominator.

$$\frac{5}{6} = \frac{20}{24} \qquad \frac{7}{8} = \frac{21}{24}$$

Then find a fraction between $\frac{20}{24}$ and $\frac{21}{24}$. Use 2×24 to find a common denominator.

$$\frac{20}{24} = \frac{40}{48} \qquad \frac{21}{24} = \frac{42}{48}$$

A fraction between $\frac{5}{6}$ and $\frac{7}{8}$ is $\frac{41}{48}$.

Find a fraction between each pair of fractions.

1. $\frac{2}{5}$ and $\frac{3}{5}$ **2.** $\frac{21}{24}$ and $\frac{22}{24}$ **3.** $\frac{1}{3}$ and $\frac{2}{3}$ **4.** $\frac{3}{7}$ and $\frac{4}{7}$

5. $\frac{1}{9}$ and $\frac{1}{6}$ **6.** $\frac{2}{5}$ and $\frac{1}{2}$ **7.** $\frac{7}{8}$ and $\frac{9}{10}$ **8.** $\frac{6}{6}$ and $\frac{7}{6}$

Chapter 11 Review/Test

Add or subtract. Write the answers in simplest form.

1. $\frac{1}{8} + \frac{3}{8}$ **2.** $\frac{3}{10} + \frac{3}{10}$

3. $\frac{11}{12} - \frac{1}{12}$ **4.** $\frac{5}{6} - \frac{1}{6}$

5. $\begin{array}{r} 4\frac{9}{16} \\ + 2\frac{1}{16} \\ \hline \end{array}$ **6.** $\begin{array}{r} 6\frac{11}{15} \\ - 1\frac{10}{15} \\ \hline \end{array}$

7. $2\frac{7}{8} + 3\frac{3}{8}$ **8.** $5\frac{4}{5} + 3\frac{3}{5}$

9. $\begin{array}{r} 9 \\ - 2\frac{1}{8} \\ \hline \end{array}$ **10.** $\begin{array}{r} 10 \\ - 2\frac{2}{3} \\ \hline \end{array}$

11. $\begin{array}{r} 6\frac{1}{3} \\ - 2\frac{2}{3} \\ \hline \end{array}$ **12.** $\begin{array}{r} 10\frac{1}{12} \\ - 5\frac{5}{12} \\ \hline \end{array}$

13. $\begin{array}{r} \frac{3}{4} \\ + \frac{1}{8} \\ \hline \end{array}$ **14.** $\begin{array}{r} \frac{9}{10} \\ - \frac{1}{5} \\ \hline \end{array}$

15. $\frac{1}{6} + \frac{1}{4}$ **16.** $\frac{1}{2} + \frac{1}{5} + \frac{3}{10}$

17. $\frac{9}{10} - \frac{1}{15}$ **18.** $\frac{3}{8} - \frac{1}{3}$

19. $7\frac{1}{3} + 3\frac{3}{4}$ **20.** $6\frac{1}{12} - 3\frac{3}{8}$

21. Is the sum $7\frac{7}{8} + 5\frac{3}{4}$ about 14?

Copy and complete.

22. $\begin{array}{r} 7 = 6\frac{\boxed{}}{5} \\ - 2\frac{2}{5} = 2\frac{2}{5} \\ \hline 4\frac{3}{5} \end{array}$ **23.** $\begin{array}{r} \frac{1}{9} = \frac{\boxed{}}{18} \\ + \frac{5}{6} = \frac{\boxed{}}{18} \\ \hline \frac{\boxed{}}{18} \end{array}$

Solve each problem.

24. A carpenter cut $\frac{1}{2}$ foot from a board that was $3\frac{1}{4}$ feet long. How long was the board after the cut?

25. A room is 20 feet long by 12 feet wide. A rug that is 15 feet long by 9 feet wide is placed in the center of the room so that equal space is left at each end. How much space will be left at each end?

Read the problem below. Then answer the question.

Julie spent $2\frac{1}{2}$ hours one day baby-sitting and $3\frac{1}{4}$ hours the next. She was paid \$2 per hour. How many hours did she work in all?

26. Which is the correct answer for the problem?

   a. $5\frac{3}{4}$ dollars

   b. $5\frac{3}{4}$ days

   c. $5\frac{3}{4}$ hours

27. **Write About Math**   What must be true for a number to be a common denominator of two fractions with different denominators?

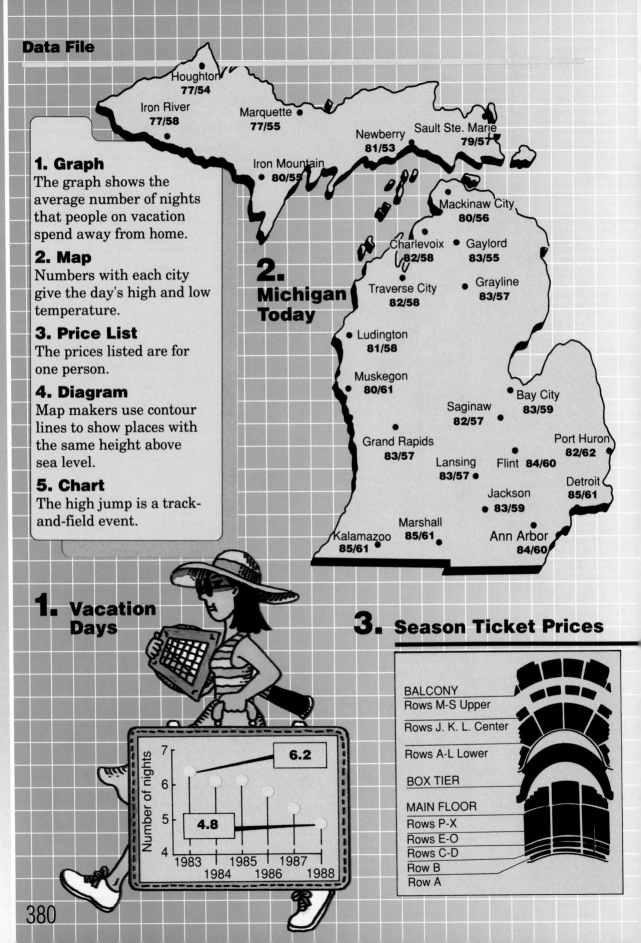

1. Graph
The graph shows the average number of nights that people on vacation spend away from home.

2. Map
Numbers with each city give the day's high and low temperature.

3. Price List
The prices listed are for one person.

4. Diagram
Map makers use contour lines to show places with the same height above sea level.

5. Chart
The high jump is a track-and-field event.

2. Michigan Today

Houghton 77/54
Iron River 77/58
Marquette 77/55
Newberry 81/53
Sault Ste. Marie 79/57
Iron Mountain 80/55
Mackinaw City 80/56
Charlevoix 82/58
Gaylord 83/55
Traverse City 82/58
Grayline 83/57
Ludington 81/58
Muskegon 80/61
Saginaw 82/57
Bay City 83/59
Grand Rapids 83/57
Lansing 83/57
Flint 84/60
Port Huron 82/62
Jackson 83/59
Detroit 85/61
Marshall 85/61
Ann Arbor 84/60
Kalamazoo 85/61

1. Vacation Days

Number of nights

6.2

4.8

1983 1984 1985 1986 1987 1988

3. Season Ticket Prices

BALCONY
Rows M-S Upper

Rows J. K. L. Center

Rows A-L Lower

BOX TIER

MAIN FLOOR
Rows P-X

Rows E-O

Rows C-D

Row B

Row A

4. **Topographic Maps**

5. **Chart of Heights**

Highest jump by a horse: 8 $\frac{1}{12}$ ft.

Normal ceiling in a house: 8 ft

Cuba's Javier Sotomayor's high jump: 8 ft (July 1989)

Professional basketball player (Manute Bol): 7 $\frac{1}{2}$ ft

Telephone booth: 7 $\frac{5}{6}$ ft

	Thursday A-B-C Series 10 Concerts	Friday A-B Series 7 Concerts	Saturday A-B Series 10 Concerts
MAIN FLOOR			
Rows A	$ 50	$ 35	$ 50
B	125	87.50	135
C-D	200	140	220
E-O	390	273	440
P-X	315	220.50	350
BALCONY			
Rows A-L	390	273	440
J-K-L (Center)	315	220.50	350
M-S	250	175	280

Cumulative Review/Test Chapters 1–11

1. Multiply.

    23
    × 41

    a. 843
    b. 64
    c. 943
    d. 115

2. Multiply.

    30 × 800

    a. 240
    b. 2,400
    c. 24,000
    d. 240,000

3. Divide.

    21)1,315

    a. 63 R2
    b. 62 R12
    c. 62 R13
    d. 67 R8

4. Subtract.

    4,826
    − 3,459

    a. 1,367
    b. 1,477
    c. 1,467
    d. 1,377

Choose the most sensible measure.

5. Length of a needle

    a. 40 m
    b. 40 mm
    c. 40 dm
    d. 40 cm

6. Find the perimeter.

    a. 200 m
    b. 30 m
    c. 50 m
    d. 60 m

7. Subtract.

    7 ft 2 in.
    − 3 ft 7 in.

    a. 4 ft 5 in.
    b. 3 ft 5 in.
    c. 3 ft 7 in.
    d. 4 ft 7 in.

8. What decimal represents three thousandths?

    a. 0.300
    b. 0.030
    c. 0.003
    d. 0.3

9. Multiply.

    2.6
    × 0.3

    a. 6.18
    b. 0.78
    c. 7.8
    d. 0.618

10. Multiply.

    0.93 × 100

    a. 9.3
    b. 93
    c. 930
    d. 9,300

11. Look for the pattern. Then give the next number in the sequence.

    3   13   12   22   21   31

    a. 30
    b. 41
    c. 32
    d. 33

12. Which ordered pair names the point labeled by A?

    a. (1, 4)
    b. (4, 1)
    c. (0, 4)
    d. (4, 0)

13. Find the rule.

A	B
2	8
3	12
4	16
5	20

    a. 4 × A = B
    b. 4 × B = A
    c. A + B = 10
    d. A ÷ 4 = B

14. What is $\frac{20}{30}$ in lowest terms?

 a. $\frac{10}{15}$ **b.** $\frac{4}{6}$ **c.** $\frac{2}{3}$ **d.** $\frac{3}{5}$

15. What is the least common denominator for $\frac{2}{3}$ and $\frac{1}{4}$?

 a. 6 **b.** 12 **c.** 8 **d.** 7

16. Which number sentence is true?

 a. $\frac{3}{8} > \frac{1}{2}$ **c.** $\frac{8}{16} = \frac{7}{15}$

 b. $7\frac{1}{5} < 8\frac{1}{3}$ **d.** $\frac{3}{4} < \frac{5}{8}$

17. Add.

 $\frac{1}{10} + \frac{1}{10}$

 a. $\frac{1}{10}$

 b. $\frac{1}{5}$

 c. $\frac{1}{100}$

 d. $\frac{1}{20}$

18. Subtract.

 $\frac{11}{12}$

 $-\frac{1}{3}$

 a. $\frac{7}{12}$

 b. $\frac{7}{24}$

 c. $\frac{10}{9}$

 d. $\frac{10}{12}$

19. Subtract.

 12

 $-7\frac{5}{8}$

 a. $4\frac{3}{8}$

 b. $5\frac{5}{8}$

 c. $4\frac{5}{8}$

 d. $5\frac{5}{8}$

20. Mrs. Hayes trimmed $\frac{1}{2}$ foot from the length of a curtain that was $4\frac{1}{4}$ feet long. How long was the curtain after she trimmed it?

 a. $3\frac{3}{4}$ feet **c.** $4\frac{1}{4}$ feet

 b. $3\frac{1}{5}$ feet **d.** $4\frac{1}{2}$ feet

Make a chart to solve the following problem.

21. Vic, Tess, Frank, and Sue each had a different snack. The choices were fruit cup, muffin, oatmeal cookies, or carrot sticks. None of the boys ate cookies. Vic and the boy who had carrot sticks have different teachers. Tess had jam on her muffin. Who had fruit cup?

 a. Frank **c.** Tess
 b. Sue **d.** Vic

22. Oranges are packed 8 to a sack. How many sacks are needed for 70 oranges?

 a. 7 sacks **c.** 6 sacks
 b. 8 sacks **d.** 9 sacks

Read the problem below. Then answer the question.

Mr. Jones bought a jacket for $95 and a sweater for $39. The sales tax was 6 cents on the dollar. What was the total cost?

23. Which method can be used to solve the problem?

 a. $95 + 39 = 134$

 b. $95 + 39 = 134$ 134
 $134 \times 0.06 = 8.04$ $\underline{+\ \ 8.04}$
                    142.04

 c. $95 \times 0.06 = 5.70$ 5.70
 $39 \times 0.06 = 2.34$ $\underline{+\ 2.34}$
                    8.04

 d. $95 + 39 + 6 = 140$

Exploring Multiplication of Fractions

Did You Know: A good way for two people to share something that needs to be cut into two parts: one person cuts the thing in two, and the other person gets the half of his or her choice.

Number-Sense Project

Estimate
What ways do people use to estimate or divide something into "equal shares"?

Gather Data
Present a series of problems to 3 people and see what methods they use to divide things into "equal shares."

Analyze and Report
Compare your findings with those of other students. How many different ways of sharing were used?

Using Pictures to Multiply Fractions

Build Understanding

Forests once covered about $\frac{3}{5}$ of the earth's land surface. Today, only about $\frac{1}{2}$ of those forest areas remain. What fraction of the earth's land surface is now covered by forests?

You can draw a picture to help you find $\frac{1}{2}$ of $\frac{3}{5}$.

First shade $\frac{3}{5}$.   Next shade $\frac{1}{2}$ of that.

In the second picture, how many equal parts are in the whole? What is the value of each of these parts? How many parts are shaded twice?

The diagrams show that $\frac{1}{2}$ of $\frac{3}{5}$ is $\frac{3}{10}$. Multiplication can be used to find a fraction of a number.

$$\frac{1}{2} \times \frac{3}{5} = \frac{3}{10}$$

About $\frac{3}{10}$ of the earth's land surface is covered by forests.

■ **Talk About Math**   Do you think you would get the same product for $\frac{1}{2} \times \frac{3}{5}$ if you shaded $\frac{1}{2}$ first? Why or why not? Draw a picture to see if your reasoning is correct.

Forests cover about one third of the land area in the United States.

Check Understanding

For another example, see Set A, pages 408–409.

Use the picture to find each product.

1. $\frac{1}{4}$ of $\frac{1}{2}$
$\frac{1}{4} \times \frac{1}{2}$

2. $\frac{3}{4}$ of $\frac{2}{5}$
$\frac{3}{4} \times \frac{2}{5}$

Practice

For More Practice, see Set A, pages 410–411.

Use the picture to find the product.

3. $\frac{1}{4}$ of $\frac{1}{3}$

$\frac{1}{4} \times \frac{1}{3}$

4. $\frac{1}{2}$ of $\frac{3}{4}$

$\frac{1}{2} \times \frac{3}{4}$

5. $\frac{2}{3}$ of $\frac{1}{6}$

$\frac{2}{3} \times \frac{1}{6}$

6. $\frac{2}{3}$ of $\frac{2}{5}$

$\frac{2}{3} \times \frac{2}{5}$

7. $\frac{5}{6}$ of $\frac{1}{4}$

$\frac{5}{6} \times \frac{1}{4}$

8. $\frac{3}{4}$ of $\frac{3}{4}$

$\frac{3}{4} \times \frac{3}{4}$

Write a number sentence that states what each picture shows.

9.

10.

11.

Draw a picture to find each product.

12. $\frac{1}{2}$ of $\frac{1}{2}$

$\frac{1}{2} \times \frac{1}{2}$

13. $\frac{1}{3}$ of $\frac{1}{4}$

$\frac{1}{3} \times \frac{1}{4}$

14. $\frac{1}{3}$ of $\frac{1}{3}$

$\frac{1}{3} \times \frac{1}{3}$

15. $\frac{2}{3}$ of $\frac{1}{2}$

$\frac{2}{3} \times \frac{1}{2}$

16. $\frac{1}{6}$ of $\frac{1}{3}$

$\frac{1}{6} \times \frac{1}{3}$

17. $\frac{5}{6}$ of $\frac{1}{2}$

$\frac{5}{6} \times \frac{1}{2}$

18. $\frac{2}{3}$ of $\frac{4}{5}$

$\frac{2}{3} \times \frac{4}{5}$

19. $\frac{4}{5}$ of $\frac{3}{5}$

$\frac{4}{5} \times \frac{3}{5}$

20. $\frac{1}{3}$ of $\frac{1}{2}$

$\frac{1}{3} \times \frac{1}{2}$

21. $\frac{2}{3}$ of $\frac{1}{4}$

$\frac{2}{3} \times \frac{1}{4}$

22. $\frac{7}{8}$ of $\frac{2}{3}$

$\frac{7}{8} \times \frac{2}{3}$

23. $\frac{1}{6}$ of $\frac{1}{4}$

$\frac{1}{6} \times \frac{1}{4}$

24. Number Sense   Is the product of any two proper fractions greater or less than either of those two fractions? Explain.

Problem Solving

Solve each problem by drawing a picture.

25. Land covers $\frac{2}{7}$ of the earth's surface. If $\frac{1}{3}$ of the land is in Asia, what fraction of the earth's surface is land in Asia?

26. About $\frac{1}{6}$ of the world's land is in North America. About $\frac{1}{8}$ of the world's land is in South America. What fraction of the world's land is in North and South America?

Multiplying Fractions

Build Understanding

George makes table tops with Dutch ceramic tiles. For one table, $\frac{3}{4}$ of the tiles have animals on them. Birds are painted on $\frac{1}{3}$ of the animal tiles. What part of the table top is animal tiles with birds painted on them?

$\frac{1}{3}$ of $\frac{3}{4}$ is $\frac{1}{3} \times \frac{3}{4}$

The picture shows that $\frac{1}{3} \times \frac{3}{4} = \frac{3}{12}$. Do you see another way to find the answer?

You could multiply numerators.

$\frac{1}{3} \times \frac{3}{4} = \frac{3}{}$

Then multiply denominators.

$\frac{1}{3} \times \frac{3}{4} = \frac{3}{12}$

On the table top, $\frac{3}{12}$ or $\frac{1}{4}$ of the tiles are animal tiles with birds painted on them.

■ **Talk About Math** Is $\frac{1}{3}$ greater than or less than 1? Why? Is $\frac{3}{4}$ greater or less than 1? Is $\frac{1}{3} \times \frac{3}{4}$ greater or less than 1? Choose another pair of fractions, each less than 1, and find the product. What can you say about the product of two fractions, each less than 1?

In the 17th century, whole walls of Dutch rooms were often covered with tiles. They were also exported to Germany to cover heating stoves.

Check Understanding

For another example, see Set B, pages 408–409.

1. How can you write $\frac{2}{3}$ of $\frac{5}{6}$ as a product?

2. How can you multiply fractions without drawing a picture?

3. Find $\frac{2}{3} \times \frac{5}{6}$ without drawing a picture.

4. Find $\frac{5}{6}$ of $\frac{2}{3}$. How does the answer compare to $\frac{2}{3}$ of $\frac{5}{6}$?

Practice

For More Practice, see Set B, pages 410–411.

Multiply.

5. $\frac{3}{4} \times \frac{5}{6}$ **6.** $\frac{1}{10} \times \frac{1}{10}$ **7.** $\frac{3}{4} \times \frac{1}{4}$ **8.** $\frac{3}{8} \times \frac{2}{3}$ **9.** $\frac{1}{6} \times \frac{5}{6}$

10. $\frac{1}{8} \times \frac{1}{4}$ **11.** $\frac{3}{5} \times \frac{7}{8}$ **12.** $\frac{1}{4} \times \frac{5}{6}$ **13.** $\frac{1}{2} \times \frac{3}{4}$ **14.** $\frac{11}{12} \times \frac{3}{4}$

15. $\frac{1}{3} \times \frac{1}{2}$ **16.** $\frac{1}{6} \times \frac{3}{4}$ **17.** $\frac{2}{5} \times \frac{2}{5}$ **18.** $\frac{8}{9} \times \frac{1}{9}$ **19.** $\frac{2}{3} \times \frac{2}{3}$

20. Number Sense You know that $\frac{1}{2} \times \frac{1}{3} = \frac{1}{6}$ and $\frac{1}{6} \times \frac{5}{6} = \frac{5}{36}$. What does $\frac{1}{2} \times \frac{1}{3} \times \frac{5}{6}$ equal?

Multiply. **Remember** to write each product in simplest form.

21. $\frac{1}{4} \times \frac{2}{5} \times \frac{3}{4}$ **22.** $\frac{2}{3} \times \frac{1}{5} \times \frac{5}{6}$ **23.** $\frac{1}{2} \times \frac{2}{3} \times \frac{3}{8}$

24. Number Sense Is the product of three fractions, each being less than 1, greater than or less than 1?

25. **Calculator** Find the decimal for each fraction in Exercise 21. Multiply the decimals.

Problem Solving

Solve the problem.

26. In the 17th century, English floor tiles were $\frac{3}{4}$-inch thick. Floor tiles now are $\frac{1}{6}$ as thick as the old tiles. How thick are floor tiles now?

A
L
G ▶ **Critical Thinking** Use +, −, or × in each ▦
E to make true sentences.
B
R
A

27. $\frac{7}{8}$ ▦ $\frac{1}{4} = \frac{5}{8}$ **28.** $\frac{1}{4}$ ▦ $\frac{2}{3} = \frac{2}{12}$ or $\frac{1}{6}$

Early Persian tiles were $10\frac{1}{2}$-inch squares. They decorated mosques and public buildings.

Skills ——— Review   pages 22–163

Find each answer.
1. 189 + 334 **2.** 1,250 ÷ 25 **3.** 3,001 − 728 **4.** 349 × 765

Multiplying Fractions and Whole Numbers

Build Understanding

A. Egg Carton Fractions
Materials: Counters
Groups: With a partner

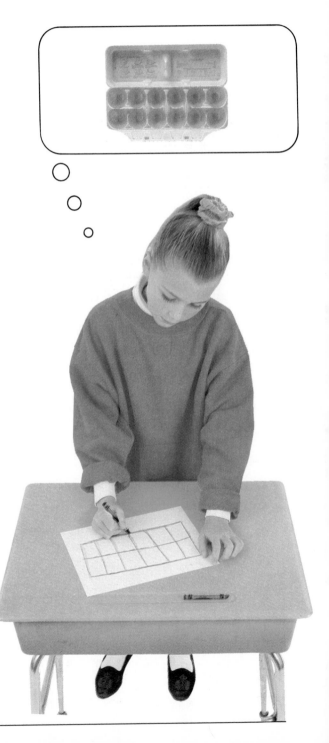

a. Draw a diagram like the picture to act as an egg carton. How many parts are in the whole egg carton?

b. Think of separating the carton into 3 equal parts. What fraction of the whole carton is each part?

c. Put counters into $\frac{1}{3}$ of the spaces. How many spaces have counters?

d. Use your answer from Step c to find $\frac{1}{3}$ of 12. Remember that $\frac{1}{3}$ of 12 means $\frac{1}{3} \times 12$.

e. Next put counters into $\frac{2}{3}$ of the spaces. What is $\frac{2}{3}$ of 12? What is $\frac{2}{3} \times 12$?

B. You can use multiplication of fractions to check your work in the activity.

Any whole number can be written as a fraction with the whole number as the numerator and 1 as the denominator.

$\frac{1}{3} \times 12 = \frac{1}{3} \times \frac{12}{1}$ Multiply the numerators.
Multiply the denominators.

$\qquad = \frac{12}{3}$

$\qquad = 4$ Write the product in simplest form.

$\frac{2}{3} \times 12 = \frac{2}{3} \times \frac{12}{1}$

$\qquad = \frac{24}{3}$

$\qquad = 8$

c. Find $\frac{3}{4}$ of 14.

$\frac{3}{4} \times 14$ Write 14 as a fraction.

$\frac{3}{4} \times \frac{14}{1} = \frac{42}{4}$ Multiply the fractions.

$= 10\frac{2}{4}$

$= 10\frac{1}{2}$ Write the product in simplest form.

■ **Talk About Math** When you multiply $\frac{1}{3} \times 5 \times 12$, is it easier to multiply $\frac{1}{3}$ and 5 first or to multiply $\frac{1}{3}$ and 12 first? Why?

Check Understanding

For another example, see Set C, pages 408–409.

Choose the best answer for Exercises 1–4.

1. To multiply a whole number and a fraction, you should first

  a. write the whole number as a fraction.

  b. write the fraction as a whole number.

  c. round the fraction to the nearest whole number.

2. To write a whole number as a fraction, you should write

  a. 1 in the numerator and the whole number in the denominator.

  b. the product of the whole number and 1.

  c. the whole number in the numerator and 1 in the denominator.

3. To multiply fractions, you should first

  a. add the numerators.

  b. multiply the numerators, then multiply the denominators.

  c. round both fractions to the nearest whole number.

  d. divide the numerator and the denominator by 1.

4. The last step when multiplying fractions is to

  a. round the fraction to the nearest whole number.

  b. write the whole number as a fraction.

  c. write the product in simplest form.

  d. write a 1 in the denominator.

Mental Math Write each whole number as a fraction.

5. 737   **6.** 1   **7.** 17

Multiply.

8. $\frac{4}{5} \times 20$ **9.** $28 \times \frac{2}{7}$

Practice

For More Practice, see Set C, pages 410–411.

Multiply. **Remember** to write the product in simplest form.

10. $\frac{3}{4} \times 12$ **11.** $\frac{7}{8} \times 24$ **12.** $15 \times \frac{3}{5}$ **13.** $\frac{1}{5} \times 2$

14. $\frac{7}{8} \times 40$ **15.** $6 \times \frac{5}{9}$ **16.** $\frac{2}{3} \times 7$ **17.** $\frac{5}{6} \times 15$

18. $\frac{4}{7} \times 14$ **19.** $\frac{3}{4} \times 3$ **20.** $9 \times \frac{4}{18}$ **21.** $\frac{1}{8} \times 32$

22. $\frac{2}{3} \times 18$ **23.** $\frac{3}{4} \times 36$ **24.** $15 \times \frac{3}{5}$ **25.** $\frac{2}{3} \times 8$

26. $\frac{7}{8} \times 24$ **27.** $15 \times \frac{1}{4}$ **28.** $5 \times \frac{3}{20}$ **29.** $\frac{4}{15} \times 60$

30. $\frac{3}{8} \times 16$ **31.** $\frac{1}{5} \times 4$ **32.** $50 \times \frac{5}{6}$ **33.** $9 \times \frac{2}{3}$

34. $6 \times \frac{7}{12}$ **35.** $\frac{3}{4} \times 16$ **36.** $15 \times \frac{4}{5}$ **37.** $\frac{3}{5} \times 4$

38. Number Sense Look at the products you found in Exercises 10–37. Are any products greater than the whole number in the exercise? Write a statement about the product of a proper fraction and a whole number.

Mixed Practice   Add, subtract, or multiply.

39. $\frac{2}{4} + \frac{1}{4}$ **40.** $\frac{2}{4} - \frac{1}{4}$ **41.** $\frac{2}{4} \times \frac{1}{4}$

42. $5 + \frac{4}{9}$ **43.** $5 - \frac{4}{9}$ **44.** $5 \times \frac{4}{9}$

45. $\frac{7}{8} + \frac{3}{4}$ **46.** $\frac{7}{8} - \frac{3}{4}$ **47.** $\frac{7}{8} \times \frac{3}{4}$

48. $\frac{1}{2} + \frac{3}{4} + \frac{5}{8}$ **49.** $\frac{1}{2} \times \frac{3}{4} \times \frac{5}{8}$ **50.** $3\frac{1}{2} - \frac{5}{9}$ **51.** $13 \times \frac{1}{4}$

52. $14\frac{2}{3} - 9\frac{5}{7}$ **53.** $8\frac{3}{4} + 9\frac{7}{9}$ **54.** $\frac{3}{5} \times 20$ **55.** $18 - \frac{5}{6}$

Problem Solving

Kristen saw signs advertising sales at almost every store in the mall. For each regular price in Problems 56–61, find how many dollars would be saved on each item during the sale.

56. Sweater $30

57. Coat $64

58. Gloves $12

59. Watch $100

60. Boots $48

61. Jeans $25

62. Critical Thinking What is the sale price for each item in Problems 56–61?

63. How much would it cost Kristen to buy a sweater, jeans, and boots at the sale price?

TIPS FOR PROBLEM SOLVERS

Think about your own thinking. Pause to ask, "How is this going to help me solve the problem?"

Midchapter ✓ **Checkup**

Use the picture to find each product.

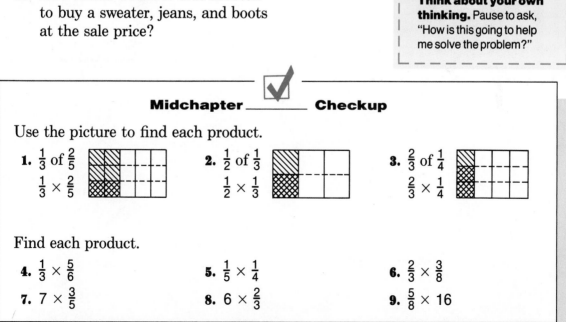

1. $\frac{1}{3}$ of $\frac{2}{5}$
$\frac{1}{3} \times \frac{2}{5}$

2. $\frac{1}{2}$ of $\frac{1}{3}$
$\frac{1}{2} \times \frac{1}{3}$

3. $\frac{2}{3}$ of $\frac{1}{4}$
$\frac{2}{3} \times \frac{1}{4}$

Find each product.

4. $\frac{1}{3} \times \frac{5}{6}$

5. $\frac{1}{5} \times \frac{1}{4}$

6. $\frac{2}{3} \times \frac{3}{8}$

7. $7 \times \frac{3}{5}$

8. $6 \times \frac{2}{3}$

9. $\frac{5}{8} \times 16$

Real-Life Decision Making

You and your friends are planning a bicycle trip in Spotted Deer Park. You will begin the ride at Winding Road Lodge at 9:00 A.M. You must be back at the lodge by 3:30 P.M. Make a schedule for your bicycle trip in the park.

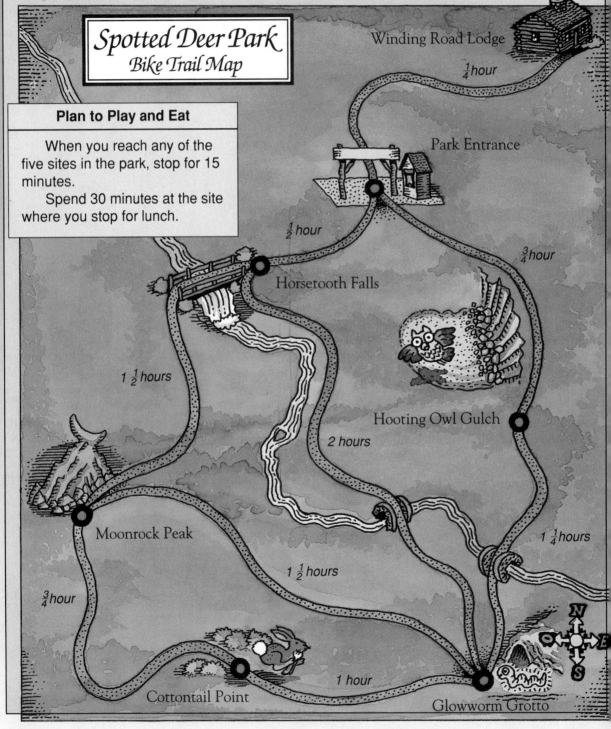

Spotted Deer Park
Bike Trail Map

Winding Road Lodge

$\frac{1}{4}$ hour

Plan to Play and Eat

When you reach any of the five sites in the park, stop for 15 minutes.

Spend 30 minutes at the site where you stop for lunch.

Park Entrance

$\frac{1}{2}$ hour

$\frac{3}{4}$ hour

Horsetooth Falls

$1\frac{1}{2}$ hours

2 hours

Hooting Owl Gulch

Moonrock Peak

$1\frac{1}{4}$ hours

$1\frac{1}{2}$ hours

$\frac{3}{4}$ hour

1 hour

Cottontail Point

Glowworm Grotto

Number-Sense Project

Look back at pages 384-385. Giving everyone an equal share is not always easy to do. Erwin and his two sisters received a package of things to be divided equally among them. What is his "equal share" in each case below?

a. 24 baseball cards

b. 5 dozen postcards

c. Two identical 12-inch strips of garden seeds

d. One $2 coupon to be used for a $5 pizza

Math-at-Home Activity

Take a survey of 12 people who live with or near you. Ask them which is the capital of Florida: Miami, Jacksonville, or Tallahassee.

Copy this circle. Make a circle graph of their answers. Use:
M or red for Miami,
J or blue for Jacksonville,
T or yellow for Tallahassee.

Which is Florida's capital?

Critical Thinking Activity

a. Who owns $\frac{1}{2}$ as much land as Michelle?

b. Who owns $\frac{1}{3}$ as much land as Christine?

c. Who owns $\frac{1}{3}$ as much land as Patrick?

b. Which two people together own $\frac{3}{8}$ of the land?

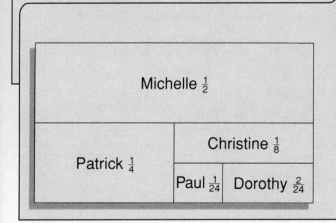

Michelle $\frac{1}{2}$		
Patrick $\frac{1}{4}$	Christine $\frac{1}{8}$	
	Paul $\frac{1}{24}$	Dorothy $\frac{2}{24}$

395

Mixed Numbers as Improper Fractions

Build Understanding

A. Sophia is having carpeting installed in her hallway. The hallway is $3\frac{1}{2}$ feet wide. How many $\frac{1}{2}$-foot-wide carpet tiles will fit across the hallway?

Think of a picture of the hallway.
Think: 1 is the same as 2 halves.
       3 is the same as 6 halves.
       So, $3\frac{1}{2}$ is the same as 7 halves.

The width of the hallway can be carpeted with 7 tiles that are $\frac{1}{2}$ foot wide.

B. Write $3\frac{1}{2}$ as an improper fraction.

$$3\frac{1}{2} = 3 + \frac{1}{2}$$
$$= \frac{3}{1} + \frac{1}{2}$$
$$= \frac{6}{2} + \frac{1}{2}$$
$$= \frac{7}{2}$$

C. A shortcut can be used to change a mixed number to an improper fraction.

$$5\frac{3}{4} = \frac{23}{4}$$

■ **Write About Math** Explain why the shortcut in Example C works. Draw a picture to help you.

Check Understanding

For another example, see Set D, pages 408–409.

1. Write both a mixed number and an improper fraction for each lettered point.

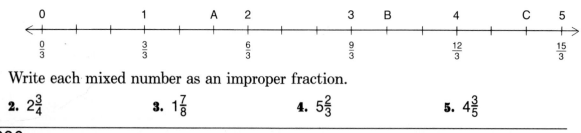

Write each mixed number as an improper fraction.

2. $2\frac{3}{4}$ **3.** $1\frac{7}{8}$ **4.** $5\frac{2}{3}$ **5.** $4\frac{3}{5}$

Practice

For More Practice, see Set D, pages 410–411.

Write each mixed number as an improper fraction.

6. $4\frac{1}{6}$ **7.** $3\frac{1}{4}$ **8.** $5\frac{3}{8}$ **9.** $16\frac{2}{3}$ **10.** $8\frac{2}{9}$ **11.** $5\frac{3}{10}$

12. $3\frac{3}{7}$ **13.** $11\frac{2}{9}$ **14.** $21\frac{2}{5}$ **15.** $14\frac{1}{3}$ **16.** $12\frac{1}{2}$ **17.** $8\frac{3}{10}$

18. $12\frac{2}{6}$ **19.** $13\frac{1}{9}$ **20.** $9\frac{7}{7}$ **21.** $6\frac{1}{4}$ **22.** $1\frac{5}{8}$ **23.** $10\frac{1}{5}$

24. $7\frac{1}{2}$ **25.** $15\frac{1}{3}$ **26.** $20\frac{3}{6}$ **27.** $2\frac{5}{10}$ **28.** $18\frac{4}{7}$ **29.** $1\frac{4}{4}$

Mixed Practice   Write each fraction as a whole or mixed number.

30. $\frac{17}{3}$ **31.** $\frac{13}{10}$ **32.** $\frac{25}{5}$ **33.** $\frac{28}{7}$ **34.** $\frac{21}{3}$ **35.** $\frac{33}{8}$

36. $\frac{16}{2}$ **37.** $\frac{25}{3}$ **38.** $\frac{29}{1}$ **39.** $\frac{21}{5}$ **40.** $\frac{21}{4}$ **41.** $\frac{54}{6}$

42. $\frac{52}{9}$ **43.** $\frac{37}{7}$ **44.** $\frac{64}{1}$ **45.** $\frac{48}{4}$ **46.** $\frac{56}{8}$ **47.** $\frac{13}{6}$

Problem Solving

Solve each problem.

48. When measuring a window for blinds, Sophia found that the window was $31\frac{3}{4}$ inches wide. Write $31\frac{3}{4}$ as an improper fraction.

49. When measuring a room for carpeting, Sophia found the room was 18 feet 5 inches long. Write 18 feet 5 inches as a mixed number. Write the mixed number as an improper fraction.

50. **Critical Thinking**   Which two statements are true about the product of a whole number that is not zero and an improper fraction?

    a. The product is between 0 and 1.
    b. The product is less than the whole number.
    c. The product is greater than or equal to the whole number.
    d. The product equals the improper fraction when the whole number is 1.

Multiplying Mixed Numbers

Build Understanding

A. To make a fishing pole, Mike uses $5\frac{2}{3}$ feet of line.
How much line does he need for 6 fishing poles?

Since the same amount of line is used for each pole, multiply.

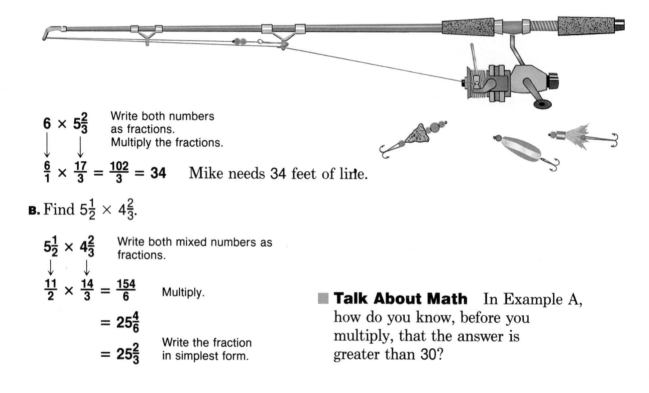

$6 \times 5\frac{2}{3}$ Write both numbers as fractions.
Multiply the fractions.

$\frac{6}{1} \times \frac{17}{3} = \frac{102}{3} = 34$ Mike needs 34 feet of line.

B. Find $5\frac{1}{2} \times 4\frac{2}{3}$.

$5\frac{1}{2} \times 4\frac{2}{3}$ Write both mixed numbers as fractions.

$\frac{11}{2} \times \frac{14}{3} = \frac{154}{6}$ Multiply.

$= 25\frac{4}{6}$

$= 25\frac{2}{3}$ Write the fraction in simplest form.

■ **Talk About Math**   In Example A, how do you know, before you multiply, that the answer is greater than 30?

Check Understanding

For another example, see Set E, pages 408–409.

Complete. **Remember** to write the product in simplest form.

1. $\frac{3}{4} \times 1\frac{1}{2} = \frac{3}{4} \times \frac{\blacksquare}{2} = \frac{\blacksquare}{8} = \blacksquare$ **2.** $2\frac{1}{3} \times 3 = \frac{\blacksquare}{3} \times \frac{\blacksquare}{1} = \frac{\blacksquare}{3} = \blacksquare$

3. $2\frac{3}{4} \times 1\frac{2}{3} = \frac{\blacksquare}{4} \times \frac{\blacksquare}{3} = \frac{\blacksquare}{12} = \blacksquare$ **4.** $4 \times 3\frac{2}{5} = \frac{\blacksquare}{1} \times \frac{\blacksquare}{5} = \frac{\blacksquare}{\blacksquare} = \blacksquare$

Multiply.

5. $\frac{2}{3} \times 6\frac{1}{2}$ **6.** $1\frac{2}{5} \times 3\frac{3}{4}$ **7.** $3 \times 3\frac{1}{2}$ **8.** $2\frac{1}{2} \times 2\frac{1}{5}$

Practice

For More Practice, see Set E, pages 410–411.

Multiply.

9. $3\frac{3}{5} \times 6\frac{1}{2}$ **10.** $2\frac{4}{5} \times 7$ **11.** $\frac{3}{4} \times 5\frac{1}{6}$ **12.** $2 \times 4\frac{5}{6}$ **13.** $3 \times 2\frac{5}{7}$

14. $4\frac{1}{3} \times 1\frac{2}{3}$ **15.** $6\frac{1}{8} \times 2\frac{2}{5}$ **16.** $5 \times 5\frac{4}{5}$ **17.** $10 \times 3\frac{2}{7}$ **18.** $\frac{1}{3} \times 6\frac{2}{3}$

19. $4\frac{3}{4} \times 2\frac{3}{8}$ **20.** $2 \times 4\frac{1}{5}$ **21.** $3 \times 2\frac{2}{3}$ **22.** $1\frac{1}{2} \times 4$ **23.** $5\frac{1}{2} \times 5\frac{1}{8} \times \frac{3}{4}$

Mixed Practice   Multiply.

24. $\frac{3}{8} \times \frac{1}{4}$ **25.** $12 \times \frac{5}{6}$ **26.** $9 \times 2\frac{4}{9}$ **27.** $2\frac{1}{3} \times 1\frac{4}{5}$ **28.** $14 \times 4\frac{5}{7}$

29. $\frac{6}{7} \times 13$ **30.** $\frac{3}{5} \times \frac{4}{10}$ **31.** $3\frac{1}{2} \times 7$ **32.** $4\frac{2}{5} \times 1\frac{1}{9}$ **33.** $\frac{3}{4} \times 4\frac{1}{3}$

34. $10 \times 5\frac{1}{4}$ **35.** $5\frac{3}{5} \times 9\frac{1}{6}$ **36.** $\frac{2}{3} \times \frac{1}{2} \times \frac{4}{7}$ **37.** $2\frac{5}{8} \times \frac{3}{4}$ **38.** $43 \times \frac{1}{2}$

39. $3\frac{1}{2} \times 6$ **40.** $\frac{1}{4} \times \frac{3}{5}$ **41.** $4\frac{1}{2} \times \frac{1}{6}$ **42.** $4 \times 3\frac{1}{2}$ **43.** $\frac{6}{7} \times 4\frac{5}{9}$

Problem Solving

Solve each problem.

44. Mike gave $\frac{1}{2}$ of a $20\frac{5}{8}$-ounce fish to his uncle. How much did his uncle's portion weigh?

45. Estimation Estimate the product of $3\frac{7}{8} \times 6\frac{4}{5}$ by rounding each number to the nearest whole number.

Explore ———— Math

46. Find these products.

   a. $\frac{3}{8} \times \frac{8}{3}$ **b.** $7 \times \frac{1}{7}$

47. What pattern do you notice in the products?

Numbers whose product is 1 are called *reciprocals.*
Find the reciprocal of each number.

48. $\frac{3}{5}$ **49.** $\frac{7}{3}$ **50.** $6\frac{2}{3}$ **51.** $5\frac{3}{4}$

Use Data from a Table

Build Understanding

Length	Weight	Time
1 foot = 12 inches 1 yard = 3 feet 1 mile = 5,280 feet	1 pound = 16 ounces 1 ton = 2,000 pounds	1 minute = 60 seconds 1 hour = 60 minutes 1 day = 24 hours

An Asian elephant weighs about $3\frac{1}{2}$ tons. It normally walks at 4 miles per hour. It can run at 25 miles per hour. What is the weight of the elephant in pounds?

Understand   QUESTION   How many pounds does an Asian elephant weigh?

FACTS   An elephant weighs $3\frac{1}{2}$ tons.

KEY IDEA   Use data from the table of weights to find the number of pounds in one ton. For $3\frac{1}{2}$ tons, there will be $3\frac{1}{2}$ times the number of pounds in one ton.

Plan and Solve   Since 1 ton is 2,000 pounds, $3\frac{1}{2}$ tons will be $3\frac{1}{2} \times 2,000$ pounds.

Paper and Pencil

$3\frac{1}{2} \times 2,000 = \frac{7}{2} \times \frac{2,000}{1}$

$= 7,000$

Calculator

3.5 $\boxed{\times}$ 2000 $\boxed{=}$ *7000.*

An Asian elephant weighs about 7,000 pounds.

Look Back   Estimate $3\frac{1}{2} \times 2,000$. $3\frac{1}{2}$ is between 3 and 4. $3 \times 2,000 = 6,000$ and $4 \times 2,000 = 8,000$. The answer is reasonable.

Elephants are classified as an endangered species.

■ **Write About Math**   What information from the tables would you use to find the weight of the elephant in ounces? Write a number sentence.

PROBLEM SOLVING GUIDE

Understand
QUESTION
FACTS
KEY IDEA

Plan and Solve
STRATEGY
ANSWER

Look Back
SENSIBLE ANSWER
ALTERNATE APPROACH

Check Understanding

1. An Asian elephant carried a load of logs for $1\frac{3}{4}$ miles. Find the distance in feet.

   $1\frac{3}{4}$ miles = $1\frac{3}{4} \times$ ▦ feet

               = ▦ feet

2. The elephant took $\frac{3}{4}$ hour to walk this distance. Find the time in minutes.

   $\frac{3}{4}$ hour = $\frac{3}{4} \times$ ▦ minutes

           = ▦ minutes

Practice

3. If an elephant walks 4 miles per hour, how far can it walk in $3\frac{5}{6}$ hours?

4. Bennie the elephant is $8\frac{2}{3}$ feet tall. What is his height in inches?

5. An elephant worked for $2\frac{2}{5}$ hours lifting logs. How many minutes was this? How many seconds was this?

6. If each elephant can carry up to 600 pounds of cargo, how many elephants are needed to carry 3,400 pounds of cargo?

7. A mother elephant weighed 6,200 pounds. This was 3,700 pounds more than her baby's weight. Find the baby's weight.

8. **Calculator** At 25 miles per hour, how many feet would an elephant run in 1 hour? How many feet would it run in 1 minute?

Choose a ⎯⎯⎯ Strategy

Roses for Everyone Jill cut some roses from her garden. James cut a dozen roses and gave $\frac{1}{2}$ of them to Jill. Then Jill gave Janelle $\frac{1}{2}$ of all the roses she had. When Jill gave Pedro 5 roses, she only had 1 left. How many roses did Jill have originally?

9. How many roses would Jill have if Pedro returned the roses?

10. If Janelle then returned her roses how many roses would Jill have?

11. If James took his roses back, how many roses would Jill have?

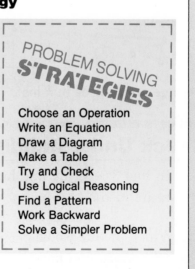

PROBLEM SOLVING STRATEGIES

Choose an Operation
Write an Equation
Draw a Diagram
Make a Table
Try and Check
Use Logical Reasoning
Find a Pattern
Work Backward
Solve a Simpler Problem

Exploring Division by Fractions

Build Understanding

A. Ben is packing lunches for his friends. He has 5 oranges. He wants to put $\frac{1}{2}$ orange into each lunch. How many lunches can have $\frac{1}{2}$ orange?

To find how many halves are in 5, divide 5 by $\frac{1}{2}$.

Use a picture to help.

$5 \div \frac{1}{2} = 10$

Ben can put $\frac{1}{2}$ orange in 10 lunches.

B. Each slice of a loaf of bread is $\frac{1}{8}$ of the loaf. How many slices are in $\frac{1}{2}$ loaf? Find how many eighths are in $\frac{1}{2}$.

Use a picture to help.

$\frac{1}{2} \div \frac{1}{8} = 4$

There are 4 slices in $\frac{1}{2}$ loaf.

■ **Talk About Math** What would you do to check the computation $153 \div 17 = 9$? How could you check the computation in Example B?

Check Understanding

For another example, see Set F, pages 408–409.

1. To find $3 \div \frac{1}{2}$, you find how many ▦ are in ▦.

2. To find $\frac{1}{2} \div \frac{1}{4}$, you find how many ▦ are in ▦.

3. Which picture would help you to find how many eighths are in $\frac{1}{4}$, or $\frac{1}{4} \div \frac{1}{8}$?

a.   b. c.

402

Practice

For More Practice, see Set F, pages 410–411.

Use the pictures to complete the divisions.

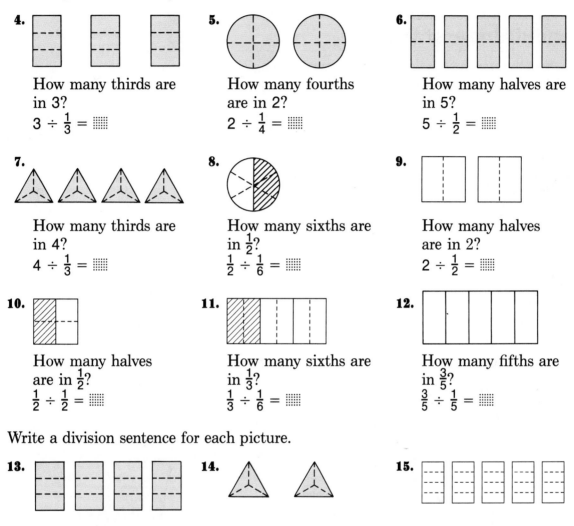

4. How many thirds are in 3?

$3 \div \frac{1}{3} = $ ▦

5. How many fourths are in 2?

$2 \div \frac{1}{4} = $ ▦

6. How many halves are in 5?

$5 \div \frac{1}{2} = $ ▦

7. How many thirds are in 4?

$4 \div \frac{1}{3} = $ ▦

8. How many sixths are in $\frac{1}{2}$?

$\frac{1}{2} \div \frac{1}{6} = $ ▦

9. How many halves are in 2?

$2 \div \frac{1}{2} = $ ▦

10. How many halves are in $\frac{1}{2}$?

$\frac{1}{2} \div \frac{1}{2} = $ ▦

11. How many sixths are in $\frac{1}{3}$?

$\frac{1}{3} \div \frac{1}{6} = $ ▦

12. How many fifths are in $\frac{3}{5}$?

$\frac{3}{5} \div \frac{1}{5} = $ ▦

Write a division sentence for each picture.

13.

14.

15.

16.

17.

18.

Problem Solving

Use a picture to solve each problem.

19. Alice has 3 melons. She wants to serve $\frac{1}{4}$ melon to each guest. How many guests will get $\frac{1}{4}$ melon?

20. In selecting a turkey, a cook should allow $\frac{1}{2}$ pound for each person being served. What is the least a turkey should weigh to feed 16 people?

Choose an Operation

Build Understanding

Stores often have sales to attract customers. They offer a discount that reduces the price of items they sell. What is the sale price of a shirt that regularly costs $18?

Understand   How much will the shirt cost on sale? The regular price is $18 and $\frac{1}{3}$ of that price will be taken off $18. The amount taken off is called the discount.

▶ **Plan and Solve**   STRATEGY   First find the amount of the discount. Find $\frac{1}{3}$ of 18.

$$\frac{1}{3} \times 18 = \frac{1}{3} \times \frac{18}{1} = \frac{18}{3} = 6$$

The amount of the discount is $6.

To find the sale price, subtract the discount from the regular price.

$$
\begin{array}{rl}
\$18 & \text{regular price} \\
-\ \ 6 & \text{discount} \\
\hline
\$12 & \text{sale price}
\end{array}
$$

ANSWER   The sale price of the shirt is $12.

Look Back   The answer is reasonable since the sale price should be less than the regular price, and $12 is less than $18.

■ **Talk About Math**   If the discount is $\frac{1}{3}$, the sale price is $\frac{2}{3}$ of the regular price. Find $\frac{2}{3}$ of $18. Is the answer the same as above?

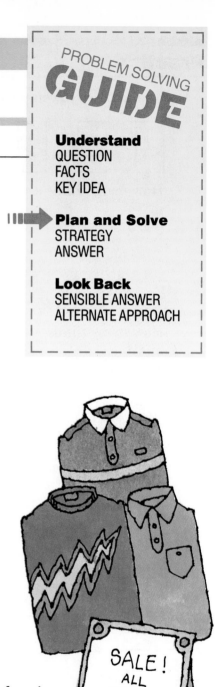

SALE! ALL ITEMS $\frac{1}{3}$ OFF

Check Understanding

The regular price of a pair of running shoes is $24.

1. What is $\frac{1}{4}$ of $24?

2. What is the amount of the discount?

3. What is the sale price?

Practice

4. Appliances are selling for $\frac{1}{4}$ off. The original price of a stove was $456. What is the amount of discount and the sale price?

5. Jeff bought a parka for $\frac{1}{3}$ off the original price, which was $36. How much was the discount? What was the sale price?

6. Originally, a pearl necklace cost $65 and a pair of earrings cost $15. Both items were on sale for $\frac{1}{4}$ off. How much would it cost for the necklace and earrings on sale?

7. Mr. Clark bought an oil filter that originally cost $14.25 for his car. The filter was marked $\frac{1}{3}$ off. How much change did he get from $10.00?

8. Fred bought a jacket on sale for $\frac{1}{3}$ off. The original price was $75. The sales tax was $0.06 on each dollar. What was the total amount Fred paid for the jacket?

9. The sale price of a sofa is $180. The original price was $240. How much is the discount? What fraction of the original price is saved?

Use Data Refer to Problems 56–61 on page 393. Find the sale price.

10. Sweater   11. Coat   12. Gloves   13. Watch   14. Boots   15. Jeans

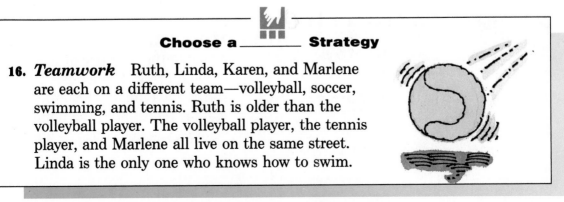

Choose a _____ Strategy

16. *Teamwork* Ruth, Linda, Karen, and Marlene are each on a different team—volleyball, soccer, swimming, and tennis. Ruth is older than the volleyball player. The volleyball player, the tennis player, and Marlene all live on the same street. Linda is the only one who knows how to swim.

Skills Review

Write a number sentence that states what each picture shows.

1.   **2.**

Draw a picture for each product.

3. $\frac{1}{2} \times \frac{1}{3}$ **4.** $\frac{3}{4} \times \frac{2}{3}$

Multiply.

5. $\frac{1}{3} \times \frac{3}{4}$ **6.** $\frac{5}{6} \times \frac{1}{4}$ **7.** $\frac{3}{8} \times \frac{2}{3}$

8. $\frac{2}{3} \times 10$ **9.** $\frac{3}{4} \times 14$ **10.** $\frac{2}{5} \times 12$

11. $3\frac{2}{5} \times \frac{1}{3}$ **12.** $4 \times 3\frac{1}{6}$

13. $2\frac{1}{2} \times 6\frac{3}{4}$ **14.** $1\frac{11}{12} \times 2$

Write each mixed number as an improper fraction.

15. $3\frac{2}{3}$ **16.** $2\frac{1}{6}$ **17.** $5\frac{3}{8}$

Use the pictures to complete the divisions.

18.

How many halves are in 4? $4 \div \frac{1}{2} = $ ▦

19.

How many fourths are in 3? $3 \div \frac{1}{4} = $ ▦

Problem-Solving Review

Solve each problem.

20. If 3 melons cost $2, how much do 2 melons cost?

21. Of the 30 people in a play, $\frac{5}{6}$ had speaking parts. How many people had speaking parts?

22. Joy and James divided equally the $13\frac{5}{8}$ pounds of berries they picked. How many pounds did each person get?

23. Larry lost $2\frac{1}{2}$ pounds per week for 6 weeks. How much weight did he lose in all?

24. Mira rode her horse for 2 hours and 20 minutes. If she rode $4\frac{1}{2}$ miles per hour, how far did she ride?

25. A protoceratops was 6 feet long. Its eggs were about 8 inches long. How many times as long as its egg was the protoceratops?

26. **Data File** Jolene wants to sew 3 pairs of shorts. Using the information on pages 528–529, find the amount of fabric and braid trim she must buy.

27. **Make a Data File** For one day, estimate the quantity of food you eat and drink. Use a chart that shows the number of calories in various foods. Find the number of calories you consumed in one day.

Round 12,805.399 to the nearest

1. thousand.   **2.** whole number.

3. tenth.   **4.** hundredth.

Find the area of each figure.

5. 10 yd, 6 yd

6. 4 cm, 6 cm

What time will it be

7. 3 h 15 min after 5:30 P.M.?

8. 2 h 50 min after 8:45 A.M.?

Complete.

9. 4 L = ▦ mL   **10.** 35 kg = ▦ g

11. 2 gal 1 qt = ▦ qt

12. 4,000 lb = ▦ T

Find the average of each group of numbers.

13. 9   5   8   5   3

14. 85   77   68   94

Compute.

15. 53.62 + 9.842 + 2.1

16. 78.3 − 64.75

17. 63.9 ÷ 3   **18.** 3.05 × 0.094

Write each mixed number as an improper fraction.

19. $3\frac{3}{4}$ **20.** $5\frac{2}{9}$ **21.** $2\frac{5}{6}$

Draw the next three figures in the pattern. Complete the table.

1 Row   2 Rows   3 Rows

22.

Number of						
Rows	1	2	3	4	5	6
Squares	1	4	9	▦	▦	▦

Describe the pattern. Then write the next four numbers.

23. 3, 9, 15, 21, . . .

24. 5, 8, 6, 9, . . .

25. 7, 14, 13, 26, . . .

Write each fraction in lowest terms.

26. $\frac{9}{27}$ **27.** $\frac{10}{25}$ **28.** $\frac{12}{18}$

Add or subtract.

29. $\frac{4}{7} + \frac{5}{7}$ **30.** $\frac{8}{9} - \frac{2}{9}$ **31.** $8 - 2\frac{3}{4}$

32. $7\frac{1}{4} - 2\frac{3}{4}$ **33.** $\frac{5}{12} + \frac{5}{6}$

34. $\frac{3}{8} + \frac{5}{6}$ **35.** $\frac{1}{3} - \frac{1}{4}$

36. $6\frac{3}{4} + 2\frac{2}{5}$ **37.** $8\frac{1}{2} - 4\frac{2}{7}$

38. Draw a picture to find $\frac{1}{4} \times \frac{2}{3}$.

Multiply.

39. $\frac{3}{5} \times \frac{1}{2}$ **40.** $\frac{5}{9} \times \frac{2}{3}$ **41.** $\frac{5}{6} \times 4$

42. $4\frac{1}{4} \times 1\frac{2}{3}$ **43.** $3\frac{1}{5} \times 2\frac{3}{4}$

Reteaching

Set A   pages 386–387

Draw a picture to find
$\frac{1}{3}$ of $\frac{3}{4}$.

First shade $\frac{3}{4}$.   Next shade $\frac{1}{3}$ of that.

Of the 12 parts in the second picture,
3 parts are shaded twice.

$\frac{1}{3}$ of $\frac{3}{4}$ is $\frac{3}{12}$, or $\frac{1}{4}$.

Remember to write the product in
simplest form.

Use the picture to find the product.

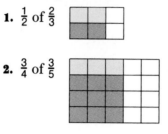

1. $\frac{1}{2}$ of $\frac{2}{3}$

2. $\frac{3}{4}$ of $\frac{3}{5}$

Set B   pages 388–389

Find $\frac{7}{8}$ of $\frac{4}{5}$.

To multiply fractions, multiply the
numerators and multiply the denominators.
Write the answer in simplest form.

$\frac{7}{8} \times \frac{4}{5} = \frac{7 \times 4}{8 \times 5}$

$\qquad = \frac{28}{40}$ or $\frac{7}{10}$

Remember that the product of two
fractions is less than 1 if both fractions
are less than 1.

Multiply.

1. $\frac{3}{5} \times \frac{3}{4}$ **2.** $\frac{1}{8} \times \frac{5}{6}$

3. $\frac{7}{8} \times \frac{2}{5}$ **4.** $\frac{3}{4} \times \frac{3}{4}$

Set C   pages 390–393

Find $\frac{3}{8}$ of 18.

$\frac{3}{8}$ of 18 means $\frac{3}{8} \times 18$.

Multiply the fractions.

$\frac{3}{8} \times \frac{18}{1} = \frac{54}{8}$ Think: $8\overline{)54}$

$\qquad = 6\frac{6}{8}$

$\qquad = 6\frac{3}{4}$

Remember that any whole number can be
written as a fraction with the whole
number as the numerator and 1 as the
denominator.

Multiply. Remember to write the product
in simplest form.

1. $\frac{5}{6} \times 18$ **2.** $\frac{3}{7} \times 21$

3. $9 \times \frac{3}{4}$ **4.** $12 \times \frac{2}{5}$

5. $16 \times \frac{3}{8}$ **6.** $\frac{3}{10} \times 22$

Set D   pages 396–397

Write $4\frac{3}{5}$ as an improper fraction.

$4\frac{3}{5} = 4 + \frac{3}{5}$

$\quad = \frac{4}{1} + \frac{3}{5}$

Rename $\frac{4}{1}$ with a denominator of 5 so it can be added to $\frac{3}{5}$.

$\quad = \frac{20}{5} + \frac{3}{5}$

$\quad = \frac{23}{5}$

Remember that when you write a mixed number as an improper fraction, you can check by writing the improper fraction as a mixed number.

Write each mixed number as an improper fraction.

1. $5\frac{1}{8}$ **2.** $9\frac{3}{5}$

3. $12\frac{3}{4}$ **4.** $16\frac{2}{3}$

Set E   pages 398–399

Find $3\frac{2}{3} \times 4\frac{1}{2}$.

To multiply with mixed numbers, write the mixed numbers as improper fractions.

$3\frac{2}{3} \times 4\frac{1}{2} = \frac{11}{3} \times \frac{9}{2}$

$\quad\quad = \frac{99}{6}$

$\quad\quad = 16\frac{3}{6}$

$\quad\quad = 16\frac{1}{2}$

Remember to write your answer in simplest form.

Multiply.

1. $2\frac{1}{2} \times 4\frac{1}{5}$ **2.** $4\frac{2}{5} \times 6$

3. $8\frac{1}{3} \times 4\frac{1}{6}$ **4.** $\frac{1}{3} \times 6\frac{1}{2}$

5. $6\frac{3}{5} \times 1\frac{2}{3}$ **6.** $\frac{1}{4} \times 8\frac{1}{2}$

7. $10 \times 4\frac{3}{5}$ **8.** $2 \times 6\frac{7}{8}$

Set F   pages 402–403

How many eighths are in 3?

Find $3 \div \frac{1}{8}$.

Draw figures to show 3 and divide each figure into 8 equal parts.

Count the total number of parts. So
$3 \div \frac{1}{8} = 24$.

Remember that you can check the answer when dividing by multiplying the quotient by the divisor. This number should be equal to the dividend.

Use the pictures to complete the divisions.

1.   **2.**

How many fourths   How many fifths
are in 3?   are in 4?

$3 \div \frac{1}{4} = $ ▦ $4 \div \frac{1}{5} = $ ▦

More Practice

Set A pages 386–387

Use the pictures to find the product.

1. $\frac{2}{3}$ of $\frac{3}{5}$

$\frac{2}{3} \times \frac{3}{5}$

2. $\frac{3}{4}$ of $\frac{4}{5}$

$\frac{3}{4} \times \frac{4}{5}$

3. $\frac{2}{3}$ of $\frac{4}{5}$

$\frac{2}{3} \times \frac{4}{5}$

Write a number sentence that states what each picture shows.

4.

5.

6.

Draw a picture to find each product.

7. $\frac{1}{2}$ of $\frac{1}{3}$

$\frac{1}{2} \times \frac{1}{3}$

8. $\frac{1}{3}$ of $\frac{1}{6}$

$\frac{1}{3} \times \frac{1}{6}$

9. $\frac{3}{4}$ of $\frac{3}{5}$

$\frac{3}{4} \times \frac{3}{5}$

10. $\frac{1}{4}$ of $\frac{2}{5}$

$\frac{1}{4} \times \frac{2}{5}$

Set B pages 388–389

Multiply.

1. $\frac{1}{4} \times \frac{1}{6}$

2. $\frac{3}{4} \times \frac{3}{8}$

3. $\frac{2}{3} \times \frac{7}{8}$

4. $\frac{2}{5} \times \frac{2}{3}$

5. $\frac{5}{6} \times \frac{3}{4}$

6. $\frac{7}{8} \times \frac{3}{4}$

7. $\frac{5}{12} \times \frac{1}{3}$

8. $\frac{1}{8} \times \frac{5}{6}$

Set C pages 390–393

Multiply. **Remember** to write the product in simplest form.

1. $\frac{1}{3} \times 21$

2. $\frac{3}{4} \times 16$

3. $24 \times \frac{7}{8}$

4. $\frac{1}{6} \times 42$

5. $\frac{2}{5} \times 20$

6. $\frac{2}{3} \times 8$

7. $\frac{5}{6} \times 10$

8. $\frac{3}{8} \times 48$

9. $\frac{2}{3} \times 6$

10. $\frac{1}{5} \times 45$

11. $\frac{3}{8} \times 32$

12. $\frac{1}{7} \times 42$

13. $\frac{7}{8} \times 16$

14. $24 \times \frac{1}{6}$

15. $\frac{2}{3} \times 10$

16. $55 \times \frac{1}{5}$

17. $\frac{1}{4} \times 33$

18. $\frac{5}{6} \times 8$

19. $24 \times \frac{3}{8}$

20. $\frac{1}{3} \times 18$

Set D   pages 396–397

Write each mixed number as an improper fraction.

1. $8\frac{1}{3}$ **2.** $5\frac{1}{4}$ **3.** $7\frac{2}{5}$ **4.** $9\frac{1}{6}$ **5.** $12\frac{2}{3}$ **6.** $14\frac{3}{5}$

Mixed Practice   Write a mixed number or a whole number for each fraction.

7. $\frac{18}{7}$ **8.** $\frac{21}{4}$ **9.** $\frac{32}{8}$ **10.** $\frac{63}{7}$ **11.** $\frac{37}{5}$ **12.** $\frac{18}{1}$

Set E   pages 398–399

Multiply. **Remember** to estimate to be sure your answer
is reasonable.

1. $2\frac{1}{2} \times 1\frac{2}{3}$ **2.** $4\frac{1}{2} \times 1\frac{7}{8}$ **3.** $1\frac{2}{3} \times 3\frac{3}{4}$ **4.** $\frac{3}{4} \times 4\frac{1}{4}$

5. $9\frac{1}{6} \times 8\frac{3}{5}$ **6.** $4\frac{2}{3} \times 3\frac{5}{8}$ **7.** $3\frac{1}{10} \times 5$ **8.** $6\frac{3}{8} \times 5\frac{1}{5}$

Mixed Practice   Multiply. **Remember** to write the product in simplest form.

9. $\frac{1}{6} \times \frac{5}{8}$ **10.** $20 \times \frac{4}{5}$ **11.** $\frac{3}{10} \times \frac{5}{6}$ **12.** $16 \times 2\frac{1}{8}$

13. $\frac{1}{3} \times 2\frac{1}{6}$ **14.** $\frac{5}{6} \times 15$ **15.** $\frac{4}{5} \times \frac{7}{8}$ **16.** $1\frac{1}{8} \times 2\frac{4}{7}$

Set F   pages 402–403

Use the pictures to complete the divisions.

1. **2.** **3.**

How many fourths are
in 5?

$5 \div \frac{1}{4} = $ ▦

How many eighths are
in 2?

$2 \div \frac{1}{8} = $ ▦

How many sixths are
in $\frac{1}{2}$?

$\frac{1}{2} \div \frac{1}{6} = $ ▦

Write a division sentence for each picture.

4.   **5.**   **6.**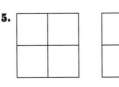

Enrichment

Shortcut in Multiplying Fractions

You can use a shortcut to find $\frac{3}{4} \times \frac{6}{7}$.

Carl multiplied like this.

Clyde used a shortcut to multiply.

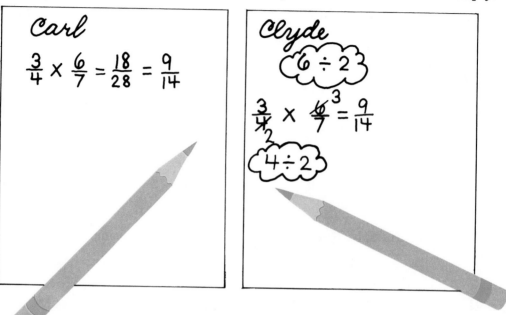

He divided one numerator and one denominator by the same number, 2.

Here is another example of how to use the shortcut.

$$5 \div 5$$
$$1$$
$$\frac{\cancel{5}}{7} \times \frac{6}{\cancel{25}} = \frac{6}{35}$$
$$5$$
$$25 \div 5$$

Multiply. Use the shortcut.

1. $\frac{2}{3} \times \frac{1}{4}$ 2. $\frac{4}{7} \times \frac{3}{4}$ 3. $\frac{3}{4} \times \frac{1}{3}$ 4. $\frac{4}{7} \times \frac{5}{12}$ 5. $\frac{3}{10} \times \frac{5}{8}$

6. $\frac{1}{2} \times \frac{2}{3}$ 7. $\frac{1}{6} \times \frac{4}{5}$ 8. $\frac{5}{12} \times \frac{8}{9}$ 9. $\frac{9}{10} \times \frac{7}{15}$ 10. $\frac{7}{25} \times \frac{10}{11}$

11. $\frac{6}{7} \times \frac{5}{9}$ 12. $\frac{5}{6} \times \frac{4}{7}$ 13. $\frac{5}{6} \times 12$ 14. $24 \times \frac{3}{8}$ 15. $16 \times \frac{3}{4}$

Chapter 12 Review/Test

1. Write a number sentence that states what the picture shows.

Multiply.

2. $\frac{1}{2} \times \frac{5}{6}$ 3. $\frac{1}{8} \times \frac{1}{8}$

4. $\frac{2}{3} \times 24$ 5. $\frac{1}{3} \times 7$

6. $7\frac{1}{2} \times \frac{1}{5}$ 7. $3\frac{1}{3} \times 1\frac{3}{4}$

Write each mixed number as an improper fraction.

8. $3\frac{1}{6}$ 9. $2\frac{3}{8}$

10. Use the picture to answer the question.

How many fourths are in 5?

11. If you find the product of two fractions, each less than 1, will the product be less than or greater than 1?

Solve each problem.

12. George has 5 quarts of juice. He will serve each guest $\frac{1}{4}$ quart of juice. How many guests will get $\frac{1}{4}$ quart of juice?

13. In one class, $\frac{1}{3}$ of the students are in the band. Of these students, $\frac{1}{2}$ are also in the chorus. What fraction of the students are in both the band and the chorus?

14. Use the table below to solve the problem.

| 1 minute = 60 seconds |
| 1 hour = 60 minutes |
| 1 day = 24 hours |

A sailboat makes a trip that lasts $2\frac{1}{2}$ days. How many hours is this?

Read the problem below. Then answer the question.

Jeffry bought a sweater on sale for $\frac{1}{3}$ off. The original price was $27. How much change did he receive from $30?

15. Which of the following statements is true?

   a. The discount is $27.

   b. The discount is $\frac{1}{3}$ of $27.

   c. The discounted price is $27.

16. **Write About Math** How do you find the product of two fractions?

Statistics, Graphing, and Probability

13

Number-Sense Project

Estimate
Predict the most common choice of a pet by people who live in in a city.

Gather Data
Show 5 people a list of pets and ask them what their first choice would be if they lived in a city.

Analyze and Report
Write several sentences to compare your prediction with the data you collected. Compare your results with those of other students.

Did You Know: A poll was taken to find the most popular choice for an exotic pet. The most common choice was a monkey, second was a lion, and there was a tie between an elephant and a tiger for third place. More than 60 animals were named, even a skunk, a hyena, and an alligator.

Collecting Data

Build Understanding

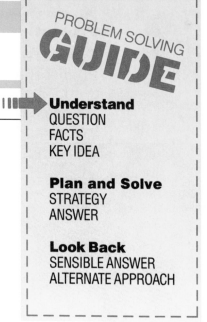

PROBLEM SOLVING GUIDE

▶ **Understand**
QUESTION
FACTS
KEY IDEA

Plan and Solve
STRATEGY
ANSWER

Look Back
SENSIBLE ANSWER
ALTERNATE APPROACH

What subjects do you think students like best?

In a national survey, students named their favorite subject. The results, in order, were math, science, gym, and art. Carmen wondered whether students in her school would choose the same subjects in the same order.

▶ **Understand** QUESTION How can Carmen collect data that she can compare with the results of the national survey?

FACTS She knows the national survey results and which subjects are taught in her school.

KEY IDEA Carmen could survey all the students in her school. Or she could ask a *sample*, a small number of students. In a random sample, all students have an equal chance of being chosen.

Plan and Solve Carmen chose four students from each room by drawing their names from a hat. She asked them, "What is your favorite subject?" She recorded the results in a frequency table.

Favorite subject	Tally	Number of students
Math	⦀⦀ ⦀⦀ ⦀⦀ ///	18
Science	⦀⦀ ⦀⦀ ////	14
Gym	⦀⦀ ⦀⦀ ⦀⦀ ⦀⦀ ////	24
Art	⦀⦀ /	6
Reading	⦀⦀ ⦀⦀ ⦀⦀	15
Social Studies	⦀⦀ ///	8

She ordered her data. In order, the favorites were gym, math, reading, and science. Her results differed from those in the national survey.

Look Back Are the frequencies and ordering correct?

■ **Talk About Math** Suppose Carmen had counted smiles during a lesson in each subject. Would that have been a good way to collect data? Why or why not? When could observation be used to collect data?

Check Understanding

1. Why do you think Carmen decided to survey only some students?

2. Why should a sample be chosen randomly?

3. How might the results have differed if Carmen had surveyed only fifth graders?

4. How might the results have differed if Carmen had surveyed all students?

5. How might the results have differed if students had chosen from a list of subjects?

Practice

For each item, tell whom you would survey and the question you would ask.

6. Favorite sport of students in your state

7. Favorite pet of people in your community

8. Favorite color of students in your class

9. Favorite food of students in your school

Choose a _____ Strategy

The Mummies Have It!

10. The class voted on what to see at the museum. Each student had one vote. Jewelry got 5 votes. Costumes got 9 votes. The mummies won by getting 6 votes more than the runner-up. These 6 votes were $\frac{1}{5}$ of all the votes cast. Sculpture got the rest of the votes. How large is the class? How many votes did each kind of exhibit get?

Organizing Data

Build Understanding

What kind of job would you like after you finish school?

A. Aki collected data for a social studies report on new jobs expected to be available in the year 2000. With her data, she prepared a table to display the information.

After looking at the table, Aki saw that she could display her information better if she put it into a **bar graph.** A bar graph is one way to display information using numbers. The display helps you to compare quantities easily. How would you find the number of new jobs in food services from the graph?

Find the bar for food services. Move down from the end of the bar to the number on the horizontal scale.

What Kind of Job...

Type of Job	Number of New Jobs
Health Offices	1,400,000
Personnel	832,000
Food Services	2,500,000
Construction	890,000
Nursing	852,000

Where the New Jobs Will Be

Number of Jobs (in millions)

Preferred Jobs

Each 👤 stands for two students.

B. Stella asked 50 students which of these jobs they preferred. The **pictograph** shows the results. A pictograph is another way to display quantities. It uses pictures or symbols.

How many students prefer personnel work?

Since 👤 stands for two students, 👤 stands for one student.

There were 13 students who preferred personnel work.

c. Earl wants to find a restaurant job in Rocky City. Rocky City is a ski resort that also has a famous summer music festival. The ***broken-line graph*** shows the number of restaurant jobs available throughout the year in Rocky City.

Restaurant Employees, Rocky City

About how many people are employed in Rocky City restaurants in August?

Find August on the horizontal scale. Move straight up to the point on the grid. From that point, move along the grid line straight across to the vertical scale.

About **600** people work in Rocky City restaurants in August.

A broken-line graph can show how quantities change over time. Only the graph points, and not the line segments in-between, show data.

■ **Talk About Math** Would you use a broken-line graph to compare the salaries for different jobs? Explain.

Check Understanding

For another example, see Set A, pages 444–445.

Use the graphs in Examples A, B, and C.

1. Could you use a pictograph instead of a bar graph for the data in Example A? Explain.

2. Could you use a broken-line graph instead of the pictograph in Example B? Explain.

3. How many more people worked in Rocky City restaurants in April than in May?

419

Practice

For More Practice, see Set A, pages 446–447.

This broken-line graph shows the number of people who worked for the city of Howesville each year.

4. In which year were the most people employed by the city?

5. In which year were the fewest people employed by the city?

6. About how many people worked for the city in 1990?

7. About how many more people worked for the city in 1989 than in 1986?

This pictograph shows how many years of school are needed for some jobs.

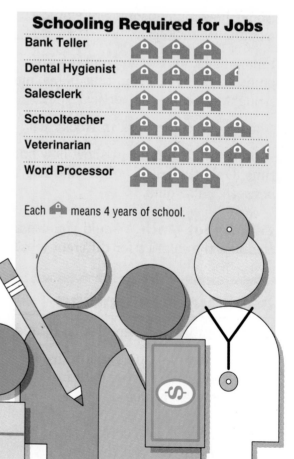

8. Which kind of work takes the longest time in school?

9. Which jobs need the least time in school?

10. How many more years of school does a veterinarian need than a dental hygienist?

11. What kind of graph would best show how the number of students who work part-time has increased over the years?

12. The weekly incomes for five types of work are as follows: Construction, $540; Mining, $637; Factory, $487; Transportation, $566; Trade, $438. Organize these data into a table. What kind of graph would you use to show these data? Why?

13. Five after-school jobs were listed in the school paper. Seven students applied for baby-sitting, 3 for dog walking, 15 for lawn mowing, 8 for newspaper delivery, and 2 for weeding. Put these data into a table. What kind of graph would you use to show the data? Why?

14. Make a graph to show the data given in Problem 12.

15. Make a graph to show the data given in Problem 13.

16. This table shows the weekly incomes for the jobs listed in Problem 13. What kind of graph would you use to show the data? Why?

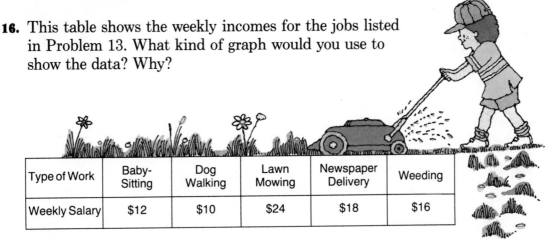

Type of Work	Baby-Sitting	Dog Walking	Lawn Mowing	Newspaper Delivery	Weeding
Weekly Salary	$12	$10	$24	$18	$16

17. Make a graph to show the data given in Problem 16.

Problem Solving

Solve these problems.

18. Number Sense In Example C, during which month were there twice as many restaurant workers as the month before?

19. Critical Thinking In Example B, about half the students Stella surveyed were female. Does this fact mean that 6 of the 12 students who chose nursing were females? Explain.

Skills _____ Review pages 326–327

Compare. Use $<$, $>$, or $=$.

1. $\frac{1}{3}$ ▦ $\frac{1}{5}$ **2.** $\frac{2}{3}$ ▦ $\frac{7}{8}$ **3.** $\frac{5}{6}$ ▦ $\frac{7}{10}$ **4.** $\frac{3}{4}$ ▦ $\frac{5}{8}$ **5.** $\frac{9}{16}$ ▦ $\frac{1}{2}$

Making a Broken-Line Graph

Build Understanding

Check the Census Counts
Materials: Ruler, grid paper

How can you tell if the number of people in your community is growing?

Every ten years the people of the United States are counted by the Bureau of the Census. This population census tells the size and other characteristics of the population. How has the size of the population of your community changed over the last 40 years?

a. *Gather data* Obtain the results of the population censuses for your community from 1950 to 1990. Ask for the data at a public library or a government office.

b. Write a title for the graph.

c. Put the years on the horizontal scale. Label the scale.

d. Decide how to round the numbers.

e. Choose numbers for the vertical scale. Be sure the smallest and largest numbers of the data fit on the graph. Write the numbers for the scale and label it.

f. Plot the points and connect them.

g. What trend does the graph show?

■ **Talk About Math** Why is this kind of graph called a broken-line graph?

The year 1990 was the 200th anniversary of the population census in the U.S.

Sometimes, to save space, go from 0 to your smallest number on the vertical scale. Draw a zigzag line to show that this interval is larger than the others.

Check Understanding

For another example, see Set B, pages 444–445.

Use your data and graph.

1. What is the size of the first interval on the vertical scale?

2. What is the size of the other intervals on the vertical scale?

3. Does the graph show the size of the population in 1965? Explain your answer.

4. Would a broken-line graph best show the difference in the sizes of the 1970 and 1990 populations?

Practice

For More Practice, see Set B, pages 446–447.

Use the table below to make two broken-line graphs showing the following. **Remember** to draw a zigzag line on the population scale to save space.

5. Size of the U.S. population, aged 5-17 years, 1960-2010, rounded to the nearest million

6. Size of the total U.S. population, 1960-2010, rounded to the nearest ten million

U S Population (in millions), 1960-2010*						
Age Range	1960	1970	1980	1990*	2000*	2010*
5-17 years	44.2	52.6	47.2	45.6	48.8	45.7
All Ages	180.7	205.1	227.8	250.4	268.3	282.6
						* projected data for 1990-2010

7. How has the population changed in the 5-17 year age range since 1960?

8. Has the size of the total population changed in the same way?

Problem Solving

Read for the facts to solve the problems.

9. The Census Bureau estimated that 1,041,400 U.S. residents were touring foreign countries on May 1, 1988. Of these, 209,900 were in Canada and 203,100 were in Mexico. How many tourists were visiting other countries on that day?

10. Use the table above. How many people does the Census Bureau expect will be living in the United States in 2010? What is the projected increase in U.S. population from 1990 to 2010?

Reading and Interpreting a Line Graph

Build Understanding

Have you ever tried to estimate how long it would take you to finish reading a book?

A **line graph** shows the rate at which something happens. This line graph shows how many book pages Ron reads in 1 hour, 2 hours, and so on, when he is reading for his own enjoyment. At this rate, how long will it take Ron to read 30 pages?

On the graph, follow the dotted line from 30 pages to the right until it meets the blue line. Follow the dotted line down from that point to the hours at the bottom.

At this rate, Ron will spend $1\frac{1}{2}$ hours reading 30 pages of his book.

Ron's Reading for Enjoyment Rate

- **Talk About Math** How is a line graph different from a broken-line graph? How are the two kinds of graphs alike?

How many books have you read for enjoyment this year?

Check Understanding

1. How long does it take Ron to read 40 pages?

2. How would you find the number of pages Ron can read in 1 hour?

3. How long do you think it takes Ron to read 50 pages?

4. How many pages does Ron read in $3\frac{1}{2}$ hours?

Practice

This graph shows how many pages Ron can carefully review when he is studying for a test. Use this graph and the one on page 424.

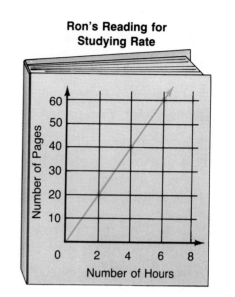

Ron's Reading for Studying Rate

5. Ron is going to study for his social studies test from 7:00 to 8:00 tonight. How many pages will he review?

6. How long would it take Ron to study 60 pages?

7. How many pages could Ron study in 4 hours?

8. The chapter Ron is studying is 30 pages long. How much time should he put aside for studying the chapter?

9. How many pages of his favorite storybook could Ron read in the same amount of time he put aside for studying 30 pages?

10. One night Ron read 40 pages from his favorite storybook. Then he studied 20 pages in his science book for a test. How long did Ron spend on these two books?

11. If Ron has 50 pages to study next week, how much time should he leave for studying on each of the five school nights?

12. If Ron studies x pages for a test, how many pages could Ron read for enjoyment in the same amount of time?

ALGEBRA

Problem Solving

Estimation Use estimation to solve each problem.

13. Ron is reading a book that has 719 pages. Use the graph on page 424. About how long will it take Ron to read the entire book?

14. Read a story for 15 minutes, and note how many pages you read. About how many pages could you read in an hour?

15. About how many hours will it take you to read 719 pages?

TIPS FOR PROBLEM SOLVERS

Compare problems to help you relate new problems to ones you've solved before.

Making a Line Graph

Treadmill at 4 Miles Per Hour		
Number of Miles	Number of Minutes	Ordered Pairs
0	0	(0,0)
1	15	(1,15)
3	▦	(3,▦)
5	▦	(▦,▦)
8	▦	(▦,▦)

Build Understanding

Walk a Mile on a Graph
Materials: Ruler, grid paper

Walking on a treadmill is good exercise. You can make a line graph to show how long it would take you to walk a certain number of miles on a treadmill set for 4 miles an hour. At this rate, you can walk 1 mile in 15 minutes.

a. Copy and complete the table.

b. Draw a grid like the one shown at the right. What labels will you use for the scales? Label them, and write a title for the graph.

c. What intervals will you use to show the minutes and the miles? Write the intervals along the scales.

d. Where will you draw the line on the graph? On your graph, plot the ordered pairs shown in your table. Draw a line to connect them.

■ **Talk About Math** Explain how you could use the graph to find how long it would take to walk a number of miles that are not shown in the table or on the graph.

Check Understanding

For another example, see Set C, pages 444–445.

Use your table and graph to answer the questions.

1. How far can you walk in 30 minutes?

2. How far can you walk in 1 hour?

3. How long will it take to walk 6 miles?

4. How long will it take to walk 9 miles?

Practice

For More Practice, see Set C, pages 446–447.

Suppose you set the speed of the treadmill at 2 miles an hour. At this rate, how many minutes would it take to walk

5. 1 mile?   **6.** 3 miles?   **7.** 6 miles?

Use the information in Exercises 5-7 to make a table showing ordered pairs for the following.

8. Time taken to walk 3 miles

9. Distance covered in 180 minutes

10. Use the data from your table to make a line graph. **Remember** to plan the intervals so the least and greatest numbers will fit on the graph.

Use your graph to answer the questions.

11. How long does it take to walk 4 miles?

12. How far can you walk in 150 minutes?

Problem Solving

Answer each question.

13. If you walked for 15 minutes at 2 miles an hour, 30 minutes at 4 miles an hour, and another 15 minutes at 2 miles an hour, how far would you walk?

14. Critical Thinking Suppose you walked for 45 minutes at 4 miles an hour. How long would your friend have to walk at 2 miles an hour to cover the same distance?

Midchapter Checkup

1. Whom would you survey and what question would you ask to find the favorite Major League baseball team of students in your school?

2. When is a broken-line graph best used?

3. What does the zigzag line on a scale of a broken-line graph mean?

4. What does a line graph show?

5. How can each point on a line graph be named?

Real-Life Decision Making

Suppose you found these two unusual types of graphs in a newspaper. They show the weekly allowance of 19 students in your town. The graphs show the same information but in different ways.

Box Plot

Stem-and Leaf Plot

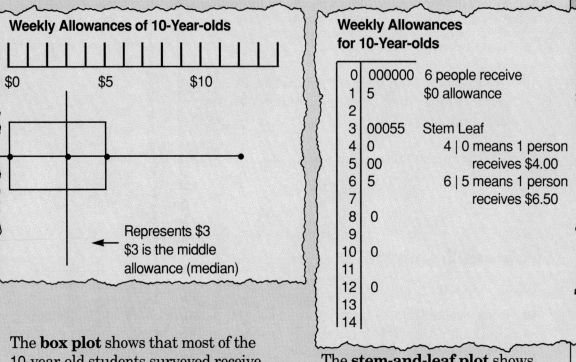

Weekly Allowances of 10-Year-olds

$0 $5 $10

Represents $3
$3 is the middle
allowance (median)

**Weekly Allowances
for 10-Year-olds**

0	000000	6 people receive
1	5	$0 allowance
2		
3	00055	Stem Leaf
4	0	4	0 means 1 person
5	00	receives $4.00
6	5	6	5 means 1 person
7		receives $6.50
8	0	
9		
10	0	
11		
12	0	
13		
14		

The **box plot** shows that most of the 10-year-old students surveyed receive from $0 to $5 weekly allowance.

The **stem-and-leaf plot** shows that the most common allowance for the 10-year-olds surveyed is $0. Three of those surveyed receive $3 and two receive $3.50.

1. You want a raise in your allowance. Decide which graph you would use to persuade your family that you should get a raise.

2. You want to ask the newspaper some questions about the people surveyed. What questions will help you decide whether the graphs are representative of most 10-year-olds?

Explore with a Computer

Use the *Graphing and Probability Workshop Project* for this activity.

At the computer, run a probability experiment. Choose to roll cubes. The computer adds the numbers that come up on each cube.

1. Have the computer roll the cubes 20 times. View the data as a **Bar graph**. Which number was rolled the most? Which number was rolled the least?

2. Predict which number would be rolled the most if you have the computer roll the cubes 200 times. Try this experiment. View the data as a **Bar graph**. Compare your prediction with the results on the computer.

3. Why do you think certain numbers are rolled more often than other numbers?

Number-Sense Project

Look back at pages 414-415.

A class collected this data. They asked a number of people what would be their first choice of a pet if they lived in a city.

Pet	Age Group		
	Child	Teen	Adult
Bird	12	14	5
Cat	36	19	42
Dog	16	12	14
Fish	12	18	6
Gerbil	5	0	0

a. Write a statement about the popularity of the gerbil as a pet according to this data.

b. Write a summary explaining the differences in the adults' choices for a pet as compared to the teenagers' choices.

c. How might the results have differed if the people surveyed did not have a list from which to choose?

Math-at-Home Activity

Try this experiment at home. Predict how many times a paper cup will land *top down* if you flip it 50 times.

Flip the cup 10 times. Record the results on a graph.

TOP UP

SIDEWAYS

TOP DOWN

0   5   10

NUMBER OF LANDINGS

Do you want to change your prediction? Continue the activity, until you have flipped the cup 50 times.

Make a Graph

Build Understanding

Len Barsky became manager of a music store, Jazz, Rock, and More, in April. He wants to show the increase in sales since he became manager.

Understand How can Len best show how sales have increased since he became manager? He knows the monthly sales from January through June. A graph is a good way to display data.

Plan and Solve STRATEGY Len needs to decide what kind of graph to make. A bar graph and a pictograph show quantities and are used to make comparisons. A broken-line graph shows changes in quantities over time.

ANSWER Len decided to make a broken-line graph. He titled the graph and labeled the scales. He rounded the monthly sales to the nearest $500 and then plotted the points to show the sales for each month.

Look Back The graph shows the increase in sales beginning in April. Are exact amounts shown? Are exact amounts necessary?

■ **Talk About Math** Is it easier to interpret data displayed in a table or in a graph? Explain.

PROBLEM SOLVING
GUIDE

Understand
QUESTION
FACTS
KEY IDEA

Plan and Solve
STRATEGY
ANSWER

Look Back
SENSIBLE ANSWER
ALTERNATE APPROACH

Total Sales, Jan.-June	
Month	Dollars
January	$3,689
February	3,402
March	3,150
April	5,287
May	8,102
June	9,608

Total Sales, Jan.-June

Check Understanding

Use the table at the right to answer Problems 1–3.

April Sales by Salesperson	
Rivera	$1,280
Jones	1,230
Dennis	1,000
Okada	1,717

1. What kind of graph would you make from the data?

2. Make a graph of the data in the table.

3. What numbers did you use as labels to show sales in dollars?

4. When would you use a pictograph instead of a bar graph?

Practice

Which kind of graph would you use for each situation? Why?

5. Number of compact discs sold by each salesperson in July

6. Total sales in one month of each of the three best-selling records

7. Number of tapes sold monthly from July through December

8. Decrease in the number of albums sold over 6 months

Answer each question.

9. During an August sale, albums were 2 for $4.00. Make a graph to show the prices of 4, 6, 8, and 10 albums.

10. What kind of graph did you make to show the data in Problem 9? Why?

Choose a ▦ Strategy

Hidden Faces

11. Each face of a cube is numbered 1 to 6 using triangles. Here are 3 views of the *same* cube. Tell what number is opposite:
    a. 5 **b.** 1 **c.** 3

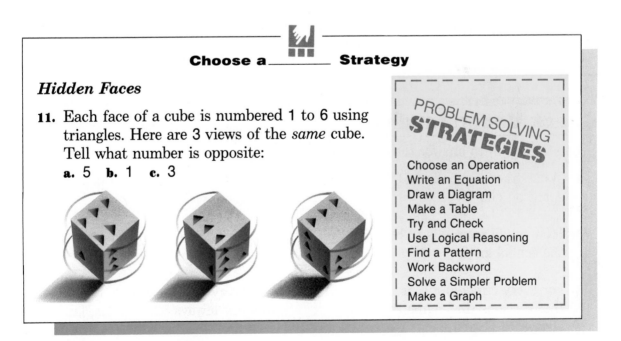

> PROBLEM SOLVING STRATEGIES
>
> Choose an Operation
> Write an Equation
> Draw a Diagram
> Make a Table
> Try and Check
> Use Logical Reasoning
> Find a Pattern
> Work Backward
> Solve a Simpler Problem
> Make a Graph

Circle Graphs

Build Understanding

A budget is a plan for spending money. Do you have a budget for your money?

A *circle graph* compares parts of a whole. This circle graph shows the budget made by the Sunnyhill School's student council. The whole circle stands for the whole amount in the budget. Each section of the circle shows how a fraction of the whole is to be spent. Since each section shows a fraction of the whole, the sum of the fractions must be 1.

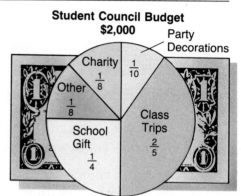

Student Council Budget
$2,000

A. On which item is the most money to be spent?

Find the largest section of the graph.

The most money is to be spent on class trips.

B. How much money is planned for party decorations?

Find $\frac{1}{10}$ of $2,000. $2,000 \div 10 = 200$

The budget shows $200 can be spent on party decorations.

■ **Talk About Math**   If the money to be spent on the school gift were $\frac{1}{5}$ of the whole $2,000, would any other sections of the graph have to change? Explain.

Check Understanding

For another example, see Set D, pages 444-445.

Use the graph to answer the questions.

1. What fraction of the $2,000 is to be spent on charity?

2. Two fifths of the $2,000 is to be spent on what item?

3. How much money is to be spent on the school gift?

4. Which is greater, the amount for charity or for the school gift?

5. For every circle graph, is the sum of the fractions that name the parts always 1? Explain.

6. For every circle graph, is the whole amount always $2,000? Explain.

Practice

For More Practice, see Set D, pages 446–447.

Juana earns $40 each week by doing chores in her neighborhood. The circle graph shows her budget for the week.

Juana's Weekly Budget

What fraction of the $40 does she budget for

7. entertainment?   **8.** snacks?

9. For which item does Juana set aside the most money?

10. What is the main idea of this circle graph?

a. How much Juana earns in a week

b. How much she spends in a week

c. How all parts of her weekly earnings are to be used

Mental Math How much money did Juana budget each week for

11. entertainment?   **12.** savings?   **13.** transportation?   **14.** snacks?

Problem Solving

Read for the facts to solve the problems.

15. How much more money does Juana put into savings than she spends on transportation?

16. Use the circle graph on page 432. How much more did the student council plan to spend on charity than on party decorations?

Calculator Use the circle graph above to answer Problems 17-19. If Juana earns $32 a week, in 52 weeks how much does she

17. earn?   **18.** save?   **19.** spend?

Skills ___ Review   pages 396–397

Write each mixed number as an improper fraction.

1. $2\frac{3}{8}$ **2.** $1\frac{7}{10}$ **3.** $4\frac{1}{2}$ **4.** $5\frac{3}{4}$ **5.** $7\frac{2}{3}$ **6.** $11\frac{3}{5}$

Line Plots in Statistics

Build Understanding

Statistics is a branch of mathematics in which data are collected, organized, and analyzed.

A. Here are quiz scores for 19 students:

90, 75, 95, 75, 95, 90, 90, 85, 80, 95,
70, 95, 95, 80, 75, 100, 65, 100, 100

These scores can be organized in a frequency table or in a *line plot*.

Score	Tally	Frequency
100	///	3
95	₩₩	5
90	///	3
85	/	1
80	//	2
75	///	3
70	/	1
65	/	1

B. The *median* is the middle number in a set of data. You can put the test scores in order to find the median.

65, 70, 75, 75, 75, 80, 80,
85, 90, 90, 90, 95, 95, 95,
95, 95, 100, 100, 100

The median is the tenth score, 90.

Line Plot of Quiz Scores for 19 Students

C. To find the *average*, or *mean*, for a set of scores, add to find the total. Then divide by the number of scores.

Hyung's quiz scores were 70, 70, 60, 80, 90, 50. What was the mean?

Hyung's mean score was 70.

D. When there is an even number of scores, the median is the mean of the two middle scores. Find the median:

75, 80, 80, 90, 95, 100

The median is 85.

E. The *mode* is the number that occurs most often in a set of data. In Example A, the mode is 95.

■ **Talk About Math** Could there ever be more than one mode? Explain.

Check Understanding

For another example, see Set E, pages 444–445.

Use the line plot for Reba's test scores to answer the questions.

Reba's Test Scores

1. How many scores are greater than 80?

2. How many scores are there in all?

3. What is the mode?

4. What is the median?

5. What is the mean?

Frequency				
4		X		
3	X	X		
2	X	X	X	
1	X	X	X	X
	70	80	90	100

Scores

Practice

For More Practice, see Set E, pages 446–447.

Use these data for Exercises 6–10:
90, 70, 60, 70, 90, 100, 80, 70, 65, 55.

6. Make a frequency table.

7. Draw a line plot.

8. Find the mean.

9. Find the median.

10. Find the mode.

Use these data for Exercises 11–15:
100, 92, 92, 96, 88, 88, 88, 96, 92, 94, 90, 88.

11. Make a frequency table.

12. Draw a line plot.

13. **Calculator** Find the mean.

14. Find the median.

15. Find the mode.

Mixed Practice Use paper and pencil or a calculator.
Find the mean, the median, and the mode for each set of data.

16. 23, 41, 31, 27, 23

17. 67, 33, 58, 66, 48, 58

18. 140, 160, 110, 110

19. 12, 19, 13, 13, 16, 13, 15, 19

20. 8, 4, 9, 8, 6, 6, 7, 11, 5, 10, 3

21. 73, 90, 78, 82, 92, 95, 84, 86

Problem Solving

Critical Thinking Solve each problem.

22. What do you think would happen to the mean in Example A if the lowest score was 75?

23. Is it possible for the mean, median, and mode for a set of data to be the same number? Explain your answer.

Outcomes

Build Understanding

Have you ever played dominoes? Variations of the game were played hundreds of years ago in Asia and Europe. The Chinese played dominoes as early as the 12th century A.D. Today, it is enjoyed in many countries.

Margo put the 12 dominoes shown on this page into a bag. Then she drew one out without looking.

When Margo draws a domino, she is *certain* to draw a domino so that the sum of the two groups of dots is greater than 0. Could she draw a domino with a sum of 6? of 5? Drawing a sum of 6 is one possible **outcome.** There are no dominoes shown with a sum of 5, so drawing a sum of 5 is *impossible.*

There is one domino with a sum of 2 and one domino with a sum of 6. So drawing a sum of 2 or drawing a sum of 6 is *equally likely.*

Only three of the dominoes are doubles, showing the same number of dots on each half. When Margo draws a domino without looking, it is *more likely* to be a domino with a different number of dots on each half than a double.

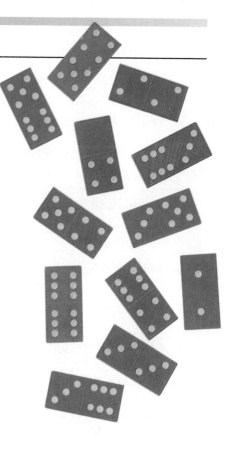

Dominoes are made from many different materials, including wood, bone, ivory, and plastic.

■ **Write About Math** If you drew one domino from the bag, is it more likely to have a sum of 9 or a sum of 10? Give a reason for your answer.

Check Understanding

For another example, see Set F, pages 444–445.

Norm draws a domino from the bag described above without looking. For each exercise, are the two outcomes equally likely? If not, which outcome is more likely?

1. Draw a sum of 8 or a sum of 6.

2. Draw an even sum or an odd sum.

3. Draw a sum less than 10 or a sum greater than 10.

4. Draw a sum of 4 or a sum not equal to 4.

Practice

For More Practice, see Set F, pages 446–447.

Mah-Jongg is a game developed in China. Thom placed these Mah-Jongg tiles face-down, mixed them up, and drew one.

5. List all the possible outcomes.

6. Is Thom more likely to draw a dragon or a bird?

7. Order all the possible outcomes from least likely to most likely.

8. Is Thom more likely to draw an animal or a character?

9. A Mah-Jongg set has 144 tiles in all. What fraction of the set is shown on this page?

Problem Solving

Solve each problem.

10. The *dreidel* is a 4-sided spinning top. Each side shows one of these Hebrew letters: ש, ה, ג, or ב. When the dreidel is spun, is one letter more likely to appear on the top? Explain your answer.

Many dreidels are made from wood or plastic. The ornate one pictured is made from silver.

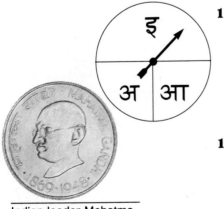

Indian leader Mahatma Gandhi is shown on this Indian coin.

11. Critical Thinking Alka spins the spinner at the left that shows the first three letters of the Hindi alphabet, which is used in India. She thinks, "It is equally likely that I will get the letter इ as the letter अ." Is Alka correct about her chances? Why or why not?

12. In a game, Ajay spins the spinner with the Hindi letters. Then he flips the coin shown at the left and gets heads or tails. List all the possible outcomes of spinning the spinner followed by flipping the coin.

Experiments

Build Understanding

The Road Home
Materials: Spinner as shown; 3-6 markers
Groups: 3-6 students

a. Each time it is your turn, choose a color and spin. If the spinner lands on the color you chose, move your marker this number of squares: red, 1; blue, 3; yellow, 5.

b. Make a table for 6 turns.

Player	Turn 1	Turn 2
	Spinner Landed on	Spinner Landed on
1		
2		

Keep track of each player's first 3 turns.

c. After each player has had 3 turns, study the table. How many times did the spinner land on red? on blue? on yellow?

d. Predict how many times the spinner will land on red, blue, and yellow during the next 3 turns. Write your predictions and continue playing. Record the spinner results in the table.

e. Compare your predictions and finished table. If everyone took 24 turns, do you think the results would be closer to your predictions? Why?

f. Think about the spinner results and play the game again. This time use what you know to try to reach Home before anyone else.

■ **Talk About Math** Explain your strategy for playing this game. How did you develop your strategy?

Check Understanding

For another example, see Set G, pages 444–445.

Use the spinner and your table to answer the questions.

1. When you spin, what color are you most likely to land on? least likely to land on? Explain your answers.

2. If you spin the spinner 30 times, how many times do you think the spinner will land on yellow?

Practice

For More Practice, see Set G, pages 446–447.

Label pieces of paper as shown. Put them in a bag and mix them up.

3. Write how many times you think you will choose each letter in 40 draws.

4. Record the results of 40 draws.

5. Were your predictions close to the results? Why might they be different?

Label pieces of paper with the numbers 1–8.

6. In 32 draws, how many times do you think you will draw a number greater than 2?

7. Record the results of 32 draws. Was your prediction close to the result?

Problem Solving

Explore ———— Math

The most common letters in English, listed in order, are **E, T, A, O, N, R, I,** and **S.** Choose two paragraphs from any book to answer the following questions.

8. Tally how many times each letter of the alphabet appears in your two paragraphs.

9. For the two paragraphs that you chose, list the eight most common letters in order.

10. Compare and contrast your results to the list of the most common letters above. Try to explain any differences.

11. If you tallied the letters on the last page of a dictionary, how would you expect the results to be different?

Fractions and Probability

Build Understanding

A. Karl puts these tiles into a bag and draws one without looking. He records the letter in a tally chart, returns the tile to the bag, and draws again. If he repeats this activity many times, what fraction of the time would you expect him to get an R?

One of the 8 tiles has an R. In many draws, you would expect about $\frac{1}{8}$ of the letters drawn to be R.

Probability tells how likely it is that an outcome will happen. The probability of an outcome is written as a fraction. The probability of drawing an R is

$$\frac{\textbf{Number of favorable outcomes}}{\textbf{Number of possible outcomes}} = \frac{\textbf{Number of tiles with R}}{\textbf{Total number of tiles}} = \frac{1}{8}$$

B. If you drew 80 times from the bag, about how many times would you expect to get a G?

The probability of drawing a G is

$$\frac{\textbf{Number of favorable outcomes}}{\textbf{Number of possible outcomes}} = \frac{\textbf{Number of tiles with G}}{\textbf{Total number of tiles}} = \frac{2}{8} = \frac{1}{4}$$

You would expect to get a G on about $\frac{1}{4}$ of 80 draws, or about 20 times.

$\frac{1}{4}$ of 80 = 20

■ **Talk About Math** Which is more likely, drawing an N or drawing an R? Would you expect the probability of drawing N to be a fraction greater or less than $\frac{1}{8}$?

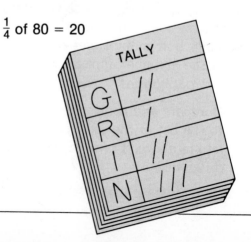

TALLY	
G	//
R	/
I	//
N	///

440

Check Understanding

For another example, see Set H, pages 444–445.

1. Karl's bag has 3 Ns, so the probability of getting an N is $\frac{3}{\ldots}$.

2. The bag has 8 tiles, so the probability of getting an I is $\frac{\ldots}{8}$.

3. About how many times would you expect to get an I in 80 draws?

4. Name two outcomes that are equally likely when Karl draws a tile.

Practice

For More Practice, see Set H, pages 446–447.

Take each of the following words one at a time. Suppose you put the tiles that spell the word in a bag and draw a letter without looking. What is the probability of getting an L?

5. GLADLY   **6.** LOLLIPOP   **7.** ELEVATOR   **8.** EXPERIMENT

The numbers 1 through 6 appear on the 6 faces of this number cube. When the cube is tossed, all the faces have the same chance to come up. Find the probability of getting each result on one toss.

9. a 5   **10.** a 2   **11.** a 6   **12.** an odd number

13. an even number   **14.** a number less than 5   **15.** a number less than 7

16. About how many times would you expect to get a 4 in 60 rolls?

Problem Solving

Critical Thinking The spinner has the names of all the members of the bicycle club. The member whose name is spun will be leader for a month. Give a reason why you think each statement below is correct or incorrect.

17. "There are more boys than girls in the club, so Jim is more likely to win than Gina."

18. "Hal won the spin last month, so this month he is less likely to win than the other members."

19. Use Data Explain how you would change the spinner on page 438 so that it is equally likely that you spin red, blue, or yellow.

20. Draw and color a spinner that shows these probabilities.

red: $\frac{3}{8}$; blue: $\frac{1}{8}$; yellow: $\frac{2}{8}$; green: $\frac{2}{8}$

441

Skills Review

1. The cost of joining five teams is as follows: soccer: $45; football: $60; swimming: $55; hockey: $85; tennis: $35. What kind of a graph would you use to show these data?

2. The table below shows the number of students at Lake School on Sept. 1 of each year. Make a broken-line graph of the data.

Year	1970	1975	1980	1985	1990
Students	550	625	675	575	650

3. How long does it take the bicyclist to go 6 miles?

Distance traveled by Bicyclist

4. How far did the bicyclist travel in 50 minutes?

5. If Pat earns $24 a week, how much more does she budget for recreation than for savings?

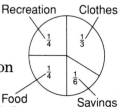

6. Make a line plot of these math test scores: 75, 85, 90, 85, 85, 100, 95, 90, 85, 80.

Brad placed these tiles facedown. Use these tiles for Exercises 7–9.

A B C C B A A D

7. He picked 1 tile. List the possible outcomes from least likely to most likely.

8. If he picks 1 tile and puts it back, how many times should he expect to get an A in 16 picks?

9. What is the probability of getting a C in one draw?

Problem-Solving Review

Solve each problem.

10. A pen and an eraser together cost about $1.10. The pen costs a dollar more than the eraser. How much does the eraser cost?

11. A company makes 3,500 softballs each day. The softballs are packed in boxes of 16. How many boxes can be filled with the softballs made in 1 day?

12. Mrs. Kraus needs $6\frac{1}{2}$ gallons of juice for the picnic. If Joe brings $2\frac{1}{2}$ gallons, Celia brings $2\frac{1}{3}$ gallons, and Lenny brings $1\frac{3}{4}$ gallons, will there be enough juice?

13. Matt practiced piano for 65 minutes on Monday and for 32 minutes on Tuesday. How many hours and minutes did he practice in all?

14. Raoul has 3 pairs of red socks and 4 pairs of blue socks. What is the probability of pulling one red pair from the drawer without looking?

15. **Data File** Using the line graph on pages 528–529, estimate the difference in population between the United States and Canada in 1850, and in 1982.

16. **Make a Data File** Each day for one week count the number of people in your class wearing blue or another color of your choice. Display the data using two different kinds of graphs.

Compare. Use $<$, $>$, or $=$.

1. 35,549 ▦ 35,459

2. 162,450 ▦ 163,450

3. 0.65 ▦ 0.650   **4.** 2.5 ▦ 2.48

5. $\frac{5}{8}$ ▦ $\frac{5}{4}$ **6.** $1\frac{2}{3}$ ▦ $2\frac{1}{4}$

Use mental math to multiply or divide.

7. 40×70 **8.** $8,000 \times 4$

9. 10×6.78 **10.** $0.47 \times 1,000$

11. $390 \div 3$ **12.** $185 \div 5$

13. $320 \div 80$ **14.** $3,600 \div 90$

Find the perimeter of each figure.

15. 2 cm | 2 cm | 2 cm | 2 cm

16. 2 yd / 3 yd / 1 yd / 7 yd / 4 yd

Find each answer.

17.   3 ft 10 in.
        $+ 4$ ft 8 in.

18.   2 lb 8 oz
          $\times$ 4

Draw the next 3 figures in each pattern.

19. ↓ ↑ → ← ↓ ↑

20. □ ○ □ ○ ○ □ ○ ○ ○

Write each decimal as a fraction or mixed number.

21. 0.5   **22.** 0.35   **23.** 2.15

Write each mixed number as an improper fraction.

24. $2\frac{2}{3}$ **25.** $6\frac{1}{2}$ **26.** $10\frac{2}{5}$

Compute.

27. $\frac{1}{4} + \frac{3}{4}$ **28.** $\frac{5}{8} - \frac{1}{4}$

29. $2\frac{1}{6} + 1\frac{2}{3}$ **30.** $8 - 3\frac{3}{5}$

31. $5\frac{2}{3} + 2\frac{7}{8}$ **32.** $9\frac{1}{4} - 5\frac{1}{2}$

33. $\frac{3}{4} \times \frac{1}{6}$ **34.** $\frac{2}{3} \times \frac{4}{5}$

35. $\frac{2}{3} \times 10$ **36.** $6 \times \frac{4}{9}$

37. $1\frac{1}{2} \times 4\frac{2}{3}$ **38.** $3\frac{3}{8} \times 2\frac{2}{3}$

39. Complete the division sentences.

▯▯ ▯▯ ▯▯ ▯▯ ▯▯

How many thirds are in 5? $5 \div \frac{1}{3} = $ ▦

Write how many times you think the spinner will land on each number in 24 spins.

8 2 / 8 4 / 8 4 / 6 6

40. 2   **41.** 4   **42.** 6   **43.** 8

Use these data for Exercises 44–48: 85, 75, 80, 95, 95, 90, 95, 70, 85, 80.

44. Make a frequency table.

45. Draw a line plot.

Find the

46. mean.   **47.** median.   **48.** mode.

Reteaching

Set A   pages 418–421

Bar graphs and pictographs can make it easy to compare quantities. A broken-line graph shows change over time.

Remember that one type of graph may be better to use than another type of graph depending, on the type of data.

What kind of graph would you use to show these data? Why?

1. The average annual rainfall in each of 5 major cities

2. The average annual rainfall in one city over the last 8 years

Set B   pages 422–423

Follow these steps to make a broken-line graph:

1. Write the title for the graph.
2. Label the horizontal scale and write the months, or years, or other time interval.
3. Label the vertical scale and write the number for the scale.
4. Plot the points and connect them.

Remember that a zigzag line can be used on the vertical scale to save space from 0 to the smallest number.

Make a broken-line graph of these data.

White House Visitors (in thousands)

Month	Jan.	Feb.	Mar.	Apr.	May	June
Number	48	60	100	180	172	168

Set C   pages 426–427

Follow these steps to make a line graph:

1. Complete a table of ordered pairs.
2. Write the title for the graph.
3. Number and label the scales.
4. Plot the ordered pairs from the table.
5. Draw a line to connect the points.

Remember to plan the intervals so the least and the greatest numbers will fit on the graph. Copy and complete this table. Then make a line graph.

Car Traveling 20 Miles Per Hour

Number of Minutes	Number of Miles	Ordered Pairs
15	5	(15, 5)
30	10	(▦, 10)
▦	20	(▦, ▦)
▦	30	(▦, ▦)

Set D   pages 432–433

This circle graph shows how a student spent each part of a weekday. The largest section is "sleeping." How many hours does $\frac{1}{3}$ represent?

$\frac{1}{3} \times 24 = 8$ hours

Remember that each section shows a fraction of the whole. So the sum of the fractions must be 1.

What fraction of a day does the student spend

1. at school?   **2.** playing?

How many hours are spent
3. studying?   **4.** playing?

Set E   pages 434–435

At the right, a frequency table and a line plot are given for these pulse rates:

70, 75, 75, 90, 80, 70, 80, 80, 75, 85, 80, 70, 85, 85, 80, 85, 80, 75, 75, 85.

In a set of data, the median is the middle number, the mean is the average, and the mode is the number that occurs most often.

Remember that there could be no mode or more than one mode in a set of data.

Pulse Rate	Frequency
70	3
75	5
80	6
85	5
90	1

Pulse Rates: 20 Students

```
6              x
5        x  x  x
4        x  x  x
3     x  x  x  x
2     x  x  x  x
1     x  x  x  x  x
   70 75 80 85 90
```
Frequency

Pulse Rates

For the set of pulse rates, find
1. the median.   2. the mean.

3. the mode.

Set F   pages 436–437

If you spin this spinner, the three possible outcomes are A, B, and C.
Remember that outcomes are not always equally likely.

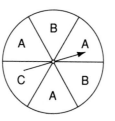

1. Are you more likely to spin an A or a B?

2. Order all the possible outcomes from least likely to most likely.

3. If there were 3 As and 3 Bs on the spinner, what could you conclude?

Set G   pages 438–439

If you spin the spinner in Set F, you are most likely to land on A, because there are more As than Bs or Cs.

Remember that each section of a spinner is the same size.
Make a spinner like the one shown in Set F.

1. Write how many times you think the spinner will land on each letter in 12 spins.

2. Record the results of 12 spins.

3. Were your predictions close to the results? Why might they be very different?

Set H   pages 440–441

If you spin the spinner in Set F, the probability of landing on C is $\frac{1}{6}$.
If you spin it 24 times, you would expect it to stop on C 4 times because

$\frac{1}{6} \times 24 = 4$.

Remember that there are 6 possible places for the spinner to stop.

What is the probability of stopping on

1. A?   2. B?

More Practice

Set A   pages 418–421

This table shows the top speed of some animals in miles per hour.

Animal	Speed
Rabbit	35
Lion	50
Elephant	25
Zebra	40
Cat	30

1. What kind of graph would you use to show the data? Why?

2. Jamie collected the following data about the top speed in miles per hour of 5 sea creatures. Sea turtle: 20; bluefish: 40; sailfish: 60; dolphin: 25; baleen whale: 20. Organize the data in a table.

3. What kind of graph would you use to show these data?

4. Make a graph to show these data.

Set B   pages 422–423

Use the table to make a broken-line graph for

1. black and white receivers.

2. color receivers.

U.S. Production of Television Receivers (in millions)

Year	1977	1978	1979	1980	1981	1982
Black/White	2.4	2.7	2.5	2.7	2.4	2.7
Color	4.7	5.3	5.2	6.2	6.7	6.9

3. How has the number of black and white receivers changed since 1977?

4. Has the number of color televisions changed in the same way?

Set C   pages 426–427

This table shows how long it would take to drive a certain number of miles.

Car Traveling 60 Miles Per Hour

Number of Minutes	Number of Miles	Ordered Pairs
0	0	(0, 0)
10	10	(10, ▦)
20	▦	(▦, ▦)
40	▦	(▦, ▦)
60	▦	(▦, ▦)

1. Copy and complete the table.

Suppose the speed is reduced to 30 miles per hour. At this rate, how many minutes would it take to drive

2. 10 miles?   3. 20 miles?   4. 60 miles?

5. Make a table like the one at the left for a car traveling 30 miles per hour. Use 0, 10, 20, 40 and 60 for the number of minutes.

6. Use the data from your table to make a line graph.

Set D   pages 432–433

Nick received $80 for his birthday. The circle graph
shows how he plans to spend this money.
What fraction of the $80 did he budget for

1. clothes?   **2.** savings?

Mental Math   How much money did Nick budget for
3. clothes?   **4.** entertainment?

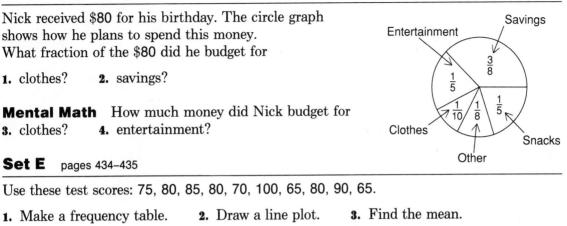

Set E   pages 434–435

Use these test scores: 75, 80, 85, 80, 70, 100, 65, 80, 90, 65.

1. Make a frequency table.   **2.** Draw a line plot.   **3.** Find the mean.

4. Find the median.   **5.** Find the mode.

Set F   pages 436–437

Amy placed these cards face down and
mixed them. Then she drew a card and
recorded the number on it.

1. Is Amy more likely to draw a 5 or
to draw a 7?

2. Order all the possible outcomes from
least likely to most likely.

| 5 | 5 | 5 | 5 | 6 |

| 6 | 7 | 7 | 7 | 8 |

3. Is Amy more likely to draw an odd number or an even number?

Set G   pages 438–439

For Exercises 1–3, make a spinner like the one shown.

1. Write how many times you think the spinner will
land on each letter in 24 spins.

2. Record the results of 24 spins.

3. Were your predictions close to the results?
Why might they be very different?

Set H   pages 440–441

Use each of the following words one at a time. Suppose
you put the tiles that spell the word in a bag and draw a
letter without looking. What is the probability of drawing
an A?

1. FLORIDA   **2.** KANSAS   **3.** ALABAMA   **4.** MONTANA

Enrichment

Order of Operations

What is the value of $9 + 4 \times 3$?

Ralph said the value was 39. Juana said it was 21.

Ralph did the addition, then the multiplication. Juana did the multiplication, then the addition. Who was right?

To avoid such confusion, mathematicians follow a standard *order of operations*.

1. First do all operations within parentheses.

$(3 + 4) \times 6 - (52 - 4) \div 6$

2. Then multiply and divide in order from left to right.

$7 \times 6 - 48 \div 6$

3. Then add and subtract in order from left to right.

$42 - 8$

34

Which operation should be done first: addition, subtraction, multiplication, or division?

1. $3 \times 4 + 12$ **2.** $27 \div (7 - 4)$ **3.** $14 - 8 \div 4 + 6$

Choose the correct value.

4. $(6 + 12) \div 3$
  a. 20   **b.** 6   **c.** 14

5. $(24 \div 6) \times 6 - (36 \div 18)$
  a. 16   **b.** 22   **c.** 12

6. $10 - 3 \times 3 + 5$
  a. 26   **b.** 56   **c.** 6

7. $24 - (16 \div 2) \times 2$
  a. 20   **b.** 32   **c.** 8

Find the value of each expression.

8. $10 - 4 \times 2$ **9.** $(6 \times 5) + (3 \times 5)$ **10.** $27 \div 3 + 9$

11. $6 + 3 \times 9 - 3$ **12.** $(15 + 5) \times 4 - 16$ **13.** $18 - 3 - 2 + 9 \times 2$

14. $(10 \times 8) \div 4 + 5$ **15.** $9 + (8 \div 2) \times (18 \div 3)$

Chapter 13 Review/Test

1. If you conducted a survey to find the favorite movie of students in your school, tell whom you would survey and the question you would ask.

2. Steve asked 20 students what their favorite pet was. The pictograph shows the results. How many students prefer a dog for a pet?

Favorite Pets

Dog	⚥ ⚥ ⚥ ⚥ ⚥	
Cat	⚥ ⚥ ⚧	Each ⚥
Bird	⚥ ⚧	stands for
Hamster	⚥	2 students

Use the table to answer the question.

Year	1986	1987	1988	1989	1990
Sales (in thousands)	$185	$200	$220	$248	$300

3. The table shows the annual sales for a company. If you were making a broken-line graph to show this data, what numbers would you use when labeling the scale for sales?

4. This graph shows the distance traveled by a train in 5 hours.

Distance traveled

Miles: 200, 160, 120, 80, 40

Number of hours: 0 1 2 3 4 5

How long does it take the train to travel 160 miles?

5. Use the line graph in Item 4. What ordered pair would you use to show how long it takes the train to travel 120 miles?

6. What kind of graph would you use to show the total sales in one month for each of five salespersons? Why?

7. If a fruit market sells $1,200 worth of fruit, how much more money did the market take in for apples than for bananas?

Fruit Sales

Apples $\frac{1}{3}$ — Bananas $\frac{1}{4}$ — Peaches $\frac{1}{8}$ — Other $\frac{7}{24}$

On 10 tests, Sarah got these scores: 80, 90, 95, 75, 90, 95, 100, 85, 95, 95.

8. Draw a line plot of her scores.

9. Find the mean of Sarah's scores.

Suppose these cards are face down.

9 6 6 9 5 9

10. Pick one card. List the possible outcomes from least to most likely.

11. If you pick one card from the cards above and then replace it, how many times would you expect to get a 9 in 24 picks?

12. What is the probability of getting a 6 in one draw?

13. Use the graph in Item 4. Alan said that the train travels 800 miles in 10 hours. Is this a reasonable answer? Why or why not?

14. **Write About Math** Can you know in advance how an experiment will turn out?

Geometry

14

Did You Know:
A group of students flew a train of kites to an altitude of 35,530 feet. About how many miles is that altitude? About how many miles of line do you think were needed to lift the kites to that altitude?

450

Number-Sense Project

Estimate
Today kites are made of many materials and come in many sizes and shapes. Guess which of these kites the adults you know might have flown.

Gather Data
Interview one or more adults. Ask them whether they have ever flown kites. If so, ask them to identify the shapes of the kites they have flown.

Analyze and Report
Use a table or a graph to summarize your results. Write a sentence telling whether your guess was accurate.

Solid Shapes

Build Understanding

Paul and Melissa used these pieces of plywood to build a ramp for their brother, Brad.

A. What do you notice about the surfaces of these objects?

All of the surfaces of these objects are flat.

What do you notice about the surfaces of these objects?

Some of the surfaces of these objects are not flat.

B. A geometric solid that has all flat surfaces is a **polyhedron**. Which of these solid shapes are polyhedrons?

Sphere   Cylinder   Cone   Triangular Prism   Rectangular Prism   Pyramid   Cube

The first three shapes are not polyhedrons because they have some curved surfaces. The other shapes have all flat surfaces, so they are polyhedrons.

C. Some polyhedrons are **prisms**.

Rectangular prism   Cube   Triangular prism

Some polyhedrons are **pyramids**.

Rectangular pyramid   Square pyramid   Triangular pyramid

D. Each surface of a polyhedron is a **face**. Two faces of a polyhedron meet to form an **edge**. The edges meet to form a **vertex**.

6 faces   12 edges   8 vertices

■ **Talk About Math** Name some everyday items that are polyhedrons. Name some everyday items that are not polyhedrons.

Check Understanding

For another example, see Set A, pages 488–489.

Tell which solid at the right Paul and Melissa could build with the pieces of plywood.

1.   **a.**   **b.**   **c.**

Tell if each solid is a polyhedron. Write *yes* or *no*.

2.   **3.**   **4.**   **5.**

Tell if each polyhedron is a prism or a pyramid.

6.   **7.**   **8.**   **9.**

10.   **11.**   **12.**   **13.**

Tell if each object in the picture below suggests a polyhedron. Write *yes* or *no*. If it is a polyhedron, tell whether it is a prism or a pyramid.

14. Tent   **15.** Paper towels   **16.** Soap bubbles   **17.** Aquarium   **18.** Number cube

Complete the table.

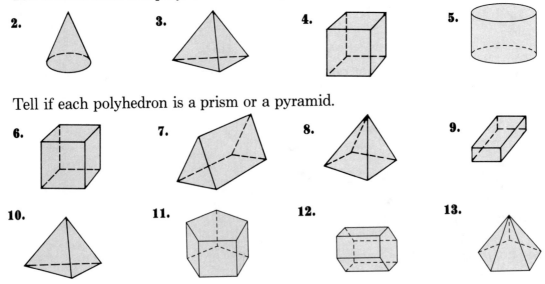

Object	Geometric solid	Number of vertices	Number of faces	Number of edges
Microwave oven		**19.**	**20.**	**21.**
Aquarium		**22.**	**23.**	**24.**
Number cube		**25.**	**26.**	**27.**
Tent		**28.**	**29.**	**30.**

Problem Solving

Tell how many pieces of plywood are needed to make each object.

31.

32.

33.

Visual Thinking   Suppose you traced each face of each solid.
Sketch all the different figures you would draw.

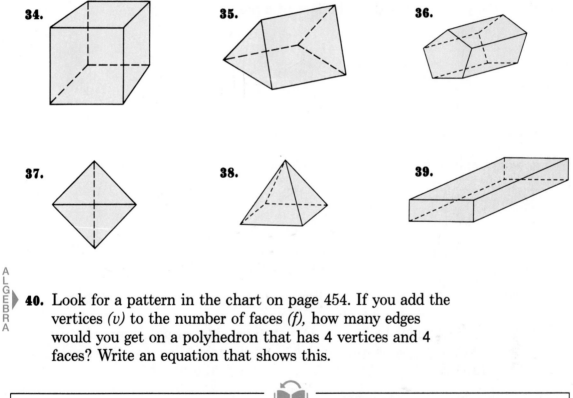

34.

35.

36.

37.

38.

39.

40. Look for a pattern in the chart on page 454. If you add the
vertices (*v*) to the number of faces (*f*), how many edges
would you get on a polyhedron that has 4 vertices and 4
faces? Write an equation that shows this.

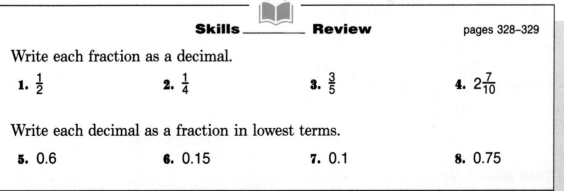

Skills _____ **Review**   pages 328–329

Write each fraction as a decimal.

1. $\frac{1}{2}$ **2.** $\frac{1}{4}$ **3.** $\frac{3}{5}$ **4.** $2\frac{7}{10}$

Write each decimal as a fraction in lowest terms.

5. 0.6   **6.** 0.15   **7.** 0.1   **8.** 0.75

Polygons

Build Understanding

A. The figures you get when you trace the faces of a polyhedron are *polygons*.

Each of these polygons could be the face of a polyhedron.

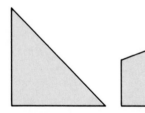

B. Polygons are named by the number of *sides* they have.

| Triangle | Quadrilateral | Pentagon | Hexagon | Octagon |

C. What makes the polygons in Example B and the polygons in Example A different?

Some of the sides of each polygon in Example A have different lengths. The sides of each polygon in Example B have the same length. The polygons in Example B are *regular polygons*.

D. Two sides of a polygon meet to form a *vertex*. How many vertices does this figure have?

This hexagon has 6 vertices.

■ **Talk About Math** What is another name for a quadrilateral that is a regular polygon?

456

Check Understanding

For another example, see Set B, pages 488–489.

Match each polygon with its name from the list below.

1. **2.** **3.** **4.** **5.**

a. Triangle **b.** Quadrilateral **c.** Pentagon **d.** Hexagon **e.** Octagon

Use the figures in Exercises 1–5 to answer Exercises 6–8.

6. Which of the figures are regular?

7. How many sides does the figure in Exercise 3 have?

8. How many vertices does the figure in Exercise 4 have?

Practice

For More Practice, see Set B, pages 490–491.

Name the polygon you see. Then tell how many sides and vertices the polygon has.

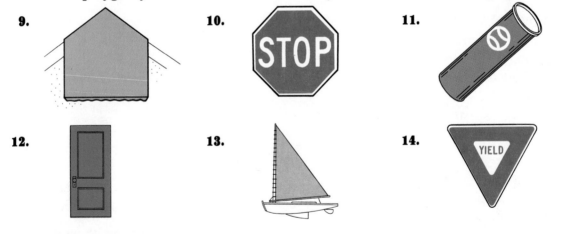

9. **10.** **11.**

12. **13.** **14.**

Problem Solving

Name the polygons you would get if you traced each face of these polyhedrons.

15.

16.

17. Critical Thinking What is the relationship between the edge of a polyhedron and the side of a polygon traced from one of the faces of the polyhedron?

Basic Geometric Ideas

Build Understanding

A. All the edges of a polyhedron and all the sides of a polygon are **segments**. A segment is part of a **line**.

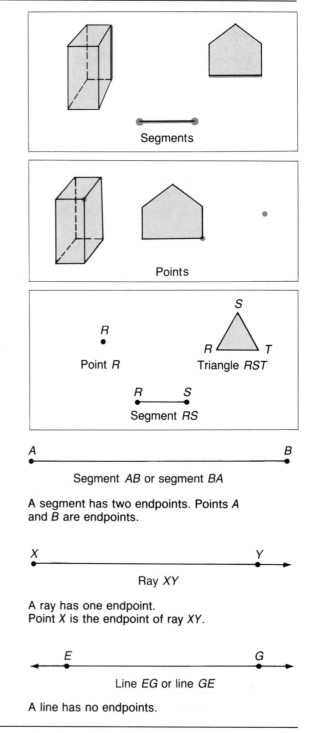

Segments

In polyhedrons and in polygons, all the segments meet at **points** called vertices. Sometimes a point is represented by a dot.

Points

Points are often labeled to help you tell them apart. Polygons and other geometric figures are often named by their points.

Point *R*

Triangle *RST*

Segment *RS*

B. You know that a segment is part of a line. How many **endpoints** does this segment have?

Segment *AB* or segment *BA*

A segment has two endpoints. Points *A* and *B* are endpoints.

A **ray** is also part of a line. A ray goes on and on in one direction. How many endpoints does this ray have?

Ray *XY*

A ray has one endpoint.
Point *X* is the endpoint of ray *XY*.

In geometry, a line goes on and on in two directions. Does a line have any endpoints?

Line *EG* or line *GE*

A line has no endpoints.

c. Parallel lines are lines that never meet.

Lines *CD* and *ST* are parallel lines.

D. Intersecting lines are lines that meet in a point.

Lines *MN* and *PQ* are intersecting lines. They meet at point *A*.

■ **Talk About Math**   In Example B, is "ray *YX*" another name for ray *XY*?

Check Understanding

For another example, see Set C, pages 488–489.

Use the figures at the right to complete these sentences.

1. Another name for line *AB* is line ▦.

2. Point C is the ▦ of ray *CD*.

3. Lines *EF* and *GH* are ▦ lines.

Practice

For More Practice, see Set C, pages 490–491.

Name each figure.

4. 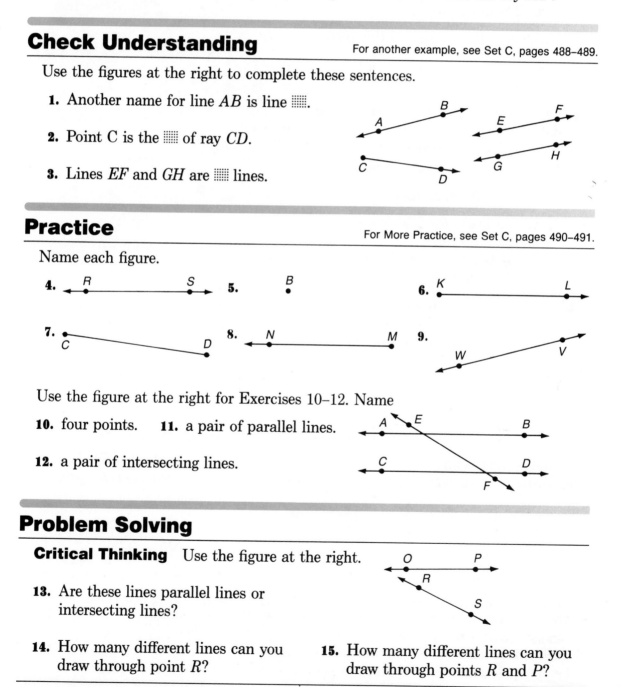   **5.**   **6.**

7.   **8.**   **9.**

Use the figure at the right for Exercises 10–12. Name

10. four points.   **11.** a pair of parallel lines.

12. a pair of intersecting lines.

Problem Solving

Critical Thinking   Use the figure at the right.

13. Are these lines parallel lines or intersecting lines?

14. How many different lines can you draw through point *R*?

15. How many different lines can you draw through points *R* and *P*?

Triangles

Build Understanding

A. Go to Any Length
Materials: Math Sketcher, paper
Groups: Groups of 4

a. Locate any three cities on this map.

b. Trace the dots that represent the locations of the three cities.

c. Draw 3 line segments connecting the dots you made. Unless the cities you selected are in a straight line, the figure you draw will be a **triangle**.

d. Label the dots *R*, *E*, and *J*.

e. In your triangle *REJ*, which is greater: the distance from *R* to *J* to *E* or the distance from *R* straight to *E*? Measure to check.

f. Practice constructing triangles using different cities on the map. Is the result you got in *Step e* true for all the triangles? Summarize your results.

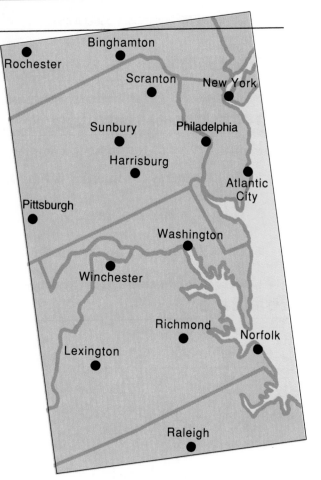

B. Triangles can be named according to the lengths of their sides.

| Triangle GHJ is an **equilateral triangle**. | Triangle DEF is an **isosceles triangle**. | Triangle ABC is a **scalene triangle**. |

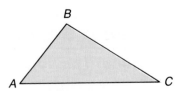

All three sides of an equilateral triangle are equal in length.

At least two sides of an isosceles triangle are equal in length.

None of the sides of a scalene triangle are equal in length.

■ **Talk About Math** Could an isosceles triangle also be an equilateral triangle? Explain your answer.

Check Understanding

For another example, see Set D, pages 488–489.

Name each triangle. Then tell whether the triangle is equilateral, isosceles, or scalene.

1. 4 in. / N \ 3 in. — M, 5 in., O

2. 2 in. / S \ 2 in. — R, 2 in., T

3. 4 in. / E \ 4 in. — D, 7 in., F

Practice

For More Practice, see Set D, pages 490–491.

Measure each side of each triangle. Then tell whether the triangle is equilateral, isosceles, or scalene.

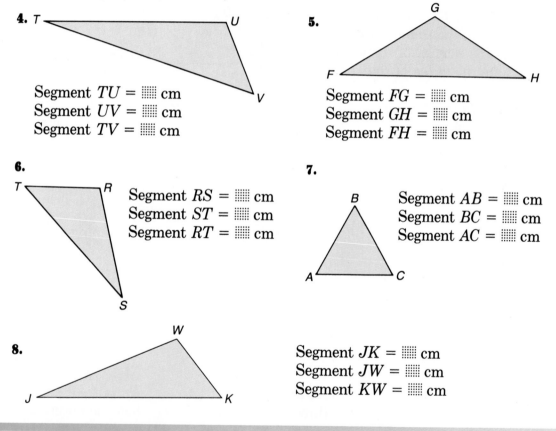

4. Segment TU = ▦ cm
Segment UV = ▦ cm
Segment TV = ▦ cm

5. Segment FG = ▦ cm
Segment GH = ▦ cm
Segment FH = ▦ cm

6. Segment RS = ▦ cm
Segment ST = ▦ cm
Segment RT = ▦ cm

7. Segment AB = ▦ cm
Segment BC = ▦ cm
Segment AC = ▦ cm

8. Segment JK = ▦ cm
Segment JW = ▦ cm
Segment KW = ▦ cm

Problem Solving

9. **Visual Thinking** On a map, a line drawn from Hilltop to Milltown measures 6 cm. A line drawn from Milltown to River City measures 7 cm. How long could a line from Hilltop to River City be?

10. **Critical Thinking** Is this statement true or false? Explain your thinking.

Every equilateral triangle is an isosceles triangle.

Angles

Build Understanding

What do you think will happen when the laser beam is pointed at a mirror?

When the laser beam hits the mirror, it bounces off and goes in another direction. The path of the laser beam suggests an **angle**.

A. Ray *ED* and ray *EF* form an angle. Both rays have the same endpoint. Point *E* is the **vertex** of the angle. The two rays are the **sides** of the angle.

Angle *DEF* or angle *FED*
∠*DEF* or ∠*FED* or ∠*E*

B. A **right angle** looks like a square corner.

An **acute angle** is smaller than a right angle.

An **obtuse angle** is larger than a right angle.

c. You have seen how the sides of a triangle can be used to classify the triangle. The angles of a triangle also can be used to classify the triangle.

A **right triangle** has one right angle.

The right angle is ∠*A*.

An **acute triangle** has three acute angles.

The acute angles are ∠*D*, ∠*E*, and ∠*F*.

An **obtuse triangle** has one obtuse angle.

The obtuse angle is ∠*J*.

■ **Talk About Math** Does an obtuse triangle have any acute angles? Does an acute triangle have any obtuse angles?

Check Understanding

For another example, see Set E, pages 488–489.

Tell whether each statement is *true* or *false*.

1. Another name for
∠*JKL* is ∠*LKJ*.

2. The vertex of ∠*RST*
is *R*.

3. A right angle is larger
than an acute angle.

4. ∠*Y* is
acute.

5. ∠*W* is
obtuse.

6. An obtuse triangle has
3 obtuse angles.

Practice

For More Practice, see Set E, pages 490–491.

Name each angle. Then tell whether the angle is right, acute, or obtuse.

7.   **8.**   **9.**

Use the figure at the right for Exercises 10–12.

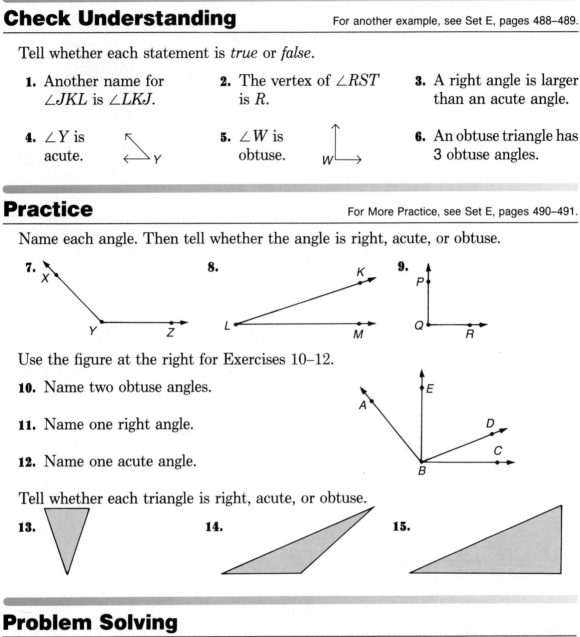

10. Name two obtuse angles.

11. Name one right angle.

12. Name one acute angle.

Tell whether each triangle is right, acute, or obtuse.

13.   **14.**   **15.**

Problem Solving

Tell whether each angle formed
by the laser beams seems to be
right, acute, or obtuse.

16.   **17.**

18. Critical Thinking Can a right
triangle also be a scalene triangle?
Explain your thinking.

19. Visual Thinking How many
lines can you draw that divide an
equilateral triangle into 2 right
triangles?

Using a Protractor

Build Understanding

Doreen uses the Math Sketcher to draw designs for a poster. She uses a **protractor** to find the measures of angles.

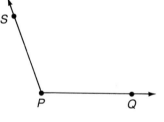

A. The unit used to measure an angle is the **degree.** A protractor is marked with 180 degrees. What is the measure of ∠XYZ?

The measure of ∠XYZ is 90°.

To find the measure of an angle with a protractor, put the center mark of the protractor on the vertex of the angle. Place the zero mark on one of the rays. Then use the scale with that zero mark to find the measure of the angle.

B. How would Doreen draw an angle with a measure of 110°?

First, draw a ray. Point P will be the vertex of the angle.

Put the center mark of a protractor on point P. Put a zero mark on the ray. Using the scale with that zero mark, mark point S at 110°.

Draw ray PS. The measure of ∠SPQ is 110°.

c. The angle in Example A is a **_right angle._** Its measure is 90°. The angle in Example B is an **_obtuse angle._** Its measure is greater than 90° and less than 180°. An **_acute angle_** has a measure of less than 90°.

What kind of angle is ∠BCD?

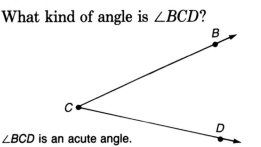

∠BCD is an acute angle.

D. What do you notice about the angles formed by these intersecting lines?

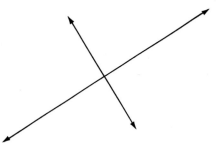

The intersecting lines form right angles. Intersecting lines that form right angles are **_perpendicular lines._**

■ **Talk About Math**   Explain why you think a protractor has two scales.

Check Understanding

Find the measure of each angle. Then tell whether the angle is right, acute, or obtuse.

1. ∠ABC

2. ∠EBC

3. ∠DBC

Use a protractor to tell whether each pair of intersecting lines is perpendicular. Answer *yes* or *no*.

4.

5.

Practice

Estimation Estimate the measure of each angle.
Then use a protractor to find the measure.

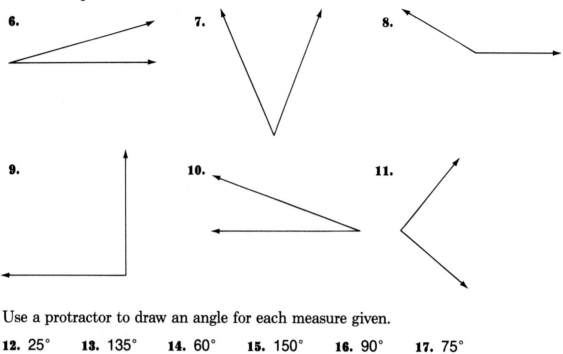

6.

7.

8.

9.

10.

11.

Use a protractor to draw an angle for each measure given.

12. 25° **13.** 135° **14.** 60° **15.** 150° **16.** 90° **17.** 75°

Problem Solving

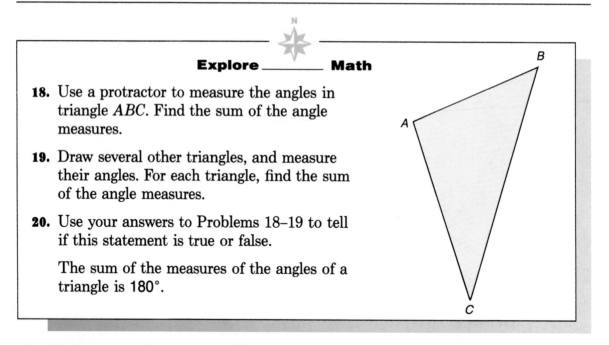

Explore ———— Math

18. Use a protractor to measure the angles in triangle *ABC*. Find the sum of the angle measures.

19. Draw several other triangles, and measure their angles. For each triangle, find the sum of the angle measures.

20. Use your answers to Problems 18–19 to tell if this statement is true or false.

The sum of the measures of the angles of a triangle is 180°.

1. Tell which of the figures below are polyhedrons.

a.

b.

c.

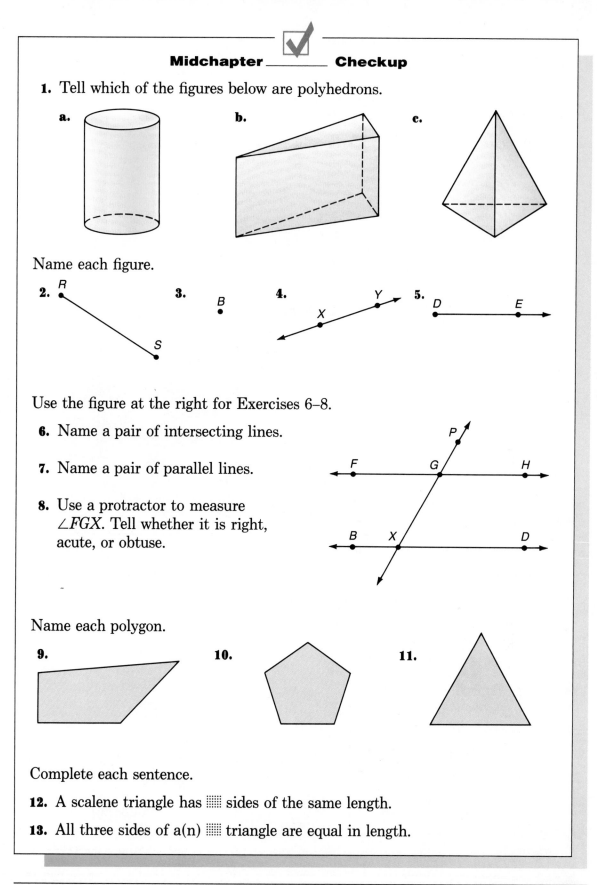

Name each figure.

2. R ... S

3. B

4. X Y

5. D E

Use the figure at the right for Exercises 6–8.

6. Name a pair of intersecting lines.

7. Name a pair of parallel lines.

8. Use a protractor to measure
∠*FGX*. Tell whether it is right,
acute, or obtuse.

Name each polygon.

9.

10.

11.

Complete each sentence.

12. A scalene triangle has ▦ sides of the same length.

13. All three sides of a(n) ▦ triangle are equal in length.

Explore as a Team

1. Which triangle do you think has the greatest perimeter?

2. Which triangle do you think has the least perimeter?

3. Work with other students to find ways to measure the perimeter of each triangle. Record the perimeter of each triangle. Were your predictions correct?

4. How many different triangles with a perimeter of 15 cm can your team find? Use only whole number measures for the lengths of the sides.

MATH
Laugh

A. What kind of triangle never makes a mistake?

B. What geometric figure represents a lost parrot?

B. Polygon
A. Right triangle
ANSWERS:

TIPS FOR **WORKING TOGETHER**

To make sure your group understands the task or solution have each group member say it in his/her own words, summarize the steps, or give an example.

Explore with a Computer

Use the *Geometry Workshop Project* for this activity.

Brett plans to be an architect. He likes to draw unusual designs of homes and floor plans like the one shown here.

1. At the computer, use the **Draw** option to create an original floor plan for a home.

2. Print a copy of your floor plan and label the rooms that make up your home.

Number-Sense Project

Look back at pages 450-451. Use the kite designs sketched at the right. Identify which kites match the descriptions below.

a. Contains at least three different triangles.

b. Contains two congruent triangles.

c. Contains a hexagon.

Math-at-Home Activity

Play *Adjacent Squares* with someone at home. Make a grid like this one.

Each player needs **12** markers. Players take turns placing markers on one or two squares at a time.

If a player covers two squares, the squares must be adjacent (share one side).

Adjacent   Not Adjacent

The player who covers the last square wins.

Quadrilaterals

Build Understanding

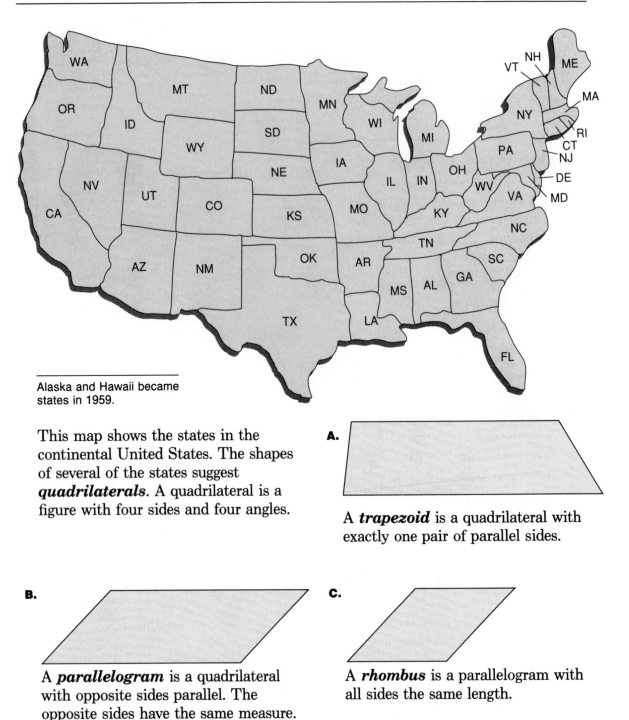

Alaska and Hawaii became
states in 1959.

This map shows the states in the
continental United States. The shapes
of several of the states suggest
quadrilaterals. A quadrilateral is a
figure with four sides and four angles.

A.

A *trapezoid* is a quadrilateral with
exactly one pair of parallel sides.

B.

A *parallelogram* is a quadrilateral
with opposite sides parallel. The
opposite sides have the same measure.

C.

A *rhombus* is a parallelogram with
all sides the same length.

D.

A *rectangle* is a parallelogram with four right angles.

E.

A *square* is a rectangle with all sides the same length.

■ **Talk About Math** Is a square always a rhombus? Is a rhombus always a square? Explain.

Check Understanding

For another example, see Set F, pages 488–489.

Use the map on page 470. Tell which quadrilateral each state suggests.

1. TN   **2.** WY   **3.** NV   **4.** CO   **5.** VT

Practice

For More Practice, see Set F, pages 490–491.

Name each quadrilateral.

6.   **7.**   **8.**   **9.**

10.   **11.**   **12.**   **13.**

14. Is this figure a quadrilateral?

15. Is this figure a trapezoid?

Problem Solving

Visual Thinking Tell which segments at the right could be put together to form each figure. Sketch the figure.

16. Parallelogram   **17.** Rhombus

18. Square   **19.** Trapezoid

Critical Thinking Write a sentence to describe

20. how a parallelogram and a rectangle are alike.

21. how a rhombus and a square can be different.

Circles

Build Understanding

A. Going in Circles
Materials: Paper clips of various sizes, two pencils
Groups: With a partner

a. Use a paper clip and two pencils as shown at the right.

b. Hold one pencil in place and move the other pencil around until you return to the beginning point.

c. The shape you drew should be a *circle*. All the points of a circle are the same distance away from the *center* of the circle. The point made by the pencil you held in place is the center of the circle.

d. Repeat these steps using a paper clip of a different length. What do you notice about the size of the circle and the length of the paper clip?

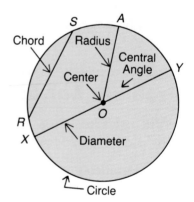

B. The circle at the right is circle *O*. The center is point *O*. A *radius* is a segment from the center to any point on the circle. Segment *OA* is a radius of this circle.

A segment through the center that connects two points on the circle is a *diameter* of the circle. Segment *XY* is a diameter of this circle.

A segment that has both endpoints on the circle is a *chord*. Segment *RS* is a chord.

An angle whose vertex is the center of the circle is a *central angle*. Angle *YOA* is a central angle.

■ **Talk About Math** Name two more radii of this circle. What can you say about the relationship between a radius and a diameter of a circle?

Check Understanding

Refer to the circle at the right. Complete each statement.

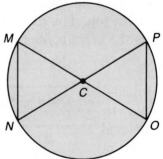

1. Point *U* is the ___?___.
2. Angle *VUW* is a ___?___.
3. Segment *UV* is a ___?___.
4. Segment *VZ* is a ___?___.
5. Segment *WZ* is a ___?___ and also a ___?___.

Practice

Use circle *C* at the right for Exercises 6–11.

6. Name each segment that is a radius.

7. Name each segment that is a diameter.

8. Name each segment that is a chord.

9. Name each central angle.

10. Name four angles in the figure that are not central angles.

11. Name four points that are the same distance from point *C*.

Can a circle have more than one
12. center?   13. diameter?   14. radius?   15. chord?   16. central angle?

Problem Solving

Use circle *O* at the right for Problems 17–19.

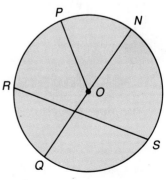

17. Can a radius be a diameter? a chord? Explain.

18. Are the angles formed by segments *RS* and *NQ* central angles? Explain.

19. Are points *N*, *P*, *S*, *Q*, and *R* the same distance from the vertex of the central angle? Explain.

20. **Use Data**   Use the circle graph on page 432. If the total number of degrees in the central angles shown is **360°**, how many degrees are there in the central angle for School Gift?

Circumference

Build Understanding

Marti makes fabric-covered containers to sell in her gift shop. Each container top has fancy piping trim along the outside edge.

A. The length of the trim Marti needs for each container is the distance around the edge of the top. The distance around a circle is the *circumference*.

B. Marti made this chart to help her find the length of trim she needs for certain containers.

Diameter of container	Approximate length of trim needed
3 in.	$9\frac{1}{2}$ in.
5 in.	$15\frac{3}{4}$ in.
8 in.	$25\frac{1}{4}$ in.
12 in.	$37\frac{3}{4}$ in.

What do you notice about the relationship between the length of trim and the diameter of the container?

The trim is always a little more than 3 times the length of the diameter.

■ **Talk About Math** How could you use what you know about the relationship between the lengths of a radius and a diameter of a circle to estimate the circumference of a circle with a radius of 15 centimeters?

Check Understanding

Complete the chart.

Radius	Diameter	Approximate circumference
5 cm	10 cm	**1.** ▦ cm
8 cm	**2.** ▦ cm	**3.** ▦ cm
4. ▦ cm	20 cm	**5.** ▦ cm
6. ▦ cm	**7.** ▦ cm	48 cm

Practice

Estimation   Find the approximate circumference of a circle
with the given diameter.

8. 12 cm   **9.** 8 mm   **10.** 7 in.   **11.** 5 m   **12.** 10 in.   **13.** 18 mm

14. 20 cm   **15.** 15 ft   **16.** 1 yd   **17.** 24 cm   **18.** 32 in.   **19.** 14 m

20. 54 in.   **21.** 72 cm   **22.** 108 cm   **23.** 16 in.   **24.** 42 in.   **25.** 132 cm

Find the approximate circumference of a circle with the given radius.

26. 5 yd   **27.** 12 mm   **28.** 11 in.   **29.** 17 m   **30.** 3 cm   **31.** 10 m

32. 1 km   **33.** 15 cm   **34.** 50 mm   **35.** 24 ft   **36.** 16 m   **37.** 2 in.

Estimation   Estimate the circumference of each object in
Exercises 38–45. **Remember** to label each unit of measure.

38. Clock with a diameter of 14 cm

39. Paint can with a diameter of 5 in.

40. Volleyball with a radius of 5 in.

41. Penny with a diameter of 19 mm

42. Table with a diameter of 45 in.

43. Popcorn tin with a radius of 17 cm

44. Plate with a diameter of 25 cm

45. Tire with a radius of 13 in.

Complete this sentence. For any circle,

46. the circumference divided by the
length of the diameter is about ▨.

Problem Solving

47. Mental Math   Will a container
top with a diameter of 9 centimeters
fit on a container with a radius of
5 centimeters?

48. A button has a diameter of
2 centimeters. Will it fit through a
buttonhole that is 1.5 centimeters
long?

49. Marti has 8 feet of trim. About
how many containers with
diameters of 5 inches can Marti
trim using the red trim?

50. Marti wants to use lace trim on
10 containers with diameters of
10 inches. How much would she
spend if lace were on sale for
10¢ per inch?

Congruent Figures

Build Understanding

Paula makes paperweights. The piece of felt she glues on the bottom of each paperweight is exactly the same size and shape as the bottom of the paperweight.

A. Figures that have the same size and shape are ***congruent***.

You can ***slide*** one triangle on top of the other triangle to see that both triangles are the same size and shape.

B. These figures are congruent.

You can ***turn*** one of these figures to see that both figures are the same size and shape.

C. These figures are congruent.

You can ***flip*** one of these figures on top of the other to see that the figures are the same size and shape.

D. The triangles are congruent because they have the same size and the same shape. The rectangles are not congruent.

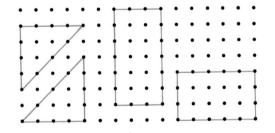

E. The diagonal segments are congruent because they have the same length. The vertical segments are not congruent.

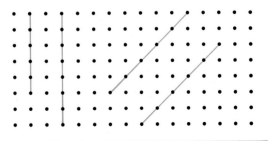

■ **Talk About Math** How could you be sure two polygons in different positions are congruent?

Check Understanding

For another example, see Set H, pages 488–489.

Tell whether the segments or figures are congruent. Write *yes* or *no*.

1.

2.

Practice

For More Practice, see Set H, pages 490–491.

Tell whether the segments or figures are congruent. Write *yes* or *no*.

3.

4.

5.

6.

7.

8.

9.

10.

11.

Problem Solving

12. For each pair of congruent figures in Exercises 6–11, how would you move one figure exactly on top of the other? Tell whether you would flip, turn, slide, or do a combination of these.

13. **Critical Thinking** In Example B on page 476, you can move the blue triangle onto the red triangle with a turn. What combination of two other moves does the same thing?

Draw a Diagram

Build Understanding

Steve Park is an architect. He is designing a tile floor. Could Steve use tiles like the one shown to make a rectangular floor with no spaces between the tiles?

Understand   QUESTION   Could tiles like the one shown be put together to form a solid rectangle?

FACTS   Only one size and shape will be used. The tiles must form a rectangle. There must be no space between tiles.

KEY IDEA   You can draw a diagram to help you answer the question.

Plan and Solve   STRATEGY   Trace the figure at the right. Then cut it out. Use the cut-out figure to draw more congruent figures. Determine if there is any way to draw the figures so that they form a solid rectangle.

ANSWER   Steve could not use the octagonal tiles for his design because they cannot be put together to form a solid rectangle.

PROBLEM SOLVING GUIDE

Understand
QUESTION
FACTS
KEY IDEA

▶ **Plan and Solve**
STRATEGY
ANSWER

Look Back
SENSIBLE ANSWER
ALTERNATE APPROACH

The smooth surface on ceramic tiles is called *glazing*.

Look Back   SENSIBLE ANSWER   You tried to arrange congruent figures to form a solid rectangle. Your answer is reasonable.

■ **Talk About Math**   What do you notice about the angles of an octagon? How could this have helped you solve the problem?

Check Understanding

Draw a diagram to help you decide whether Steve could use tiles of each shape for a solid rectangular floor. Write *yes* or *no*.

1.   2.   3.

Practice

Trace each of these figures. Then cut out your tracings. Which figures can be put together to form a

4. square?

5. rectangle?

6. parallelogram?

7. trapezoid?

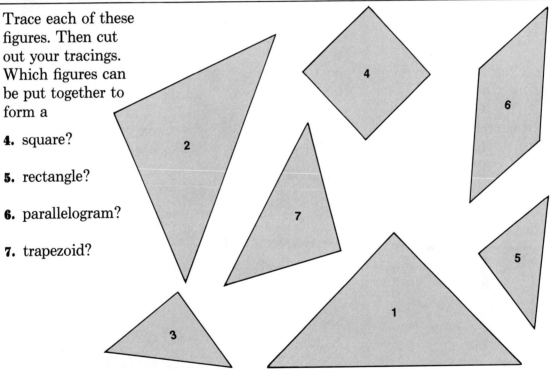

8. Steve is designing a floor with tiles all of the same shape and color. He can use tiles in shapes of triangles, squares, or rectangles. The tiles can be black, gray, or white. How many choices does Steve have for the floor?

9. For a mosaic wall design, Steve used one third as many blue tiles as red tiles, twice as many yellow tiles as red tiles, and 20 fewer yellow tiles than green tiles. He used 50 green tiles. How many red, blue, and yellow tiles did he use?

Symmetry

Build Understanding

Countries all over the world use *symbols* every day. They are used in their written languages, flags, packaging, and transportation.

National symbols are used to identify countries. The maple leaf shown here is a national symbol of Canada. Another national symbol of Canada is the beaver.

Where could you fold the maple leaf so that the two parts match exactly?

The maple leaf appears on the Canadian flag, which was adopted in 1965.

A fold line drawn vertically down the middle of the maple leaf gives two matching parts.

A. If a figure can be folded so that one part fits exactly over the other part, then the figure has **symmetry**. The fold line is a **line of symmetry**.

The maple leaf has one line of symmetry.

B. Some figures have more than one line of symmetry.

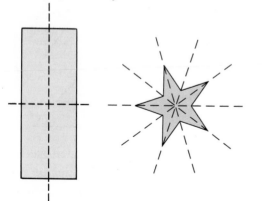

C. Does this figure have a line of symmetry?

The figure cannot be folded to make two matching parts. Some figures have no line of symmetry.

■ **Talk About Math**   If a figure has symmetry, are the matching parts congruent? Explain your answer.

Check Understanding

For another example, see Set I, pages 488–489.

How many lines of symmetry does each figure have?

1. 2. 3. 4. 5. 6.

Practice

For More Practice, see Set I, pages 490–491.

The symbols below are from different countries or American Indian nations. How many lines of symmetry does each have?

7. England

8. United States

9. Ancient China

10. Menominee Indians

11. Kenya

12. Peru

13. Imperial family, Japan

14. France

15. Trace the figures in Exercises 5 and 6. Then draw the lines of symmetry.

Problem Solving

Solve each problem.

16. Japan is called the *land of the rising sun*. Its flag has a large red circle. How many lines of symmetry does a circle have?

17. At the right, the dashed line is a line of symmetry. Trace the figure and the dashed line. Then draw the other part of the figure. The completed figure is an Arapaho symbol which is used to decorate musical instruments.

TIPS FOR PROBLEM SOLVERS

Compare problems to help you relate new problems to ones you've solved before.

481

Similar Figures

Build Understanding

Ismael is an artist. His friend Alice wanted him to paint a mural for her new restaurant. The small image Ismael placed in his slide projector and the large image that appears on the wall suggest *similar figures*.

A. Similar figures have the same shape but not necessarily the same size. Are these triangles similar?

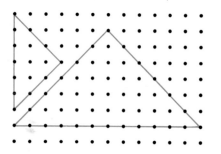

Both figures have the same shape. Each side of the large triangle is twice as long as the corresponding side of the small triangle. The triangles are similar.

B. Are these rectangles similar?

The second rectangle is twice as wide as the first rectangle, but it is not twice as long. They are not similar figures.

■ **Talk About Math**   Are congruent figures similar? Explain your answer.

Check Understanding

Tell whether the figures are similar. Write *yes* or *no*.

1.   **2.**   **3.**

Practice

Tell whether the figures are similar. Write *yes* or *no*.

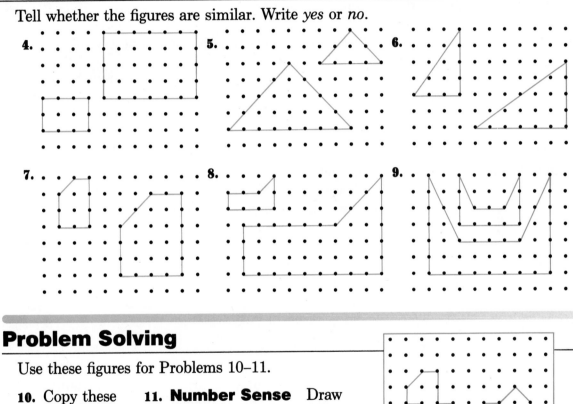

4.   **5.**   **6.**

7.   **8.**   **9.**

Problem Solving

Use these figures for Problems 10–11.

10. Copy these figures onto grid paper.

11. Number Sense Draw similar figures with sides that are three times as long.

Reading ———— Math

Vocabulary Complete each sentence.

1. Congruent segments have equal ▦.

2. A quadrilateral has ▦ sides.

3. An ▦ triangle has one obtuse angle.

4. A unit used to measure angles is the ▦.

Find a Pattern

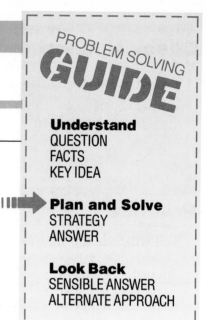

PROBLEM SOLVING
GUIDE

Understand
QUESTION
FACTS
KEY IDEA

➤ **Plan and Solve**
STRATEGY
ANSWER

Look Back
SENSIBLE ANSWER
ALTERNATE APPROACH

Build Understanding

In Ms. Sanford's geometry class, the students learned that a **_diagonal_** is a segment that connects one vertex of a polygon to another vertex but is not a side of the polygon. One question on a quiz was: How many diagonals does a heptagon have?

Understand How many different segments can be drawn that connect the vertices of a heptagon but are not sides of the heptagon? A heptagon is a seven-sided polygon.

➤ **Plan and Solve** STRATEGY Drawing the heptagon and all the diagonals might get confusing. Start with a polygon with fewer sides and see if there is a pattern in the number of diagonals as the number of sides increases.

Triangle	Quadrilateral	Pentagon	Hexagon	Heptagon
3 sides	4 sides	5 sides	6 sides	7 sides
0 diagonals	2 diagonals	5 diagonals	9 diagonals	

There are 2 more diagonals in a quadrilateral than a triangle. There are 3 more diagonals in a pentagon than a quadrilateral. There are 4 more diagonals in a hexagon than a pentagon. Continuing the pattern, a heptagon will have 5 more diagonals than a hexagon.

ANSWER   A heptagon has 14 diagonals.

Look Back You could draw a picture of a heptagon with its diagonals. Be sure you draw all the diagonals and have counted all of them.

■ **Talk About Math** Explain how you would find how many diagonals a decagon has. A decagon is a 10-sided polygon.

Check Understanding

How many triangles can you make by drawing diagonals from one vertex of a decagon? Start by drawing polygons with fewer sides. How many triangles can you make in a

1. quadrilateral? **2.** pentagon? **3.** hexagon?

Use the pattern you found in Problems 1–3 to complete this table.

Number of sides	4	5	6	7	8	9	10
Number of triangles	**4.** ▦	**5.** ▦	**6.** ▦	**7.** ▦	**8.** ▦	**9.** ▦	**10.** ▦

Practice

If you measure the three angles in any triangle and find the sum of the measures, the total is 180°. What is the sum of the angle measures of a decagon? Start with a polygon with fewer sides. Use the pattern you found in Problems 1–10 for the number of triangles in each polygon. What is the sum of the angle measures

11. of a quadrilateral? **12.** of a pentagon? **13.** of a decagon?

14. How many triangles can you make by drawing diagonals from one vertex of a 100-sided polygon?

15. 🖩 **Calculator** What is the sum of the angle measures of a 100-sided polygon?

Choose a ▟▟▟ Strategy

Green or Not? There are 27 small white cubes in the large cube. The top, bottom, and four sides of the large cube are painted green. How many of the small cubes have

16. no faces that are painted green?

17. 1 green face?

18. 2 green faces?

19. 3 green faces?

PROBLEM SOLVING
STRATEGIES

Choose an Operation
Write an Equation
Draw a Diagram
Make a Table
Try and Check
Use Logical Reasoning
Find a Pattern
Work Backward
Solve a Simpler Problem
Make a Graph

Skills Review

Name each figure.

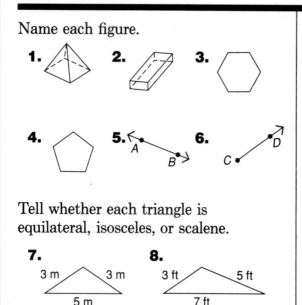

1.

2.

3.

4.

5. A B

6. C D

Tell whether each triangle is equilateral, isosceles, or scalene.

7.

3 m   3 m

5 m

8.

3 ft   5 ft

7 ft

9. Use a protractor to measure the angle.

10. Tell whether the angle above is right, acute, or obtuse.

Name each quadrilateral.

11.

12.

13. Write *true* or *false*. A radius is a segment through the center of a circle that connects two points on the circle.

14. Estimate the circumference of a circle with a radius of 6 feet.

Write *yes* or *no*. Are the figures
15. congruent?   **16.** similar?

17. Draw a rectangle. Then draw the lines of symmetry.

Problem-Solving Review

Solve each problem.

18. Marco is making a mask from an 8-inch diameter paper plate. He has 28 inches of yarn. Does he have enough yarn to put around the circumference of the mask?

19. Glenn went to lunch after he went to the library and before he went to the bookstore. Right after lunch, he went to the bank. The post office was his first stop. List Glenn's stops from first to last.

20. Photo reprints cost $0.65 each. Can Darryl have 15 reprints made for less than $10?

21. A circular swimming pool has a diameter of 30 feet. If Mike swims along the edge of the pool, about how many times should he swim around the pool to swim $\frac{1}{4}$ mile (1,320 feet)?

22. What two numbers have a sum of 34 and a product of 285?

23. **Data File** George wants to make the lantern kite shown on pages 528–529. If the diameter of each circle is 12 in. long, about how many inches will the circumference of each circle be?

24. **Make a Data File** Find the regulation size of balls used in at least five different sports. List them in order from smallest to largest in circumference.

List from least to greatest.

1. 6,075   6,750   6,570

2. 93,261   9,326   9,623

3. 0.579   0.597   0.795

4. 35.24   35.42   35.6

5. $\frac{3}{8}$ $\frac{1}{4}$ $\frac{1}{2}$ **6.** $\frac{5}{6}$ $\frac{2}{3}$ $\frac{4}{9}$

Estimate each answer.

7. 7,821 + 4,925   **8.** 54 + 46 + 51

9. 9,345 − 829   **10.** 5,250 − 4,198

11. 103 × 87   **12.** 2 × 27 × 5

13. 5,721 ÷ 72   **14.** 7,896 ÷ 81

Find the area of each figure.

15. 10 ft / 10 ft   **16.** 4 cm / 8 cm

Describe the pattern. Then write the next four numbers.

17. 4, 12, 36, 108, . . .

18. 5, 9, 8, 12, 11, . . .

Compute.

19. $\frac{5}{8} + \frac{2}{3}$ **20.** $4\frac{1}{4} + 3\frac{1}{2}$

21. $6 - 2\frac{2}{5}$ **22.** $3\frac{1}{6} - 1\frac{1}{2}$

23. $\frac{2}{7} \times \frac{3}{4}$ **24.** $\frac{1}{3} \times 15$

25. $2\frac{1}{2} \times 3\frac{1}{3}$ **26.** $5\frac{3}{5} \times 2\frac{1}{2}$

The number of students who ate school lunch last week is as follows: Monday: 125; Tuesday: 110; Wednesday: 145; Thursday: 150; Friday: 105.

27. What kind of a graph would you use to show the data above? Why?

28. Make a graph to show the data.

If Joe spent $240, how much money was spent on

29. lunch?

30. clothes?

31. recreation?   **32.** gifts?

Suppose you put tiles that spell the word STATISTICS in a bag and draw a tile without looking. On one draw, what is the probability of getting

33. an S?   **34.** an I? **35.** an A?

Use the figure at the right for Exercises 36–41.

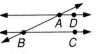

36. Name a line.   **37.** Name a ray

38. Name a pair of parallel lines.

39. Name a pair of intersecting lines.

40. Measure ∠ABC with a protractor.

41. Is ∠ABC right, acute, or obtuse?

Name each polygon.

42. △   **43.**   **44.**

Reteaching

Set A   pages 452–455

A geometric solid that has all flat surfaces is a polyhedron. Each surface of a polyhedron is a face. Two faces meet to form an edge, and three or more edges meet to form a vertex.

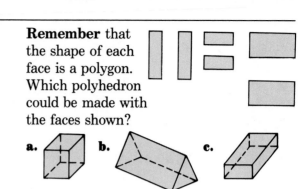

Remember that the shape of each face is a polygon. Which polyhedron could be made with the faces shown?

a.   **b.**   **c.**

Set B   pages 456–457

The pyramid in Set A above shows two types of polygons. Four of the faces are triangular. The bottom face is square.

Remember that two sides of a polygon meet to form a vertex. This polygon has

1. ▦ sides.

2. ▦ vertices.

3. What kind of polygon is this?

Set C   pages 458–459

A segment is named by its two endpoints.

A ————• B

Segment *AB* or segment *BA*

A line is named by two points on it. A line has no endpoints.

C   *D*

Line *CD* or line *DC*

A ray is named by its endpoint and one other point on it.

E   *F*

Ray *EF*

Remember that the endpoint of a ray is the point named first.

Use this figure for the exercises.

1. Name two rays with endpoint *A*.

2. Name two lines passing through *C*.

Set D   pages 460–461

Here are three types of triangles.

Equilateral   Isosceles   Scalene

6 cm / 6 cm / 6 cm   8 cm / 8 cm / 6 cm   7 cm / 12 cm / 10 cm

All sides equal   Two sides equal   No sides equal

Remember that an equilateral triangle is also an isosceles triangle.

1. Segment *AB* = ▦ cm

2. Segment *BC* = ▦ cm

3. Segment *AC* = ▦ cm

4. What type is triangle ABC?

Set E pages 462–463

A right angle looks like a square corner. A corner of a book page forms a right angle.

An acute angle is smaller than a right angle.

An obtuse angle is larger than a right angle.

Remember that when using 3 points to name an angle, the vertex is always the middle point. Which angle is

1. obtuse?

2. right?

3. acute?

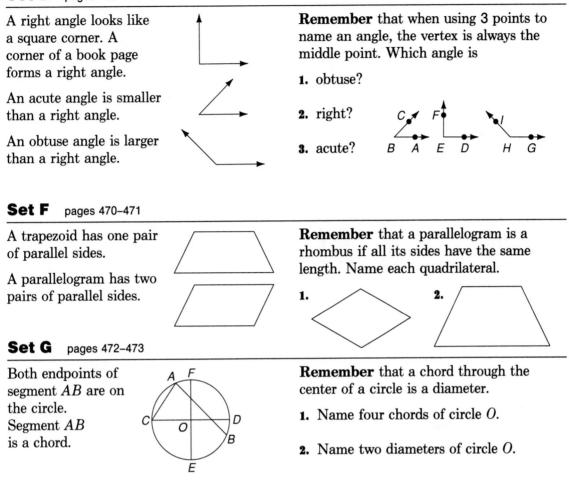

Set F pages 470–471

A trapezoid has one pair of parallel sides.

A parallelogram has two pairs of parallel sides.

Remember that a parallelogram is a rhombus if all its sides have the same length. Name each quadrilateral.

1.   **2.**

Set G pages 472–473

Both endpoints of segment *AB* are on the circle. Segment *AB* is a chord.

Remember that a chord through the center of a circle is a diameter.

1. Name four chords of circle *O*.

2. Name two diameters of circle *O*.

Set H pages 476–477

Some ways of moving a polygon are: *Slide:* Move it in any direction, as if on a sled. *Flip:* Flip it over a line, as if turning a page in a book. *Turn:* Turn it on a vertex, as if the vertex was nailed down.

Remember that congruent figures have the same size and shape. Would you slide, flip, or turn one figure to show it is congruent to the other?

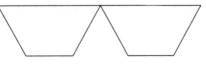

Set I pages 480–481

A square has 4 lines of symmetry because there are 4 ways to fold it so that one half of the figure fits the other half exactly.

Remember that a figure may have 0, 1, or more lines of symmetry. How many lines of symmetry does each figure have?

1.   **2.**

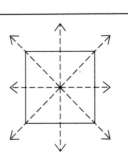

More Practice

Set A pages 452–455

This rectangular prism has

1. ▦ faces.

2. ▦ vertices.

3. ▦ edges.

This triangular prism has

4. ▦ faces.

5. ▦ vertices.

6. ▦ edges.

Set B pages 456–457

Tell which polygon you see. Then tell how many sides and vertices each polygon has.

1.

STOP

2.

3.

ROAD
CONSTRUCTION
AHEAD

Set C pages 458–459

Use the figure at the right for Exercises 1–4.

1. Name a ray.

2. Name a line.

3. Name a pair of intersecting lines.

4. Name a pair of parallel lines.

Set D pages 460–461

Measure each side of each triangle. Then tell whether the triangle is equilateral, isosceles, or scalene.

1. Segment AB = ▦ cm

   Segment AC = ▦ cm

   Segment BC = ▦ cm

2. Segment DE = ▦ cm

   Segment DF = ▦ cm

   Segment EF = ▦ cm

Set E pages 462–463

Use the figure at the right for Exercises 1–3.

1. Name two right angles.

2. Name one acute angle.

3. Name two obtuse angles.

Set F pages 470–471

Name each quadrilateral.

1.

2.

3.

Set G pages 472–473

Use circle O for Exercises 1–4. Name each segment that is

1. a radius.

2. a chord.

3. a diameter.

4. Name each central angle of circle O.

Set H pages 476–477

Tell whether the figures are congruent. Write *yes* or *no*.

1.

2.

3.

4. For each pair of congruent figures in Exercises 1–3, tell whether you would flip, slide, or turn one figure to show it is congruent to the other figure.

Set I pages 480–481

Copy each figure. Draw each line of symmetry. How many lines of symmetry does each figure have?

1.

2.

3.

Enrichment

Surface Area

To find the *surface area* of a solid shape, add the areas of all the faces.

Find the surface area of this prism. Think of the figure as being taken apart.

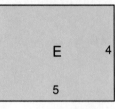

Make a table showing the area of each face. **Remember** to multiply the length and width to find the area of each rectangle.

	Face	Length (ft)	Width (ft)	Area (sq ft)
1.	A	4	3	⊞
2.	B	5	4	⊞
3.	C	4	3	⊞
4.	D	5	3	⊞
5.	E	5	4	⊞
6.	F	5	3	⊞

7. What is the surface area of the figure?

Find the surface area to answer each question.

8. How much wrapping paper is needed to cover this box?

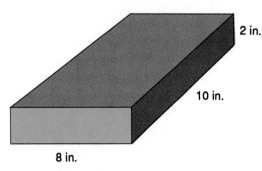

9. How much paint is needed to cover this container?

Chapter 14 Review/Test

Is each polyhedron a prism or a pyramid?

1.

2.

How many sides does each have?

3. Pentagon

4. Octagon

Name each figure.

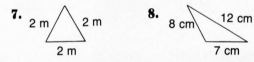

5. R S

6. X Y

Tell whether each triangle is *equilateral, isosceles,* or *scalene.*

7. 2 m 2 m 2 m

8. 8 cm 12 cm 7 cm

Use a protractor to measure each angle. Then tell whether the angle is *right, acute,* or *obtuse.*

9.

10.

11. Use a protractor to draw an angle with a measure of 30°.

Name each quadrilateral.

12.

13.

14. Estimate the circumference of a circle with a diameter of 12 inches.

15. A diameter is a segment from the center of a circle to any point on the circle. Write *yes* or *no.*

16. Are the figures congruent? Write *yes* or *no.*

17. Could tiles like the ones shown cover a floor with no spaces between the tiles?

18. How many lines of symmetry does the figure at the right have?

19. Are the figures similar? Write *yes* or *no.*

Read the problem below. Then answer Items 20–21.

How many cuts would be made on a pizza shaped like a pentagon if cuts are made on all the diagonals?

20. Which is another way of asking the question in the problem?

  a. How many pieces of pizza can be cut from a pizza shaped like a pentagon?

  b. How many sides in a pentagon?

  c. How many diagonals does a pentagon have?

21. Solve the problem.

22. **Write About Math** Can parallel lines ever be perpendicular to each other? Why or why not?

Ratio, Proportion, and Percent

15

Did You Know: Early bikes were called high wheelers. Those "wheels" moved on a direct drive system. There were no chains to make a gear system. Each turn of the pedal made the wheel go around one time.

Number-Sense Project

Estimate
Using the fastest gear, estimate how many times the back wheel of a bike will go around (without coasting) when you move the pedal so it makes one revolution.

Gather Data
Ask a student to hold up the back wheel of a bike while you turn the pedal around one time. Hold a finger against the tire to keep the wheel from coasting. Count the number of revolutions.

Analyze and Report
Count the number of back tire revolutions for one turn of the pedal using the highest and lowest gears. Make a table or graph to show your results. Share your results with other students.

Meaning of Ratio

Build Understanding

The students at Washington School held a talent show. The first act of the show featured 5 singers and 2 dancers.

A. A *ratio* is one way to compare two quantities. The ratio of singers to dancers is 5 to 2. This ratio can be written as 5 to 2 or 5 : 2.

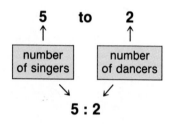

5 : 2

The order of comparison is important.

The ratio of dancers to singers is 2 to 5. This ratio is written 2 to 5 or 2 : 5.

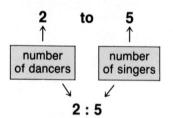

2 : 5

B. A ratio can compare a part to a total. The first act of the talent show featured a total of 7 performers. The ratio of singers to performers is 5 to 7. The ratio is written as 5 to 7 or 5 : 7.

The ratio of dancers to performers is 2 to 7. The ratio is written as 2 to 7 or 2 : 7.

■ **Talk About Math** If you know the ratio of boys to girls is 3 to 4, how do you find the ratio of girls to boys? of boys to the total number of performers? How do you decide which number to write first in a ratio?

Check Understanding

For another example, see Set A, pages 522–523.

The performers in the second act of the talent show were jugglers and musicians. Write each ratio.

1. Jugglers to musicians

2. Musicians to jugglers

3. Musicians to performers

4. Jugglers to performers

Practice

For More Practice, see Set A, pages 524–525.

The musicians for the third act needed drums, guitars, and trumpets. Write each ratio.

5. Guitars to trumpets

6. Drums to instruments

7. Guitars to instruments

8. Instruments to trumpets

Suppose students used 5 red, 4 blue, and 2 white rolls of streamers to decorate the stage. Explain each ratio.

9. 5 : 2   10. 4 : 5   11. 2 : 4   12. 5 : 11   13. 4 : 11

14. A package of streamers costs 97 cents. There are 3 rolls in a package. Write the ratio of rolls to cents.

Problem Solving

15. Kevin needs 7 rolls of red and 8 rolls of white streamers. Packages are sold containing 3 rolls of a single color. How many packages of each color does he need to buy?

16. The only coins Kevin has are quarters and dimes. The ratio of his dimes to his coins is 7 : 23. How much money does he have? Does he have enough to buy the streamers he needs? Use the information in Exercises 14 and 15.

Equal Ratios

Build Understanding

One of the water rides at Colossal Park has boats that look like logs. Each log can hold 5 people.

A. Ratio Rides
Materials: Pencils, unit cubes
Groups: With a partner

a. Use small objects to represent riders. Use pencils to represent logs. Show the ratio of riders to logs, 5 : 1.

b. Show the ratio of riders to logs when there are 2 logs and 10 riders.

The ratio is 5 riders to 1 log, or 5 : 1, and 10 riders to 2 logs, or 10 : 2.

The ratio 10 : 2 is equal to the ratio 5 : 1.

c. Use your materials to find another ratio equal to 5 : 1 when there are 4 full logs.

d. How many ratios can you find equal to 5 : 1?

B. You can use pictures to write a list of equal ratios. There are 3 triangular flags and 2 square flags on each post.

3:2   3:2   3:2   3:2   3:2

|___ 6:4 ___|

|___ 9:6 ___|

|___ 12:8 ___|

|___ 15:10 ___|

■ **Talk About Math**
Suppose the first number in a ratio is greater than the second. In an equal ratio, will the first number also be greater than the second? Explain.

1. In another ride, there are 4 riders to a car. Use objects to complete.

   Riders : Cars

   4 : 1   8 : ▦   ▦ : ▦   ▦ : ▦   ▦ : ▦

2. If each car holds 3 riders, use the picture to complete the list of equal ratios.

   Car : Riders

   1 : 3   2 : ▦   ▦ : 9   4 : ▦   ▦ : ▦

Practice

For More Practice, see Set B, pages 524–525.

Use the picture to write a list of equal ratios.

3. Each stack has 1 green and 2 red stars.

   Red stars : Green stars

   2 : 1   4 : ▦   ▦ : 3   ▦ : 4   ▦ : ▦

4. 4 red stripes and 3 blue stripes are on each T-shirt.

   Red stripes : Blue stripes

   4 : 3   ▦ : 6   12 : ▦   16 : ▦   ▦ : ▦

5. Each ride lasts 10 seconds and goes 90 meters.

   Seconds : Meters

   10 : 90   ▦ : 180   30 : ▦   ▦ : ▦   ▦ : ▦

6. It costs $5 to rent a paddle boat for 30 minutes.

   Dollars : Minutes

   5 : 30   ▦ : ▦   ▦ : ▦   ▦ : ▦   ▦ : ▦

Problem Solving

Visual Thinking   Two fences each measure 40 feet. Each has a post every 10 feet. One is in a straight line. The other forms a square.

7. Are the ratios for the number of feet of fence to the number of posts the same for both fences? Why or why not?

8. How many posts are needed for an 80-foot straight fence? for an 80-foot fence in the shape of a square?

A
L
G
E
B
R
A

Finding Equal Ratios

Build Understanding

A. Leland owns the Bicycle Fix-it Shop. He can repair 4 bicycles in 2 hours. The ratio of bicycles to hours can be written in three different ways.

4 to 2   **4 : 2** $\dfrac{4}{2}$

B. This ratio can be used to find the number of bicycles Leland can repair during different amounts of time.

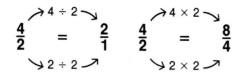

$$\dfrac{4}{2} = \dfrac{2}{1} \qquad \dfrac{4}{2} = \dfrac{8}{4}$$

$4 \div 2$ and $2 \div 2$ 4×2 and 2×2

C. Find d in $\dfrac{2}{3} = \dfrac{12}{d}$.

$$\dfrac{2}{3} = \dfrac{12}{d}$$

$$\dfrac{2}{3} = \dfrac{12}{18}$$

2×6 and 3×6 Since $2 \times 6 = 12$, multiply 3×6 to find d.

$$d = 18$$

■ **Talk About Math** $\dfrac{3}{5}$ and $\dfrac{6}{10}$ are equal ratios. How are the first terms related? How are the second terms related?

Check Understanding

For another example, see Set C, pages 522–523.

Tell how to find the equal ratios.

1. $\dfrac{4}{5} = \dfrac{16}{20}$ Multiply 4 and 5 by ▦.

2. $\dfrac{24}{21} = \dfrac{8}{7}$ Divide 24 and 21 by ▦.

3. $\dfrac{9}{4} = \dfrac{18}{8}$ Multiply 9 and 4 by ▦.

Find each equal ratio.

4. $\dfrac{3}{4} = \dfrac{}{8} = \dfrac{9}{} = \dfrac{}{16} = \dfrac{15}{}$

5. $\dfrac{4}{5} = \dfrac{f}{10}$

6. $\dfrac{14}{42} = \dfrac{2}{p}$

Practice

For More Practice, see Set C, pages 524–525.

Complete each list of equal ratios.

7. $\frac{2}{7} = \frac{▦}{14} = \frac{6}{▦} = \frac{▦}{28} = \frac{▦}{35}$

8. $\frac{5}{8} = \frac{10}{▦} = \frac{▦}{24} = \frac{▦}{32} = \frac{25}{▦}$

9. $\frac{4}{5} = \frac{▦}{10} = \frac{12}{▦} = \frac{▦}{20} = \frac{20}{▦}$

10. $\frac{11}{12} = \frac{22}{▦} = \frac{▦}{36} = \frac{▦}{48} = \frac{55}{▦}$

Find each equal ratio.

11. $\frac{5}{2} = \frac{10}{t}$ **12.** $\frac{3}{4} = \frac{c}{12}$ **13.** $\frac{9}{5} = \frac{27}{m}$ **14.** $\frac{4}{3} = \frac{v}{15}$ **15.** $\frac{3}{2} = \frac{b}{18}$

16. $\frac{5}{6} = \frac{40}{n}$ **17.** $\frac{7}{11} = \frac{s}{33}$ **18.** $\frac{4}{7} = \frac{28}{f}$ **19.** $\frac{3}{10} = \frac{9}{w}$ **20.** $\frac{3}{13} = \frac{15}{x}$

21. $\frac{2}{15} = \frac{14}{a}$ **22.** $\frac{5}{8} = \frac{100}{a}$ **23.** $\frac{17}{3} = \frac{z}{15}$ **24.** $\frac{12}{15} = \frac{36}{g}$ **25.** $\frac{14}{30} = \frac{k}{90}$

Multiply or divide to find the equal ratio.

26. Buy 2 brake pads for $7. $\frac{2}{7} = \frac{6}{▦}$

27. Spend 132 minutes to assemble 4 bicycles. $\frac{132}{4} = \frac{▦}{1}$

28. Write 4 equal ratios. Replace 3 mirrors in 10 minutes.

29. Write 3 equal ratios. Spend $6 for 48 wheel spokes.

Problem Solving

30. Leland can stack 9 bicycle tires on each rack at the shop. How many racks does he need to stack 36 bicycle tires?

31. Leland orders 8 new 18-inch bicycle tires for every 5 new 26-inch bicycle tires. If 25 of the 26-inch tires were ordered, how many 18-inch tires were ordered?

Skills ———— **Review**   pages 214–267

Add, subtract, or multiply.

1. $\begin{array}{r} 0.72 \\ + 0.49 \end{array}$ **2.** $\begin{array}{r} 0.72 \\ \times 0.49 \end{array}$ **3.** $\begin{array}{r} 0.72 \\ - 0.49 \end{array}$ **4.** $\begin{array}{r} 5.68 \\ - 0.204 \end{array}$ **5.** $\begin{array}{r} 0.205 \\ \times \quad 92 \end{array}$ **6.** $\begin{array}{r} 0.809 \\ + 15.2 \end{array}$

7. $82.4 + 3.65$ **8.** $19.5 - 14.7$ **9.** 3.2×7.91 **10.** 1.4×0.07

Proportions

Build Understanding

A. The most common colors worn by Major League baseball teams are listed in the chart. The Rockford Little League has 4 teams that wear orange and 12 teams that wear blue on their uniforms. Is the ratio of teams that wear orange to teams that wear blue the same for both leagues?

Color	Number of Teams
Blue	18
White	17
Red	15
Orange	6
Yellow	6

Major League
Orange → $\dfrac{6}{18} = \dfrac{12}{36}$
Blue ⟶

Little League
Orange → $\dfrac{4}{12} = \dfrac{8}{24} = \dfrac{12}{36}$
Blue ⟶

Since each list of equal ratios shows 12 orange and 36 blue, the ratios 6:18 and 4:12 are equal.

$\dfrac{6}{18} = \dfrac{4}{12}$

6×12 and 4×18 are **cross-products** of these two ratios.
$6 \times 12 = 72$ and $4 \times 18 = 72$.

If two ratios are equal, their cross-products are equal.
Two ratios that are equal form a **proportion.**

B. If the Rockford Little League wanted to have the same ratio of red to blue on their uniforms as the Major Leagues do, how many teams would wear red? Cross-products can be used to find a missing number in a proportion.

Major League   Little League

Red → $\dfrac{15}{18} = \dfrac{u}{12}$
Blue →

Write a proportion. Use u for the missing number.

$18 \times u = 15 \times 12$

Find the cross-products. Since the ratios are equal, the cross-products are equal.

$18 \times u = 180$

Multiply.

$u = 180 \div 18$ Divide to find u.

$u = 10$

The Rockford Little League would have 10 teams wearing red.

■ **Talk About Math**   Why is the proportion $\frac{15}{18} = \frac{12}{u}$ not correct for Example B?

Check Understanding

For another example, see Set D, pages 522–523.

1. Tell if the ratios are equal.

$\dfrac{4}{3}$ $\dfrac{9}{6}$

2. Solve using cross-products.

$\dfrac{6}{15} = \dfrac{w}{10}$

Solve each proportion using cross-products.

3. $\frac{2}{a} = \frac{3}{15}$ **4.** $\frac{x}{6} = \frac{3}{9}$ **5.** $\frac{4}{6} = \frac{14}{e}$ **6.** $\frac{c}{8} = \frac{9}{12}$ **7.** $\frac{20}{6} = \frac{10}{z}$

8. $\frac{4}{16} = \frac{3}{m}$ **9.** $\frac{2}{b} = \frac{5}{20}$ **10.** $\frac{9}{15} = \frac{12}{w}$ **11.** $\frac{n}{18} = \frac{16}{36}$ **12.** $\frac{12}{40} = \frac{18}{d}$

13. $\frac{6}{14} = \frac{h}{42}$ **14.** $\frac{1}{k} = \frac{17}{51}$ **15.** $\frac{2}{12} = \frac{5}{x}$ **16.** $\frac{b}{5} = \frac{9}{15}$ **17.** $\frac{4}{8} = \frac{5}{z}$

18. $\frac{5}{v} = \frac{9}{27}$ **19.** $\frac{6}{5} = \frac{c}{30}$ **20.** $\frac{24}{8} = \frac{w}{3}$ **21.** $\frac{4}{e} = \frac{28}{7}$ **22.** $\frac{r}{36} = \frac{15}{12}$

23. $\frac{2}{3} = \frac{14}{y}$ **24.** $\frac{12}{16} = \frac{d}{4}$ **25.** $\frac{3}{m} = \frac{4}{12}$ **26.** $\frac{f}{6} = \frac{5}{10}$ **27.** $\frac{12}{l} = \frac{9}{6}$

28. Number Sense Would the missing number in the proportion $\frac{15}{20} = \frac{12}{f}$ be greater than or less than 12? How do you know?

For Exercises 29–38, tell whether you would use paper and pencil or mental math. Then solve the proportion.

29. $\frac{5}{v} = \frac{10}{12}$ **30.** $\frac{a}{8} = \frac{8}{64}$ **31.** $\frac{10}{6} = \frac{15}{j}$ **32.** $\frac{6}{y} = \frac{7}{14}$ **33.** $\frac{k}{12} = \frac{3}{2}$

34. $\frac{20}{8} = \frac{25}{i}$ **35.** $\frac{t}{15} = \frac{20}{50}$ **36.** $\frac{21}{g} = \frac{2}{10}$ **37.** $\frac{27}{18} = \frac{n}{4}$ **38.** $\frac{36}{24} = \frac{15}{p}$

Problem Solving

39. The league can buy 15 pairs of baseball socks for $20. How much would 24 pairs of socks cost?

40. Gerry bought a baseball cap for $4.70 and a bat for $8.65. How much change will he get from $20?

41. The Rockford Twins practice 4 times in 7 days. How many times will they practice in 2 weeks?

42. Sam bought 6 baseballs for $14. How many baseballs can he buy for $21?

A
L
G
E
B
R
A

Write an Equation

Build Understanding

Totem poles are carved by Alaskan and Northwest Coast Indian tribes. Many totem poles tell historical stories. In a **scale drawing** of a totem pole, 2 inches represented 15 feet. What is the actual height of the totem pole?

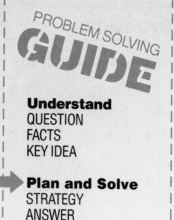

PROBLEM SOLVING
GUIDE

Understand
QUESTION
FACTS
KEY IDEA

▶ **Plan and Solve**
STRATEGY
ANSWER

Look Back
SENSIBLE ANSWER
ALTERNATE APPROACH

Understand   How tall is the actual totem pole? In the picture, it is 5 inches tall. The scale in the drawing is the ratio of 2 inches to 15 feet. It compares drawing height to actual height.

Plan and Solve   STRATEGY   Write a ratio for the totem pole to compare drawing height to actual height. Write a proportion using the two ratios.

Scale   Totem pole
$$\frac{2}{15} = \frac{5}{c}$$ ← Drawing (inches)
← Actual (feet)

Solve the proportion.

Paper and Pencil   📱 **Calculator**

Find the cross-products. $2 \times c = 15 \times 5$ $15 \boxed{\times} 5$

Multiply. $2 \times c = 75$ $\boxed{\div} 2 \boxed{=} \; 37.5$

Divide. $c = 37\frac{1}{2}$

ANSWER   The actual height of the totem pole is $37\frac{1}{2}$ feet.

Look Back   The drawing height of 5 inches is a little more than twice the 2 inches in the scale. The actual height is more than twice the 15 feet in the scale. The answer is reasonable.

■ **Talk About Math**   Could you also solve the problem with the proportion $\frac{15}{2} = \frac{c}{5}$? with the proportion $\frac{2}{15} = \frac{c}{5}$? Explain why or why not.

The salmon on this totem pole represents the importance of fish as a source of food for Indians.

504

Check Understanding

Measure each carving. Use the scale 2 cm → 1 m.

1. Which of these proportions will not help you find the actual height of the eagle? Why?

   a. $\frac{2}{1} = \frac{t}{4}$ **b.** $\frac{2}{1} = \frac{4}{t}$ **c.** $\frac{2}{4} = \frac{1}{t}$

Find the actual height of

2. the eagle.

3. the beaver.

Eagle   Beaver

Practice

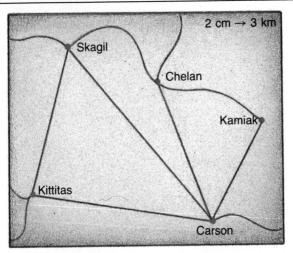

2 cm → 3 km

Skagil

Chelan

Kamiak

Kittitas

Carson

Measure the map distance to find the actual distance between Carson and the other Indian villages. **Remember** to use a proportion to find the actual distance.

4. Skagil   5. Chelan

6. Kittitas   7. Kamiak

8. A 40-foot totem pole weighs about 3,000 pounds. About how much would a 70-foot pole with the same circumference weigh?

9. A tree trunk 70 feet long was used for a totem pole. If the ratio of the portion of the pole above ground to the portion below ground is $\frac{6}{1}$, how much of the pole is above ground?

10. In a scale drawing of a *moai* statue, 2 inches represent 12 feet. The actual height of the largest statue is 33 feet. What is the height of its scale drawing?

About 800 *moai* statues can be found on Easter Island. These giant stone carvings, some 1,000 years old, range in size from 6 feet to 33 feet and can weigh as much as 85 tons.

Problem Solving WORKSHOP

Explore as a Team

1. Work with another student to cut a piece of string the same length as your height.

2. How many times will that length of string wrap around your head, wrist, elbow, knee, and ankle?

3. Record your results. Write a ratio to compare the number of times the string wraps safely around your head, wrist, and so on, to 1 (the number of times the string reaches your height).

	Number of times string wraps around	Number of times string reaches your height	Ratio
Head		1	
Wrist		1	

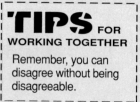

TIPS FOR
WORKING TOGETHER
Remember, you can disagree without being disagreeable.

Explore with a Computer

Use the *Spreadsheet Workshop Project* for this activity.

Mary and Helen volunteer to read articles to senior citizens. Each week Mary visits 2 people for 1 hour each. Helen visits 3 people for 45 minutes each.

	People Visited	Minutes Each	Minutes/ Week	Hours/ Month
Mary				
Helen				

1. At the computer, enter this data in the spreadsheet. Who volunteers more time each month? How much more?

2. Find the ratio of the minutes Mary visits each person to the minutes Helen visits each person.

Real-Life Decision Making

You want to buy Puffy Crunch Popcorn. Your mother says you can buy it if you can prove that it is a better buy than Movie Time Popcorn. Is Puffy Crunch a better buy? Why?

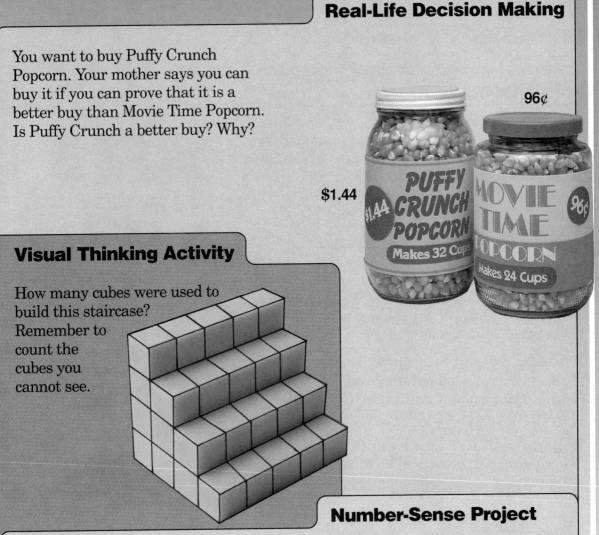

96¢

$1.44

Visual Thinking Activity

How many cubes were used to build this staircase? Remember to count the cubes you cannot see.

Number-Sense Project

Look back at pages 494-495.

Most bicycles use gears consisting of a chain and different size sprockets. The size of the sprocket is determined by the number of teeth.

a. The high gear formed by this sprocket setup has a ratio of 54:14. Would the back wheel make more than one revolution or less than one revolution each time you turn the pedals?

Gear Ratio:

Number of teeth in front sprocket
————————————
Number of teeth in rear sprocket

b. Based on the 54:14 ratio, describe what the back wheel does every time there is a complete revolution of the pedals.

507

Ratios and Percents

Build Understanding

A newspaper poll asked 100 children, ages 5 to 12, what they wanted to be when they grew up. They were asked to pick one of the choices in the chart. The chart shows how many children selected each choice.

A. Grown-up Percents
Materials: Grid paper, 5 different color crayons or markers
Groups: With a partner

a. Outline a 10-by-10 grid. How many squares are enclosed in the outline?

b. Using a different color for each choice, show the number of children who made each choice by coloring squares in the grid. Color one square for each child.

c. Copy the chart. For each choice write a ratio comparing the number of children who selected that choice to the total number of children polled.

What do you want to be when you grow up?	
Happily married	38
Rich	24
Healthy	19
Surrounded by friends	14
Other	5
Total children polled	100

B. When a number is compared to 100, the comparison can be written as a ratio, or as a ***percent***. Percent means *per one hundred*. The symbol for percent is %.

The selection of the choice *Happily married* by 38 of the 100 children can be shown in different ways.

The grid shows 38 out of 100 squares colored.

The ratio of children who made this choice to the total is written 38 to 100, or 38:100, or $\frac{38}{100}$.

The percent of children who made this choice is written 38%.

■ **Talk About Math** On a 10-by-10 grid, how many squares would be colored to show 100%? How many squares would be colored to show 0%?

508

Check Understanding

For another example, see Set E, pages 522–523.

1. Write $\frac{3}{100}$ as a percent.

2. Write 62% as a ratio.

Practice

For More Practice, see Set E, pages 524–525.

Write each ratio as a percent.

3. $\frac{18}{100}$　　**4.** $\frac{50}{100}$　　**5.** $\frac{5}{100}$　　**6.** $\frac{100}{100}$　　**7.** $\frac{27}{100}$　　**8.** $\frac{20}{100}$

9. 2 to 100　　**10.** 75 to 100　　**11.** 1 to 100　　**12.** 43 to 100

13. 25:100　　**14.** 43:100　　**15.** 99:100　　**16.** 32:100

Write each percent as a ratio in fraction form.

17. 26%　　**18.** 7%　　**19.** 67%　　**20.** 90%　　**21.** 9%　　**22.** 1%

23. 39%　　**24.** 19%　　**25.** 82%　　**26.** 29%　　**27.** 16%　　**28.** 12%

Problem Solving

Out of 100 cars, 13 are sports cars. Of the 13 sports cars, 9 are red. What percent of the cars are

29. sports cars?　　**30.** not sports cars?　　**31.** red sports cars?

32. Critical Thinking If 20% of all the cars are black, can you say that 20% of the sports cars are black? Explain.

33. Estimation About 10% of the sports cars are blue. Explain why this is only an estimate.

Midchapter ✓ Checkup

For Exercises 1–3, find each equal ratio.

1. $\frac{21}{42} = \frac{7}{x}$　　**2.** $5:2 = 10:$▦　　**3.** $\frac{7}{3} = \frac{▦}{6} = \frac{21}{▦} = \frac{▦}{▦}$

4. Tell the cross-products for $\frac{7}{12}$ and $\frac{6}{9}$.

5. Write 27% as a ratio.

6. In the map on page 505, measure the distance between Kittitas and Skagil. Then use a proportion to find the actual distance.

Percents and Fractions

Build Understanding

For a science project, Melanie counted and identified birds that came near her home.

OBSERVATIONS ON APRIL 12	
Robins	15
Wrens	24
Cardinals	12
Mourning Doves	9
Total	60

A. Of the birds that Melanie saw, 15 out of 60, or $\frac{1}{4}$ of the birds, were robins. What percent of the birds were robins?

Since percent means *per hundred*, find an equal fraction with a denominator of 100.

Fraction $\longrightarrow$ Percent

$$\frac{1}{4} \overset{\times 25}{\underset{\times 25}{=}} \frac{25}{100} = 25\%$$

25% of the birds were robins.

B. Write 40% as a fraction with a denominator of 100. Then write the fraction in lowest terms.

Percent $\longrightarrow$ Fraction

$$40\% = \frac{40}{100} \overset{\div 20}{\underset{\div 20}{=}} \frac{2}{5}$$

The cardinal is the state bird of 7 states in the U.S.

■ **Talk About Math** Melanie saw no woodpeckers. What fraction is that? What percent is it?

Check Understanding

For another example, see Set F, pages 522–523.

Complete.

1. $\frac{7}{10} = \frac{\text{▦}}{100}$
   $= \text{▦}\%$

2. $\frac{3}{4} = \frac{\text{▦}}{100}$
   $= \text{▦}\%$

3. $\frac{3}{5} = \frac{\text{▦}}{100}$
   $= \text{▦}\%$

4. Write a percent for $\frac{4}{5}$.

5. Write a fraction in lowest terms for 25%.

Practice

For More Practice, see Set F, pages 524–525.

Write each percent as a fraction in lowest terms.

6. 27% **7.** 13% **8.** 1% **9.** 30% **10.** 50% **11.** 45% **12.** 4% **13.** 100%

14. 3% **15.** 62% **16.** 80% **17.** 2% **18.** 7% **19.** 16% **20.** 5% **21.** 10%

Write each fraction as a percent.

22. $\frac{23}{100}$ **23.** $\frac{9}{100}$ **24.** $\frac{81}{100}$ **25.** $\frac{14}{100}$ **26.** $\frac{33}{100}$ **27.** $\frac{47}{100}$ **28.** $\frac{50}{100}$ **29.** $\frac{1}{100}$

30. $\frac{3}{10}$ **31.** $\frac{19}{20}$ **32.** $\frac{6}{10}$ **33.** $\frac{40}{40}$ **34.** $\frac{3}{30}$ **35.** $\frac{9}{25}$ **36.** $\frac{25}{50}$ **37.** $\frac{1}{10}$

38. $\frac{4}{25}$ **39.** $\frac{1}{5}$ **40.** $\frac{1}{4}$ **41.** $\frac{1}{50}$ **42.** $\frac{17}{25}$ **43.** $\frac{35}{70}$ **44.** $\frac{27}{45}$ **45.** $\frac{14}{35}$

46. Number Sense What fraction and percent would describe the situation in which all the birds Melanie saw were sparrows?

Problem Solving

Melanie put her second day's observation in a circle graph. Use it to find these percents.

47. Woodpeckers   **48.** Blue jays

49. Wrens   **50.** Cardinals

51. Robins   **52.** Doves

53. Only 5% of the children did science projects on birds. What fraction did not do projects on birds?

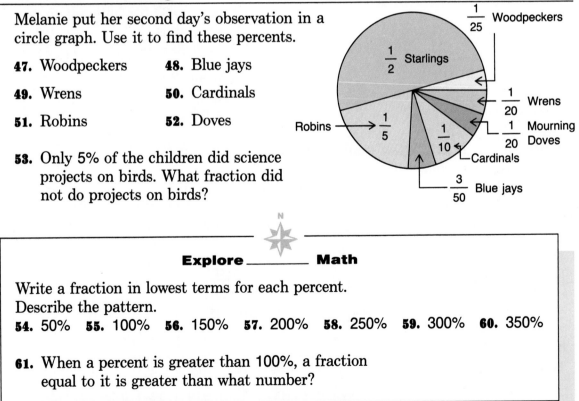

Explore ———— Math

Write a fraction in lowest terms for each percent.
Describe the pattern.

54. 50% **55.** 100% **56.** 150% **57.** 200% **58.** 250% **59.** 300% **60.** 350%

61. When a percent is greater than 100%, a fraction equal to it is greater than what number?

Percents and Decimals

Build Understanding

Many states charge a sales tax on items you buy. A tax of $0.06 on each dollar spent is a ratio of 6 cents to 100 cents. A sales tax is often named as a percent.

A. Decimals that name hundredths can easily be written as percents. Remember that percent means *per hundred.*

$$0.06 = \frac{6}{100} = 6\%$$

A tax of $0.06 on a dollar is a 6% tax.

B. Write 0.4 as a percent. First find the equal decimal in hundredths.

Think: $\frac{4}{10} = \frac{40}{100}$

$$0.4 = 0.40 = 40\%$$

C. Percents can be written as decimals.

30% means 30 per hundred or 30 hundredths.
$$30\% = 0.30 = 0.3$$

9% means 9 per hundred or 9 hundredths.
$$9\% = 0.09$$

■ **Talk About Math** How would you write 140% as a decimal? How would you show it using 10-by-10 grids?

Check Understanding

For another example, see Set G, pages 522–523.

Write a decimal and a percent for each picture.

1. **2.** **3.** **4.**

5. Complete the table.

Percent	50%	7%	▦	▦	▦
Decimal	▦	▦	0.29	0.3	0.03

Practice

For More Practice, see Set G, pages 524–525.

Write each percent as a decimal.

6. 23%   **7.** 94%   **8.** 45%   **9.** 6%   **10.** 1%   **11.** 9%

12. 90%   **13.** 25%   **14.** 99%   **15.** 80%   **16.** 100%   **17.** 10%

Write each decimal as a percent.

18. 0.43   **19.** 0.65   **20.** 0.91   **21.** 0.19   **22.** 0.07   **23.** 0.04

24. 0.5   **25.** 0.3   **26.** 0.02   **27.** 0.1   **28.** 0.10   **29.** 1.00

Mixed Practice   Complete the table.

Percent	**30.** ▒	30%	**33.** ▒	**35.** ▒	**36.** ▒	5%
Decimal	0.2	**31.** ▒	0.25	0.75	0.44	**38.** ▒
Lowest Terms Fraction	$\frac{1}{5}$	**32.** ▒	**34.** ▒	$\frac{3}{4}$	**37.** ▒	**39.** ▒

Problem Solving

40. Judy's state charges a 3% sales tax on food items. Toni's state charges a 5% sales tax on food items. How much more on every dollar does Judy save than Toni on food purchases?

41. Critical Thinking During weekend sales, Big Bob sells items at 60% of the regular price. During the Giant Sale at the end of the year, items are sold at 60% *off* the regular price. How much more on every dollar will you save if you buy an item at the Giant Sale instead of buying it at a weekend sale?

TIPS FOR PROBLEM SOLVERS

Compare problems to help you relate new problems to ones you've solved before.

60%

513

Finding a Percent of a Number

Build Understanding

Mr. and Mrs. Rivera and their children had lunch at the Blue Peacock Restaurant. Their total bill was $25.

In restaurants, people leave a tip for the person who serves them. The usual tip is 15% of the cost of the food. What is the tip on $25?

Since 15% means 15¢ for each dollar, find 15% of 25.

Write the percent as a decimal.	Then multiply.
15% = 0.15	$$\begin{array}{r} 25 \\ \times\,0.15 \\ \hline 125 \\ 250 \\ \hline 3.75 \end{array}$$

The tip is $3.75. The Riveras left $3.75 for the tip.

■ **Talk About Math** How could you do the computation in the example using a calculator? Try to use the ⬚% key.

Receipt:

2	chicken dinners:	12.50
1	chef salad:	3.65
1	spaghetti dinner:	5.25
4	beverages:	3.60
	Subtotal:	$25.00
	sales tax:	
	total:	

Check Understanding

For another example, see Set H, pages 522–523.

Find the percent of each number.

1. 8% of 90

2. 12% of 70

3. 7% of 45

4. 50% of 83

5. 40% of 19

6. 75% of 86

7. 30% of 210

8. 60% of 185

Practice

For More Practice, see Set H, pages 524–525.

Find the percent of each number.

9. 10% of 50   **10.** 80% of 35   **11.** 75% of 12   **12.** 6% of 300

13. 60% of 300   **14.** 40% of 18   **15.** 4% of 150   **16.** 7% of 70

17. 35% of 70   **18.** 5% of 36   **19.** 90% of 150   **20.** 1% of 18

Number Sense Write >, <, or =.

21. 100% of 65 ▦ 65   **22.** 85% of 65 ▦ 65   **23.** 125% of 65 ▦ 65

24. 50% of 45 ▦ 45   **25.** 99% of 87 ▦ 87   **26.** 25% of 40 ▦ 40

Problem Solving

Solve each problem.

27. Mr. Rivera's state charges a 6% sales tax. What is the amount of tax he paid on his bill of $25?

28. What was the cost of the food and tax for the Riveras' meal? What was the total cost including the tip as well?

Use Data Use the data in the table on page 84.

29. 75% of 1 foot = ▦ inches

30. 50% of 1 mile = ▦ yards

31. 20% of 1 mile = ▦ feet

32. 25% of 1 yard = ▦ inches

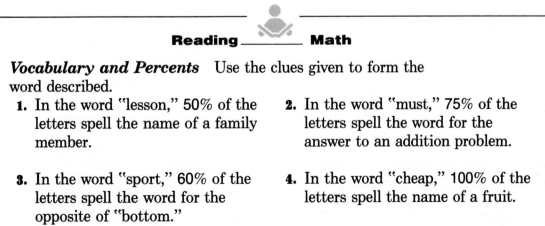

Reading —— Math

Vocabulary and Percents Use the clues given to form the word described.

1. In the word "lesson," 50% of the letters spell the name of a family member.

2. In the word "must," 75% of the letters spell the word for the answer to an addition problem.

3. In the word "sport," 60% of the letters spell the word for the opposite of "bottom."

4. In the word "cheap," 100% of the letters spell the name of a fruit.

515

Estimating a Percent of a Number

Build Understanding

The United States Census Bureau estimates that 18% of the population will be between 5 and 17 years old in 2000. If the city of Oak Hill, West Virginia, has a population of 7,800 in 2000, about how many people will be in the 5-to-17 age group?

To find an estimate of the population, use numbers compatible with the percent and the population. Compatible numbers are close to the original numbers and are easy to use in computation.

18% is about 20%.
7,800 is about 8,000.

A. Find 20% of 8,000 to estimate the population.

$$\begin{array}{r} 8{,}000 \\ \times\ \ 0.20 \\ \hline 1{,}600.00 \end{array}$$

Write 20% as a decimal. Then multiply.

2000 Population Estimate

18%
5 to 17
years old

B. You can also use a fraction to estimate the population. Find 20% of 8,000.

$\frac{1}{5}$ **of 8,000**   Write 20% as a fraction.
$20\% = \frac{20}{100} = \frac{1}{5}$

$\frac{1}{5} \times \frac{8{,}000}{1} = \frac{8{,}000}{5} = 1{,}600$

Oak Hill will have about 1,600 people in the 5-to-17 age group.

■ **Talk About Math**   Here is a chart of useful percent-fraction equivalents.

$10\% = \frac{1}{10}$ $20\% = \frac{1}{5}$ $25\% = \frac{1}{4}$ $50\% = \frac{1}{2}$

What fraction would you use to estimate 50% of a number? 20% of a number? How could you find a fraction equal to 60%? equal to 75%?

Check Understanding

For another example, see Set I, pages 522–523.

1. Name a compatible number for 48%.

2. Name a fraction for the compatible number in Exercise 1.

3. Estimate 26% of 81.

Practice

For More Practice, see Set I, pages 524–525.

Estimate each answer. **Remember** to use compatible numbers.

4. 9% of 21　　**5.** 26% of 97　　**6.** 73% of 101　　**7.** 53% of 997

8. 19% of 79　　**9.** 96% of 220　　**10.** 12% of 3,014　　**11.** 52% of 629

12. 31% of 62　　**13.** 8% of 1,785　　**14.** 22% of 514　　**15.** 49% of 874

16. 74% of 82　　**17.** 27% of 7,922　　**18.** 11% of 37　　**19.** 68% of 9,351

20. 43% of 501　　**21.** 62% of 5,973　　**22.** 84% of 78　　**23.** 91% of 12

24. 9% of $29　　**25.** 32% of $819　　**26.** 26% of $587　　**27.** 98% of $52.30

Problem Solving

Use the table for Problems 28–31.
Estimate these populations in 1990.

28. Between 45 and 62 years old in Orlando

29. Between 20 and 44 years old in Memphis

30. What percentage of the population is over 64 years of age?

31. About how many fewer people, ages 5 to 19, were in Ocala than in Wichita?

1990 Census

8% of the population: under 5 years of age
21%: between 5 and 19 years old
40%: between 20 and 44 years old
19%: between 45 and 64 years old

Metropolitan Area	Population
Burlington, Vermont	137,079
Grand Rapids, Michigan	688,399
Orlando, Florida	1,072,748
Wichita, Kansas	485,270
Ocala, Florida	194,833
Louisville, Kentucky	952,662
Memphis, Tennessee	981,747

Explore ——— Math

Find the percent of each number. What do you notice about each pair of answers? Describe a method you could use to find the percent of the numbers mentally.

32. What is 50% of 80?　80% of 50?　　**33.** What is 25% of 40?　40% of 25?

Mental Math　Exchange the percent and the number to compute mentally.

34. 22% of 50　　**35.** 88% of 25　　**36.** 12% of 75　　**37.** 45% of 20

Too Much or Too Little Information

PROBLEM SOLVING GUIDE

Understand
QUESTION
FACTS
KEY IDEA

Plan and Solve
STRATEGY
ANSWER

Look Back
SENSIBLE ANSWER
ALTERNATE APPROACH

Build Understanding

Rosa earns $2 per hour babysitting. The regular price of a hat she wants to buy is $16. How much will the hat cost with a 30% discount?

Understand QUESTION What is the sale price of the hat?

FACTS The regular price is $16. The discount is 30%. The fact that Rosa earns $2 per hour babysitting is extra information.

KEY IDEA A discount is an amount taken off the regular price. To find the sale price, subtract the discount from the regular price.

Plan and Solve Find 30% of $16 to find the amount of discount.

Paper and Pencil

$$\begin{array}{r} 16 \\ \times\,0.30 \\ \hline 4.80 \end{array}$$

▦ Calculator

Press: **16** $\times$ **30** %

Display: *4.8*

The discount is $4.80. Subtract to find the sale price.

$$\begin{array}{r} 16.00 \\ -\ \ 4.80 \\ \hline 11.20 \end{array}$$

Press: **16** $-$ **4.8** $=$

Display: *11.2*

The hat will cost $11.20 on sale.

Look Back The answer is reasonable. A discount of 50% would be the same as half price. 30% is less than 50%. The discount of $4.80 is less than half of $16.

■ **Talk About Math** If the question had asked whether Rosa had enough money to buy the hat, could you have answered it? What additional information would you need?

Check Understanding

Use the information in the Example. Solve each problem. If there is not enough information given, write *too little information*.

1. Joanna worked 10 hours delivering newspapers last week. How much money will she have left if she buys the same hat on sale?

2. After another week, the same hat will sell for a price of 40% off the regular price. What will be the new sale price?

Practice

Solve each problem. If there is not enough information given, write *too little information*.

3. Mary bought a blouse on sale for $14. The discount was 30%. How much change did she get from $20?

4. Blair wanted to buy jeans at 20% off the original $40 price. How much did the jeans cost on sale?

5. Sue's Sneaker Den has 18 different brands of sneakers in stock. 65% of the sneakers were low-cuts. What percent of the sneakers were high-tops?

6. The Clothes Closet was having a year-end sale. Julie bought 2 pairs of slacks. The regular price was $16.95 for each pair. What was the sale price?

Choose a _____ Strategy

Speedy Discount

7. What is the price of a $150 10-speed bicycle with a 20% discount?

8. If you pay cash, there is a 5% discount off the sale price. What is the price of the bike with a 20% discount followed by a 5% discount for cash?

9. Is a 20% discount followed by a 5% discount the same as a 25% discount?

PROBLEM SOLVING STRATEGIES

Choose an Operation
Write an Equation
Draw a Diagram
Make a Table
Try and Check
Use Logical Reasoning
Find a Pattern
Work Backward
Solve a Simpler Problem
Make a Graph

Skills Review

1. There were 3 apples and 4 oranges in a bowl. Write the ratio of oranges to fruit.

2. Each banner has 3 black dots and 2 white dots. Use the pictures to complete the equal ratios.

black : white   3 : 2   6 : ▒   9 : ▒

3. Complete the equal ratios.

$\frac{3}{5} = \frac{▒}{10} = \frac{9}{▒} = \frac{12}{▒} = \frac{▒}{25}$

Use cross-products to solve.

4. $\frac{3}{4} = \frac{n}{8}$ **5.** $\frac{4}{5} = \frac{20}{n}$ **6.** $\frac{3}{15} = \frac{n}{45}$

Write each ratio as a percent.

7. $\frac{27}{100}$ **8.** $\frac{6}{100}$ **9.** 30 : 100

Write each percent as a fraction in lowest terms.

10. 37%   **11.** 40%   **12.** 5%

13. Write $\frac{8}{50}$ as a percent.

Write each percent as a decimal.

14. 35%   **15.** 2%   **16.** 100%

Write each decimal as a percent.

17. 0.56   **18.** 0.05   **19.** 0.2

Find the percent of each number.

20. 30% of 60   **21.** 5% of 140

Estimate each answer.

22. 48% of 80   **23.** 74% of 200

Problem-Solving Review

Solve each problem.

24. Two pencils cost $0.25. How much do 12 pencils cost?

25. Joe's garden is 30 feet long and 10 feet wide. He wants the rows to be $2\frac{1}{2}$ feet apart. In each row he will leave 2 feet between plants. To plant the most plants, should he plant the rows to run the length or the width of his garden?

26. Juan bought 8 pens for $6. How many pens can he buy for $15?

27. A recipe calls for 3 cups of water for every 2 cups of fruit juice. How many cups of water are needed for 6 cups of juice?

28. The distance from the lodge to the river is $1\frac{1}{2}$ inches on a map. If the map scale is 1 inch equals 6 miles, how far is it from the lodge to the river?

29. A newspaper story reported that 60% of the 40 people surveyed played an instrument. How many of the people surveyed did not play an instrument?

30. **Data File** A survey asked 1,000 consumers what is their favorite color for sneakers. Using the chart on pages 528–529, find how many people would have bought black sneakers.

31. **Make a Data File** Find at least six examples of "2 for" or "3 for" advertisements. For each one, make a table to show the cost of up to 12 items.

Tell what the 2 in each number means.

1. 6,123,750

2. 52,678,590,000

3. 0.526

4. 15.29

5. 5.6812

6. 98.47302

Multiply or divide.

7. 805 × 46

8. 756 × 184

9. 3 × 4.75

10. 5.23 × 72.164

11. 6)1,543

12. 78)6,798

13. 12.36 ÷ 3

14. 0.945 ÷ 9

Find the volume of each figure.

15.

16.

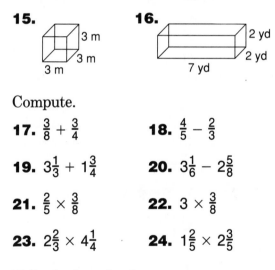

Compute.

17. $\frac{3}{8} + \frac{3}{4}$

18. $\frac{4}{5} - \frac{2}{3}$

19. $3\frac{1}{3} + 1\frac{3}{4}$

20. $3\frac{1}{6} - 2\frac{5}{8}$

21. $\frac{2}{5} \times \frac{3}{8}$

22. $3 \times \frac{3}{8}$

23. $2\frac{2}{3} \times 4\frac{1}{4}$

24. $1\frac{2}{5} \times 2\frac{3}{5}$

Tell whether the figures are *congruent* or *similar*.

25.

26.

The graph below shows Anne's walking record. Use the graph for Items 27–29.

27. How many miles does Anne walk in 3 days?

28. How many days does it take for Anne to walk 10 miles?

29. What ordered pair shows how far Anne walks in 2 days?

The numbers 1–6 are on the faces of a cube. Find the probability getting each result on one roll.

30. 4

31. An odd number

Name each figure.

32.

33.

34.

35.

36. Use a protractor to draw an angle of 120°.

37. Is the angle you drew in Item 36 right, acute, or obtuse?

Use cross-products to solve.

38. $\frac{8}{12} = \frac{n}{3}$

39. $\frac{3}{8} = \frac{n}{24}$

Write each percent as a decimal.

40. 75%

41. 6%

42. 50%

Write each decimal as a percent.

43. 0.78

44. 0.03

45. 0.8

Reteaching
Set A pages 496–497

The U.S. flag has 7 red stripes and 6 white stripes. You can write four ratios to compare the stripes.
Red stripes to white stripes   7 : 6
White stripes to red stripes   6 : 7
Red stripes to total stripes   7 : 13
White stripes to total stripes   6 : 13

Remember that the order in which you compare two quantities is important. The pet shop has 4 canaries and 6 parakeets. Write the following ratios.

1. Canaries to parakeets

2. Parakeets to canaries

3. Canaries to the total number of birds

Set B pages 498–499

At Ace Sports, there are 3 tennis balls in a can. No matter how many cans you buy, the ratio of cans to tennis balls stays the same.

Number of cans to number of balls

Number of cans $\overset{\nearrow 1 : 3 \nwarrow}{\searrow 2 : 6 \swarrow}$ Number of balls

The ratio 1 : 3 equals the ratio 2 : 6.

Remember that there is no end to the number of ratios that you can find that equal a given ratio.

Use the picture to write a list of equal ratios.

The car goes 20 miles on 1 gallon of gas.

1 Gal	1 Gal	1 Gal	1 Gal
20	40	60	80

Miles : gallons 20:1   40:▒   ▒:3   ▒:▒

Set C pages 500–501

Find n in $\frac{7}{3} = \frac{28}{n}$.

Since $7 \times 4 = 28$, multiply 3 by 4 to find n.

$$n = 12$$

Remember that both multiplication and division can be used to find equal ratios.

Find each equal ratio.

1. $\frac{5}{2} = \frac{15}{c}$ **2.** $\frac{12}{20} = \frac{t}{5}$

3. $\frac{5}{6} = \frac{w}{30}$ **4.** $\frac{3}{8} = \frac{18}{g}$

Set D pages 502–503

Solve this proportion.

$\frac{6}{14} = \frac{9}{z}$

Use cross-products.

$6 \times z = 14 \times 9$
$6 \times z = 126$
$z = 126 \div 6$
$z = 21$

Remember to check the answer by replacing the variable in the proportion. Then see if the cross-products are equal.

Solve each proportion using cross-products.

1. $\frac{n}{6} = \frac{6}{9}$ **2.** $\frac{8}{10} = \frac{12}{p}$

3. $\frac{6}{b} = \frac{9}{12}$ **4.** $\frac{12}{9} = \frac{s}{12}$

Set E   pages 508–509

In a poll of 100 people, 55 chose red as their favorite color. What percent of these people liked red the best?

When a number is compared to 100, the comparison can be written as a ratio or as a percent.

$$\dfrac{\text{Number who chose red} \rightarrow 55}{\text{Number polled} \rightarrow 100}, \text{ or } 55\%$$

Remember that percent means per hundred.

Write each ratio as a percent.

1. $\frac{20}{100}$ 2. $\frac{37}{100}$

3. $\frac{4}{100}$ 4. $\frac{10}{100}$

5. 3 to 100   6. 49 : 100

Set F   pages 510–511

Write 38% as a fraction in lowest terms. Write the percent as a fraction with a denominator of 100. Then reduce the fraction to lowest terms.

$$38\% = \dfrac{38}{100} \overset{\div 2}{\underset{\div 2}{\longrightarrow}} \dfrac{19}{50}$$

Remember that you reduce a fraction to lowest terms by dividing the numerator and denominator by common factors.

Write each percent as a fraction in lowest terms.

1. 22%   2. 60%   3. 47%   4. 75%

Set G   pages 512–513

Write 56% as a decimal.

56% means 56 per hundred or 56 hundredths. So

$$56\% = 0.56$$

Remember that per hundred means hundredths.

Write each percent as a decimal.

1. 32%   2. 68%   3. 4%

Set H   pages 514–515

Find 6% of 80.
Write 6% as a decimal. $6\% = 0.06$
Then multiply:

$$\begin{array}{r} 80 \\ \times\, 0.06 \\ \hline 4.80 \end{array}$$

Remember to place the decimal point in the product.

Find the percent of each number.

1. 20% of 60   2. 8% of 40

Set I   pages 516–517

Estimate 73% of 310.
Use compatible numbers.
73% is about 75%.   310 is about 300.

Find 75% of 300.
Using decimals: $300 \times 0.75 = 225$
Using fractions: $300 \times \frac{3}{4} = 225$

Remember that the actual answer will be greater than the estimate if both compatible numbers are smaller than the given numbers.

Estimate each answer.

1. 12% of 47   2. 23% of 95

3. 48% of 63   4. 98% of 77

More Practice

Set A   pages 496–497

Write each ratio.

1. Circles to triangles

2. Triangles to circles

3. Circles to all the figures

4. Triangles to all the figures

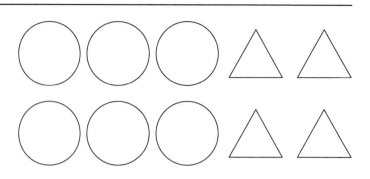

Set B   pages 498–499

Use the pictures to write a list of equal ratios.

1. You can rent 3 movie videos for $5.

   Dollars : videos

$5	$5	$5	$5	$5
3	6	9	12	15
5:3	▦:6	15:▦	▦:12	▦:▦

2. A pump pumps 4 gallons every 10 minutes.

   Gallons : minutes

4	8	12	16	20
4:10	▦:20	12:▦	▦:40	▦:▦

Set C   pages 500–501

Complete each list of equal ratios.

1. $\frac{3}{8} = \frac{▦}{16} = \frac{9}{▦} = \frac{▦}{32} = \frac{▦}{40}$

2. $\frac{5}{6} = \frac{10}{▦} = \frac{▦}{18} = \frac{▦}{24} = \frac{25}{▦}$

Find each equal ratio.

3. $\frac{3}{2} = \frac{18}{a}$

4. $\frac{5}{8} = \frac{n}{48}$

5. $\frac{3}{7} = \frac{27}{v}$

6. $\frac{2}{3} = \frac{m}{39}$

7. $\frac{5}{4} \times \frac{45}{q}$

Multiply or divide to find the equal ratio.

8. Use 2 cups of flour to make 16 muffins $\frac{2}{16} = \frac{▦}{48}$

9. Spend 96 minutes to balance 16 tires $\frac{96}{16} = \frac{▦}{1}$

Set D   pages 502–503

Solve each proportion using cross-products.

1. $\frac{4}{d} = \frac{18}{27}$

2. $\frac{6}{8} = \frac{9}{y}$

3. $\frac{n}{12} = \frac{10}{5}$

4. $\frac{k}{12} = \frac{15}{20}$

5. $\frac{f}{30} = \frac{16}{20}$

6. $\frac{14}{24} = \frac{21}{f}$

7. $\frac{5}{4} = \frac{x}{20}$

8. $\frac{16}{6} = \frac{c}{9}$

9. $\frac{10}{3} = \frac{o}{12}$

10. $\frac{16}{s} = \frac{40}{35}$

Set E   pages 508–509

Write each ratio as a percent.

1. $\frac{22}{100}$ **2.** $\frac{60}{100}$ **3.** $\frac{3}{100}$ **4.** $\frac{39}{100}$ **5.** $\frac{9}{100}$ **6.** $\frac{99}{100}$

7. 4 to 100   **8.** 35 to 100   **9.** 66 : 100   **10.** 82 : 100

Write a ratio for each percent.

11. 29%   **12.** 6%   **13.** 51%   **14.** 80%   **15.** 2%   **16.** 18%

Set F   pages 510–511

Write each percent as a fraction in lowest terms.

1. 25%   **2.** 27%   **3.** 3%   **4.** 40%   **5.** 90%   **6.** 64%

Write each fraction as a percent.

7. $\frac{8}{100}$ **8.** $\frac{32}{100}$ **9.** $\frac{72}{100}$ **10.** $\frac{4}{10}$ **11.** $\frac{3}{20}$ **12.** $\frac{3}{5}$

Set G   pages 512–513

Write each percent as a decimal.

1. 28%   **2.** 39%   **3.** 53%   **4.** 2%   **5.** 50%   **6.** 7%

Write each decimal as a percent.

7. 0.38   **8.** 0.84   **9.** 0.52   **10.** 0.05   **11.** 0.2   **12.** 0.20

Set H   pages 514–515

Find the percent of each number.

1. 90% of 60   **2.** 10% of 80   **3.** 50% of 120   **4.** 4% of 400

5. 30% of 200   **6.** 8% of 110   **7.** 6% of 200   **8.** 45% of 90

9. 75% of 40   **10.** 1% of 26   **11.** 80% of 160   **12.** 2% of 52

Number Sense   Write >, <, or =.

13. 25% of 8 ⬚ 25   **14.** 90% of 82 ⬚ 82   **15.** 10% of 40 ⬚ 3

Set I   pages 516–517

Estimate each answer.

1. 19% of 43   **2.** 8% of 54   **3.** 23% of 82   **4.** 97% of 340

5. 54% of 92   **6.** 11% of 78   **7.** 78% of 202   **8.** 27% of 155

Enrichment

Making a Circle Graph

A *circle graph* shows how parts make up a whole or 100%. The sections of the circle are parts representing percents.

The graph at the right shows the percent of pages in a home catalog that advertises different kinds of products.

Advertising Pages

1. The most pages of advertising were for women's fashions. What percent of the pages advertised women's fashions?

2. Which products had the fewest pages of advertising? What percent of the total pages was it?

3. Which two kinds of products have the same number of pages of advertising? What is the percent of these two together?

4. What percent of the catalog was used to advertise children's clothing?

You can make a circle graph. Each mark on the circle below shows one tenth or 10% of the circle. To draw the circle graph that shows the percent of Help Wanted ads in the daily newspaper for different types of jobs, do this:

5. Trace the circle.

6. Using the marks as your guide, draw lines from the center of the circle to the outside to show the following percents. Label each section. The first one is done for you.

    a. 25% Office Help

    b. 20% Food Services

    c. 30% Health Services

    d. 10% Maintenance

    e. 10% Construction

    f. 5% Other

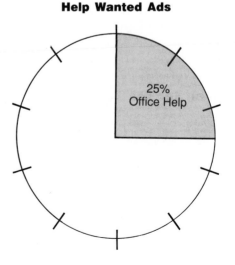

Help Wanted Ads

25%
Office Help

Chapter 15 Review/Test

1. The price of paper towels is $2 for 3 rolls. Write the ratio of rolls to dollars.

2. Each basket holds 4 pears. Use the pictures to write two more equal ratios.

   1:4   ▦:8   ▦:12

3. Complete the list of equal ratios.
$$\frac{3}{8} = \frac{6}{▦} = \frac{▦}{24} = \frac{▦}{32}$$

Solve each proportion using cross-products.

4. $\frac{9}{10} = \frac{n}{20}$ 5. $\frac{12}{16} = \frac{9}{n}$

Write each ratio as a percent.

6. $\frac{87}{100}$ 7. 98:100

Write each percent as a fraction in lowest terms.

8. 31%   9. 60%

Write each fraction as a percent.

10. $\frac{3}{10}$ 11. $\frac{3}{4}$

Write each percent as a decimal.

12. 79%   13. 46%

Write each decimal as a percent.

14. 0.33   15. 0.07

Find the percent of each number.

16. 10% of 60   17. 5% of 16

Estimate each percent.

18. 21% of 41   19. 49% of 98

20. A survey showed that 58 people out of 100 watch a certain television program. What percent is this?

Read the problem below. Choose the equation you can use to solve the problem. Then solve the problem.

21. A book showed a scale drawing of a room in which 2 inches represented 15 feet. In the drawing the room was 3 inches long. What was the actual length of the room?

   a. $\frac{2}{15} = \frac{3}{n}$ b. $\frac{2}{15} = \frac{n}{3}$

Read the problem below. Then answer the question.

Jason bought 3 cassettes that were on sale. The original price for each cassette was $9.98. How much did he pay?

22. Is there *too much* or *too little* information given to solve the problem?

23. **Write About Math** If the cross-products of two ratios are equal, what do you know about the ratios?

DATA FILE

1. **Favorite Sneaker Color**

Red 2%

Blue 5%

Gray 5%

Black 9%

Other 10%

White 69%

1. Chart
The chart shows the results of a survey of 1,000 consumers.

2. Graph
The dotted parts show the projected growth in population.

3. List
The pattern lists the amount of fabric, braid, and elastic needed for different sizes.

4. Diagram
The kite is made with 3 circles of bamboo supported by strips crossing in the center.

5. Drawing
This is the floor plan of a split-level house. The measurement 10' 4" means 10 feet 4 inches.

2. **Population Growth**

POPULATION GROWTH

— United States
— Canada

Millions of people

Years

3. Sewing Pattern

Shorts are encased in fold over braid and have elastic waistline casing.

Top has neck and armholes encased in fold over braid.

BODY MEASUREMENTS

Chest		22	23	24	25	Inches
Waist		$20\frac{1}{2}$	21	$21\frac{1}{2}$	22	Inches
Hip		—	24	25	26	Inches
Back-neck to waist		9	$9\frac{1}{2}$	10	$10\frac{1}{2}$	Inches
Sizes		3	4	5	6	
Shorts	60 in. wide	$\frac{3}{8}$	$\frac{3}{8}$	$\frac{3}{8}$	$\frac{3}{8}$	Yards
Knitted fold over braid $\frac{3}{8}$ in. wide		$1\frac{3}{8}$	$1\frac{3}{8}$	$1\frac{3}{8}$	$1\frac{3}{8}$	Yards
Pajama Elastic-$\frac{5}{8}$ yd of $\frac{3}{4}$in. wide						
Top	60 in. wide	$\frac{1}{2}$	$\frac{1}{2}$	$\frac{1}{2}$	$\frac{1}{2}$	Yard
Knitted fold over braid $\frac{5}{8}$ in. wide		$1\frac{5}{8}$	$1\frac{5}{8}$	$1\frac{5}{8}$	$1\frac{5}{8}$	Yards

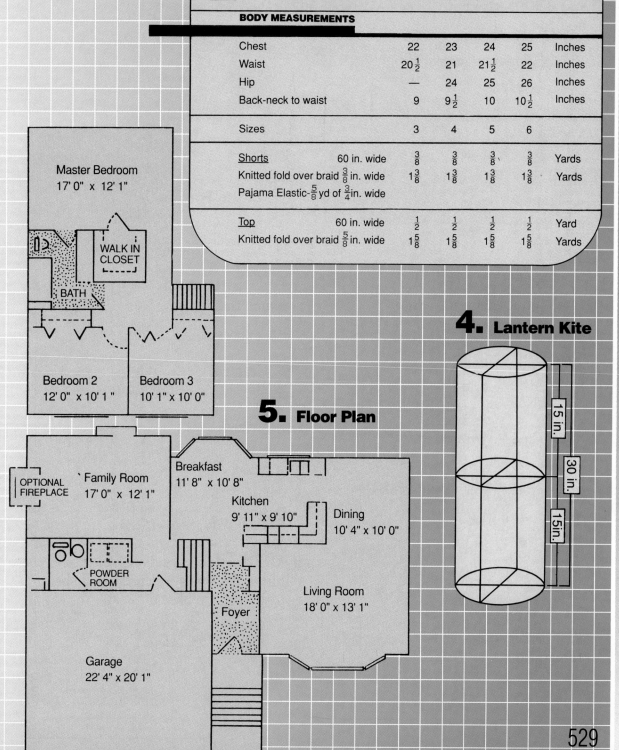

Master Bedroom
17' 0" x 12' 1"

WALK IN CLOSET

BATH

Bedroom 2
12' 0" x 10' 1"

Bedroom 3
10' 1" x 10' 0"

5. Floor Plan

OPTIONAL FIREPLACE

Family Room
17' 0" x 12' 1"

Breakfast
11' 8" x 10' 8"

Kitchen
9' 11" x 9' 10"

Dining
10' 4" x 10' 0"

POWDER ROOM

Foyer

Living Room
18' 0" x 13' 1"

Garage
22' 4" x 20' 1"

4. Lantern Kite

15 in.

30 in.

15 in.

Cumulative Review/Test Chapters 1–15

1. Multiply.

$$\begin{array}{r} 32 \\ \times\, 58 \\ \hline \end{array}$$

  a. 1,336   **c.** 1,856
  b. 1,646   **d.** 1,214

2. Find the missing addend.

$518 + n = 736$

  a. 118   **c.** 1,254
  b. 218   **d.** 1,244

3. What does the 4 in 1.347 mean?

  a. 4 tenths   **c.** 4 thousandths
  b. 4 hundredths   **d.** 4 hundreds

4. What is the least common denominator for $\frac{2}{3}$ and $\frac{2}{5}$?

  a. 15   **c.** 30
  b. 8   **d.** 5

5. Add.

$\frac{5}{6} + \frac{7}{9}$

  a. $\frac{1}{18}$
  b. $1\frac{11}{18}$
  c. $\frac{14}{15}$
  d. $1\frac{1}{2}$

6. What is $\frac{12}{18}$ written in lowest terms?

  a. $\frac{2}{3}$ **c.** $\frac{6}{9}$
  b. $\frac{1}{3}$ **d.** $\frac{1}{12}$

7. Divide.

$3,661 \div 9$

  a. 46 R7   **c.** 406 R7
  b. 406 R3   **d.** 47 R7

8. Multiply.

$\frac{1}{3} \times \frac{2}{5}$

  a. $\frac{2}{8}$
  b. $\frac{3}{8}$
  c. $\frac{2}{15}$
  d. $\frac{5}{6}$

9. Subtract.

$$\begin{array}{r} \$87.46 \\ -\ 85.57 \\ \hline \end{array}$$

  a. \$1.89   **c.** \$2.99
  b. \$0.89   **d.** \$2.89

10. Multiply.

$1\frac{2}{3} \times \frac{3}{5}$

  a. $\frac{8}{15}$
  b. $1\frac{6}{15}$
  c. $2\frac{7}{9}$
  d. 1

11. Name the figure.

  a. Segment   **c.** Line
  b. Ray   **d.** Vertex

12. Multiply.

$$\begin{array}{r} 0.046 \\ \times\, 0.004 \\ \hline \end{array}$$

  a. 0.0184   **c.** 0.00184
  b. 0.000184   **d.** 0.184

13. Ms. Martino's state charges a sales tax of 8%. How much tax will she pay on a purchase of \$100?

  a. \$8.00   **c.** \$0.80
  b. \$80   **d.** \$0.08

14. Which triangle is equilateral?

a. 8 ft 8 ft 10 ft
c. 2 in. 4 in. 3 in.
b. 7 m 7 m 7 m
d. 3 cm 5 cm 4 cm

15. Mark, Juan, Nora, and Miko helped collect money to sponsor a school fair. Mark raised $\frac{1}{2}$ as much as Juan. Nora raised $\frac{1}{3}$ as much as Juan but $4 more than Miko. Miko raised $12. How much did Mark collect?

a. $16   **c.** $24
b. $48   **d.** $40

16. Solve the proportion.

$$\frac{8}{10} = \frac{4}{n}$$

a. 10   **c.** 3.2
b. 8   **d.** 5

17. Which division sentence is shown by the picture?

a. $3 \div \frac{1}{4} = 12$ **c.** $12 \div \frac{1}{2} = 6$
b. $\frac{1}{4} \div 3 = 12$ **d.** $3 \div 12 = 4$

18. What is 62% written as a fraction in lowest terms?

a. $\frac{62}{100}$ **c.** $\frac{31}{50}$
b. $\frac{31}{100}$ **d.** $\frac{62}{25}$

19. Sheila bought a dress for $\frac{1}{3}$ off the original price. The original price was $39. How much change did she receive from $50?

a. $13   **c.** $26
b. $24   **d.** $37

20. The graph shows the number of miles traveled by a car in 5 hours.

Distance traveled

How far did the car go in 4 hours?

a. 50 miles   **c.** 150 miles
b. 100 miles   **d.** 200 miles

Read the problem below. Then answer the question.

The All-City Swatters play 74 baseball games each year. They won 47 games in 1987, 68 games in 1988, 54 games in 1989, and 67 games in 1990. What was the mean number of games won by the Swatters for these 4 years?

21. What is the correct answer?

a. 59 teams   **c.** 59 losses
b. 59 games   **d.** 59 players

22. Suppose you place the five cards shown below face down and pick one without looking. What is the probability of picking a 2?

a. 2   **b.** $\frac{2}{5}$ **c.** $\frac{2}{4}$ **d.** $\frac{1}{4}$

Whole Numbers Through Hundred-Thousands

Review

The standard form of the number three hundred twenty-four thousand, seven hundred sixteen is 324,716. The comma separates the number into the thousands period and the ones period.

thousands period			ones period		
hundred-thousands	ten-thousands	thousands	hundreds	tens	ones
3	2	4	7	1	6

Practice

Tell which digits are in the thousands period in each number.

1. 403,248   **2.** 36,975   **3.** 916,720   **4.** 3,062

Tell what the 6 in each number means.

5. 276,503   **6.** 567,224   **7.** 42,765   **8.** 602,431

Write each number in words.

9. 226,700   **10.** 79,462   **11.** 913,810   **12.** 4,136

13. 168,204   **14.** 380,566   **15.** 48,013   **16.** 506,742

What number is 10,000 more? 1,000 less?

17. 3,002   **18.** 79,401   **19.** 123,421   **20.** 90,742

21. 68,450   **22.** 495,700   **23.** 428,000   **24.** 300,050

Write each number in standard form.

25. Fifty thousand, fifty

26. Forty-five thousand, one

27. Four hundred fifty-three thousand, two hundred ninety-eight

28. Three hundred thirty-seven thousand, twenty-seven

Comparing and Ordering Numbers

Review

A. Compare 2,301 and 2,320. Use > or <.

2,301 ⣿ 2,320
    The thousands digits are the same.
    The hundreds digits are the same.
    Compare the tens.
    0 tens is less than 2 tens.

2,301 < 2,320   2,301 is less than 2,320.

B. List the numbers 6,587, 5,742, and 5,683 in order from least to greatest.

5,683 < 5,742   Compare the numbers
5,742 < 6,587   two at a time.

5,683 5,742 6,587

Practice

Compare these numbers. Use >, <.

1. 641 ⣿ 582

2. 198 ⣿ 219

3. 753 ⣿ 735

4. 345 ⣿ 362

5. 823 ⣿ 328

6. 472 ⣿ 412

7. 749 ⣿ 794

8. 2,753 ⣿ 2,548

9. 7,346 ⣿ 7,463

10. 5,483 ⣿ 5,427

11. 3,862 ⣿ 3,892

12. 4,375 ⣿ 4,372

13. 5,831 ⣿ 6,854

14. 3,148 ⣿ 3,143

15. 8,344 ⣿ 8,234

List the numbers in order from least to greatest.

16. 73 85 67

17. 43 34 39

18. 857 875 837

19. 685 653 638

20. 721 689 719

21. 206 260 200

22. 1,764 3,851 2,735

23. 2,753 3,465 2,956

24. 8,357 8,372 7,328

25. 3,042 3,205 4,320

26. 4,981 4,672 4,913

27. 5,701 5,077 5,071

28. 356 653 365 366 553 563

29. 1,674 768 678 756 1,763

Addition and Subtraction Basic Facts

Review

John has 3 apples and 7 oranges.

A. How many pieces of fruit does he have?

Find 3 + 7.

$$\begin{array}{r} 3 \\ +7 \\ \hline 10 \end{array}$$ Addend Addend Sum

$$\begin{array}{r} 7 \\ +3 \\ \hline 10 \end{array}$$

He has 10 pieces of fruit.

B. How many more oranges does he have than apples?

Find 7 − 3.

$$\begin{array}{r} 7 \\ -3 \\ \hline 4 \end{array}$$ Minuend Subtrahend Difference

He has 4 more oranges than apples.

Practice

Find each sum or difference.

1. $\begin{array}{r} 4 \\ +5 \end{array}$ 2. $\begin{array}{r} 9 \\ +8 \end{array}$ 3. $\begin{array}{r} 6 \\ +2 \end{array}$ 4. $\begin{array}{r} 9 \\ -3 \end{array}$ 5. $\begin{array}{r} 8 \\ -0 \end{array}$ 6. $\begin{array}{r} 11 \\ -6 \end{array}$

7. $\begin{array}{r} 12 \\ -9 \end{array}$ 8. $\begin{array}{r} 1 \\ +2 \end{array}$ 9. $\begin{array}{r} 8 \\ +5 \end{array}$ 10. $\begin{array}{r} 5 \\ -4 \end{array}$ 11. $\begin{array}{r} 17 \\ -8 \end{array}$ 12. $\begin{array}{r} 6 \\ +9 \end{array}$

13. 0 + 3   14. 4 + 6   15. 6 + 7   16. 9 + 2   17. 7 + 8   18. 3 + 4

19. 7 − 1   20. 16 − 7   21. 10 − 5   22. 12 − 8   23. 13 − 7   24. 16 − 9

25. 4 − 0   26. 14 − 9   27. 4 + 8   28. 7 + 3   29. 13 − 5   30. 7 − 2

31. 4 + 4   32. 9 + 5   33. 16 − 8   34. 15 − 8   35. 3 + 8   36. 2 + 3

37. 6 + 0   38. 4 + 2   39. 14 − 7   40. 18 − 9   41. 6 + 5   42. 7 + 2

43. 8 + 9   44. 9 + 1   45. 11 − 3   46. 8 + 2   47. 10 − 3   48. 11 − 7

49. 5 − 5   50. 9 − 5   51. 8 − 6   52. 6 + 7   53. 8 + 4   54. 9 + 9

Adding and Subtracting Money

Review

Add or subtract money the same way you add or
subtract whole numbers.

A. Find $13.55 + $1.25.

B. Find $23.50 − $12.98.

$$\begin{array}{r} \$13.55 \\ +1.25 \\ \hline \$14.80 \end{array}$$

Use the decimal point
to line up dollars and cents.
Write the decimal point and
dollar sign in the answer.

$$\begin{array}{r} \$23.50 \\ -12.98 \\ \hline \$10.52 \end{array}$$

Practice

Find each sum or difference.

1. $$\begin{array}{r} \$13.34 \\ +1.87 \\ \hline \end{array}$$
2. $$\begin{array}{r} \$27.45 \\ +6.98 \\ \hline \end{array}$$
3. $$\begin{array}{r} \$3.52 \\ +9.64 \\ \hline \end{array}$$
4. $$\begin{array}{r} \$34.86 \\ +19.92 \\ \hline \end{array}$$
5. $$\begin{array}{r} \$46.95 \\ +81.63 \\ \hline \end{array}$$

6. $$\begin{array}{r} \$10.00 \\ -7.63 \\ \hline \end{array}$$
7. $$\begin{array}{r} \$14.61 \\ -1.87 \\ \hline \end{array}$$
8. $$\begin{array}{r} \$32.65 \\ -17.98 \\ \hline \end{array}$$
9. $$\begin{array}{r} \$22.50 \\ -11.16 \\ \hline \end{array}$$
10. $$\begin{array}{r} \$57.75 \\ -32.07 \\ \hline \end{array}$$

11. $$\begin{array}{r} \$26.89 \\ +30.68 \\ \hline \end{array}$$
12. $$\begin{array}{r} \$68.97 \\ +7.23 \\ \hline \end{array}$$
13. $$\begin{array}{r} \$89.53 \\ -34.62 \\ \hline \end{array}$$
14. $$\begin{array}{r} \$20.02 \\ -12.47 \\ \hline \end{array}$$
15. $$\begin{array}{r} \$50.75 \\ -21.75 \\ \hline \end{array}$$

16. $$\begin{array}{r} \$0.97 \\ 11.54 \\ +23.02 \\ \hline \end{array}$$
17. $$\begin{array}{r} \$63.62 \\ 7.47 \\ +3.89 \\ \hline \end{array}$$
18. $$\begin{array}{r} \$6.99 \\ 0.27 \\ +13.15 \\ \hline \end{array}$$
19. $$\begin{array}{r} \$79.18 \\ 32.82 \\ +8.47 \\ \hline \end{array}$$
20. $$\begin{array}{r} \$14.19 \\ 23.20 \\ +10.98 \\ \hline \end{array}$$

21. $0.37 + $7.73

22. $23.99 − $4.99

23. $34.86 − $19.92

24. $50.75 − $1.99

25. $12.71 + $6.92

26. $33.50 − $18.98

27. $16.15 + $40.21

28. $3.99 + $45.90

29. $55.32 − $14.90

30. $32.09 + $41.32

31. $56.66 − $42.19

32. $0.98 + $90.56

33. $4.82 + $12.65 + $8.99 + $72.36

34. $4.50 + $2.75 + $8.25 + $10.50

35. $10.19 + $0.97 + $1.25 + $4.55

36. $3.12 + $14.15 + $5.67 + $2.39

Addition and Subtraction Families of Facts

Review

Number sentences that are related make up a family of facts.

A. Write a family of facts using 6, 8, and 14.

$6 + 8 = 14$ $14 - 8 = 6$
$8 + 6 = 14$ $14 - 6 = 8$

B. Find the missing number.

$6 + \boxed{} = 14$

$\boxed{} + 6 = 14$, $14 - 6 = \boxed{}$, and $14 - \boxed{} = 6$
are from the same fact family as $6 + \boxed{} = 14$.
Since $14 - 6 = 8$, the missing addend is 8.

Practice

Write a family of facts using the given numbers.

1. 3, 5, 8 **2.** 4, 7, 11 **3.** 6, 6, 12 **4.** 7, 0, 7 **5.** 9, 1, 10

6. 8, 1, 9 **7.** 2, 8, 10 **8.** 3, 3, 6 **9.** 9, 4, 13 **10.** 0, 9, 9

11. 7, 5, 12 **12.** 6, 9, 15 **13.** 7, 7, 14 **14.** 1, 3, 4 **15.** 9, 9, 18

16. 4, 5, 9 **17.** 3, 7, 10 **18.** 6, 7, 13 **19.** 3, 8, 11 **20.** 9, 7, 16

Use a family of facts to help you find the missing number.

21. $\boxed{} + 3 = 7$ **22.** $4 + \boxed{} = 10$ **23.** $\boxed{} - 5 = 5$ **24.** $16 - \boxed{} = 9$

25. $\boxed{} + 8 = 11$ **26.** $16 - \boxed{} = 8$ **27.** $\boxed{} - 9 = 5$ **28.** $4 + \boxed{} = 8$

29. $13 - \boxed{} = 8$ **30.** $\boxed{} + 8 = 12$ **31.** $\boxed{} + 2 = 11$ **32.** $\boxed{} - 4 = 1$

33. $\boxed{} + 2 = 8$ **34.** $\boxed{} - 0 = 8$ **35.** $11 - \boxed{} = 5$ **36.** $\boxed{} + 8 = 17$

37. $12 - \boxed{} = 5$ **38.** $3 + \boxed{} = 10$ **39.** $\boxed{} + 9 = 18$ **40.** $\boxed{} - 3 = 6$

41. $\boxed{} + 4 = 9$ **42.** $7 - \boxed{} = 4$ **43.** $9 + \boxed{} = 12$ **44.** $7 + \boxed{} = 13$

Multiplication Basic Facts

Review

How many balloons are in the picture?
There are 4 groups with 5 balloons in each group.

$4 \times 5 = 20$
     └─ Product
There are 20 balloons.

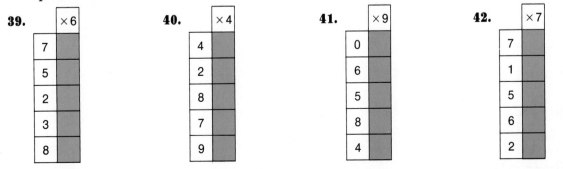

Practice

Find each product.

1. $\begin{array}{r} 7 \\ \times 1 \\ \hline \end{array}$	**2.** $\begin{array}{r} 7 \\ \times 6 \\ \hline \end{array}$	**3.** $\begin{array}{r} 4 \\ \times 0 \\ \hline \end{array}$	**4.** $\begin{array}{r} 6 \\ \times 2 \\ \hline \end{array}$	**5.** $\begin{array}{r} 8 \\ \times 7 \\ \hline \end{array}$	**6.** $\begin{array}{r} 1 \\ \times 3 \\ \hline \end{array}$
7. $\begin{array}{r} 8 \\ \times 5 \\ \hline \end{array}$	**8.** $\begin{array}{r} 5 \\ \times 9 \\ \hline \end{array}$	**9.** $\begin{array}{r} 9 \\ \times 6 \\ \hline \end{array}$	**10.** $\begin{array}{r} 8 \\ \times 3 \\ \hline \end{array}$	**11.** $\begin{array}{r} 9 \\ \times 3 \\ \hline \end{array}$	**12.** $\begin{array}{r} 5 \\ \times 7 \\ \hline \end{array}$
13. $\begin{array}{r} 7 \\ \times 8 \\ \hline \end{array}$	**14.** $\begin{array}{r} 9 \\ \times 9 \\ \hline \end{array}$	**15.** $\begin{array}{r} 6 \\ \times 6 \\ \hline \end{array}$	**16.** $\begin{array}{r} 4 \\ \times 7 \\ \hline \end{array}$	**17.** $\begin{array}{r} 8 \\ \times 2 \\ \hline \end{array}$	**18.** $\begin{array}{r} 7 \\ \times 9 \\ \hline \end{array}$

19. 8×5 **20.** 2×8 **21.** 9×5 **22.** 4×8 **23.** 6×5

24. 9×8 **25.** 4×3 **26.** 2×9 **27.** 3×7 **28.** 4×6

29. 3×8 **30.** 9×7 **31.** 6×5 **32.** 4×5 **33.** 6×4

34. 6×8 **35.** 8×8 **36.** 7×7 **37.** 3×9 **38.** 5×5

Complete each table.

39.

	$\times 6$
7	
5	
2	
3	
8	

40.

	$\times 4$
4	
2	
8	
7	
9	

41.

	$\times 9$
0	
6	
5	
8	
4	

42.

	$\times 7$
7	
1	
5	
6	
2	

Measuring in Inches

Review

Measured to the nearest inch, this key is about 2 inches long.

Most rulers do not show fraction names. But you need to know the fractions on a ruler when reading measurements to the nearest half inch and quarter inch. Remember that $\frac{1}{2}$ inch is the same as $\frac{2}{4}$ inch.

To the nearest half inch, the key is about $1\frac{1}{2}$ inches long.

To the nearest quarter inch, the key is about $1\frac{3}{4}$ inches long.

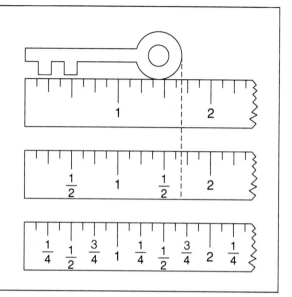

Practice

Measure each line segment below to the nearest

1. inch. **2.** half inch. **3.** quarter inch.

a. ———————

b. ———————

c. ———————

d. ———

e. ——

f. ———

g. ———————

h. ———————

Use a ruler to draw a segment

4. 4 inches long. **5.** $5\frac{3}{4}$ inches long. **6.** $3\frac{1}{2}$ inches long.

7. $1\frac{1}{4}$ inches long. **8.** $\frac{3}{4}$ inch long. **9.** $2\frac{1}{4}$ inches long.

Measuring in Centimeters

Review

Measure the length of the lace to the nearest centimeter.

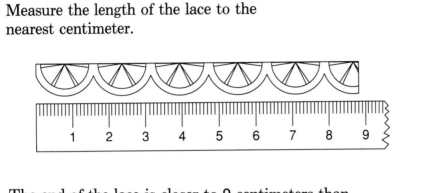

The end of the lace is closer to **9** centimeters than 8 centimeters. To the nearest centimeter, the lace is about **9** centimeters long.

Practice

Measure each line segment to the nearest centimeter.

Use a metric ruler to draw line segments of the following lengths.

10. 6 centimeters   **11.** 5 centimeters   **12.** 8 centimeters

13. 10 centimeters   **14.** 2 centimeters   **15.** 4 centimeters

16. 1 centimeter   **17.** 9 centimeters   **18.** 15 centimeters

Division Basic Facts

Review

Jane needs 15 buttons. The buttons are packaged in groups of 3. How many packages does she need?

Use division to find how many groups of 3.

$15 \div 3 = 5 \leftarrow$ Quotient

She needs to buy 5 packages of buttons.

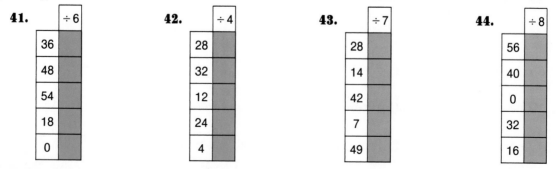

Practice

Find each quotient.

1. $2\overline{)4}$ **2.** $6\overline{)12}$ **3.** $4\overline{)16}$ **4.** $3\overline{)18}$ **5.** $6\overline{)24}$

6. $4\overline{)8}$ **7.** $3\overline{)27}$ **8.** $2\overline{)14}$ **9.** $5\overline{)15}$ **10.** $6\overline{)6}$

11. $12 \div 3$ **12.** $9 \div 3$ **13.** $6 \div 2$ **14.** $18 \div 9$ **15.** $0 \div 7$

16. $56 \div 7$ **17.** $30 \div 6$ **18.** $7 \div 1$ **19.** $24 \div 8$ **20.** $72 \div 9$

21. $72 \div 8$ **22.** $48 \div 8$ **23.** $64 \div 8$ **24.** $40 \div 5$ **25.** $36 \div 9$

26. $63 \div 9$ **27.** $35 \div 5$ **28.** $5 \div 1$ **29.** $45 \div 5$ **30.** $21 \div 7$

31. $42 \div 6$ **32.** $20 \div 4$ **33.** $36 \div 4$ **34.** $27 \div 9$ **35.** $81 \div 9$

36. $8 \div 8$ **37.** $30 \div 5$ **38.** $45 \div 9$ **39.** $63 \div 7$ **40.** $54 \div 9$

Complete each table.

41.

	÷ 6
36	
48	
54	
18	
0	

42.

	÷ 4
28	
32	
12	
24	
4	

43.

	÷ 7
28	
14	
42	
7	
49	

44.

	÷ 8
56	
40	
0	
32	
16	

Multiplication and Division Families of Facts

Review

Four number sentences can be written for this array.

$6 \times 4 = 24$ 6 rows of 4 is 24.

$4 \times 6 = 24$ 4 columns of 6 is 24.

$24 \div 4 = 6$ 24 divided into rows of 4 is 6 rows.

$24 \div 6 = 4$ 24 divided into columns of 6 is 4 columns.

These four number sentences form a family of facts.

Practice

Write the family of facts for each picture.

1.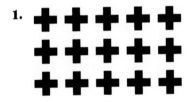

2.

Write the other facts from each family.

3. $4 \times 5 = 20$ **4.** $8 \times 3 = 24$ **5.** $18 \div 3 = 6$ **6.** $12 \div 4 = 3$

7. $28 \div 4 = 7$ **8.** $5 \times 6 = 30$ **9.** $16 \div 4 = 4$ **10.** $9 \times 5 = 45$

Write the multiplication and division family of facts
for each set of numbers.

11. 4, 36, 9   **12.** 56, 8, 7   **13.** 5, 8, 40   **14.** 12, 6, 2

15. 7, 49, 7   **16.** 48, 6, 8   **17.** 1, 8, 8   **18.** 3, 7, 21

19. 72, 8, 9   **20.** 9, 54, 6   **21.** 4, 8, 32   **22.** 63, 7, 9

23. 27, 3, 9   **24.** 9, 81, 9   **25.** 7, 5, 35   **26.** 7, 42, 6

Meaning of Equal Fractions

Review

Find 4 equal fractions for $\frac{1}{2}$.

Compare the fraction strip that shows 2 halves with each of the other fraction strips.

$\frac{1}{2} = \frac{2}{4}$ $\frac{1}{2} = \frac{3}{6}$

$\frac{1}{2} = \frac{4}{8}$ $\frac{1}{2} = \frac{5}{10}$

Practice

Use the fraction strips above to find equal fractions. Write the fraction.

1. 4 equal fractions for $\frac{2}{4}$

2. 1 equal fraction for $\frac{6}{8}$

Use the fraction strips to write equal fractions for the amount shaded.

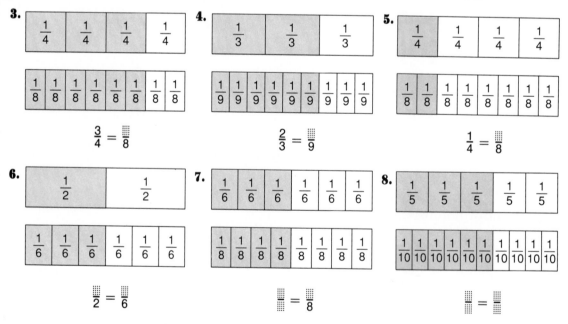

3. $\frac{3}{4} = \frac{}{8}$

4. $\frac{2}{3} = \frac{}{9}$

5. $\frac{1}{4} = \frac{}{8}$

6. $\frac{}{2} = \frac{}{6}$

7. $\frac{}{} = \frac{}{8}$

8. $\frac{}{} = \frac{}{}$

Pictographs

Review

The pictograph shows the number of students in each grade at Hilldale School who are members of the bicycle club. How many of the members are in fifth grade?

Each ☺ stands for 2 students. So, 6 ☺ stand for 6 × 2 students, or 12 students.

The bicycle club has 12 members in the fifth grade.

Number of Bicycle Club Members

Second Grade	☺
Third Grade	☺ ☺
Fourth Grade	☺ ☺ ☺ ☺ ☺
Fifth Grade	☺ ☺ ☺ ☺ ☺ ☺
Sixth Grade	☺ ☺ ☺

Each ☺ stands for 2 students.

Practice

Use the pictograph above to answer questions 1–8.

How many members are in

1. second grade?   2. third grade?   3. fourth grade?   4. sixth grade?

5. Which grade has the most students who belong to the bicycle club?

6. Which grade has the fewest students who belong to the bicycle club?

7. Does second grade or fourth grade have more students who belong to the bicycle club?

8. How many students at Hilldale School belong to the bicycle club?

9. Make a pictograph to show the data in the table.
   Remember to
   a. title the graph.
   b. list the items that the data are about.
   c. decide on a picture.
   d. decide how many each picture will stand for.

Favorite Dog Survey	
Type of dog	Number of votes
Beagle	9
Poodle	6
Collie	15
Golden Retriever	12

Bar Graphs

Review

The bar graph shows the favorite colors of students in Ernie's fifth grade class.

How many students like purple best?

The bar for purple stops at 5.
So, 5 students like purple best.

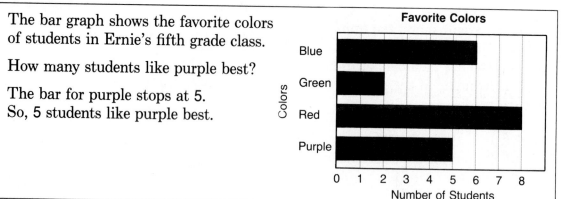

Practice

Use the bar graph above to answer questions 1–6.

1. How many students like green best?

2. How many students like red best?

3. How many students like blue best?

4. Which color is liked best?

5. Which color is liked the least?

6. Do more students like purple or blue best?

7. Make a bar graph to show the data in the table. Remember to
   a. title the graph.
   b. list the items the data are about.
   c. decide how to label the number scale.
      To label the scale, you can count by 1s or 2s or 3s and so on.

Number of Tickets Sold	
Alan	16
Alice	10
Aaron	4
Beth	8
Bart	2
Chad	14

Broken-Line Graphs

Review

The broken-line graph shows the number of aluminum cans saved by Jim's family for recycling during the first week of April. How many cans did Jim's family save on April 2?

Find April 2 along the bottom of the grid. Follow the grid line for April 2 straight up to the graph point.

Follow the grid line across to the number of cans.

They saved 6 cans on April 2.

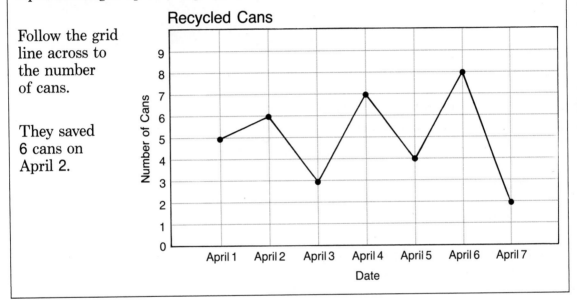

Practice

Use the broken-line graph above to answer each question.
How many cans were saved on

1. April 1?   2. April 5?   3. April 3?   4. April 7?

5. On what date were 7 cans saved?   6. On what date were 8 cans saved?

7. On what date were the most cans saved?   8. On what date were the fewest cans saved?

9. How many more cans were saved on April 4 than on April 5?   10. Were more cans saved on April 6 than on April 1?

11. What was the total number of cans saved on April 1 and April 2?   12. What was the total number of cans saved?

Independent Study Handbook

Contents

546   How to Use a Calculator
548   Problem-Solving Help File
550   Mental Math Strategies
552   Estimation Strategies
554   Math Study Skills
556   Working in Groups
557   Tables
558   Glossary

How to Use a Calculator

Calculators are used in everyday life at home and at work. They save time when solving problems with large numbers or problems with many numbers. *Remember*:

▶ **Do** estimate to check whether you pushed the correct buttons.

▶ **Don't** use a calculator when paper and pencil or mental math is faster.

Calculator displays

▶ **Number of digits** How many digits will your calculator display? If you press 99,999 × 99,999 to generate a number with more digits than the display can show, most calculators will show some kind of "error" message.

▶ **Unnecessary zeros** If you add 2.10 and 3.20, does your display show 5.3 or 5.30? Calculators usually drop unnecessary zeros.

▶ **Rounding** If you divide 2 by 3, do you see 0.6666666 or 0.6666667? Many calculators drop any digits after 8 digits, rather than round.

Calculator keys

Square Root
Finds the square root of the display.

Percent
Helps do percent problems.

Change Sign
Changes the display from positive to negative or negative to positive.

Memory Recall
Displays what is in memory. Push it twice to clear the memory.

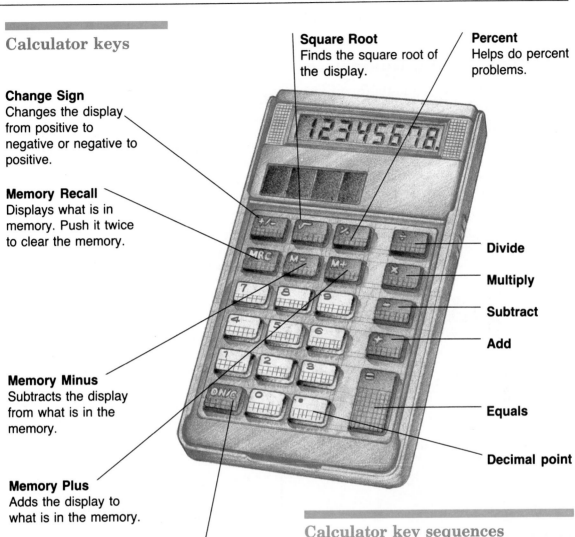

Divide

Multiply

Subtract

Add

Memory Minus
Subtracts the display from what is in the memory.

Equals

Decimal point

Memory Plus
Adds the display to what is in the memory.

On-Off, Clear
Turns the calculator on. Press it once to clear the last number entered. Press it twice to clear everything.

Calculator key sequences

▶ **Order of operations** Press 2 ⊞ 3 ⊠ 4 ⊟. If you get 20, your calculator does operations in the order they are pressed. If you get 14, your calculator does multiplication before addition.

▶ **Automatic constant** Press 2 ⊞ 3 ⊟ ⊟ ⊟ ⊟. Then press 2 ⊠ 3 ⊟ ⊟ ⊟ ⊟. If your calculator keeps adding 3 or multiplying by 2, your calculator has an automatic constant.

Problem-Solving Help File

Use these pages when you need help with problem solving.

Problem-Solving Guide

There is no recipe or magic formula for solving problems. But keeping a problem-solving guide in mind can help you become a better problem solver.

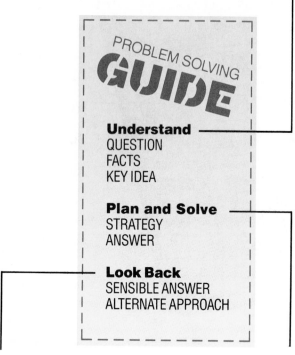

PROBLEM SOLVING GUIDE

Understand
QUESTION
FACTS
KEY IDEA

Plan and Solve
STRATEGY
ANSWER

Look Back
SENSIBLE ANSWER
ALTERNATE APPROACH

Understand
QUESTION
▶ What are you asked to find?
▶ Try to state the question in your own words.
▶ Is an exact answer needed?

FACTS
▶ What facts are given?
▶ Is there too much or too little information?
▶ Is data needed from a picture, table, graph?
▶ Do you need to collect some data?

KEY IDEA
▶ How are the facts and the question related?
▶ Are there groups that are part of a whole?
▶ Are two groups being compared?
▶ Are there groups that are joining or separating?
▶ Are there groups of the same size?

Plan and Solve
STRATEGY
▶ What can you do to solve the problem?
▶ Can the problem be solved by computing?
▶ Estimate the answer.
▶ Choose a strategy. Try another, if needed.

ANSWER
▶ Give the answer in a sentence.
▶ Do you need to interpret a remainder?
▶ Is rounding needed?

Look Back
SENSIBLE ANSWER
▶ Did you check your work?
▶ Did you use all the needed data?
▶ Does your answer have the correct units?
▶ Is your answer close to the estimate?
▶ Is your answer reasonable for the situation?

ALTERNATE APPROACH
▶ Is there another way to get the same answer?
▶ Could you use the same strategy differently?
▶ Would another strategy be faster or simpler?

Problem-Solving Strategies

You might think of problem-solving strategies as problem-solving tools that you own and use when needed. One or more strategies might be used for a problem. And if one strategy doesn't work, try another one.

PROBLEM SOLVING STRATEGIES

Choose an Operation
Write an Equation
Draw a Diagram
Make a Table
Try and Check
Use Logical Reasoning
Find a Pattern
Work Backward
Solve a Simpler Problem
Make a Graph

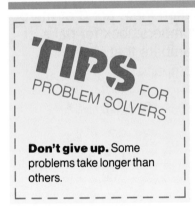

TIPS FOR PROBLEM SOLVERS

Don't give up. Some problems take longer than others.

Problem-Solving Behaviors and Attitudes

When you solve problems, do you give up quickly or lack confidence? Behaviors and attitudes can affect your work. So, remember these tips. They can help you become a better problem solver.

Tips for Problem Solvers

- ▶ **Don't give up.** Some problems take longer than others.

- ▶ **Be flexible.** If you get stuck, try another idea.

- ▶ **Be confident** so you can do your best.

- ▶ **Take risks.** Try your hunches. They often work.

- ▶ **Brainstorm to get started**—one idea will lead to another.

- ▶ **Visualize the problem** in your mind to help you understand it better.

- ▶ **Compare problems** to help you relate new problems to ones you've solved before.

- ▶ **Think about your thinking.** Pause to ask, "How is this going to help me solve the problem?"

- ▶ **Share your thinking with others.** Explaining your ideas helps you think better.

- ▶ **Organize your work** to help you think clearly.

Mental Math Strategies

Often the best calculator is your own mind. For simple calculations, mental math can be better than paper and pencil or a calculator. To sharpen your mental math skills, use the mental computation strategies shown on these pages.

Breaking Apart Numbers

Break apart one or more numbers to get numbers that are easier to use.

54 + 23
$54 + 20 + 3$ Break apart 23.
$74 + 3$
77

87 × 2
$(80 + 7) \times 2$ Break apart 87.
$(80 \times 2) + (7 \times 2)$ Use the distributive
$160 + 14$ property.
174

35 + 48
$(30 + 5) + (40 + 8)$ Break apart 35 and 48.
$(30 + 40) + (5 + 8)$ Regroup the numbers.
$70 + 13$
83

Compatible Numbers

Compatible numbers are pairs of numbers that are easy to use. Look for numbers like 1, 10, 100 or 3, 30, 300 that are easy to use.

40 + 30   **28 × 10**
70   280

180 ÷ 60
3

When there are 3 or more numbers, look for pairs of numbers that are compatible.

3 + 48 + 7
$3 + 7 + 48$
$10 + 48$
58

$\frac{1}{3} \times 7 \times 12$
$\frac{1}{3} \times 12 \times 7$
4×7
28

Using Equivalent Forms

Divide to find "fraction of."

$\frac{1}{3} \times 180$

$180 \div 3$

$\quad 60$

Change decimals or percents to fractions to get a number that is easier to use.

25% of 32

$\frac{1}{4}$ of 32

$32 \div 4$

$\quad 8$

Compensation

Change one number to make it easy to use. Then change the answer to compensate.

57 + 29

$57 + 30 = 87$ Add 1 to 29 to get 30.

$87 - 1 = 86$ Subtract 1 from the answer.

165 − 97

$165 - 100 = 65$ Add 3 to 97 to get 100.

$65 + 3 = 68$ Add 3 to the answer.

Change one number to make it easy to use. Then change the other number to compensate.

66 + 19

$65 + 20$ Add 1 to 19 and subtract

$\quad 85$ 1 from 66.

157 − 98   Add 2 to 98 and to 157.

$159 - 100$

$\quad 59$

Estimation Strategies

In everyday life, an exact answer is often unnecessary. For example, you can estimate while shopping to see if you have enough money.

When you do need an exact answer, estimation helps you find possible errors. Estimation is especially important for checking whether you pushed a wrong button on a calculator.

To help you make good estimates, use the estimation strategies shown on these pages.

Front-End Digits

Use just the first digit in each number to help you make an estimate.

173	100
421	400
+348	**+300**
	800

Since 73 + 21 + 48 is about 100, you can also adjust the estimate by adding 100 to get 900.

$$4\frac{1}{2} + 6\frac{5}{8} + 2\frac{1}{3}$$
$$4 + 6 + 2$$
$$12$$

Rounding

Round to one nonzero digit.

425	400
×28	× 30
	12,000

Round to the same place.

28.45	28
− 3.79	− 4
	24

$$13\frac{1}{4} + 8\frac{7}{8}$$
$$13 + 9$$
$$22$$

Round to the nearest half.

$$\frac{3}{8} + 2\frac{5}{8} + \frac{1}{4}$$
$$\frac{1}{2} + 2\frac{1}{2} + \frac{1}{2}$$
$$3\frac{1}{2}$$

Round both numbers up and both numbers down to get a range.

57 × 84
$60 \times 90 = 5,400$
$50 \times 80 = 4,000$

57 × 84 is between 4,000 and 5,400.

Substituting Compatible Numbers

Use numbers that are close to the original numbers.

23)476

24)480 or 23)460 or 25)500

23)476 is about 20.

24 × 78 × 4

25 × 78 × 4

100 × 78

24 × 78 × 4 is about 7,800.

$\frac{1}{3} \times$ **187**

$\frac{1}{3} \times 180$

$\frac{1}{3} \times 187$ is about 60.

26% of 32

25% of 32

$\frac{1}{4} \times 32$

26% of 32 is about 8.

Clustering

Look for groups of numbers that are close to the same number.

6,278	Each number
6,589	is about 6,000,
5,893	so the sum is
+6,134	about
	4 × 6,000 or
	24,000.

$4\frac{7}{8} + 5\frac{1}{5} + 4\frac{2}{3}$

Each number is about 5, so the sum is about 3 × 5 or 15.

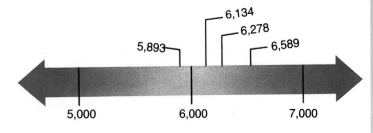

Comparing to a Reference Point

Compare the numbers to numbers you can work with easily.

346	Both numbers are less than 500, so the
+438	sum is less than 1,000.

$\frac{5}{8} + \frac{3}{5}$ Both numbers are greater than $\frac{1}{2}$, so the sum is greater than 1.

Math Study Skills

Try these math study skills to help you do your best.

Before a Lesson

▶ **Preview the lesson.** Look over the lesson to see what it's about.

▶ **Set a purpose.** Are you about to learn a new topic or revisit a familiar one?

▶ **Recall what you know.** What have you learned about this topic previously?

Build Understanding

Reading the lesson

▶ **Read slowly.** Don't try to read a math book as fast as a story book.

▶ **Learn vocabulary and symbols.** Note new math terms and symbols. Use the glossary and index. Watch for words like "product" that have other meanings outside of math.

▶ **Read diagrams, tables, graphs.** Use a ruler to help you read rows and columns.

▶ **Do the examples.** Work the examples yourself as you go through them.

Doing Activities

▶ **Use materials.** Keep the materials organized. Use them to explore new ideas.

▶ **Work with others.** When you work with others, use the tips for working together given on page 556.

Build Understandir

A. A market gets boxes o 24 heads in each box. heads of lettuce are in

Since each box contai same number of he

Check Understanding

Trying on your own

▶ **Note what you don't understand.** When you try some exercises, be aware of what you don't understand.

▶ **Reread the lesson.** When you don't understand, reread the "Build Understanding" section.

Preventing errors

▶ **Find another example.** When you need another example, turn to the "Reteaching" set at the back of the chapter.

▶ **Try again.** Keep trying until you feel you understand.

Practice and Problem Solving

Reading the exercises

▶ **Read directions.** Read carefully.

▶ **Read word problems.** Read slowly and reread, if needed.

Doing written work

▶ **Show your work.** Record what you did. Make your paper easy to follow and the answer easy to find.

▶ **Check your work.** Read what you write.

▶ **Find more practice.** Use the "More Practice" at the back of the chapter when needed.

After a Lesson

▶ **Look back.** Summarize the lesson. Would you be able to teach it to another student?

▶ **Connect to other lessons.** Think about how this lesson is related to other lessons.

Check Understanding

Copy and comple   chart.

×		7
4	1. ■	
40	7.	

Working in Groups

When you do math working with others, you'll learn more math, you'll learn how to work as a team, and you'll enjoy math more.

Roles for Group Members

When you work in a group, it can be helpful for each person to have a role. Some roles are:

TIPS FOR WORKING TOGETHER

You can disagree without being disagreeable.

▶ **Reporter**—This person summarizes the group's thinking.

▶ **Encourager**—This person encourages group members to take part and to work together well.

▶ **Recorder**—This person records the group's work.

▶ **Checker**—This person asks group members to explain their thinking or may ask others if they agree.

▶ **Materials Manager**—This person gets any materials that are needed and returns them at the end of class.

Tips for Working Together

Here are some tips for working well with others in a group.

▶ Involve your whole group. Help everyone to participate.

▶ Help keep your group on task.

▶ To make sure your group understands the task or solution, have each group member say it in his or her own words, summarize the steps, or give an example.

▶ Work as a group. If you understand, help another group member. Don't work ahead of the others.

▶ Be a good tutor. Make up similar problems or easier ones to help someone understand.

▶ When you are unsure, ask someone in your group for help or say you don't understand.

▶ Tell someone when he or she does or says something that helps you.

▶ Don't decide by voting. Try to understand which might be the best solution and why.

▶ Remember, you can disagree without being disagreeable.

Tables

Metric System

Length

10 millimeters (mm)	= 1 centimeter (cm)
10 centimeters 100 millimeters	= 1 decimeter (dm)
10 decimeters 100 centimeters	= 1 meter (m)
1,000 meters	= 1 kilometer (km)

Area

100 square millimeters (mm^2)	= 1 square centimeter (cm^2)
10,000 square centimeters	= 1 square meter (m^2)
100 square meters	= 1 are (a)
10,000 square meters	= 1 hectare (ha)

Volume

1,000 cubic millimeters (mm^3)	= 1 cubic centimeter (cm^3)
1,000 cubic centimeters	= 1 cubic decimeter (dm^3)
1,000,000 cubic centimeters	= 1 cubic meter (m^3)

Mass (weight)

1,000 milligrams (mg)	= 1 gram (g)
1,000 grams	= 1 kilogram (kg)
1,000 kilograms	= 1 metric ton (t)

Capacity

1,000 milliliters (mL)	= 1 liter (L)

Time

60 seconds	= 1 minute
60 minutes	= 1 hour
24 hours	= 1 day
7 days	= 1 week
365 days 52 weeks 12 months	= 1 year
366 days	= 1 leap year

Addition-Subtraction Table

+	0	1	2	3	4	5	6	7	8	9
0	0	1	2	3	4	5	6	7	8	9
1	1	2	3	4	5	6	7	8	9	10
2	2	3	4	5	6	7	8	9	10	11
3	3	4	5	6	7	8	9	10	11	12
4	4	5	6	7	8	9	10	11	12	13
5	5	6	7	8	9	10	11	12	13	14
6	6	7	8	9	10	11	12	13	14	15
7	7	8	9	10	11	12	13	14	15	16
8	8	9	10	11	12	13	14	15	16	17
9	9	10	11	12	13	14	15	16	17	18

Multiplication-Division Table

×	1	2	3	4	5	6	7	8	9
1	1	2	3	4	5	6	7	8	9
2	2	4	6	8	10	12	14	16	18
3	3	6	9	12	15	18	21	24	27
4	4	8	12	16	20	24	28	32	36
5	5	10	15	20	25	30	35	40	45
6	6	12	18	24	30	36	42	48	54
7	7	14	21	28	35	42	49	56	63
8	8	16	24	32	40	48	56	64	72
9	9	18	27	36	45	54	63	72	81

Customary System

Length

12 inches (in.)	= 1 foot (ft)
3 feet 36 inches	= 1 yard (yd)
1,760 yards 5,280 feet	= 1 mile (mi)
6,076 feet	= 1 nautical mile

Area

144 square inches (sq in.)	= 1 square foot (sq ft)
9 square feet	= 1 square yard (sq yd)
4,840 square yards	= 1 acre (A)

Volume

1,728 cubic inches (cu in.)	= 1 cubic foot (cu ft)
27 cubic feet	= 1 cubic yard (cu yd)

Weight

16 ounces (oz)	= 1 pound (lb)
2,000 pounds	= 1 ton (T)

Capacity

8 fluid ounces (fl oz)	= 1 cup (c)
2 cups	= 1 pint (pt)
2 pints	= 1 quart (qt)
4 quarts	= 1 gallon (gal)

Glossary

Acute angle An angle with a measure less than 90°.

Acute triangle Triangle with three acute angles.

Add To find the total by putting together two or more quantities.

Angle (∠) Two rays with the same endpoint.

Area A number given in square units that indicates the size of the inside of a plane figure.

Associative property (Grouping property) The way in which addends (or factors) are grouped does not affect the sum (or product).
(7 + 2) + 5 = 7 + (2 + 5)
(7 × 2) × 5 = 7 × (2 × 5)

Average A number obtained by dividing the sum of two or more addends by the number of addends.

Base (Geometry) A name used for a side of a polygon or surface of a solid figure.

Betweenness property For any two numbers, there is another number between them.

Box plot A way of displaying data to show the median values.

Breaking apart numbers Changing the form of a number so it is easier to use when computing. 23 can be changed to 20 + 3.

Broken-line graph A drawing that shows how quantities change over time.

Central angle An angle with its vertex at the center of a circle.

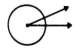

Chord A segment with both endpoints on a circle. A diameter is a special chord.

Circle A plane figure with all points the same distance from a given point called the *center*.

Circle graph A drawing that compares the parts of a quantity with the whole quantity.

Circumference The distance around a circle.

Clustering An estimation method used when all the numbers are close to the same number.

Combinations of numbers Computing by using numbers in an order that makes the computation easier.

Common denominator A common multiple of two or more denominators. A common denominator for $\frac{1}{6}$ and $\frac{3}{8}$ is 48.

Common factor A number that is a factor of two or more numbers. A common factor of 6 and 12 is 3.

Common multiple A number that is a multiple of two or more numbers.

Commutative property (Order property) The order in which numbers are added (or multiplied) does not affect the sum (or product).
4 + 6 = 6 + 4
4 × 6 = 6 × 4

Compass An instrument used for drawing circles and for doing geometric constructions.

Compatible number A number close to the number in a problem being solved that is easy to use in mental computation.

Compensation Changing a number by adding to it, or subtracting from it, so it is easier to use when computing. Then changing the answer to make up for the change.

Complements Two numbers with a sum that has only the digit 9.

Composite number A whole number, greater than 0, that has more than two factors.

Cone A solid figure formed by connecting a circle to a point not in the plane of the circle.

Congruent figures Figures with the same size and shape.

Coordinates *See* ordered pair.

Cross-products The cross-products of the ratios $\frac{3}{4}$ and $\frac{9}{12}$ are 3 × 12 and 4 × 9.

Cube A prism with all square faces.

Customary units of measure A system for measuring length in *inches, feet, yards,* and *miles;* capacity in *cups, pints, quarts,* and *gallons;* weight in *ounces, pounds,* and *tons;* temperature in *degrees Fahrenheit.*

Cylinder A solid figure with two circular bases that are parallel and congruent.

Data A collection of gathered information that has not been organized.

Daylight-saving time Time that is one hour ahead of standard time.

Decimal A number that names a whole and/or fractional parts with denominators of 10 (*tenths*), 100 (*hundredths*), or 1,000 (*thousandths*). In standard form, a point separates the whole number and fraction parts.

Degree (of an angle) A unit for measuring angles.

Denominator The number below the line in a fraction. It names the number of equal parts or objects.

Diagonal A segment with two nonadjacent vertices of a polygon as its endpoints.

Diameter In a circle, a segment that passes through the center and that has both endpoints on the circle.

Difference The number found by subtracting one number from another.

Digit One of the symbols used for writing numbers: 0, 1, 2, 3, 4, 5, 6, 7, 8, and 9.

Distributive property When a factor is a sum, multiplying each addend before adding does not change the product.

Divide To separate a total amount into an equal number of groups, or into groups of equal size.

Dividend A number that is divided by another number.

Divisible One number is divisible by another if the remainder is zero after dividing.

Divisor The number by which another number is divided.

Edge Segment where two faces of a polyhedron meet.

Endpoint The point at the end of a segment or a ray.

Equal decimals Decimals that name the same number. 1.8 and 1.80 are equal decimals.

Equal fractions Fractions that name the same number. $\frac{2}{3}$ and $\frac{8}{12}$ are equal fractions.

Equation A number sentence used to show how the parts of a problem are related.

Equilateral triangle Triangle with three congruent sides.

Estimate A number about the same as another number. A name used for a calculation not requiring an exact answer.

Even number A whole number with 0, 2, 4, 6, or 8 in the ones place.

Expanded form A way to write a number to show the value of each digit.

Face Flat surface that is part of a polyhedron.

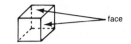

Factor (1) A number to be multiplied. (2) A number that divides evenly into a given second number is a factor of that number.

Favorable outcome A result in a probability experiment that meets a specific condition.

Flip A change in location of a figure by flipping it over a line, creating a mirror image (reflection) of the figure.

Fraction A number that names a part of a whole or of a set. It is written in the form $\frac{a}{b}$.

Frequency The number of times a certain item occurs in a set of data.

Front-end digit The digit in a number that has the greatest place value.

Graph A drawing used to show information in an organized way. Some types of graphs are *bar graphs* and *pictographs*.

Greatest common factor (1) The greatest number that is a factor of two or more numbers. (2) The greatest number that divides two or more numbers with no remainder.

Hexagon A six-sided polygon.

Improper fraction A fraction whose numerator is greater than or equal to its denominator.

Inequality A number sentence using the greater than (>) or less than (<) symbol.

Integers The whole numbers and their opposites. Some integers are +3, -3, 0, +16, -16.

Intersecting lines Lines that meet at a point.

Isosceles triangle Triangle with two congruent sides.

Least common denominator (LCD) The least common multiple of the denominators of two or more fractions. The least common denominator of $\frac{1}{2}$ and $\frac{2}{3}$ is 6.

Least common multiple (LCM) The smallest number that is a common multiple of two given numbers. The least common multiple for 6 and 8 is 24.

Line A set of points continuing without end in opposite directions.

Line graph A drawing that shows the rate at which something happens.

Line plot A graph that uses Xs to show information and compare quantities.

Line of symmetry A line on which a figure can be folded into two congruent parts.

Lowest terms A fraction for which 1 is the greatest common factor of both the numerator and the denominator.

Mean Average of a group of numbers. The mean of 2, 4, 5, 6, 6 is 23 ÷ 5, or 4.6.

Median The middle number in a group of numbers when the numbers are listed in order. The median of 2, 4, 5, 6, 6 is 5.

Metric units of measure A system for measuring length in *millimeters, centimeters, decimeters, meters,* and *kilometers;* capacity in *milliliters* and *liters;* mass in *grams* and *kilograms;* temperature in *degrees Celsius.*

Mixed number A number that has a whole number part and a fraction part.

Mode Number that occurs most often in a set of data.

Multiple The number that is the product of a number and a whole number.

Multiply To find the total by putting together groups of equal size, or to find the number that is "times as many" as another number.

Negative number A number less than 0, such as -5 or -10.

Numerator The number above the line in a fraction. It names the number of objects or parts under consideration.

Obtuse angle An angle with a measure greater than 90° and less than 180°.

Obtuse triangle Triangle with one obtuse angle.

Octagon An eight-sided polygon.

Odd number A whole number with 1, 3, 5, 7, or 9 in the ones place.

Ordered pair Two numbers arranged so there is a first number and a second number, used to locate a point on a grid.

Order of operations Rules for finding the value of an expression.

Outcome A possible result in a probability experiment.

Palindrome A set of letters that read the same forward and backward.

Parallel lines Lines in a plane that never meet.

Parallelogram A quadrilateral with opposite sides parallel and congruent.

Pattern A general idea by which things can be arranged or events can happen in an organized way.

Pentagon A five-sided polygon.

Percent (%) A ratio that compares a number to 100. 45% means 45 hundredths.

Perimeter The sum of the lengths of the sides of a polygon.

Period A group of three digits in a number separated by a comma.

Perpendicular lines Lines that intersect to form right angles.

Place value The number each digit represents is determined by the position the digit occupies.

Plane A flat surface that extends without end in all directions.

Plot To find the location of a point on a grid using an ordered pair.

Point An exact location in space.

Polygon A closed plane figure made by line segments.

Polyhedron A solid figure made of flat surfaces called *faces*. Each face is a polygon.

Polyomino A figure made of squares that are the same size. Each square shares at least one of its sides with another square.

Positive number A number greater than 0, such as $+35$.

Prime factorization A number written as the product of prime numbers. $30 = 2 \times 3 \times 5$

Prime number A whole number, greater than 1, that has exactly two factors: itself and 1.

Prism A polyhedron with two parallel, congruent faces, called *bases*. All other faces are parallelograms.

triangular prism

bases

rectangular prism

Probability A number from 0 to 1 that tells how likely it is that a given event will occur. The closer to 1, the *more likely* the event is to occur. The closer to 0, the *less likely* it is to occur.

Product The number found by multiplying numbers.

Proper fraction A fraction that is less than 1.

Property of one The product of one and a number is that number.

Property of zero The sum of zero and a number is that number. The product of zero and a number is zero.

Proportion A statement that two ratios are equal. $\frac{2}{5} = \frac{12}{30}$

Protractor An instrument used to measure angles.

Pyramid The solid figure formed by connecting points of a polygon to a point not in the plane of the polygon. The polygon and its interior is the *base*.

triangular pyramid

rectangular pyramid

Quadrilateral A four-sided polygon.

Quotient The answer after dividing one number by another.

Radius (1) In a circle, a segment that connects the center of the circle with a point on the circle. (2) The distance from the center to a point on the circle.

radius

Range (1) The difference between the greatest and the least numbers in a set of data. (2) An estimate consisting of a greater and lesser possible answer.

Rate A ratio that compares one quantity to a different kind of quantity.

Ratio A pair of numbers that expresses a rate or a comparison.

Ray A set of points that has one endpoint and that extends without end in one direction.

Reciprocals Two numbers whose product is 1. $\frac{3}{4}$ and $\frac{4}{3}$ are reciprocals because $\frac{3}{4} \times \frac{4}{3} = 1$.

Rectangle A parallelogram with four right angles.

Reference point When estimating, a number used for comparison with other numbers.

Regular polygon A polygon with all sides congruent and all angles congruent.

Repeating decimal A decimal in which one or more digits keep repeating, such as 0.518181818...

Remainder The number that is left over after dividing.

Rhombus A parallelogram with four congruent sides.

Right angle An angle with a measure of 90°.

Right triangle Triangle with one right angle.

Rounded number A number expressed to the nearest 10, 100, 1,000, and so on. 368 rounded to the nearest 10 is 370; rounded to the nearest 100 is 400.

Sample Part of a group upon which an experiment or survey is conducted.

Scale drawing A drawing made so that distances in the drawing are proportional to actual distances.

Scalene triangle Triangle with no congruent sides.

Segment Two points and the straight path between them.

Sequence A set of numbers formed by a pattern.

Side (1) A seqment used to form a polygon. (2) A ray used to form an angle.

Similar figures Figures with the same shape but not necessarily the same size.

Slide A change in location of a figure by moving it without turning it.

Solid figure A figure with three dimensions: length, width, and height.

Special numbers Numbers like 1, 10, 100, or 3, 30, 300 that are easy to use when computing mentally.

Sphere A solid figure with all points the same distance from a given point called the *center*.

Square (Geometry) A rectangle with four congruent sides. (Numeration) To multiply a number by itself.

Square numbers A sequence of numbers that can be shown by dots arranged in the shape of a square.

Standard form The notation for writing numbers using the digits 0-9 and each place represents a power of ten.

Statistics Numerical facts that are collected, organized, and analyzed.

Stem-and-leaf plot A way to display numerical data in which tens digits (stems) appear in a vertical line and ones digits (leaves) appear in horizontal lines.

Subtract To find how many are left when some are taken away, or to compare two quantities.

Sum The number found by adding numbers.

Surface area The sum of the areas of all the surfaces of a solid figure.

Symmetric figure A plane figure that can be folded in half so the two halves match.

Terminating decimal A decimal with an exact number of nonzero digits, such as 0.375.

Terms The numerator and denominator of a fraction.

Trapezoid A quadrilateral with one pair of parallel sides.

Tree diagram An organized way to list all possible outcomes of an experiment.

Triangle A three-sided polygon.

Turn A change in location of a figure by moving it around a given point.

Unit fraction A fraction with a numerator of one.

Vertex (1) The common endpoint of two rays that form an angle. (2) The point of intersection of two sides of a polygon. (3) The point of intersection of the edges of a polyhedron.

Volume A number given in cubic units that indicates the size of the inside of a space figure.

Whole number One of the numbers 0, 1, 2, 3, and so on.

GLOSSARY

561

Index

Acre, 214
Activities, 14, 46, 96, 138, 154,
    182, 216, 252, 268, 284,
    324, 360, 390, 422, 426,
    438, 460, 472, 498, 508
Acute angle, 462–463
Addends, 12
    missing, 34–35, 41, 536
    three or more, 12–17, 343,
        347, 349
Addition
    associative property, 16–17
    commutative property, 16–17
    decimals, 232–233
    equations, 34, 41, 137, 536
    estimating, 12–13, 228–229
    families of facts, 34–35, 536
    fractions (different
        denominators), 356–367,
        360–363
    fractions (same
        denominators), 342–343
    fractions (three addends),
        342–343, 356–357, 360–363
    integers, 114
    meaning of, 17, 534
    missing addends, 34–35, 41,
        536
    mixed numbers, 346–349,
        366–367
    money, 22–23, 232–233, 535
    number sense, 14–19, 22–23
    patterns, 23, 31
    property of zero, 16–17
    renaming, 14–17, 22–23, 535
    three or more addends,
        16–17, 22–23, 342–343,
        347–349, 356–357, 360–363
    three or more digits, 16–17,
        22–23, 535
    two digits, 14–17
    whole numbers, 14–17,
        22–23, 534, 536
Adjust estimates. See
    Estimation strategies in
    computation
Adjust quotients. See
    Estimation strategies in
    computation
Algebra
    equations, 32–35, 41, 55,
        136–139, 143, 145, 147,
        169, 235, 296–297, 311,
        502–505, 524
    function tables, 296–297,
        537, 540
    graphing, 292–293, 296–297
    inequalities, 55, 220, 246,

327, 335, 337, 421, 525
integers, 114
order of operations, 448
properties, 16–17, 56–57, 389
variable, 32–35, 41, 47,
    136–139, 143, 145, 147,
    153, 169, 321, 502–505
Alternate solutions, 10–11,
    102–103, 190, 371, 404
Alternate strategies. See
    Decision making; Problem-
    solving skills
Angle, 462–467, 470, 473,
    476–477.
Applications. See Connections
Appropriate units of measure
    See Measurement
Area
    customary units, 94–97, 100–103
    estimating, 20, 109
    irregular figures, 102–103
    metric units, 94–97, 100–103
    and perimeter, 95, 98–99
    rectangle, 96–97
    square, 96–97, 109
    surface area, 492
    triangle, 100–101
Array, 287, 537, 540–541
Art connection. See
    Connections
Associative (grouping) property
    of addition, 16–17
    of multiplication, 56–57
Average, 128, 134–135,
    434–435, 443

Bar graph, 21, 418–421,
    430–431, 544
Basic facts/basic fact strategies
    addition/subtraction, 534, 536
    division, 540–541
    multiplication, 537, 541
Between, 378
Billions place, 4–5
Box plot, 428
Break apart numbers. See
    Mental-math strategies
Broken line graph, 419–423,
    430–431
Budget, 432–433

Calculator
    key sequences, 132–135,
        234–235, 328–329
    number and operation keys,
        54–55, 132–133

in problem solving, 22–23,
    54–55, 90–91, 286–287,
    432–433, 514–515
reading a display, 50–51
to reinforce concepts, 6–7,
    22–23, 37, 50–51, 54–55,
    90–91, 134–135, 162–163,
    190–191, 250–251, 264–265,
    328–329, 432–433, 514–515
special keys, 134–135,
    162–163, 514–515
Capacity, 188–191
Career connection
    animal caretaker, 190–191
    architect, 478–479
    bicycle repairer, 500–501
    bicycle shop owner, 500–501
    butcher, 366–367
    carpenter, 314–315, 464–467
    chicken farmer, 316–317
    city planner, 94–95, 290–291
    commissioner of public works,
        130–131
    computer salesperson, 330–331
    dairy store owner, 68–69
    farmer, 316–317
    forest ranger, 150–151
    hardware and lumber yard
        clerk, 200–201
    music store manager,
        430–431
    park designer, 94–95
    reservations clerk, 104–105
    roofing contractor, 102–103
    salesperson, 186–187,
        200–201, 330–331
    sign painter, 82–83
    store clerk, 186–187, 200–201
    store manager, 430–431
    store owner, 68–69, 474–475,
        500–501
    zoo employee, 190–191
Celsius, 106–107
Census. See Data collection
Center of a circle, 472–473
Centimeter, 86–89, 539
    cubic, 94–97, 100–101
    square, 184–187
Central angle, 472–473
Certain event, 436–437
Check computation
    division, 122–123, 402
    subtraction, 26–27, 344
Choose an alternate strategy.
    See Decision making;
    Problem-solving strategies
Choose a computation method,
    22, 32, 58–59, 66–68, 71,

131, 133–136, 155–157, 159, 162–163, 166–167, 169–170, 235, 267
Choose an operation. See Problem-solving strategies
Choose a sensible measure. See Estimation strategies
Choose a strategy, 33, 36, 69, 72, 99, 108, 125, 140, 165, 171, 172, 203, 204, 231, 236, 257, 271, 272, 295, 298, 323, 331, 332, 359, 371, 372, 401, 405, 406, 417, 431, 437, 442, 485, 486, 519, 520
Chord, 473
Circle, 472–473, 491
Circle graphs, 432–433, 526
Circumference, 474–475
Classify and sort. See Data collection and analysis; Critical thinking
Classify shapes, 456–457, 460–461, 470–471
Clock, 104–105
Clustering. See Estimation strategies in computation
Collect and analyze data. See Data collection and analysis; Problem-solving skills
Combinations, 52–53
Common denominator, 324–325
Common factor, 312–313
Common multiple, 47, 324
Commutative (order) property
of addition, 16–17
of multiplication, 56–57, 386
Compare numbers
decimals, 220–221
fractions, 326–327
whole numbers, 6–7, 533
Compatible number. See Mental-math strategies
Compensation. See Mental-math strategies
Composite number, 242
Computation
addition, 14–15, 22–23, 232–233, 235, 342–343, 346–349, 356–357, 360–363, 366–367, 534–536
division, 122–123, 130–133, 146, 150–151, 154–159, 162–163, 166–169, 268–269, 402–403
multiplication, 48–51, 54–57, 66–67, 70–71, 252–255, 258–259, 264–267, 388–393, 398–399, 412
subtraction, 26–31, 234–235, 344–347, 350–353, 356–357, 364–365,

368–369, 534–536
Computation method. See Choose a computation method
Computer
constructions, 93, 469
graphic models, 319, 355
number patterns, 93, 129
organizing data and graphing, 21, 291, 429
probability simulations, 429
problem-solving applications, 21, 223, 262, 291, 355, 469
spreadsheets, 129, 223, 262, 506
Conclusions. See Data collection and analysis; Critical thinking
Concrete representations,
area, 94–95
decimals, 216, 252–254, 268–269
division, 138, 154, 268–269
fractions, 318, 324–325, 360, 364, 390
geometric solids, 182–183, 192, 222
measurement, 83, 87, 95, 96, 506
money, 252–254, 268–269
multiplication, 138, 252–254
patterns, 298
percent, 508–509
probability, 438–439
ratio, 498–499
subtraction, 364
Cone, 452–455
Congruence, 476–477
Connections
art, 182–183, 216–217, 320–321, 476–477, 482–483
careers. See Career connection
consumer topics. See Consumer connections/topics
health, 32–33, 166–167, 196–197, 232–233, 426–427
multicultural. See Multicultural connection
music, 34–35, 122–123, 350–351
reading, 84–85, 184–185, 424–425
science, 70–71, 156–157, 202–203, 226–227, 260–261, 296–297, 322–323, 352–353, 400–401, 462–463, 510–511
social studies, 4–7, 48–49, 292–293, 312–313, 328–329, 386–387, 418–423, 470–471, 516–517
Consumer connections/topics
budgets, 432–433
discounts, 404–405, 513
earning money/income, 257, 268–269, 518–519
measurement, 396–397
product choices, 52–53
purchasing, 52–55, 58–59,

188–189, 230–231, 255–257, 266–267, 270–271, 294–295, 404–405, 503, 513
sales tax, 266–267, 270–271, 512–513
shopping, 52–53
transportation, 162–163
unit pricing, 188–189
weights, 194–195, 294–295
Coordinate graphing, 292–297
Coordinate plane, 292–293
Count backward, 16–17, 28–29
Counting choices, 52–53
Critical thinking
classify and sort, 6–7, 16–17, 46–47, 86–87, 198–199, 282–283, 290, 308–309, 314–317, 330–331, 398–399, 452–453, 464–466, 472–473
develop alternatives, 10–11, 102–103
draw conclusions, 8–9, 12–13, 16–17, 30–33, 46–47, 50–51, 62–63, 66–67, 70–71, 82–83, 88–89, 94–97, 100–101, 104–107, 124–125, 130–131, 156–159, 168–169, 196–197, 202–203, 252–255, 266–267, 286–287, 312–315, 320–321, 398–399, 404–405, 422–423, 426–427, 430–431, 434–435, 460–461, 478–481, 496–497, 504–505
evaluate evidence and conclusions, 16–17, 23, 25, 31, 47, 49–50, 53–54, 62, 95, 98–100, 103, 105, 123, 128, 136, 153, 162, 164, 168, 170–171, 182, 186, 192, 223, 224–225, 230–231, 233, 253, 284, 318, 331, 348, 350, 368, 386, 392, 397, 416–417, 420–421, 424–425, 428, 432–433, 435, 438–439, 440–441, 457, 459, 466, 474, 479, 484–485, 496, 507, 518
explain reasoning/justifying answers, 4–5, 14–15, 17–19, 23–30, 32, 47, 50–51, 56–57, 62, 64–65, 68, 85, 88, 94, 100, 104, 106, 122, 124, 130, 132, 134, 153, 154, 156, 166, 169, 183, 184, 200, 220, 226, 229, 234, 251, 256, 258, 260–261, 262, 287, 294, 310, 316, 321, 325, 326, 344, 346, 361, 366, 388, 391, 396, 398, 419, 426, 430, 436, 471, 477, 480, 498, 503–504

find/extend/use patterns, 4–5, 46–47, 90–91, 282–289, 484–485

generalizations, 6–9, 12–15, 18–19, 24–25, 30–31, 46–49, 52–55, 64–65, 82–83, 86–87, 94–95, 106–107, 122–123, 134–137, 166–171, 186–187, 194–195, 218–219, 256–259, 284–289, 292–297, 310–313, 320–321, 324–325, 342–347, 356–357, 360–367, 390–393, 402–403, 416–421, 424–427, 432–433, 440–441, 456–457, 462–466, 470–471, 498–499, 518–519

graphs and charts, reason with, 98–99, 202–203, 294–295, 400–401, 430–431

inductive reasoning, 4–5, 24–25, 46–55, 62–67, 70–71, 82–85, 94–95, 98–105, 122–123, 158–159, 162–171, 186–189, 194–197, 202–203, 218–219, 228–229, 260–261, 266–271, 295–296, 310–313, 330–331, 344–347, 350–353, 356–363, 388–389, 400–401, 404–405, 418–421, 424–427, 430–439, 462–466, 472–473, 476–477, 480–481, 484–485, 496–501, 508–509

logic, 6–7, 12–13, 22–23, 32–33, 46–47, 56–57, 62–71, 84–87, 90–91, 94–97, 104–105, 122–123, 126–127, 130–131, 134–139, 156–157, 164–165, 168–171, 184–185, 190–191, 198–201, 230–231, 258–259, 286–287, 316–317, 322–323, 356–357, 396–397, 404–405, 426–427, 432–433, 436–441, 460–461, 470–471, 482–483, 502–503

order and sequence, 4–9, 56–57, 220–221, 282–287, 299, 326–327

predictions, make and test, 3, 45, 81, 121, 124–125, 149, 181, 213, 249, 281, 307, 341, 385, 415, 436–439, 495

use number sense, 4–9, 14–19, 22–27, 30–33, 46–49, 54–57, 62–63, 66–69, 82–91, 96–97, 104–105, 122–125, 132–135, 150–159, 166–169, 182–183, 200–203, 214–221, 226–229, 250–255, 258–261, 266–269, 282–283, 286–287, 296–297, 307–317, 319–329, 342–353, 360–371, 386–393, 396–405,

418–421, 434–435, 482–483, 496–497, 502–505, 508–520

Cross-curriculum connections. *See* Connections

Cross-products, 502–503

Cube, 182–183, 222, 453–455

Cubic measures, 184–187

Cumulative review and tests
    skills, 37, 73, 109, 118–119, 141, 173, 205, 237, 246, 273, 299, 333, 373, 382, 407, 443, 487, 521, 530
    problem solving 37, 73, 109, 141, 173, 205, 237, 273, 299, 333, 373, 407, 443, 487, 521

Cup, 188–189

Customary (English) system of measures
    adding/subtracting 200–201
    area, 94–97, 100–101
    capacity, 188–189
    conversion within the system, 84–85, 188–189, 194–195, 200–201, 397, 400–401
    estimation, 87, 91, 97, 189–191, 195, 197
    estimation strategies, 321
    Fahrenheit, 106–107
    length, 82–85
    measuring in, 82, 341, 538
    perimeter, 90–91
    volume, 184, 187
    weight, 194–195

Cylinder, 453

Daily-life connection. *See* Career and Consumer connections

Data collection and analysis
    collect and organize data, 3, 21, 45, 61, 81, 108, 121, 140, 149, 204, 223, 307, 332, 341, 372, 385, 406, 415, 421, 424–425, 434–435, 442, 451, 495
    conduct surveys, 3, 61, 281, 395, 415–417, 442, 451
    draw conclusions from data, 45, 61, 81, 127, 149, 161, 192, 193, 223, 249, 263, 272, 307, 319, 341, 355, 415–427, 430–433, 436–441, 451, 506–507, 520, 543–545
    find statistical measures, 128, 140, 172, 434–435
    make frequency tables, 160, 307, 406, 416–417, 434–435, 438–439, 451, 495
    make predictions, 21, 61, 129, 160, 223, 262, 298, 415, 422–427, 429,

432–441, 451, 507

sampling, 416–417

summarize results, 3, 36, 45, 63, 72, 81, 108, 172, 181, 192, 213, 236, 249, 272, 281, 298, 341, 372, 385, 406, 428, 442, 451, 520

use graphs to display data, 21, 61, 213, 307, 416–427, 430–433, 442, 451, 495, 543–545

use simulations, 355, 434–441, 520

Data file, 36, 72, 108, 140, 172, 204, 236, 272, 298, 332, 372, 406, 442, 486, 520

Daylight-saving time, 105

Decimals
    adding, 232–233
    comparing, 220–221, 223
    counting decimal places, 252–256
    dividing, 268–269
    equal, 214–215, 220–221, 278
    estimating, 228–229, 260–261
    and fractions, 214–215, 328–329
    hundred-thousandths, 250–251
    hundredths, 214–215
    and measurement, 223, 278
    and mixed numbers, 333, 373
    money, 214–215, 218–219, 252–256
    multiplying, 252–255, 258–259, 264–267
    number sense, 214–221, 226–229, 234–235, 250–255, 258–261, 266–269
    on the number line, 220–221, 226–227
    ordering, 220–221
    and percents, 512–513
    place value, 214–219, 250–251
    problem solving, 221, 224–225, 230–231, 233, 235, 255–257, 259, 265, 267, 269–273
    in quotients, 268–269
    repeating, 338
    rounding, 226–227
    subtracting, 234–235
    ten-thousandths, 250–251
    tenths, 214–215
    terminating, 338
    thousandths, 216–217
    zeros in the product, 266–267

Decimeter, 86–89

Decision making
    choose an alternate strategy, 33, 69, 99, 125, 165, 171, 203, 231, 257, 271, 295, 323, 331, 358–359, 371, 401, 405, 417, 431, 437,

485, 519
choose a computation
method, 22, 32, 58–59,
66–68, 71, 131, 133–136,
155–157, 159, 162–163,
166–167, 169–170, 235, 267
choose an operation, 36, 68,
72, 108, 140, 170, 172,
204, 236, 256, 271, 272,
298, 332, 372, 442, 486,
520
decide if an answer is
reasonable, 10–11, 18–19,
32–33, 68–69, 98–99,
136–137, 170, 171, 198–199,
224–225, 230–231, 256–257,
270–271, 294–295, 400–401,
404–405, 478–479, 504–505
decide when to estimate,
64–65, 430–431
use inductive reasoning, 4–5,
24–25, 46–55, 62–67,
70–71, 82–85, 94–95,
98–105, 122–123, 154–155,
158–159, 162–171, 182–183,
186–189, 194–197, 202–203,
218–219, 224–225, 228–229,
260–261, 266–271, 284–285,
295–296, 310–313, 324–325,
330–331, 344–347, 350–353,
356–363, 370–371, 388–389,
400–401, 404–405, 418–421,
424–427, 430–439, 462–466,
472–473, 476–477, 480–481,
484–485, 496–501, 508–509
Degrees
of an angle, 464–467
temperature, 106–107
Denominator, 308–313, 321,
328–329, 334–337,
342–345, 388–389
least common, 324–327,
356–357, 360–369
Develop alternatives. See
Critical thinking
Diagram, 478–479
Diameter, 473
Difference. See Subtraction
Digits and place value, 4–5,
214–219, 250–251
Discount, 404–405, 518–519
Distributive property, 56–57
Dividend. See Division
Divisibility, 178
Division
adjusting quotients, 156–157
averages, 134–135, 434–435,
443
basic fact strategies, 540–541
basic facts, 540–541
checking, 122–123, 402
decimals, 268–269
divisibility rules, 178

in equations, 173
estimation, 152–153, 158–159
families of facts, 138–139,
150–151, 541
finding averages, 134–135,
434–435, 443
and fractions, 316–317, 333
by fractions, 402–403
interpret remainder, 164–165
inverse operations, 138–139,
150–151
large numbers, 130–131
meaning of, 122–123, 540–541
missing factors, 138–139
and mixed numbers, 316–317
money, 130–131, 164–165,
170–171
number sense, 122–125,
132–135, 138–139, 150–159,
162–163, 166–169
one-digit divisors, 122–139
quotients as improper fractions
and mixed numbers, 316–317
relationship to multiplication,
138–139
remainders, 122–123, 164–165
rounding divisors, 156–159
short division, 146
three-digit quotients, 166–167
two-digit divisors, 154–169
two-digit quotients, 162–163
with zero and one, 168–169
zero in the quotient, 132,
168–169
Divisor, 152
Draw a picture or diagram. See
Problem-solving strategies
Draw conclusions. See Critical
thinking

E dge, 453–455
Eighth inch, 82–83
Elapsed time, 104–105
Endpoint, 458–459
Enrichment. In every chapter
Equal decimals, 214–215,
218–221, 278
Equal fractions, 310–311, 542
Equal ratios, 498–503
Equally likely outcome,
436–437
Equations. See also Formulas;
Problem-solving strategies
addition/subtraction, 32–35
missing addends, 34–35, 41
missing factors, 138–139,
143, 145, 147
multiplication and division,
136–139, 143, 145, 147
in problem solving, 32–35,
136–139
proportions, 500–503, 524

writing, 32–33
Equilateral triangle, 460–461
Equivalent expressions,
214–215, 328–329
Equivalent forms. See Mental-
math strategies
Equivalent fractions. See Equal
fractions
Estimation
addition, 12–13, 15, 22–23,
228–229, 346–347, 366–367
angle measures, 466
area, 20
average, 128, 434–435
capacity, 189, 191
circumference, 475
with compatible numbers, 155
decimals, 228–229, 252–255
differences, 24–25, 27
distance, 83
division, 126–127, 152–153,
155, 158–159, 166, 169
with fractions and mixed
numbers, 320–321, 329,
391, 392, 398
length, 82–83, 86–87
measurement, 20–21, 83, 87,
189, 190–191, 195, 196, 321
mixed numbers, 326–328,
366–369
money, 270–271
multiplication, 62–63, 260–261
one-digit quotients, 122
percent, 516–517
in problem solving, 64–65
products. See Multiplication
quotients. See Division
subtraction, 24–25, 27,
346–347
sums, 12–13, 15, 22
two-digit quotients, 126–127
Estimation strategies in
computation
adjust estimates, 22–23,
346–347
adjust quotients, 156–159
clustering, 12–13
compare to a reference point,
12–13, 320–321
decide when to estimate,
64–65, 430–431
front-end digits, 12–13,
22–25, 27, 54–55, 228–229
range, 12–13, 62–63
rounding, 12–13, 24–25,
62–63, 260–261, 320–321
substitute compatible
numbers, 62–63, 152–153,
260–261
Estimation strategies in
measurement
compare to something with
a known measure, 82–83,

86–87, 188–191, 194–197
with graphs and tables,
418–419, 424–427, 430–433
sampling/predicting, 416–417
sensible measures, 82–83,
86–87, 188–191, 194–197
Estimation strategies in problem
solving
deciding when to estimate,
64–65
giving sensible answers,
18–19
Evaluate evidence and
conclusions. *See* Critical
thinking
Even number, 147, 242
Event. *See* Probability
Expanded form, 4–5
Experimental probability,
438–439
Experiments
concrete representation, 438
fractions in, 440–441
in probability, 438–439
and sampling, 416–417
Explain reasoning and justify
answers. *See* Critical
thinking
Explore Math, 23, 31, 53, 101,
135, 163, 201, 219, 267,
287, 313, 363, 399, 439,
466, 511, 517
Explore Math at Home, 61, 161,
193, 290, 395, 429, 469
Explore as a Team, 20, 60, 128,
192, 222, 291, 318, 354,
468, 506
Extend patterns. *See* Critical
thinking

Face, 182–183
Factor
common, 312–313
missing, 138–139
prime, 304
Factorization (prime), 304
Fahrenheit, 106–107
Families of facts, 34–35,
138–139, 150–151,
158–159, 536, 541
Favorable outcome, 440–441
Figurate number, 60
First-quadrant graphing,
292–293, 296–297
Flip (reflection), 476–477
Foot, 97, 186–187
Formulas
area of a rectangle, 96–97
area of a triangle, 100–101
perimeter, 90–91

volume of a rectangular
prism, 186–187
Fractions. *See also* Mixed
numbers
adding, 342–343, 356–357,
360–363, 366–367
adding three addends,
342–343, 356–357, 360–363
betweenness, 378
common denominator,
324–325
comparing, 326–327
and decimals, 214–215,
328–329
denominator, 308–313, 321,
324–329, 334–337, 342–345,
356–357, 360–369, 388–389
density, 378
division, 402–403
equal (equivalent), 310–311,
542
estimation, 320–321
estimation strategies,
346–349, 366–367
in experiments, 440–441
finding fractional parts,
308–309, 332
improper, 314–317, 396–397
least common denominator,
324–325
lowest terms, 312–313
meaning of, 308–309
in measurement, 82, 86, 306,
314, 332, 340, 538
mental computation
strategies, 360–363
multiplying, 386–393, 412
multiplying by whole
numbers, 390–393
number line, 308, 310,
314–315, 320–321, 335,
342–345, 378, 396–397
number sense, 307–317,
320–329, 342–343, 346–349,
358–363, 366–367, 370–371,
386–393, 496–505
numerator, 308–313, 321,
342–345, 363, 388–389
ordering, 326–327
parts of a set, 308–309
parts of a whole, 308–309
and percent, 510–511
and probability, 440–441
as quotients, 316–317
reciprocals, 399
rounding, 320–321
subtraction, 344–347,
356–359, 364–365, 368–369
unit, 363
Frequency distribution. *See*
Data collection and analysis
Front-end digits. *See*
Estimation strategies in

computation
Functions, 284–285, 296–297,
537, 540

Gallon, 188–189
Games, 290, 354, 469
Gather data. *See* Data collection
and analysis; Problem-
solving strategies
patterns, 284–285, 296–297,
537, 540
tables, 296–297, 537, 540
Generalize. *See* Critical thinking
Geometry
acute angle, 462–463
angle, 462–463
angles of a triangle, 462–463,
466
area of a rectangle, 96–97,
109
area of a square, 96–97, 109
area of a triangle, 100–101
center of a circle, 472–473
central angle, 472–473
chord, 472–473
circle, 472–473
circumference, 474–475
classifying triangles, 460–461
cone, 452–455
congruent angles/figures,
476–477
cube, 182–183, 453–455
cylinder, 452–455
degree, 464–467
diameter, 472–473
edge, 453–455
endpoint, 458–459
equilateral triangle, 460–461
face, 453–455
flip, 476–477
hexagon, 456–457
intersecting lines, 458–459
isosceles triangle, 460–461
line, 458–459
line of symmetry, 480–481
obtuse angle, 462–463
octagon, 456–457
parallel lines, 458–459
parallelogram, 470–471
patterns for three-dimensional
figures, 182–183, 222
pentagon, 456–457
perimeter, 90–91, 98–99, 109
perpendicular lines, 464–465
plane figures, 456–461,
470–477
point, 458–459
polygon, 456–457
polyhedron, 453–455
polyomino, 210
prism, 182–183, 453–455

problem solving, 90–91, 97–99, 101–103, 457, 461, 463, 466, 471, 473, 475, 477–479, 481, 483–485
protractor, 464–467
pyramid, 452–455
quadrilateral, 456–457, 470–471
radius, 472–473
ray, 458–459
rectangle, 470–471
reflection (flip), 476–477
regular polygon, 456–457
rhombus, 470–471
right angle, 462–463
rotation (turn), 476–477
scalene triangle, 460–461
segment, 458–459
side, 456–457, 462–463
similar figures, 482–483
slide, 476–477
sphere, 452–455
square, 470–471
surface area, 492
symmetry, 480–481
tessellations, 478–479
three-dimensional figures, 182–183, 222, 452–455
transformations (flips, slides, turns), 476–477
translation (slide), 476–477
trapezoid, 470–471
triangle, 456–457, 460–461
turn, 476–477
two-dimensional figures, 456–461, 470–477
vertex, 453–455, 458–459, 462–463
volume, 184–187
Glossary, 558–561
Gram, 196–197
Graphical representations
  betweenness, 378
  comparisons, 21, 48
  cost/weight relationship, 294–295, 305
  interpreting graphs, 294–295, 305, 332, 372, 418–419, 420–421, 424–425, 428, 432, 444, 447, 449
  list all possible choices, 52–53
  location, 290–293
  making graphs, 395, 422–423, 426–427, 431, 434–435, 444–449, 520
  number line, 378
  ordered pairs, 290–293, 296–297, 303, 305
  time/distance, 296–297
Graphs
  bar, 21, 418–421, 430, 544
  box plot, 428
  broken-line, 418–423,

430–431, 545
  circle, 432–433, 526
  line, 294–295, 424–427
  make a, 430–431, 526
  on a number line, 220–221
  ordered pairs, 292–293, 296–297
  pictograph, 172, 418–421, 543
  stem-and-leaf, 428
Greater than (>), 55, 220–221, 246, 327, 335, 337, 421, 525
Greatest common factor, 312–313
Grouping (associative) property, 16–17, 56–57

Half inch, 82–83, 86
Health connection. See Connections
Height, 100–101
Hexagon, 456–457
Hour, 104–105
Hundreds place, 4–5
Hundred-thousands/millions/billions place, 4–5
Hundred-thousandths place, 250
Hundredths place, 214–215

Identify too much or too little information. See Problem-solving skills
Identity property, 48–49
Impossible event, 436–437
Improper fraction, 314–317
Inch, 82–85, 538
  cubic, 184–187
  fractions of, 314–315
  square, 94–97, 100–103
Income, 257, 268–269, 518–519
Independent Study Handbook, 546–561
Indirect measurement, 504–505
Inductive reasoning. See Critical thinking
Inequalities. See Greater than; Less than
Integers, 114
Interpret data. See Data collection and analysis
Interpret the remainder. See Problem-solving skills
Intersecting lines, 459
Inverse operations
  addition/subtraction, 34–35
  multiplication/division, 138–139, 150–151, 158–159
Irregular shapes, 102–103
Isosceles triangle, 460–461

Kilogram, 196–197
Kilometer, 86–89

Lattice multiplication, 78
Least common denominator, 324–325
Least common multiple, 47, 324–325
Length, 82–89
Less than (<), 55, 220, 246, 327, 335, 337, 421, 525
Line, 458–459
  intersecting, 459
  parallel, 459
  perpendicular, 465–467
  of symmetry, 480–481
Line graph, 424–427, 438–439
Line plot, 434–435
Line segment. See Segment
Line of symmetry, 480–481
Liquid measure. See Capacity
List outcomes, 436–437
Liter, 190–191
Locate points, 220–221, 292–293, 296–297
Logic. See Critical thinking
Logical reasoning. See Critical thinking; Problem-solving strategies
Lowest terms of fractions, 312–313

Make a diagram, graph, or table. See Problem-solving strategies
Make generalizations. See Critical thinking
Make and test predictions. See Critical thinking; Data collection and analysis
Manipulatives. See Concrete representations
Mass, 196–197
Math at Home, 61, 161, 193, 290, 395, 429, 469
Mathematical reasoning. See Critical thinking; Decision making; Problem solving; Visual thinking
Mean, 434–435
Measurement
  angle, 464–466
  appropriate units, 83, 85, 87, 89, 107, 189, 191, 195, 197
  area, 94–97, 100–103
  capacity, 188–191
  circumference, 474–475
  computation with, 84–85, 88–91, 96–105
  conversion within a system, 84–85, 88–89, 188–191, 196–197, 200–201, 278, 400–401
  customary units, 82–85,

188–189, 194–195, 538
with decimals, 223, 278
equal customary measures,
  84–85, 400–401
equal metric measures, 88–89,
  278
estimation, 20, 83, 107, 189,
  190, 191, 195, 196
with fractions, 82–83, 86–87,
  306–307, 314–315, 332,
  340–341, 538
length, 82–89
mass, 196–197
metric units, 86–89,
  190–191, 196–197, 539
with mixed numbers, 314–315
number sense, 188–197
perimeter, 90–91, 291, 468
problem solving, 83, 85, 87,
  89, 91, 93, 95, 97–99, 101,
  105, 107, 183, 185, 187,
  189, 191, 195, 197, 201–204
surface area, 492
temperature, 106–107, 202–203
time, 104–105, 201, 400–401
volume, 184–187
weight, 194–195, 400–401
Measures of central tendency.
  See Mean; Median; Mode
Median, 434–435
Mental math
  choosing when to use, 317
  differences, 26, 28–29, 255
  fractions, 329, 348–349,
    361–362, 366–367
  measurement, 191, 201
  problem solving, 17, 29, 49,
    57, 127, 151, 255, 295, 433
  products, 48–49, 51, 56–57,
    159, 258–259, 391–393, 433
  quotients, 126, 133, 150
  sums, 16–17, 22–23, 232,
    348–349, 361–362, 366–367
Mental-math strategies
  associative property, 16–17,
    56–57
  break apart numbers, 16–17,
    28–29, 56–57, 126–127,
    150–151
  commutative property, 16–17,
    56–57
  compatible numbers, 16–17,
    28–29, 126–127, 150–151
  compensation, 22–23, 28–29,
    56–57, 126–127, 252–255
  distributive property, 56–57
  equivalent forms, 516–517
  multiples of 10, 100, and
    1,000, 48–49, 54–55,
    150–151, 258–259
Meter, 86–89
Metric system of measures, 86,
  190, 196, 223, 539

area, 94–97, 100–101
capacity, 190–191
Celsius, 106–107
conversion within the system,
  88, 190, 196, 223, 278
equal measures, 278
estimation, 87, 190, 196
length, 86–89
liquid measure, 190–191
mass, 196–197
measuring in, 223, 539
perimeter, 90–91
volume, 184–187
Mile, 82–85
Milliliter, 190–191
Millimeter, 86–89
Millions, 4–5
Minute, 104–105
Missing terms
  addends, 34–35, 41, 136–137
  factors, 138–139
Mixed number
  adding, 346–349, 366–367
  comparing, 326–327
  and decimals, 328–329, 333,
    338, 373
  estimation, 320–321,
    346–349, 366–367
  as improper fractions,
    314–317, 396–397
  meaning of, 314–317
  in measurement, 82–83,
    86–87, 314–317, 538
  mental computation
    strategies, 348–349,
    366–367
  multiplying, 398–401
  number line, 308–311,
    314–315, 320–321
  ordering, 326–327
  and percents, 510–511
  pictorial representations,
    314–315
  and quotients, 316–317
  subtracting, 346–347,
    352–353, 368–369
  subtracting from a whole
    number, 350–361
Mixed Practice, 27, 31, 67, 133,
  159, 197, 235, 255, 259,
  261, 293, 311, 345, 351, 362,
  369, 392, 397, 399, 513
Mode, 434–435
Money
  adding and subtracting,
    230–231, 233, 235
  column addition, 233
  concrete representations,
    252–253, 268–269
  and decimals, 252–255,
    268–269
  discounts, 404–405
  division, 130–131, 164–165,

170–171
estimating differences,
  228–229, 234–235
estimating sums, 228–229,
  232–233, 270–271
and fractions, 393, 404–407
mental computation
  strategies, 22–23, 50–51
multiplying, 50–51, 54–57,
  270–271, 393, 404–405
place value, 214–215
problem solving, 50, 55–57,
  132–133, 171, 215, 230–231,
  252, 255–257, 261–262, 265,
  267–273, 393, 404–407
renaming, 214–215, 232–233,
  252–255, 268–269
rounding, 232–235, 252–255
unit prices, 130–131, 172
Multicultural connection
  American Indian baskets, 8–9
  ancient numeration, 218–219
  animals, 136–137
  cultural symbols, 480–481,
    504–505
  fabric designs, 282–283
  flags, 308–309
  food, 194–195, 342–343
  games, 258–259, 426–427
  kites, 100–101
  Mexican peppers, 50–51
  Moroccan crafts, 26–27
  names, 168–169
  tiles, 388–389
Multiple
  common, 46–47
  least common, 324–325
Multiple-step problems. *See*
  Problem-solving skills
Multiplication
  associative property, 56–57
  basic facts, 138–139, 150–151,
    158–159, 537, 541
  common multiples, 46–47,
    324–325
  commutative property, 56–57,
    386
  by a decimal, 264–265
  decimals by 10, 100, or
    1,000, 258–259
  decimals by a whole number,
    252–255
  distributive property, 56–57
  equations, 138–139
  estimating products, 62–63,
    252, 260–261
  factors, 138–139
  families of facts, 138–139,
    150–151, 158–159, 541
  to find equal ratios, 500–501
  fractions, 386–393, 412
  fractions and whole numbers,
    390–393

identity property (informally
   used), 48
lattice multiplication, 78
least common multiple,
   46–47, 324–325
meaning of, 537
mental, 56–57
missing factors, 138–139
mixed numbers, 398–399
money, 50–51, 54–57,
   270–271, 392–393, 404–405
multiples, 46–49
multiples of ten, 48–49,
   54–55, 258–259
number sense, 46–49, 54–57,
   62–63, 66–69, 386–393,
   396–405
one-digit factors, 50–51
prime factorization, 304
property of one, 48–49
property of zero, 48, 54
renaming in, 50–51
special products, 48–49,
   54–55, 258–259
three-digit factors, 70–71
three factors, 56–57
two-digit factors, 66–67
zeros in the product, 266–267
Music connection. *See*
   Connections

Negative integer, 114
Nonroutine problems, 2–3, 20–21,
   44–45, 60–61, 80–81,
   92–93, 120–121, 128–129,
   148–149, 160–161, 180–181,
   192–193, 212–213, 222–223,
   248–249, 262–263, 280–281,
   290–291, 306–307, 318–319,
   340–341, 354–355, 384–385,
   394–395, 414–415, 428–429,
   450–451, 468–469, 494–495
Not equally likely outcomes. *See*
   Probability
Number. *See* Number theory;
   Whole numbers;
   Fractions; Decimals;
   Integers
Number line
   adding fractions, 343
   estimating fractions, 320
   mixed numbers, 320
   ordering decimals, 220–221
   renaming fractions, 396
   rounding decimals, 226–227
   rounding fractions, 320
   subtracting fractions, 344–345
   whole numbers, 8–9
Number pair. *See* Ordered pair
Number pattern, 60, 284–289
Number relationships, 286–287,
   296–297

Number sense
   effects of operations, 10–17,
      26–33, 46–47, 54–57,
      61–63, 66–67, 84–85,
      104–105, 124–125, 132–133,
      150–153, 166–169, 232–233,
      252–255, 260–261, 286–287,
      322–323, 342–347, 358–363,
      370–371, 385–393, 398–399,
      402–403, 514–515, 518–519
   meaning of decimals, 214–221,
      223, 226–227, 234–235,
      250–251, 258–259, 266–267
   meaning of fractions,
      308–311, 314–317, 342–345,
      350–353, 360–365, 368–369
   meaning of integers, 114
   meaning of percent, 508–513
   meaning of whole numbers,
      4–5, 8–9, 14–15, 26–27,
      30–31, 122–123, 132–133
   number relationships, 6–9,
      14–17, 22–27, 34–35,
      46–49, 68–71, 82–83,
      86–91, 96–97, 104–105,
      122–127, 150–159, 164–165,
      170–171, 182–183, 200–201,
      296–297, 310–313, 319–329,
      346–349, 366–367, 398–401,
      418–421, 474–475, 482–483,
      496–505, 508–511, 516–517
   projects, 21, 61, 93, 129, 160,
      193, 223, 263, 290, 319,
      341, 355, 385, 395, 415,
      429, 451, 469, 507
   relative magnitude of
      numbers, 6–9, 12–13,
      18–19, 24–27, 30–31,
      46–51, 61–63, 84–89, 93,
      104–105, 129, 134–135,
      154–160, 162–163, 188–189,
      194–195, 214–215, 218–219,
      226–229, 258–261, 268–269,
      319–321, 346–349, 352–353,
      360–363, 386–393, 398–399,
      418–421, 440–441, 482–485,
      500–503, 512–513, 516–520
Number sentence. *See* Equation
Number theory
   common multiples, 46, 324
   composite numbers, 242
   divisibility rules, 178
   even and odd, 242, 386–387
   factors, 138–139
   greatest common factor,
      312–313
   least common multiple,
      46–47, 324–325
   multiples, 46–49, 354
   prime factorization, 304
   prime numbers, 242
Numeration
   decimals, 214–219, 250–251

   Roman, 42
   standard form, 4–5, 42
   whole numbers, 4–5
Numerator, 308–309

Obtuse angle, 462–463
Octagon, 456–457
Odd number, 47, 242
One, property of, 48–49
Ones place, 4–5
Order numbers, 6–7, 56–57,
   220–221, 326–327
Order (commutative) property,
   16–17, 56–57, 386
Order of operations, 448
Ordered pairs, 292, 296
Ordering and sequencing. *See*
   Critical thinking
Organize data. *See* Data
   collection and analysis
Ounce, 194–195
Outcome. *See* Probability

Palindrome, 14–15
Parallel, 458–459
Parallelogram, 470–471
Parentheses, in order of
   operations, 16–17
Patterns. *See also* Critical
      thinking; Problem-solving
      strategies
   finding 288–289
   in figurate numbers, 60
   with figures, 60, 182–183,
      282–285
   multiplication, 284–285
   with numbers, 60, 282–287
   with objects, 282–285
   in sequences, 286–287
   skip counting, 242
   square numbers, 60
   in tables, 284–285
Pentagon, 456–457
Percent
   and circle graphs, 526
   concrete representations,
      508–509
   and decimals, 512–513
   discounts, 521
   estimating, 516–517
   finding a percent of a number,
      506, 514–515
   and fractions, 508–511
   greater than 100%, 512–515
   meaning of, 510–511
   mental computation
      strategies, 516–517
   number sense, 508–520
   pictorial representations,
      510–512
   and ratio, 508–509

tax, 521
Perimeter, 90–91, 95, 98, 109, 291, 468
Period, in place value, 4–5
Perpendicular, 465–467
Pictograph, 418–421, 544
Pictorial representations
  angles, 462–466
  area, 94–97, 100–103, 110
  circles, 472–473, 474
  congruency, 482–483, 491
  decimals, 214–215, 218, 220, 226, 232, 263, 328, 512
  division, 122, 402–403
  draw a diagram, 478–479
  fractions, 308–310, 314–315, 320, 328, 342–345, 350–351, 352, 356, 386–389, 396, 402–403, 511, 531
  geometry, 184–187, 452–485
  lines, segments, rays, 458, 467, 488, 490, 493
  map reading, 394
  measurement, 82, 86, 90–91, 94–95, 100–103
  mixed numbers, 350–352, 355, 356, 396
  multiplication, 264, 386–389
  patterns, 282–283, 289–290, 300, 302, 305
  percent, 510–512
  polygons, 456–457, 460–461, 466–469, 470–471, 488–493
  polyhedron, 183–187, 452–455
  polyominoes, 210
  probability, 437, 440–441, 445, 447, 449
  ratio, 496–497, 499–501, 524, 527
  solid figures, 453–455
  subtraction, 344–345, 350–352, 356, 364
  surface area, 492
  symmetry, 480–481, 489, 491, 493
  temperature, 106–107
  time, 104
  visual thinking, 160, 455
Pint, 188–189
Place value
  chart, 4–5, 38, 214–219
  and decimals, 214–219
  division, 154
  expanded form, 4–5
  and money, 214–215
  periods, 4–5, 218–219, 250–251
  standard form, 4–5, 42
  through hundred-billions, 4–5
Plane, 292–293
Plane figure. See Geometry
Point, 458–459

ordered pairs, 292–293
Polygon, 456–458, 460–461, 470–471, 476–477
Polyhedron, 453–455
Polyomino, 210
Positive integer, 114
Possible outcome. See Probability
Pound, 194–195
Practice. See Midchapter Checkup; Problem-solving review; Skills review
Pre-algebra. See Algebra
Predictions. See Critical thinking; Data collection and analysis
Prime factorization, 304
Prime number, 242
Prism, 182–183, 453–455
Probability, 436–441
  counting choices, 52–53
  events, certain, possible, impossible, 436–437
  experimental, 438–439
  finding, 440–441
  listing, 436–437
  meaning, 436–437
  outcomes, equally likely, more likely, less likely, 436–437
  predictions, 128, 438–439
  theoretical, 438–441
  tree diagram, 52–53
  of zero and one, 440–441
Problem solving. See also Problem-solving skills; Problem-solving strategies
  addition, 23, 31, 33, 35, 69, 72, 137, 155, 171, 486
  area, 95, 97, 101, 140
  average, 135, 140, 151, 160, 167, 317
  customary units, 83, 85, 90, 101, 155, 157, 185, 187, 189, 195, 229, 236, 263, 265, 321, 323, 327, 332, 347, 352, 357, 363, 367, 371, 399, 401, 406, 486
  decimals, 217, 219, 221, 227, 257, 259, 263
  discounts, 393, 405, 513, 519, 521
  division, 127, 131, 133, 135, 137, 140, 151, 165, 167, 169, 171, 257, 317, 331, 403, 442
  fractions, 309, 311, 313, 315, 317, 323, 325, 329, 332, 345, 372, 387, 389, 393, 395, 397, 399, 401, 403
  geometry, 459, 461, 463, 466, 471, 473, 475, 481, 483, 485, 486
  graphing, 293, 297, 332, 372, 421, 425, 428
  length, 263, 315, 321, 349,

353, 357, 359, 369, 371, 372, 401, 406
  mental math, 16, 29, 36, 57, 63, 151
  metric units, 87, 89, 90, 99, 101, 185, 187, 191, 197
  money, 55, 72, 92, 108, 131, 133, 140, 153, 160, 189, 215, 231, 236, 255, 257, 262, 265, 267, 269, 270, 272, 323, 331, 332, 371, 393, 405, 406, 442, 486, 503, 515, 519, 520
  multiplication, 47, 49, 51, 57, 59, 67, 69, 71, 72, 123, 137, 140, 160, 169, 171, 257, 259, 265, 331, 486
  nonroutine problems. See Nonroutine problems
  number relationships, 125, 127, 139, 140, 155, 159
  patterns, 283, 285, 287, 289, 290, 298
  percent, 509, 511, 513, 515, 517, 519, 520, 521
  perimeter, 90–91, 95, 99, 108, 140, 298, 372
  probability, 437, 439, 441
  ratio, 497, 499, 501, 503
  subtraction, 10–11, 29, 31, 33, 35, 36, 69, 71, 137, 140, 171, 197, 257
  tax, 267, 272, 513, 515, 521
  temperature, 107, 203, 227
  time, 105, 108, 140, 155, 201, 203, 233, 235, 236, 255, 317, 343, 345, 351, 357, 372, 401, 427, 442
  two-step problems, 31, 35, 55, 72, 153, 187, 195, 255, 262, 423
  volume, 185, 187
  weight, 157, 195, 197, 236, 259, 272, 323, 363, 367, 399, 401, 406
Problem-solving guide, 10–11
Problem-Solving Review, 36, 72, 108, 140, 172, 204, 236, 273, 298, 332, 372, 406, 442, 486, 520
Problem-solving skills
  collect data, 416–417
  decide when an estimate is enough, 64–65
  give sensible answers, 18–19
  interpret the remainder, 164–165, 330–331
  multiple-step problems, 270–271
  too little information, 230–231, 518–519
  too much information, 230–231, 518–519

use alternate strategies, 358–359
use data from a graph, 294–295
use data from a picture, 102–103
use data from a table, 202–203
Problem-solving strategies. *See also* Choose a strategy
choose an operation, 68–69, 170–171, 256–257, 404–405
draw a diagram, 52–53, 478–479
find a pattern, 288–289, 484–485
make a graph, 430–431
make a table, 98–99
solve a simpler problem, 370–371
try and check, 124–125, 198–199
use reasoning, 224–225
work backward, 322–323
write an equation, 32–33, 136–137, 504–505
Problem-solving tips, 17, 57, 95, 127, 157, 187, 221, 255, 289, 329, 343, 393, 425, 481, 513
Problem-Solving Workshop. In every chapter.
Product. *See* Multiplication
Proper fraction, 314–315
Properties of operations
associative, 16–17, 56–57
commutative, 16–17, 56–57
distributive, 56–57
of one, 48–49
of zero, 16–17, 48–49, 54–55
Proportion
cross-products in, 502–503
meaning, 502–503
and percents, 508–509
solving, 502–505
Protractor, 464–467
Purchases, 52–55, 58–59, 188–189, 194
Pyramid, 453–455

Quadrilateral, 456–457, 470–471
Quart, 188–189
Quarter inch, 82–83
Quotient. *See* Division

Radius, 472–473
Range in estimation. *See* Estimation strategies in computation
Ratio. *See also* Proportion

concrete materials, 499
cross-products, 502–505
equal, 498–501
in equations, 500–505
meaning of, 496–497
and percents, 508–509
problem solving, 497, 499, 501, 503
and scale drawing, 504–505
solving proportions, 502–503
Rational number. *See* Fractions; Mixed numbers
Ray, 458–459
Reading connection. *See* Connections
Reading Math, 9, 55, 131, 153, 183, 251, 297, 321, 369, 483, 515
Real-Life Decision Making, 21, 92, 161, 262, 318, 394, 428, 507
Reasoning. *See* Critical thinking; Decision making; Problem solving; Visual thinking
Reciprocal, 399
Rectangle, 96–97, 109, 470–471
Rectangular prism, 182–183, 452–453
Reflection (flip), 476–477
Regular polygon, 456–457
Relative magnitude of numbers, 4–9, 114, 220–221, 284–287, 326
Remainder, 164–165, 330–331
Repeating decimals, 338
Representations. *See* Algebraic, Concrete, Graphic, and Pictorial representations
Review
cumulative, 37, 73, 109, 118–119, 141, 173, 205, 237, 246–247, 273, 299, 333, 373, 382–383, 407, 443, 487, 521, 530–531
mid-chapter, 19, 59, 91, 127, 159, 191, 221, 261, 289, 317, 353, 393, 427, 467, 505
problem solving, 36, 72, 108, 140, 172, 204, 236, 272, 298, 332, 372, 406, 442, 486, 520
skills, 29, 36, 63, 72, 103, 108, 137, 140, 167, 172, 197, 204, 229, 236, 255, 272, 283, 298, 315, 332, 365, 372, 389, 406, 421, 433, 442, 455, 486, 501, 520
Review appendix, 532–545
Rhombus, 470–471
Right angle, 462–463
Roman numeral, 42
Rotation(turn).*See*Transformations

Rounding numbers
decimals, 226–227
money, 232–235, 252–255
whole numbers, 8–9
Rounding to estimate. *See* Estimation strategies in computation
Rules, 296–297

Sample and predict. *See* Data collection and analysis; Estimation strategies in measurement
Saving
Scale drawing, 504–505
Scalene triangle, 460–461
Schedules and timetables, 18–19, 270–271
Science connection. *See* Connections
Second, 104–105
Segment, 458–459
congruent, 476
Sensible answer. *See* Problem-solving skills
Sensible measures. *See* Estimation strategies in measurement; Measurement
Short division, 146
Side, 456–458, 462–463
Similarity, 482–483
Skills Review, 29, 36, 63, 72, 108, 137, 140, 167, 172, 197, 204, 229, 236, 255, 272, 283, 298, 332, 365, 372, 389, 406, 421, 433, 442, 455, 486, 501, 520
Slide (translation), 476–477
Social studies connection. *See* Connections
Solid shapes. *See* Geometry
Solve a simpler problem. *See* Problem-solving strategies
Spatial perception. *See* Visual thinking
Sphere, 453–455
Spreadsheet, 129, 223, 263, 506
Square, 96–97, 109, 470–471
Square measures, 94–103
Standard form, 4–5
Standard time, 105
Statistics
average, 128, 134–135, 434–435, 443
bar graphs, 21, 418–421, 430–431, 544
broken-line graphs, 419–423, 430–431, 545
collecting data, 416–419
experiments, 438–439
frequency table, 416–417, 434–435, 438–439

INDEX

graphs and tables, 416–421, 424–425
interpreting, 418–421, 424–425
line plots, 434–435
mean, median, mode, 434–435
number pairs, 92–93, 296–297
organizing data, 418, 434
outcomes, 436–437, 440–441
probability, 436–441
sampling, 416–417
surveys, 416–417
tallying, 416–417
Stem-and-leaf plot, 428
Strategies. *See* Estimation, Mental-math, and Problem-solving strategies
Study skills, 554–555
Subtraction *See also* Estimation computation strategies; Mental math strategies; Representations
checking, 26–27, 344
decimals, 234–235
equations, 32–33
estimating, 24–25, 228–229
families of facts, 34–35, 536
fractions 344–345, 356–357, 364–365, 368–369
fractions from whole numbers, 350–351
integers, 114
inverse operations, 34–35
meaning of, 24–27, 534
mental computation strategies, 28–29, 34–35
missing addends, 34–35
mixed numbers, 346–347, 350–353, 356–357, 368–369
mixed numbers from a whole number, 350–351
money, 535
number sense, 24–25, 30–31, 344–347, 350–353, 358–359, 364–365, 368–371
patterns, 31
renaming, 26–27, 30–31, 352–353
three or more digits, 26–27, 30–31, 535
two digits, 26–27
whole numbers, 26–27, 30–31, 534–536
zero in, 26–27
Sum. *See* Addition
Summarize results. *See* Data collection and analysis
Surface area, 492
Survey. *See* Data collection
Symmetry, 480–481

Tables, 98–99, 116–117, 160, 180–181, 188–189,
202–203, 263, 270–271, 296–297, 400–401, 416–421, 423, 424–427, 430, 434–435, 537, 540
Talk/Write About Math. In every lesson
Tallying and tally charts, 160, 416, 434–435, 440
Taxes, 266, 270, 512
Temperature, 106–107, 114, 202–203
Tens place, 4–5
Ten-thousands/millions/billions place, 4–5
Tenths place, 214–215
Terminating decimal, 338
Tessellations, 478–479
Tests
chapter, 43, 79, 115, 147, 179, 211, 243, 279, 305, 339, 379, 413, 449, 493, 527
cumulative, 118–119, 246–247, 382–383, 530–531
Theoretical probability. *See* Probability
Thermometer, 114
Thousands place, 4–5
Thousandths place, 216–217
Time
daylight saving time, 105
elapsed, 104–105, 307
standard time, 105
time tables, 18–19, 270–271
Timetables and schedules, 18–19, 270–271
Tips for problem solvers. *See* Problem-solving tips
Tips for working together. *See* Work together
Ton, 194–195
Too much or too little information. *See* Problem-solving skills
Transformations, 476–477
Translation (slide), 476–477
Transportation, 162
Trapezoid, 470–471
Tree diagram, 52–53
Triangle, 100–101, 109, 456–457
Triangular prism, 453–455
Try and check. *See* Problem-solving strategies
Turn (rotation). *See* Transformations

Unit fraction, 363
Unit prices, 130–131
Units of measure. *See* Customary and Metric systems of measures

Variable, 32–35, 41, 47, 136–139, 143, 145, 147, 153, 169, 502–505, 524
Vertex, 453–455, 458–459, 462–463
Visual thinking
spatial perception, 46–47, 68–69, 82–83, 86–87, 94–97, 100–103, 182–189, 193, 216–217, 222–223, 232–233, 264–265, 282–285, 291, 320–321, 358–363, 386–387, 395, 402–403, 430–433, 452–459, 462–463, 470–481, 484–485, 498–499, 508–513, 520
visual perception, 86–87, 93, 100, 160, 182–187, 507
Vocabulary. *See* Glossary
Volume, 184–187, 205

Weight
customary units, 194–195
metric units, 196–197
Whole numbers
addition, 14–15, 534
comparing, 6–7, 543
dividing, 122–123, 126–127, 130–133, 540–541
multiplication, 48–51, 54–57, 537
number line, 8–9
number sense, 4–9
ordering, 6–7, 533
rounding, 8–9
subtraction, 26–27, 30–31, 534, 536
through hundred-billions, 4–5
uses of, 37
writing, 4–5
Work backward. *See* Problem-solving strategies
Work together, 20, 60, 128, 192, 222, 291, 318, 354, 468, 506
Write an equation. *See* Equations; Problem-solving strategies
Write/Talk About Math. In every lesson
Write a problem, 34, 54, 138, 150, 253, 265, 282, 324, 339, 400, 413

Yard, 82–85

Zero
as a factor, 48
identity property, 16
in the product, 266–267
in the quotient, 168

ACKNOWLEDGMENTS

Design

Cover and Special Features: SHELDON COTLER + ASSOCIATES
Art Direction and Production/ Core Lessons: Taurins Design Associates, Inc./NYC
Rosa + Wesley Design Associates, Jack Weiss Associates

Photographs

Cover: Richard Chesnut, Fred Schenk xi (tl): Richard Hutchings, InfoEdit xi (bl): Stephen Frisch, Stock Boston xi (l): Brent Jones xi (br) Lawrence Migdale xv (t): Courtesy Compaq Computer Corporation xvi (t): Lawrence Migdale xx-1: Charles Gupton, Click/Chicago/Tony Stone ScottForesman photographs by: Richard Chesnut 61, 129, 160, 180–181, 193, 222, 223, 244, 245, 262, 306–307, 318, 373, 395, 507, 528–529; Arie deZanger 44–45, 120–121, 161, 262, 299, 340–341, 384–385, 506; Fred Schenk 80–81, 327, 319, 450–451; unless otherwise acknowledged, all photographs are the property of ScottForesman. Clare Aich: 24, 52, 86, 105, 134, 154, 155, 163, 165, 196, 210, 224, 225, 250, 252, 268, 284, 309, 320, 338, 464, 465, 474, 475, 478, 502, 503, 512, 513 AlaskaStock: S. Nelson 504; Jeff Schultz 137 Animals Animals: Breck P. Kent 150 Peter Arnold, Inc.: Stephen J. Kraseman 414–415; Putnam 168 Craig Aurness: 150 The Bettmann Archive: 494–495 Cameramann Int'l: Milt and Joan Mann 194, 437 Woodfin Camp: Marc & Evelyne Bernheim 136 Cherokee Historical Assn.: 9 Click/Chicago/Tony Stone: Chris Baker 244 Bruce Coleman: Ellen Beach 50 Duomo: Paul J. Sutton 44–45; Steve E. Sutton 244, 245 Ellis Wildlife Collection: Ken Deitcher 414–415; Gerry Ellis 44–45, 116, 117, 414–415 Focus on Sports: 369 FPG: Joel Elkins 44–45; Gerald L. French 280–281; Richard Laird 280–281; John Turner 44–45 Judy Gurovitz: 30, 132, 133 Richard Hutchings: 14, 16, 28, 126, 184, 254, 256, 260, 288, 289, 296, 316, 390, 424, 425, 472 The Image Bank: 92; Charles Allen 2–3; Alan Becker 2–3; Luis Castaneda 521; Francois Dardelet 120–121; Grant V. Faint 296; Heintz Fischer 120–121; Larry Dale Gordon 46; Janeart LTD. 2–3; Elyse Lewin 2–3; Jon Love 2–3; Burton McNeely 65; Margaret W. Peterson 2–3; Steve Proehl 148–149; Sobel/Klonsky 516; Harald Sund 148–149; Maria Taglienti 2–3; Lars Ternblad 2–3; A. Upitis 70 The Image Works: Bob Daemmrich 234; Ron Morecraft: 12, 62, 68, 146, 242, 266, 284, 402, 438, 439, 440, 441 Wolfgang Kaehler: 505 Museum of the American Indian, Heye Foundation: 8 NASA: 244, 245 Odyssey: R. Frerck 7, 26 Photo Researchers, Inc.: Bartlett 195; Treat Davidson 225; Richard Hutchings 225; Pat & Tom Leeson 151 Private Collection: 283 From New York Road Map © 1990 by Rand McNally & Company, R.L. 90-S-5: 116, 117, 280, 281 Stock Boston: John Coletti 280–281; Owen Franken 259; Jerry Howard 131; William Johnson 162; J.C. Lejeune 389; Mike Mazzaschi 278, 342; Pasley 258; Seth Resnick 122 Stock House: Steve Dalton 487 The Stock Market: 21; Paul Barton 494–495; Bill Bernstein 414–415; Michael Kevin Daly 494–495; Smith Garner 494–495; Mark Gibson 244, 345, Ted Horowitz 44–45, 212–213; Michael Newler 212–213; Gabe Palmer 494–495; Otto Rogge 414–415; Sohm/Chromosohm 507; Michael Tamborrino 148–149 From PACIFIC AND SOUTHEAST ASIAN COOKING by Raphael Steinberg and the Editors of TIME-LIFE BOOKS. Photo by Anthony Blake. Copyright © 1970 Time Life Books Inc. All rights reserved. Used by permission: 51 United Nations: 219, 308 U.S.A. Rivers: John Blaustein 64 Daffy Duck is a trademark of Warner Bros., Inc. © 1989 Warner Bros., Inc. All rights reserved.

Illustrations

Elizabeth Allen, Ron Becker, Dolores Bego, Eliot Bergman, Lee Lee Brazeal, Dan Bridy, Lloyd Birmingham, David Cain, Chi Chung, Darch Clampitt, Jim Deigan, Jim Delapine, Nancy Didion, Paul Dolan, Mac Evans, David Febland, Mark Fisher, Janice Fried, Susan Gray, Franklin Hammond, Fred Harsh, Steve Henry, Mark Herman, Dave Joly, Mark Kaplan, Robert Korta, Andy Levine, Ron Lieberman, Mike Muir, James Needham, Eileen Mueller Neill, Julie Pace, Earl Parker, Bob Pepper, Brenda Pepper, Nikolai Punin, Bob Radigan, Ellen Rixford, Joe Rogers, Claudia Sargent, Sandra Shap, Dan Siculan, Deborah Sims, Susan Skoorka, Suzanne Snider, Kirsten Soderlind, Susan Swan, Phyllis Tarlow, John Trotta, Rhonda Voo, John Walter Jr.

Data

pp. 116–117, Tables, "The right size bat for boys," "The right size bat for girls," and "Bat Facts: Long and short of it" from USA Today, August 3, 1989. Copyright © 1989 USA Today. Adapted with permission.

ScottForesman Staff

ScottForesman gratefully acknowledges the contributions of the following individuals.

Editorial

Karen Usiskin, Janice Ziebka, Therese Smith, Clare Froemel, Nancy Baty, Jean Tucknott, Christine Rakow, Iromie Fernando

Design

Barbara Schneider, Virginia Pierce, George Roth, David Dumo, Tom Gorman

Production

Mary Lou Beals, Joy Kelly, Barbara Albright, Kathy Oberfranc, Lois Nelson, Fran Simon, Sally Buehne, Cynthia Clampitt

Marketing

Cathie Dillender, Nan Simpson, Muffet Fox

Business

Elizabeth A. Dietz, Elizabeth R. Semro

Picture Research/Photo Studio

Nina Page, Rosemary Hunter, John Moore, Phoebe Novak

Photo Lab/Keyline

Marilyn Sullivan, Mark Spears, Madeline Oton-Tarpey, Gwen Plogman